A Macintosh® Journey

with Guided Projects for

- Microsoft® Word 4
- Microsoft® Excel 2.2
- HyperCard™ 1.2
- FileMaker® II
- MacDraw® II
- MacPaint® 2.0

John Dilbeck   Nicki Fink

The Benjamin/Cummings Publishing Company, Inc.

Redwood City, California • Menlo Park, California
Reading, Massachusetts • New York • Don Mills, Ontario
Wokingham, U.K. • Amsterdam • Bonn • Sydney
Singapore • Tokyo • Madrid • San Juan

Sponsoring Editor: Michelle Baxter
Developmental Editor: Evelyn Spire
Production Coordinator: Cathy Lewis
Copy Editor: Anna Huff
Sr. Manufacturing Coordinator: Merry Free Osborn
Cover: Detta Penna
Production Service: Fog Press
Film Output: The Courier Connection
Cover Art: Michael Swain

Library of Congress Cataloging-in-Publication Data

Dilbeck, John.
     A Macintosh journey: with guided projects for Microsoft Word 4,
  Microsoft Excel 2.2, HyperCard 1.2, FileMaker II, MacDraw II,
  MacPaint 2.0 / John Dilbeck, Nicki Fink
       p. cm.
     Includes index.
     ISBN 0-8053-1260-9
     1. Macintosh (Computer)—Programming.   I. Fink, Nicki.
  II. Title.
  QA76.8.M3D548   1991
  005.265—dc20   90-28794
                                      CIP

ISBN 0-8053-1260-9

12345678910-MU-9594939291

The Benjamin/Cummings Publishing Company, Inc.
390 Bridge Parkway
Redwood City, California 94065

Special Introductory Offer

15% Package Discount for:

A Macintosh Journey with Guided Projects
and
Reference Guide to Your Macintosh

One of the best tools you can give your students is Benjamin/Cummings' new **Reference Guide to Your Macintosh.** And now when you order our special *Macintosh Journey Package,* your students get **A Macintosh Journey,** plus the **Reference Guide** at a considerable savings off the regular price!

A Reference Guide
to Your Macintosh

John Dilbeck   Nicki Fink

A Reference Guide to Your Macintosh is a handy at-your-fingertips resource for all your students' Macintosh questions. Part I - *A Mini Manual* - explains everything from the Macintosh's "desk accessories," to how to format a disk.
Part II - *How to Buy Your Own Macintosh* - provides a buyer's checklist to help students assess their microcomputer needs, and includes a complete review of Macintosh hardware products.

(0-8053-1264- 1/softcover/96 pages/1991)

Features:

•Gives students a complete tour of the Macintosh, with easy-to-understand descriptions of icons, menus, the CHOOSER, the system folder and much more.

•Provides clear, concise explanations of frequently used computer terms including windows, hard disks, and CD-ROM.

•Offers *Timesaver Tips* and *Cautions* to help students use the Macintosh more efficiently and avoid common mistakes.

•Includes plenty of helpful figures, sample screens, and illustrations.

•Provides a buyer's guide to the latest Macintosh models and a Buyer's Checklist.

For more information about Benjamin/Cummings' special Macintosh Journey Package, contact your local Benjamin/Cummings sales representative or call 800/447-2226.

The Benjamin/Cummings Publishing Company, Inc.
390 Bridge Parkway
Redwood City, California 94065

Preface

Within these pages are thirty projects to guide your introduction to the Apple Macintosh. We developed these projects after several years of teaching a broad range of students, from novices to computer programmers. While many of these projects help you create useful items, all will provide you with a fresh look at organizing your world, allowing you to be creative and to enjoy your journey as you master individual software packages. *A Macintosh Journey with Guided Projects* provides step-by-step instructions to individuals interested in learning to use an Apple Macintosh at school, in the office, or at home. It is an introduction to using many popular software packages available for the Macintosh—Microsoft Word, Microsoft Excel, MacPaint, MacDraw II, FileMaker II, and HyperCard.

Each of the five parts of our book begins with a brief chapter on the basic concepts of computing, graphics, word processing, spreadsheets and information management software. The application chapter(s) that follow are a series of projects that reinforce learning by building upon the successful completion of the previous project. However, each application chapter is independent of the others. You may choose to skip an entire application package, or learn the packages in any order you require.

The Application chapters are structured on this model:

- Objectives
- Two-to-Four hands-on Projects with each completed Project provided
- Visual integration of Icons, Command Key Equivalents, Menus,
- Dialog boxes and Screens
- Enhanced selected screens as checkpoints for your work
- Suggested points to quit and instructions for starting up again
- Cautions and Warnings for beginning computer users
- Suggested points to Save Your Work
- Summary with Key Terms
- Command Key Equivalents and Shortcuts Summary Table
- Additional Project(s) for independent study

Conventions Used in This Book

You will see lines in the applications chapters that are formatted as follows.

⌘-S    Choose **Save** from the File menu.

The arrow indicates that this is an action step that the reader should perform. Command key equivalents and keyboard shortcuts for these actions, when available, are listed in the left column.

Ancillaries

- *Reference Guide to Your Macintosh* by John Dilbeck and Nicki Fink. A brief guide in two parts:
  1. A Mini Manual (essential information and practical tips for beginning computer users); and
  2. How to Buy Your Own Macintosh (a concise overview of Macintosh hardware) with Buyer's Checklist.
- *Instructor's Manual to Accompany A Macintosh Journey* by Ann Quade with Lecture Outlines, Project Summaries, Teaching Hints and Test Questions.
- Macintosh Journey Projects disk. An optional disk with data files and project graphics.

About the Authors

John L. Dilbeck and Nicki Fink have been teaching computer applications and programming courses at Tri-County Community College for many years. Both are professional programmers, who after using a variety of different computers, have become avid Macintosh enthusiasts who enjoy guiding others in learning to use the Macintosh.

Reviewer Acknowledgements

We gratefully acknowledge the participation of the following reviewers:

Michael Bieber, *Boston College*
Nan Bowman, *College of San Mateo*
Walter Chesbro, *Santa Rosa Junior College*
Clifford Clark, *Napa Valley Community College*
Lee Erker, *Tri-County Community College*
Victoria Fouts, *St. Petersburg Community College*
Raymond Freese, *St. Louis University*
James Gips, *Boston College*
John Hawkins, *Dartmouth College*
Bipin Indurkhya, *Boston University*

Chas de La, *Purdue University*
Yvonne Loest, *Ventura Unified School District*
Lewis Miller, *Canada College*
Steven Mullins, *Purdue University*
Chris Peters, *Clemson University*
Ann Quade, *Mankato State University*
Sherrill Rabe, *American River Community College*
Edward Stewart, *Austin Community College*
Patricia Tormey, *University of Wisconsin-Madison*
Debra Trantina, *Arizona State University*

Acknowledgements

The authors appreciate the contributions of the staff at Benjamin/Cummings Publishing Company, including Michelle Baxter, Cathy Lewis, Lisa Weber, Deborah Hunter, and Stacey Treco. We also thank Evelyn Spire and Nancy Canning of Editorial Arts, who skillfully guided, organized, and molded our rough drafts into a complete book.

We also wish to thank the developers of the hardware and software presented in this book: Apple Computer, Inc., Claris Corporation, and Microsoft Corporation. We use their products every day for educational, professional, personal, and recreational purposes.

Additional thanks go to the many people who contributed to the completion of this book, *some* of whom are: George Kelischek, Leon Tatham, Jim Bell, Marsha Szczepanski, June Brooks, Judy Baker, Dr. Robert McCoy, Ken Fox, and all the students at Tri-County Community College who took our Macintosh Applications course and offered criticisms and suggestions for improvements.

We thank our spouses, who put up with us while this project was being completed:

Gene Jole, for his support, encouragement, and endurance when he had to eat his own cooking and fish by himself.

Kathleen Dilbeck, not only for her support and encouragement, but also for her invaluable help and the many long hours she spent proofreading, working through projects, and word processing (not to mention living in a house where the grass wasn't mowed all summer).

Lastly, we thank Mattie Lee Dilbeck for reading every draft and working through every project as *A Macintosh Journey* evolved. Her devotion to this project, her lifelong search for knowledge, and the values she represents have been an inspiration to us both. We dedicate this book to Mattie Lee Dilbeck.

Although as much care as possible was taken in the production of this book, errors will undoubtedly surface. We take full responsibility for any errors and we welcome your comments and suggestions. Write to us in care of Computer Information Systems Editor, Benjamin/Cummings Publishing Company, 390 Bridge Parkway, Redwood City, California, 94065. We will respond to letters with a return address.

A Macintosh® Journey
with Guided Projects
Contents

Part I: Introduction to Using the Macintosh

Part I teaches you the basics of using the Macintosh and introduces you to some of the concepts, terminology, and procedures that are standard on this computer.

The concepts include the Macintosh user interface and its components: the desktop, windows, buttons, menus, and icons. You will learn to use the Finder, format a disk, create and move folders, use menus, open a program and quit from it, and be able to identify the parts of the desktop and windows.

You will learn the background information necessary to interact with the Mac and to use programs that implement the standard Macintosh interface.

Chapter 1: Getting Started

What You Will Learn in This Chapter

After reading this chapter and completing the projects in it, you should be able to:

- Identify the parts of the Macintosh desktop and windows

- Maneuver around the desktop

- Use the keyboard and mouse

- Issue commands from menus

- Open and close windows

- Open a program and quit from it

- Format a data disk

- Create and move folders

- Duplicate documents, folders, and disks

- Organize documents, folders, and disks

- Erase documents and folders

The Macintosh is one of the easiest of all computers to use. You can learn the basic operations of the system in less than an hour. The programs you will be using—graphics, word processing, spreadsheets, information managers, and others—all share a common method of operation. Once you learn the standard methods of interacting with the Mac, you will be on your way to knowing how to use these other programs as well.

The Macintosh introduced a *graphical user interface*. Instead of typing commands to the Macintosh, you interact with it using icons, windows, menus, buttons, and a mouse.

When you first start a Macintosh, it runs a program named *Finder*, which allows you to run programs, copy and erase documents, format disks, find files, tell the computer when you are ready to quit, and many other tasks.

THE DESKTOP

The Finder presents a view of the system known as the *desktop* (see Figure 1-1).

Figure 1-1   The desktop

In most offices you can usually find items that you already know how to use. These items could include such things as clocks, calculators, note pads, file folders, and trash cans. By building on your real-world skills and knowledge, the Macintosh lets you interact easily with the computer as you perform tasks that are similar to equivalent tasks in an office.

The desktop metaphor is one of the reasons the Macintosh is easy to learn to use. If you want to file a document, you already know how to put it into a file folder and then put the file folder into a filing cabinet. On the Macintosh you also put a document into a folder, and the folder is contained in a disk.

Applications

You already know how to drop something into a folder, open a folder, take something out of a folder, close a folder, and store a folder or throw it away. The Macintosh lets you build on your real-world experience as you work in the Mac's desktop. You can prepare a document, store it on a disk, place it into a folder with similar documents, move it into a different folder, place it on the desktop, and throw it away.

Trash

On the Macintosh, there are no arcane commands that you have to learn to do these things with documents. If you want to throw something away, you already have practice putting it into a trash can. On the Macintosh, you can discard a document by selecting its icon and dragging the icon into the *Trash*.

The desktop allows you to control the Macintosh and tell it what to do. At the same time, the computer will be communicating with you, so you can see the results of your actions. For example, when you place a document in the Trash, the Trash icon changes to a bulging trash can to show that something is in it.

There are two *icons* (pictures representing objects) showing on the screen (see Figure 1-1). One icon is named My Hard Disk and the other is named Trash.

My Hard Disk contains the programs and documents currently available for use. The Trash allows you to discard (erase) any documents you no longer need. (Since the Trash has straight—as opposed to bulging— sides, you know it is empty.)

In addition to allowing you to organize your disks and dispose of unwanted documents, the desktop enables you to start application programs. Many popular programs are available for use on the Macintosh. One of the first programs written for the Macintosh is named MacPaint. This program allows you to create and modify graphics on your computer.

For the next several pages you will be led through the process of finding, starting, and quitting MacPaint. Read along, and follow the process without trying the steps yourself. Your disk will probably be organized differently from what is demonstrated here, and it could get confusing if you were to try to follow along at this point. In Project 1, however, you will work through a brief tutorial to learn how to work with the desktop. *(Later, in Chapter 4, you will learn how to use MacPaint.)*

USING THE MOUSE

Most of the actions on the desktop are initiated using the *mouse*. The *pointer* on the screen is controlled by moving the mouse on a desk or table. Pull the mouse toward you and it moves the pointer down on the screen. Push the mouse away from you and the pointer moves up. Moving the mouse left or right causes the pointer to move in a corresponding direction on the screen.

The mouse has a single button on its top. There are four main ways to use the mouse and its button.

Click   Press down on the *mouse button*, and then release it.

Double-click   Click the mouse button twice in rapid succession without moving the mouse.

Drag   Press the mouse button and keep holding it down while you move the mouse to a new location. Then release the button.

Shift-click   While you are pressing the *Shift key* on the keyboard, click the mouse button.

The pointer changes shape depending upon what you are doing at any particular moment. When you are working on the desktop, you will be using the *arrow pointer* most of the time. This is the shape it will be when you are working with the icons and controls on the desktop. If you select an icon and then move the pointer over the icon's name, the pointer will change to the *I-beam pointer,* which indicates that you can now change the name of the icon if you wish. When you tell the Macintosh to perform some operation that may take more than a second or two, the pointer will usually change to a *wristwatch pointer*, which essentially means, "Wait a minute, I'm busy."

Figure 1-2 shows the pointers that you will see most frequently when working on the desktop.

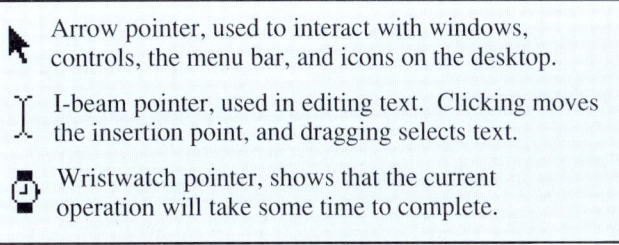

Figure 1-2   Pointers used when working on the desktop

ISSUING A COMMAND

Issuing a command is a two-step process. First you select an object, and then you tell the computer what to do to it. You can also issue a command when more than one object is selected.

In the top right corner of Figure 1-1 is the icon of a disk named My Hard Disk (yours will probably say something else). You want to open this disk to see what is in it. The easiest way to do this is to move the mouse pointer so that the tip of the arrow is touching the disk icon. Then, without moving the mouse, double-click on the icon.

As soon as you double-click on it, the disk icon opens a window, as shown in Figure 1-3. This window shows six icons representing *folders*. The *System Folder* icon has a picture of a Macintosh on it, which means that it is the folder containing all the necessary files for the Macintosh to operate. All the other folders look alike, but each has a different name.

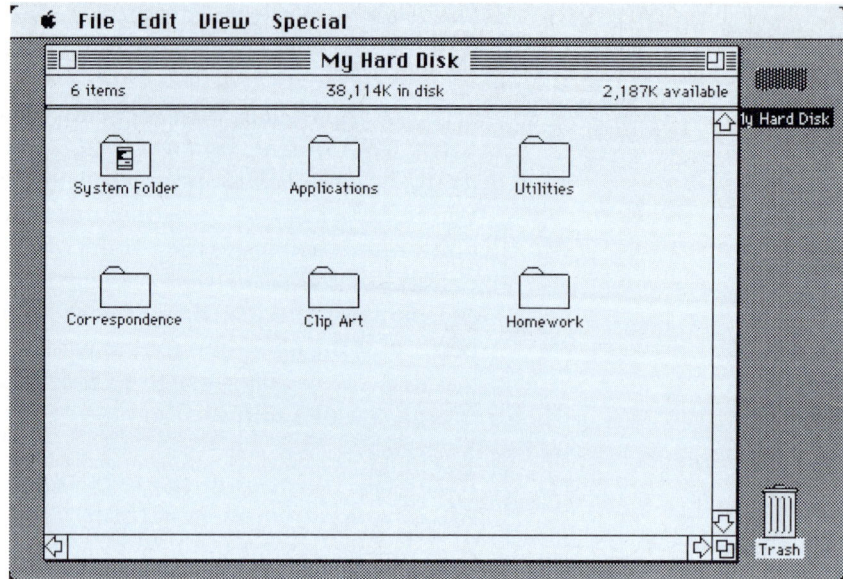

Figure 1-3   The window for My Hard Disk

Every hard disk is probably organized differently. Some have more or fewer folders than this one.

TWO TYPES OF PROGRAMS

There are two main types of computer programs. *System programs* are used to control the system, and they are stored in the System Folder on a Macintosh. The desktop on a Macintosh computer is provided by a system program known as the Finder.

Application programs are used by a person to perform a task. MacPaint is used to draw images, so it is an application program. On this hard disk, MacPaint is located in the Applications folder.

Your next step is to open the Applications folder by double-clicking on its icon.

When you double-click on the Applications folder, the Finder opens the folder and shows its *directory window* (see Figure 1-4), which contains six more folders. This directory window shows all the documents and folders contained in the Applications folder just opened.

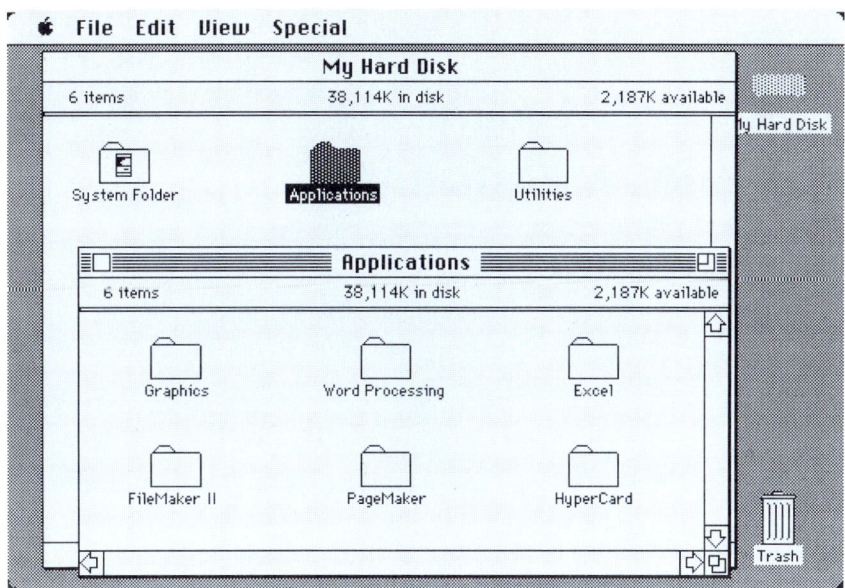

Figure 1-4   Directory window for the Applications folder

FOLDERS WITHIN FOLDERS

The process of storing folders within folders is known as *nesting*. Nesting allows you to store large quantities of information on a disk and still be able to find it quickly.

MacPaint is a graphics program, so you will find it inside the Graphics folder. Opening the Graphics folder reveals other folders and documents (see Figure 1-5).

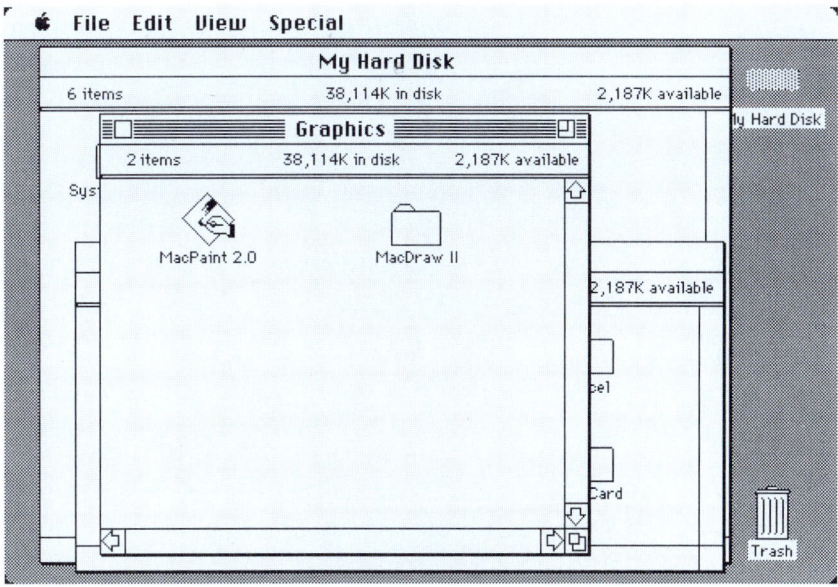

Figure 1-5   The Graphics folder's contents

The Graphics folder contains two items, including one with an icon representing a hand painting on a sheet of paper. This is the icon for MacPaint. It is named MacPaint 2.0.

RUNNING A PROGRAM

MacPaint 2.0

Let's tell the Finder to run MacPaint. You have already seen that you can open a disk by double-clicking on its icon, and you can open a folder by double-clicking on its icon. This would lead you to guess that you can open MacPaint by double-clicking on its icon, and you would be correct.

Pointing to an icon and double-clicking is actually a shortcut method preferred by many Macintosh users. The standard method for opening a document or folder, or for running a program, is to select the icon, and then choose the **Open** command from the File menu. Many people who are new to the Macintosh prefer this method, at least until they become comfortable using the mouse and double-clicking.

Another shortcut method for opening a document or folder, or for running a program, involves using a *Command-key equivalent.*

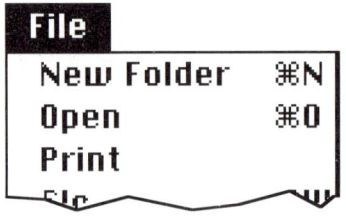

As you can see in the top portion of the File menu (at left), the Open command has something to its right in the menu. There is a cloverleaf symbol and the letter "O". The cloverleaf symbol represents the *Command key* on the keyboard. In the Finder, the process of pressing the "O" key while the Command key is held down is equivalent to choosing the **Open** command from the File menu.

In the remainder of this book, Command-key equivalents are shown as Command-O (with the "O" replaced by the appropriate key). You also can see from the menu that Command-N is equivalent to choosing **New Folder** from the File menu. The Print command does not have a Command-key equivalent in Finder, but it may in other programs.

When you open MacPaint, it runs the application, creates a blank document, and presents you with the view shown in Figure 1-6. As you can see, the pointer has changed to the shape of a pencil, but if you move the pointer up to the menu bar, it will change back to the arrow pointer, which is used to select commands from a menu.

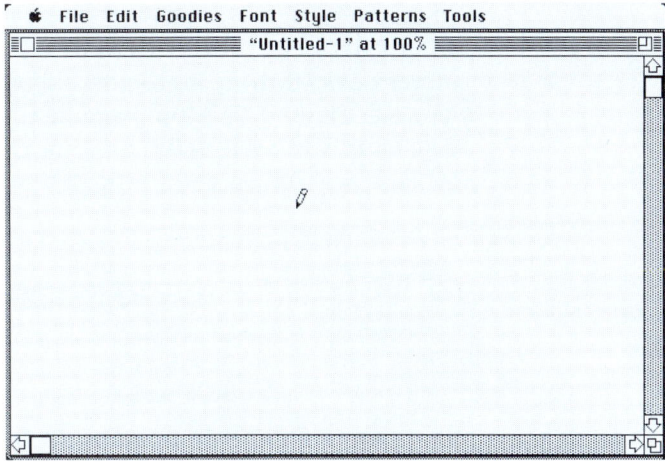

Figure 1-6 The opening screen of MacPaint

You will learn how to use MacPaint in Chapter 4. Now that you opened MacPaint, how do you tell the Macintosh that you don't want to use it anymore?

When you are first learning to use the mouse, you may feel uncomfortable with it and have trouble pointing to the icon you want. If you accidentally open an application that you don't want to use, you should have no problem quitting the program, even if you don't know how to use that program yet.

QUITTING A PROGRAM

The main thing that makes the Macintosh easy to use is the consistency of commands given to all programs. You will tell MacPaint to quit the same way you tell almost all Macintosh programs to quit.

To do this, you will use one of the commands in a *menu*. On the top of the screen is a *menu bar* that lists eight menu names. The first is the *Apple* ( ) *menu*, and the next two are the *File menu* and the *Edit menu*. These three menus are standard on all Macintosh programs (except games and special-purpose programs).

A *file* is computer terminology for a collection of information. In Macintosh terminology a file is also called a *document*. The File menu allows you to control operations concerning a document, including the ability to tell the program to quit.

Let's tell MacPaint to quit and return to the desktop. To do this, move the mouse pointer so that it touches the File menu. Pressing the mouse button pulls the menu down onto the screen. While you are still pressing the button, drag the mouse toward you until it selects the *menu item* you want.

When a menu item is selected, it is *highlighted*. This means that the white parts in the item turn black, and vice versa. Continue dragging the pointer down until it highlights the word **Quit** at the bottom of the menu (see Figure 1-7). Stop dragging the mouse, and release the button while **Quit** is still selected. The command will blink several times, and MacPaint will return you to the desktop.

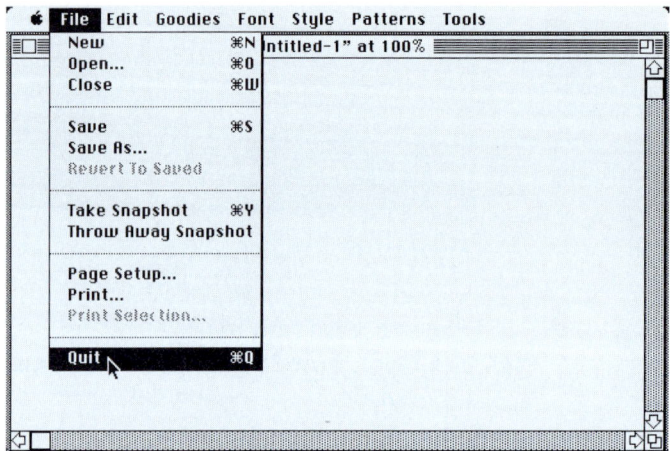

Figure 1-7   Selecting the Quit command from the File menu

(Most programs allow you to quit by typing Command-Q.)

That's all there is to issuing a command using the Macintosh's *pull-down menus*.

CLOSING OPEN FOLDERS

The Finder now returns you to the same place you were before you launched MacPaint. Now you want to close all the folders and return to an uncluttered desktop. There are several ways to do this.

The easiest way is to click in the window's *close box* (see Figure 1-8). Notice that the pointer in the figure is in a small square box to the left of the Graphics folder title.

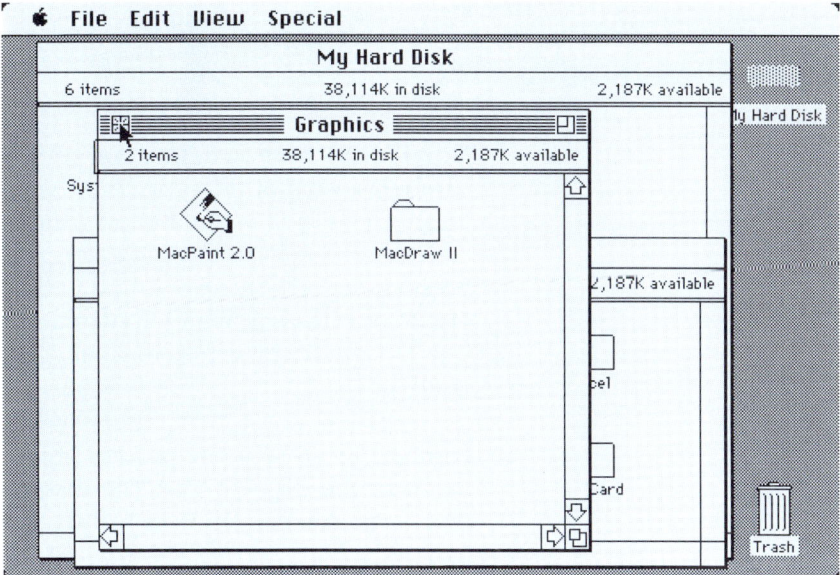

Figure 1-8   Closing a window with the close box

Each *window* has a *title bar* at its top. Most also have a close box on the left and a *zoom box* on the right side of the title bar.

As its name implies, the close box causes the window to close. The screen should return to the same appearance it had before you opened the folder that is represented by the window.

The zoom box, if it is present, causes the window to zoom to a larger size. Some application programs cause the window to fill the screen when the zoom box is clicked. Others cause the window to get larger, but not to fill the entire screen. If you click in the zoom box a second time, most applications will return the window to the size it was before you first clicked in the zoom box.

You can also see in Figure 1-8 that the Graphics folder window has several horizontal lines in its title bar, but the window named My Hard Disk does not. The presence of the horizontal lines tells you that a window is the *active window*.

A standard feature of the Macintosh user interface is that actions occur in the active window. There is another way to close a window that will illustrate this. Instead of clicking in the close box of a window, you can go to the File menu and choose **Close**. This will cause only the active window to close and will have no effect on any others that may be present.

There is another way to close windows that is even easier and faster if you want to close all open windows on the desktop. First, position the pointer so that it is in the close box of the active window. Then hold down the *Option key* and click in the close box. This tells the Finder to close the active window, make the next one active, close it, and continue this process until all the windows are closed and the desktop once again looks like Figure 1-1.

Project 1: Preparing a Data Disk

Now it's time for you to give it a try. Since you will probably be working through several of the projects presented later in the book, it is a good idea for you to *format a disk* on which to store your work.

You may be working on a computer that has a *hard disk*, or you may have only *floppy disks* on which to work. Either way, you will need to know how to format a disk, to keep a spare copy, or *backup*, of your important work.

Formatting a disk is the process of letting the computer magnetically organize the disk, so that the disk can store your information and retrieve it. You can think of formatting as setting up a file cabinet and hanging folders, in which you can store real information at a later time. Many different computers use 3.5-inch disks, and each type of computer has a different routine that it uses to format the disk for its pattern of storage.

You will need a blank disk, or one you can erase, to proceed with this project.

A paragraph shown indented with a right-pointing arrow (such as the next one) is the indication that you are to do what is stated in that paragraph. Paragraphs that are italicized (such as this one) are comments to the reader, hints, or mild warnings.

➠ The first thing you need to do is have your computer turned on. If you are working on a Mac that has an external hard disk, turn on the power to the disk drive and then to the computer. If you are working with a floppy-based system, turn on the computer and insert a system disk.

Since most readers will probably be using a Macintosh with a hard disk, that is the basic configuration assumed for the projects. We will also assume that you will be storing these projects on a floppy disk rather than the hard disk. If you are using a system that does not have a hard disk, you will need to remember to insert a startup disk *into your computer that contains the system and applications you will need to complete the particular project. For the projects in this chapter, you will need a startup disk containing a System Folder and a blank disk.*

You should also have a copy, or access to a copy, of the Macintosh Journey Projects *disk. If you are in a class that has adopted this book, your teacher should have one or more copies available for you to use. If you purchased this book to learn on your own, you will find a card with instructions for obtaining this disk attached inside the rear cover. You don't absolutely need the* Projects *disk to complete the projects in* A Macintosh Journey, *but in a few projects, such as this one, the disk will make it easier.*

When your computer is started, you will see a desktop similar to the one in Figure 1-9. Your desktop may look different, depending on the number and type of disk drives you have attached to your system.

Figure 1-9   The desktop

➡ Your system will have one or more 3.5-inch floppy disk drives. When you and your Macintosh are ready, insert a blank disk into any available drive.

If the disk you inserted is blank or has been formatted on a different type of computer, you will see a *dialog box* like the one in Figure 1-10.

Figure 1-10   Unreadable disk notice

This dialog box allows you to respond in one of three ways. If you insert a disk that has valid data on it and receive this notice, immediately click the **Eject** button. This means that something is wrong with the disk or the way the data is stored on it. If you do not know how to correct the situation, take the disk to someone who may be able to recover your data.

The other two buttons, One-Sided and Two-Sided, are there so you can tell the Mac how you want the disk to be formatted. Many single-sided disk drives are still in use, and these drives can read disks that are formatted for 400K storage only. If you want to use the disk you are formatting in a drive that reads 400K disks, you must click **One-Sided**.

If your disk drive stores and reads 800K disks, you should click **Two-Sided**.

(If you are using a Macintosh with a "SuperDrive" you will see one of two dialog boxes, depending upon whether you inserted a DSDD (double-sided, double density) or high-density disk into the drive. If you put a DSDD disk (the most common one) into the drive, you will see the dialog shown in Figure 1-10. If you inserted a high-density disk into the drive, the computer can recognize this and will show the same dialog box with only two choices: Eject or Initialize. Macintoshes without a SuperDrive are not able to read high-density disks.)

➡ You probably will want to format (*initialize*) the disk for use in an 800K disk drive, so click **Two-Sided**.

If you are using System 6.0 or later, the Macintosh will then respond with another dialog box (see Figure 1-11).

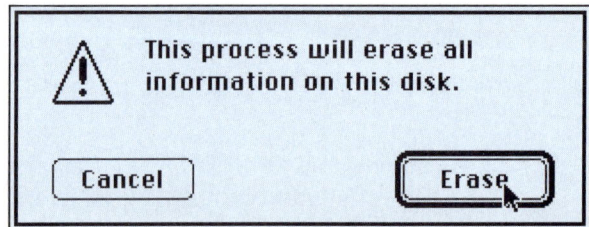

Figure 1-11   Warning against erasing contents of disk

➡ This should be a blank disk; you don't have to be concerned with losing any information, so click **Erase**.

Before formatting your disk, the computer asks for a name to assign to the disk (see Figure 1-12). If you are using this textbook in a classroom setting, you probably should have your name as part of the disk's name so that even if the label were to come off, someone could recognize the disk as yours by inserting it into the computer and reading the disk's name.

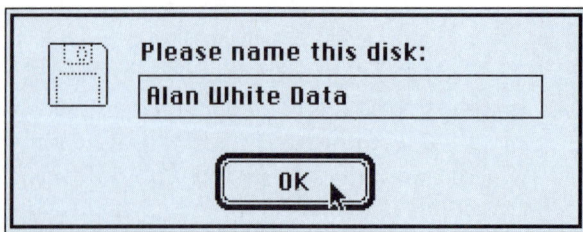

Figure 1-12   Naming your disk

➡ Enter your name, followed by the word **Data** for the disk's name. Click **OK**.

For the next few seconds, the Macintosh will format the disk and then verify that the formatting process worked correctly. If the initialization was successful, the icon of your disk will show on the desktop (see Figure 1-13).

Figure 1-13   Formatted disk's icon on the desktop

Don't worry if part of the name goes off the side of the screen. The full name is still there. However, if this appearance bothers you, you can either drag the icon a little to the left or use shorter names or abbreviations. If you want to move the disk icon, you move the mouse pointer to the icon, press the button, and then drag the disk to the left while the button is held down. When you release the mouse button, the icon will move to its new location and stay there.

If the initialization was not successful, you will receive a notice that the initialization failed. At that point, you have the option of trying it again or using a different disk. Sometimes a disk will format correctly the second time. If the initialization still fails, you should use another disk.

If the initialization fails, you may want to discard the disk now, before you save important information onto it. All disks eventually fail, so discarding one that does not format correctly may save you from losing valuable time and information later.

➡ Open your disk's directory window by double-clicking on its icon.

Another way to open a disk's directory window is to click once on the disk's icon to select it. Then type Command-O to open the disk. It is your choice whether to issue a command with the mouse and menu or with a Command-key equivalent.

As you can see in Figure 1-14, no documents are currently located on this newly formatted disk. The status line just below the window's name shows that there are 0 items on the disk. Seven kilobytes of storage are already used by the system, which has reserved a portion of the disk for directory information and a place to store how the directory window will appear on the desktop.

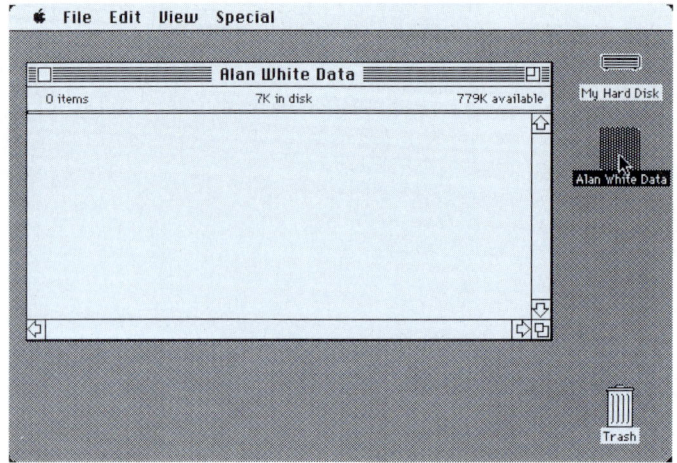

Figure 1-14   Directory window of newly initialized disk

⌘-W   ➧   Close the window by clicking in the close box, the small white rectangle at the left end of the title bar just above "0 items."

The symbol to the left of the instruction above represents Command-W, which is the Command-key equivalent for closing the active window. Throughout the book we will usually indicate a Command-key equivalent (also known as a keyboard equivalent) when one exists. It will be your option to select from the menu or issue the command from the keyboard.

DUPLICATING A DISK

The next part of this project involves copying the documents in the *Macintosh Journey Projects* disk onto your newly formatted data disk. If you do not have that disk, you can read along and complete only the parts that do not depend on having the *Projects* disk.

All Macintosh computers have at least one floppy *disk drive*, and some have two or more. For this project, we will assume that your Macintosh has a hard disk and one floppy drive.

Pat yourself on the back if you noticed there is a problem arising. You have two disks and only one floppy disk drive. How can you copy one disk onto the other with only one drive?

Duplicating one disk onto another is a fairly easy process, even if you only have one drive. (If you have two floppy drives, of course, it is fast and easy.)

Ejecting a Disk and Still Showing Its Icon

The first step is to eject your data disk from the drive in such a way that the Macintosh will still remember it. Then you can insert the *Projects* disk and drag its icon onto your data disk's icon, even though the data disk is not currently in the drive.

As was stated before when you were learning how to start MacPaint, doing something on a Macintosh usually involves two steps: selecting an object and then issuing the command that will affect that object.

First, select the object. . .

➧ Select your data disk by moving the pointer so that the tip touches your data disk's icon, and then click the mouse button once.

And then issue the command. . .

⌘-E ➧ Eject your data disk by choosing **Eject** from the File menu, and then remove the disk from the drive.

This will eject the disk and leave its icon showing on the desktop. Notice that there is now a gray pattern in your data disk's icon (see Figure 1-15). An icon that looks like this is known as a *dimmed* icon. This indicates that the Mac remembers the disk but that it is not currently in a disk drive.

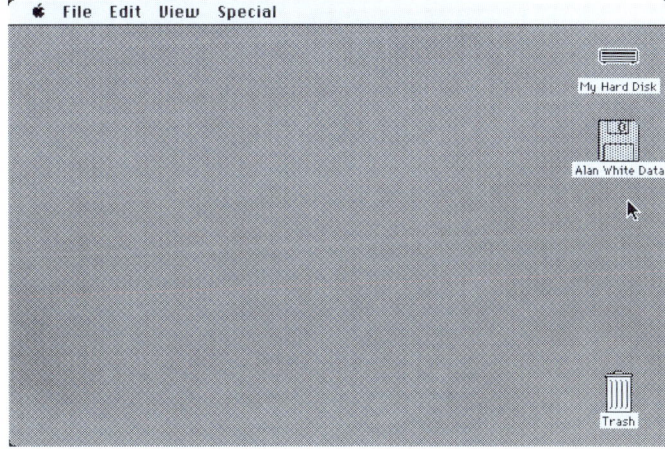

Figure 1-15   Disks not presently in a drive have dimmed icons.

Copying the *Projects* Disk onto the Data Disk

You have to insert the document disk, so you can copy the information stored on it.

➡ Insert the *Macintosh Journey Projects* disk into the drive.

Another icon, representing the *Projects* disk, will appear on the desktop below the icon of your data disk. Now that both icons are visible on the screen, you have largely overcome the problem of two disks and only one drive.

Since both disks are formatted the same (double-sided or 800K), you can copy the *Projects* disk onto your data disk by dragging the icon representing the *Projects* disk onto the icon of the data disk and then releasing the mouse button.

➡ Move the mouse pointer so the tip is on the *Macintosh Journey Projects* icon.

➡ Press the mouse button and, while keeping the button pressed, move the mouse forward so the outline of the *Projects* disk icon moves up on the screen. When the pointer is on your data disk icon, the data disk icon will change appearance, indicating that you have chosen it as the disk onto which the documents will be copied. Release the mouse button to start the copying process.

When copying from one disk to another, the disks are usually referred to as the *source* and *destination* disks. Since you are copying *from* the *Projects* disk, it is the source disk. The data disk is the destination disk, because it is the *destination* of the files being copied.

If you have correctly told the Macintosh to copy the files on the *Projects* disk onto your data disk, a dialog box (see Figure 1-16) will appear asking if you want to completely replace the contents of your data disk with the contents of the *Projects* disk.

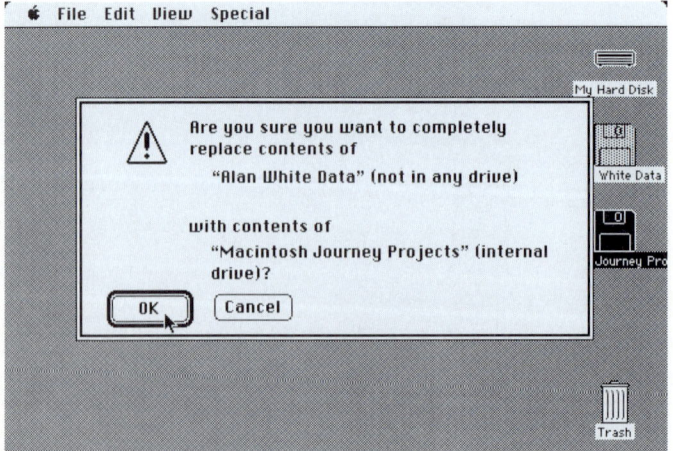

Figure 1-16   Dialog box to confirm disk duplication

Enter or Return   ➡   This is what you want to do, so click **OK**.

The dark oval around the OK button shows that it is the *default* button. Pressing the *Enter* or *Return key* is interpreted the same as clicking the default button.

Once you give the Mac your permission to replace the contents of the data disk with the contents of the *Projects* disk, a new dialog box will appear showing the progress of copying the disk. This process begins with reading the information on the *Projects* disk.

When the computer has read all the information on the disk, or all that it can contain in memory, it will eject the *Projects* disk and ask you to insert your data disk. It will then continue the copying process by writing information to your data disk.

Depending on how much information is on the source disk and the amount of main memory in the Macintosh you are using, you may be asked to swap disks one or more times. When the computer is finished copying the information from the *Projects* disk, the operation will end with your data disk in the computer's disk drive.

(If you have two or more floppy disk drives, you can insert both disks into the computer at the same time and then drag the *Projects* disk's icon onto the data disk. The copying operation will proceed without requiring any disk swapping.)

Warning: You can use this process of dragging a disk's icon onto another disk whenever you want to duplicate all of the information on one disk onto another. This process will erase the information on the destination disk, so be sure this is what you really want to do before you tell the Mac it is okay to completely replace the destination disk's contents.

This process will only work if both disks are formatted the same. This restriction is there to insure the safety of your information. You would *never* want to completely replace the contents of a hard disk with the contents of a floppy disk.

COPYING A DOCUMENT

There is another way to copy one or more documents from one disk onto another one without replacing the entire contents of the destination disk.

Just as you can drag a disk onto another disk to make a complete disk duplicate, you can drag one or more selected documents from one disk onto another disk.

Let's drag one file from the *Projects* disk onto your data disk. You will drag the Mystery Document onto your disk. The process of duplicating the disk that you just completed has already placed this file on your disk. The Macintosh will recognize this and ask if you want to replace a file with the same name as the selected file.

Only one file with a particular name may exist on a disk or in a folder. If you copy another file with the same name, the Mac would have to erase the one already on the disk. There is potential that this situation could be accidentally encountered and would result in the loss of the original file. Therefore, the Mac asks your permission before it continues. If you have any doubt about the contents of the files in question, tell the Mac to cancel the copy operation and determine if this is what you really want to do by looking at the contents of both documents.

In this case, you already know that it is okay to replace the document, so you will tell the Mac to go ahead with the operation.

Notice that the icons of both disks are still on the desktop. You can look at the contents of the *Projects* disk by double-clicking on its icon. Then you will copy the Mystery Document onto your data disk again.

➟   Double-click on the *Macintosh Journey Projects* disk icon. You may be prompted to swap disks one or more times. If the icons are dimmed, eject your data disk and insert the *Projects* disk.

The directory window opens, and you will see the Mystery Document in the fourth row of icons.

➟   Click on the **Mystery Document** and then drag it onto the icon of your data disk (see Figure 1-17).

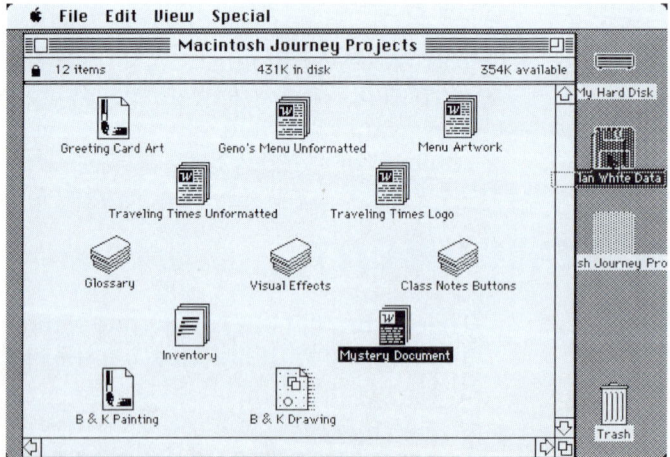

Figure 1-17   Copying one file to another disk

The process of copying the file will involve at least one disk swap (if you are using only one floppy drive). As soon as the computer determines that a document with the same name already exists on your data disk, it will ask if you want to continue (see Figure 1-18).

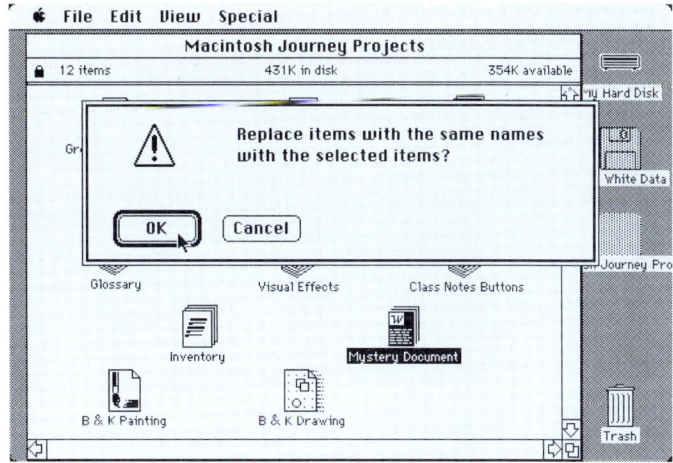

Figure 1-18   Dialog box for permission to replace a document on data disk

Enter or Return   ➠   Since you are sure you want to replace the Mystery Document, click **OK**.

You will see a dialog box showing the progress of the copy operation and may be asked to swap disks one or more times.

If a document named Mystery Document had not already been stored on your data disk, the Macintosh would not have encountered a situation with the potential for losing data. In that case, it would not have asked permission before copying the file. It will only ask permission before engaging in a copy operation that may erase information.

Of course, once you tell it to proceed, the Macintosh will replace the original document, so be sure you know what you are doing before you tell the computer to continue.

Ejecting a Disk and Removing Its Icon

Now that you have copied the files from the *Macintosh Journey Projects* disk, you are finished with it and can eject it (if it is in the computer) and remove its icon from the desktop.

Whenever you are finished using a disk, you should tell the computer to eject the disk and remove the disk's icon from the desktop. It doesn't matter if the disk is in the computer or not.

➠   Drag the *Projects* disk icon onto the **Trash** and release the mouse button.

This will not erase the disk; it just tells the computer that you are finished using the disk for now and to forget what it knows about that disk. Not only does this remove the icon from the desktop, it also frees some of the computer's memory for other uses.

➡ Double-click on your data disk icon to open its directory window.

You can now see, as shown in Figure 1-19, that the Mystery Document icon is out of place. It may not be in the position shown, but it should be located in the first available position in the top row.

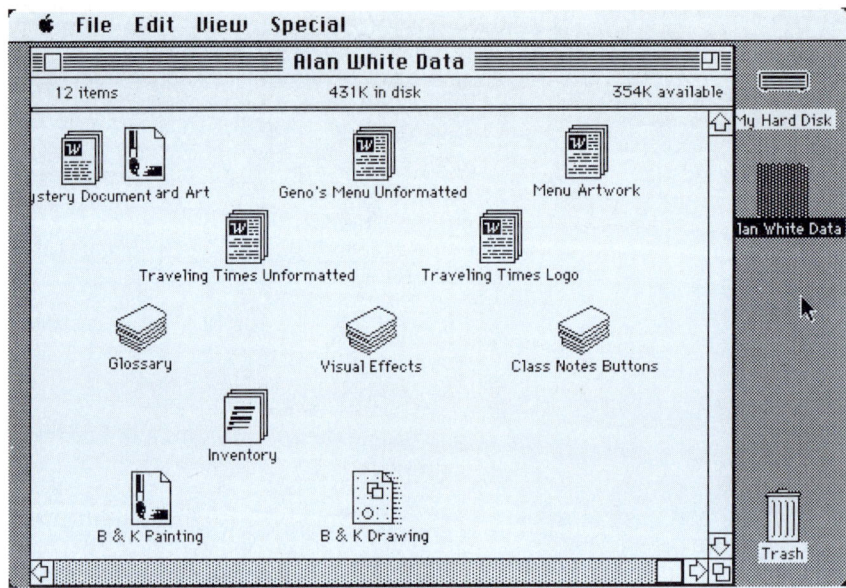

Figure 1-19   Mystery Document's icon is out of place.

When you duplicated the entire *Projects* disk onto your data disk, the icons were placed in this window the same as they were on the original disk. However, when you copied the Mystery Document onto the disk individually, its icon was placed in the first available position.

Since this is not where we want the icon, you can move it to its original position. (Note: It is not important to try to place the icon precisely, just get it in its approximate position.)

Moving a Document's Icon

You have already seen that you can copy a document from one disk onto another one by dragging the document's icon onto the destination disk. This does not erase the file from the source disk.

If you drag a document icon around inside the same window, it does not copy the file; it just changes the location where the icon will be displayed. If you drag the icon onto a folder on the same disk, it does not copy the file and place a copy into the folder; it moves the document into the folder and removes it from its previous location.

In a few minutes, you will move a file into a folder, but for now just move the Mystery Document's icon to the fourth row of icons (see Figure 1-20).

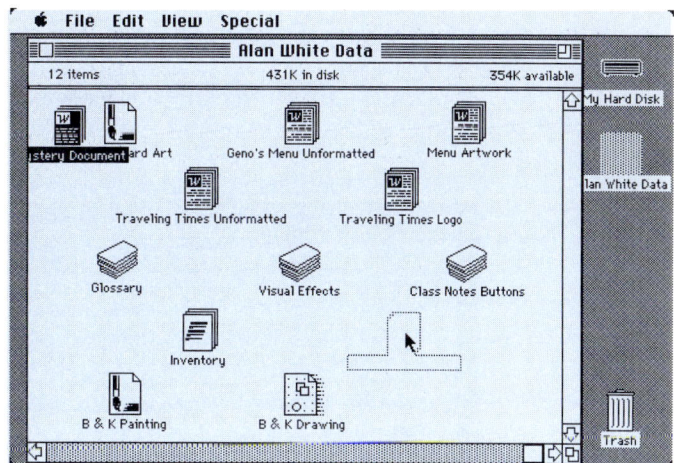

Figure 1-20   Moving a file's icon to a different location

➡ Drag the **Mystery Document** icon to its new position and release it. Be sure to keep the mouse pointer inside the directory window of your data disk.

Notice, when you drag the icon, that a gray outline of the icon moves with the pointer. This is to show the position the icon will assume if you release the mouse button. It enables you to move and place icons accurately in the window.

If you release the mouse button before you have the icon where you want it, just drag it again until you get it to its proper new location.

TAKING DIFFERENT VIEWS OF A DIRECTORY WINDOW

Up until now you have been viewing the directory window using icons. This is only one way you can view the contents of a disk or folder.

Every application uses a particular icon to represent its documents. Each of these icons is different from the others. When you become familiar with the different icons, this is a convenient way to find and access the document in which you are interested.

There are times, however, when it is more convenient to view the directory in other ways. Two of the other most useful views are by date and by name.

By Date

Viewing a disk or folder window by date shows all the documents sorted by reverse chronological order based on the last time each document was modified (see Figure 1-21). If you want to quickly find a document you worked on recently, it is convenient to view by date so that the most recently modified files are shown first.

➡ Choose **by Date** from the View menu.

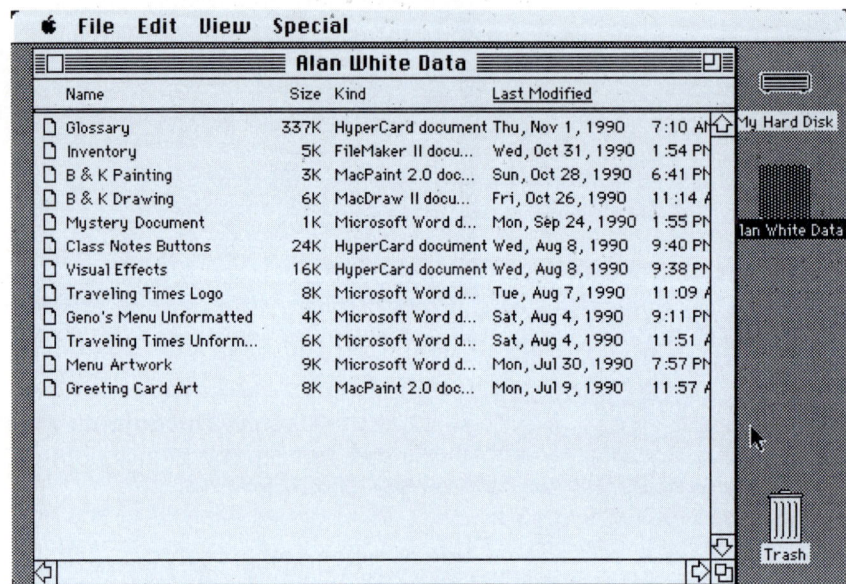

Figure 1-21   Viewing your data disk by date

Another convenient way to view the window's contents is by name.

By Name

Viewing a disk or folder window by name shows all the documents sorted alphabetically by name (see Figure 1-22). If you want to quickly find a document and you know its name, the view by name option may be helpful.

➡ Choose **by Name** from the View menu.

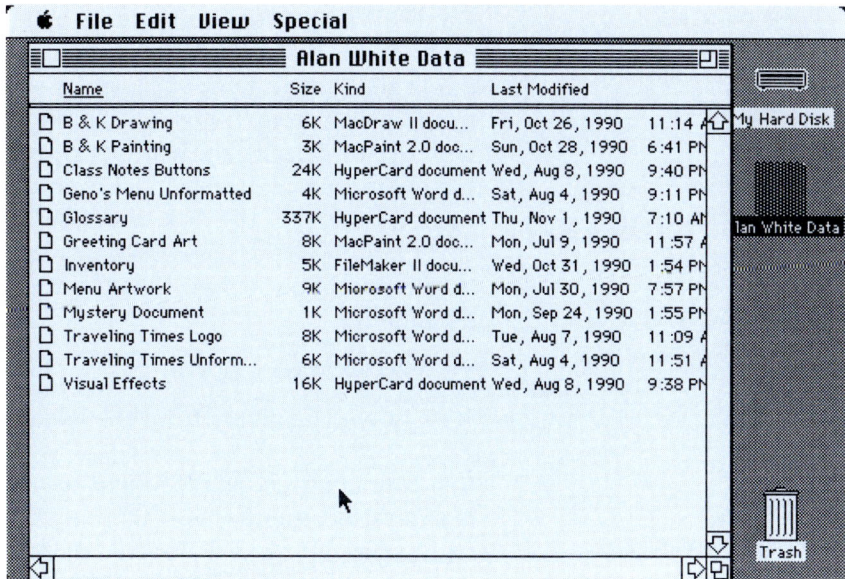

Figure 1-22   Viewing your data disk by name

By Icon

You will find all of these methods of viewing the directory window useful.

➡ Choose **by Icon** from the View menu to change back to the original view of the disk's directory.

This is the Macintosh's default view. When you format a new disk, it will automatically be viewed by icon. Next time you insert the disk, the view will be the same as it was the last time you used it.

DUPLICATING A DOCUMENT

Now you will learn how to create an exact duplicate of a document. This is useful if you want to make a backup copy of a document on the same disk before you try an operation that might result in damage to the current state of the document. For example, you might want to duplicate a spreadsheet before sorting it, backup a complex drawing before modifying it, or backup a long word processing document before starting an involved formatting process.

Copying a document and duplicating a document are similar, but use different mechanisms. Copying a document involves making a new copy of the document on a different disk. To copy a document, click on its icon and drag it to a different disk. The Finder will then create a copy of the file, with the same name, on the other disk.

Duplicating a document involves making a new copy of the document on the same disk and in the same folder as the original document. To duplicate a document, click on its icon, and then choose **Duplicate** from the File menu (or use Command-D). The Finder will then create a copy of the file, with the words "Copy of " added to the beginning of the file's name. Since the original file, and the new copy of it, are located at the same level on the disk, they must have different names.

In this case, you will go through the steps involved in duplicating a document.

⟹ Select **Mystery Document** by clicking on its icon.

⌘-D   ⟹ Choose **Duplicate** from the File menu.

In a couple of seconds, you will see a new document named Copy of Mystery Document appear in your disk's directory window just below and to the right of the selected document (see Figure 1-23). The new document is selected so you can change its name if you want.

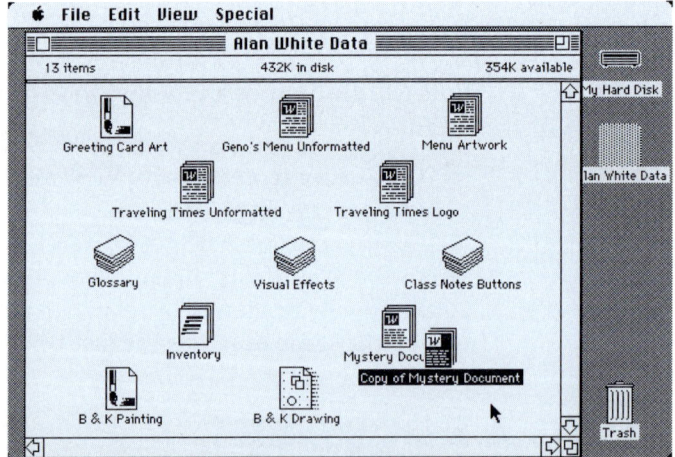

Figure 1-23   The new copy of the Mystery Document

That's all you will be doing with this new document for a few minutes.

⟹ Deselect the Copy of Mystery Document icon by clicking in the white area of the window.

CREATING A NEW FOLDER

Now you will create and place a folder on your disk. This will allow you to organize the storage of the projects you will later create. You may decide that you would like to organize your disk differently later. Feel free to customize it so that it works best for you, but for now, try it like this.

⌘-N ➡ Create a new folder by choosing **New Folder** from the File menu (see Figure 1-24).

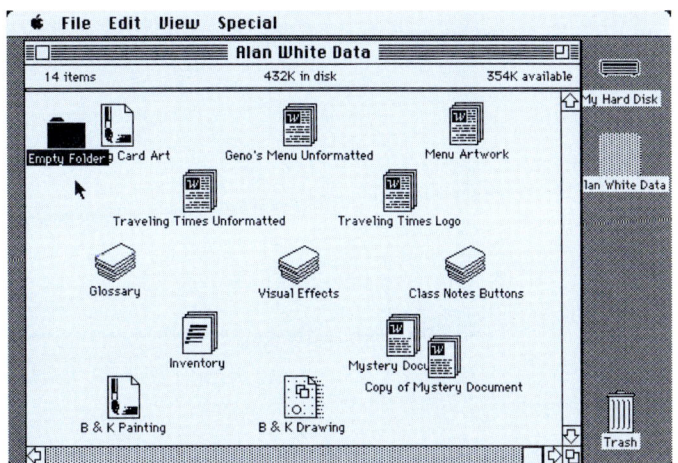

Figure 1-24 Creating a new folder on your disk

This will create a new folder on your disk labeled Empty Folder.

➡ Do not click anywhere yet.

When the Empty Folder is created, it is automatically selected so you can easily change its name.

➡ Rename the folder Final Projects by typing this name on the keyboard. As you type, you will see the name change.

If you make any typing mistakes, use the Backspace key (Delete key on some keyboards) to erase the mistake and retype the name.

➡ Move the **Final Projects** folder to the last row just below and to the right of the two Mystery Documents.

➡ Deselect the folder by clicking in the white area of the window.

You may have to resize the window so the folder will fit and be visible.

When you finish, the new folder will be named Final Projects and will be in the lower right side of the window (see Figure 1-25).

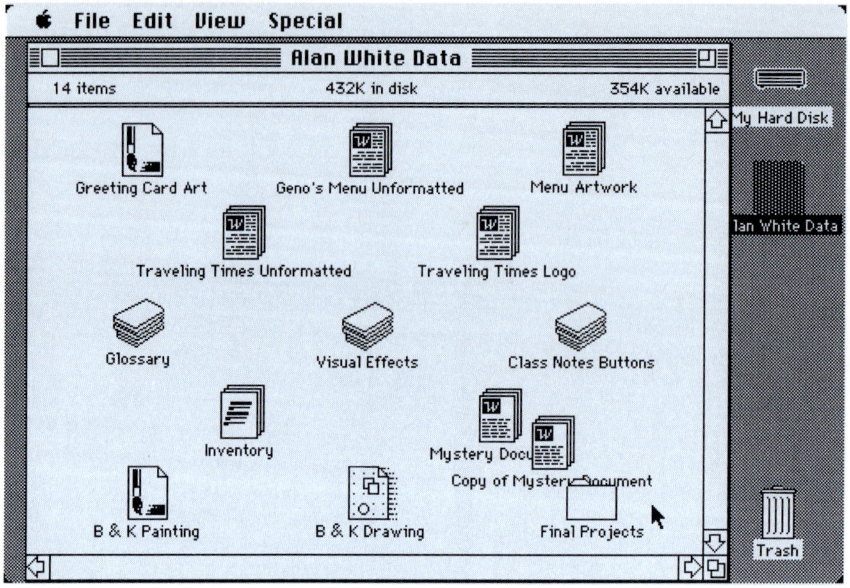

Figure 1-25   New Final Projects folder

DRAGGING A DOCUMENT INTO A FOLDER

The main use for folders is to help you organize many files on a disk by placing them into folders where you will be able to locate them as you need to access the information they contain.

Putting a document into a folder is a matter of dragging its icon onto the icon of the folder and releasing the mouse button.

➡ Using what you have learned, drag the icon representing **Copy of Mystery Document** into the **Final Projects** folder.

The Final Projects folder will be highlighted when the cursor gets on top of it. When you release the mouse button the Copy of Mystery Document icon will disappear.

How can you tell if the document was really moved into the folder? Open the folder and take a look.

➡ Double-click on the **Final Projects** folder to open its directory window.

When the window opens, part of the document's name may be missing on the left. If it is, you can click in the left scroll arrow so that the entire name becomes visible.

Your screen should now look like the one shown in Figure 1-26.

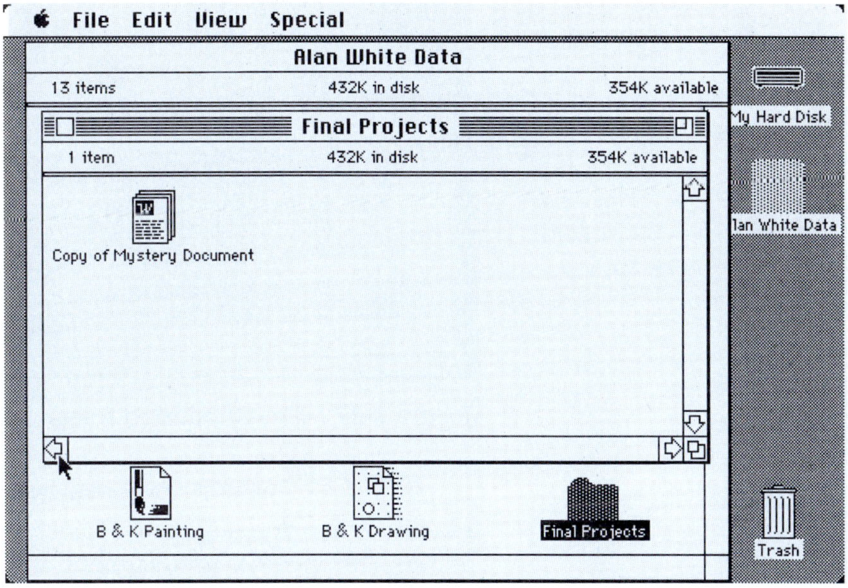

Figure 1-26   The document after dragging it into the folder

Now that you have verified that the document is really inside the folder, you can close the folder.

⌘-W   ➥   Close the window by choosing **Close** from the File menu or by clicking in the window's close box.

DUPLICATING A FOLDER

You have seen how easy it is to duplicate a disk and a document. Now let's duplicate a folder. Duplicating a folder is very similar to duplicating a document.

➥   Select the **Final Projects** folder.

⌘-D   ➥   Choose **Duplicate** from the File menu.

In a couple of seconds you will see another folder appear on your desktop. (see Figure 1-27).

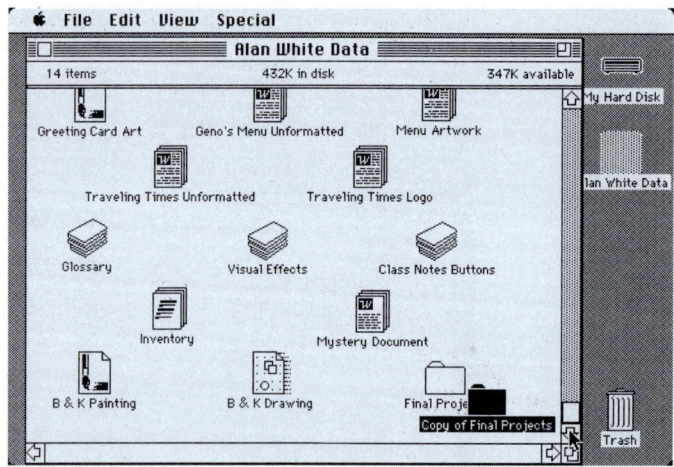

Figure 1-27 The duplicated folder

Duplicating a folder is similar to duplicating a document, but not exactly. When you duplicate a folder, its entire contents are duplicated as well. This includes all documents in the folder and even other folders and their contents that are located within the selected folder.

This means that you now have two documents named Copy of Mystery Document. One is contained in the Final Projects folder, and the other is in Copy of Final Projects.

If the folder you select for duplication has a lot of information in it, the duplication process may result in more information than the disk has room to store. In this case, your Macintosh will inform you and will terminate the duplication process.

ERASING A FOLDER AND ITS CONTENTS

This is all you will be doing with the Copy of Final Projects folder and its contents, so you can now erase it from your disk.

➡ Drag the icon of the **Copy of Final Projects** folder into the **Trash** and release it there.

Be sure that the Trash is highlighted (turns black) before you release the mouse button; otherwise, the folder will be placed close to the Trash but will not go into it. You can tell if you were successful in putting the folder into the Trash in a couple of ways.

If the folder icon disappears and the sides of the Trash bulge, the folder was placed inside the Trash (see Figure 1-28). If you can still see the folder icon next to the Trash, the folder is just on top of the Trash and not inside it.

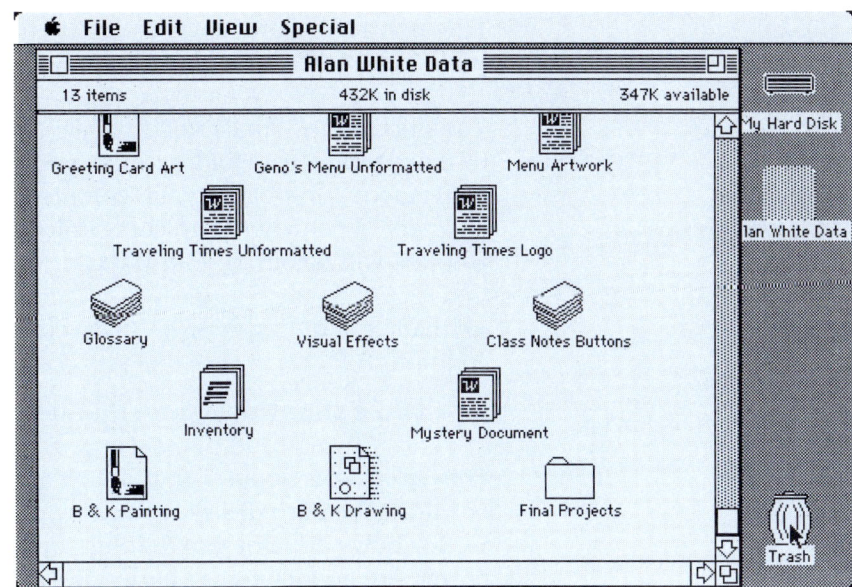

Figure 1-28   The Trash bulges when there is something inside it.

Warning: Dragging a folder into the trash will erase not only the folder, but also all of its contents. This includes any folders it contains and all of their contents. Before dragging a folder into the Trash, be sure that it does not contain other folders whose information you want to keep. You can accidentally erase a lot of information from your disk by not being aware of what is inside a folder before putting it in the Trash.

As long as the Trash's sides still bulge, you can open the Trash and remove any of its contents by dragging the icon(s) back where you want it. When the Trash is emptied, the files that were in the Trash are erased from the disk and cannot be retrieved.

There are several ways to empty the Trash. You can choose **Empty Trash** from the Special menu, start any application, or choose **Shut Down** from the Special menu. All of these methods empty the Trash and erase whatever was inside it.

In this case, you know what is in the Trash, and you are sure you want to delete it.

➧   Select **Empty Trash** from the Special menu.

➧   Click the up scroll arrow to make the top row of icons visible again.

ERASING A DOCUMENT

You have learned how to duplicate documents, disks, and folders. You have learned to move an icon around inside a window. You can move a document into a folder, and you know how to erase unwanted information.

➧   Using what you have learned, open the **Final Projects** folder and drag **Copy of Mystery Document** into the **Trash**. Empty the Trash and close the **Final Projects** folder.

This will leave your data disk set up for completing the rest of the projects in *A Macintosh Journey*.

You still have the Final Projects folder on your data disk. You do not have to make use of this folder unless you want to, but you might find it convenient for storing your completed projects from the following chapters. When you complete a project, you can drag it into this folder where it will be out of your way.

All that remains in this project is to eject your data disk and turn off the computer.

➡ Choose **Shut Down** from the Special menu.

This ejects any floppies that are in any of the Mac's disk drives and positions the hard disks for shutting down. A Mac Plus, SE, Classic, or SE/30 shows a dialog box telling you that you can now turn off the power. Any model in the Mac II series automatically shuts the power off to the computer.

Congratulations! You have completed this project.

This completes your quick tour of using the Macintosh and setting up a data disk. Although the Finder and other programs on the Mac do much more than you have seen so far, you have touched on many of the basics you need to know to get started.

For more detailed information on using the Macintosh, see *Reference Guide to Your Macintosh*, a reference that covers Macintosh subjects in alphabetical order by topic. It also includes an overview of Macintosh systems. Refer to the glossary in this book for defnitions of key terms used in this book.

If you want more background about computers in general, continue with Chapter 2.

If you are anxious to start working, turn to Part II and continue there.

SUMMARY

- The Macintosh employs a graphical user interface consisting of windows, menus, icons, dialog boxes, buttons, and the use of a mouse for a person to interact with the computer.

- Windows have title bars, close boxes, and zoom boxes. A window contains information that varies depending on the application that created the window.

- Only the topmost window is active, and all action takes place in the active window. Active windows are indicated by title bars and other visible controls, such as scroll bars, that are not present in inactive windows.

- Disks are used to store information in a form that is readable by computers. Disks must be formatted, or initialized, before they can be used to store this information.

- Disks are organized by the use of folders on the Macintosh. Folders may be placed inside other folders, a process that is known as nesting.

- Moving the mouse moves a pointer on the screen and allows the user to interact with the computer by pointing at icons that represent objects and by clicking, dragging, or double-clicking the button on the mouse. The pointer changes shape depending upon the task being performed. In some applications, the pointer can take many shapes.

- To issue a command to the Macintosh, point at a menu name, pull down the menu, and select a menu item from the list. Command-key equivalents are combinations of key presses that substitute for using the menus to issue commands with the mouse.

- The Finder is an application that allows the user to organize and rearrange the storage of information on disks, to copy and move files and folders, and to open applications. The Finder is the program that provides the desktop when you first start your Mac.

KEY TERMS

active window
Apple menu
application program
arrow pointer

backup

click
close box
Command key
Command-key equivalent

default
desktop
destination disk
dialog box
dimmed
directory window
disk drive
document
double-click
dragging an icon
DSDD disk

Edit menu
Enter key

file
File menu
Finder
floppy disk
folders
formatting a disk

graphical user interface

hard disk
high-density disk
highlight

I-beam pointer
icon
initialize

menu
menu bar
menu item
mouse
mouse button

nesting folders

Option key

pointer
pull-down menus

Return key

scroll bar
Shift key
Shift-click
source disk
startup disk
System Folder
system program

title bar
Trash
window
wristwatch pointer
zoom box

COMMAND KEYS AND SHORTCUTS

File Menu			**Edit Menu**		
New Folder	⌘ -N		Undo	⌘ -Z	
Open	⌘ -O		Cut	⌘ -X	
Close	⌘ -W		Copy	⌘ -C	
Duplicate	⌘ -D		Paste	⌘ -V	
			Select All	⌘ -A	

Chapter 2: Computer Concepts

What You Will Learn in This Chapter

After reading this chapter, you should be able to:

- Understand some of the concepts and terminology applicable to personal computing

- Name the two main categories of software

- Name the standard parts of a computer system

- Name the most common peripherals attached to a computer

If you are new to computers, this section should help you understand some of the concepts and terminology used in data processing. If you already have experience with computers and are anxious to start working, you might want to skip the general discussion and go straight to Part II.

A BRIEF OVERVIEW OF TERMS

In personal computing, as in all other technical areas, a standard terminology is used by the people working in that field. Sometimes the terms are used only in a particular area. Other times, words take on a different meaning when they are used as technical jargon from when they are used in ordinary conversation. The computer field is filled with examples of these words and phrases.

Some examples of terms that have a different meaning when referring to computers and the use of computers are: bug (error), debug (find and correct errors), and bomb or crash (the program encounters a problem and stops working properly). This is only a small sample of a large group of such words.

In addition to redefining some words, the computer industry constantly uses acronyms, such as ROM (read-only memory), RAM (random access memory), SCSI (small computer system interface), GUI (graphical user interface), and WYSIWYG (what you see is what you get).

Believe it or not, almost all of the computer-related acronyms you will encounter are pronounceable, and in ordinary speech those of us who use this terminology pronounce them; we don't spell them as you might expect. For example, RAM and ROM are obviously pronounceable, SCSI is pronounced "scuzzy," GUI is "gooey," and WYSIWYG is spoken as "wissy-wig" or "wizzy-wig."

You will encounter a number of these terms in any book that discusses computers. Many are defined and explained in the following sections of this chapter.

PARTS OF A COMPUTER SYSTEM

There are three main components of a computer system: hardware, software, and people.

You may be so new to using computers that you don't know how to turn one on, or you may have many years of experience with other computers. Either way, you are about to set out on a journey that will increase your knowledge of computers and enhance your skills in using them.

Hardware and software are the terms used for equipment and programs, respectively. Many people have a difficult time at first understanding what these terms mean. The *hardware* part is easy. If you can touch it, it's hardware. The equipment that makes up the system is the hardware.

Software

Software is a little more difficult to grasp because it is an abstraction. Information and methods for solving problems are known as software. When using a computer, you process data (or facts) to produce information. The methods for solving problems or performing tasks are called *algorithms*. When you combine data and proper algorithms you produce a *program*. All of these—data, information, algorithms, and programs—are known as software. This is one of the reasons it can be a confusing term. However, *most* of the time software means a computer program.

A computer program is a set of steps for the computer to follow to arrive at a particular goal. Part of these instructions allow the computer to interact with you—the user. Other instructions tell the computer to accept data, modify it, output it, and store it for further use.

Usually, when someone refers to software, they mean a program, such as Microsoft Word or MacPaint. Since "software" and "program" are synonymous, it is redundant to call something a software program.

Software is divided into two categories: *system software* and *application software*.

System Software

System software is a program that controls the interaction among different parts of the computer system or between the user and the system. It allows you to find information on the disk, make copies of it, and send it to the printer as well as many other tasks. The *Finder* is the system software on the Macintosh that allows you to control the system and the information it contains.

Application Software

Application software is designed to allow you to complete a task. If you want to write a letter or a book, you use a word processor, such as Microsoft Word. To produce a budget or cash flow analysis, you use a spreadsheet, such as Excel. If you have a list of customer information, you store it using a database or file management program, such as FileMaker or HyperCard.

All of these are examples of applications. They are not designed to facilitate your interaction with the computer system; they are designed to allow you to complete a task.

Application software on the Macintosh is available for purchase from many third-party companies. This means that neither you nor Apple Computer produced this program. If you want to do the tasks a program allows, you can purchase the program from whomever produced it— Microsoft, Claris, Apple, and so on—and use it on your computer.

Hardware

The software tells the hardware how to do tasks. The hardware performs the operations and handles the flow of information. The hardware comprises a central processing unit, memory, storage, and input/output peripherals.

Central Processing Unit

The *central processing unit*, or *CPU*, is the part of the computer that processes information. This is the part of the computer that controls data flow and the interaction among other hardware components. It performs arithmetic calculations and logical operations.

The CPU accesses and controls the computer's memory and directs the flow of information into the system and out of it. The CPU performs the tasks that convert data into the information you need from the system.

In a microcomputer, this CPU is on a single *microprocessor*. You may have heard of a microprocessor being referred to as a "computer chip." The MC68000 is the microprocessor, or brain, used in the first generation of Macintosh computers (128K, 512K, 512Ke, Plus, SE, and Classic) and the

Macintosh Portable. The "sixty-eight thousand" is produced by Motorola, and it and its descendants provide the computing power for the Macintosh line of computers.

The second generation of Macintosh computers (Mac II, Mac LC) uses a newer and more powerful processor—the MC68020. The "sixty-eight-oh-twenty" runs at a faster speed and processes information more quickly than the 68000. This in turn was followed by the MC68030, which is even more powerful and faster and is found in the Macintosh SE/30, IIx, IIcx, IIci, IIsi, and IIfx computers.

Newer and more powerful microprocessors are in the works (such as the MC68040), and Apple will undoubtedly introduce computers that use them as they become available. Change is inevitable in the world of computers.

Memory

Memory in a computer is a group of integrated circuits where information can be stored and from which the CPU can access and read this information.

There are essentially two types of computer memory: *ROM* and *RAM*. *ROM* means *read-only memory*. This is a type of *permanent* storage. ROM retains its contents even when the power is removed from the system. However, it cannot be modified by a user. Once the information is stored in ROM it stays there for the life of the chip. On the Macintosh, the instructions that produce windows, pull-down menus, and other parts of the Macintosh user interface are stored mostly in ROM.

The second type of memory is *RAM*, or *random access memory*. It is not truly random access; it is really direct access, but probably nobody wanted to call it DAM memory. (If computers really had random access memory, it would be quite a trick to get any work done.)

Whatever the name, RAM is the changeable memory used to store the information the system is currently processing. This memory is *temporary* (or volatile) storage only. If the power to the computer goes out for a fraction of a second, this memory is erased. When you see the lights blink in a room where people are using computers, it is not uncommon to hear various socially unacceptable phrases uttered by users who have not recently saved their work onto disks. Any work done since the last time it was saved is usually lost.

*(There is a simple way to protect yourself from losing your work when the power goes out. All you have to do is save your work every ten or fifteen minutes. Get into the habit of doing this. In fact, since many applications support Command-S as the equivalent of choosing **Save**, many Mac users have learned to type this command routinely as they work. You hardly ever hear this group groaning and moaning about losing a day's work when the power goes out!)*

Several arcane-sounding terms are used to describe various amounts of memory. These terms apply to both ROM and RAM.

You have probably heard of *bits* and *bytes*. *Bit* is the contraction for BInary digiT. Computers don't process English, or words or numbers as you are familiar with them. Everything the computer does is in the form of a code. Many ingenious people have devised codes for all types of data storage and representation.

All the computer knows is high voltage or low voltage, on or off, positive or negative. Each of these groups is composed of exactly two conditions. The computer works using binary numbers, which allow only the digits 0 and 1. (This is also known as the base two number system.) For most purposes, one bit is not very useful, so eight bits are combined into a byte.

A *byte* is the smallest unit of storage for most uses. For example, each of the letters that compose this sentence is stored in the computer as one byte. Even the blank spaces are stored as a single character in one byte of the computer's memory.

Often, you need to store more than a few bytes of information, so bytes are grouped into larger units. The next unit of storage commonly used is the *kilobyte*. This is not 1,000 bytes as you might expect; it is 1,024 bytes. (1,024 is a round number in the base two number system: 10000000000_2, which is the binary representation for 2 raised to the 10th power.) You should remember that kilo- (as in kilobyte) means 1,024, not 1,000, when referring to computer storage, even though you will probably tend to think of it as roughly 1,000.

The next unit of storage is the *megabyte*. This is approximately one million bytes (1,024 x 1,024 = 1,048,576). Since humans can't easily remember these kinds of numbers, we don't like to be concerned with the extra 48,000 bytes or so. Megabyte is easier to pronounce and remember, anyway.

Input and Output

If a computer is going to process information, there has to be some means for entering information into the computer and getting it back.

Information is *input* into the computer (reading data) and is *output* from the computer (writing data).

Many forms of input and output are available to computers, depending on which peripherals are attached to the computer. A *peripheral* is a device that is external to the CPU and that allows the computer to interact with the outside world or to store information for later retrieval. Peripherals may be mounted externally to the computer by means of *cables* or may be internally mounted inside the computer's case, where they are connected by cables or by being plugged into *expansion ports* or *expansion slots*.

Expansion slots are places where peripherals may be attached to the computer by plugging in additional electronic circuit boards, and these slots are located inside the computer's case. *Expansion ports* allow peripherals to be attached by means of a cable and may be located internally or externally.

All microcomputers have at least one main *electronic circuit board*. This board holds the microprocessor and other electronic components that make up the computer. The SE and Mac II series of computers all have at least one expansion slot that allows the addition of other circuit boards designed for special purposes. For example, many Macintosh computers are now equipped with large monitors that are capable of displaying one, or even two, letter-size pages at actual size. These monitors require a video card that plugs into an expansion slot on the computer's main circuit board.

The most common peripherals attached to a Macintosh computer are a mouse, keyboard, monitor, printer, modem, disk drive, and tape drive.

Mouse

A *mouse* is a hand-held device that slides on a desktop and allows you to control the position of a *pointer* on the computer screen. The pointer indicates where the next action will take place if you click the mouse button.

A mouse used with the Macintosh has only one button. When you press and release the button, it tells the Macintosh that you want to do something at the position where the pointer is located on the screen.

Most computer systems other than the Macintosh make the user interact mostly through the keyboard, and that can be very frustrating if you are not a touch typist. On the Macintosh, most of your interactions will involve pointing at something and clicking the mouse button.

Although the mouse is the most common pointing device for the Macintosh, many people use alternate devices, such as *trackballs*, which consist of balls mounted in a stationary housing. Moving your hand over the ball causes the pointer to move in the same direction. The Macintosh Portable has a trackball, and they are available for attachment to other Macs as well.

Keyboard

The *keyboard* is used for entering text. Unless you are actually entering text, you don't need to use the keyboard at all. Some people prefer to keep their hands on the keyboard, so most Macintosh programs provide keyboard equivalents to using the mouse and pulling down menus. These keyboard equivalents are also known as *Command-key equivalents*. They allow you to issue commands using the Command key. For example, Command-S often means Save. When a Command key equivalent is available for a particular command, it is listed next to the command on the right side of the menu. Other keyboard shortcuts and Command-key equivalents are listed in the manual for each program.

Monitors

A *monitor* is the TV screen used with a computer. You also will hear this referred to as a *CRT* (cathode ray tube) or sometimes as a *VDT* (video display terminal).

The monitor is the output device you will use the most when working on a Macintosh. As you type, draw, paint, calculate, or compose pages, you will see the results of your actions on the monitor.

This almost instantaneous feedback is what allows you to interact so intuitively with the Mac. As you do something with the mouse or keyboard, it is shown on the screen. As the computer performs an operation, you can quickly see the results.

Some models of the Macintosh only support black-and-white monitors. All Macs in the original-shaped case (128K, 512K, 512Ke, Plus, SE, SE/30, Mac Classic) and the Mac Portable come equipped with a built-in black-and-white monitor. The SE, SE/30, and Portable also have slots or ports that make it easy to add other monitors that support color, or that can display a full letter-size page of text or more.

The modular Macintosh computers (II, IIx, IIcx, IIci, IIfx, LC, IIsi) do not come bundled with a monitor. You can choose to add a black-and-white or a color monitor. In fact, if you can afford it, you can add both, or even several of them in any combination to all of these models but the LC and IIsi. Drawbacks to adding extra monitors, however, include the amount of extra RAM required to use them and the delay caused by updating more than one screen.

The standard Macintosh screen has a resolution of 72 dots per inch. *Dots per inch* (*dpi*) refers to the number of dots that are displayed horizontally and vertically by the screen in one inch. As this number (5,184 dots per square inch) increases, so does the resolution of the device. *Resolution* is a measure of how well a device can produce an image. Higher resolution produces clearer images. (The Mac screen, at 72 dpi, has a resolution of 5,184 dots per square inch; a LaserWriter, at 300 dpi, has a resolution of 90,000 dots per square inch. The number of horizontal and vertical dots per inch is a little over 4 times greater, and the resolution improves by a factor of a little more than 16.)

Each dot on the screen is known as a *pixel* (picture element) and is used to represent the information you see. The Macintosh screen uses square pixels so that when a circle or square is drawn on the screen, that is what you see. Many other computers use rectangular pixels that are taller than they are wide, because they were designed for use with text rather than graphics.

Printers

When you have information that you want to preserve or send to someone, you can print it on paper. This is known as *hard copy. Soft copy* is what you see on the screen. It is called soft because it is changeable and transitory.

There are many types of printers. On the Macintosh, you are mostly concerned with two types of printers: ImageWriters and LaserWriters.

The *ImageWriter* is a *dot-matrix printer* capable of printing text and graphics at a resolution of 72 or 144 dpi, depending upon whether you choose *faster* or *better* quality when you print. *Faster* printing uses lower resolution. *Better* uses higher resolution but prints much slower.

The *LaserWriter* was a dramatic development in printer technology when it was introduced. It offered, and continues to offer, much higher resolution than any dot-matrix printer and its output is often referred to as near-typeset quality. The LaserWriter prints 300 dots per inch and supports the *PostScript* page description language, which is a programming language designed to facilitate graphics printing and provide smooth outline fonts. (This includes text, since the characters printed by PostScript are mathematical descriptions of the shapes used to represent those characters.)

LaserWriters come equipped with a set of built-in, high-quality fonts. The LaserWriter Plus, IINT, Personal IINT, IINTX, and Personal IINTX all come with 11 fonts in 35 typefaces. If the font you want to use is not included in this selection, you can download others from your computer. The LaserWriter IINT and IINTX can use more additional, *downloadable* fonts due to their increased RAM. The LaserWriter IINTX also offers the option of attaching a hard disk to the printer so that additional fonts will be readily accessible to the printer.

Modems

Modems are devices that allow computers to communicate with each other over the phone lines. The speed of this communication is increasing. The standard communication speed was 300 *baud* (about 30 characters per second) just a few years ago. Then it went to 1200 baud, and now many people are using 2400, 4800, and 9600 baud over normal phone lines.

If you have a computer, a modem, and communication software, you can access other computers around the world. In computer-to-computer communication, both users have to have a modem and communication software, but you don't have to have the same type of computer. In fact, dissimilar computers, such as IBM PCs and Macs, can communicate using modems. Many people are using their computers and modems to transmit and receive electronic mail.

Storage

Because RAM is temporary memory, you must have some other way to retain information after you turn off the computer. For this purpose you generally use some type of magnetic mass storage such as disks or tapes.

On the Macintosh, *hard disk drives* are the primary form of data storage because of their ability to hold large amounts of information. You should keep a copy of what is on your hard disk, and backing up the information to floppy disks is very popular because every Macintosh has at least one floppy disk drive. *Tape drives*, however, are becoming more widely available and are increasingly popular because they hold so much more information than floppy disks, and backing up using a tape drive is much faster and easier.

Most information is distributed on 3.5-inch *floppy disks* in the Macintosh world. These disks are not really floppy, because they are enclosed in a hard plastic case. Most people just refer to them as disks.

Disks are called permanent, or nonvolatile, storage. However, do not make the mistake of thinking that once you have stored your data on a disk that it will be available forever. Although the information on a disk is nonvolatile, the disk itself has an unpredictable lifetime. Disk technology, in its simplest terms, is a method of storing information magnetically onto very small metallic particles glued to plastic (disks) or aluminum (hard disks). Anything that damages the surface of the disk will cause you to lose any information that might be stored there, and it can even cause you to lose all of the information on that disk.

For this reason, it is standard practice to make *backups* of your information. You can copy a document onto two or more disks. If one of them goes bad, you can use the other backup copy. If you do not have a backup copy, you will probably lose whatever information was stored on that disk.

The number of backups you make, and the frequency with which you make them, depends on how valuable the information is and how difficult it would be to recover or reproduce. Accounting information or important strategic planning documents for a whole company should be backed up frequently.

SUMMARY

- A computer system is composed of memory (ROM and RAM), a central processing unit (CPU), input and output devices, storage devices, and other attached peripherals.

- Computer systems can be divided into two major categories: software and hardware.

- There are two types of software: system software and application software. System software allows various parts of the computer system to interact. Application software is used to solve a problem or perform a task, such as writing a letter or planning a budget.

- Common peripherals attached to a Macintosh computer include a mouse, keyboard, monitor, printer, modem, and storage devices such as disk and tape drives.

- Two main types of printers are most commonly used on microcomputer systems: dot-matrix and laser. Dot-matrix printers have the advantages of being able to produce multiple copies on multipart forms, many can print in color, and they can print on continuous forms such as computer paper, mailing labels, 3x5 cards, and pre-printed checks. Laser printers have the advantages of being faster, quieter, and producing better quality output, but they accept only cut-sheet paper and cannot print on multipart forms.

- Most computer information is stored on hard disks. Since the life of a disk is indeterminate, data is backed up on floppy disks and/or tape cartridges. Floppy disks have the advantage of being available on all computer systems, but backing up large quantities of data is a slow, boring process when using them. Tape drives are optional and cost more, but they have the advantage of being faster and easier to use, and a cartridge stores much more information than a floppy disk.

KEY TERMS

algorithms
application software

backup
baud
bit
byte

cable
Command-key equivalent
CPU (central processing unit)
CRT (cathode ray tube)

dot-matrix printer
dpi (dots per inch)

electronic circuit board
expansion port
expansion slot

Finder
floppy disk
hard copy
hard disk drive
hardware

input
ImageWriter

keyboard
kilobyte

LaserWriter

megabyte
memory
microprocessor
modem
monitor (also called CRT or VDT)
mouse

output   soft copy
                                          software
peripheral   system software
pixel
pointer   tape drive
PostScript   trackball
printer
program   VDT (video display terminal)

RAM (random access memory)
resolution
ROM (read-only memory)

Part II: Graphics

Part II introduces Macintosh graphics.

Chapter 3 presents the basic concepts of graphics applications.

Chapter 4 introduces you to using MacPaint. MacPaint was the first graphics application created for the Macintosh, and it is both fun and easy to use. You will create some drawings of your own in this chapter and copy some existing MacPaint artwork into your drawing.

Chapter 5 teaches you how to use MacDraw II. MacDraw II's ease of use and high quality output make it one of the most popular drawing programs for the Macintosh. You will create drawings using some of MacDraw II's text and layout capabilities.

Chapter 3: Graphics Concepts

What You Will Learn in This Chapter

After reading this chapter, you should be able to:

- See that there is a familiar drawing environment used in a graphics application

- List some uses for computer graphics

- Understand the differences between bitmapped and object-oriented graphics

Most people don't associate fun with a computer, but drawing with a graphics application is just that—fun. The combination of using the mouse, the Macintosh's screen resolution, its graphical user interface, and the LaserWriter creates an environment of easy-to-use, high-quality graphics.

Just how do you go about drawing with a computer? Graphics applications make it easy by providing a familiar environment—your screen acts as the paper, and you have available the various tools you would need for any drawing, such as pencils and paint brushes. You can draw lines and shapes, even perfectly straight lines and perfect circles and squares, without having any special skills. You can paint lines and fill shapes using an array of patterns. Not only can you draw objects in varying shapes and sizes, but you can erase, move, duplicate, flip, invert, rotate, shrink, and stretch your creations. Once you have created your masterpieces, you can save them and copy them into other drawings and other types of documents.

There are endless uses for computer graphics. You can create noteworthy greeting cards, announcements, invitations, signs, posters, and letterheads. You can illustrate term papers and reports, create logos, and design floor plans. You can create decorative mailing labels and illustrated newsletters. Graphics can also make a business presentation impressive. Your imagination is all that limits your uses of a graphics application.

If you don't have the interest or the talent to create freehand drawings, you can use some of the thousands of drawings available from firms whose artists produce some useful libraries of clip art. There are also public domain drawings available from users groups and public domain libraries. Creativity and drawing ability are not prerequisites for using and enjoying a graphics application.

BITMAPPED GRAPHICS

There are basically two types of graphics applications: paint (bitmapped) programs and draw (object-oriented) programs.

Painted, or *bitmapped*, shapes are a collection of dots. Drawing with a painting program consists of turning on or off a series of dots on the screen. If the dot is on, it is black; if the dot is off, it is white.

To modify a shape created in a paint program, you must turn off, or "erase," the dots from the part of the shape that you want to modify. The concepts of painting with a program such as this are relatively easy to understand, and even beginners can quickly master bitmapped drawing techniques.

A dot is also called a *pixel*, for "picture element." A pixel is stored internally as a bit, and a map of these bits and their on or off status is stored for each drawing, hence the term "bitmapped."

The Macintosh screen displays 72 dots per inch, measured both horizontally and vertically, giving each square inch 5,184 dots that can each be either on or off. Paint programs such as MacPaint use each of these pixels to compose the drawing page.

The main drawback of paint programs is the resulting jagged lines and edges of some of the objects when they are printed. This is often referred to as the *jaggies*. Figure 3-1 illustrates the difference between the output of a bitmapped drawing and that of an object-oriented drawing. Notice the jagged curves of the bitmapped drawing on the left.

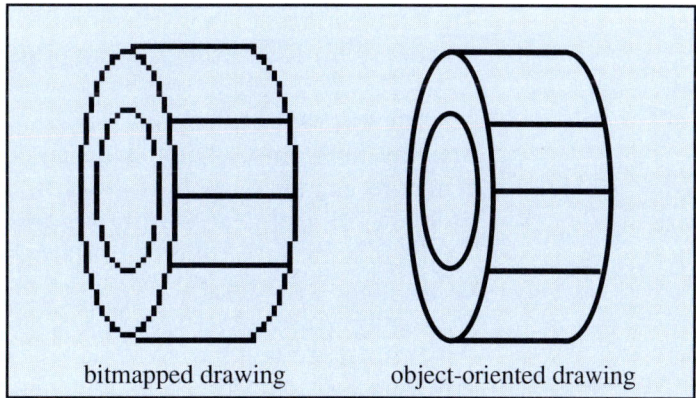

bitmapped drawing   object-oriented drawing

Figure 3-1   Comparison of bitmapped and object-oriented output

There are many excellent paint programs on the market, some of which are more sophisticated that others. MacPaint, FullPaint, DeskPaint, Studio/1, Studio/8, PixelPaint, and SuperPaint are all paint programs of varying degrees of sophistication and difficulty. Studio/8, DeskPaint, PixelPaint, and SuperPaint support color. SuperPaint uses two layers to allow you to paint bitmapped objects on one layer and object-oriented objects on the other.

The bitmapped paint program you'll be using in Chapter 4 is MacPaint.

OBJECT-ORIENTED GRAPHICS

In an *object-oriented* drawing program, each object in the drawing is stored as mathematical information in the computer rather than as a collection of dots.

In an object-oriented drawing you can move one item on top of the other and the "foreground" item does not "erase" the item it obscures, like it would in a bitmapped program. You also use a different technique to edit object-oriented images. Objects cannot be edited dot-by-dot as bitmapped images can. Modifying an object-oriented item is easier, since you can resize an item and change its fill pattern, line pattern, and thickness without redrawing it.

Using an object-oriented program is different from using a bitmapped program, and object-oriented programs are generally more sophisticated. Also, the output of object-oriented graphics programs is generally superior to that of bitmapped programs. This is because object-oriented drawing programs use the attributes of each object to create an image that contains as many dots per inch as the printer can produce. Therefore, images to be printed on the LaserWriter will be converted to 300 dots per inch before they are printed.

MacDraw II, SuperPaint, and DeskDraw are examples of object-oriented drawing programs. There are also some sophisticated 3D drawing programs available, such as Pro 3D. Two professional level drawing programs for technical illustrators and artists are Aldus Freehand and Adobe Illustrator. While technically object-oriented, these programs create graphics using the *PostScript* printer description language and work only with PostScript printers, such as the Apple LaserWriter. In PostScript graphics, the description of each drawing element is stored in PostScript, which is the same language that a PostScript printer uses.

You'll be exploring some of the many object-oriented features of MacDraw II in Chapter 5.

SUMMARY

- The mouse, the Macintosh's screen resolution and its graphical user interface, and the LaserWriter have created an environment of easy-to-use and high-quality graphics.

- Graphics applications provide a familiar drawing environment. Your screen acts as the paper or canvas and you have available the various tools you would need for any drawing, such as pencils and paint brushes.

- Drawings created in a graphics application can be saved and copied into other drawings and into other types of documents.

- There are many uses for computer graphics. You can create greeting cards, announcements, invitations, signs, posters, logos, and letterheads. You can illustrate term papers and reports, design floor plans, and incorporate graphics into business presentations. Your imagination is all that limits your uses of a graphics application.

- There are basically two types of graphics applications: paint (bitmapped) programs and draw (object-oriented) programs.

- Bitmapped shapes are drawn by turning on or off a series of dots on the screen. If the dot is on, it is black; if the dot is off, it is white. To modify a shape created in a bitmapped graphics program, you must turn off, or "erase," the dots from the part of the shape that you want to modify.

- In an object-oriented drawing program each object in the drawing is stored as mathematical information in the computer rather than as a collection of dots. It is easier to modify an object-oriented item, since you can resize an item and change its fill pattern without redrawing it.

- The output of an object-oriented graphics application is usually superior to that of a bitmapped application.

KEY TERMS

bitmapped

jaggies

object-oriented

pixel
PostScript

Chapter 4: MacPaint 2.0

What You Will Learn in This Chapter

After reading this chapter and completing the projects in it, you should be able to:

- Position tear-off menus on the drawing window

- Select, move, and duplicate objects

- Use the Shift key for horizontal and vertical constraints

- Change line weights with the border palette

- Draw objects filled with a selected pattern

- Draw lines and unfilled ovals, circles, and rectangles

- Use Zoom In and Zoom Out for detailed drawing

- Position the drawing using the grabber tool and the scroll bars

- Use different brush shapes and patterns

- Copy drawings to the Clipboard

- Paste drawings into a document from the Clipboard

- Use the Flip Horizontal and Rotate commands

- Fill objects using the paint bucket tool

- Add text to a drawing using the text tool

- Save and print documents

MacPaint was one of the first two applications available on the Macintosh, and it set the standard for bitmapped graphics on this computer. These standards are still in effect today, which means users can transfer graphic images for most applications to almost every other application.

Imagine drawing a picture using only the keys on a typewriter and no other tools. Producing graphics on a computer prior to the introduction of the microcomputer just ten years ago was essentially like producing pictures on a typewriter. Using this method of character-based graphics, your picture was formed with whatever characters were available. MacPaint is a good example of just how far we've progressed in the field of computer graphics in the last decade or so.

Instead of trying to paint a picture with a typewriter, wouldn't it be easier to use tools you're already familiar with? Most people started their artistic endeavors using crayons, and when they learned to stay inside the lines they progressed to colored pencils, watercolor sets, charcoal, or pen and ink. With each new tool that was adopted, they were able to overlay new skills on top of the skills that were developed using crayons.

MacPaint allows you to take skills you've already developed and apply them to computer graphics. MacPaint provides tools that you are familiar with, such as pencils, brushes, erasers, and spray cans, and introduces new tools such as those for producing geometric shapes and straight lines.

Remember as a child when you watched your favorite cartoon character on TV and you were amazed and entertained when he or she threw a bucket of plaid paint on a wall? You knew, even as a child, that this couldn't be done in the real world. However, using a Macintosh and MacPaint, if you want to throw a bucket of plaid paint on a wall, you can.

MacPaint 2.0 is the second generation of this program and has all the original features as well as some very interesting new abilities. This chapter will start you on your journey to discovering the fascinating capabilities of MacPaint.

STARTING MACPAINT

MacPaint 2.0

➡ Double-click on the MacPaint 2.0 icon to open a new, untitled drawing window.

Every new document has the title "'Untitled-1' at 100%" until you save it for the first time and give it a name.

The drawing window shows only a part of the 8- by 10-inch area available for drawing.

A *menu bar* runs across the top of the screen:

| ⬥ File Edit Goodies Font Style Patterns Tools |

You'll learn about each menu as you get to it.

GETTING HELP

Many applications provide online help for quick reference when you are using different tools and commands. Unfortunately, MacPaint is not one of these programs. The reference manual you get when you purchase MacPaint is very comprehensive, however, and includes a tutorial as well as detailed descriptions of the features of each tool and command.

SAVING YOUR WORK

The first time you save your document, MacPaint asks you, by way of the dialog box shown in Figure 4-1, where you want your document saved and what you want it to be named. After you have saved it the first time, the next time you choose **Save**, MacPaint assumes you want the document to be saved in the same place and under the same name. Be careful about saving your document in the correct place the first time you save it so you can find it later. The save process is much quicker the second and subsequent times, because you are not prompted for any additional information.

Unfortunately, sometimes people are not careful, and they occasionally lose their work because they save it but do not think about where they are saving it and then can't find it again. Clicking the **Drive** button (see Figure 4-1) toggles between one or more floppy drives and hard drives, depending on the hardware you are using. The Save dialog box shows the name of the floppy disk or hard drive as that drive is selected. You are saving your document on the selected disk or hard drive with the name showing in the Save dialog box. In the dialog box shown in Figure 4-1, the name of the disk, Connie Barlow, is shown in two places. Always be aware of where you are saving your work.

The Save As command is similar to the Save command, except that it enables you to give your document a different name and save it in a different location. Every time you choose **Save As** from the File menu, you are prompted with the dialog box shown in Figure 4-1. This is the same dialog box you see the first time you save your document.

When you use the Save As command and you attempt to save the document with the same name and in the same location as before, you will be asked if you want to replace the old document. This is because no two files in a particular location can have the same name. If you want to save different versions of the same document, use the Save As command and give the document a different name and/or location.

Save your work often—at least every ten minutes, so you never lose more than ten minutes of work. The Command-key equivalent of the Save command, Command-S, is a helpful shortcut. Always save your work before printing.

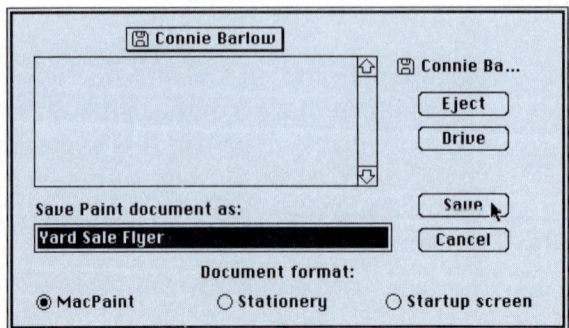

Figure 4-1   The Save dialog box

Be aware that you can save a document before you actually type anything into it, and that many people do it this way. However, you will be given explicit instructions for saving your work at appropriate times throughout the projects in this chapter.

USING MACPAINT'S TOOLS

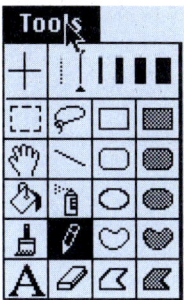

➠ Click **Tools** in the menu bar.

This shows you the *toolbox*. The toolbox is what is referred to as a *tear-off menu*. It can be placed and moved to wherever it is most accessible on the screen. Placing the toolbox on the screen gives you faster access to the different tools and allows you to see at a glance which tool is selected. You can move the toolbox to a different place on your screen if it gets in your way.

To tear off the toolbox, click and drag downward until the cursor goes past its bottom edge. When you do this, the outline of the toolbox follows the cursor around on the screen, as shown in Figure 4-2. Wherever you stop and release the mouse button, the toolbox will remain. The *patterns palette* is also a tear-off menu.

➠ Tear the toolbox off the menu bar and position it in the bottom right portion of the screen, as shown in Figure 4-2.

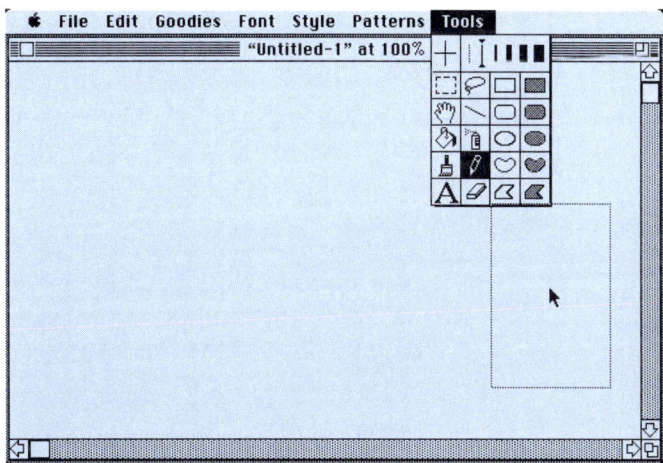

Figure 4-2   The Tools menu is a tear-off menu.

Now that you've got the Tools menu positioned, you'll learn how each tool works, and you'll get practice working with each one before you start the actual project.

Drawing Lines

 The *pencil* is the tool that is automatically selected when you open a new, untitled drawing window. It is used to draw a one-pixel-wide line. You can tell it is selected because it is *highlighted.* When the pencil is selected, the pointer becomes a pencil when positioned over the drawing area.

➡ Hold down the mouse button while you drag the pencil across the drawing window in the direction you want to draw. Release the mouse button when the line is the length you want it to be.

The pencil tool draws a freehand line. The line you draw will be crooked, but you get the idea of how the pencil works. Draw a few lines with the pencil to get the feel of it.

 The *line tool* is used to draw straight lines. When the line tool is selected, the pointer becomes a *cross-beam* (+). As you draw a line you can control the length of the line and its position on the screen. When the line is positioned and sized like you want then you release the mouse button.

➡ Select the line tool by clicking on it in the toolbox.

➡ Hold the mouse button down while you drag the pointer across the drawing window, and release the mouse button when the line is the desired length and angle.

Practice drawing a few more lines with this tool.

Using the Eraser

 Now is a good time to learn how the *eraser tool* works, because you can use it to clear the screen of the lines you just drew. When you select the eraser by clicking on it, the pointer becomes a small square. To erase, hold down the mouse button while dragging across the object you want to erase.

CAUTION Caution: double-clicking on the eraser in the toolbox erases the entire screen. This is a great shortcut if you want to clear your screen. Be sure to click only once on the eraser to select it when you don't want to erase the whole screen.

➡ To get rid of the lines you practiced drawing, double-click on the eraser tool to clear the whole screen, or drag the eraser across the lines to erase them.

Drawing Shapes

MacPaint provides several tools for easily drawing a variety of shapes.

Rectangles and Squares

Unfilled and *filled* rectangles and unfilled and filled *rounded rectangles* allow you to draw rectangles and squares. The unfilled rectangle draws hollow rectangles and squares, and the filled rectangle draws rectangles and squares that are filled with the currently selected pattern in the Patterns menu. The rounded rectangles work the same way, except that they have rounded corners. The pointer becomes a cross-beam when you select any of these shapes.

➠ Click on the unfilled rectangle tool in the toolbox to select it, and then place the cursor in the upper left corner of the screen.

➠ Hold down the mouse button and drag diagonally to the bottom center of the screen, and then release the mouse button.

You use the filled rectangle tools in the same manner.

➠ To change the currently selected pattern, choose **Patterns** from the menu bar, and drag down to the pattern on the palette that you want to use. Release the mouse button while the pointer is on the desired pattern.

If you choose **Patterns** again from the menu bar, you'll see that the wider box on the left side of the first row reflects the *currently selected pattern*, as shown in Figure 4-3.

Figure 4-3   The currently selected pattern in the Patterns menu

➠ Click on the filled rounded rectangle, and draw a rectangle in the same manner as you did the hollow rectangle. It is filled with the pattern that you select or with the default pattern.

To draw a perfect square, hold down the Shift key while using the rectangle tools.

➠ Draw a few filled and unfilled squares, rectangles, rounded squares, and rounded rectangles for practice, and then clear the screen with the eraser tool when you're ready to go on.

Ovals and Circles

The unfilled and filled ovals are used to draw ovals and circles. The unfilled oval draws hollow ovals and circles, and the filled oval draws ovals and circles that are filled with the selected pattern. The pointer becomes a cross-beam when you select either of these shapes.

➡ Click on the filled oval tool in the toolbox to select it, select a pattern from the Patterns menu, and then place the pointer in the center of the screen.

➡ Hold down the mouse button and drag diagonally to create an oval. Release the mouse button when the oval is the shape and size you want.

To draw a perfect circle, hold down the Shift key when using either of the oval tools.

➡ Draw several circles and ovals using both of these tools, and then use the eraser to clear the screen when you are ready to go on.

Freehand Shapes

The unfilled and filled *freehand tools* allow you to draw curved irregular freehand shapes, either filled with the currently selected pattern or hollow. The pointer becomes a cross-beam when you select either of these tools.

➡ Click on the filled freehand tool in the toolbox to select it, and then hold down the mouse button while you drag the pointer to create the shape of a banana on the screen. Release the mouse button when the lines are connected to close the shape.

Polygons

The unfilled and filled *polygon tools* allow you to create angular shapes consisting of different angles and short connected lines, such as L-shapes and stars, either filled with the currently selected pattern or hollow. When you select either of these tools the pointer becomes a cross-beam.

➡ Select the unfilled polygon tool from the toolbox, and click once on the screen to create a starting point for your polygon.

➡ Move the pointer about one inch to the right, and then click again to *anchor* that line.

➡ Move the pointer in a different direction this time, and click again to anchor the new line, as shown in Figure 4-4.

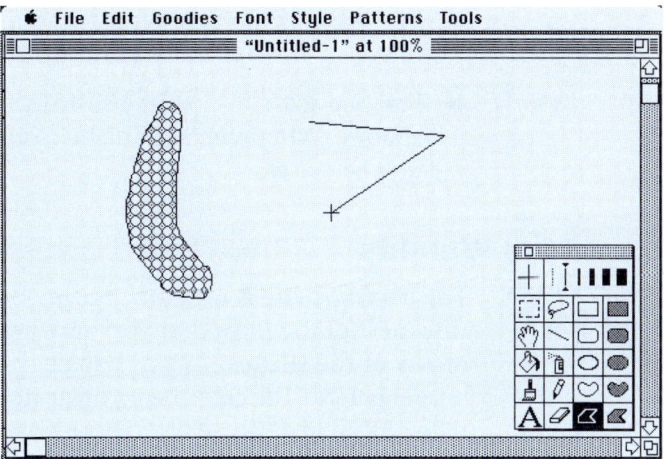

Figure 4-4   Shapes drawn with the freehand and polygon tools

➡ When you've drawn all the angles and lines that you'd like in this polygon, double-click on the screen where the last line should end to finish the polygon and release the polygon tool.

When you've finished practicing with these tools, use the eraser to clear the screen.

Painting

The *spray can tool* is used to spray a "mist" of the currently selected pattern onto the drawing area. You can make the mist more dense by moving the pointer repeatedly over the same area. The pointer changes to a series of small dots when this tool is selected.

➡ Click on the spray can in the toolbox to select it, and then move the pointer into the drawing window.

➡ Hold down the mouse button and drag the pointer across the screen, moving the mouse in a side-to-side motion. Release the mouse button when you've painted the desired area.

When you've finished experimenting with this tool, double-click on the eraser tool to clear the screen.

The *paint brush tool* lets you paint brush-strokes of the selected pattern. There are many *brush shapes* available. You access them by double-clicking on the paint brush tool. The pointer changes to the currently selected brush shape when this tool is selected.

➡ Double-click on the paint brush tool in the toolbox to display the selection of brush shapes available.

➡ Click once on any of the brush shapes to select it, and then position the pointer in the drawing window.

➡ Try writing your first name by holding down the mouse button and dragging the pointer around in the drawing window.

➡ Practice with the paint brush using different patterns and brush shapes. When you are finished, clear the screen by double-clicking on the eraser.

Using Different Line Weights

The *border palette* is used to change the weight of a line. It affects the thickness of the lines that you draw with the line tool and the borders of any of the shapes. When you click on one of the *line weights* in the border palette, the cross-beam indicator on the left of the border palette reflects the currently selected horizontal and vertical weights of the line. The position of the small triangle above the line controls the vertical line weight, and the position of the triangle below the line controls the horizontal line weight, as shown in Figure 4-5.

Figure 4-5   Different horizontal and vertical line weights

Entering Text

The *text tool* allows you to add text to a drawing. The text characters are created in the type style, or *font*, that is selected from the Font menu. The options in the Style menu also apply to the text you type. When you select the text tool, the pointer changes to an *I-beam*.

➡ Click on the text tool to select it, and then move the pointer into the drawing window.

➡ Click in the center of the drawing window to set the insertion point.

The *insertion point* is where the text will begin on the screen, and it is represented by a small, blinking vertical line.

➡ Choose a font of your choice from the Font menu by dragging to a font name and releasing the mouse button.

➡ Choose one of the larger font sizes from the Style menu by dragging to a size and releasing the mouse button.

Font sizes are shown in *points*. Since there are 72 points, or dots, per inch on the Macintosh screen, a 72-point character is 1 inch high, and 36-point type is $1/2$ inch high.

➡ Type your name. If you make an error, press the Backspace key (Delete key on some keyboards) to delete the incorrect characters and then retype. To go to another line, press the Return key.

MacPaint's text capabilities are very limited. As long as you do not click the mouse button to reset the insertion point, you can backspace to delete and correct mistakes. Once you have moved on to another tool or have clicked elsewhere on the screen, you can no longer use the Backspace key to delete characters—at that point you must retype.

Selecting Objects

In MacPaint, as in most Macintosh applications, you have to point out an object that you want to do something with, and then you either issue a command or take some action with the mouse. You *select* something as a means of pointing it out. For example, to copy an object you select it first, and then you choose **Copy** from the Edit menu. If you didn't select the object first, MacPaint would not know what you wanted to copy.

Two tools are used to select objects in MacPaint: the selection rectangle and the lasso.

Selection Rectangle

 To use the *selection rectangle*, also called the *selection marquee*, you click and drag through an object in a diagonal manner to encompass the selection with a dotted rectangle. The border of the rectangle surrounding the object will look animated—the effect has been described as looking like *marching ants*. The pointer changes to a dotted cross-beam when this tool is selected (see Figure 4-6).

➡ Click on the selection rectangle in the toolbox to select it.

➡ Beginning slightly above and to the left of the name you just typed, click and drag diagonally to slightly below and to the right of your name, and then release the mouse button. See Figure 4-6.

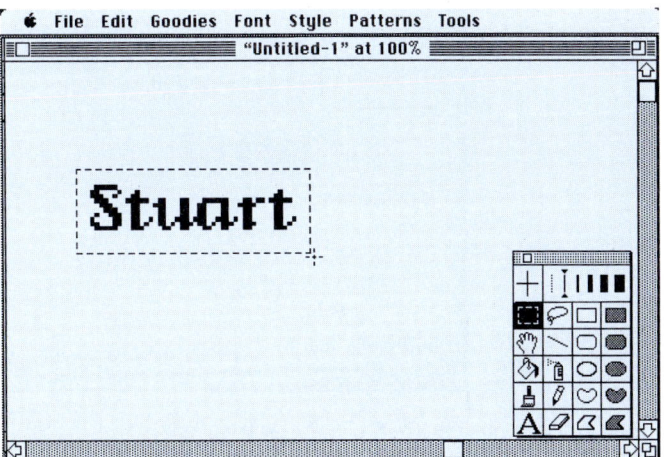

Figure 4-6   Selecting with the selection rectangle

Your name and the white space around it within the dotted rectangle are now selected.

➡ Now that the object is selected you can click within the border of the dotted rectangle and drag to reposition your name on the screen.

To *deselect* a selected object, click somewhere on the screen (outside the selected area) or click on a tool in the toolbox.

➡ Click somewhere outside the selected area to deselect your name.

You can also select the entire contents of your window by double-clicking the selection rectangle in the toolbox.

Lasso

 The other tool used for selecting objects is the *lasso*. The pointer changes to a lasso when this tool is selected (see Figure 4-7).

The difference between the selection rectangle and the lasso is that the selection rectangle also selects all the area inside the rectangle, including the white space surrounding an object, whereas the lasso shrinks to the exact size of the object and selects *only* the object.

➡ Click on the lasso in the toolbox to select it.

➡ While holding down the mouse button, move the lasso around your name on the screen. The line it creates must completely encircle the object you are selecting and must not cut into the object.

When you release the mouse button, the name you selected looks animated, as shown in Figure 4-7.

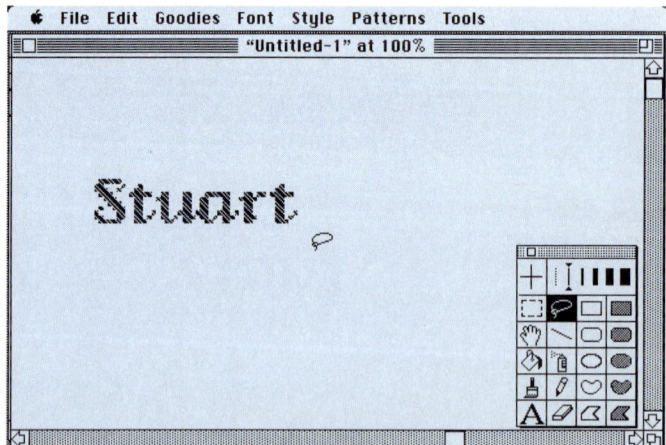

Figure 4-7   Selecting with the lasso

Clicking elsewhere on the screen or in the toolbox will deselect anything that you select with the lasso.

⇒   Without pressing the mouse button, position the pointer on the selected name until the pointer changes from a lasso to an arrow.

If you click while the pointer is not an arrow, it will deselect the selected object. You will need to encircle the object with the lasso again to select it.

⇒   Once the pointer changes to an arrow, click and drag to reposition your name on the screen, and then click somewhere else on the screen to deselect your name.

Whether you use the selection rectangle or the lasso to select objects depends on whether you want the area surrounding the object selected also. The selection rectangle is easier to use, but sometimes you will need the precision afforded by the lasso.

The Grabber

The *grabber tool* is not really used for selecting, but it is used to drag a portion of the window into view. The pointer changes to a hand when this tool is selected.

⇒   Click on the grabber in the toolbox to select it.

⇒   Position the hand on the screen, and then click and drag to shift the position of the page on the screen.

Filling Objects

Filling an object with a pattern involves using the Patterns menu and the paint bucket. The Patterns menu is used to select the pattern that you want to fill the object with.

Patterns Menu

The Patterns menu is a tear-off menu like the toolbox. You can position it anywhere on your screen so you can easily access any of the patterns it contains. The currently selected pattern is shown in the wide box in the upper left portion of the Patterns menu. You click on a pattern to make it the currently selected pattern.

⇒   Choose **Patterns** from the menu bar and select a pattern of your choice by dragging to a pattern and releasing the mouse button when the pointer is on the pattern you want.

Paint Bucket

 The *paint bucket* is used to fill a hollow shape with a pattern. You select the paint bucket and move it so that the drip of the paint bucket is inside the shape to be filled with the selected pattern; then you click once to fill the shape. Be sure there are no *leaks*, or gaps in the border of the shape you are filling, or the paint will "spill out" and fill the background area.

➡ Click on the unfilled rectangle tool to select that tool, and then draw a hollow rectangle about the size of a matchbox somewhere on the screen.

➡ Click on the paint bucket in the toolbox, and, without holding down the mouse button, position the drip of the paint bucket inside the rectangle. Click the mouse button once.

This fills your shape with the selected pattern. Use the eraser to clear the screen when you've finished experimenting with this tool.

Project 1: Creating a Flyer

This project teaches you how to use MacPaint to create a flyer advertising a yard sale. You'll use most of the tools in MacPaint's toolbox to create the different shapes and pictures, and you'll use the text tool to create the body of the yard sale flyer. The completed project is shown in Figure 4-8.

Trash and Treasure
Yard Sale

4712 Blount Ave.N.W.
(5th house on right)

Friday – Saturday – Sunday
April 7, 8, 9 from 9:00–5:00

Rain or Shine!!!

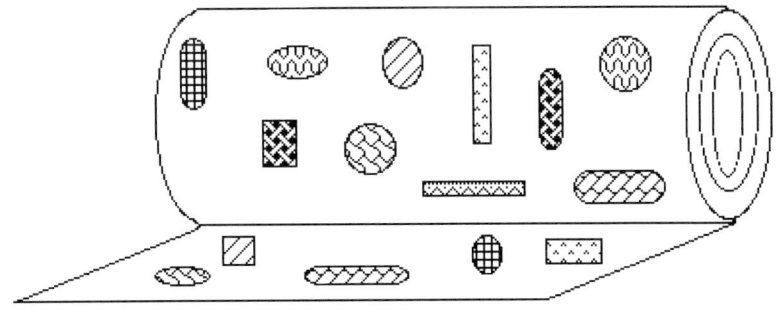

Figure 4-8   Final output of Project 1

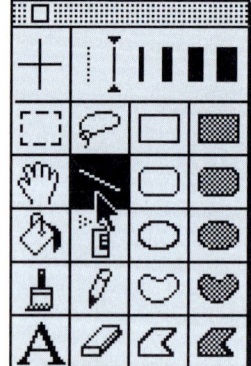

You'll begin the project by drawing the garbage can in the upper left corner of the flyer.

⇒ Select the line tool by clicking on it.

To draw the sides of the garbage can, you'll draw one line and then you'll select it, duplicate it, and flip it horizontally.

⇒ Beginning in the upper left corner of the screen, click and drag the pointer down, angling slightly to the right, to create a line about 2 ½ inches long, as shown in Figure 4-9.

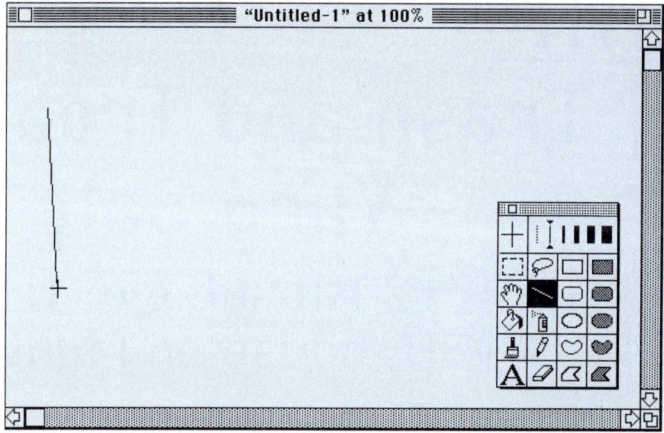

Figure 4-9   Drawing the first line

  ⇒ Next, select the selection rectangle by clicking on it.

⇒ Place the pointer just above and to the left of the line you just drew and, while holding down the mouse button, drag to the bottom right of the line so that a dotted rectangle completely encompasses the line. See Figure 4-10.

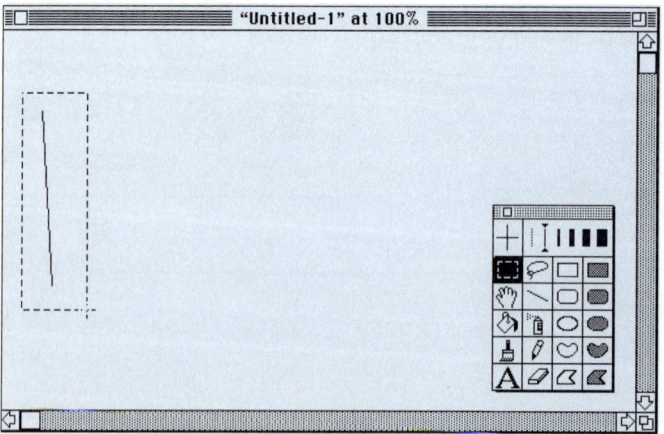

Figure 4-10   Using the selection rectangle

Now the line you drew is selected.

If you press the Backspace key (or choose **Clear** or **Cut** from the Edit menu) while an object is selected, you erase that object from the drawing.

DUPLICATING OBJECTS

Now you'll *duplicate* the line you just selected.

There are a couple of ways to duplicate objects in MacPaint. In each case, the object you want to duplicate must be selected first.

⌘-C   One way to duplicate an object is to choose **Copy** from the Edit menu. This copies it to the *Clipboard*, which is an area in memory that contains the most recently copied or cut item. After copying an object to the Clipboard, you click in your drawing window where you want the

⌘-V   duplicate to be placed, and then you choose **Paste** from the Edit menu. The duplicate object is then pasted into your drawing.

Using the Option Key

Another way to duplicate an object in MacPaint is to hold down the Option key while dragging the selected object to a different position on the screen. This leaves the original object in place and the object you drag becomes the duplicate.

Using the Shift Key

The Shift key is used with the Option key when the duplicate object is to be aligned vertically or horizontally to the original—for example, to *align* objects along their bottom edge, as you want to do in this case.

The Shift key has many other uses. It is used to *constrain* a motion vertically or horizontally. To draw a straight line, you hold down the Shift key while using the line tool. To draw a circle, you hold down the Shift key while using the oval tool. To draw a square, you hold down the Shift key while using the rectangle tool. To erase in a straight line, you hold down the Shift key while using the eraser.

You want the duplicate line you're about to make to align with the original line along the bottom. You'll use the Shift-Option combination to accomplish this.

➡ Press and hold down the Shift and Option keys.

➡ Move the pointer into the selection rectangle that surrounds the line on the screen. While holding down the Option and Shift keys, hold down the mouse button. Now drag the mouse to the right. When the duplicated object is where you want it, release the mouse button. See Figure 4-11.

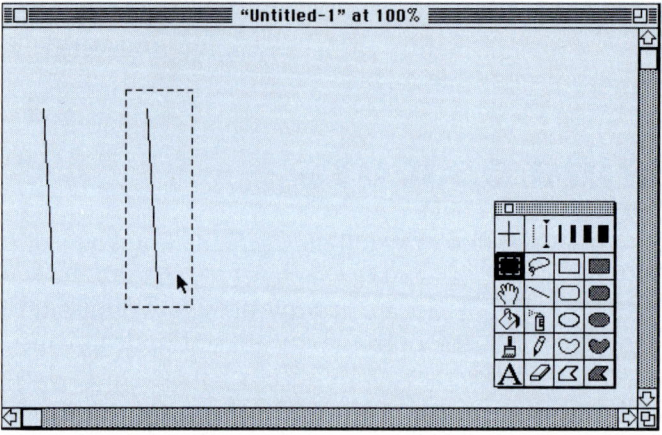

Figure 4-11   Duplicating an object

FLIPPING OBJECTS

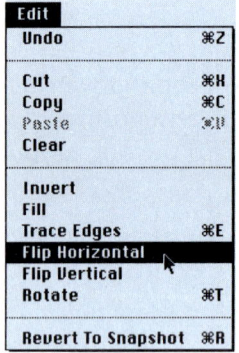

➡ While the duplicated line is still selected, choose **Flip Horizontal** from the Edit menu.

If you deselected the duplicate line by clicking somewhere else on the screen, you must select it again so you can flip it.

Flipping this line horizontally makes the duplicate line have an angle that is the mirror image of the first one. Now you have drawn both sides of the garbage can.

➡ Click on the line tool to select that tool.

➡ To connect the two lines to form the bottom of the garbage can, move the pointer to one end, hold down the Shift key, and draw a horizontal line connecting the bottom ends of the lines, as shown in Figure 4-12.

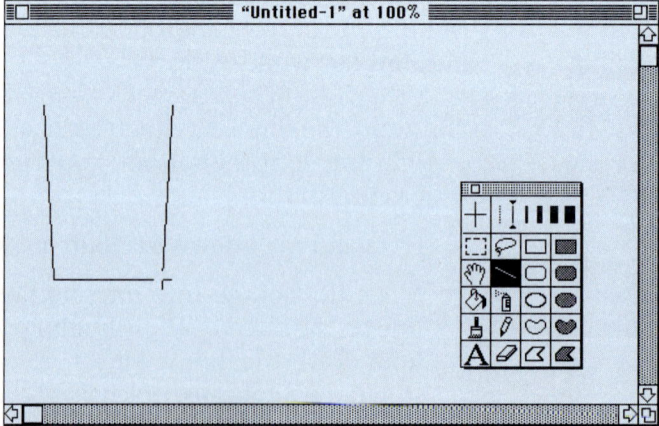

Figure 4-12   Using the Shift key with the line tool

SAVING THE DOCUMENT

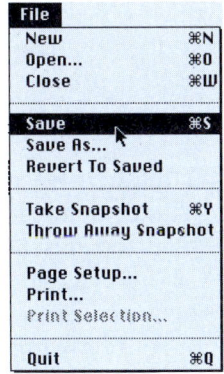

⇒ Choose **Save** from the File menu.

You'll be presented with a dialog box similar to the one shown in Figure 4-13.

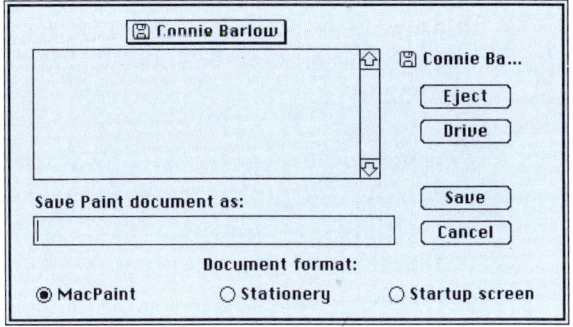

Figure 4-13   The Save dialog box

When saving a MacPaint document, you can choose one of three document formats, as shown at the bottom of the dialog box in Figure 4-13. MacPaint format is the preset option, and it causes the document to be saved as a MacPaint picture. The Stationery option lets you save the document as a template that records the page setup, menu positions, and other preferences. The Startup screen option lets you save the MacPaint drawing as a startup screen that is displayed when you turn on your Macintosh. You will use the default MacPaint format for the projects in this book.

It is important that you save your work in a place where you know it will be when you go back to modify or print that document later. If you are using a data disk, be sure you save your work on it. Since you probably named your data disk when you initialized it, you will want that name to be at the top of the dialog box when it is presented to you, where "Connie Barlow" is showing in Figure 4-13.

⇒ If necessary, click the **Drive** button to switch drives until the name of your disk is showing at the top of the window, as shown in Figure 4-13.

⇒ In the box marked Save Paint document as:, type the name that you want this document to have when it is saved: **Yard Sale Flyer**. Then click the **Save** button.

Your document will no longer be named Untitled, as it has been up to this point—it will come back on the screen with the name Yard Sale Flyer.

After you've named and saved the document once, when you next choose **Save**, it will automatically be saved with the same name, and in the same location, as when you originally saved it.

CORRECTING MISTAKES

As you are working through this assignment, it is likely that you may accidentally do something in the drawing window that you would like to undo. MacPaint gives you a couple of options to use to fix your drawing.

There are several ways to erase in MacPaint. You can erase all or part of an unwanted drawing with the eraser tool. You drag the eraser across an object to erase it, or you can double-click on the eraser tool in the toolbox to erase the entire screen.

Another way to get rid of an unwanted part of your drawing is to select it with the selection rectangle or the lasso and then press the Backspace key (Delete on some keyboards). You can also use the Cut or Clear command from the Edit menu to remove the selected object from the drawing.

When typing with the text tool, you can press the Backspace key to delete the characters you just typed, as long as you haven't clicked elsewhere on the screen or selected another tool. If you have done either of these things, you have to erase the text in some other way and retype it.

Using the Undo Command

One way to undo your *last* action is with the *Undo Command* from the Edit menu. This command allows you to undo the effects created on the drawing window with the *last action of the mouse*. Immediately after you realize you did something in the drawing window that you didn't want to do, and before clicking anywhere else with the mouse, choose **Undo** from the Edit menu. The key words here are *"before clicking anywhere else in the drawing window,"* because MacPaint will consider the last clicking action the one to be undone.

Using the Revert To Saved Command

Another way to correct a mistake takes a certain amount of forethought. *If you always remember to save your document whenever you create anything in it that you definitely do not want to lose,* you'll have no problem using the *Revert To Saved* command in the File menu. This command brings back to the drawing window the last version you saved on disk. Use this command especially when you are trying something that you are not sure will work. Save your work first, experiment, and then you can always use Revert To Saved if your experiment didn't work. No matter how badly you mess up, if you save your work whenever you make a significant change to your drawing window, you can always go back to that last saved version using the Revert To Saved command.

When you choose **Revert To Saved** from the File menu, you are presented with the dialog box shown in Figure 4-14. Clicking **OK** will restore the last saved version from your disk; clicking **Cancel** will cancel the command.

Figure 4-14   Revert To Saved dialog box

Now you're ready to draw thicker vertical lines on the garbage can.

CHANGING THE LINE WEIGHT

You change the line weight by clicking on one of the other weights in the border palette at the top of the toolbox.

➡ Click on the fourth line weight from the left.

➡ While holding down the Shift key so that the line will be straight, draw a thick, straight line down the center of the garbage can, stopping before you touch the bottom line, as shown in Figure 4-15.

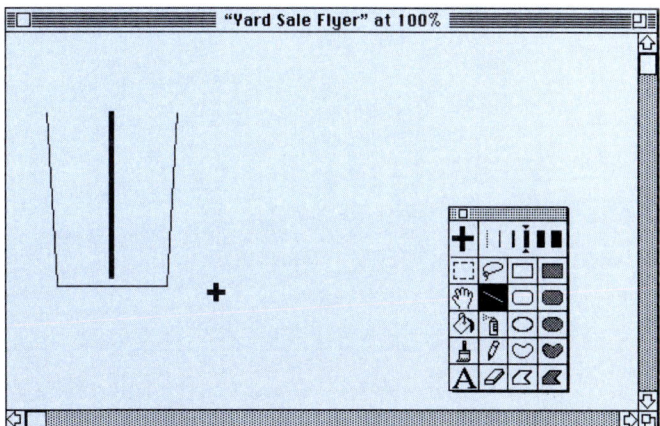

Figure 4-15   Drawing a vertical line with the Shift key

➡ Without using the Shift key, draw some lines on either side of this straight line, spaced about the same distance apart.

Next you'll draw the lid to the garbage can.

➡ Change the line weight back to the second one in the border palette, where the pointer is in Figure 4-16.

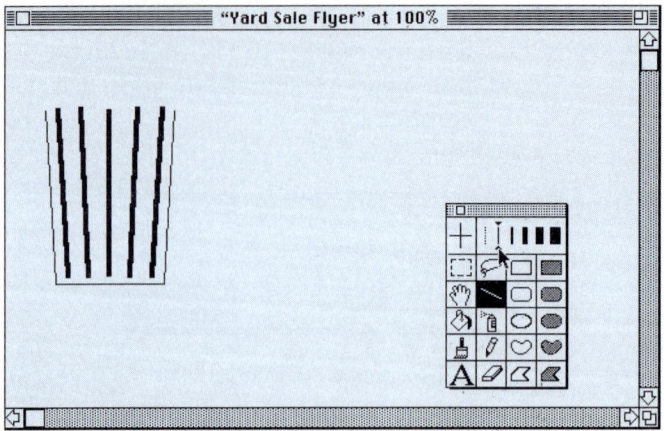

Figure 4-16   Changing the line weight

 ⇒ Select the unfilled oval tool from the toolbox.

⇒ Place the pointer above the garbage can on the upper left, and click and drag to the right to make an oval about the same size as the opening of the garbage can. Do this about 1/2 inch above the can, so you can place the oval on top of the can after it is done, as shown in Figure 4-17.

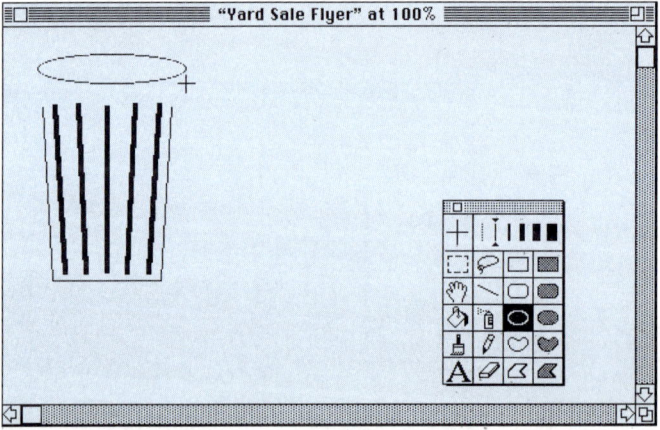

Figure 4-17   Using the unfilled oval tool

SELECTING OBJECTS IN YOUR DRAWING

If you experimented with the lasso and the selection rectangle in the first part of this chapter, you'll recall the difference between them—the selection rectangle also selects all the area inside the rectangle, including the white space surrounding an object, whereas the lasso shrinks to the exact size of the object and selects *only* the object. You want to use the lasso in this case because you want to select only the oval, not any space around it.

 ⇒ Click on the lasso.

➡ While holding down the mouse button, move the lasso around the oval. This line must completely encircle the object you are selecting and must not cut into the object. See Figure 4-18.

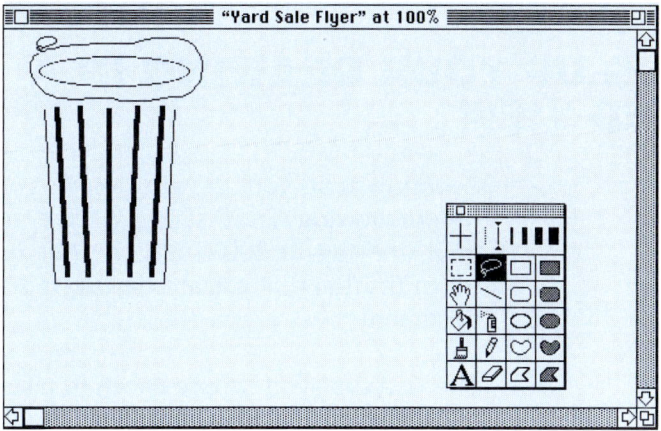

Figure 4-18   Using the lasso tool

When selecting with the lasso, you create a line around the object you are selecting. If you release the mouse button without moving the lasso back to the starting point of that line, MacPaint will close the gap and finish the line between the point where you pressed the mouse button and the point where you released it. This line will be a straight line.

➡ Without pressing the mouse button, position the pointer on the object until the pointer changes to an arrow.

If you click while the pointer is not an arrow, you will deselect the selected object. You will need to encircle the object with the lasso again to select it.

➡ Click and drag the oval down to form the lid of the garbage can, as shown in Figure 4-19. Don't worry about the lines showing through the lid—you'll clean them up in a minute.

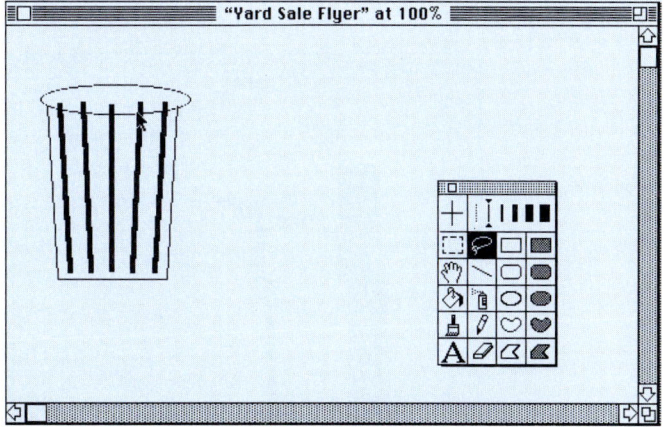

Figure 4-19   Placing the lid on the garbage can

Now is a good time to save your work.

⌘-S ➡ Choose **Save** from the File menu.

Now you need to clean up any overlapping lines on your garbage can lid.

TOUCHING UP YOUR DRAWING IN A MAGNIFIED VIEW

Zooming in on your drawing allows you to work in detail on any part of your drawing. The first time you use the *Zoom In command* you *magnify* your drawing to 200%. In the *title bar* of the window the percent magnification that you are viewing is displayed next to the name of the document.

The next time you choose **Zoom In** takes you to a 400% magnification, and the next time to 800%, or what was originally called *FatBits*. (FatBits is the term used throughout this chapter when referring to the 800% magnification view.) Each level of the Zoom In magnification can be useful for different purposes. FatBits gives you the ability to work in the greatest detail.

  ➡ Click on the pencil tool to select it, and then click once on the lid of the garbage can.

MacPaint zooms in to the most recent point clicked on the screen. Clicking on the lid of the garbage can will enable you to zoom in to precisely that spot.

⌘-M ➡ Choose **Zoom In** from the Goodies menu.

⌘-M ➡ Choose **Zoom In** twice more in succession.

You should now be viewing your document in FatBits, as shown in Figure 4-20.

A shortcut for getting directly to FatBits is double-clicking on the pencil tool.

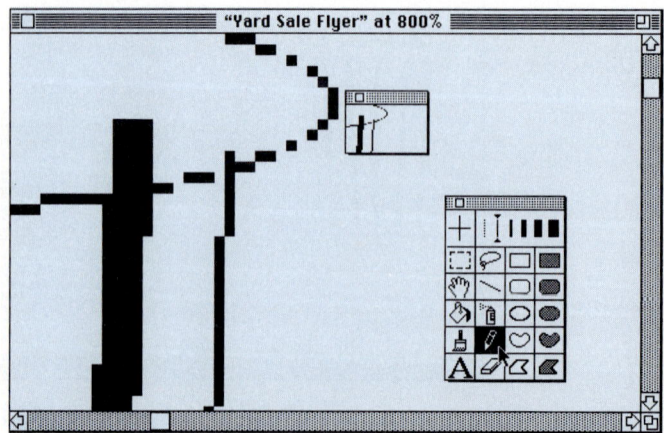

Figure 4-20   Working in FatBits

Notice the small *actual size window*. This reflects your drawing as it appears in the actual (100%) size. You can reposition this actual size window by dragging it around by its title bar, or you can get rid of it by clicking in its close box. If you want to see the actual size window again after closing it, choose **Show Actual Size** from the Goodies Menu.

 ⇒ Select the eraser tool.

While you are pressing the mouse button, the eraser is active. When you release the mouse button, the eraser does not erase.

Caution: *Double-clicking on the eraser will erase the entire screen.* If you accidentally double-click on the eraser, you can always choose **Undo** from the Edit menu.

⇒ Erase the dot created when you clicked on the lid with the pencil, and then the parts of the thick lines that are on the lid, as shown in Figure 4-21.

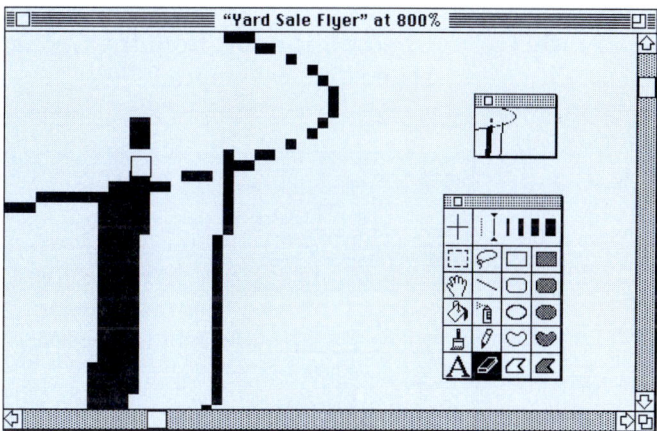

Figure 4-21   Erasing in FatBits

 ⇒ To move to a different portion of the drawing, select the grabber tool.

If you click and drag with this tool selected, it moves the portion of the drawing that you want to work with into view. Imagine it shifting the page across the screen.

⇒ Continue touching up your drawing in this manner until all the parts of the lines that overlapped onto the oval lid have been eliminated.

This is a good time to clean up any overlapping lines that you may have drawn when you drew the base of the garbage can.

 You can erase one dot (or *pixel*) at a time with the pencil tool. If you click in a white area with the pencil it will leave a black dot, and if you click on a black dot that dot will change to white (erasing the dot). All the tools work in the FatBits window and in all the magnification views, but the pencil is probably the most useful in FatBits since you can work at the level of the individual pixel.

⇒ When you are finished cleaning up the garbage can in FatBits, double-click on the pencil tool to take you back to the normal 100% size drawing. You can also use the *Zoom Out command* from the Goodies menu, but that takes you back to 100% size in stages, and it requires choosing **Zoom Out** three times.

Since you've made changes to your drawing that you don't want to lose, now is a good time to save your work.

⌘-S ⇒ Choose **Save** from the File menu.

SHORTCUTS

Double-clicking on the pencil tool is a shortcut when using FatBits. If you would like to learn more MacPaint shortcuts, you can always access a help screen called Shortcuts.

⌘-H ⇒ Choose **Shortcuts** from the Goodies menu. The screen shown in Figure 4-22 will appear.

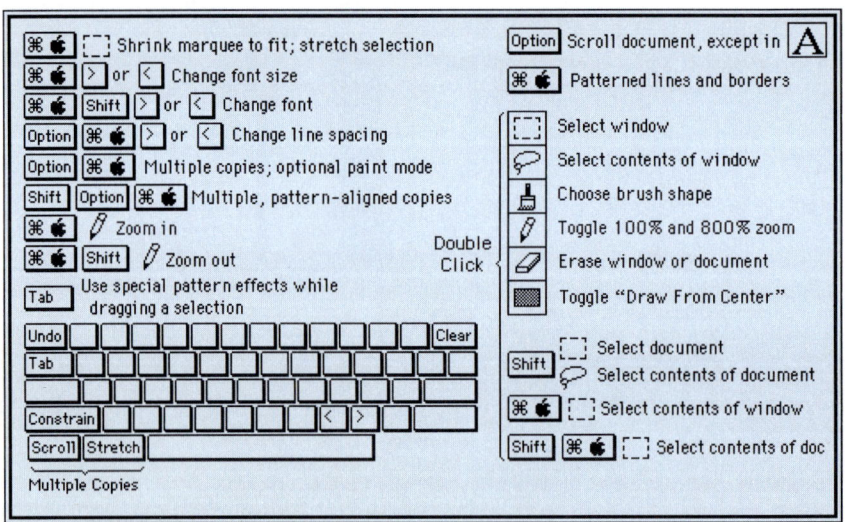

Figure 4-22 The Shortcuts screen

⇒ To return to your drawing window, click anywhere in the Shortcuts screen.

Try out some of these shortcuts. Whenever you need to refresh your memory while working in MacPaint, you can access this option.

ADDING ELEMENTS TO YOUR DRAWING

The last thing you need to do to your garbage can is to put handles on both sides and on the lid.

Drawing Filled Rectangles

You'll use the filled rectangle tool to draw the handles.

➡ Click on the filled rectangle tool in the toolbox.

Since filled rectangle means the object will be filled with a pattern, you'll need to select a pattern with which to fill it.

➡ Choose **Patterns** from the menu bar, and drag the pointer to the first dotted pattern on the second row in the pattern palette to select that pattern for your filled rectangle (see Figure 4-23).

Figure 4-23   Selecting a pattern

➡ Using the filled rectangle tool, draw a small rectangle near the center of the screen, about the size of the one shown in Figure 4-24.

If the toolbox gets in your way, you can move it to a new location by dragging its title bar.

➡ After drawing the rectangle, choose the selection rectangle and select the rectangle you just drew, as in Figure 4-24.

You will duplicate this rectangle so you have a total of three, and then you'll use them as handles for the garbage can sides and lid.

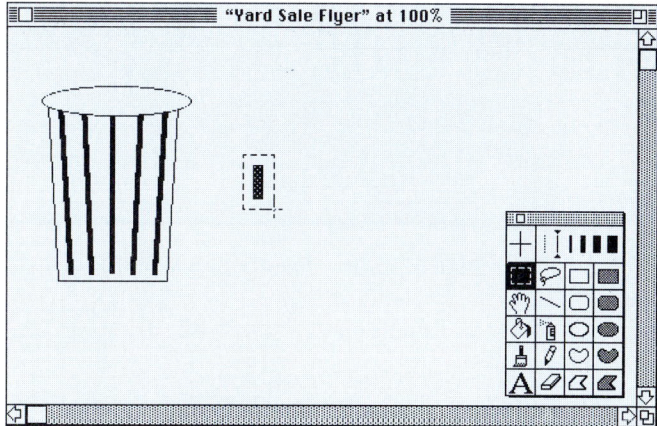

Figure 4-24   Selecting a rectangle

➠ To duplicate this rectangle, hold down the Option key and press the mouse button and drag the selected rectangle. Wherever you release your mouse button, it will leave a duplicate behind. Make three duplicate rectangles, as shown in Figure 4-25.

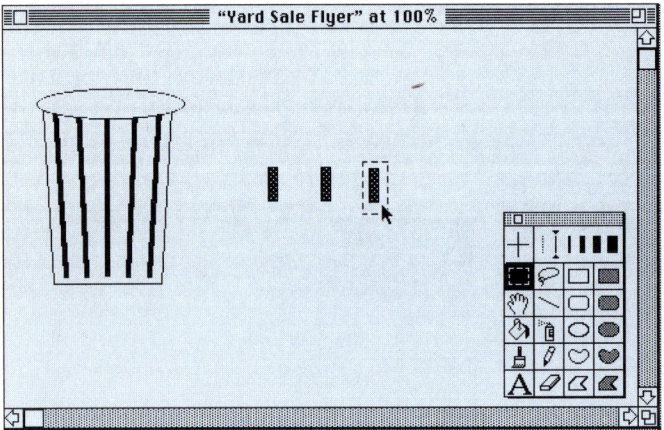

Figure 4-25   Duplicating rectangles

Rotating an Object

➠ While the last of the three rectangles is still selected, choose **Rotate** from the Edit menu.

This will cause the selected object to *rotate* 90° counterclockwise, as shown in Figure 4-26. You'll use this rotated rectangle for the handle on the lid.

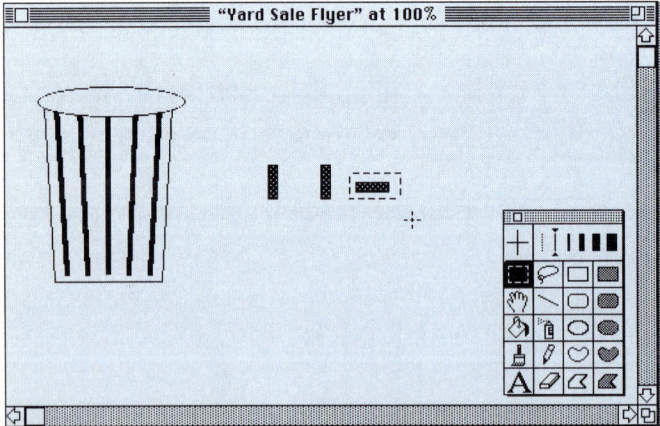

Figure 4-26   Rotating a rectangle

 ➠ Select the lasso, and encircle the first of the three small rectangles.

➡ Move that rectangle to the left side of the garbage can and position it against the can as a handle, as shown in Figure 4-27.

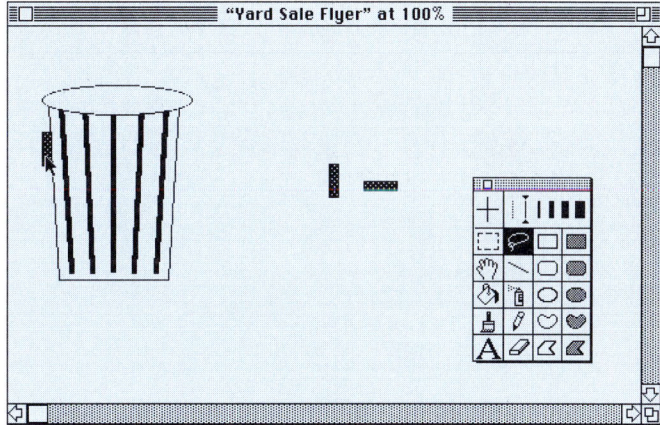

Figure 4-27 Placing the left garbage can handle

➡ Place the other handle on the right side of the garbage can and the horizontal handle on the lid, as shown in Figure 4-28.

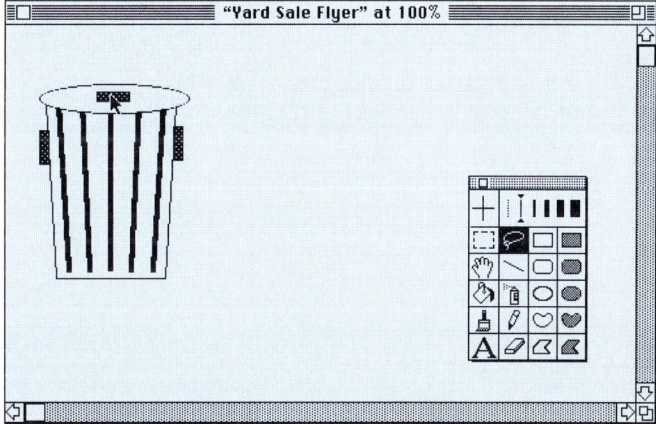

Figure 4-28 Finished garbage can

Your garbage can is complete.

➡ Save your document now by choosing **Save** from the File menu.

Drawing Unfilled Rectangles

The next object to draw is the box of toys.

➡ Move the toolbox to the left side of the screen by dragging in its
title bar, so you can draw in the right side of the screen. In the *scroll
bar* at the bottom of the screen, drag the *scroll box* to the far right so
you'll be working in the right side of the window, as shown in
Figure 4-29.

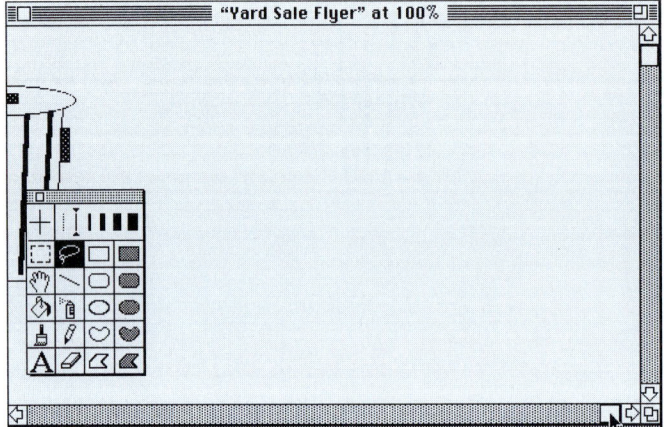

Figure 4-29 Move the toolbox and drag the scroll box

➡ Select the unfilled rectangle tool.

➡ Draw a rectangle about 3 inches long and 1 inch high.

➡ Use the line tool to draw the box flaps on either side of the box, so
your box looks similar to the one shown in Figure 4-30.

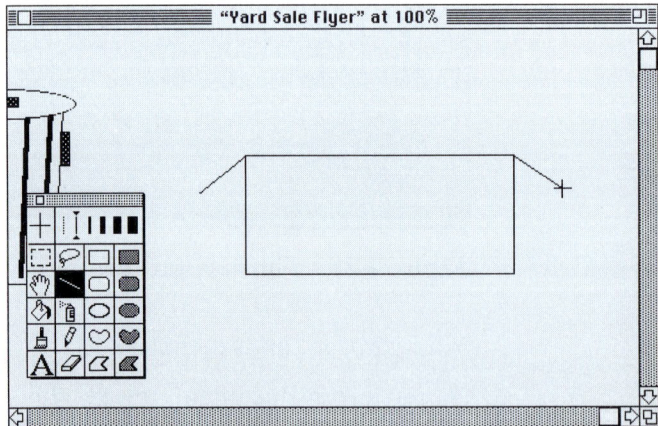

Figure 4-30 Drawing the box and flaps

 ➡ To draw the teddy bear's head, select the unfilled oval tool. While
holding down the Shift key to get a circle, draw a circle about 1 inch
in diameter, as shown in Figure 4-31.

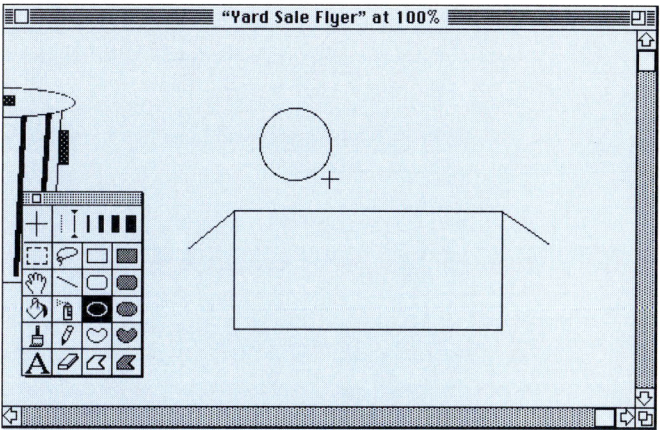

Figure 4-31   Drawing a teddy bear head

Painting with Different Brush Shapes

To draw the ears, nose and eyes on the teddy bear, you'll use some of the paint brush shapes.

➠ Double-click on the paint brush tool.

This brings up a box showing the available brush shapes (see Figure 4-32).

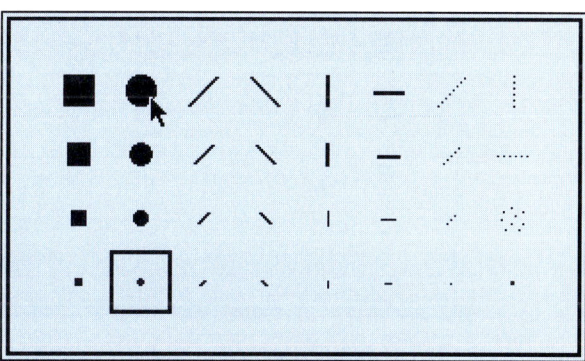

Figure 4-32   Paint brush shapes

➠ Select the largest round brush shape, second from the left on the top row (where the pointer is in Figure 4-32), by clicking on that shape.

Since the current pattern is the one you used to draw the handles on the garbage can, you need to change the pattern back to black.

➠ Click to select solid black on the patterns palette, which is next to the currently selected pattern on the top row.

➡ Draw two ears and two eyes on the teddy bear by clicking this brush shape where you want the black circles. See Figure 4-33.

Figure 4-33   Drawing the teddy bear's ears and eyes

 ➡ Double-click on the paint brush tool again, and this time select the circle that is second from left in the third row down, as shown by the pointer in Figure 4-34.

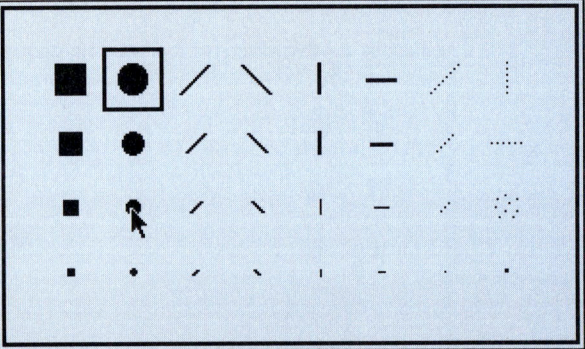

Figure 4-34   Selecting a different brush shape

➡ Draw the nose with this brush shape.

➡ Select the white pattern from the patterns palette.

This is the pattern you'll be using with the paint brush to create the white in the eyes.

➡ Using the white brush shape, click inside each eye of the teddy bear to produce an "eyeball" effect, as shown in Figure 4-35.

Figure 4-35   Adding the teddy bear's eyes

 ⟹ To draw the ball, select the unfilled oval tool. Hold down the Shift key and draw a circle about 2 inches in diameter, like the one shown in Figure 4-36.

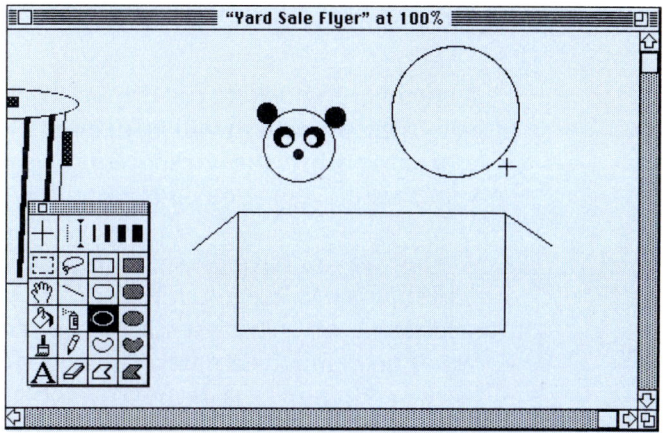

Figure 4-36   Drawing the ball

Filling an Object with a Pattern

Next you'll use the paint bucket tool to fill the ball with a pattern.

 ⟹ Select the paint bucket tool.

⟹ Select a pattern of your choice from the Patterns menu.

It's always a good idea to save your work prior to painting with the paint bucket, since you can accidentally click in the wrong portion of your drawing and fill your whole screen with the selected pattern. For instance, if you used the paint bucket tool inside the garbage can lid, it would paint the whole screen because the oval tool often leaves gaps that the paint can "leak" through. You can use **Undo** from the Edit menu if you don't click somewhere else first.

⌘-S ⟹ Choose **Save** from the File menu.

⟹ Position the drip portion of the paint bucket within the boundaries of the circle you just drew, and then click.

The circle fills with the selected pattern, as shown in Figure 4-37.

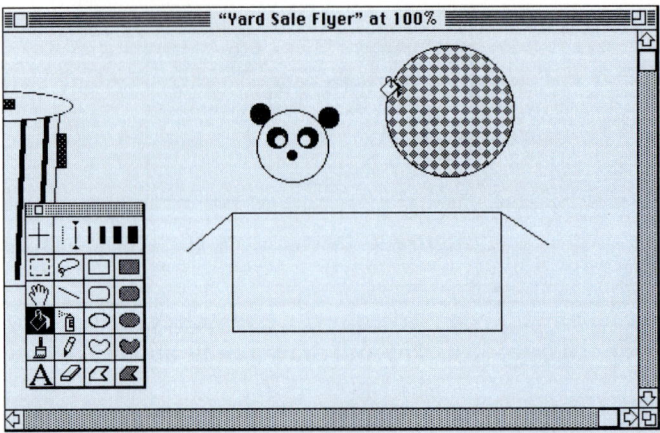

Figure 4-37   Filling the ball

Remember that where the drip of the bucket is positioned determines where the fill pattern will be painted. Each tool has a *hot spot*, and the end of the drip is the hot spot for the paint bucket tool. You need to be very careful where you click when the paint bucket tool is selected.

As soon as you have finished filling the desired object, always select a tool that is less likely to mess you up, such as the pencil or one of the selection tools. That way, if you accidentally click on the screen, you won't do as much damage. The same holds true with the eraser tool—select a different, less destructive tool when you're finished using it.

Moving Objects

Once you've completed the teddy bear's head and the ball, the box needs to be positioned so it looks as though those objects are in the box.

➧ Using the lasso tool, encircle the entire box to select it, as shown in Figure 4-38.

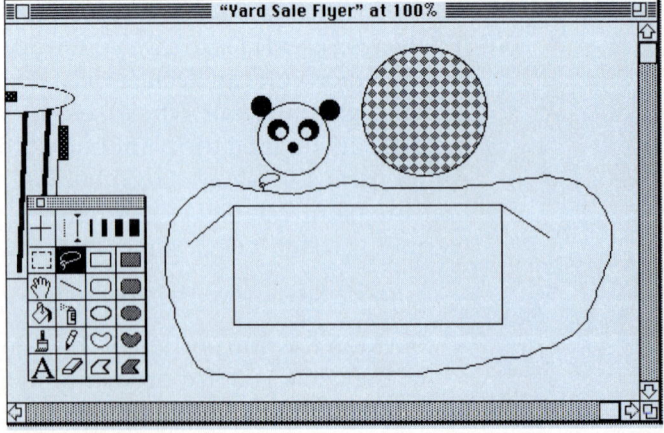

Figure 4-38   Selecting the box with the lasso

➠ Drag the selected box up so that it partially covers the teddy bear's nose.

Now the teddy bear and ball appear to be in the box, as shown in Figure 4-39.

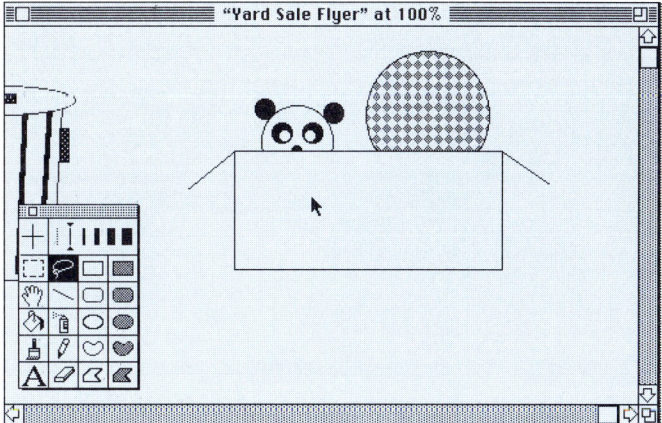

Figure 4-39 The toys appear to be in the box

Drawing Text

The last step to finish this box of toys is to add text to it.

There are two ways to add text to a MacPaint drawing—by drawing it or by typing it. You'll draw the text on the toy box using the paint brush tool, and in a few minutes you'll type the text in the middle of the flyer using the text tool.

➠ Select the paint brush tool, but double-click on it so the selection of paint brush shapes is also displayed. Select the brush pattern that is fourth from the left in the bottom row, as shown in Figure 4-40.

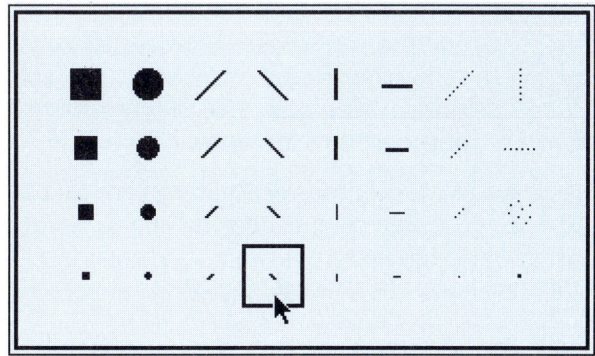

Figure 4-40 Selecting a different paint brush shape

⟹ Change the currently selected pattern to any shade of gray from the patterns palette.

⟹ Position the paint brush inside the box, on the left side, and write **Toys** across the front of the box. See Figure 4-41.

Figure 4-41   Box of toys completed

⌘-S   ⟹ Choose **Save** from the File menu.

Drawing and Filling Additional Objects

That completes the box of toys. Next you'll draw the gaudy roll of carpeting such as you'd find only at a yard sale.

⌘-L   ⟹ Choose **Zoom Out** from the Goodies menu.

This will show you the drawing at 50% of its actual size and a gray area that represents the area outside the drawing.

⟹ Drag the toolbox over to the gray area so it doesn't obscure the drawing area.

Zooming out to 50% view allows you to see three-fourths of the picture at one time so that you can get an idea of the overall effect. All the tools work in 50% view. Use the vertical scroll bar to move a different portion of the picture into view.

⟹ Using the vertical scroll bar on the right, drag the scroll box all the way to the bottom of the scroll bar so the bottom edge of the drawing is visible, as shown in Figure 4-42.

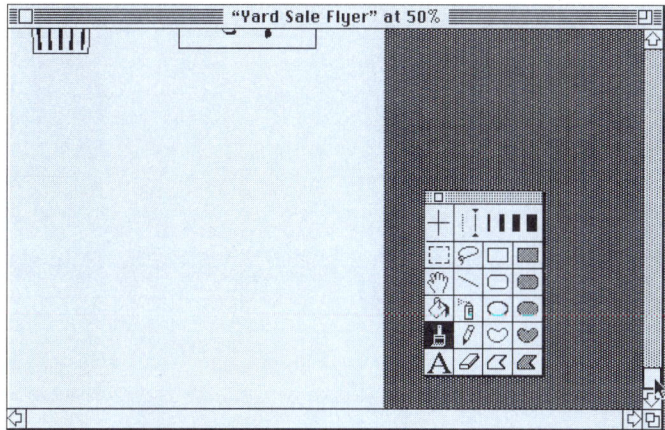

Figure 4-42   Moving to the bottom of the drawing

  ➠ Select the unfilled oval tool, and draw an oval in the bottom right portion of the page, about 1 inch from the bottom.

➠ Select the oval using the selection rectangle or the lasso, and duplicate it by holding down Option-Shift while dragging. Place the duplicate 3 or 4 inches to the left of the original oval, as shown in Figure 4-43.

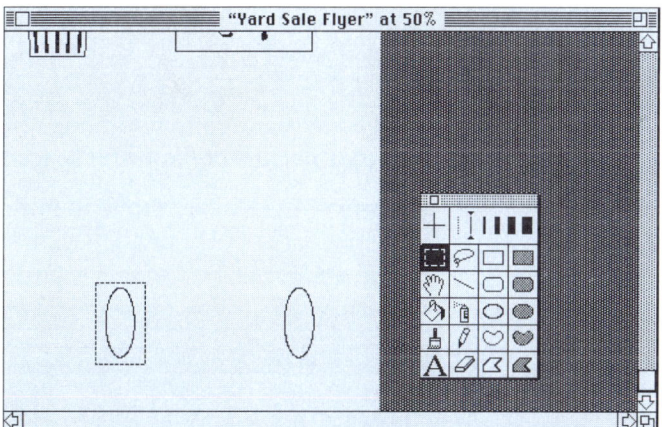

Figure 4-43   Drawing and copying ovals

  ➠ Using the line tool, with the Shift key held down, connect both ovals on the top and bottom, as shown in Figure 4-44.

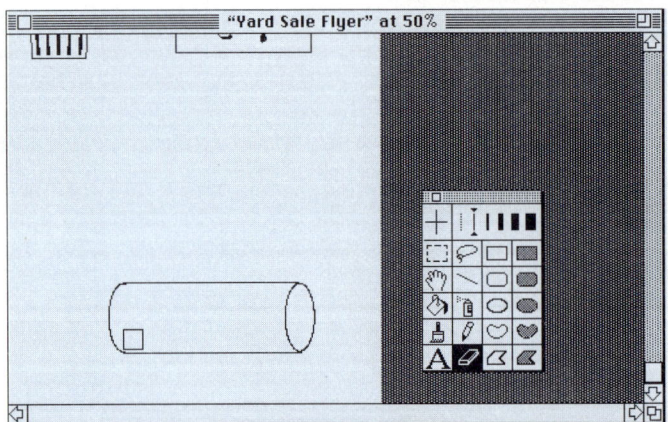

Figure 4-44   Creating the cylinder

 ➡ Use the eraser to erase the inside portion of the left oval. You should now have a cylinder lying on its side.

Now is a good time to save your work.

⌘-S ➡ Choose **Save** from the File menu.

⌘-M ➡ Choose **Zoom In** from the Goodies menu so you can draw the details more easily.

 ➡ Position the toolbox so it is not in the way, and then select the unfilled oval tool.

You may have to drag the scroll box to the bottom of the vertical scroll bar to view the cylinder and the space beneath it.

➡ Draw two more ovals above the cylinder, one slightly smaller than the other and both smaller than the original oval, as shown in Figure 4-45.

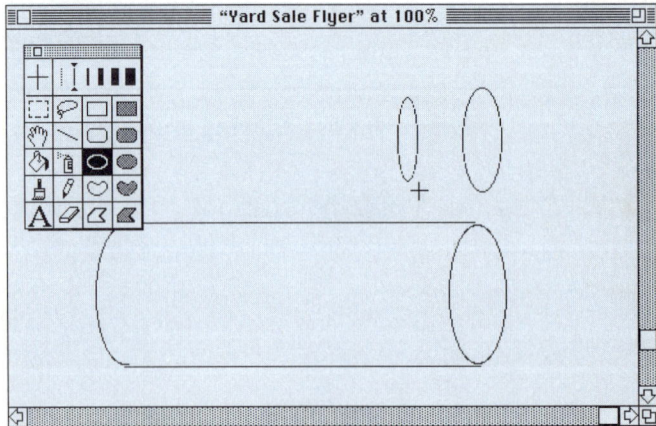

Figure 4-45   Drawing additional ovals

➡ Select the smallest oval with the lasso, and drag it so that it is inside the next largest oval, as shown in Figure 4-46.

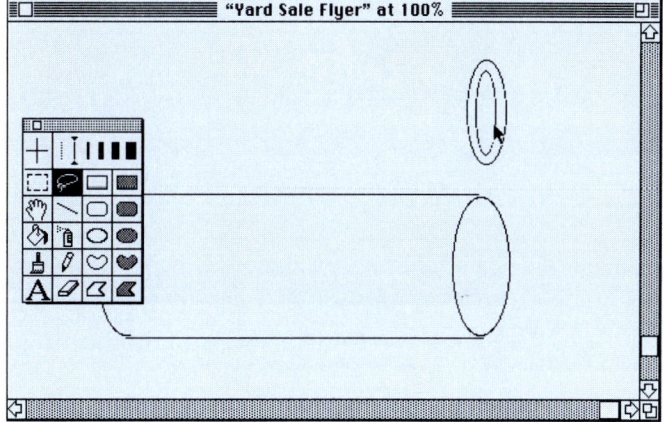

Figure 4-46 Positioning the smaller oval

➡ Select both of those two ovals and place them inside the oval at the end of the cylinder, as shown in Figure 4-47.

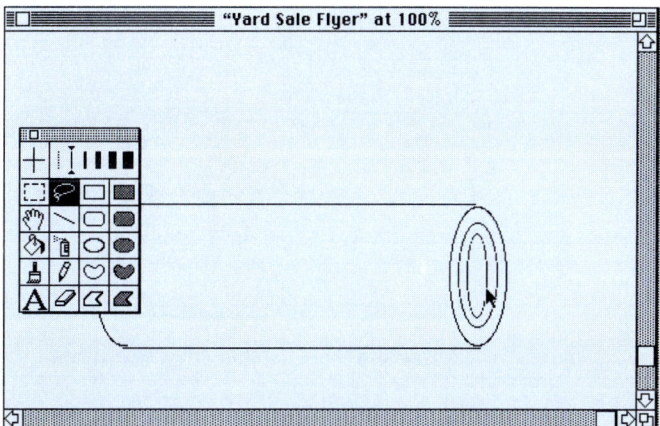

Figure 4-47 Placing ovals to simulate a rolled rug

➡ Using the line tool, draw a diagonal line underneath the three ovals, as shown in Figure 4-48.

➡ Duplicate that line by selecting it with the lasso and then dragging it while holding down the Option-Shift keys. Place the duplicate line on the other end of the cylinder, as shown in Figure 4-48.

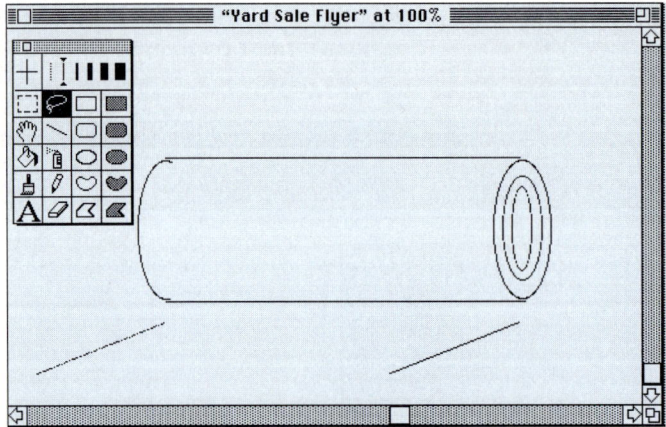

Figure 4-48 Drawing and duplicating lines

➡ Holding down the Shift key, draw a horizontal line to connect the ends of the two diagonal lines, as shown in Figure 4-49.

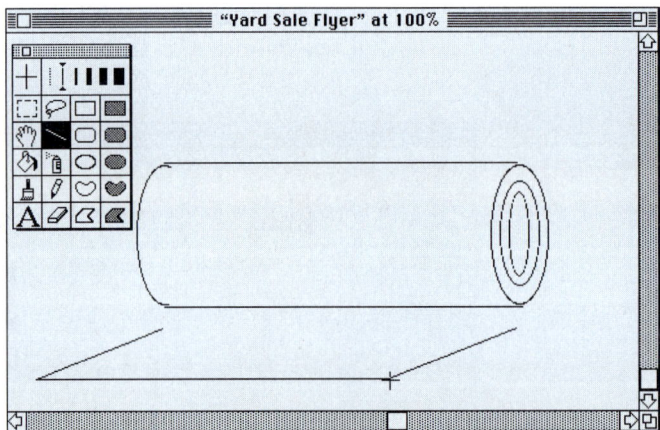

Figure 4-49   Connecting the lines

 ➡ Select that group of three lines with the lasso and drag the lines up to the cylinder to form the unrolled piece of carpet, as shown in Figure 4-50.

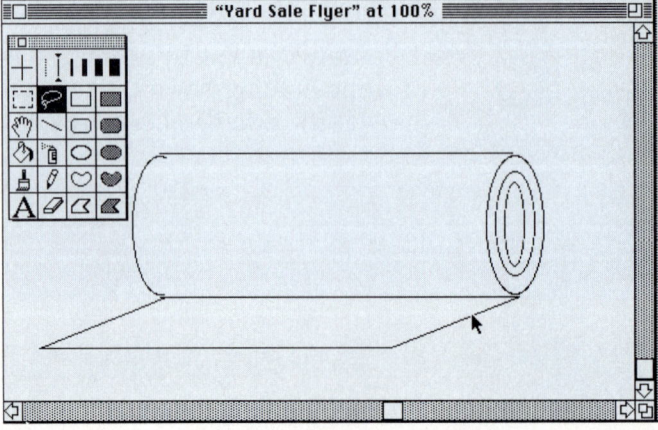

Figure 4-50   Creating the flap of the rug

⌘-S ➠ Save your work now before you add the pattern to the carpet.

➠ To create a pattern on the carpet, use any combination of filled or unfilled ovals, circles, rectangles, squares, and rounded rectangles. If you use unfilled shapes, select the paint bucket and choose different patterns with which to fill the shapes.

Take a good look at your roll of carpeting. If you have any lines that don't connect, use FatBits (double-click on the pencil tool) and clean up any lines that need it.

Typing Text

The last thing needed to complete your yard sale flyer is the text.

⌘-L ➠ Zoom out to 50% size again, and position the toolbox in the gray area.

  ➠ Select the text tool, which is indicated by the "A" in the bottom left corner of the toolbox.

When you move the pointer into the drawing window, notice that it is now an I-beam.

➠ Center the I-beam pointer in the area below the top two drawings and click to set the insertion point, as shown in Figure 4-51.

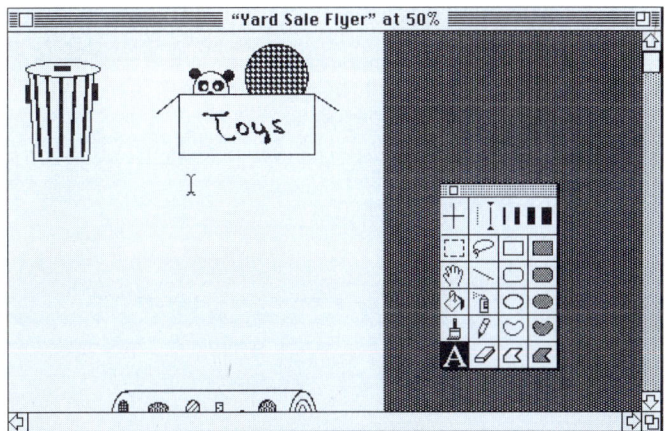

Figure 4-51   Setting the insertion point for text entry

➠ Choose **36 point** from the Style menu. Go back to the Style menu and choose **Bold**, and go back again and choose **Align Middle**. (See Figure 4-52.)

If you do not have 36 point available, choose another large size.

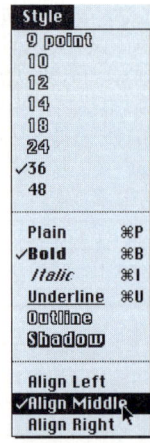

Figure 4-52   The selected options on the Style menu

➡ Type **Trash and Treasure**, press the Return key, and then type **Yard Sale**. (See Figure 4-53.)

If you make any errors while typing, press the Backspace key to delete the character and then retype it.

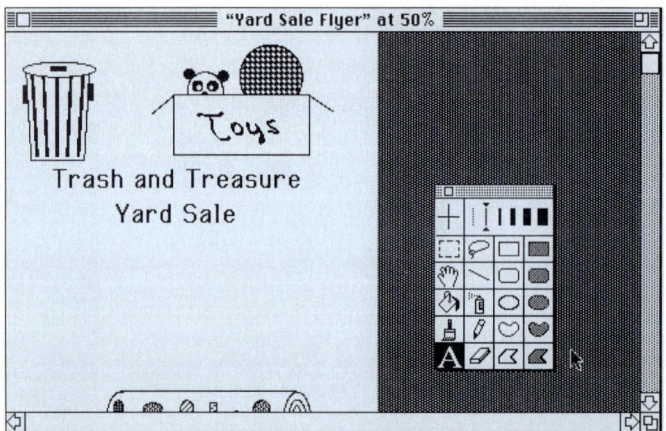

Figure 4-53   Adding text

➡ Click in the line beneath Yard Sale, under the "d", and then choose **24 point** from the Style menu.

If you do not have 24 point available, select the next smaller size from the first size you used. You will still be typing in bold text.

➡ Type the street address, **4712 Blount Ave. N.W.** Press Return, and on the next line type **(5th house on right)**. See Figure 4-54.

Figure 4-54   Adding the address and location

➡ Finish up by typing **Friday - Saturday - Sunday** on one line and **April 7, 8, 9 from 9:00-5:00** on the next line. Press Return again to make a blank line, and then type **Rain or Shine!!!** on the next line. Your screen should look like the one shown in Figure 4-55.

Figure 4-55   Completion of text entry

PRINTING YOUR DOCUMENT

Now you're done with the yard sale flyer—it's ready to print. There is no need to zoom in again to take your drawing back to its 100% size, because MacPaint will open your document at 100% each time, no matter what view it was in when you last worked with it.

It's a good habit to save your work before printing it.

⌘-S ➥ Save your work by choosing **Save** from the File menu.

➥ Choose **Print** from the File menu.

Your dialog box for the Print command may not look exactly like the one shown in Figure 4-56, since this box is for a LaserWriter. The dialog box for an ImageWriter is similar, and clicking OK and accepting all the default settings will print your document as well.

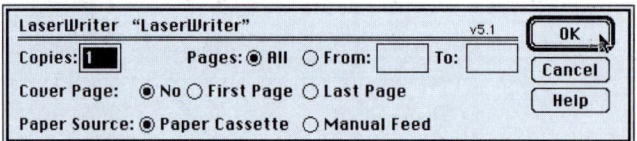

Figure 4-56   LaserWriter Print dialog box

The Copies box in the Print dialog box specifies the number of copies to print. The Pages options specify whether to print all pages of a multipage document or just certain pages in a multipage document. The Cover Page option, which is only available for the LaserWriter and is for use when more than one Macintosh prints to a single shared printer, lets you print a page identifying your document. The Paper Source option, also only available to the LaserWriter, lets you specify whether to print from the paper cassette or from the manual feed slot.

The Cancel button is used to cancel the Print command. Clicking the Help button will present you with information about printing your document. The OK button accepts the settings in the dialog box and executes the Print command.

Return ➥ Click **OK** in the dialog box to print one copy.

⌘-Q ➥ To exit MacPaint, choose **Quit** from the File menu. If you want to continue working with the next project, just close the document to remain in MacPaint.

Project 2: Creating a Greeting Card

In this project you'll create a greeting card that combines what you learned in the first project with MacPaint's copy and paste features.

Let your creativity be your guide. The *Macintosh Journey Projects* disk that accompanies this book includes the artwork for this project. If you desire, however, you can let these instructions be a guideline for creating your own, individually designed greeting card.

The finished greeting card from this project is shown in Figure 4-57. When it is folded, it will open as a greeting card does.

It's a shame you're
going to look so silly
in that hat!!

You've achieved your goal
and deserve to be
recognized for your
accomplishment.

We'll be proud when
you get your diploma . . .

Cheapo Cards Company
$17.50

Figure 4-57   Final output of Project 2

MacPaint 2.0

➡ Double-click on the MacPaint 2.0 icon to open a new, untitled drawing window. If you did not quit MacPaint after finishing the first project, choose **New** from the File menu to open a new, untitled document.

Since you're going to be working on an 8- by 10-inch area, you will be folding the finished printed sheet to open and close as a greeting card does—showing a message (and drawing) on the front, other messages and drawings on the inside, and even a price and "created by" message on the back. You'll start by drawing some lines on the page that will act as boundaries for each of the four sections of the card: the front, inside left, inside right, and back.

It's easier to get a proportional view of your entire drawing page by viewing it at 50% size.

⌘-L ➡ Choose **Zoom Out** from the Goodies menu.

DRAWING GUIDE LINES

➡ Tear off the toolbox and place it in the gray area of the screen. See Figure 4-58.

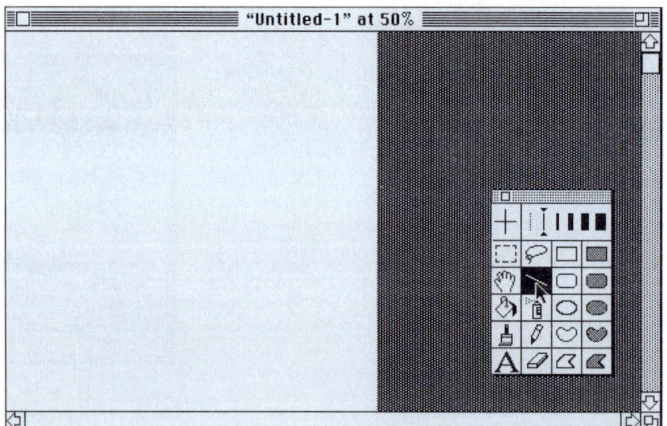

Figure 4-58   Placement of the toolbox at 50% size

➡ Select the line tool.

➡ Holding down the Shift key to constrain the line vertically, position the pointer at the center of the top of the page (approximately) and draw a line to divide the page in half vertically, as shown in Figure 4-59.

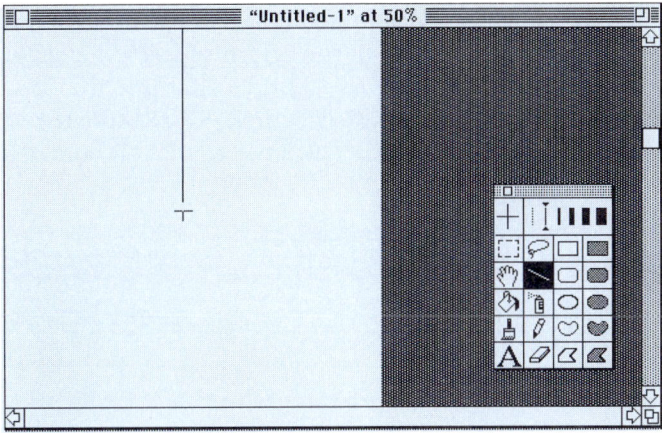

Figure 4-59   Dividing the page vertically

Notice the vertical scroll bar at the right of your screen. The scroll box moves down as your line is drawn, indicating your position relative to the entire page. When the scroll box is all the way at the bottom of the scroll bar, your vertical line is complete.

When you have finished drawing the line, be sure to release the mouse button *before* you release the Shift key. Otherwise, if you move your pointer to the left or to the right as you are drawing, the line will *snap* to the pointer when you release the Shift key.

You'll notice that you don't have a horizontal scroll bar when you're viewing at 50% size. This is because the width of the page is entirely visible in this view.

➡ Drag the vertical scroll box to the center of the scroll bar, as shown in Figure 4-60.

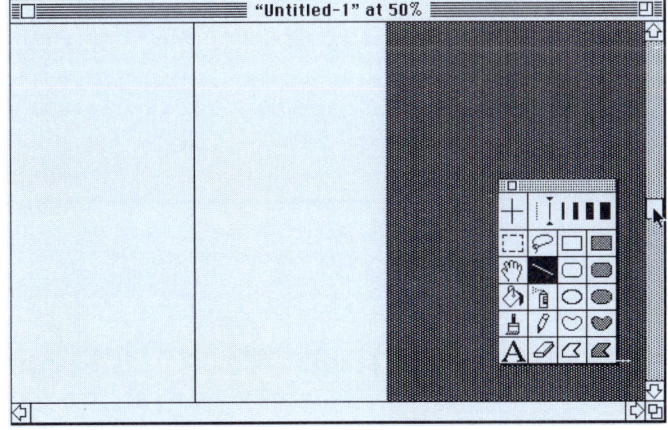

Figure 4-60   Moving the scroll box in the scroll bar

This positions the page so that you are looking at the middle portion of it. The very top and very bottom are not visible on the screen.

➡ Holding down the Shift key, place the cross-beam pointer of the line
   tool in the center of the left edge of the page, and drag to the right
   to create a horizontal line that intersects the vertical line you just
   drew (see Figure 4-61). Be sure to release the mouse button *before* you
   release the Shift key when you are finished drawing the line.

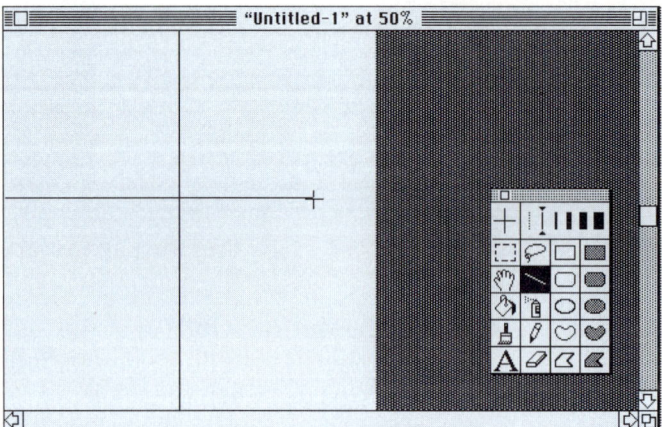

Figure 4-61   Dividing the page into quarters

As explained earlier, the greeting card contains four sections that you'll
be working with. Now that you have marked these boundaries on your
page with *guide lines*, it's easier to understand how your card will be
created using the guide lines as fold lines, as shown in Figure 4-62.

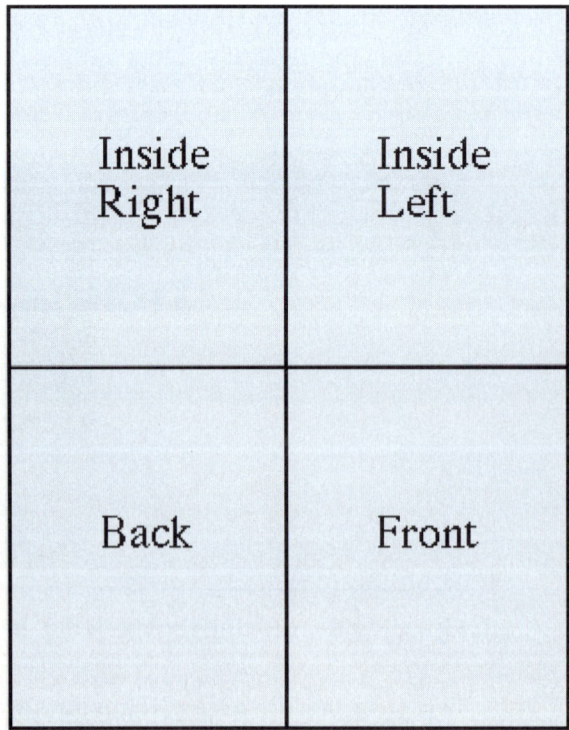

Figure 4-62   Greeting card layout—unfolded

Whatever you place on the lower right corner of the drawing, in the rectangle that is labeled "Front" in Figure 4-63, will be displayed on the front of your card once it is folded. Anything that you place on the lower left side of the page will be displayed on the back of the folded card. Take a piece of paper and try folding it.

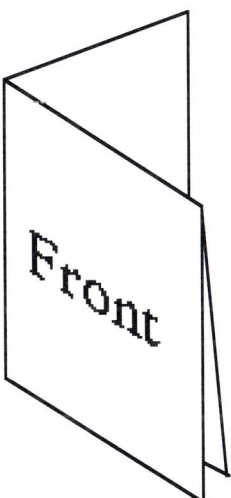

Figure 4-63   Folded greeting card

The two sections that will be in the center of the greeting card, those marked "Inside Right" and "Inside Left" in Figure 4-62, will need to have any drawing or text turned upside down so that when the page is folded to form the card, the images are positioned correctly. You'll learn how to do this in the instructions for this project.

SAVING THE DOCUMENT

Now is a good time to save what you have done so far and to name your document.

⌘-S ➡ Choose **Save** from the File menu.

➡ If necessary, click the **Drive** button until your name, or whatever name you gave your data disk, is showing at the top of the screen, where "Connie Barlow" is showing in Figure 4-64.

➡ Type **Greeting Card** in the box marked Save Paint document as:, and then click **Save**.

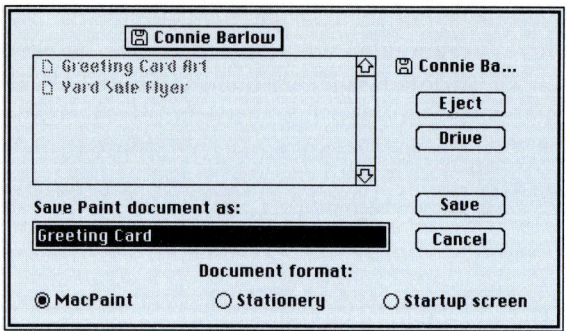

Figure 4-64   Saving the document Greeting Card

COPYING AND PASTING AN EXISTING GRAPHIC

Now that you have created the layout of the card, you'll place a graphic on the front of the card. On the *Macintosh Journey Projects* disk is a MacPaint document entitled Greeting Card Art.

(If you are using this book in a classroom environment, check with the instructor to ensure that this document has been made available to you.)

Opening the Document

First you'll open the document that contains the artwork.

⌘-O   ➡ To open an existing piece of artwork, choose **Open** from the File menu.

Your screen shows a dialog box that lists the MacPaint documents available to be opened, as shown in Figure 4-65.

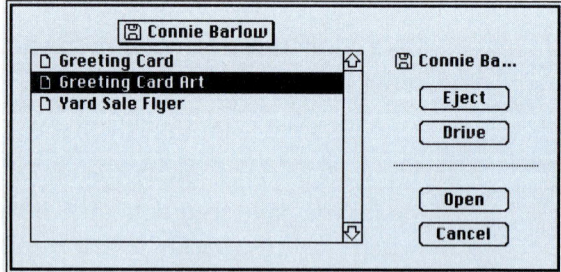

Figure 4-65   The Open dialog box

➡ Click the **Drive** button, if necessary, to view the contents of the disk that contains Greeting Card Art.

➡ Select **Greeting Card Art** from the list by clicking on it, and then click the **Open** button. A faster way to open a document is to double-click on its name in the list.

Your screen should now show the Greeting Card Art document, and your greeting card should peek out from beneath it, as shown in Figure 4-66.

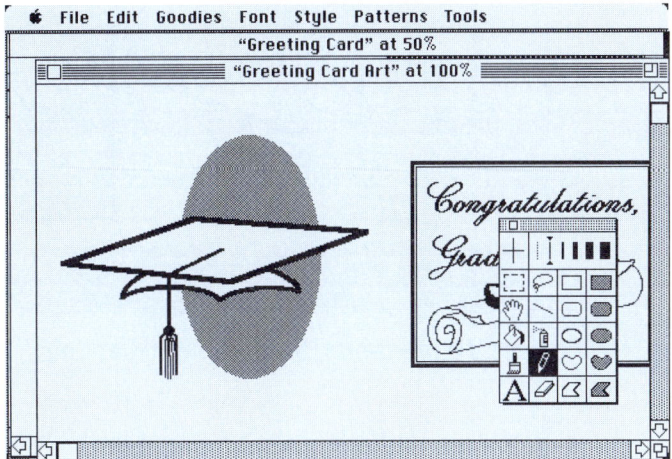

Figure 4-66   Greeting Card Art

➠   Drag the toolbox by its title bar to reposition it on the left side of the screen, and use the bottom scroll bar to scroll so that the entire Congratulations Grad box is showing, as in Figure 4-67.

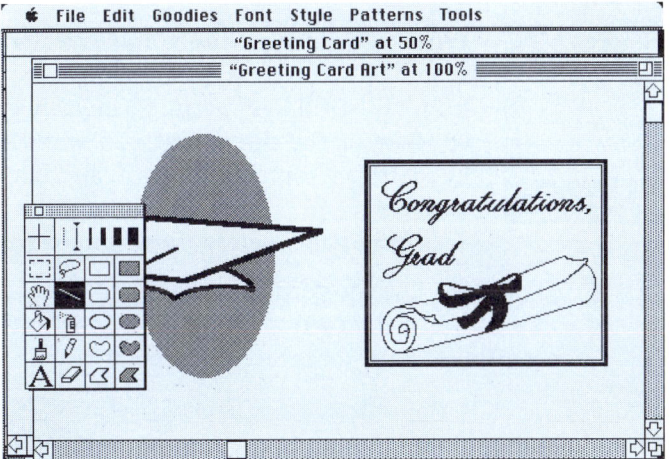

Fgure 4-67   Positioning the toolbox and the scroll bar

Selecting the Artwork You Want to Copy

Congratulations Grad will go on the front of the card. To use it in your greeting card, you'll select it and then *copy* it to the Clipboard.

   ➠   Click on the selection rectangle, and then select the **Congratulations Grad** rectangle, as shown in Figure 4-68.

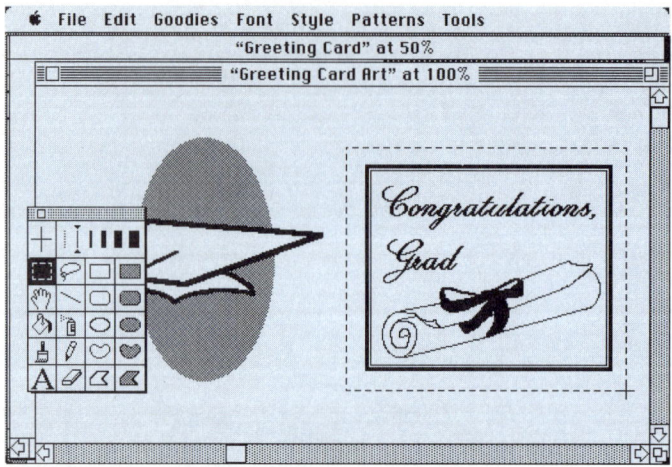

Figure 4-68   Selecting the drawing

⌘-C   ➡   With the desired drawing selected, choose **Copy** from the Edit menu.

Activating Your Document

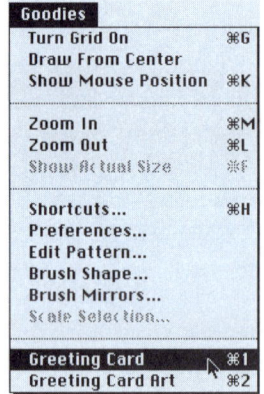

➡   To make your greeting card the *active* drawing (or active window), choose **Greeting Card** from the Goodies menu, or click on any part of its window.

The Greeting Card window moves to the topmost position.

Whenever you have more than one window open in MacPaint, you can switch between them by choosing the name of the document you want from the Goodies menu. You can also just click anywhere in the window of the document you want active, and that document will move to the topmost position and become active.

Your original Greeting Card should now be showing on the screen.

➡   Use the vertical scroll bar to scroll down so the entire front section of the card is showing, as in Figure 4-69.

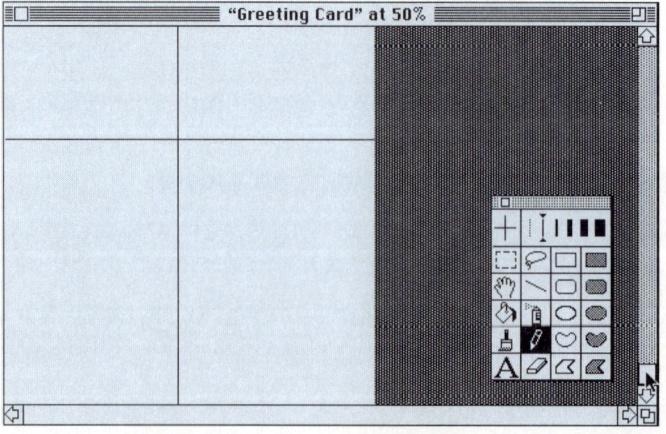

Figure 4-69   Scrolling to view the front section of the card

Pasting the Artwork into Your Document

Now you'll *paste* the drawing that was copied to the Clipboard into your MacPaint document.

⌘-V   ➧   Choose **Paste** from the Edit menu.

Your screen should look like the one shown in Figure 4-70.

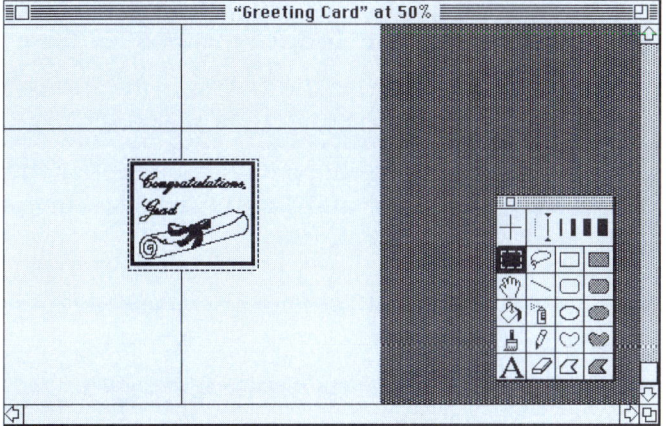

Figure 4-70   Pasting the drawing into the document

The drawing will appear in the center of the card, and it will be selected—notice the "marching ants" around the border of the drawing.

Positioning the Artwork

Now that you have copied and pasted the Congratulations Grad artwork, you can put it where you want it.

➧   Position the pointer on top of the drawing and click and drag, placing the drawing in the top portion of the area reserved for the front of the card (see Figure 4-71).

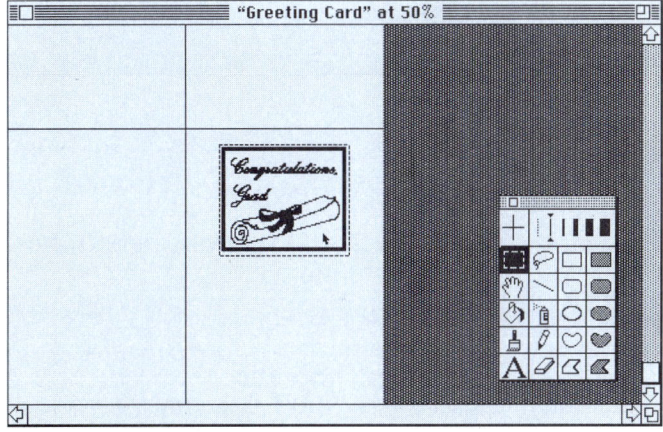

Figure 4-71   Positioning the drawing on the card

⌘-S ➡ Now is a good time to save your greeting card. Choose **Save** from the File menu.

ADDING TEXT

Now that the drawing is positioned on the front of the card, you can finish the front by typing your message on it.

⌘-M ➡ Since it is easier to see your typed message at 100% size, choose **Zoom In** from the Goodies menu.

➡ Position the toolbox in the lower left corner of the screen by clicking on the title bar of the toolbox and dragging it.

➡ Drag the scroll box in the horizontal scroll bar all the way to the right, and drag the scroll box in the vertical scroll bar all the way to the bottom.

This will ensure that you are working in the lower right corner of the page.

  ➡ Select the text tool.

➡ Position the insertion point in the center of the front section of the card, just beneath the drawing, and click to set the insertion point, as shown in Figure 4-72.

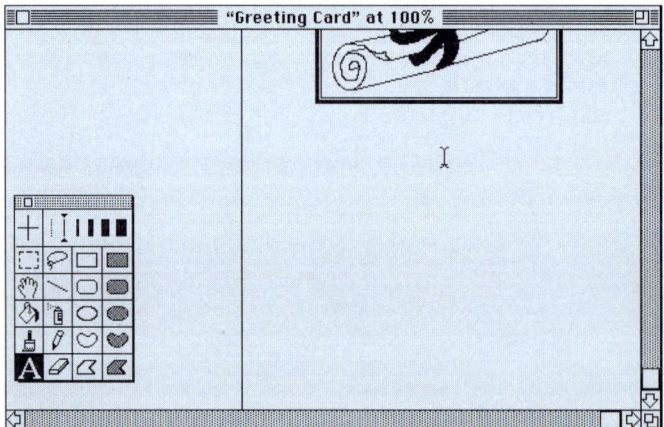

Figure 4-72 Centering the insertion point under the drawing

➡ Choose **New York** from the Font menu.

➡ Choose the following options from the Style menu:
    14 point
    Bold
    Italic
    Align Middle
    (This will take four trips to the Style menu.)

You can be sure that you have the right selections, because they will have checkmarks next to them. See Figure 4-73. If you accidentally select the wrong item, you can choose it again to deselect it.

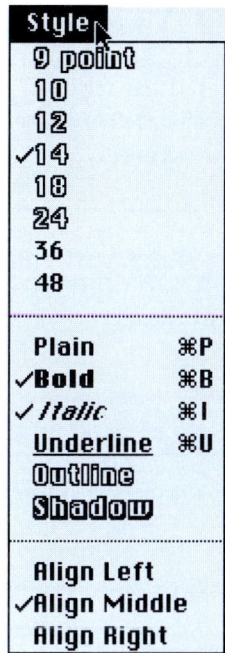

Figure 4-73   The settings in the Style menu

➡ Now type the following lines on the card (press Return where
   indicated):
   You've achieved your goal (press Return)
   and deserve to be (press Return)
   recognized for your (press Return)
   accomplishment. (press Return <u>twice</u>)
   We'll be proud when (press Return)
   you get your diploma . . . (press Return)

Your screen should look similar to the one shown in Figure 4-74.

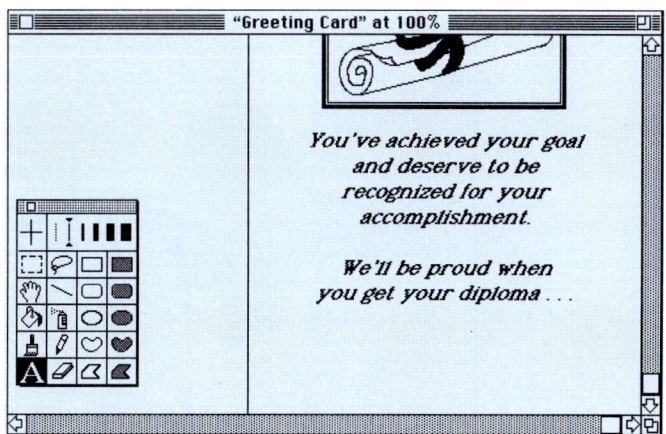

Figure 4-74   Text on the front of the card

⌘-S   ➡ Save your work by choosing **Save** from the File menu.

ADDING MORE ARTWORK TO YOUR DOCUMENT

Now you have completed the front of the card. Next you'll copy and paste the graduation cap art from Greeting Card Art into the "inside right" section of the document.

➡ Choose **Greeting Card Art** from the Goodies menu.

➡ When you're viewing the Greeting Card Art document, move the toolbox to the right part of the screen, and drag the bottom scroll box to the left. You should be viewing the entire cap, as shown in Figure 4-75.

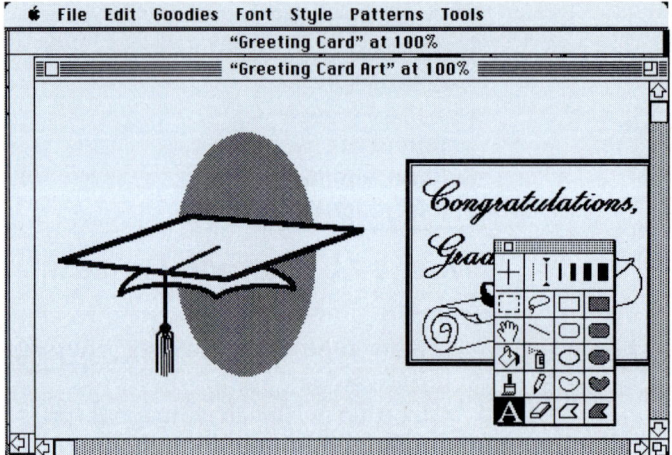

Figure 4-75   Positioning the art in the window

 ➡ Click on the selection rectangle, and then select the entire cap, as shown in Figure 4-76.

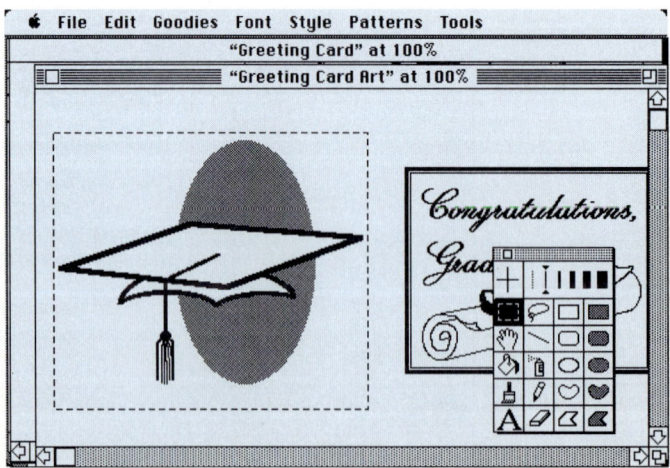

Figure 4-76   Selecting the cap

⌘-C ➡ Choose **Copy** from the Edit menu to copy the selection to the Clipboard.

Now that you've copied the second drawing to the Clipboard, you no longer need to have the Greeting Card Art document open.

⌘-W ➧ Close Greeting Card Art by clicking in its close box or by choosing **Close** from the File menu.

➧ Click **No** in the dialog box that asks if you want to save changes to the document before closing.

WORKING IN ANOTHER PORTION OF THE DOCUMENT

Now you'll position your greeting card so you can work in another portion of it.

⌘-L ➧ Choose **Zoom Out** from the Goodies menu to view your card at 50% size. Drag the toolbox into the gray area at the right side of the screen.

⌘-V ➧ Choose **Paste** from the Edit menu.

This will cause the drawing of the cap to be placed in the center of the document. The drawing will automatically be selected.

➧ Position the drawing in the center of the upper left section, and then click elsewhere on the screen to deselect the drawing. See Figure 4-77.

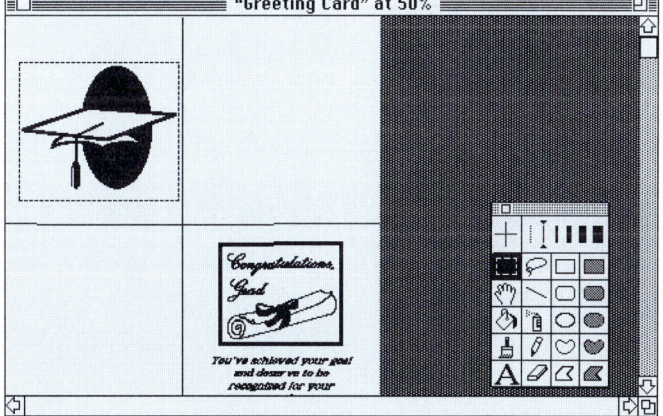

Figure 4-77   Positioning the second piece of artwork on the card

ROTATING THE ARTWORK

Since everything in the top section of the page must be upside down so that it will be positioned properly when the paper is folded as a card, you'll rotate the graduation cap artwork.

  ➧ Select the graduation cap artwork with the selection rectangle.

Any item you choose to rotate or flip horizontally or vertically must first be selected with the selection rectangle, *not with the lasso.*

⌘-T ➡ Choose **Rotate** from the Edit menu.

This causes the selected drawing to be rotated 90°. Since you want the cap rotated 180°, you will rotate it again.

⌘-T ➡ Choose **Rotate** from the Edit menu.

Now that the drawing has been turned upside down, your drawings should have the same placement as those shown in Figure 4-78.

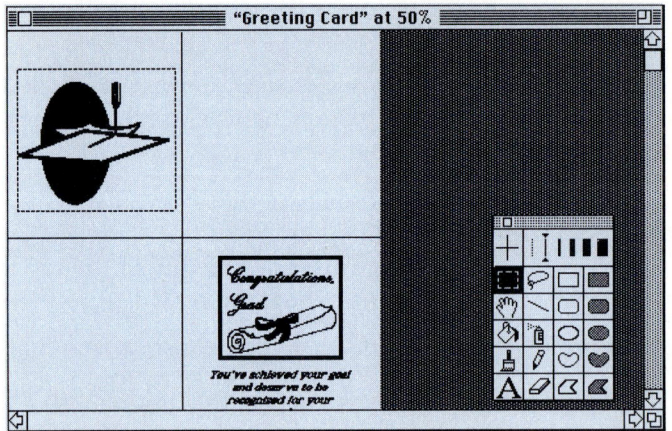

Figure 4-78   The rotated cap

⌘-S ➡ Save your work now by choosing **Save** from the File menu.

ROTATING TEXT

Now you'll type the text in the "inside left" section of the card.

➡ Choose **Zoom In** from the Goodies menu to go to 100% size.

⌘-M ➡ Position the horizontal scroll box to the far right in the scroll bar, and position the vertical scroll box at the top of the scroll bar, as they are positioned in Figure 4-79.

This will ensure that you are working in the upper right portion of the page.

  ➡ Move the toolbox to the left side of the screen so it's out of the way, and then select the text tool.

➡ Position the pointer in the center of the right side of the screen, as shown in Figure 4-79, and click to set the insertion point.

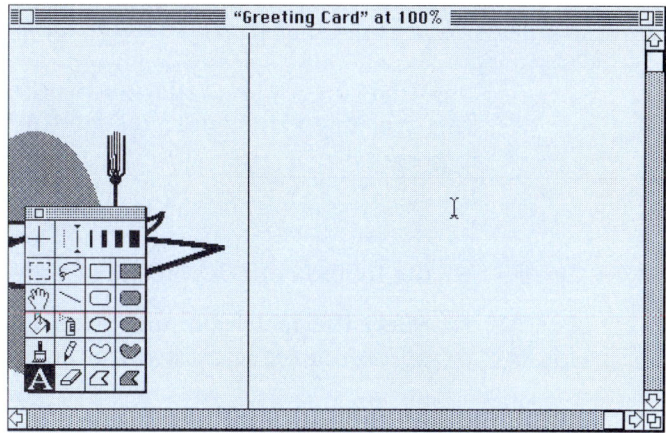

Figure 4-79 Setting the insertion point

➡ Select **18 point** from the Style menu. Then go back and select **Italic** to remove the checkmark beside it, which deselects it.

➡ Type the following, pressing Return where indicated:
   It's a shame you're (press Return)
   going to look so silly (press Return)
   in that hat!! (press Return)

➡ Save your work.

Now you need to select the text so that you can rotate it, as you did the drawing of the cap.

➡ Select the text with the selection rectangle, and then choose **Rotate** twice in succession from the Edit menu.

Your screen should now look like the one shown in Figure 4-80.

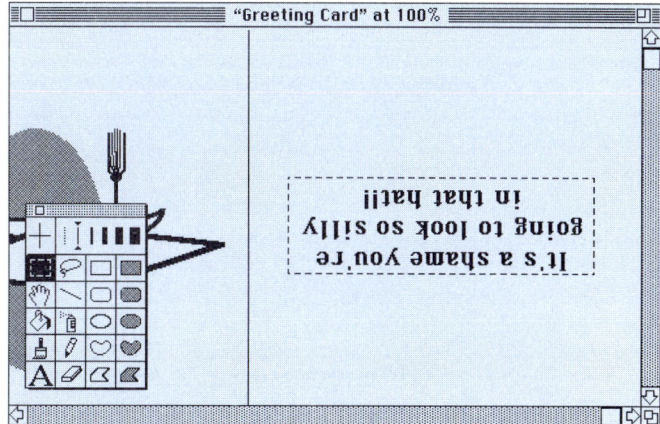

Figure 4-80 Rotating the text

➡ Once the text is rotated 180°, click somewhere else on the screen to deselect the text.

ADDING A PERSONALIZED MESSAGE

Now that you've placed all the artwork and have typed all the text in the card, you may want to put a "created by" message on the back of the card to personalize it.

➡ Drag the scroll box to the far left in the horizontal scroll bar, and to the bottom in the vertical scroll bar, as shown in Figure 4-81. Drag the toolbox out of your way to the right side of the screen.

➡ Select the text tool, and then position the pointer in the lower portion of the left side of the screen, as shown in Figure 4-81.

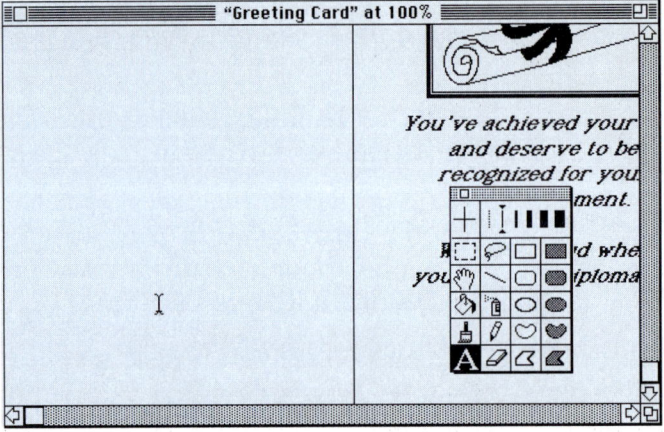

Figure 4-81   Positioning the pointer on the back of the card

➡ Choose **9 point** from the Style menu.

➡ Type **Cheapo Cards Company** and press Return.

➡ Type **$17.50**, or whatever you feel is a good price for your masterpiece (see Figure 4-82).

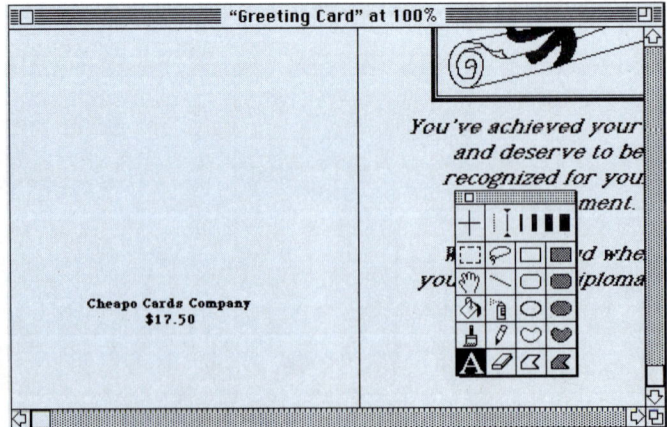

Figure 4-82   Finishing the back of the card

ERASING THE GUIDE LINES

All that remains to be done now is to erase the guide lines that you drew to partition the four sections of the card for folding.

➠ Save your work.

➠ Choose **Zoom Out** from the Goodies menu so you'll be viewing the card at 50% size.

 ➠ Select the eraser tool. While holding down the Shift key, use the eraser to erase the lines.

Using the Shift key with the eraser will constrain the eraser's movement horizontally or vertically, depending on which way you move first, thus reducing the risk of erasing other parts of the card.

If your lines are close to images or text, you may need to zoom in to FatBits to delete the lines with more precision. Refer to the first project in this chapter, if necessary, to refresh your memory about using FatBits.

➠ After you've erased the lines, be sure to save your work.

Now you're ready to print your card.

PRINTING THE DOCUMENT

➠ Choose **Print** from the File menu.

The Print dialog box will look similar to the one shown in Figure 4-83.

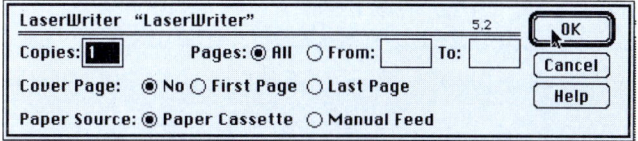

Figure 4-83   The Print dialog box

➠ Click **OK** to accept the default settings.

➠ Using the fold lines shown in Figure 4-62 as a guide, fold the page to form a greeting card.

➠ If any of the drawings or text are not placed the way you'd like them to be, select the item and reposition it to your satisfaction. Then reprint the page.

➠ Choose **Quit** from the File menu to exit MacPaint. If you want to stay in MacPaint and continue with the additional projects, close the Greeting Card document.

SUMMARY

- MacPaint provides familiar tools for creating drawing effects. The tools are found in the toolbox, which is a tear-off menu that can be positioned wherever you like in the drawing window. You select a tool by clicking on it in the toolbox. A selected tool is highlighted.

- Lines are drawn using the line tool and the pencil tool. The pencil tool draws a freehand one-pixel-wide line, and the line tool draws a straight line.

- Shapes are drawn using the oval tool, the rectangle tool, the rounded rectangle tool, the freehand tool, and the polygon tool. Shapes can be drawn either unfilled or filled with the currently selected pattern.

- The Shift key constrains the movement of many of the tools. It is used to draw perfect squares, perfect circles, and straight lines. It also constrains the movement of the eraser to horizontal or vertical movements.

- The eraser is used to erase all or part of an object from the drawing window. Double-clicking the eraser tool erases the entire contents of the drawing window.

- You select a pattern by clicking on a pattern in the Patterns menu, which is also a tear-off menu that can be positioned anywhere on the screen.

- Painting is done with the spray can tool and the paint brush tool. The spray can tool paints a "mist", and the paint brush tool paints in the shape of any of the many available brush shapes. Both of these tools paint in the currently selected pattern.

- The border palette is used to change the vertical and horizontal weights of lines drawn with the line tool or in the border of a shape.

- Text can be drawn either with the pencil tool or with the paint brush tool or typed using the text tool. The options in the Style menu and Font menu apply to the text typed with the text tool.

- Objects are selected using the selection rectangle or the lasso. The difference between the selection rectangle and the lasso is that the selection rectangle also selects the area inside the rectangle, including the white space surrounding an object, whereas the lasso shrinks to the exact size of the object and selects only the object. An item must be selected before you can issue a command that will affect it—to copy or move it, for example.

- The paint bucket tool is used to fill an object with the currently selected pattern from the Patterns menu.

- Once an object is drawn, you can modify it in several ways. For example, you can flip an object vertically or horizontally, rotate it, duplicate it, or delete it.

- The Zoom In command allows you to work in a magnified view of your drawing, which takes you in 200% increments up to 800% view. The details of the drawing can be modified with more precision in 800% view, because you can erase or add one pixel at a time.

KEY TERMS

active window
actual size window
align
anchor

border palette
brush shapes

Clipboard
constrain
copy
cross-beam pointer
currently selected pattern

deselect
duplicate

eraser tool

FatBits
filled
flip
font
freehand tools

grabber tool
guide lines

highlighted
hot spot

I-beam pointer
insertion point

lasso selection tool
leaks
line tool
line weight

magnify
marching ants
menu bar

paint bucket tool
paint brush tool
paste
Patterns menu
pencil tool
pixel
points, point size
polygon tools

Revert To Saved command
rotate
rounded rectangles

scroll bar
scroll box
select
selection marquee
selection rectangle
snap
spray can tool

tear-off menu
text tool
title bar
toolbox

Undo command
unfilled

Zoom In command
Zoom Out command

MACPAINT COMMAND KEYS AND SHORTCUTS

File Menu

New	⌘ -N
Open	⌘ -O
Close	⌘ -W
Save	⌘ -S
Quit	⌘ -Q

Edit Menu

Undo	⌘ -Z
Cut	⌘ -X
Copy	⌘ -C
Paste	⌘ -V
Rotate	⌘ -T

Goodies Menu

Zoom In	⌘ -M
Zoom Out	⌘ -L
Shortcuts	⌘ -H

Style Menu

Bold	⌘ -B
Italics	⌘ -I
Underline	⌘ -U

Shortcuts Window

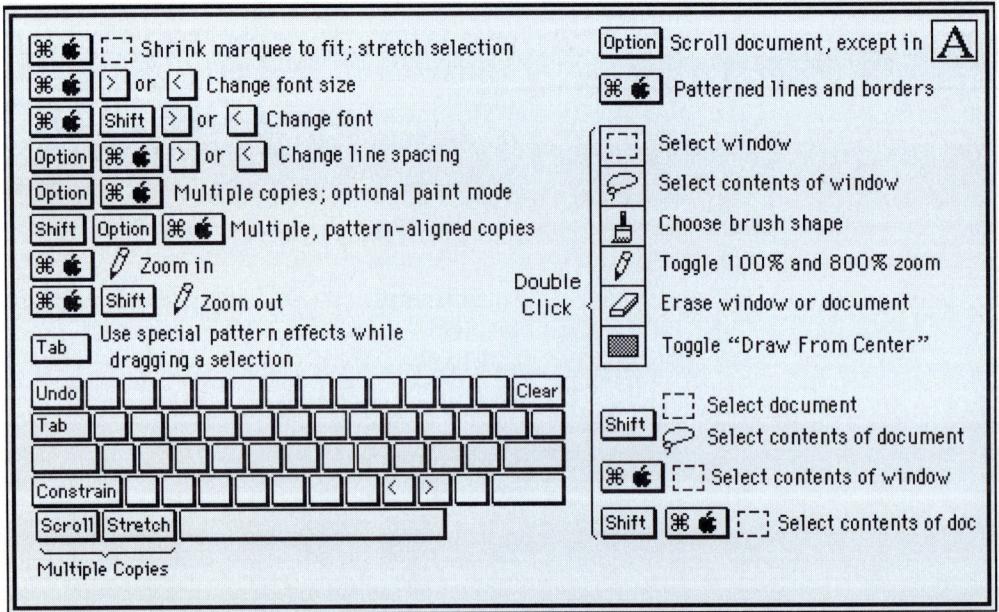

Additional Projects

The following projects are accompanied by briefer instructions than those you have previously completed in this chapter. They require that you apply what you learned in the first two projects. If necessary, refer to "Using MacPaint's Tools" at the beginning of this chapter for information and instructions about using any tools that you aren't familiar with. Experiment with the shortcuts available from the Goodies menu.

You will not be reminded to save your work—you should be developing good saving habits of your own by now.

Project 3: Drawing Perspective

Everybody dreams of having a lot of money, and this project gives you that chance. You'll use the polygon tool to draw the bills and the oval tool to draw the coins to achieve a look of perspective in the drawing. The finished project is shown in Figure 4-84.

Figure 4-84   Final output for Project 3

 ➡ Use the polygon tool to draw the shape of the bill in the lower left part of the screen, as shown in Figure 4-85.

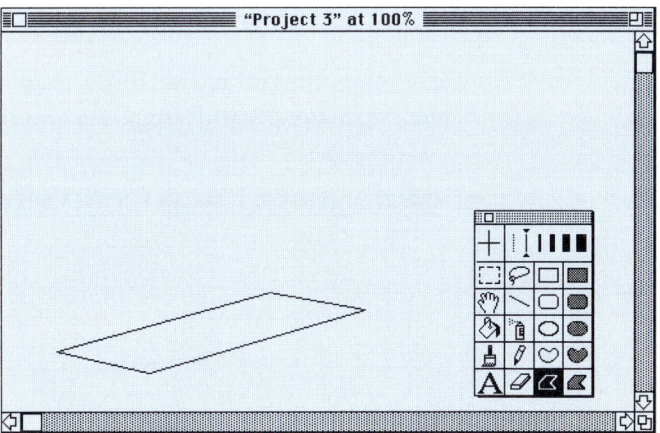

Figure 4-85   The bill drawn with the polygon tool

 ➡ Select the polygon with the selection rectangle, and then choose **Trace Edges** from the Edit menu.

The Trace Edges command traces the edges of the selected object, as shown in Figure 4-86. When you use this command, the object must be selected with the selection rectangle, not the lasso.

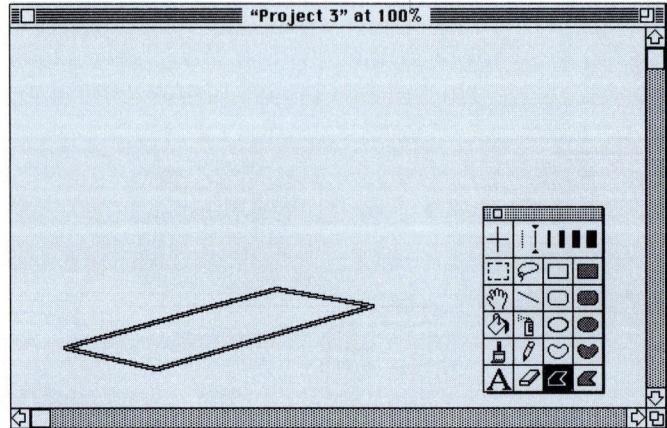

Figure 4-86   The bill with the edges traced

 ⇒ Erase the top and right outline of the bill, so the bill looks "thick."

Zoom in to clean up the corners of the bill using the following shortcut to zero in on a particular area.

 ⇒ Select the pencil tool, and then hold down the Command key.

The pointer turns into a small magnifying glass when you move it into the drawing area.

⇒ Click on the area you want to edit in a magnified view.

The view is magnified in 200% increments each time you click the screen with the magnifying glass. See Figure 4-87.

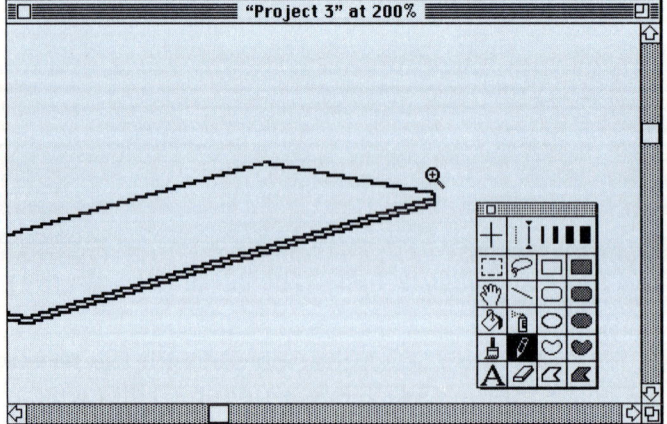

Figure 4-87   Zooming in to the selected area

➡ To create the border on the face of the bill, select a heavier line weight from the border palette, and select a gray pattern.

 ➡ Select the polygon tool.

➡ Hold down the Command key while drawing the border on the top of the bill to get a patterned line.

Holding down the Command key while drawing a line or shape draws the border in the currently selected pattern.

 ➡ Use the oval tool to draw the ovals and any other design you want on the top of the bill.

Next you'll create the "stack" of bills.

 ➡ Select the bill with the lasso.

➡ Hold down the Option and Command keys, and drag the bill toward the menu bar at the top of the screen. See Figure 4-88.

The Option-Command keys allow you to make multiple copies of the selected object. If you don't like the effect you get with your first try, use the Undo command and try again until the stack is to your liking.

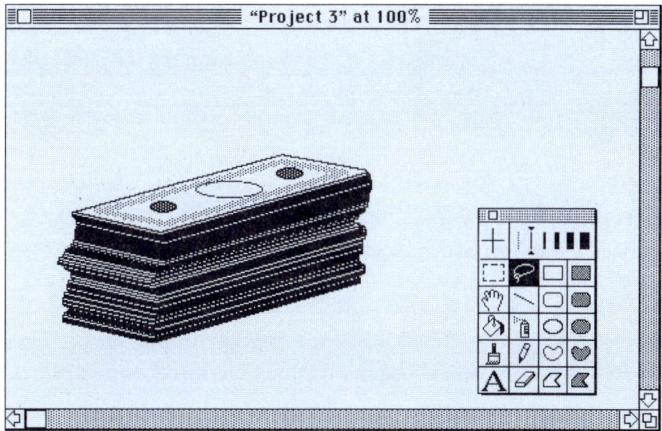

Figure 4-88   The stack of bills

 ➡ To draw the coins, draw an oval with the oval tool and then duplicate it.

➡ Zoom in to work in greater detail on the rest of the coin.

 ➡ Place one oval on top of the other. Erase where they overlap, as shown in Figure 4-89.

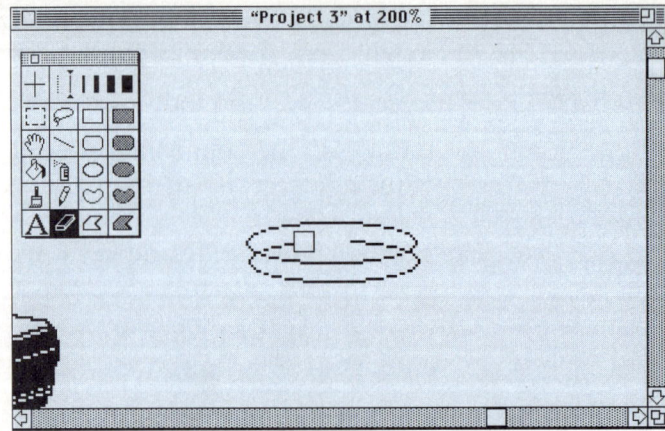

Figure 4-89   Erasing the overlapping ovals

➟ Connect the two ovals with a vertical line on each side to form a coin.

➟ Close up all the gaps in the borders of the ovals.

 ➟ Fill the edge of the coin (the space between the two ovals) with the paint bucket using the vertical line pattern in the Patterns menu, as shown in Figure 4-90.

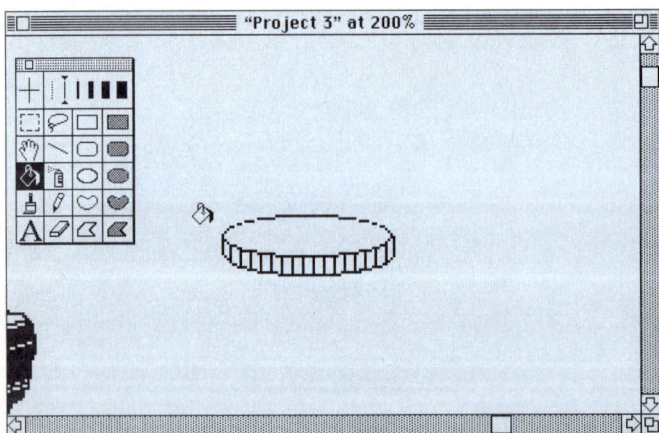

Figure 4-90   Filling the edge of the coin with the paint bucket

➟ Choose **Draw From Center** from the Goodies menu.

You'll use this option to draw the oval on the face of the coin. The Draw From Center command allows you to draw shapes from the center instead of from the edge. This usually makes drawing shapes in a particular location easier. When Draw From Center is in effect, you'll see small crosses in the center of some of the tools in the toolbox. To turn off Draw From Center, choose **Draw From Edge** from the Goodies menu.

 ➟ Select the oval tool, and then position the cross-beam pointer in the center of the face of the coin.

➠ Drag to create an oval slightly smaller than the face of the coin.

 ➠ Use the pencil tool in FatBits to draw a face or other design on the coin.

 ➠ Select the coin with the lasso and, using the Option key, duplicate the coin to form several stacks of coins.

➠ Position the coin stacks around the stack of bills.

Project 4: Creating a Logo

In this project you'll put together a few simple shapes—a polygon, two circles, and some lines—to create a logo. You'll also create some special effects with the eraser tool and with the Invert command. The finished project is shown in Figure 4-91.

Figure 4-91   Final output for Project 4

 ➠ Select the line tool, and then select the third line weight on the border palette.

➠ Hold down the Shift key to constrain the line to a 45° angle and draw six lines each about 2 inches long.

If you rest the bottom of the cross-beam pointer on one line as you draw the next one it helps you keep an equal distance between each line.

 ➠ Select the group of lines with the selection rectangle, and use the Option key to duplicate them, as shown in Figure 4-92.

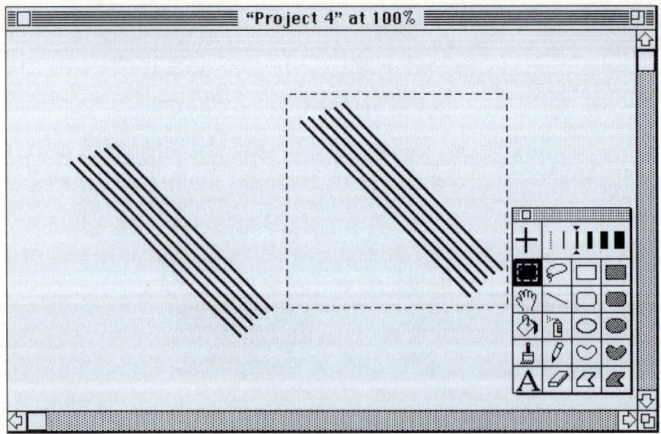

Figure 4-92   Duplicating the group of lines

➠   While the duplicate lines are still selected, choose **Flip Horizontal** from the Edit menu.

Now you'll duplicate these flipped lines to form the background of the arrow.

    ➠   Select the top part of the duplicated lines with the lasso. Using the Option key, place a duplicate of that portion on either side of the group of lines, as shown in Figure 4-93.

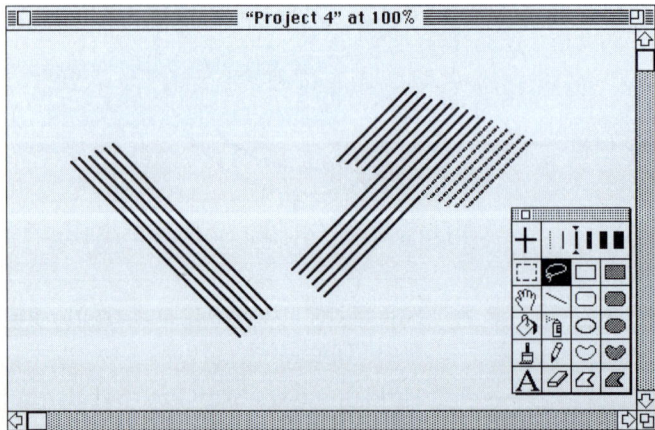

Figure 4-93   Duplicating the lines for the arrow background

    ➠   Zoom in to 200% size, and then use the polygon tool to draw the arrow, as shown in Figure 4-94.

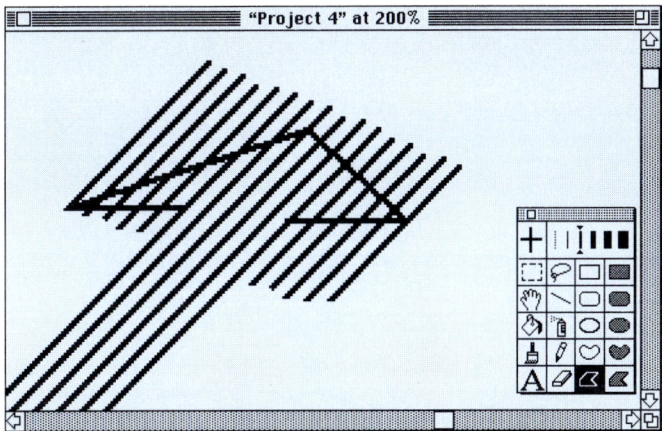

Figure 4-94   Creating the arrow with the polygon tool

➡ Zoom in to 400% or larger, and use the eraser and the pencil to erase all the lines that extend beyond the outline of the arrow.

 ➡ Zoom out to 100% size and select the eraser tool. Hold down the Shift key to constrain the eraser's movement, and erase the top of the left group of lines, as shown in Figure 4-95.

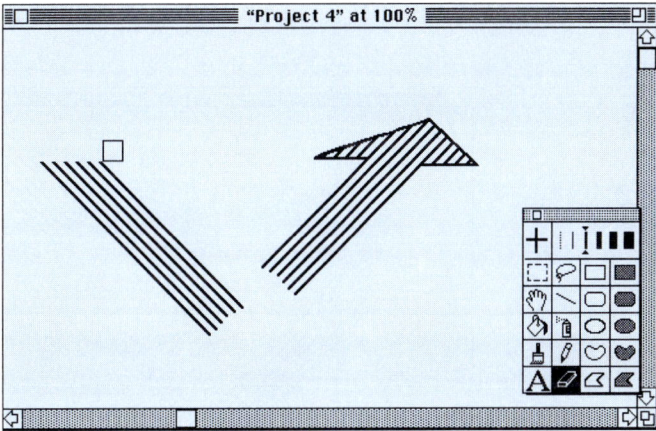

Figure 4-95   Erasing the lines horizontally

➡ Hold down the Shift key to erase first vertically and then horizontally so the bottom of the left group of lines forms a point, as shown in Figure 4-96.

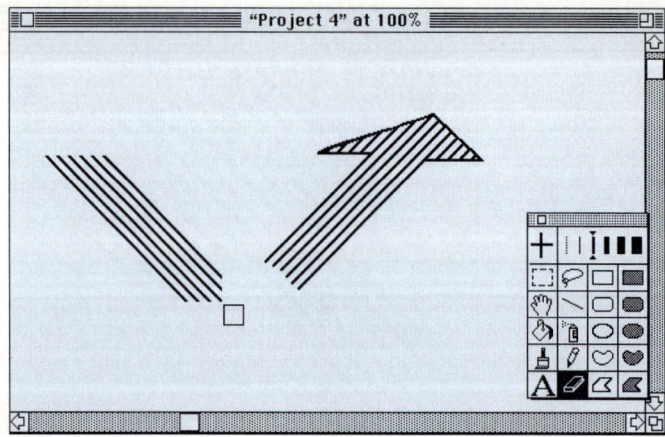

Figure 4-96   Erasing to form a point

➡ Select one group of lines and move them away from the other so you'll have room to work. Scroll the screen so you're not working on top of the lines.

 ➡ Use the oval tool with the Shift key to create a circle about 1 ³/₄ inches wide.

 ➡ Select that circle with the lasso and place it on top of the group of lines that forms the arrow, as shown in Figure 4-97.

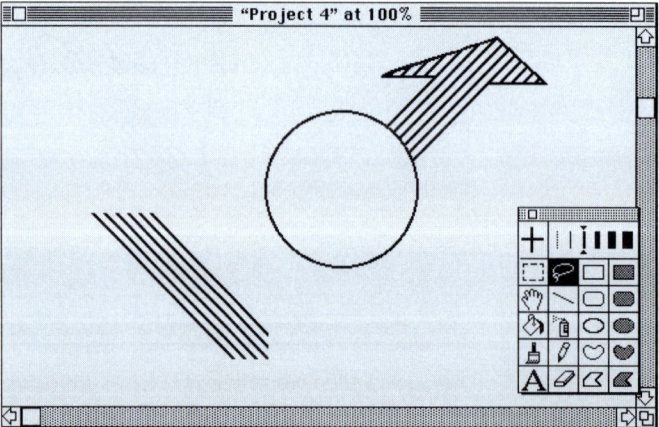

Figure 4-97   Positioning the circle on the arrow

➡ Select **Draw From Center** from the Goodies menu, and then draw another slightly smaller circle inside the first one.

 ➡ Select the left group of lines with the lasso, and place them on the circles, as shown in Figure 4-98.

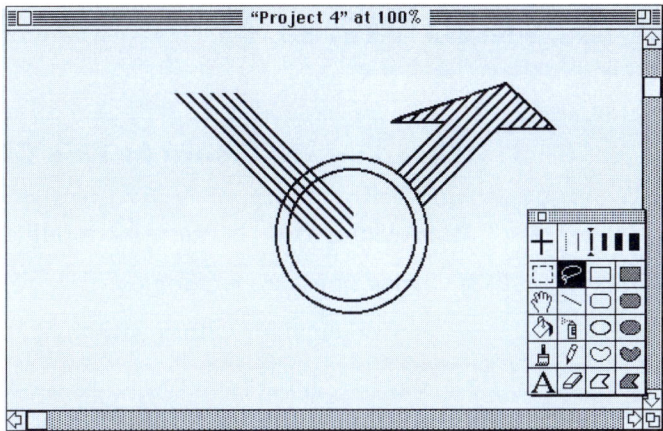

Figure 4-98   Positioning the lines on the circles

    ⇒   Zoom in to FatBits and use the pencil tool to erase the parts of the circles that show through the lines.

⇒   Zoom out to 100% size.

Now you'll type the text for the logo.

    ⇒   Select the text tool and set the insertion point away from the rest of the drawing.

⇒   Type **Stanford Recycling Center** in a bold, 18 point font of your choice (the example uses Helvetica).

    ⇒   Select the text with the selection rectangle. Select only a small amount of the background with the text, as shown in Figure 4-99.

Stanford Recycling Center

Figure 4-99   Selecting the background with the text

⇒   Choose **Invert** from the Edit menu.

The Invert command changes black dots to white and white dots to black in a selected area.

⇒   Position the text on the logo. Refer to the finished logo shown in Figure 4-91 at the beginning of this project.

Chapter 5: MacDraw II

What You Will Learn in This Chapter

After reading this chapter, you should be able to:

- Draw lines and rectangles

- Resize rectangles, lines, and text

- Use the Shift key to constrain lines horizontally and vertically

- Draw objects filled with a selected pattern

- Change line weights from the Pen menu

- Add text to a drawing using the text tool

- Change the style and font of text

- Reposition objects and text

- Group objects to form a composite object

- Save and print documents

- Select and move multiple objects at one time

- Change the fill pattern of selected objects

- Change the line pattern of selected lines

- Fill the text background with a pattern

- Move objects in their stacking order

- Use Autogrid for precise alignment of objects

- Align objects to one another

- Use the zoom controls to view a larger portion of the drawing

MacPaint works like using a pen, pencil, or brush on paper to create your drawing. If you want to modify an object in MacPaint, you "erase" by changing a black dot to white. If you move or draw a shape on top of another in a bitmapped drawing program such as MacPaint, the shape beneath is removed because the dots are changed to represent the one that was drawn or moved on top. No record of the one beneath remains, just as if you had erased it from the paper.

MacDraw II works more like cutting objects out of construction paper and then arranging them to form a picture. If you draw or place an object on top of another in an object-oriented drawing program such as MacDraw II, the item beneath still remains. You can move aside the one on top and the shape underneath is unchanged, just as it would be with shapes cut out of construction paper, because object-oriented drawing programs store a definition of each object's location, shape, size, and depth level.

MacDraw II's drawing surface can be 69 square feet, compared with MacPaint's 80 square inches. MacDraw II's grid and ruler allow you to precisely place objects on the drawing page. A less sophisticated grid is available in MacPaint, but a ruler is not. In MacDraw II you can edit text in more of a word processing fashion, where you can select text and then type over it to modify it, and you can control the placement of the insertion point. MacPaint's text editing is very limited—you can either correct errors by backspacing while typing or erase the text and retype.

Since the printed output of MacDraw II and most object-oriented programs is superior to that of paint programs, MacDraw II is popular among draftspersons as well as artists. Although MacDraw II is a powerful drawing program with many features that exceed the scope of this book, you'll use many of the tools of this object-oriented drawing program to create some introductory and intermediate level drawings.

MacDraw II is best for jobs that involve a lot of text and text editing, or ones that require precise placement and alignment of objects, or ones that require smooth, high-quality output. Freehand drawing and quick illustrations are easier in MacPaint. In working through these projects, you'll see some of the differences, advantages, and disadvantages of working with a bitmapped graphics program vs. an object-oriented graphics program.

STARTING MACDRAW II

MacDraw II

➡ Double-click on the MacDraw II icon to open a new, untitled drawing window.

Every new document has the title "Untitled-Layer#1" until you save it for the first time and give it a name.

The drawing window shows only a part of the available drawing area, which is preset to a single page for a new document. The drawings you'll be creating in the projects in this chapter will fit on one page, although a MacDraw II drawing can be as large as 69 square feet.

A *menu bar* runs across the top of the screen:

```
 ⬤  File  Edit  Layout  Arrange  Pen  Font  Size  Style
```

You'll learn about many of the options on the menus as you work through the projects.

GETTING HELP

Many applications provide online help for quick reference when you are using different tools and commands. Unfortunately, MacDraw II is not one of these programs. The reference manual that you get when you purchase MacDraw II is very comprehensive, however, and includes a tutorial as well as detailed descriptions of the features of each tool and command.

SAVING YOUR WORK

The first time you save your document, MacDraw II asks you, by way of the dialog box shown in Figure 5-1, where you want your document saved and what you want it to be named. After you have saved a document the first time, the next time you choose **Save**, MacDraw II assumes that you want the document to be saved in the same place and under the same name. Be careful about saving your document in the correct place the first time you save it so you can find it later. The save process is much quicker the second and subsequent times, because you are not prompted for any additional information.

Unfortunately, sometimes people are not careful, and they occasionally lose their work because they save it but do not think about where they are saving it and then can't find it again. Clicking the **Drive** button (see Figure 5-1) toggles between one or more floppy drives and hard drives, depending on the hardware you are using. The Save dialog box shows the name of the floppy disk or hard drive as that drive is selected. You are saving your document on the selected disk or hard drive with the name showing in the Save dialog box. In the dialog box shown in Figure 5-1, the name of the disk, Pamela Gurnari, is shown in two places. Always be aware of where you are saving your work.

The Save As command is similar to the Save command, except that it enables you to give your document a different name and save it in a different location. Every time you choose **Save As** from the File menu, you are prompted with the dialog box shown in Figure 5-1. This is the same dialog box you see the first time you save your document.

When you use the Save As command and you attempt to save the document with the same name and in the same location as before, you will be asked if you want to replace the old document. This is because no two files in a particular location can have the same name. If you want to save different versions of the same document, use the Save As command and give the document a different name and/or location.

Save your work often—at least every ten minutes, so you never lose more than ten minutes of work. The Command-key equivalent of the Save command, Command-S, is a helpful shortcut. Practice it often, and it will become automatic. Always save your work before printing.

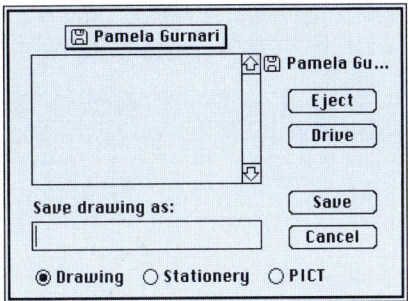

Figure 5-1   The Save dialog box

Be aware that you can save a document before you actually type anything into it, and that many people do it this way. However, you will be given instructions for saving your work at appropriate times throughout the projects in this chapter.

USING MACDRAW'S TOOLS

The *tools palette* shows the drawing tools that you can use to create graphics. The nine icons in the tools palette represent the types of objects that the tools create.

The pointer changes to a *cross-beam* when it moves into the drawing window, which is the *grid* you see on the screen. The cross-beam and the *gridlines* make it easier to position objects.

To draw an object, you first *select* a tool by clicking on it. After you've drawn an object, black squares called *handles* appear around the object. The *selection arrow* (at the top of the tools palette) becomes automatically *active*, and the tool you drew with is no longer active. You can manipulate the object with the selection arrow.

A tool becomes *highlighted* in gray when you select it by clicking once on it. It becomes highlighted in black when you click twice on it. When it is highlighted in black, it remains the selected tool after you complete an action with it, rather than automatically defaulting to the selection arrow.

Now you'll get some practice with each of these tools before beginning Project 1.

Text Tool

The *text tool* is used for typing text. Not only does text typed in MacDraw II print in a very high quality, it is also easy to change parts of words or sentences.

➡ Select the text tool by double-clicking on it.

Double-clicking on the text tool will keep it active until you select another tool.

➡ Click in the center of the screen to set the *insertion point* for where the text will begin, and then type **Using the text tool.**

➡ Click and drag through the word **the** in the line you just typed. (You can also double-click on a word to select it.)

The selected word becomes highlighted, as shown in Figure 5-2.

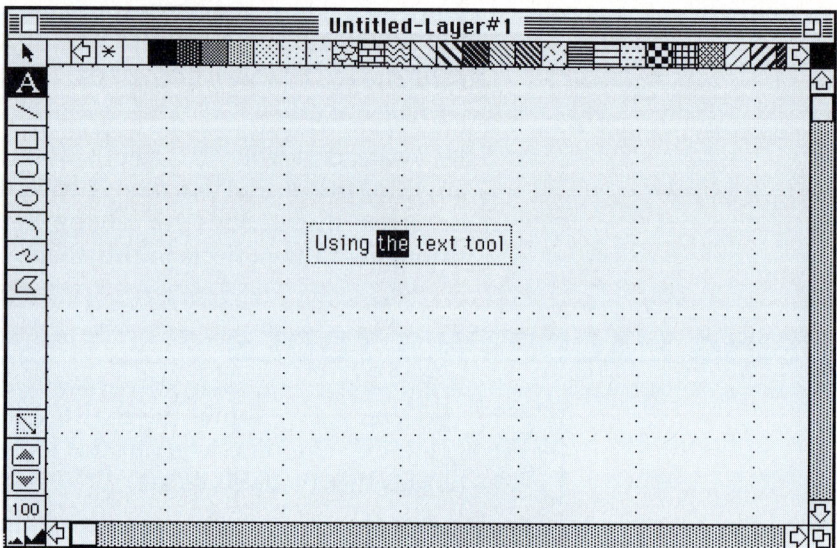

Figure 5-2   Selecting a word with the text tool

➡ Type **MacDraw II's** to replace the word "the" that you highlighted.

Your sentence now reads "Using MacDraw II's text tool".

You can reposition text on the screen without having to retype it. You use the selection arrow for this.

 ➡ Click on the selection arrow to select it, and then click anywhere on the text you just typed.

Notice that small black squares, called *handles*, appear around the block of text. The presence of these handles indicates that the object is selected.

➡ Click on the text with the selection arrow, but don't click on one of the handles.

➡ Drag the text to another part of the screen, and then release the mouse button.

Your text should be positioned in another part of the screen.

To delete an object, you select it by clicking on it, and then you press the Backspace key (Delete key on some keyboards).

➡ Select the text (if it is not already selected), and then press the Backspace key.

Line Tool

The *line tool* is used to draw straight lines. The width of the line is controlled by the Pen menu. You'll learn more about the Pen menu later, in Project 1.

➠   Select the line tool, and then draw a line about 2 inches long.

When you release the mouse button, the line is selected, as shown by the handles on either end.

Now you'll lengthen the line you just drew.

➠   Click on the line's right handle with the selection arrow and drag about ¹/₂ inch to the right, and then release the mouse button, as shown in Figure 5-3.

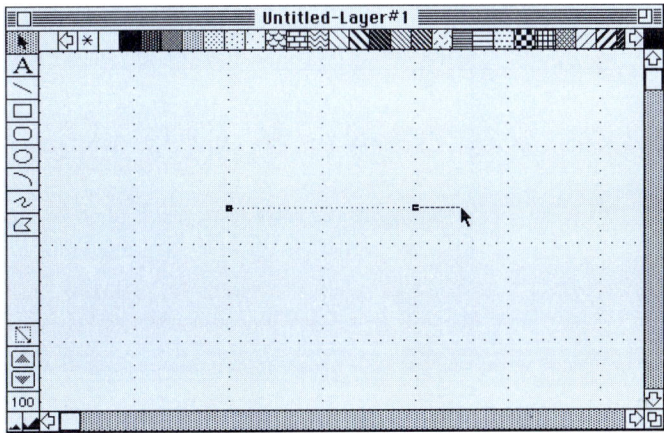

Figure 5-3   Resizing the line

Your line should now be lengthened by ¹/₂ inch.

You can shorten a line in the same manner.

➠   Practice drawing and resizing some lines now, and when you are ready to go on to the next tool, select the lines and then delete them using the Backspace key.

Rectangle and Rounded Rectangle Tools

The rectangle and rounded rectangle tools allow you to draw rectangles and squares, filled with a pattern that you select. Any MacDraw II object that you create can have its size changed, its border changed, and its fill pattern changed. You'll experiment with the rectangle border later in this chapter. To resize an object, you drag the handles on its boundary. When the mouse button is released, the object takes on its new size.

➠   Select one of the patterns in the *pattern palette* at the top of the drawing window, and then select the rectangle tool.

It doesn't matter whether you select the pattern or the tool first. To select a pattern from the pattern palette, just click on the pattern. You'll learn more about the pattern palette in a few minutes.

➡ Click and drag in a diagonal manner from upper left to bottom right, and release the mouse button when you have a rectangle.

When you release the mouse button, the rectangle is selected. Your screen shows the rectangle filled with the pattern you chose before you drew the rectangle. You can also change the pattern of an object after you draw it.

➡ While the rectangle you just drew is still selected, click on the white pattern in the pattern palette.

This causes the pattern in the rectangle to change to white.

To change the size of an object, click on one of the handles. Drag toward the object to make it smaller, and drag away from it to make it larger.

➡ Click on one of the handles of the selected rectangle, and drag toward the rectangle to make it smaller, as shown in Figure 5-4.

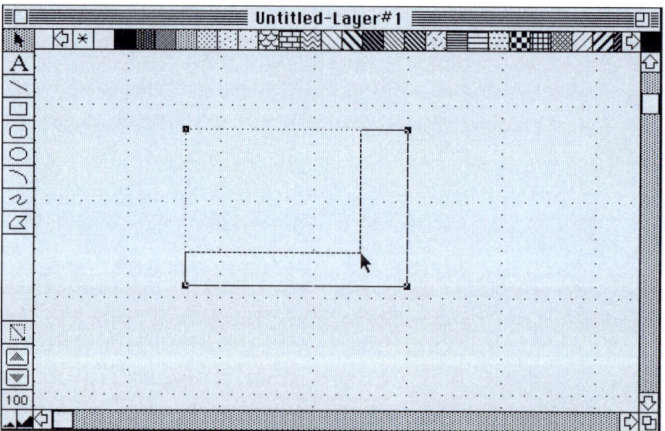

Figure 5-4   Resizing the rectangle

If you want to move an object to reposition it, don't place the pointer on one of the handles—place it on another part of the object and drag to the new position.

➡ Drag to reposition the rectangle on another part of the screen (do not drag by one of the handles).

➡ Delete the rectangle by pressing the Backspace key when the rectangle is selected.

To draw a perfect square, hold down the Shift key when drawing with either the rectangle or rounded rectangle.

Corner/Center Control

 In many cases, you will need to control the placement of the center point of the object you are drawing. MacDraw lets you control it using the *corner/center control*, which appears below the tool palette. The rectangles and lines you just drew were drawn from the corner.

➠ Click once on the corner/center control.

 The control changes to represent an object drawn from the center.

 ➠ Select the rounded rectangle tool.

➠ Position the pointer in the center of the screen. Hold down the Shift key while dragging to create a rounded square that is drawn from the center.

If you click once on the corner/center control, it becomes center/corner; if you click it again, it goes back to corner/center.

Practice drawing some other rectangles and squares, from the center and from the corner. Practice resizing the rectangles you draw by dragging one of the handles. Delete the objects when you are ready to go on to the next tool.

Oval Tool

 The oval tool is used to draw ovals and circles filled with a pattern of your choice. Like the rectangles, you can change the border thickness and pattern of the oval either before you draw it or after, and you can resize the oval or circle by dragging one if its handles. The corner/center control is also useful with the oval tool.

To create a perfect circle, hold down the Shift key when you draw with the oval tool.

 ➠ Check to see that the corner/center control is set to draw from the center.

 ➠ Double-click on the oval tool to select it if you want to draw more than one object.

The oval tool is highlighted in black to show that it will be selected until you choose another tool.

➠ Position the pointer in the center of the screen, hold down the Shift key, and click and drag to draw a circle about 2 inches across.

➠ Position the pointer at the same center point that you just used to create the first circle, and use the Shift key again to draw a circle about 1 inch across.

You should have one circle centered inside of the other circle, as shown in Figure 5-5.

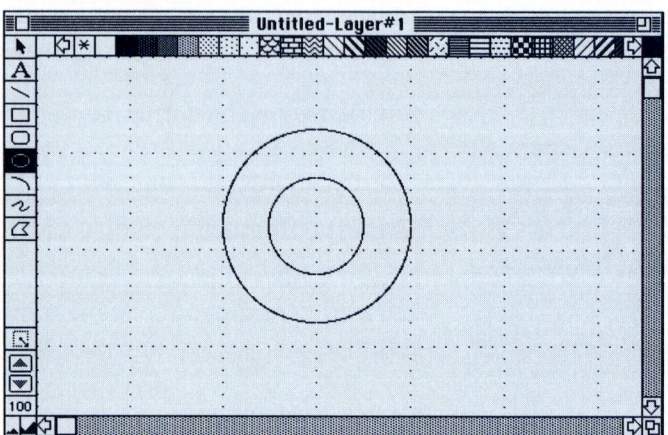

Figure 5-5   One circle centered inside of the other

Practice drawing additional circles and ovals using the corner/center control and different patterns. Delete the objects from your screen before going on to the next tool.

 ➠ Set the corner/center control back to "draw from corner" before going on.

Arc Tool

 The *arc tool* is used to draw part of a circle or part of an *ellipse*. When it is used in conjunction with the Shift key, the result is a quarter of a circle. You can change the thickness of the border of the arc before you draw it, but you fill it with a pattern after it is drawn. When an arc is filled with a pattern, it takes on a pie-shaped appearance.

➠ Click on the arc tool to select it.

➠ Click and drag to create an arc.

The direction in which you move the mouse while drawing the arc determines the shape of the arc. Figure 5-6 shows several arcs and the direction the mouse was moved when they were drawn.

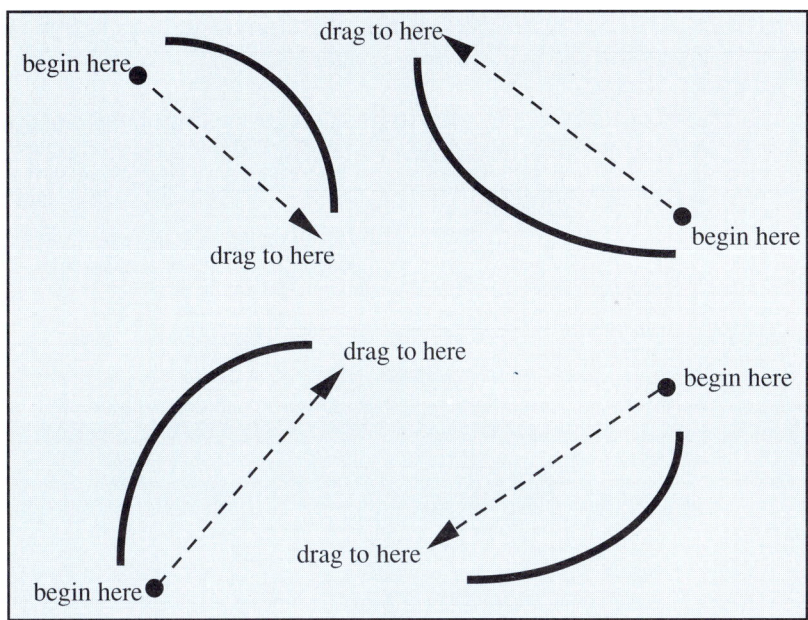

Figure 5-6   Arc shapes created by different mouse directions

➡ Click on a pattern in the pattern palette to fill the arc with that
   pattern.

Practice drawing some arcs by dragging in different directions to see
how the direction affects the shape of the arc. Use the Shift key to create
quarter-circles. Clear the screen before going on to the next tool.

Freehand Drawing Tool

 The *freehand tool* allows you to draw an irregular or curved freehand
shape similar to that created with a pencil. Freehand shapes do not fill
with a pattern as you draw them, but you can select a freehand shape
and fill it with a pattern after it is drawn. You can also change the border
thickness and border pattern. As with the other shapes you've learned
about, you can resize an object drawn with the freehand tool by
dragging one of its handles.

After you draw a freehand object, MacDraw II automatically *smooths* the
shape to get rid of any jagged lines.

➡ Click on the freehand tool to select it, and then position the pointer
   in the drawing window.

➡ With the mouse button held down, click and drag to create the
   shape of a fish or your favorite animal. Do not release the mouse
   button until the shape is completed.

When you release the mouse button, the shape is smoothed, and
handles appear that enclose the shape in a rectangular border.

➡ While the shape is still selected, click to select a pattern from the pattern pallet.

The shape you drew should be selected and filled with a pattern, as shown in Figure 5-7.

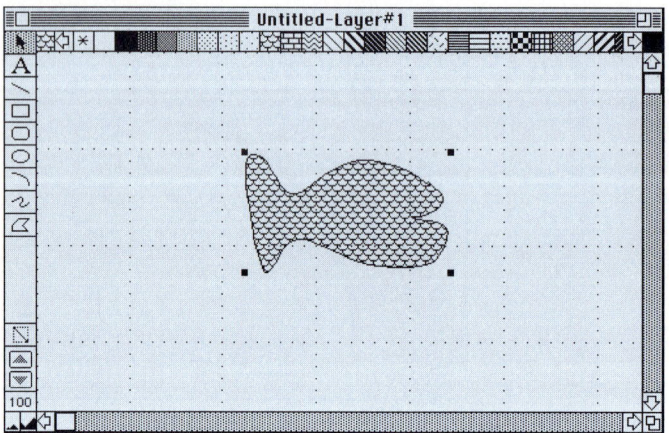

Figure 5-7   The freehand shape selected and filled with a pattern

Smoothing and Unsmoothing

If you don't want the object you drew with the freehand tool to be smoothed, you can use the *Unsmooth command* from the Edit menu to tell MacDraw to leave the object in angular form.

⌘-Shift-E   ➡ Select the animal you drew if it is not still selected, and choose **Unsmooth** from the Edit menu.

Now the shape appears as it would if it had not been smoothed after you drew it. To smooth the drawing again, choose **Smooth** from the Edit menu.

Reshaping

You can also use the *Reshape command* to change the shape of an object drawn with the freehand tool. When you choose this command from the Edit menu, handles are placed along the length of the border of the object, and you can drag those handles to change the object's shape. When a freehand object has been unsmoothed, you can also add extra handles by clicking on the outline of the shape.

⌘-R   ➡ Select the shape you drew if it is not already selected, and choose **Reshape** from the Edit menu.

The pointer changes to a small square with a cross-beam in it.

➡ Click and drag one of the handles on the border of the shape, and then release the mouse button.

Figure 5-8 shows the fish with its head reshaped.

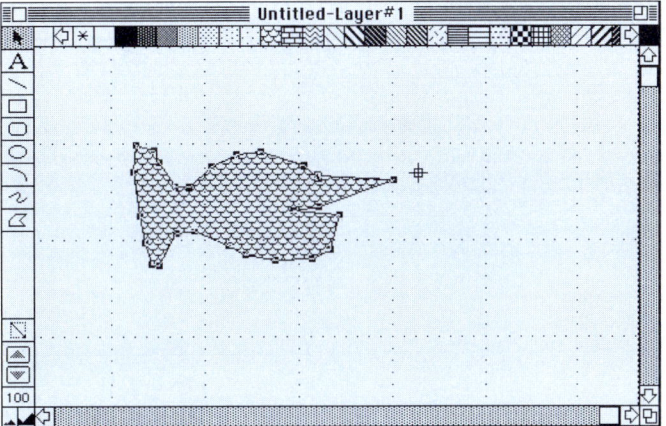

Figure 5-8   Reshaping the fish's head

➡ Continue to reshape your drawing, and then click on another part of the screen to stop reshaping. If your drawing is still unsmoothed, choose **Smooth** from the Edit menu.

When you are finished perfecting your drawing, clear your screen before going on to the next tool.

Polygon Tool

The *polygon tool* is used to draw shapes that are composed of straight lines and angles. After the polygon is drawn, you can fill it with a pattern. You can also modify a polygon's border thickness and border pattern.

This tool is similar to the freehand tool, since you can use the Smooth, Unsmooth, and Reshape commands with polygons as well. When you draw a polygon, it is not automatically smoothed as a freehand shape is.

➡ Select the polygon tool, and then click once in the center of the screen to set the starting point of the polygon.

You do not drag while using the polygon tool; you just click to direct the line between the two points it is connecting.

➠   Now click an inch or so to the right of the starting point. A line will follow the pointer on the screen.

➠   Click to create several more points and lines, and then double-click to finish drawing the shape.

Figure 5-9 shows a shape drawn with the polygon tool.

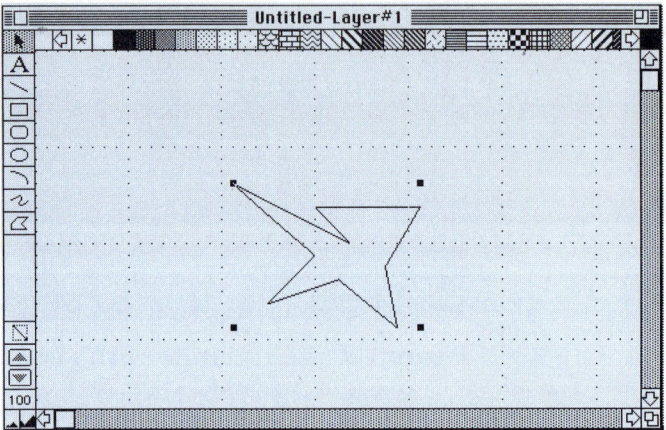

Figure 5-9   A shape drawn with the polygon tool

⌘-E   ➠   Choose **Smooth** from the Edit menu.

Figure 5-10 shows the same shape after it has been smoothed.

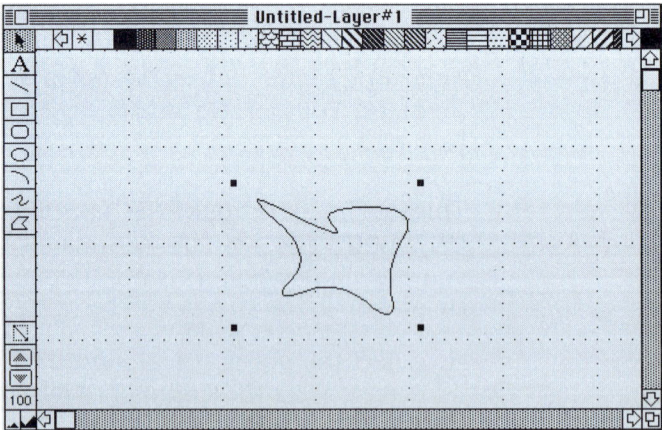

Figure 5-10   A smoothed shape drawn with the polygon tool

Practice using the polygon tool. Use the Reshape command from the Edit menu to modify the shape.

➧   Do not clear the screen, because you'll use the shapes to practice with the selection arrow.

Selection Arrow

The selection arrow is automatically active when you open a new untitled drawing window. You've already used it for selecting and resizing objects and text.

There are several ways to select an object (any shape you create in MacDraw is considered an object, including text). One way that you've already used is to click on the object with the selection arrow.

Another way to select with the selection arrow is to click and drag the selection arrow around an object, which draws a dotted rectangle around the object. The object must be completely enclosed by the rectangle for it to be selected. This method is especially helpful when you select multiple objects. You click and drag around a group of objects, and all that are completely enclosed by the dotted rectangle become selected and can be manipulated together. You can tell that the objects are selected because their handles will show.

➧   If you do not have more than one object on your screen, draw a few now.

➧   Click at the top left of the group of drawings and drag diagonally to the bottom right, so that all the drawings are enclosed by a dotted rectangle. See Figure 5-11.

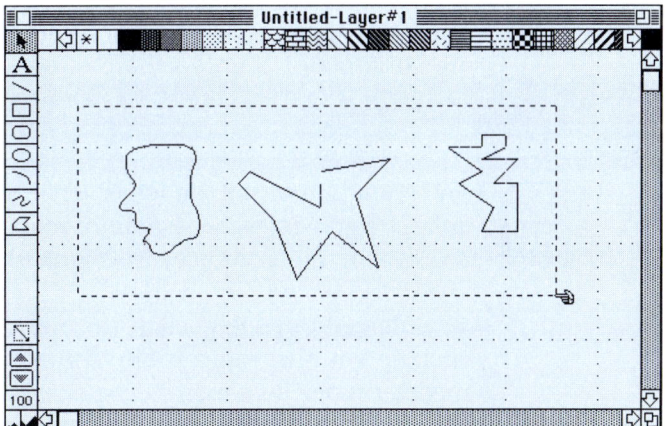

Figure 5-11   Dragging through multiple objects

When you release the mouse button all objects that were completely enclosed by the dotted rectangle are selected, as shown in Figure 5-12.

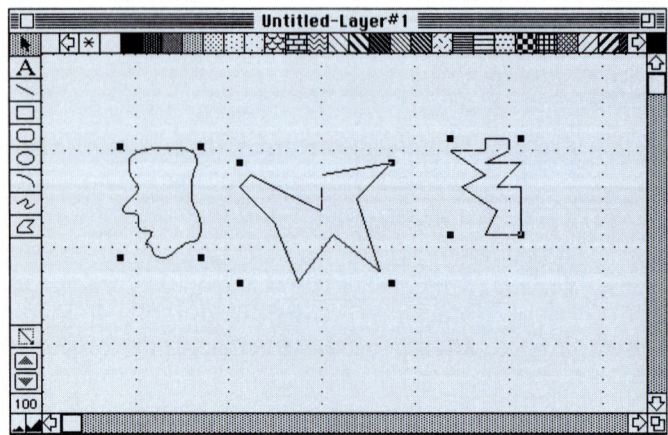

Figure 5-12   All objects selected

⟾   Click somewhere on the screen to deselect the objects, but don't delete them yet. You'll use them in a minute.

Layer Controls

The *layer controls* appear at the bottom of the tools palette, and they enable you to move between the *layers* in a MacDraw document. Working with layers in MacDraw II is similar to working with transparent film. You can create many layers in a document and work with each as a separate drawing or view them all at once in a specific stacking order. Due to the introductory nature of this book, we have not included any projects that use MacDraw's layers. All MacDraw documents consist of one layer—Layer #1—unless you specify otherwise. The layer controls are not functional unless there is more than one layer in a document.

Zoom Controls

The *zoom controls* in the lower left corner of the screen allow you to enlarge a drawing to see details or reduce it so you can see more of it on the screen. The zoom controls look like mountains.

To enlarge your view, click the right zoom control. You can keep clicking on the right zoom control to magnify up to 3200% in predetermined increments. The *zoom percentage box* just above the zoom controls shows at what percent you are currently viewing the document. The right zoom control dims when the drawing has reached its maximum viewing size. The left zoom control works the same way for reducing the viewing size, enabling you to reduce the drawing to 3.12% in predetermined increments. To bring the drawing back to its original size, click the zoom percentage box. You can edit your drawing at any zoom level.

→ Click the right zoom control to enlarge the view of your document to 200%.

 Notice that the zoom percentage box now reads "200".

→ Use the zoom controls to experiment with reducing and magnifying the view of your document. When you are finished, click on the zoom percentage box to return the view to 100%.

Pattern Palette

The *pattern palette*, at the top of the screen, allows you to *fill* an existing object with a pattern and to fill an object as you draw it.

To fill an existing object, click on the object to select it. Handles appear to show that the object is selected. Select the desired pattern from the palette. You can change the pattern whenever the object is selected.

To create a new filled object, select a drawing tool, select a pattern from the palette, and then draw the object.

 The *fill pattern box*, at the far left of the palette and to the left of the arrow, reflects the currently selected fill pattern. MacDraw's preset fill pattern is white. An object filled with white blocks the view of objects behind it. You can use the left and right *scroll arrows* on the pattern palette to view other patterns.

 The *line pattern box* is at the far right of the pattern palette and to the right of the arrow, and it reflects the currently selected line pattern. To draw a patterned line, you click the line pattern box and choose a pattern before you draw. MacDraw's default line pattern is black. To change the line pattern of an existing line, the line must be selected first. Then you click the line pattern box and select the pattern you want to use.

→ Select one of the objects in your drawing, and then select a pattern in the pattern palette to change the fill pattern.

→ With that same object still selected, click on the line pattern box at the far right of the pattern palette, and then select the same pattern that you used as a fill pattern.

The object should now have the same line and fill patterns.

Experiment with different line and fill patterns, and then delete all the objects on the screen.

→ Before continuing with the rest of the project, change the line pattern to black and the fill pattern to white.

AUTOGRID ON/OFF

The *Autogrid* feature of MacDraw II controls where you draw objects in a document and what size the objects can be.

When you first open an untitled MacDraw II drawing window, Autogrid is automatically turned on. This means that when you draw an object, it will *snap* to the grid increments on the screen.

Using Autogrid ensures that your objects are placed on the drawing's grid and makes it easier to *align* objects. When you move objects, they will always align to the divisions of the grid. You cannot place or draw objects between these grid divisions as long as Autogrid is on.

To have MacDraw II ignore the grid, choose **Turn Autogrid Off** from the Layout menu. This allows you to place and draw objects anywhere on the screen. Placement of objects can be more precise when you work with Autogrid off.

There will be times when it will be easier to draw and place objects with Autogrid on and times when you'll want to turn off the Autogrid feature.

The screen looks the same whether Autogrid is on or off. The presence of the gridlines in an untitled drawing window is controlled by a different command.

HIDE/SHOW GRIDLINES

When you first open an untitled drawing window, the *gridlines* automatically show. The gridlines are composed of dots that represent where Autogrid will *constrain* your objects, and they can be used as guides to help you place objects accurately. Gridlines do not appear when the document is printed.

To hide the gridlines, choose **Hide Gridlines** from the Layout menu. Hide Gridlines is not available on the menu unless gridlines are showing on the screen.

HIDE/SHOW RULERS

When you first open an untitled document, the *rulers* are not turned on. If you want to use them, you have to turn them on.

➡ Choose **Show Rulers** from the Layout menu.

A ruler now runs along the top and left sides of the drawing window, as shown in Figure 5-13.

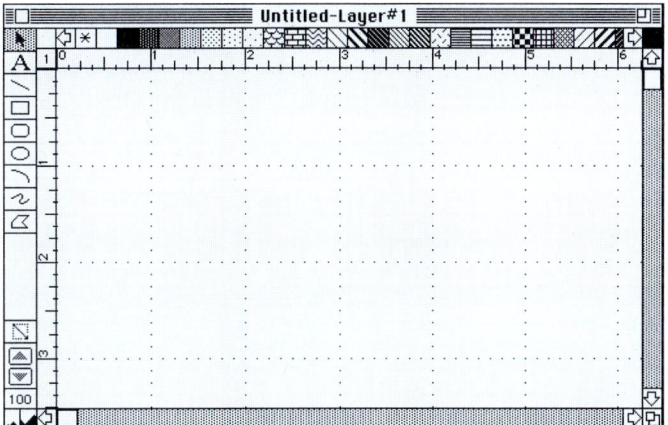

Figure 5-13   The MacDraw window with rulers showing

The current *ruler settings* control the spacing of the grid that is in effect when you begin to draw. The default ruler settings set the grid to $1/8$-inch increments, and you can see the incremental markers on the ruler.

Project 1: Creating a Form

This assignment shows you how to create a telephone message form using MacDraw II. You'll use the rectangle tool to create the background border and message option box and the line tool to create the lines in the form. The text tool will be used to create text that will be repositioned in the body of the form. Once you've completed the form, you'll duplicate the entire message slip so that four will print on a page.

The finished project is shown in Figure 5-14 .

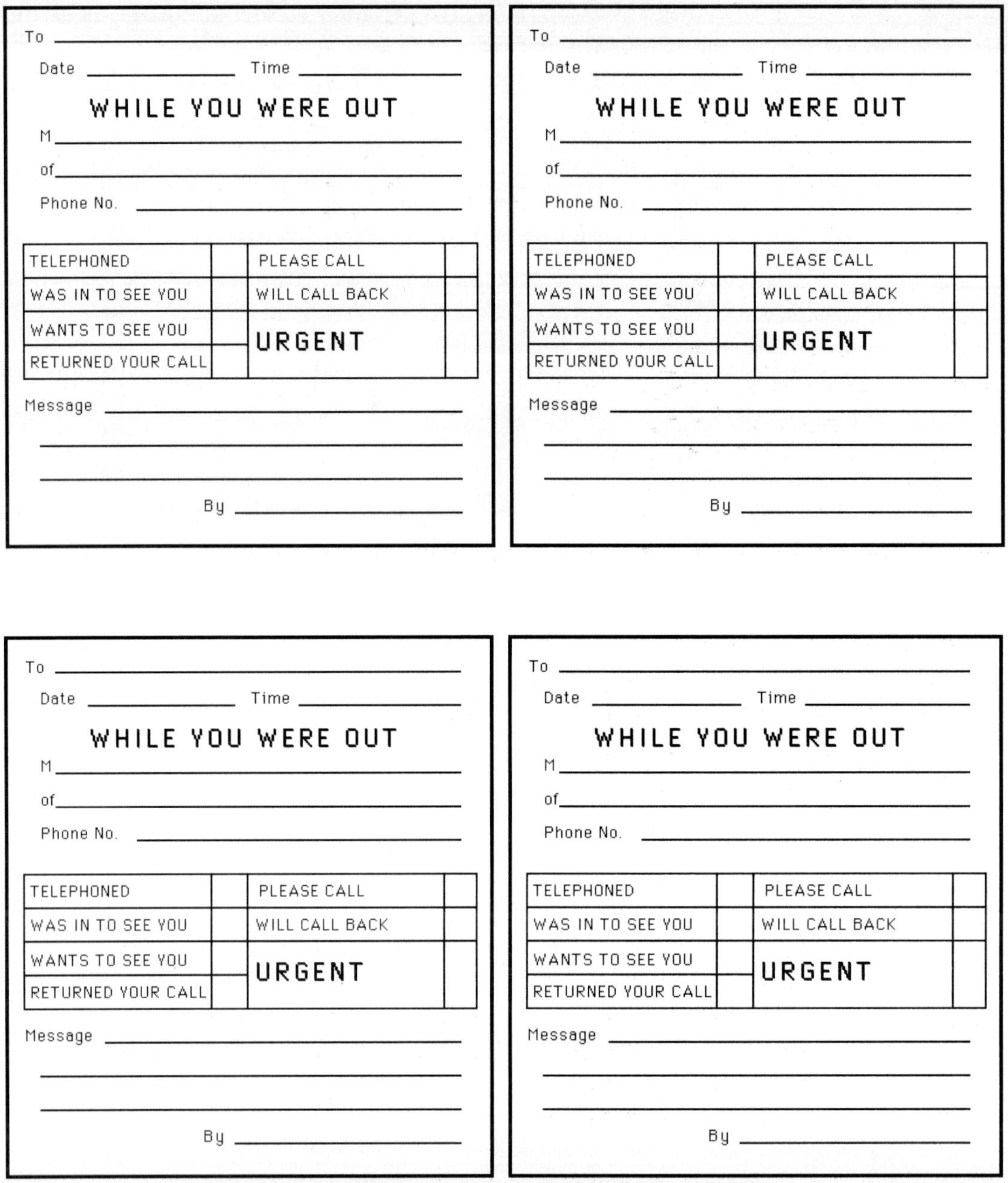

To _____
Date _____ Time _____
WHILE YOU WERE OUT
M_____
of_____
Phone No. _____

TELEPHONED		PLEASE CALL	
WAS IN TO SEE YOU		WILL CALL BACK	
WANTS TO SEE YOU		**URGENT**	
RETURNED YOUR CALL			

Message _____
_____
_____
By _____

To _____
Date _____ Time _____
WHILE YOU WERE OUT
M_____
of_____
Phone No. _____

TELEPHONED		PLEASE CALL	
WAS IN TO SEE YOU		WILL CALL BACK	
WANTS TO SEE YOU		**URGENT**	
RETURNED YOUR CALL			

Message _____
_____
_____
By _____

To _____
Date _____ Time _____
WHILE YOU WERE OUT
M_____
of_____
Phone No. _____

TELEPHONED		PLEASE CALL	
WAS IN TO SEE YOU		WILL CALL BACK	
WANTS TO SEE YOU		**URGENT**	
RETURNED YOUR CALL			

Message _____
_____
_____
By _____

To _____
Date _____ Time _____
WHILE YOU WERE OUT
M_____
of_____
Phone No. _____

TELEPHONED		PLEASE CALL	
WAS IN TO SEE YOU		WILL CALL BACK	
WANTS TO SEE YOU		**URGENT**	
RETURNED YOUR CALL			

Message _____
_____
_____
By _____

Figure 5-14   Final output of Project 1

⇒ Before you begin the project, your screen should be showing the rulers at the top and left of the drawing window. If they are not showing, choose **Show Rulers** from the Layout menu.

 ⇒ The corner/center control should be set to drawing from the corner. If it is not, click once on the control to change it.

⇒ The line pattern should be black, and the fill pattern should be white. If they are not, refer to the information about the pattern palette earlier in this chapter for instructions about changing the fill and line patterns.

⇒ If necessary, clear the screen of your practice drawings.

DRAWING AND FILLING A RECTANGLE

The first part of the form that you'll draw is the rectangle that is the border.

 ⇒ Select the rectangle tool.

⇒ Using the top and side rulers as guides, place the pointer at $1/4$ inch on the top (horizontal) ruler and $1/4$ inch on the left (vertical) ruler.

⇒ Click and drag to form a rectangle that ends at 4 inches on the horizontal ruler and 4 $1/4$ inches on the vertical ruler.

The view of the rectangle you are creating will automatically scroll when you drag the cursor past the bottom edge of the window to reach the 4 $1/4$-inch mark. Figure 5-15 shows the drawing window after it has scrolled, with the vertical *scroll box* in about the middle of the screen.

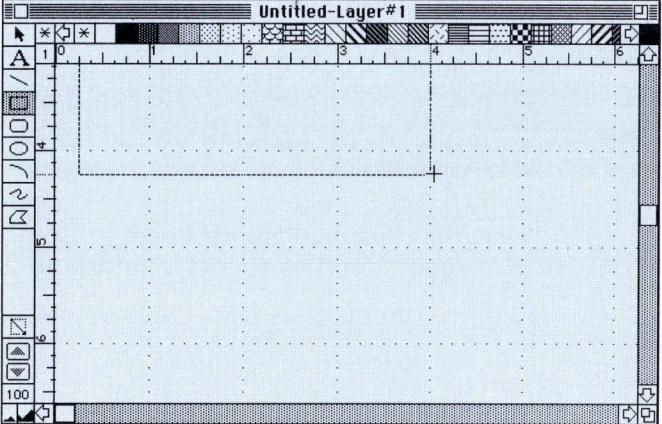

Figure 5-15   Scrolling to view the bottom of the rectangle

If you make an error and want to delete the whole rectangle, press Backspace (or Delete on some keyboards) while the object is selected. This works for any object that you create in MacDraw. You cannot erase part of an object in MacDraw.

Next you'll change the fill pattern of the rectangle you just drew.

 The empty fill pattern creates *transparent objects*, which lets objects underneath show through.

When you select an object that is filled with a transparent pattern, you must click on its border to select it. If an object is filled with any other pattern, including white, you can click anywhere on the object to select it. White is the default fill pattern (except with polygons and freehand shapes, which are filled with the transparent pattern).

➧ If the rectangle you created is not already selected, select it by clicking anywhere on it. Since you want the rectangle to be transparent, select the empty fill pattern from the pattern palette, as shown in Figure 5-16.

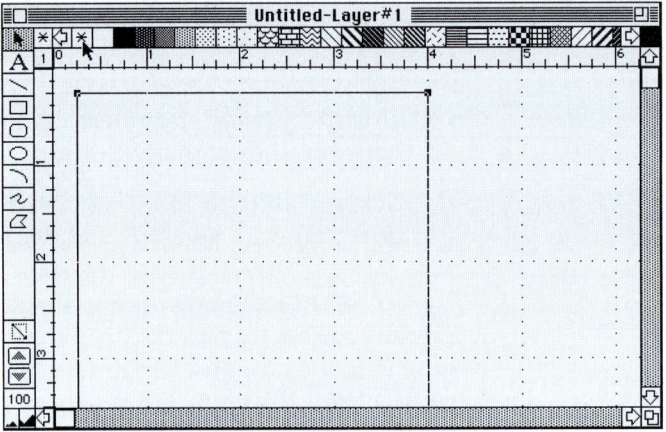

Figure 5-16   Changing fill pattern to empty

Now is a good time to save what you have done so far.

SAVING THE DOCUMENT

You save a document the same way in all standard Macintosh applications, by choosing **Save** from the File menu.

⌘-S ➧ Choose **Save** from the File menu.

➧ In the resulting dialog box, click the **Drive** button, if necessary, to be sure that your name is showing where "Pamela Gurnari" is showing in Figure 5-17 or that you are saving to the correct drive and folder.

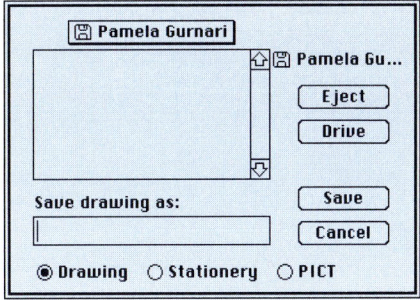

Figure 5-17   The Save dialog box

When saving a MacDraw II document, you can choose one of three document formats. They are shown in the bottom of the dialog box in Figure 5-17. *Drawing format* is the preset option, and it causes the document to be saved as a MacDraw picture. The Stationery option lets you save the document as a template that records settings, drawing elements, and other preferences. The PICT option saves the drawing in a special format so you can transfer the drawing to another application that uses the PICT file format. You will use the default Drawing format for the projects in this book.

➠ Type the name of this document as **Telephone Message Slip**, and then click the **Save** button.

The name at the top of your document is now "Telephone Message Slip-Layer#1".

SELECTING OBJECTS

Earlier in this chapter you learned two ways to select objects: by clicking on an object with the selection arrow and by dragging completely around one or more objects with the selection arrow. The second method is useful for selecting multiple objects at one time.

You can also select multiple objects by using the Shift-click method. Hold down the Shift key and click on each successive object that you want to select. If you do not hold down the Shift key, each object will be *deselected* when you select the next one.

⌘-A   To select all the objects in the drawing window, choose **Select All** from the Edit menu.

MOVING OBJECTS

To move an object, you select it and then drag the object to its new location. (Do not click on one of the handles to drag it, because that will resize it.) An outline of the object follows the pointer. When you release the mouse button, the object will be in its new location.

To move multiple objects at one time, you first select the objects using one of the methods described above. Then, dragging any one of the group of objects will move all the selected objects at one time. Be sure to click on one of the selected objects or you will deselect all you have chosen.

DELETING OBJECTS

The most straightforward way to delete an object from the drawing is to select it and then press the Backspace key. Another way to delete an object after selecting it is to choose **Cut** or **Clear** from the Edit menu. To delete the entire drawing, choose **Select All** from the Edit menu and then press the Backspace key.

⌘-Z   To undo a change made to your screen, whether you mistakenly delete an object or you don't like the results of a change to an object, immediately choose **Undo** from the Edit menu. Undo will undo the last command or the last action of the mouse.

CREATING LINES OF VARYING WEIGHTS

You can use a variety of *line weights* in MacDraw. The weights of lines are measured in points—the higher the *point size*, the heavier the line weight (the thicker the line). To create a new line of a certain size, or to create a shape that has a certain size border, select the appropriate tool, and then select the point size from the *Pen menu*. This line width will be used for all lines and shapes you draw until you select a different point size. The preset line weight in MacDraw is 1 point.

To change the line weight of an existing line or shape, you first select the object. The object will have handles around it to show it is selected. Once it is selected, you can choose a different point size from the Pen menu. The line weight then changes to the point size you selected.

You'll change the line weight of the rectangle you just drew.

⇒   Select the rectangle if it is not already selected, and then choose **2 point** from the Pen menu. Notice that the border of the rectangle becomes thicker.

Next you'll draw the lines in the message form.

 ⇒   To draw the lines for the message form, double-click on the line tool.

This will enable you to draw more than one line without having to reselect the line tool each time.

⇒   Choose **1 point** from the Pen menu.

⇒   At $^1/_4$ inch from the top of the rectangle ($^1/_2$ inch on the vertical ruler) draw a horizontal line inside the rectangle beginning at $^3/_8$ inch from the rectangle ($^5/_8$ inch on the horizontal ruler), and end it at $^1/_4$ inch before the end of the rectangle, which will be at the $3^3/_4$-inch mark on the horizontal ruler. See Figure 5-18.

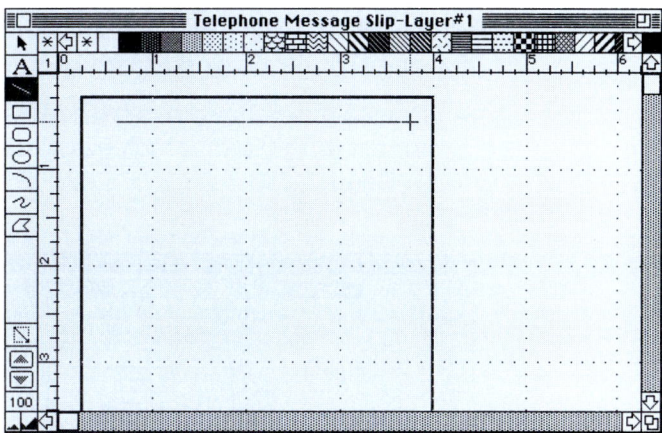

Figure 5-18   Drawing a horizontal line

⇒ $^1/_4$ inch beneath that line, draw two more shorter lines. Begin the first at $^7/_8$ inches on the horizontal ruler and end it at the 2 inch mark. Start the one next to it at $2^1/_2$ inches on the horizontal ruler and end it at the $3^3/_4$-inch mark.

You should now have two more lines in your rectangle, like those shown in Figure 5-19.

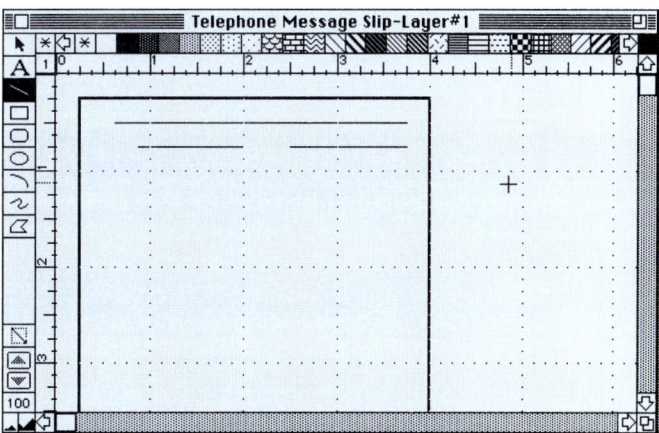

Figure 5-19   The second set of lines

Since you want two more lines the same length as the first line you drew, you'll make two copies of that line and position them in the rectangle.

 ⇒   Click on the selection arrow.

⌘-D ⇒   Click anywhere on the first line to select it, and then choose **Duplicate** from the Edit menu.

The duplicate line will be placed slightly below and to the right of the original line, and it will automatically be selected.

The *Duplicate command* places a copy of the selected object in the drawing. The Copy command places a copy of the selected object in the Clipboard, and you use the Paste command to paste the object in the drawing. Duplicate works like a combination Copy/Paste command.

➨ Drag that new line down to the $1\frac{1}{4}$-inch mark on the vertical ruler, so that it is placed $\frac{1}{2}$ inch below the short lines above it, as shown in Figure 5-20.

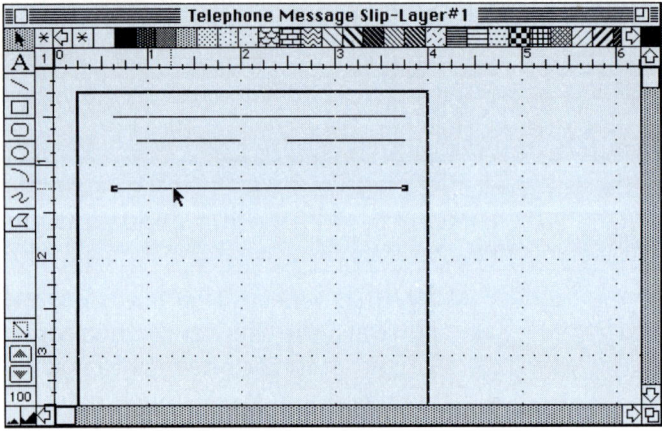

Figure 5-20   Positioning the duplicate line

➨ Click somewhere else on the screen to deselect the new line.

➨ Select the bottom line again and duplicate it in the same manner.

➨ Place the duplicate line $\frac{1}{4}$ inch beneath the last line.

➨ Duplicate the line one more time and place it $\frac{1}{4}$ inch beneath the one above it, so your drawing has three duplicate lines $\frac{1}{4}$ inch apart, as shown in Figure 5-21.

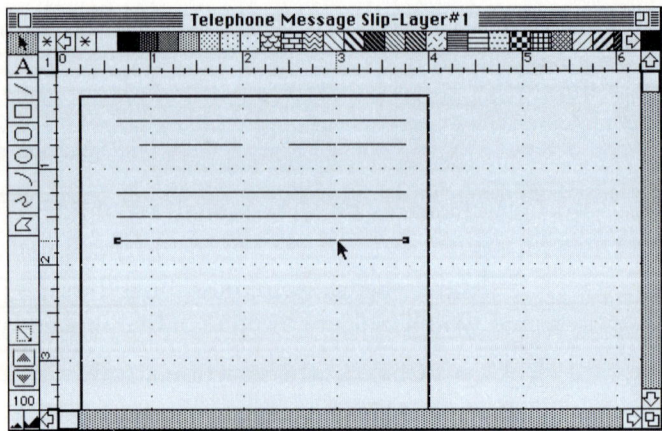

Figure 5-21   Duplicating lines

Now you'll *resize* the last line to make it slightly shorter than the one above it.

➠ If it's not already selected, select the last line and then click on its left handle. Drag to the right so it is ⁵/₈ inch shorter than the one above it, as shown in Figure 5-22.

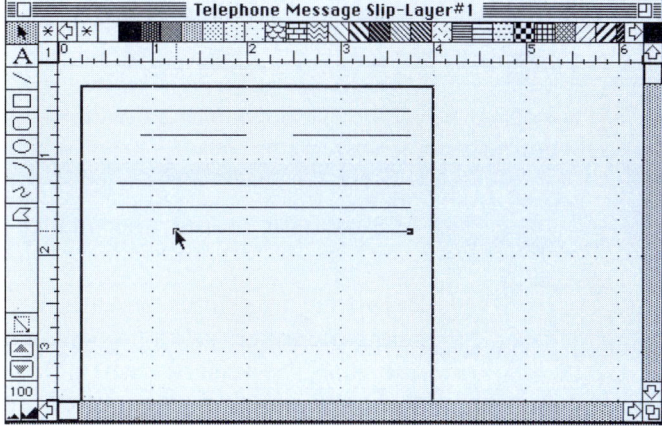

Figure 5-22   Resizing a line

The next step is to draw another rectangle for the message options.

 ➠ Select the rectangle tool.

➠ Beginning at the 2-inch mark on the vertical ruler and ³/₈ inches on the horizontal ruler, click and drag to form a rectangle that is 1 inch deep and that extends to 3⁷/₈ inches on the horizontal ruler. See Figure 5-23.

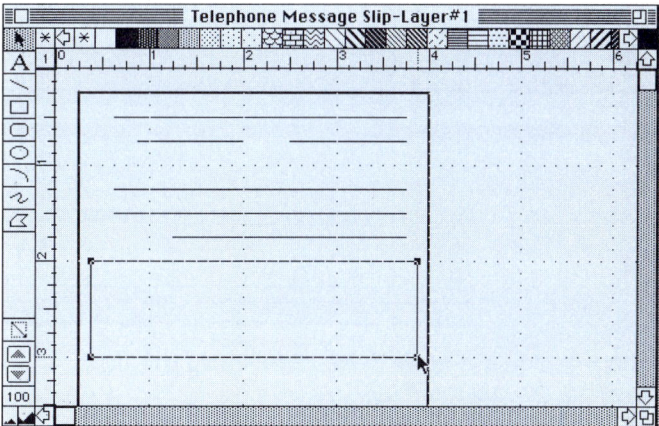

Figure 5-23   Drawing the second rectangle

 ➠ Double-click on the line tool and draw three horizontal lines within that rectangle, ¹/₄ inch apart and the entire length of the inner rectangle, as shown in Figure 5-24.

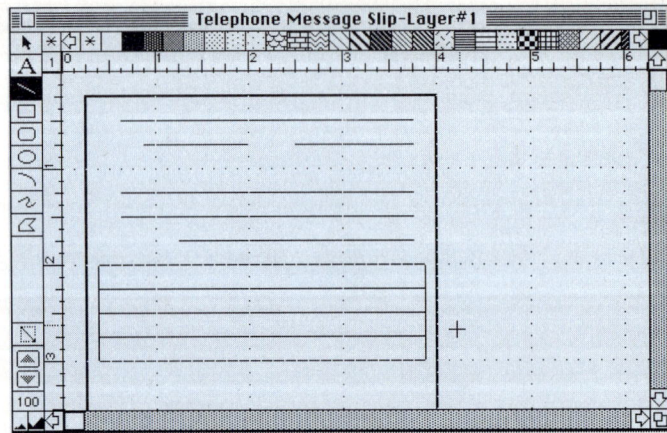

Figure 5-24   The lines in the smaller rectangle

➠ Draw four more lines beneath the rectangle, beginning at $^1/_4$ inch
    below the inner rectangle. There should be $^1/_4$ inch between each
    line. Start the first at 1 inch on the horizontal ruler and end it at the
    $3^3/_4$ -inch mark. See Figure 5-25.

➠ The next two lines should begin at $^1/_2$ inch on the horizontal ruler
    and also end at $3^3/_4$ inches.

➠ The last line should start at 2 inches on the horizontal ruler and end
    at $3^3/_4$ inches.

Your lines should look like those shown in Figure 5-25.

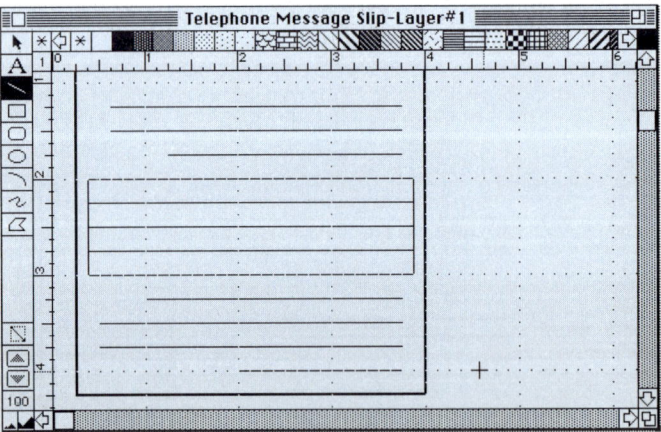

Figure 5-25   Finishing the lines

➠ If you've not already saved your work, do so now by choosing **Save**
    from the File menu.

ADDING TEXT

The next task is to type the text. To create text, you select the text tool. The pointer changes to an I-beam and is used to set the place where the text begins.

Once you enter the text, it becomes a separate object that you can select like any other object. Once you select it, you can drag it around the screen to reposition it. You can also place text on top of an object.

➠ Double-click on the text tool.

➠ Choose **Geneva** from the Font menu.

➠ Choose **9 point** from the Size menu.

➠ Click in the blank area to the right of your partially completed message slip and type the word **To**.

➠ Click next to that word and type **Date**. See Figure 5-26.

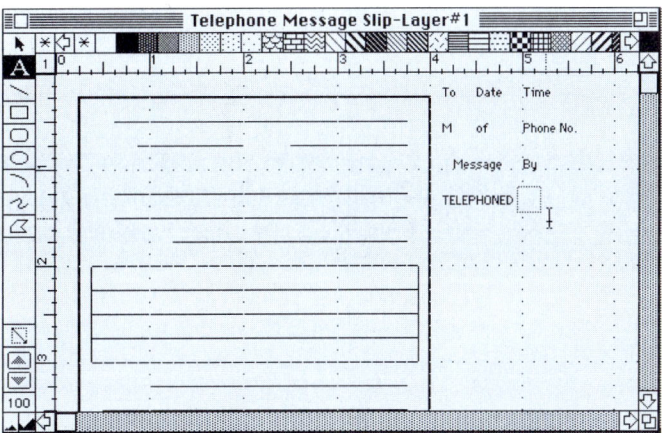

Figure 5-26   Adding text

➠ Continue in this manner: Type a word, and then click next to or beneath it to create each word as a separate object. Type the following words:
Time
M
of
Phone No.
Message
By

➠ Type the following in all caps, also as separate objects:
TELEPHONED
WAS IN TO SEE YOU
WANTS TO SEE YOU
RETURNED YOUR CALL
PLEASE CALL
WILL CALL BACK
URGENT
WHILE YOU WERE OUT

⌘-S ➡ Save your work now.

 ➡ If you used the Caps Lock key when you typed the last words, be sure to press the Caps Lock key again to release it.

When the Caps Lock key is down, it constrains the movement of the pointer and restricts where you can draw and position objects on the screen.

Another kind of text used in MacDraw II is *paragraph text*. It uses text wrap around and confines text to specific areas. To create a paragraph, select the text tool, and then drag the pointer to create a temporary text box. You don't need to set an insertion point because MacDraw will enter the text beginning at the blinking I-beam. When you are finished entering the text, clicking anywhere on the screen removes the temporary text box and leaves the paragraph automatically selected with handles until you click somewhere else. Dragging any handle will resize the margins of the paragraph. You can move the paragraph by clicking in it and dragging it around on the screen.

EDITING TEXT

To edit text, you use the text tool. To select text you'd like to edit, first click on the text tool, and then drag across the text you want to change. You can also double-click on a single word to select it. This will highlight the text. You can then type new text over the selected text.

To delete text, select it with the text tool in the same manner as above and then press the Backspace key or choose **Cut** or **Clear** from the Edit menu.

To insert text, you position the pointer in the line of text where you want to insert a character, word, or words, and then you click to set the insertion point. As you type, the rest of the text moves, or *wraps*, to make room for the inserted characters.

FORMATTING TEXT

You can format any text that you create using the options in the Font, Size, and Style menus. To select text for formatting, you can either wipe through it using the text tool, or you can select the text block using the selection arrow.

The phrases "URGENT" and "WHILE YOU WERE OUT" need to be changed to a larger, bold font.

  ➡ Choose the selection arrow and click on the word **URGENT**. Drag the handle on the bottom right of the word so that a longer rectangle is created for the word, as shown in Figure 5-27.

This will allow you to change to a larger font and still keep the words from going on to more than one line.

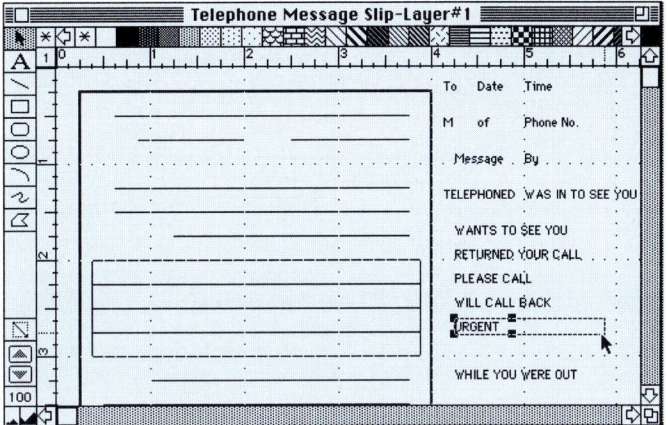

Figure 5-27   Resizing the text box

⌘-B   ➡   While **URGENT** is still selected, choose **Bold** from the Style menu, and choose **14 point** from the Size menu. See Figure 5-28.

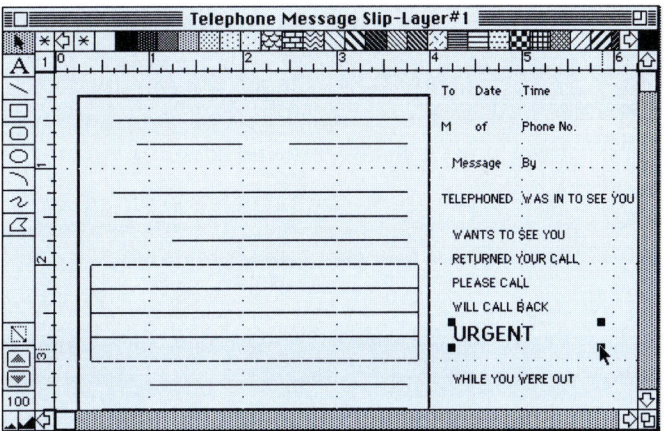

Figure 5-28   Changing the text size and style

➡   Go through the same procedure for "WHILE YOU WERE OUT".

REPOSITIONING TEXT

Now that you have created and formatted the text, you'll position it on the message slip.

➡   To make it easier to position the text precisely, choose **Turn Autogrid Off** from the Layout menu.

➡ Now you can select each text block individually and position it next to the appropriate line. Do this with all the text except what goes in the message options blocks (the text that is in all caps). See Figure 5-29.

To see how the text should be positioned, refer to Figure 5-14 at the beginning of this project.

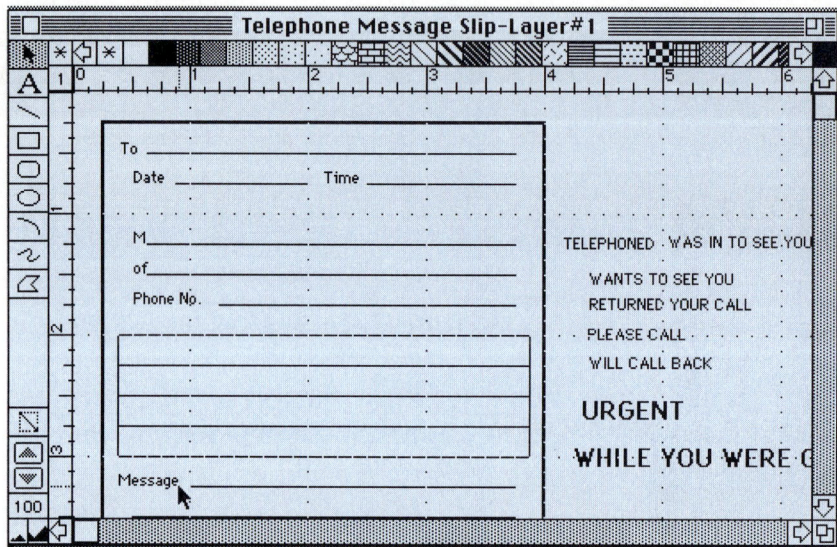

Figure 5-29   Repositioning text

⌘-S   ➡ Choose **Save** from the File menu.

➡ To determine how long to make the message options blocks, place TELEPHONED, WAS IN TO SEE YOU, WANTS TO SEE YOU, and RETURNED YOUR CALL in the areas shown in Figure 5-30.

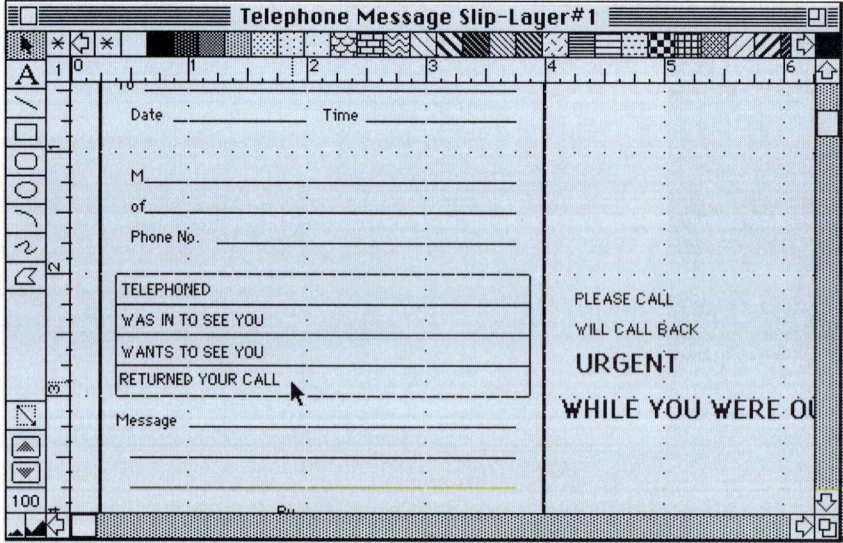

Figure 5-30   Moving more text

➡ Do this by selecting each text block individually and dragging it to its new location.

ADDING AND DUPLICATING LINES

Now you can determine where the vertical lines need to be placed within the inner rectangle.

➡ Select the line tool, and then draw a vertical line beginning after RETURNED YOUR CALL. Make that line the same height as the rectangle, as shown in Figure 5-31.

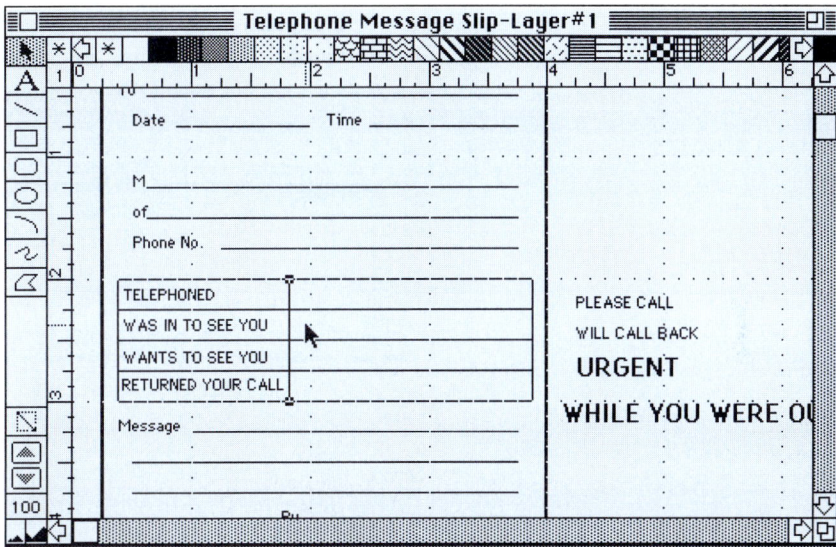

Figure 5-31   Drawing the first vertical line

⌘-D ➡ To duplicate that line, choose **Duplicate** from the Edit menu.

➡ Place the duplicate line about ¹/₄ inch to the right of the original, as shown in Figure 5-32.

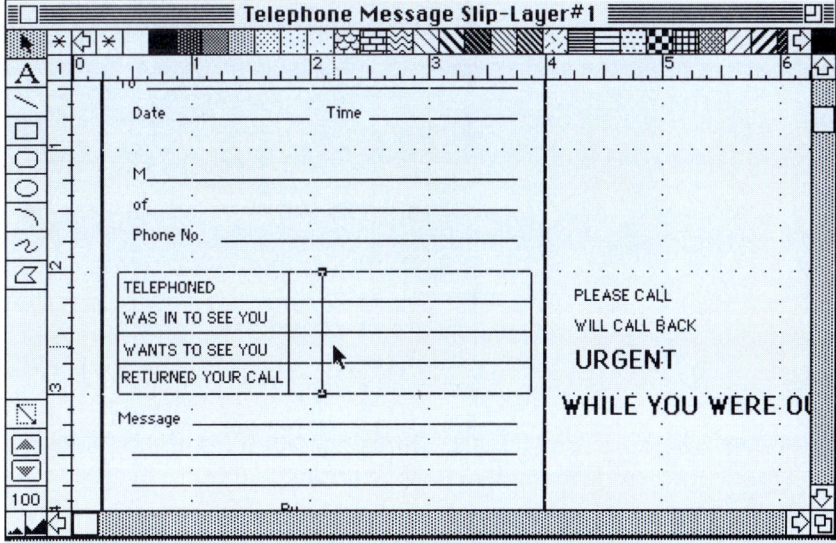

Figure 5-32   Duplicating the vertical line

⌘-D ➡ Duplicate the line again in the same manner, and place it about ¼ inch from the edge of the rectangle, as shown in Figure 5-33.

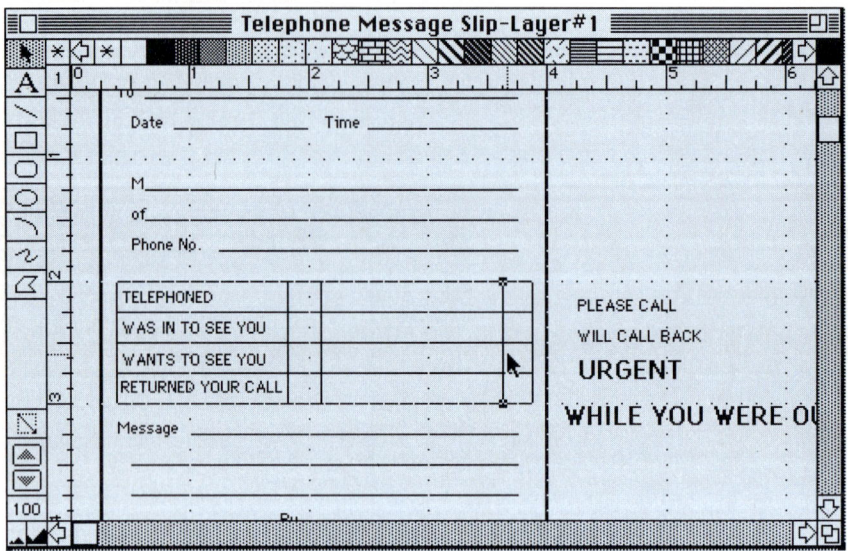

Figure 5-33 Duplicating the line again

➡ Select the line between WANTS TO SEE YOU and RETURNED YOUR CALL. Shorten that line by dragging on the right handle so that it stops at the second vertical line, as shown in Figure 5-34.

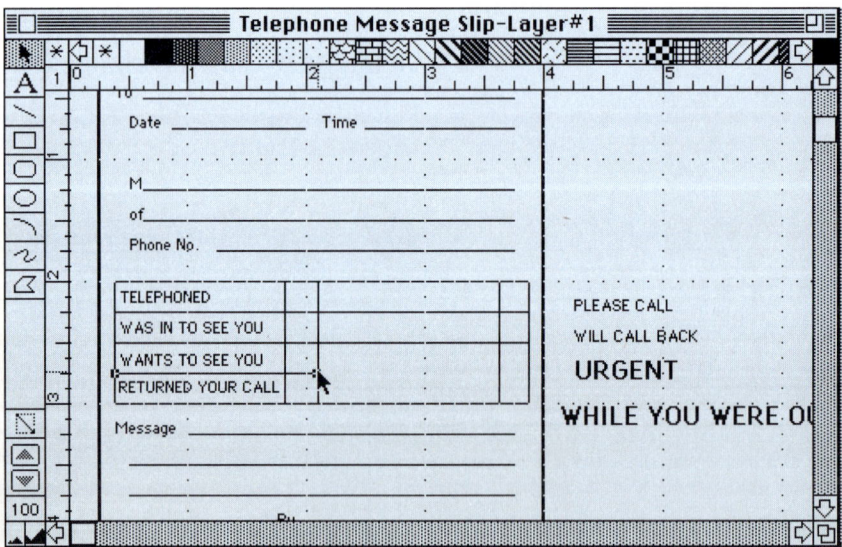

Figure 5-34 Making room for URGENT

➡ Now you can place the remainder of the text into the form in the appropriate places.

⌘-S ➡ Choose **Save** from the File menu.

You can place as many message forms on a page as will fit, to save paper and printing costs. Four message forms will fit on one page, so that is how you'll print them. Now that you've completed the first message form, creating the other ones is easy.

USING THE ZOOM CONTROLS

You'll use the zoom controls to reduce your view of the drawing and see more of it on the screen.

➠ Click once on the left zoom control to reduce your view to 50%.

The zoom percentage box now shows "50". This enables you to see more of your drawing at one time.

⌘-A   ➠ Choose **Select All** from the Edit menu.

You have just told MacDraw to select every object in your drawing.

GROUPING OBJECTS

Grouping consolidates a set of objects into one combined object. This enables you to manipulate the group as a single object. It also allows you to set each object's position in relation to other objects in the group.

⌘-G   ➠ Choose **Group** from the Arrange menu.

Now all the lines, text, and rectangles that make up the message form are grouped as one object, and only one set of handles appears around the whole form. See Figure 5-35.

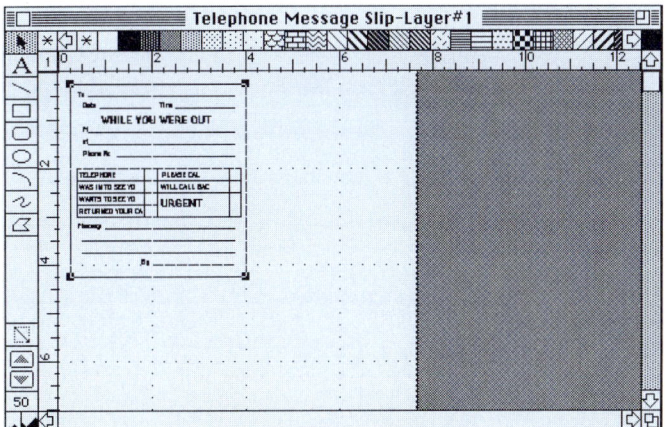

Figure 5-35   The grouped object

Once you group several objects, you cannot change a single object in the group. To make changes to individual parts of an object, you must first select the grouped object, and then choose **Ungroup** from the Arrange menu.

DUPLICATING OBJECTS

Next you'll move the message form so you can fit two forms side-by-side on the page, and then you'll duplicate the message form.

➠ Drag the message form as far as it will go to the left edge of the document, as shown in Figure 5-36.

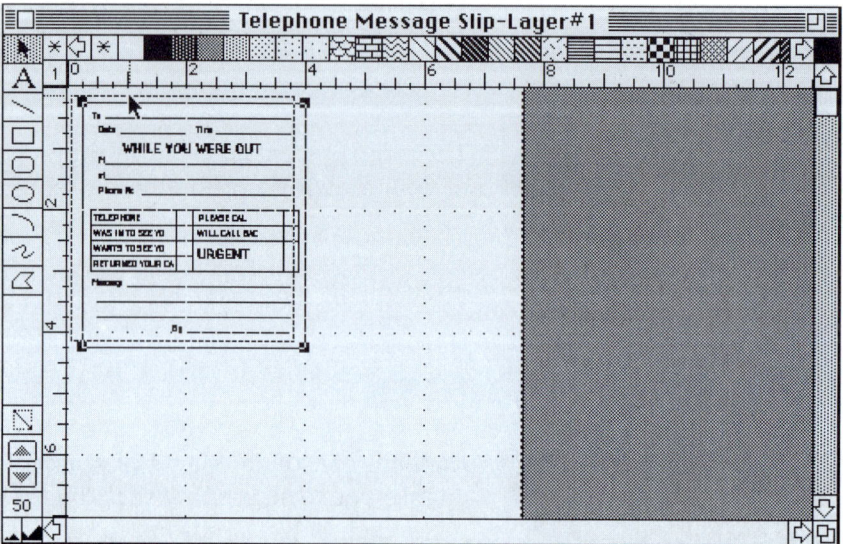

Figure 5-36   Moving the form to the left edge of the page

⌘-D ➠ Choose **Duplicate** from the Edit menu.

➠ Drag the duplicate message form and place it to the right of the original, as shown in Figure 5-37.

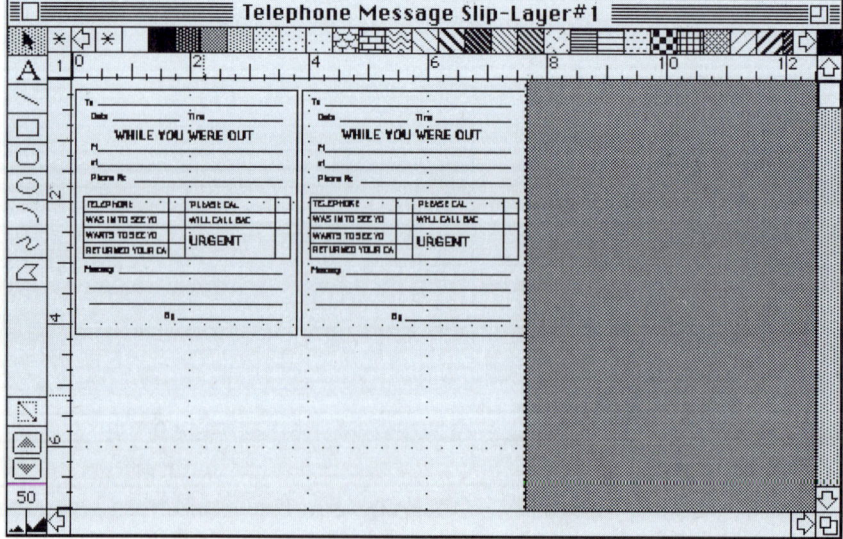

Figure 5-37   Placing the duplicate message form

⌘-A ➡ Select both message forms by choosing **Select All** from the Edit menu.

⌘-D ➡ Choose **Duplicate** from the Edit menu.

➡ Position the two duplicates on the bottom portion of the page, as shown in Figure 5-38.

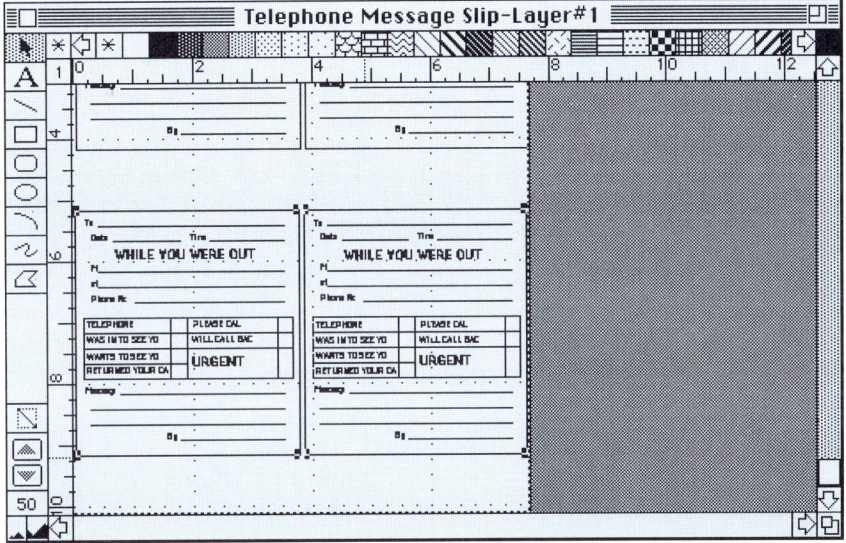

Figure 5-38   Placing two more duplicate forms

Now you have four telephone message forms in one document.

PRINTING THE DOCUMENT

Before you print the document, save your work.

➡ Choose **Save** from the File menu.

➡ Choose **Print** from the File menu. Click **OK** to accept the default print options and print one copy.

Compare your printed document with the one shown in Figure 5-14.

⌘-Q ➡ To exit MacDraw, choose **Quit** from the File menu. To continue working on the next exercise and remain in MacDraw, close the document by clicking in its close box.

Project 2: Creating an Organizational Chart

In this project you'll create a corporate organizational chart. You'll use some of the tools and commands that you learned about in the first project, and you'll also learn handy ways to create some special effects. You'll learn about pen and fill patterns and about aligning and arranging objects. The finished organizational chart is shown in Figure 5-39.

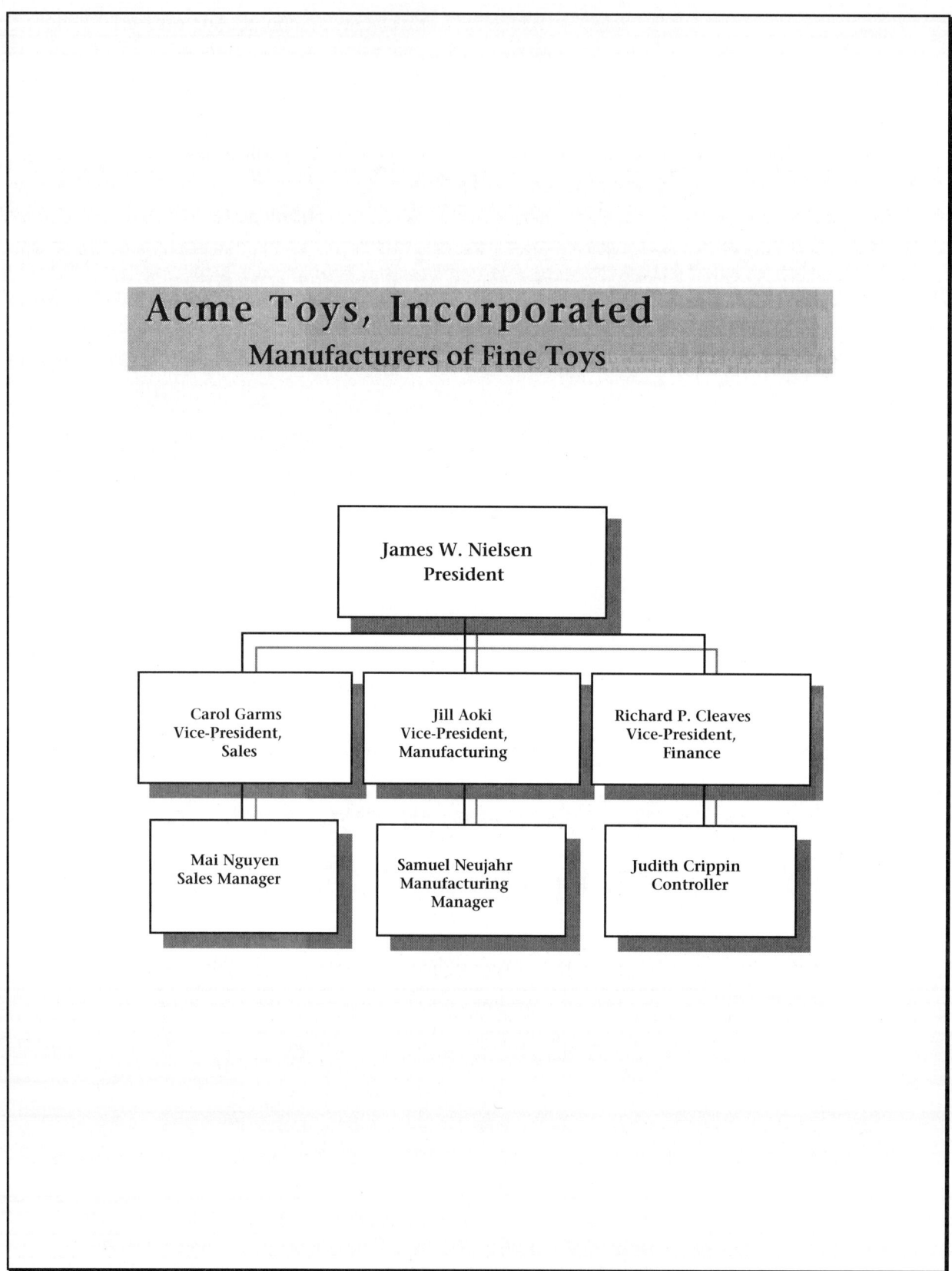

Figure 5-39   Final output of Project 2

MacDraw II

⇒ Double-click on the MacDraw II icon to open a new, untitled drawing window. If you did not exit MacDraw after working on the previous project, choose **New** from the File menu to get a new, untitled drawing window.

Keep in mind that if you need to delete an object, select it and press the Backspace key (Delete key on some keyboards).

⇒ Select **Show Rulers** from the Layout menu.

You will be using the rulers to determine the size and spacing of the objects in your organizational chart.

DISPLAYING THE SIZE OF AN OBJECT

A handy feature in MacDraw II is the *Show Size command.* The size of any object you draw is immediately reflected on the bottom of the screen as you draw it. Also, any time you click on the border of an object after it is drawn, it shows you the size of that object.

⇒ Choose **Show Size** from the Layout menu.

 ⇒ Select the rectangle tool.

⇒ Create a rectangle 2 inches wide and 1 inch high.

Notice that the size of the rectangle is displayed at the bottom of the screen as you draw it, as shown in Figure 5-40.

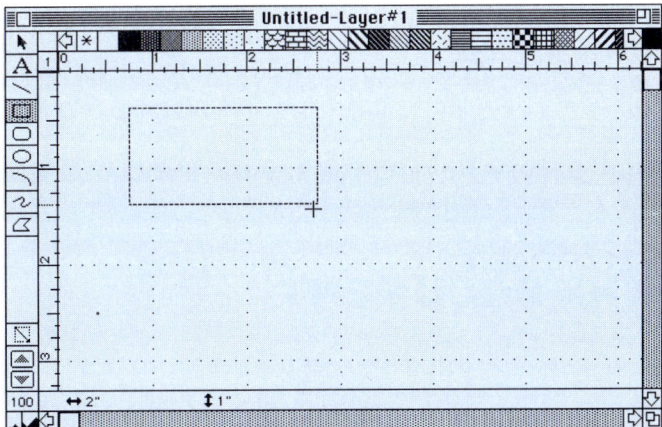

Figure 5-40   Using the Show Size feature

⇒ If you clicked elsewhere on the screen after you drew the rectangle, click anywhere on the rectangle to select it.

CHANGING LINE WEIGHTS

⇒ To change the thickness of the lines forming the rectangle, choose **2 point** from the *Pen menu*, as shown in Figure 5-41.

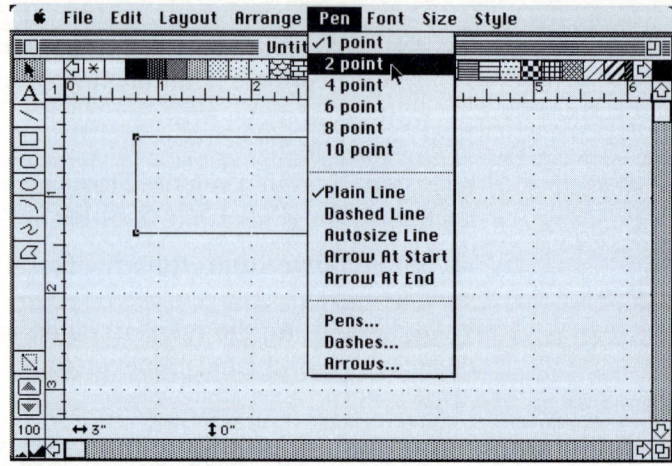

Figure 5-41   The Pen menu

You learned about line weights in Project 1. The Pen menu also offers different line styles.

Plain Line, which is checked in the Pen menu shown in Figure 5-41, is the default line style. The Dashed Line option creates a dashed line, and you can customize the dash size and space between dashes by choosing **Dashes** from the Pen Menu.

An Autosize Line has the line's length automatically printed in the middle. Autosize Lines are used for drawing dimension lines that show the measurement of objects in a drawing, such as in a floor plan.

The Arrow At Start and Arrow At End options enable you to draw lines that begin or end (or both) with arrowheads. You can modify the shape of the arrowhead by choosing **Arrows** from the Pen menu.

You can use any combination of line weights, dashes, arrows, and dimensions on any line you draw.

SAVING THE DOCUMENT

Before you get too deep into this project, it's a good idea to save what you've done so far and give the drawing a name.

⌘-S   ➡   Choose **Save** from the File menu.

Remember to be careful about where you are saving your document. Always verify that the name of the disk (or folder) that you want your document saved on is showing at the top of the Save dialog box—in this case, where "Pamela Gurnari" is showing in Figure 5-42. If necessary, click the **Drive** button so that you are viewing the correct name.

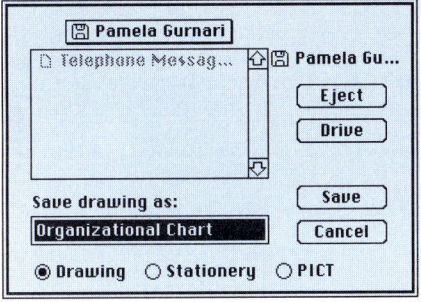

Figure 5-42   The Save dialog box

➠ Type **Organizational Chart** in the Save drawing as: box, and then click the **Save** button.

Your drawing window should now have the name of your document and the current layer showing at the top: Organizational Chart-Layer#1.

ADDING TEXT

Now you need to add some text inside the box you just drew. The first name and title will be the company president's name.

➠ Click on the text tool to select it, and then click inside the rectangle in approximately the center of it.

➠ Choose **New York** from the Font menu, and then choose **12 point** from the Size menu.

⌘-B   ➠ Choose **Bold** and then **Center** from the Style menu.

➠ Type the following text in the block, pressing return where indicated:
James W. Nielsen (press Return)
President

Your screen should look like the one shown in Figure 5-43.

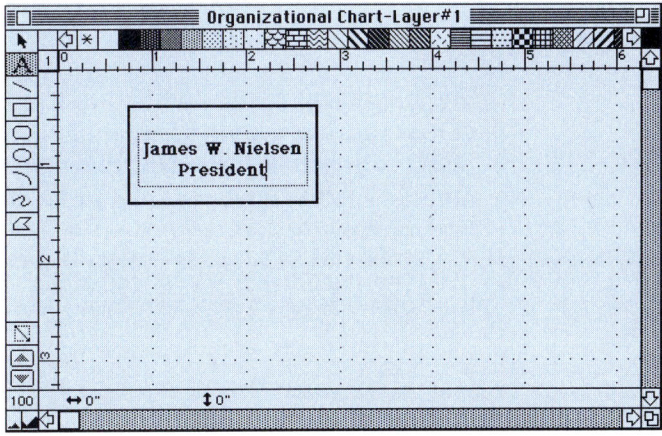

Figure 5-43   Adding text to the rectangle

➠ Click somewhere else on the screen to deselect the text tool.

SELECTING OBJECTS

 ⇒ To select both the box and the text within it, place the selection arrow above and to the left of the box and drag diagonally past the bottom right corner of the box.

A dotted rectangle is created around the objects, as shown in Figure 5-44. When you release the mouse button, all objects within the temporary rectangle are selected. All objects that are selected will have handles showing.

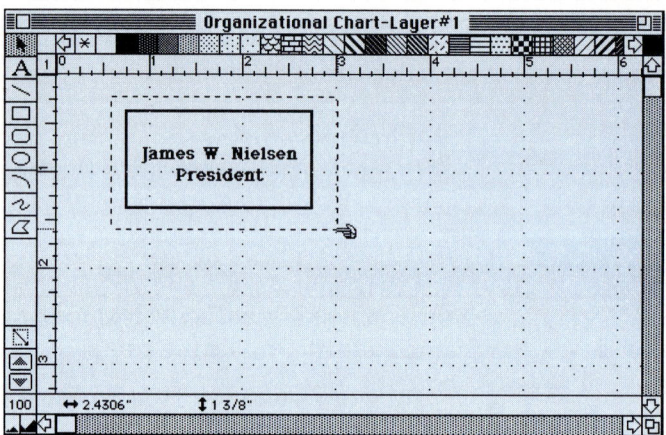

Figure 5-44   Selecting multiple objects

Selecting multiple objects is not the same as grouping objects. Grouping objects creates one composite object made up of all the objects that are selected when the Group command is invoked. Selecting multiple objects enables you to work with all selected objects at one time, but each can still be selected separately.

Next you'll center the text within the rectangle.

CENTERING TEXT WITHIN A RECTANGLE

The Alignment command allows you to align and distribute selected objects with each other or with the grid. *Aligning* refers to moving selected objects so that their boundaries line up in a specified manner. *Distributing* objects spaces them evenly in a document, either vertically or horizontally.

⇒ Choose **Alignment** from the Arrange menu.

⇒ In the resulting dialog box, select **Align** and **Center** from the right portion of the box, and select **Align** and **Center** from the bottom of the box, as shown in Figure 5-45.

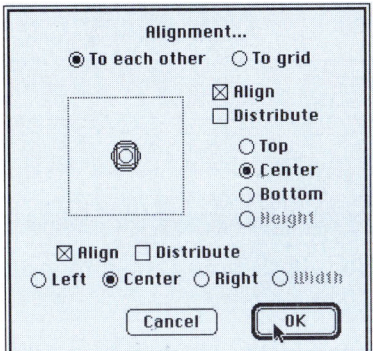

Figure 5-45   The Alignment dialog box

The settings you just chose for this dialog box told MacDraw to align the objects to the center both vertically and horizontally. Notice that the small diagram in the dialog box shows you the effect these settings will have on the objects.

⇒ Click **OK** to accept the changes you've made to the dialog box.

Now you'll use the box you just drew as a template for the others, since it is already the correct size and has the text centered within it. To do so, you'll duplicate it.

DUPLICATING USING AUTOMATIC ALIGNMENT

You'll duplicate the box as well as the name inside it, even though you'll change the names in just a moment, because you want the text to retain the same formatting characteristics (New York font, bold, and centered) when you retype a different name.

⌘-D ⇒ If both the text and the rectangle are not already selected, select them now, and then choose **Duplicate** from the Edit menu.

⇒ Click on the duplicate set of objects, but not on any of their handles. Drag them to the lower left side of the screen, as shown in Figure 5-46.

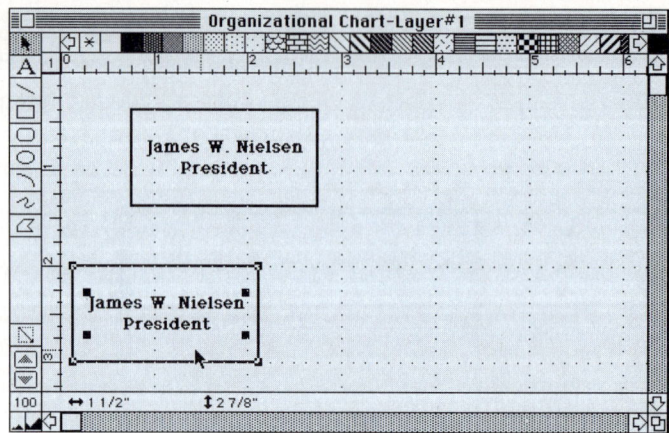

Figure 5-46   Positioning the duplicate objects

➠   Click on another part of the screen to deselect the objects.

MacDraw "remembers" where you placed the last duplicate object with
reference to the original as long as you do not deselect the duplicate
object. This feature is one of the reasons that MacDraw works well for
creating business forms and charts. You can create horizontal, vertical,
and diagonal rows of identical objects without having to draw each
object separately or copy them and then align them in a row. When you
position the duplicate object, you establish the spacing and direction of
the row, and each duplicate is positioned and aligned automatically.
You'll use this feature to create the rest of the boxes in the second row
of the organizational chart.

➠   Select the duplicate box and text within it that you just positioned
     in the lower left corner of the screen.

⌘-D   ➠   Choose **Duplicate** from the Edit menu.

When you position the duplicate that you just created, you'll establish
the direction and spacing of the second row of objects.

➠   Position the second duplicate box to the right of the original and
     align the top edges of both objects, as shown in Figure 5-47.

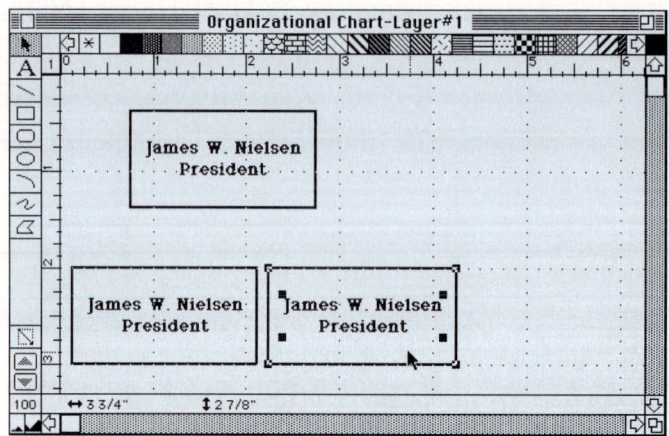

Figure 5-47   Positioning the second duplicate box

⌘-D ➠ While the object is still selected, choose **Duplicate** from the Edit menu.

Notice how that action caused the next copy to be placed to the right of the center block. The box is automatically aligned according to its relative position to the first, as shown in Figure 5-48.

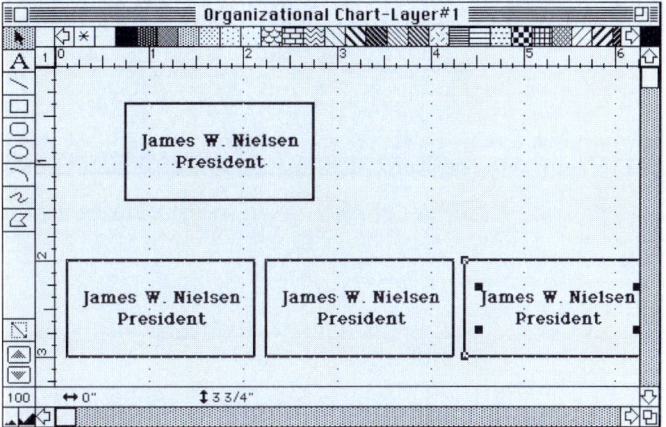

Figure 5-48 Automatically positioning the copy

⌘-S ➠ Save your work by choosing **Save** from the File menu.

MODIFYING MULTIPLE OBJECTS AT ONCE

Now that you have the row of boxes drawn, you need to change the names in each box. First you'll change the text in all three boxes on the second row to 10 point type.

➠ Click somewhere outside the currently selected box to deselect it.

➠ While holding down the Shift key, click on the name in each of the three lower boxes so the text in all three boxes is selected.

➠ Select **10 point** from the Size menu.

Notice that the change takes effect on all the selected text. It does not affect the text in the top box.

  ➠ Select the text tool.

Double-clicking on a tool selects it and keeps it active until you click on another tool.

EDITING TEXT

Now you'll change the names in each box in the second row.

➠ Drag through the name in the first block to select it, as shown in Figure 5-49.

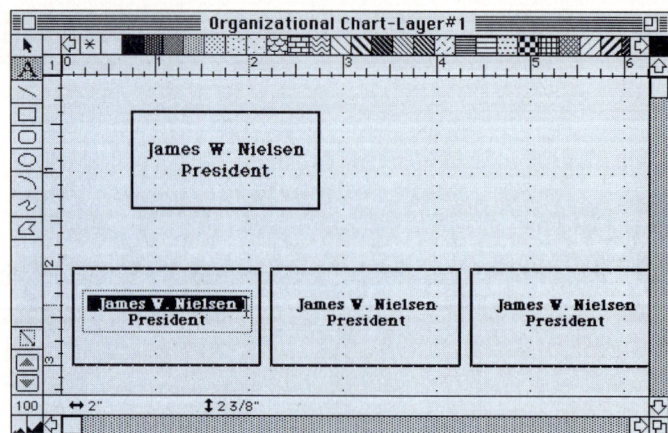

Figure 5-49   Selecting the name in the box

Feel free to type names of people who mean something to you. The following names are suggestions; you can use whatever names you think of.

⟶ Type **Carol Garms** to replace the president's name.

⟶ Select **President** in the same box, and type:
   Vice-President,
   Sales

Press Return if you need to go to a new line within the box.

⟶ Continuing in this same manner, change the name and the title in the middle box to:
   Jill Aoki
   Vice-President,
   Manufacturing

⟶ Change the name and the title in the last box to:
   Richard P. Cleaves
   Vice-President,
   Finance

Your boxes should look similar to the ones shown in Figure 5-50.

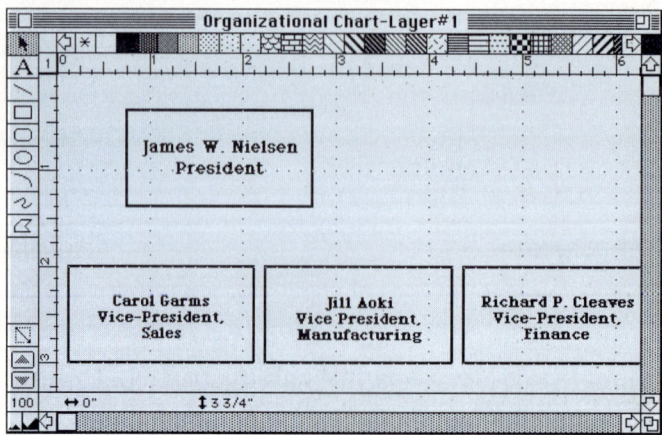

Figure 5-50   The edited boxes

Now that you have created the second row of boxes, using the first as a template, you need to change the single box in the top row, the President's box, so that it is larger than the others.

➡ Select the President's box.

➡ Click on the handle in the lower right corner of the President's box, and drag to the right. When the dimensions in the size bar at the bottom of the screen are $2^1/_2$" by 1", release the mouse button.

This makes the box $^1/_2$ inch wider than the others.

FORMATTING TEXT

Now you can center the text within the box.

➡ While holding down the Shift key, click on the border of the President's box, and then click on the text in the box so that both the box and the text are selected.

Using the Shift key while selecting objects allows you to select more than one object at a time.

⌘-K ➡ To center the text within the box, choose **Align** from the Arrange menu.

⌘-G ➡ With the box and text within it selected, choose **Group** from the Arrange menu.

This groups the centered text and the box as one object.

You did not have to change the alignment specifications as you did when you first aligned the text, since the alignment specifications remain the same until you change them. The Alignment command allows you to change the alignment specifications, and the Align command allows you to align objects based on the last alignment specifications you set.

⌘-S ➡ Save your document.

USING THE ZOOM CONTROLS

Now view the drawing in 50% size so you can finish adding the other boxes and position them properly on the page.

 ➡ Click the left zoom control to reduce your drawing to 50% size.

You will see "50" in the zoom percentage box.

DUPLICATING MULTIPLE OBJECTS

You'll duplicate the three boxes in the second row and place the duplicates in a row at the bottom.

➠ Select the row of three boxes by dragging around all three boxes with the selection arrow, as shown in Figure 5-51.

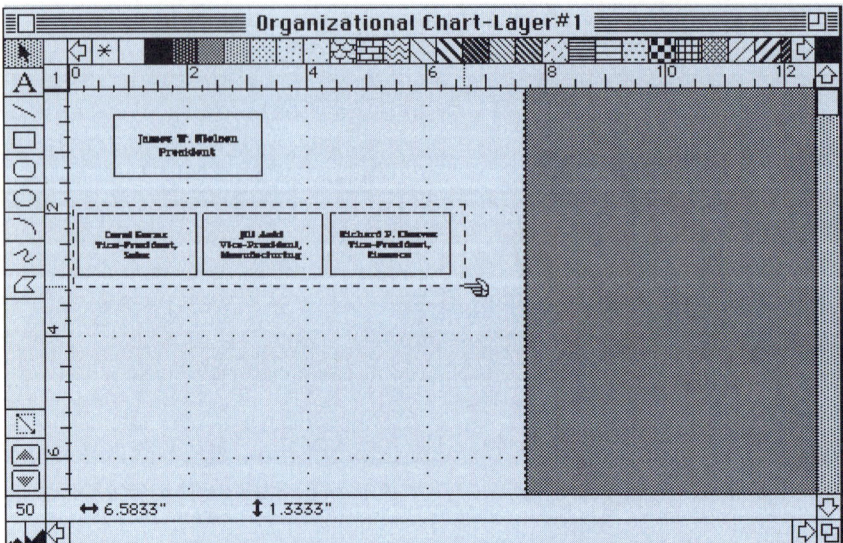

Figure 5-51   Selecting the bottom row of boxes

⌘-D ➠ Choose **Duplicate** from the Edit menu.

➠ Position the duplicate boxes directly beneath the first row of three boxes, as shown in Figure 5-52.

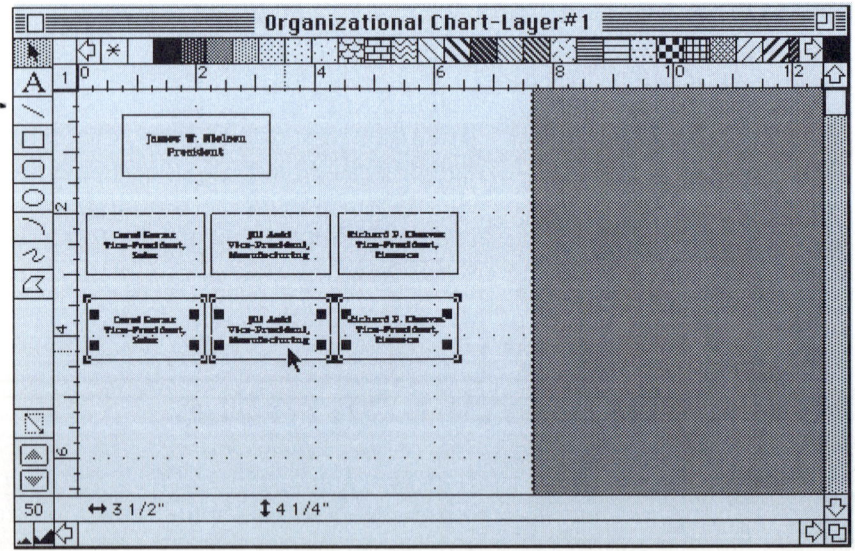

Figure 5-52   Positioning the duplicate boxes

➠ Click elsewhere on the screen to deselect the three boxes and the text within them.

RESIZING MULTIPLE OBJECTS

Next you'll reduce the size of the bottom three boxes.

→ Hold down the Shift key and click on the border of each of the bottom three boxes.

This will select just the boxes, not the text within them.

→ Now reduce the size of all three boxes by dragging to the left the lower right corner of any box, until the size bar at the bottom of the window shows that the box has been reduced to $1^3/_4$ inches by 1 inch, as shown in Figure 5-53.

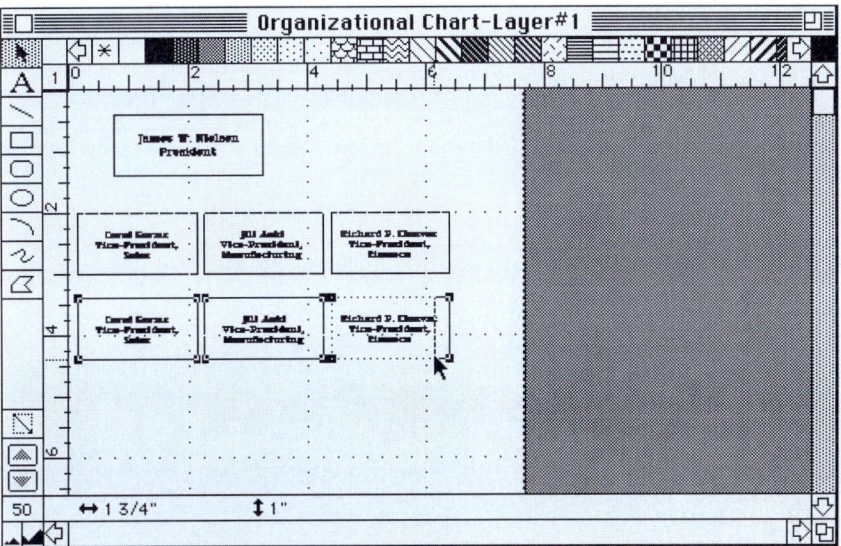

Figure 5-53   Resizing multiple objects

When you release the mouse button, all three boxes are reduced to the same size. See Figure 5-54.

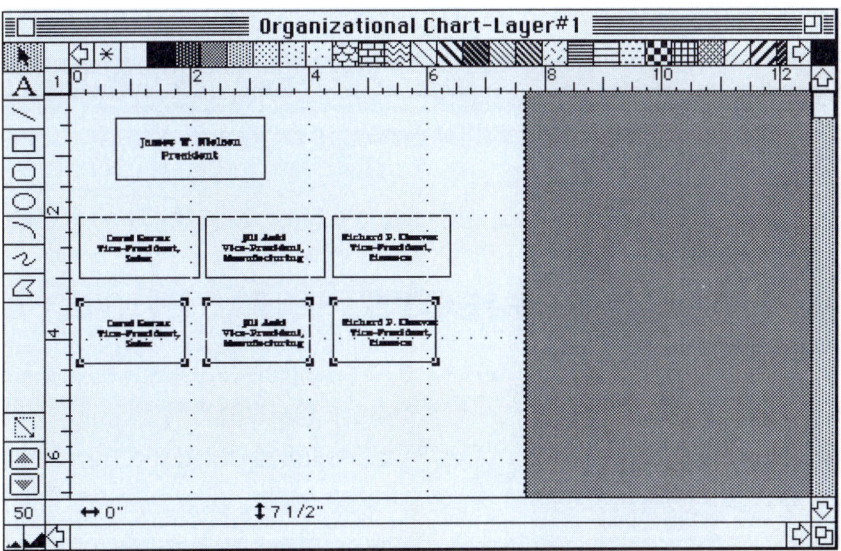

Figure 5-54   The resized boxes

➠ Use the zoom control to enlarge the drawing to 100% size. Then use the scroll boxes to position the screen so you are viewing the smaller three boxes.

Change the names and titles as you did with the middle row of boxes. Use names of your choice or the suggested ones that follow.

➠ Change the first box so that it contains the following name and title:
Mai Nguyen
Sales Manager

➠ Change the text in the middle box to the following:
Samuel Neujahr
Manufacturing Manager

➠ Change the text in the third box to read:
Judith Crippin
Controller

Your boxes should now look similar to the ones shown in Figure 5-55.

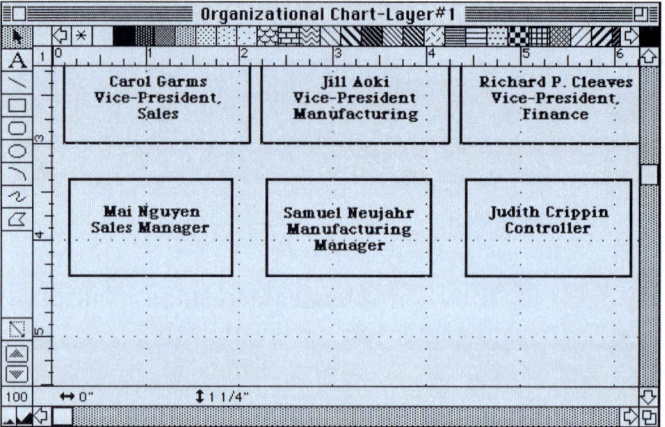

Figure 5-55   The names in the bottom row of boxes

➠ Click somewhere on the screen to deselect the three boxes.

⌘-S ➠ Choose **Save** from the File menu.

GROUPING OBJECTS

The next step is to center the text inside each box and then group the box and the text in it.

➠ While holding down the Shift key, select the first box in the middle row and then the text inside that box.

⌘-K ➠ Choose **Align** from the Arrange menu.

This centers the text inside the box, based on the last settings you made in the Alignment dialog box.

⌘-G ➠ Choose **Group** from the Arrange menu.

This groups the text and the box so that MacDraw views the box and the name in it as one object, not two.

➠ Click somewhere on the screen to deselect the grouped box and text object.

Deselecting the previous box is an important step. If you do not deselect it first, when you Shift-click to select the next box and text, the box you just grouped will be included in your centering and grouping operation.

➠ Continue centering the text within each box, and then group the centered text and box. Be sure to deselect each box after you group it and before you select the next box and text.

➠ When you are finished centering text and grouping each box with the name within it, use the zoom control to return to 50% size.

ALIGNING OBJECTS

Now that you can view all the boxes, you need to align them to one another.

➠ Select the top box and drag it to the center of the top row.

Use the horizontal ruler to help you determine the approximate center.

➠ Shift-click to select the box in the top row, the center one in the second row, and the center one in the bottom row so that all three are selected at the same time, as shown in Figure 5-56.

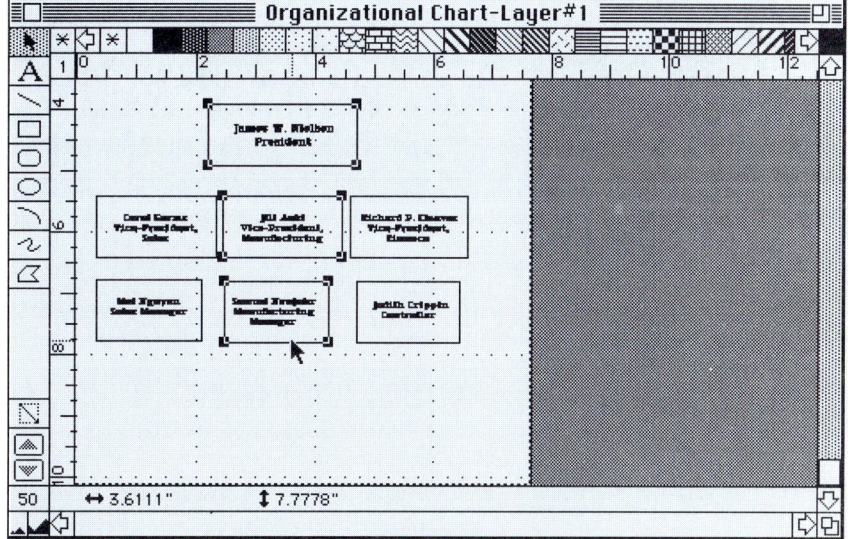

Figure 5-56   Selecting the three center boxes

➠ Choose **Alignment** from the Arrange menu. The Alignment dialog box will show on your screen.

➠ In the upper right section of the dialog box, beneath the words "To grid", click **Align** to remove the "X". This should leave both the Align and Distribute boxes without an "X" in them.

➠ Next, be sure there is an "X" in the Align box that runs horizontally across the bottom of the dialog box. Beneath that, click **Center**.

Your completed dialog box should look like the one shown in Figure 5-57.

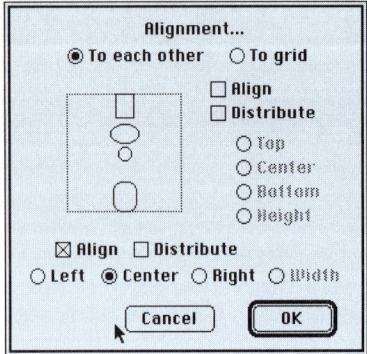

Figure 5-57   The Alignment dialog box

The settings in this dialog box tell MacDraw that you do not want to do any horizontal alignment or distribution, just vertical alignment.

Return   ➠ Click **OK** to accept those settings once you have determined that they are correct.

The three boxes you selected are now aligned vertically.

➠ Click somewhere on the screen to deselect the boxes you just aligned, and then Shift-click to select the first box in the second row and the first box in the third row.

⌘-K   ➠ Choose **Align** from the Arrange menu.

The alignment settings you selected last time will still be in effect.

➠ Click somewhere on the screen to deselect the boxes you just aligned, and then Shift-click to select the last box in the second row and the last box in the third row.

⌘-K   ➠ Choose **Align** again from the Arrange menu.

Now you need to draw the lines to connect the boxes in your organizational chart.

    ➠ Select the line tool.

➠ Place the pointer in the center of the top box, and while holding down the Shift key to constrain the line vertically, drag down to draw a straight line to the center of the middle box in the bottom row, as shown in Figure 5-58.

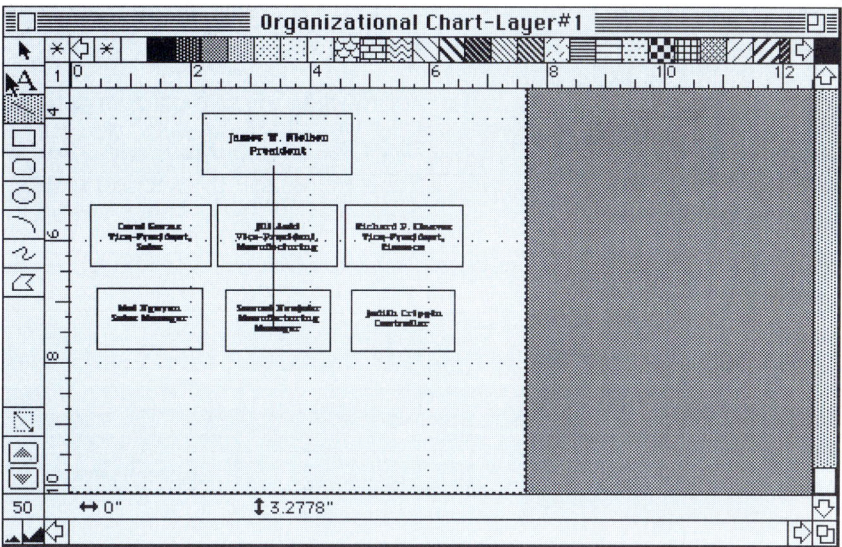

Figure 5-58   Draw the first connecting line

MOVING OBJECTS TO THE BACK

The order in which objects appear on the screen, in front of or behind each other, is called the *stacking order*. The line you just drew needs to be positioned behind the boxes in the chart. You'll change its position in the stacking order now.

➡ Select the line you just drew if you deselected it, and then choose **Move To Back** from the Arrange menu.

Now the line appears to be behind the boxes.

➡ Draw two more vertical lines through the boxes on either side, as shown in Figure 5-59.

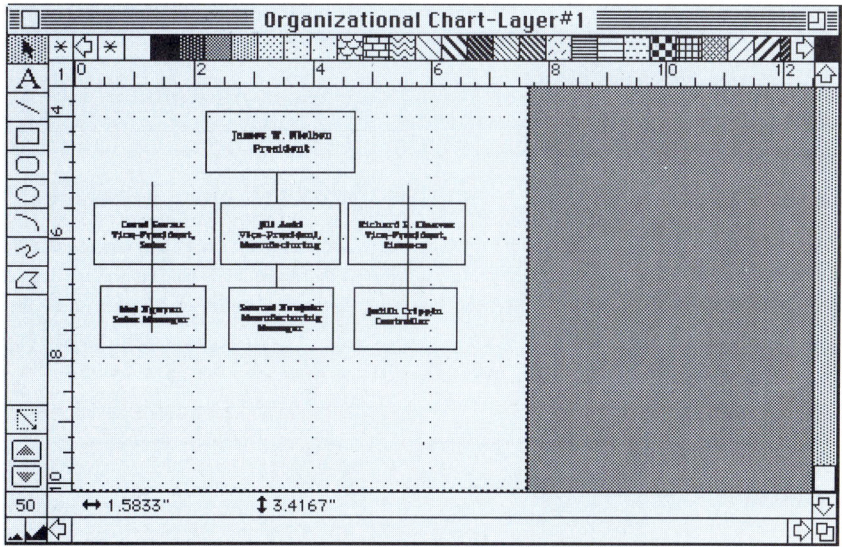

Figure 5-59   Draw two more lines

➡ With both lines selected, move them to the back by choosing **Move To Back** from the Arrange menu.

➡ Zoom to 100% size using the zoom control.

➡ Draw the horizontal line to connect the three vertical lines between the top box and the second row of boxes, as shown in Figure 5-60. If necessary, change the length of any line that does not meet precisely.

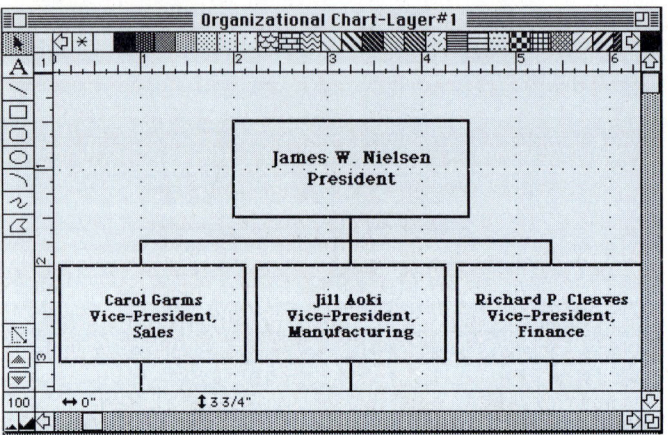

Figure 5-60   The horizontal connecting line

⌘-S ➡ Now is a good time to save all your work, if you haven't already done so.

CREATING A DROP SHADOW

Next you'll proceed with the steps to create a shadowed effect behind the boxes of the chart.

First you need to group all the elements in your existing chart as one object.

⌘-A ➡ Choose **Select All** from the Edit menu.

⌘-G ➡ Choose **Group** from the Arrange menu.

➡ Use the zoom control to reduce the view to 50% size.

➡ Drag the whole chart to the bottom portion of the screen, about a half-inch from the bottom, as shown in Figure 5-61.

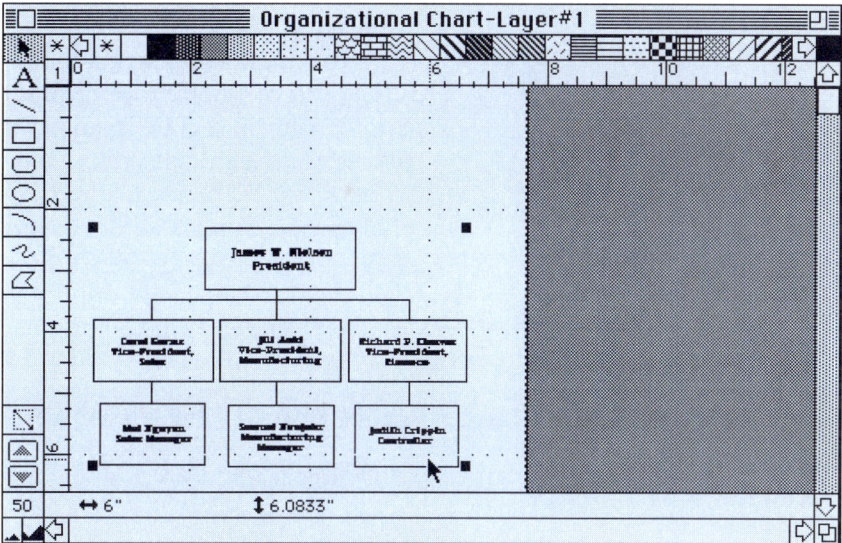

Figure 5-61   Reposition the group

⌘-D   ➡   Choose **Duplicate** from the Edit menu.

This places a duplicate of your grouped chart on top of the original, and the duplicate is selected.

Changing the Fill Pattern

➡   Without deselecting the duplicate object, click to select a medium gray pattern on the pattern palette, as shown at the top of Figure 5-62.

This will cause the duplicate boxes to be filled with gray. See Figure 5-62.

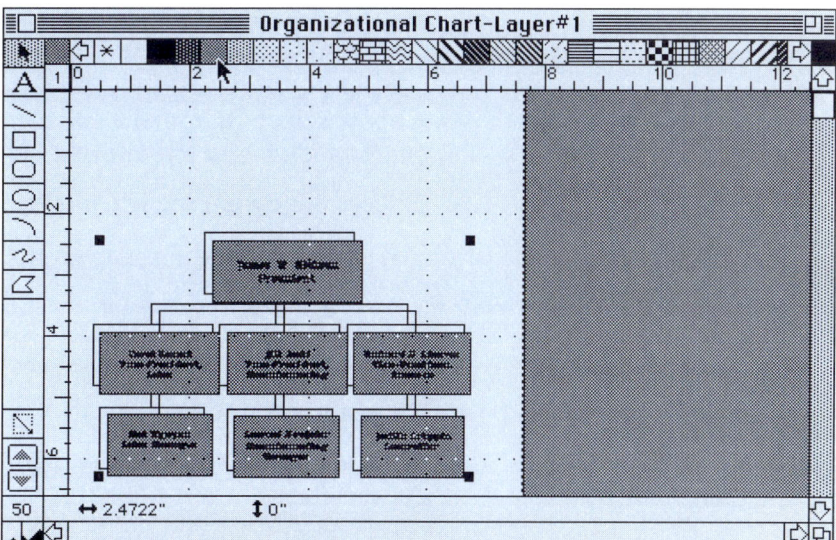

Figure 5-62   Changing the fill pattern to gray

Changing the Line Pattern

 ➠ While the duplicate chart is still selected, click on the far right square in the pattern palette to indicate that you are referring to the line pattern, and then click again on the same shade of gray that you selected for the fill pattern.

This changes the duplicate lines to gray also.

Next you need to move the duplicate object so that it appears to be peeking out from beneath the original boxes, to produce a shadowed effect.

➠ Choose **Move To Back** from the Arrange menu.

Your drawing should look like the one shown in Figure 5-63.

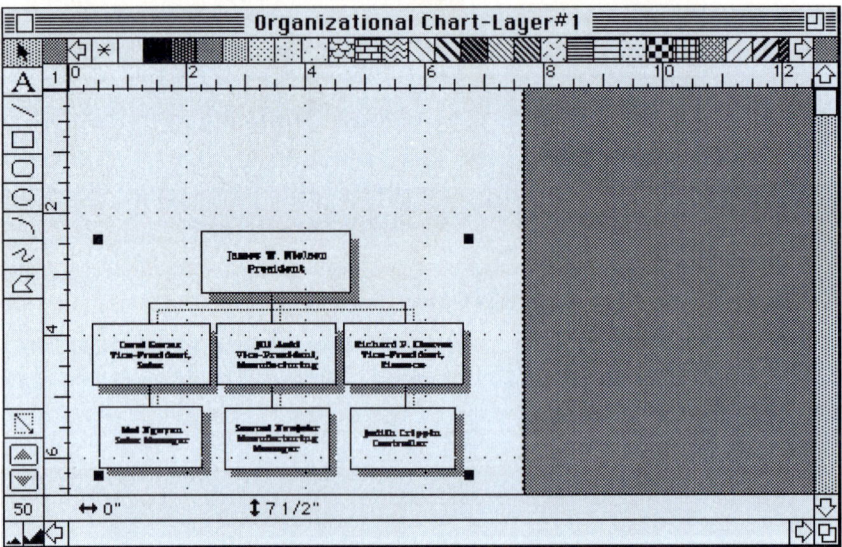

Figure 5-63   Creating a shadowed effect

⌘-A   ⌘-G   ➠ Choose **Select All** from the Edit menu, and then choose **Group** from the Arrange menu to group the shadowed chart as one object.

⌘-S   ➠ Choose **Save** from the File menu.

USING DIFFERENT TEXT STYLES

Next you'll put the company name at the top of the chart.

 ➠ Select the text tool.

➠ Select **24 point** from the Size menu, and choose **Shadow** from the Style menu.

➠ Position the pointer in the center of the top portion of the screen, and type **Acme Toys, Incorporated**. Then press Return.

The next line in the chart title will have smaller text and will not be shadowed.

⮕ Choose **18 point** from the Size menu, and choose **Shadow** from the Style menu to deselect it.

⮕ Type **Manufacturers of Fine Toys** on that line.

CHANGING THE TEXT BACKGROUND

Now you'll change the background of the text to make it stand out on the page.

⮕ While your text is still selected, select a shade of gray from the pattern palette, lighter than the one that you used for the shadows of the chart boxes.

This produces a light gray background for the title, as shown in Figure 5-64.

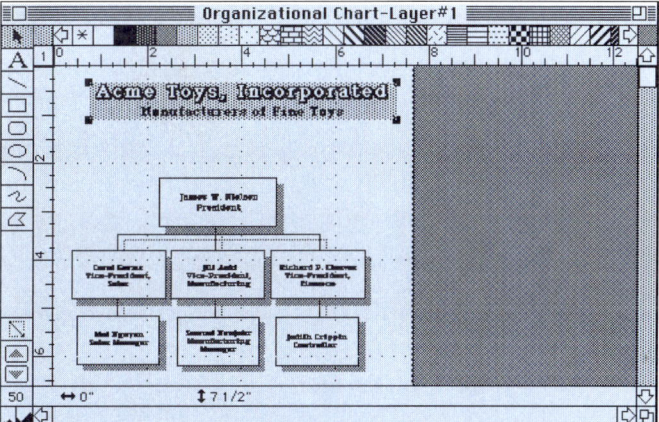

Figure 5-64   Title with light gray background

⮕ To align the title vertically to the chart, select both the chart and the title by Shift-clicking.

⮕ Choose **Alignment** from the Arrange menu. Make sure that the settings in the resulting dialog box are for vertical alignment, like the ones in the dialog box shown in Figure 5-65.

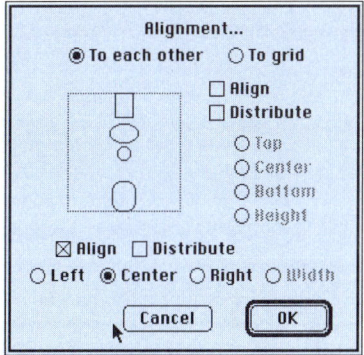

Figure 5-65   Alignment dialog box

Now you'll group the centered title with the chart.

⌘-G   ➠ While everything is still selected, choose **Group** from the Arrange menu.

➠ Click somewhere else in the screen to deselect the objects.

Finally, you'll center the chart on the page.

CENTERING THE CHART ON THE PAGE

You're going to draw a rectangle around the whole page, and then you'll align the chart to the rectangle. After the chart is centered in the rectangle, you'll delete the rectangle.

 ➠ Select empty fill, the transparent pattern, from the pattern palette.

 ➠ Click on the far right square of the pattern palette to indicate that you are referring to the line pattern, and then click on the solid black pattern.

➠ Select **Turn Autogrid Off** from the Layout menu to enable you to place your box precisely on the screen.

 ➠ Select the rectangle tool, and then draw a box around the entire drawing page, keeping as close to the edges as possible.

As you draw the bottom edge of the box and you drag the pointer off the bottom of the drawing window, notice how the scroll box in the vertical scroll bar moves all the way to the bottom of the scroll bar, as shown in Figure 5-66. This indicates that you are at the bottom of the drawing page.

➠ Do not release the mouse button until the rectangle reaches the bottom of the drawing page. See Figure 5-66.

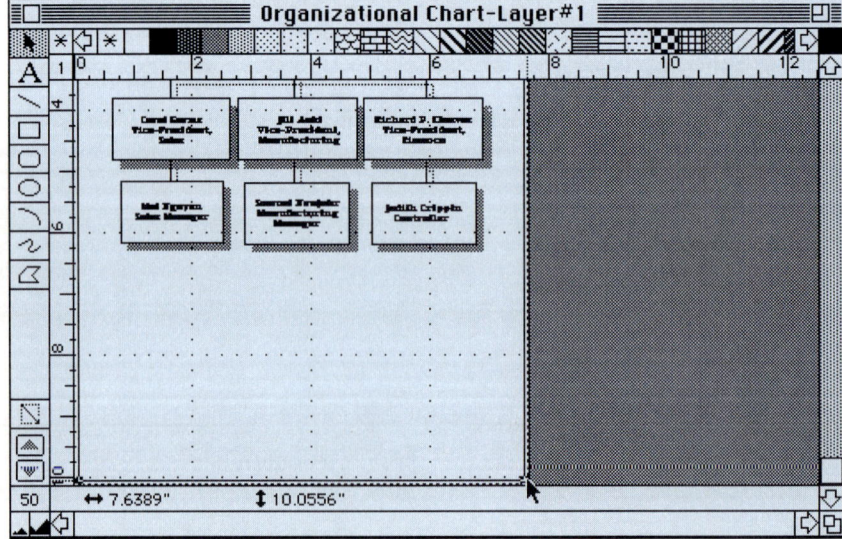

Figure 5-66   Draw a box around entire drawing page

⇒   Shift-click to select the chart, so that both the rectangle around the
     page and the chart are selected.

Now you'll set the alignment so that the objects are centered vertically
and horizontally.

⇒   Choose **Alignment** from the Arrange menu. Make sure the settings
     in the resulting dialog box match the ones shown in Figure 5-67, and
     then click **OK**.

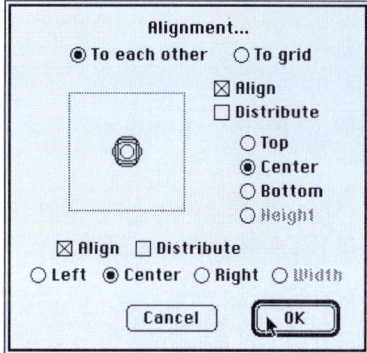

Figure 5-67   Alignment dialog box

Now your chart is aligned to the center of the page.

⇒   Choose **Save** from the File menu.

Now that you have centered the chart and title on the page, you no
longer need the large rectangle you just drew.

⇒   Click somewhere on the screen to deselect both objects, and then
     click on the rectangle to select it. Press the Backspace key (Delete on
     some keyboards) to remove the rectangle.

VIEWING THE ENTIRE PAGE

The entire drawing is not visible in 50% size, but you can see it all in
25% size.

⇒   To view the entire page, click on the left zoom control to reduce the
     drawing to 25%.

The screen should look similar to the one shown in Figure 5-68.

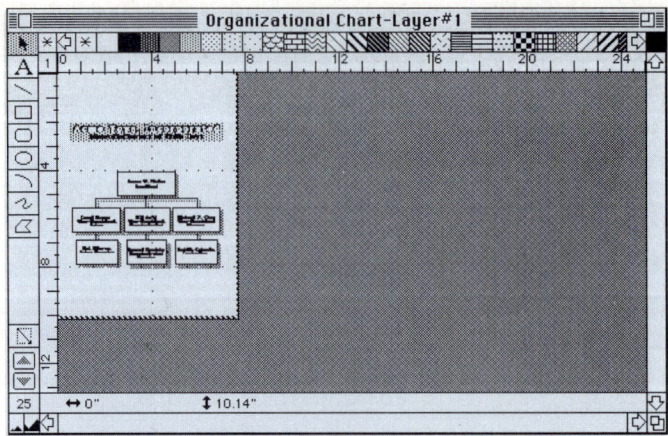

Figure 5-68   Organizational chart at 25% size

⌘-S   ➠   Before you print the organizational chart, save it one last time.

➠   Choose **Print** from the File menu.

Return   ➠   Click **OK** to accept the default settings of the dialog box, and print one copy of the document.

➠   Compare your printed organizational chart with the one in Figure 5-39 at the beginning of this project.

If you need to modify a part of the chart or a misspelled name, you must ungroup as many times as needed until the object you want to modify is accessible. As you created this chart, you grouped on many different levels, so you will have to ungroup several times to access individual objects in the chart.

⌘-Q   ➠   To exit MacDraw II, choose **Quit** from the File menu. If you intend to continue with the additional projects, just close the document and don't quit MacDraw II.

SUMMARY

• MacDraw II's tool palette contains the drawing tools that you use to create the objects in a drawing. You select a tool by clicking on it, and the tool reverts to the selection arrow after each use. To keep a tool active, you double-click on it.

• All objects created in MacDraw II, including text, lines, and shapes, can be filled with a pattern, resized, duplicated, deleted, and moved.

• You create text using the text tool. The options in the Font, Size, and Style menus apply to the text typed with the text tool. You can change and insert characters or words in MacDraw without retyping, and you can drag text to a new location in a document.

• Lines are drawn using the line tool. You can change the weight of a line before you begin drawing it or after it is drawn. The Pen menu is used to change the weight of lines drawn with the line tool and the borders of any shape drawn with the shape tools. You can also change the pattern of any line or border. The different line styles available on the Pen menu affect lines and not borders of shapes.

- Shapes are drawn using the oval tool, the rectangle tool, the rounded rectangle tool, the freehand tool, and the polygon tool. Shapes can be drawn either unfilled or filled with a pattern. A shape can be resized and moved after it is drawn.

- Autogrid controls where you draw an object and what size it can be. Using Autogrid makes it easier to align objects, but you cannot place or draw objects between grid divisions when Autogrid is on. The gridlines in a drawing represent where Autogrid will constrain the placement of objects. Horizontal and vertical rulers also enable you to control the size and placement of objects.

- The fill and line patterns are controlled with the fill pattern box and the line pattern box on the pattern palette.

- You select an object by clicking on it with the selection arrow. You can select multiple objects at one time using either the Shift-click method, by dragging through multiple objects with the selection arrow, or by choosing **Select All** from the Edit menu. Once you have selected multiple objects, you can manipulate them (resize, move, delete, duplicate, and fill them) all at one time.

- The zoom controls allow you to enlarge a drawing to see details or reduce it so you can see more of it on the screen. You can magnify a drawing up to 3,200% in predetermined increments and reduce a drawing to 3.12% in predetermined increments. You can edit a drawing at any zoom level.

- Grouping consolidates a set of objects into one combined object, which enables you to manipulate them as a single object. It also allows you to set the position of an object in relation to other objects in the group.

- You can align and distribute objects in relation to other objects using the Alignment command from the Arrange menu.

KEY TERMS

active
align, aligning
arc tool
Autogrid

constrain
corner/center control
cross-beam pointer

deselect
distributing
Drawing format
Duplicate command

ellipse

fill
fill pattern box
freehand tool

grid
gridlines
grouping

handle
highlighted

insertion point

layer controls
layers
line pattern box
line tool
line weights

menu bar

paragraph text
pattern palette

Pen menu   smooth
point size   snap
polygon tool   stacking order

Reshape command   text tool
resize   tools palette
rulers   transparent objects
ruler settings
                                                  Unsmooth command
scroll arrows
scroll box   wrap, text wrap
select
selection arrow   zoom controls
Show Size command   zoom percentage box

MACDRAW II COMMAND KEYS AND SHORTCUTS

File Menu   **Arrange Menu**
New   ⌘ -N   Move To Front   ⌘-Shift-F
Open   ⌘ -O   Move To Back   ⌘-Shift-J
Close   ⌘ -W   Align   ⌘ -K
Save   ⌘ -S   Alignment   ⌘-Shift-K
Quit   ⌘ -Q   Rotate   ⌘ -T
                                                  Group   ⌘ -G
                                                  Ungroup   ⌘-Shift-G
Edit Menu   Ungroup
Undo   ⌘ -Z
Cut   ⌘ -X   **Style Menu**
Copy   ⌘ -C   Bold   ⌘ -B
Paste   ⌘ -V   Italic   ⌘ -I
Duplicate   ⌘ -D   Underline   ⌘ -U
Select All   ⌘ -A
Reshape   ⌘ -R
Smooth   ⌘ -E
Unsmooth   ⌘-Shift-E

Additional Projects

The following projects are accompanied by briefer instructions than those you have previously completed in this chapter. They require that you apply what you learned in the first two projects. If necessary, refer to "Using MacDraw's Tools" at the beginning of this chapter for information and instructions about using any tools that you aren't familiar with.

You will not be reminded to save your work—you should be thinking of that on your own by now.

PROJECT 3: DRAWING A WHISTLE

This project makes use of the polygon tool, the circle, the corner/center control, and the Reshape command. You'll use the zoom controls to work in a magnified view of your drawing, and you'll use the Rotate command to rotate text. The finished whistle is shown in Figure 5-69.

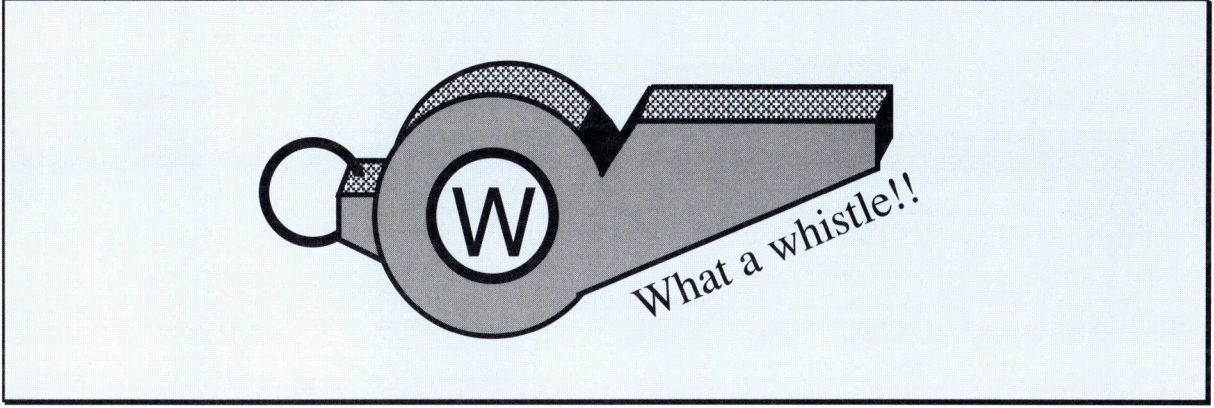

Figure 5-69   Final output for Project 3

➠ Choose **Turn Autogrid Off** from the Layout menu.

  ➠ Select the oval tool.

➠ Hold down the Shift key and draw a circle about 1 inch in diameter.

➠ Use the polygon tool to draw the mouthpiece extension, as shown in Figure 5-70.

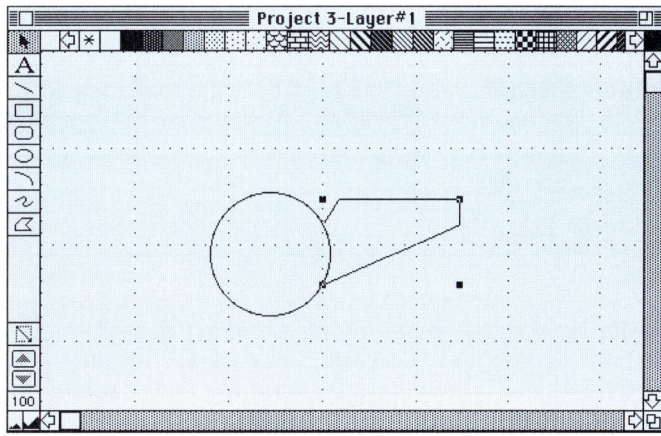

Figure 5-70   Drawing the mouthpiece of the whistle

Now that you have drawn both shapes, you need to examine them and make sure they are touching.

⟹ With the polygon shape selected, use the zoom control to magnify the view to 400%.

⌘-R   ⟹ Choose **Reshape** from the Edit menu.

⟹ Drag the endpoints of the polygon so they touch the circle. See Figure 5-71.

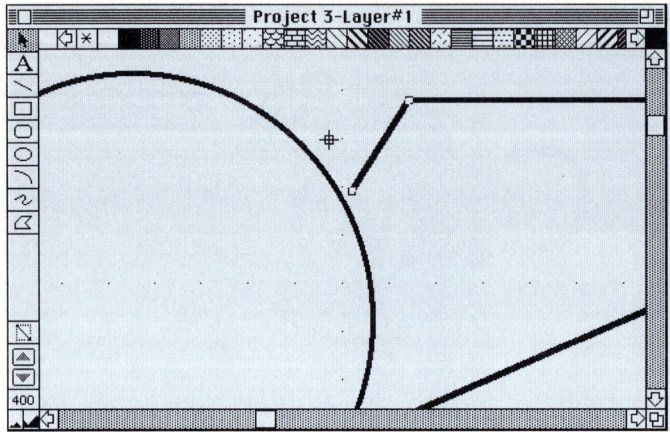

Figure 5-71   Reshaping the endpoints of the polygon

⟹ Click the zoom percentage box to return to 100% viewing size.

⌘-G   ⟹ Select the circle and the polygon shapes, and then choose **Group** from the Arrange menu.

⌘-D   ⟹ With the grouped objects still selected, choose **Duplicate** from the Edit menu.

⟹ Position the duplicate object slightly lower and to the left of the original, as shown in Figure 5-72.

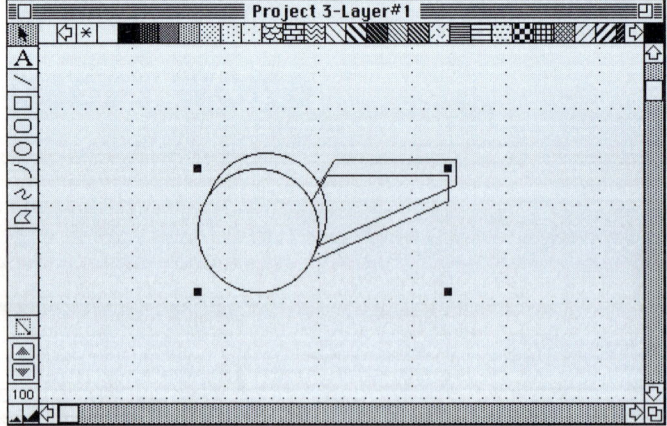

Figure 5-72   Positioning the duplicate object

→ Fill the front object with a gray pattern and the one behind with a different pattern.

Now you'll change the borders of these objects to a heavier line weight.

→ Select both objects and choose **2 point** from the Pen menu. See Figure 5-73.

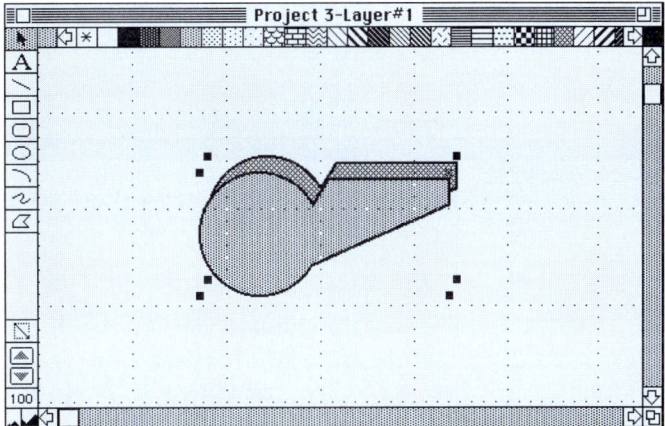

Figure 5-73   Changing the line weight of the borders

→ Use the zoom control to magnify the view to 400%.

 → Draw the whistle "opening" on the mouthpiece with the polygon tool, and fill the shape with black, as shown in Figure 5-74.

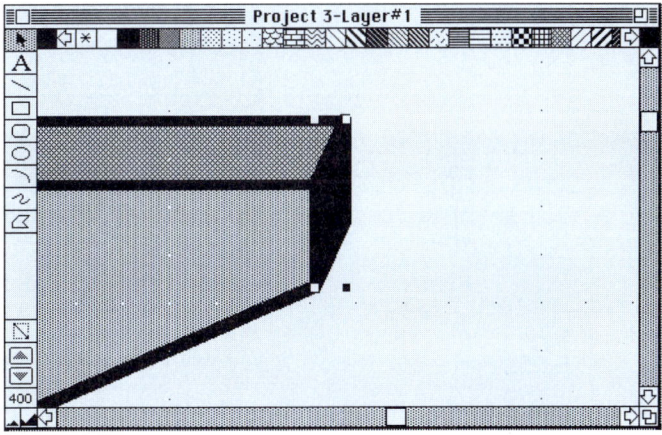

Figure 5-74   Drawing a polygon for the end "opening"

⌘-R → Use the Reshape command as necessary to make the four points of the "opening" shape match the points on the end of the whistle.

 → Move to the other "opening" area of the whistle and use the polygon tool to create that shape. Reshape as necessary, and fill it with black. See Figure 5-75.

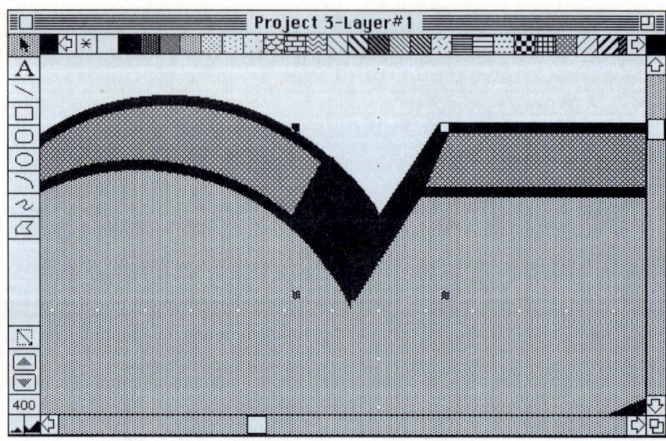

Figure 5-75   Creating the other "opening" with the polygon tool

➠ Use the zoom control to change the view to 200% size.

 ➠ Draw the shape that holds the ring with the polygon tool. Fill it with the same pattern as the front of the whistle.

⌘-J ➠ Choose **Move Backward** from the Arrange menu so the border of the circle is not obscured by the shape. See Figure 5-76.

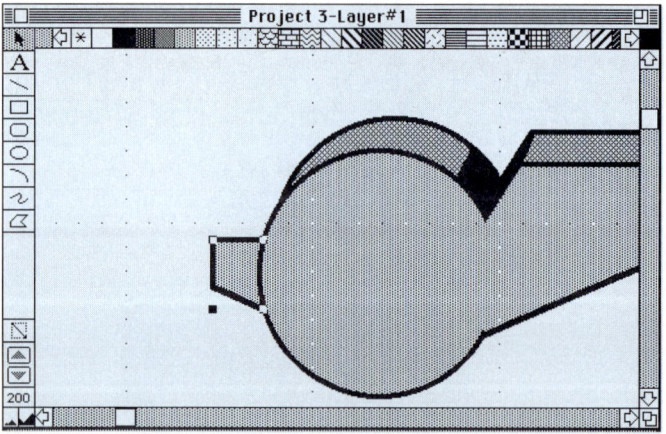

Figure 5-76   Positioning the small polygon

 ➠ Use the Shift key with the oval tool to draw the circle for the ring.

 ➠ Fill the circle with the empty fill, or transparent, pattern.

➠ Choose **4 point** from the Pen menu to give the ring a heavier border.

⌘-J ➠ Place the ring on top of the small polygon you just drew, and then choose **Move Backward** from the Arrange menu.

The ring now appears to be behind the polygon, as shown in Figure 5-77.

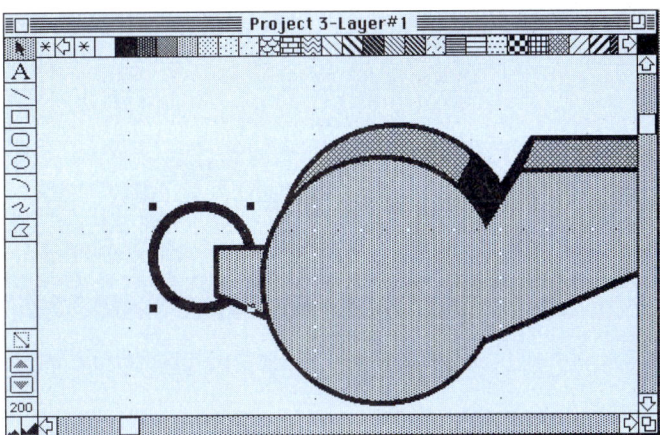

Figure 5-77   Moving the ring behind the polygon

➡ Click somewhere to deselect the ring, and then choose **2 point** from the Pen menu.

 ➡ Use the polygon tool to draw the piece on top of the ring. Fill it with the same pattern as the back of the whistle.

⌘-Shift-J ➡ Choose **Move to Back** from the Arrange menu to place this polygon in the back of the stacking order, as shown in Figure 5-78.

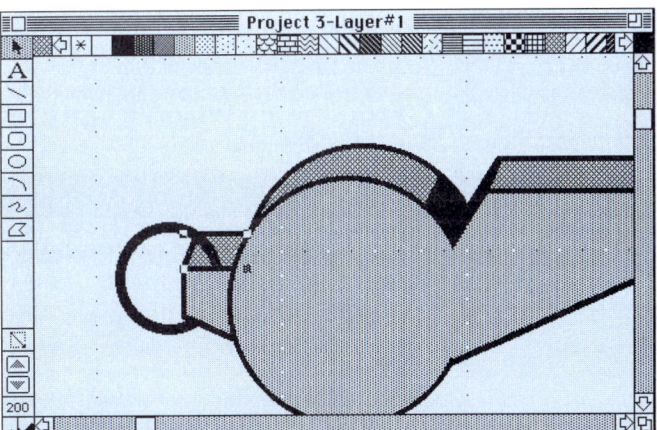

Figure 5-78   Moving the top polygon behind the ring

➡ Use the zoom control to view the drawing at 400% magnification.

➡ To make the ring appear to be going through the top polygon, draw a small rectangle with the same fill pattern and line pattern as the back of the whistle, as shown in Figure 5-79.

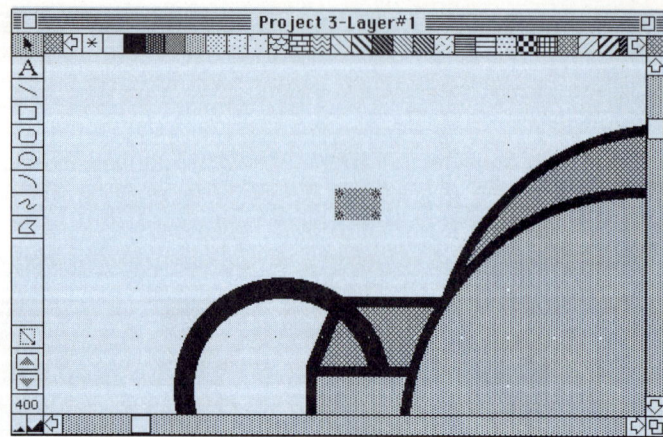

Figure 5-79   The small rectangle used to "erase" part of the ring

➡ Place the rectangle so that it obscures part of the ring, in effect "erasing" it.

➡ Change the line pattern to black and the fill pattern to white.

➡ Choose **4 point** from the Pen menu.

➡ Set the corner/center control to draw from center.

➡ Draw a small white circle in the center of the main circle, about a half-inch in diameter.

➡ Set the corner/center control to draw from corner.

➡ Choose a font of your choice and 24 or 36 point size.

➡ Use the text tool to type your initial, and then place the initial in the center of the white circle.

➡ Type the words **What a whistle!!** in a font of your choice and in 14 or 18 point size.

⌘-T ➡ Choose **Rotate** from the Arrange menu while the text is selected.

➡ Position the X pointer at the end of the word and drag in a circular motion to rotate the text. The text will pivot around the end opposite from where you place the pointer, as shown in Figure 5-80.

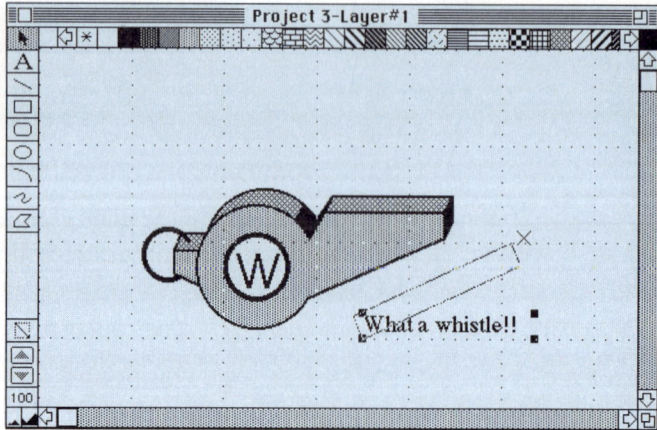

Figure 5-80   Rotating text

➡ Place the text at the same angle as the underside of the whistle.

Compare your finished whistle with the one shown in Figure 5-69.

Project 4: Drawing a Still Life

This project uses the freehand tool, the arc tool, the Reshape command, and the Smooth and Unsmooth commands. The finished drawing is shown in Figure 5-81. It shows some suggested foods to draw, but you can use your imagination. Some other ideas for food shapes that would be interesting to draw and that would exercise your creativity are breakfast foods, carrot slices, rolls, beverages, pasta, fish, and sandwiches.

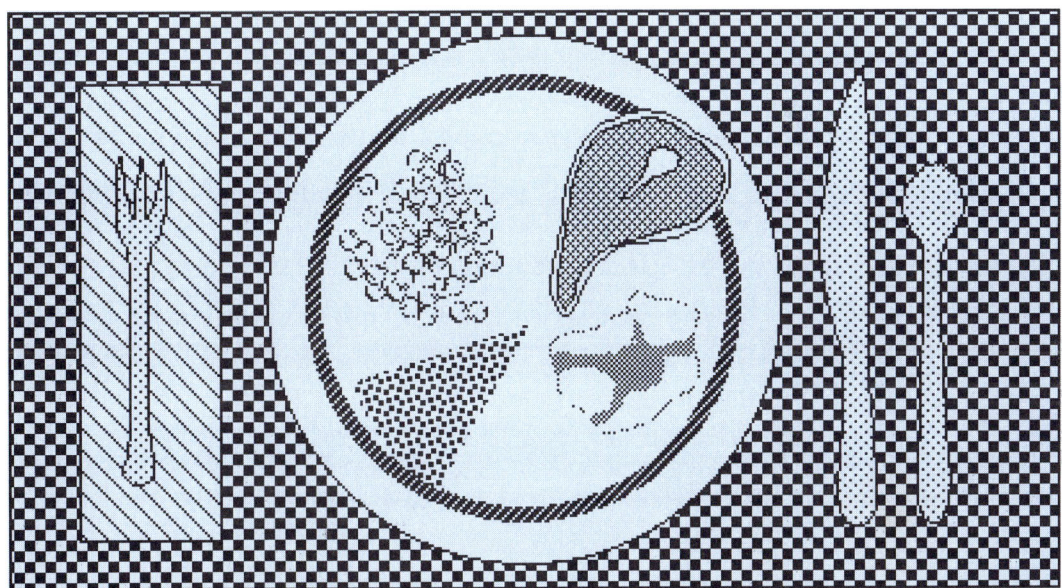

Figure 5-81   Final output for Project 4

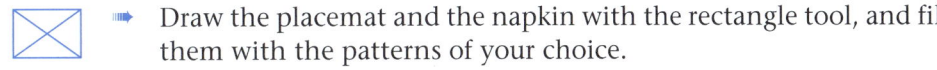 ➡ Draw the placemat and the napkin with the rectangle tool, and fill them with the patterns of your choice.

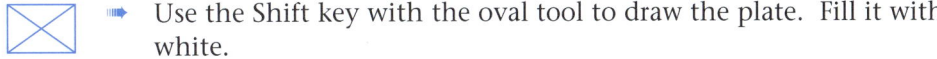 ➡ Use the Shift key with the oval tool to draw the plate. Fill it with white.

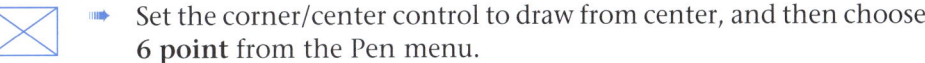 ➡ Set the corner/center control to draw from center, and then choose **6 point** from the Pen menu.

➡ Set the line pattern to a pattern of your choice, and then draw the border on the plate. See Figure 5-82.

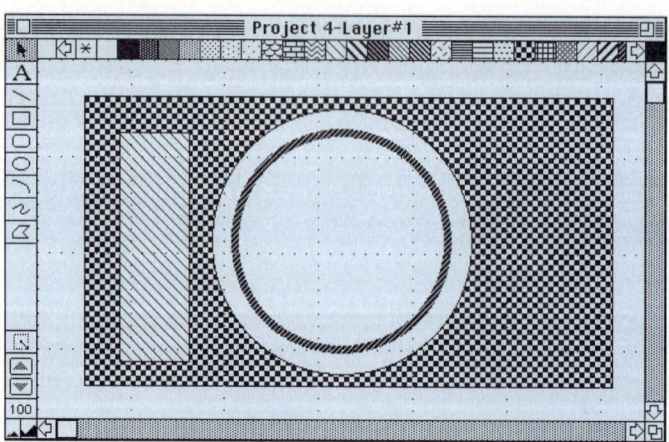

Figure 5-82   Using a 6-point line weight for the plate border

⌘-G   ➡   Select the placemat, napkin, plate, and border, and then choose **Group** from the Arrange menu.

        ➡   Click somewhere to deselect the object, and then change the pen size by choosing **1 point** from the Pen menu.

        ➡   Change the line pattern to black and the fill pattern to white.

   ➡   Scroll to the area to the right of the placemat, and then select the freehand tool.

        ➡   Draw the shape of a knife, as shown in Figure 5-83. Don't worry if it doesn't look too good—you'll use the Reshape command to fix it.

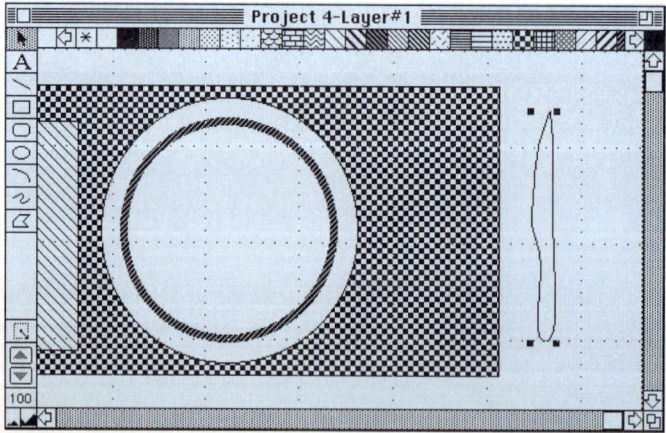

Figure 5-83   Drawing the shape of the knife

        ➡   Choose **Turn Autogrid Off** from the Layout menu.

        ➡   Use the zoom controls to view the drawing at 400% magnification.

⌘-R   ⌘-Shift-E   ➡   With the knife selected, choose **Unsmooth** and then **Reshape** from the Edit menu.

➡ Add new points on the border of the shape by clicking and move existing points as needed until the shape resembles a knife. See Figure 5-84.

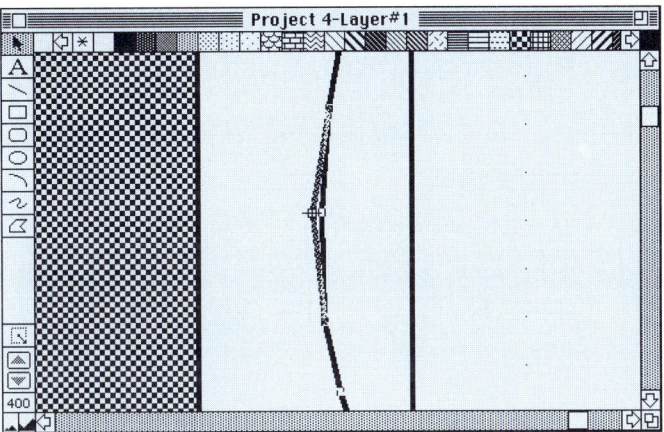

Figure 5-84   Moving a point on the knife shape

To remove a point from the border of the shape, hold down the Option key and click on the unwanted point.

➡ Click in the zoom percentage box to return to 100% size.

⌘-E ➡ Choose **Smooth** from the Edit menu, and click on the selection arrow to stop reshaping.

If your knife does not satisfy you, continue unsmoothing, reshaping, and smoothing it until it looks the way you want it to.

➡ When it is to your liking, fill the knife with a light gray pattern and position it on the placemat to the right of the plate. See Figure 5-85.

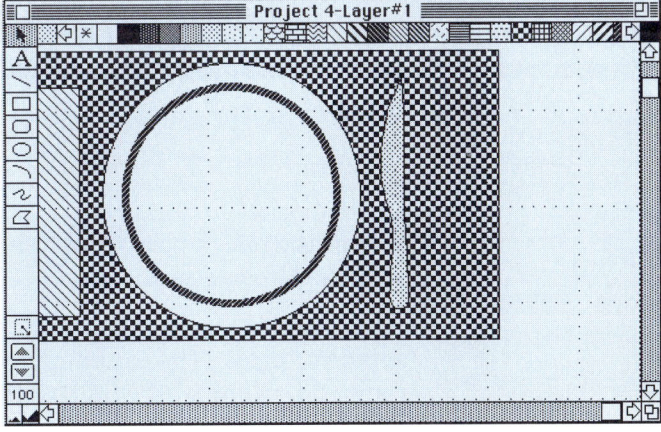

Figure 5-85   Position the completed knife on the placemat

➠ Create the spoon in the same manner and position it on the placemat next to the knife. See Figure 5-86.

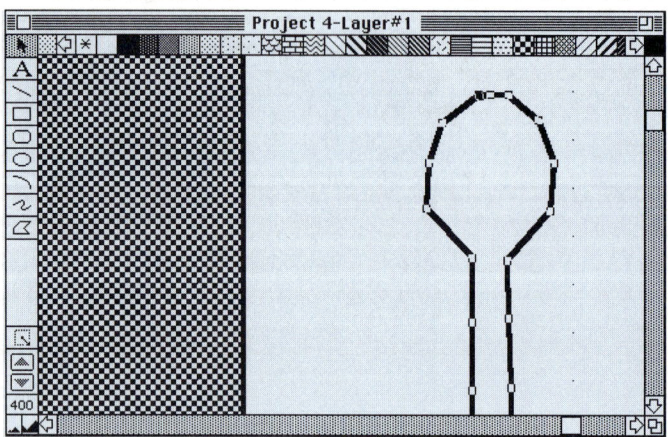

Figure 5-86   Creating and reshaping the spoon

➠ Create the fork in the same way and then place it on the napkin. See Figure 5-87.

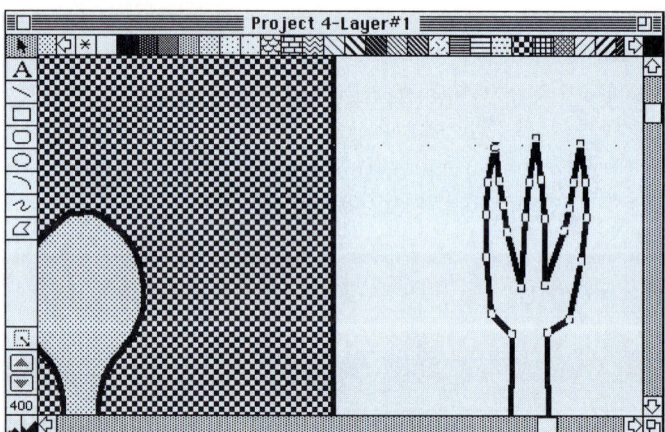

Figure 5-87   Creating and reshaping the fork

➠ Use the zoom controls to view the drawing at 200% size.

➠ To draw the pile of peas, draw a small circle with a light fill pattern and a gray line pattern.

➠ Duplicate the circles repeatedly, and position them to form a helping of peas. (The Command-key equivalent for the Duplicate command, Command-D, is useful for multiple duplications.) See Figure 5-88.

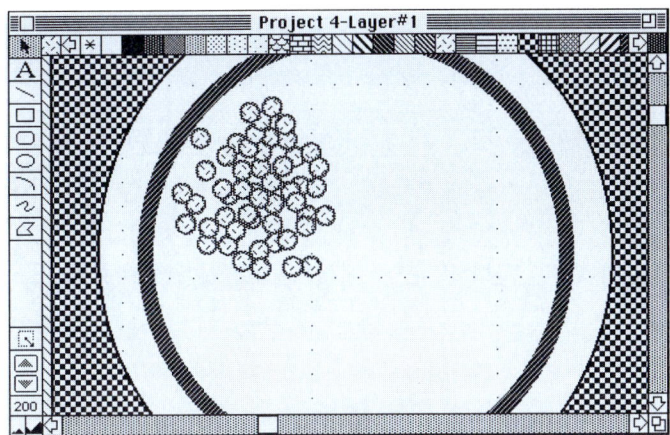

Figure 5-88   Duplicating circles to form the peas

⇒   Switch between the different magnification views to suit your drawing needs.

⇒   Draw the meat with the freehand tool.

⇒   Draw the basic shape of the meat filled with white, and then draw a slightly smaller shape inside of it filled with a light pattern. See Figure 5-89.

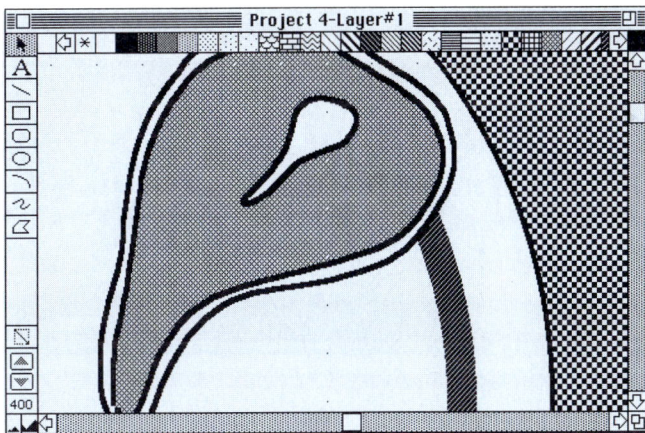

Figure 5-89   Creating the meat shape

⇒   Draw the potatoes with the freehand tool using a gray line pattern.

⇒   Draw the gravy with the freehand tool using the same gray line and fill pattern. See Figure 5-90.

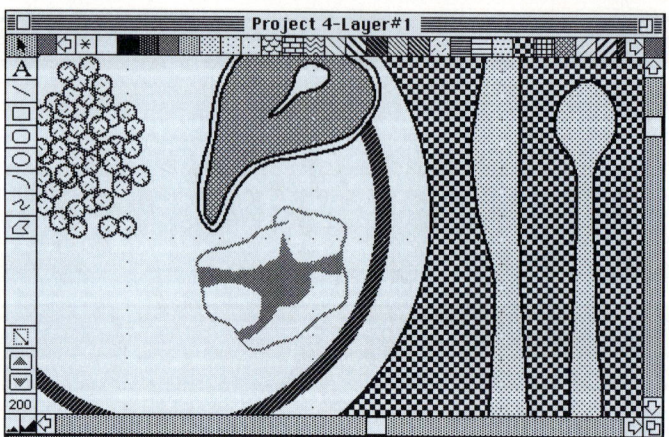

Figure 5-90   Creating the mashed potatoes and gravy.

   ⇒   Draw the wedge of cornbread with the arc tool, and after it is drawn fill it with a pattern.

⌘-T   ⇒   Use the Rotate command to help you position the cornbread on the plate. See Figure 5-91.

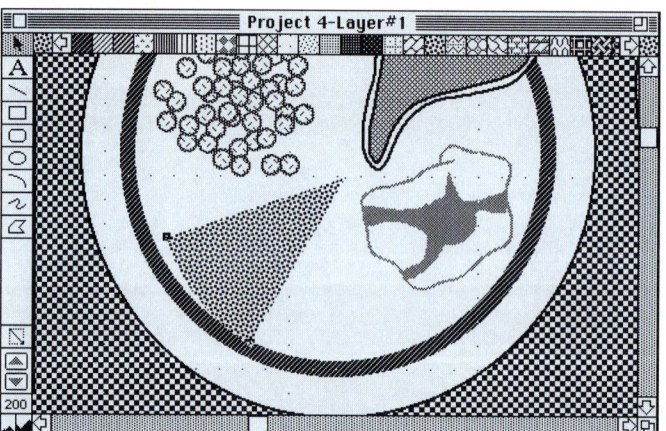

Figure 5-91   The cornbread slice created with the arc tool

If you need to make a smaller "slice," reshape the arc using the Reshape command.

Compare your finished drawing with the one shown in Figure 5-81.

Part III: Word Processing

Part III: Word Processing introduces you to word processing on the Macintosh.

Chapter 6 presents the basic concepts of word processing applications. Chapter 7 introduces you to Microsoft Word, one of the most sophisticated and widely used word processing applications on the Macintosh. You will create several kinds of documents in this chapter, including a menu and a newsletter, using Microsoft Word's desktop publishing capabilities.

Chapter 6: Word Processing Concepts

What You Will Learn in This Chapter

After reading this chapter, you will understand:

- The four areas of word processing: entering text, editing, formatting, and printing

- The computer definition of a paragraph

- The concept of "word wrap"

- The differences between using a typewriter and a word processor

- The use of formatting to change the appearance of a document

- The use of the search and replace feature

- The use of a spelling checker and its limitations

W*ord processing* is the process of using a computer to help automate the production of documents through *text entry*, *editing*, *formatting*, and *printing*.

In its simplest form, word processing is similar to using a typewriter. Whatever you type on the keyboard is printed on the page. Using a word processor is much easier than using a typewriter because changes to a document are easier to make. You don't have to retype the entire page if you want to change a few words or paragraphs or if you want to change the spacing or the margins.

As you produce a document on a typewriter, you must make quick, irrevocable decisions about how you want the document to look. For example, where will you end a line? If a word doesn't fit on a line, should you hyphenate it, erase it and put it on the next line, or just hit the margin release and hope you can cram the word in? How many more lines will fit on the page? If you type an incorrect letter, should you erase it, type over it, or ignore it? How can you fix a sentence in which you left out a word?

Word processing relieves you of many of these worries and allows you to concentrate on producing your best document. Basically four processes are used in word processing to produce a document: entering text, editing, formatting, and printing. The order in which these processes are used is not fixed—you can enter all the text and edit and format later, or format and edit as you enter the text, or use any order that you choose. The projects in this section use a sequence of first entering the text and then editing, formatting, and finally printing.

ENTERING TEXT

Word processing always begins with basic text entry. But entering text is different on a word processor than it is on a typewriter. A typewriter commits each keystroke immediately to paper. A word processor records what you type and shows it to you on the computer's screen. Since most word processors include easy ways to edit your text and many include *spelling checkers*, you don't have to worry about typing everything correctly. Just start typing. If you make mistakes, you can correct them later.

When you create a document with a word processor and then save it on your disk, you are saving it as a *file*. A *file* is a collection of characters, and that is actually what your document is. A document can consist of any number of characters, words, sentences, paragraphs, or pages—you are limited only by the amount of storage space available on your disk. The terms *file* and *document* are interchangeable in word processing.

Another advantage of a word processor is that it relieves you of the worry of having to decide if you can fit another word at the end of the current line. With a typewriter the typist must keep track of the margins—at the end of a line you use the carriage return to advance to the next line. With a word processor the program keeps track of the margins. If the word doesn't fit on the line, the word processor will automatically move the word down to the next line. This process is called *word wrap*. Some word processors even look up the word in a *hyphenation dictionary*, insert a hyphen in the appropriate place, and put the rest of the word on the next line.

Word wrap is one of the main things that touch typists have to adjust to when they are first learning to use a word processor. *When you enter text, do not press the Return key at the end of each line.* Learn to press Return only at the end of a paragraph. The computer meaning of a *paragraph* is text that is followed by a *hard carriage return* (pressing Return). A paragraph can consist of one or more characters, words, or sentences.

Just as you don't have to think about where to end a line, you don't have to think about where to end a page. When you reach the end of the page, the word processor automatically adds a new page at the end of the document; you just continue typing, and your new work is automatically entered on this new page.

When you have all the text entered, you may discover misspelled words, grammatical errors, missing or extra words, or even paragraphs out of place. These can all be easily corrected during another step in producing your document: *editing*.

EDITING

Editing is the process of adding, deleting, and modifying the text that you or someone else has entered. A word processor gives you tools that help you correct and format your document.

If you left out a word, you can click the mouse at the point in the line where the word belongs to set the insertion point and then type the word. The computer moves all the text that follows this new word to the right. When a word no longer fits at the end of the line, it wraps to the next line, and the rest of the paragraph readjusts, or *reformats*, automatically.

If you find a word that should not be in the document, you can select the word and delete it. The paragraph will be reformatted automatically. The words that follow move back to the left, or even from one line to the line above it, if there is room.

As with a typewriter, you can backspace to delete unwanted characters, but that is the long way. The beauty of deleting with a word processor is that you can select the word or words and just start typing over them. You can be much more efficient with your time and avoid unnecessary steps.

For example, if a sentence (or paragraph, page, or section) doesn't say what you want it to say, you can select that text and replace it by typing new text. Any selected text will be deleted automatically when you type new words. The paragraphs that are affected will be reformatted.

These are powerful editing features. Once you have used a word processor you will probably never want to go back to using a typewriter.

Two more important editing features are *cutting* and *pasting*. If a paragraph would make more sense somewhere else in your document, you can select that paragraph, cut it out of the document, indicate where you'd like it to be placed, and paste it into your document at that location. The word processor will relocate the text, close the gap that was created when the text was removed, make room for the text where you paste it, and automatically readjust all affected parts of the document. And you don't have to retype the whole document!

Searching and Replacing

Very helpful in the editing process is the *search and replace* feature, which allows you to search for a particular character or group of characters and replace those characters with something else. For example, you can search for a misspelled name such as Mr. Smith and replace all occurrences of it with the correct spelling of Mr. Smythe. The search and replace feature finds each occurrence in your document of whatever characters (or words or groups of words) you are searching for and replaces those characters with what you specify.

You can even search for specific formatting characters, such as tabs and spaces, and replace them with other formatting characters to help automate word processing tasks.

Spell Checking

Also helpful in the editing process is having the spelling in a document checked for you. A *spelling checker* determines if a word is spelled correctly by comparing each word in a document with the entries in its dictionary. If the word matches a dictionary entry, the spelling checker considers the word correct. If the word is not in the dictionary, that word is considered misspelled. Be aware, however, that all spelling checker dictionaries have limitations. Microsoft Word's dictionary contains about 130,000 entries, but, like most program-supplied dictionaries, proper names, acronyms, and obscure terms are not included.

Don't depend on a spelling checker to do all your proofreading for you. Spelling checkers only find words that they don't recognize. The word it finds may be correct, but the spelling checker's dictionary doesn't contain it. Or the word in the document may be wrong, but it is a legal word. For instance, a spelling checker will know that "their" is spelled correctly and won't be able to tell you that the word should be "there" for a particular context. The spelling checker only knows correct spelling, not correct usage. It doesn't know the difference between "flower" and "flour," for example. Spell checking is not an automatic process—it simply provides suggestions that the user needs to consider before changing the word in question.

There are programs that check grammatical structure, but they are beyond the scope of this book.

FORMATTING

Formatting a document involves determining how your pages will appear when printed. You can decide to change the margins of the page; change the font, size, and style of type throughout the whole document; or change single characters or words in the document. You can use multiple columns. Your document can be printed tall on the page like the usual letter, which is called *portrait orientation*, or you can turn the page sideways so the document prints out with the long side of the paper being the top of the page, which is called *landscape orientation*.

Some of these decisions have already been made by the creators of the word processing program. These preset selections are called *defaults*. They have been previously set to the most common use for your convenience. As you become more familiar with a program you can change some of the settings to suit your work style and preferences.

For instance, Microsoft Word will assume that you want a new document to be printed vertically, to have 1-inch top and bottom margins and $1^1/_4$-inch left and right margins, to print in one column of text that is 6 inches wide, and to use New York font, set for 12-point size and normal style.

If you don't do anything, Microsoft Word will use these settings. However, if you want to print in three columns, with the page turned sideways, using Times font in 10-point bold, you can easily do this.

Another example of a default setting is in Word's *ruler*. It is set to measure in inches, but a designer may want to measure in picas. Word processors usually allow you to change the defaults either for a single file or for the program in general.

Default settings do not limit you. They are there to help your document conform to conventional document formats and to help you get started easily without having to think about a lot of settings. The decision to accept a default setting or to override it is entirely up to you. When you become more proficient with Word, you can customize the program to suit your preferences.

PRINTING

Printing your document involves getting the words on the paper. Once you have entered, edited, formatted, and checked the text, you tell the computer the correct type of printer to use. Then you tell the program to print the document. The program sends the document to the printer. This process is automatic whether the document is 1 page or, in the case of this book, more than 700 pages.

SUMMARY

- Word processing is the process of using a computer to create documents through text entry, editing, formatting, and printing.

- Text entry is the process of typing the text into a document.

- Word wrap is the concept of the computer keeping track of the margins of a document.

- A paragraph is any character or group of characters that is followed by a hard return (pressing the Return key).

- A word processor is easier to use than a typewriter because a word processor allows you to make changes to a document without having to retype it.

- The search and replace feature of a word processor locates every occurrence of a selected character or group of characters in a document and replaces it with the character or group of characters that you choose.

- A spelling checker locates words in a document that do not match the entries in its dictionary. It does not catch grammatical errors or misuse of words. It is not a replacement for proofreading.

- Formatting refers to the appearance of the printed page.

- Page size, page orientation, margins, paragraph spacing, line spacing, and character formats are all governed by the formatting capabilities of a word processor.

- Printing a document involves issuing a command to the word processing program to send a document to a selected printer.

KEY TERMS

cutting

defaults
document

editing

file
formatting

hard carriage return, hard return
hyphenation dictionary

landscape orientation

paragraph
pasting
portrait orientation
printing

reformat
ruler

search and replace
spelling checker

text entry

word processing
word wrap

Chapter 7: Microsoft Word 4

What You Will Learn in This Chapter

After reading this chapter and completing the projects in it, you should be able to:

- Select, delete, and edit text

- Change character formats of text

- Move text

- Use the Find and Change features

- Check the spelling of a document

- Format a paragraph

- Format a document

- Insert tabs, tab leaders, and borders

- Add page numbers

- Adjust margins

- Save and print documents

- Open multiple documents

- Incorporate graphics and text

- Create and apply styles

- Create and modify tables

- Create multicolumn documents using sections

- Create headers and footers

- Create print merge documents

Word processing is probably the most widely used application on a microcomputer. If your creativity has been hindered by writing with pencil and paper or by using a typewriter, you will enjoy the benefits of using the Macintosh for word processing.

Like other Macintosh applications, Microsoft Word uses pull-down menus, windows, a mouse, and many of the features you will encounter throughout your use of the Macintosh.

Microsoft Word uses five formatting domains: the character, paragraph, table, section, and document.

The *character* is the smallest unit in the document. Characters consist of letters of the alphabet, punctuation marks, numbers, and symbols. Each character can be formatted individually, and groups of characters, such as words and sentences, can be formatted in one operation.

A *paragraph* is a collection of characters that is followed by a hard return (pressing the Return key). A paragraph can consist of just a few characters, many sentences, or even a blank line. Any changes you make to the paragraph formatting affect the entire paragraph that is selected or that contains the insertion point. The character and paragraph are the basic units in Microsoft Word. You'll have the opportunity to work with many different character and paragraph formats throughout this chapter.

A *table*, also called a cell table, consists of rows and columns of *cells*, and each cell can contain characters and paragraphs that have different formatting characteristics. You'll learn more about tables in Project 3 of this chapter.

A *section* consists of one or more paragraphs and is followed by a *section marker*. A document can be divided into many sections, and each section can even be formatted with a different page layout, such as different numbers of columns. Each document contains at least one section. Project 4 in this chapter covers sections in detail.

The *document* is the largest unit, and it consists of the document itself. When a document is formatted, all formatting pertains to the entire document. Some examples of document formatting include page margins and printing preparation. You'll work with document formatting at different times throughout this chapter.

STARTING MICROSOFT WORD

Microsoft Word

Starting Microsoft Word is just like starting the other applications you've worked with—you locate the application's icon and double-click on it.

➡   Double-click on the Microsoft Word icon on your disk.

This will start Microsoft Word and open a new document entitled "Untitled1".

GETTING HELP

While you are working in Microsoft Word, it is likely you'll want to make use of the additional information supplied in the online Help file. The material in the Help file is presented in concise, easily understood terms.

You can activate Help by choosing **About Word** from the Apple menu and then clicking the **Help** button, or you can choose **Help** from the Window menu. In either case, assuming that the Help file is present on the computer and in the correct location, Word displays the Help window, as shown in Figure 7-1.

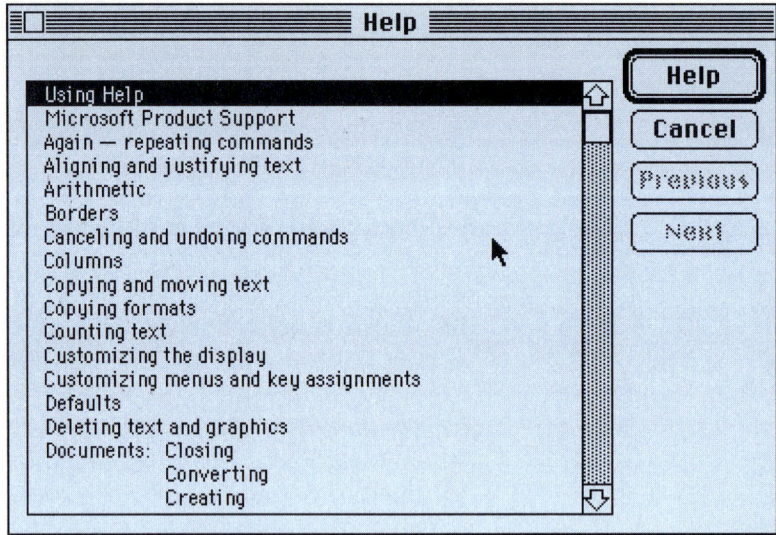

Figure 7-1   The Help window

You scroll through a list of topics that is organized alphabetically, and select the topic you want to read about. Either double-click on the topic name or click once to select the topic and then click on the **Help** button. When you've selected a topic, Word presents information about that topic.

When you are finished reading the information, you can either click the **Next** button to continue getting help or you can click the **Previous** button to go back to the previous topic. When you are finished using the Help window, you can close it by clicking its close box, or click the **Cancel** button. Either way, you are returned to where you left off in your Microsoft Word document.

In Figure 7-2, the topic selected for additional information was **Formatting: Paragraph**. The page number below the **Next** button indicates what page to reference in the program documentation for greater detail about that topic.

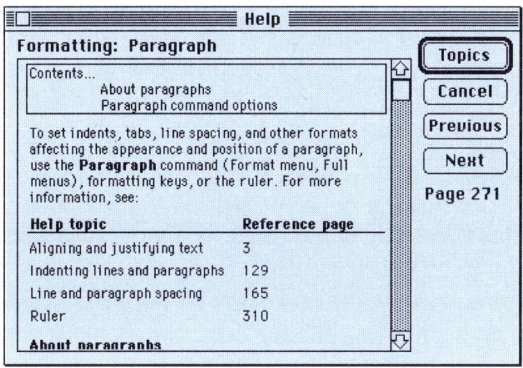

Figure 7-2   A Help topic selected

⌘-?   You can also get *context-sensitive help* on a specific command or option without scrolling through the list of available topics. To do this, press Command-?, and your pointer turns into a large question mark. When you use that question mark to select a command from one of the menus, to click an icon on the ruler, or to use a key sequence that invokes a command, the Help dialog box is presented displaying the relevant topic. This also works for getting help about an open dialog box.

With an *extended keyboard*—one that has function keys, arrow and direction keys, and other keys—you can use the Help key on the keyboard to get help and the Esc key to get out of Help.

For more information about using Help, select **Using Help** from the list of topics presented in the Help dialog box.

SAVING YOUR WORK

The first time you save your document, Microsoft Word asks you, by way of the dialog box shown in Figure 7-3, where you want your document saved and what you want it to be named. After you have saved a document the first time, the next time you choose **Save**, Word assumes that you want the document to be saved in the same place and under the same name. Be careful about saving your document in the correct place the first time you save it so you can find it later. The Save process is much quicker the second and subsequent times, because you are not prompted for any additional information.

Unfortunately, sometimes people are not careful, and they occasionally lose their work because they saved it where they couldn't find it when they needed it later. Clicking the **Drive** button repeatedly moves between one or more floppy drives and hard drives, depending on the hardware you are using. The Save dialog box shows the name of the floppy disk or hard drive as that drive is selected. Your document will be saved on the selected disk or hard drive with the name showing in the Save dialog box. In the dialog box shown in Figure 7-3, the name of the disk, Carolyn Phillips, is shown in two places. Always be aware of where you are saving your work.

The Save As command is similar to the Save command, except that it gives you the option to give your document a different name and save it in a different location. Every time you choose **Save As** from the File menu, you are prompted with the dialog box shown in Figure 7-3. This is the same dialog box you see the first time you save your document.

When you use the Save As command and you attempt to save the document with the same name and in the same location as before, you will be asked if you want to replace the old document. This is because no two files in a particular location can have the same name. If you want to save different versions of the same document, use the Save As command and give the document a different name and/or location.

Save your work often. Save at least every ten minutes, so you never lose more than ten minutes of work. The Command-key equivalent of the Save command, Command-S, is a helpful shortcut. Always save your work before printing.

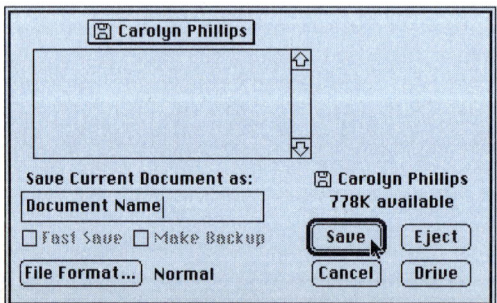

Figure 7-3   The Save dialog box

Be aware that you can save a document before you actually type anything into it, and that many people do it this way. However, you will be given explicit instructions for saving your work at appropriate times throughout the projects.

USING SHORT MENUS AND FULL MENUS

Microsoft Word provides two sets of menus: Short Menus and Full Menus. *Short Menus* provides commands for routine word processing tasks and is intended to make the program less intimidating for beginners. *Full Menus* allows you to make use of all the Short Menu commands as well as of additional commands for more advanced word processing tasks.

When Microsoft Word is in Short Menus mode, you'll see **Full Menus** on the Edit menu. Also, when in Short Menus mode, there will not be as many settings to choose from on the ruler. To switch to Full Menus mode, choose **Full Menus** from the Edit menu. If Microsoft Word is in Full Menus mode, you'll be able to choose **Short Menus** from the Edit menu. In the projects in this chapter, you will be working in Full Menus mode.

Project 1: Creating a Business Memorandum

In this first project you will produce a business memorandum. You will enter text, set tabs on the ruler, change several formatting characteristics, add page numbers, and print your document.

As with all projects, read the entire project before starting. This will give you an overview of what you will encounter and may save you the work of having to backtrack if you make mistakes.

Figure 7-4 shows the completed memorandum.

Acme Manufacturing, Inc.
12366 Coyote Lane
Dust Ring, OR 23366

MEMORANDUM

TO: Larry Cassella, Eastern District Sales Manager
FROM: Karin Jole, Vice President of Sales
DATE: July 17, 1993
SUBJECT: January through June Sales Report

Based on a compilation of your recently submitted sales reports, the following shows the sales totals (in thousands of dollars) of our small parts product line for the first half of the year:

Widgets	$746
Gadgets	$564
DooDads	$395
Total	$1,705

As you can see from the figures, Widgets continue to be our top seller, and Gadgets are moving along at the rate we expected. Although DooDads don't seem to be selling too well, they are a seasonal product and we expect to see rapid gains through late fall and into early winter.

Sales for the year closely match anticipated figures, and Widgets are running about 10 percent above projections. I am happy with the numbers at this point and feel our recent successes are due, in part, to the current "Give It All You've Got" sales campaign that has been implemented among the sales force.

In the most recent tally of this sales campaign, four of the eleven people in your sales district are already eligible for the Las Vegas trip. Two others are close to qualifying, and eight of the eleven have already won their monogrammed Acme briefcases. I want you to congratulate these people for me, Larry. I'll be speaking to them personally when we have the district sales meeting in September.

1

Figure 7-4   Page 1 of the completed memorandum

Our President, S. W. Acme, has indicated to me that he is very pleased with the results of this sales campaign. He made the following comment during the recent shareholders' meeting, and I am pleased to pass it on to you:

> *Our sales force is the backbone of our industry, and we now have the best in the history of Acme Manufacturing. These and women are dedicated workers, without whom we could not be showing the profits that we are today.*

I'm sure you'll make the President's remarks known to your sales staff, Larry. I know your people are deserving of this praise.

To achieve projections on Gadgets we need to begin our promotions for the fall. We can plan our television and magazine advertising strategies during the sales projection meeting early next week. If you have any questions prior to that, please call me.

2

Figure 7-4 (continued)   Page 2 of the completed memorandum

TYPING IN THE TEXT

⌘-N   If you don't have a document window open, follow the instructions for opening a new document under "Starting Microsoft Word" earlier in this chapter.

In the upper left corner of the document window there is a vertical line on the screen. This line flashes to draw your attention. It is called the *insertion point* and shows the location where the next character you type will appear. Since no text has been entered into this document, the insertion point is at the top left corner of the text area on the page, as shown in Figure 7-5.

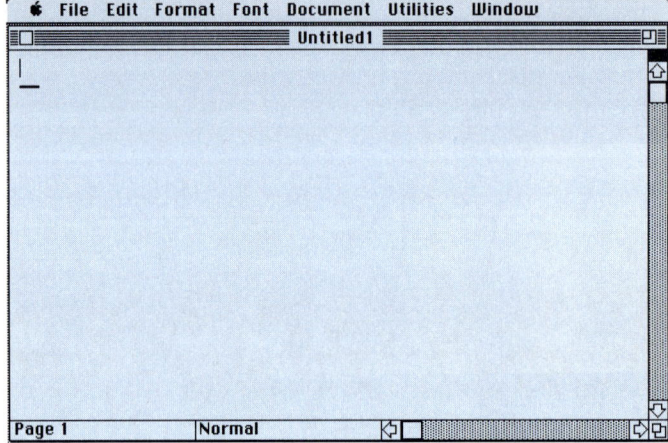

Figure 7-5   The untitled document and the insertion point

Notice that the pointer changes shape when you move the mouse to different parts of the screen. Whenever you move the mouse pointer over the text area of the window, the pointer changes to the *I-beam pointer*. This signifies to you that you are in a text editing area, and clicking the mouse button while the pointer has this shape will set the insertion point to a new location.

➡   Choose the font for the document. If you are using a LaserWriter, choose **Times** and **14 point** from the Font menu. If you are using an ImageWriter **New York** is the default font, and that is fine for this project. Leave the font at the default values of 12 point and plain text style if you are using an ImageWriter.

There are two types of fonts: bitmapped fonts and laser fonts. The output device you will be printing to affects your choice of fonts because a laser font will print best on a LaserWriter, and, if you are using an ImageWriter, a bitmapped font will print best. In addition, the printed output will have the best quality if you choose a font size that is defined in the System file. These defined sizes are called outline fonts and are displayed in the size portion of the Font menu in outlined lettering. Times is a laser font, and New York is a standard ImageWriter bitmapped font.

At the start of each project in this chapter a LaserWriter font and an ImageWriter font will be suggested for you to use. Base your choice on the printer you will be using.

The example in this project uses the New York font.

You need to verify that you are using Full Menus. If you are using Full Menus, **Short Menus** will be an option on the Edit menu. If **Full Menus** shows on the Edit menu, select **Full Menus**.

➡ Choose **Edit** in the menu bar and hold down the mouse button.

➡ If **Short Menus** is showing at the bottom of the Edit menu, release the mouse button without making a selection from the menu.

➡ If **Full Menus** is showing at the bottom of the Edit menu, select **Full Menus**.

Now you should be working in Full Menus mode, which is the mode you'll be using in all the projects in this chapter.

In this project you'll type the entire document without any special formatting, and once it's typed you'll format the document. If you make any errors as you type, use the Backspace key (Delete key on some keyboards) to remove the character or word and then retype it.

➡ Type the following, pressing Return where indicated:

Acme Manufacturing, Inc.   (press Return)
12366 Coyote Lane   (press Return)
Dust Ring, OR 23366   (press Return three times)

➡ Type **MEMORANDUM** in all caps, and then press Return three times.

The first Return is to end the line, and the second and third are to create two blank lines.

Now you'll type the memo heads, and you'll use the Tab key to separate the heads from the names. You'll use the default tab stops for now, which are at half-inch intervals. Each time you press the Tab key, the insertion point will move 1/2 inch to the right.

Don't worry about the names lining up at this point. You'll change that later.

➡ Type **TO:** in all caps, and then press the Tab key.

➡ Type **Larry Cassella, Eastern District Sales Manager**, and then press Return.

➡ Type **FROM:**, press the Tab key, and then type **Karin Jole, Vice President of Sales**. Press Return.

➡ Type **DATE:**, press the Tab key, and then type **July 17, 1993**. Press Return.

➡ Type **SUBJECT:**, press the Tab key, and then type **January through June Sales Report**. Press Return three times, so that two blank lines are between the memo heads and the body of the memo.

Your screen should now look like the one in Figure 7-6.

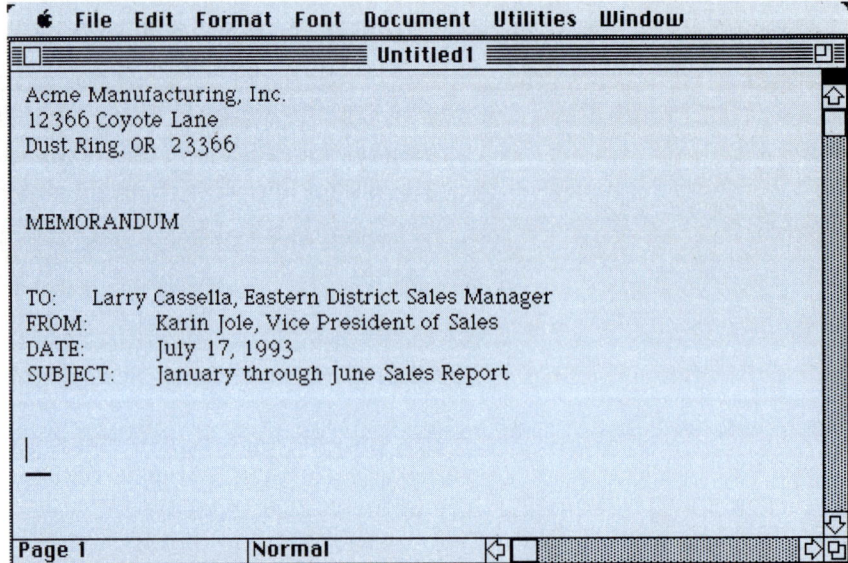

Figure 7-6   The first part of the memorandum

It's a good idea to save your work at this point.

SAVING THE DOCUMENT

Be careful about saving your document in the correct place the first time you save it so you can find it later. The Save process is much quicker the second and subsequent times, because you are not prompted for any additional information.

Save your work often—save at least every ten minutes, so you never lose more than ten minutes of work. The Command-key equivalent of the Save command, Command-S, is a helpful shortcut.

⌘-S ➡ Choose **Save** from the File menu.

➡ Click the **Drive** button, if necessary, to switch drives until the name of your data disk is showing at the top of the Save dialog box, where **Carolyn Phillips** is in Figure 7-7.

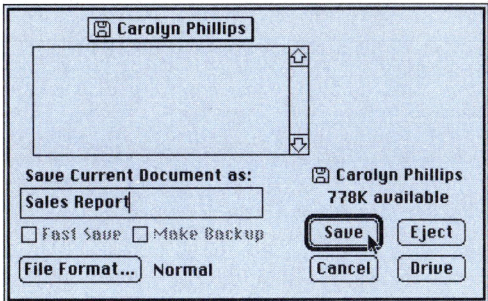

Figure 7-7   The Save dialog box

➠   Type **Sales Report** as the name of your document, and then click the **Save** button. See Figure 7-7.

Now you'll continue typing the body of the memo.

➠   Type the first paragraph of the memo, allowing word wrap to move the text onto the next line as the words reach the right margin. Do not press Return until you've typed the last word in the paragraph:

Based on a compilation of your recently submitted sales reports, the following shows our sales totals (in thousands of dollars) of our small parts product line for the first half of the year:

Notice how, when a word doesn't fit on the line, it drops to the next line automatically. Word wrap enables you to concentrate on your typing and not have to worry about the end of each line.

For the next four lines (the sales figures), you'll use the Tab key to type the two columns of text. You'll format them properly when you've finished typing the memorandum.

➠   Type **Widgets**, press the Tab key, and then type **$746**.

➠   Hold down the Shift key while pressing Return.

The Shift-Return combination is called a *soft return*, because it causes the insertion point to move to the next line but does not start a new paragraph. The next line you type will be considered part of the same paragraph. The new-line command enables you to format all the lines of a paragraph by setting the insertion point anywhere within one of the lines and then selecting the desired formatting options. In this case, it will make it easier to format the four lines in these tabbed columns since you'll be able to work with them as one paragraph. You'll see how this works in a few minutes.

➠   Type **Gadgets**, press the Tab key, and then type **$564**. Press Shift-Return.

➠   Type **DooDads**, press the Tab key, and then type **$395**. Press Shift-Return.

➠   Type **Total**, press the Tab key, and then type **$1,705**. Press Return.

If you scroll to see the last text that you typed, your screen should look like the one shown in Figure 7-8.

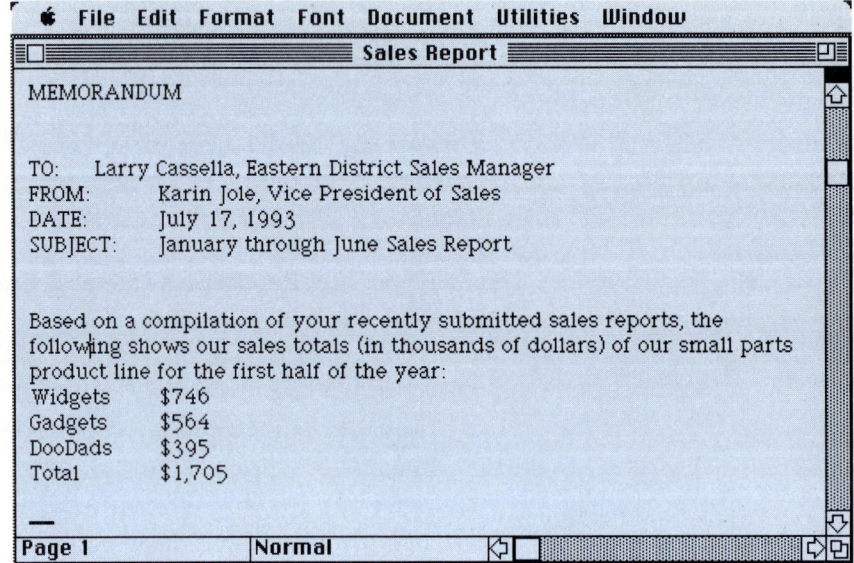

Figure 7-8   The tabbed columns

➡ Type the following three paragraphs, letting word wrap move the words to the next line when they reach the right margin. Press Return only at the end of each paragraph. Press the Return key only once after you've finished typing each paragraph in the document. You'll format the paragraphs with a space between them later:

Sales for the year closely match anticipated figures, and Widgets are running about 10 percent above projections. I am happy with the numbers at this point and feel our recent successes are due, in part, to the current "Give It All You've Got" sales campaign that has been implemented among the sales force.

As you can see from the figures, Widgets continue to be our top seller, and Gadgets are moving along at the rate we expected. Although DooDads don't seem to be selling too well, they are a seasonal product and we expect to see rapid gains through late fall and into early winter.

In the most recent tally of this sales campaign, four of the eleven people in your sales district are already eligible for the Las Vegas trip. Two others are close to qualifying, and eight of the eleven have already won their monogrammed Acme briefcases. I want you to congratulate these people for me, Larry. I'll be speaking to them personally when we have our district sales meeting in September.

⌘-S   ➡ Choose **Save** from the File menu.

➡ Type the following four paragraphs to complete the text entry of your document:

Our President, S. W. Acme, has indicated to me that he is very pleased with the results of this sales campaign. He made the following comment during the recent shareholders' meeting, and I am pleased to pass it on to you:

"Our sales force is the backbone of our industry, and we now have the best in the history of Acme Manufacturing. These men and women are dedicated workers, without whom we could not be showing the profits that we are today."

I'm sure you'll make the President's remarks known to your sales staff, Larry. I know your people are deserving of this praise.

To achieve projections on Gadgets we need to begin our promotions for the fall. We can plan our television and magazine advertising strategies during our sales projection meeting early next week. If you have any questions prior to that, please call me.

You've completed one phase of word processing: creating the document. Now that you've typed the body of the letter, save your work again.

⌘-S ➡ Choose **Save** from the File menu.

EDITING THE DOCUMENT

The next phase of word processing on this document is editing. Editing covers a lot of area, but basically it means making sure the document says what you want it to say and that it is error-free.

Show ¶ is a command that can be very useful when you are editing your document.

Using Show ¶/Hide ¶

Every time you press a key on your keyboard, a character is inserted into your document in that position. Pressing the Return key at the end of a line is an instruction that tells the program to drop down one line and go back to the left margin. Microsoft Word stores a paragraph's formatting characteristics with the paragraph marker at the end of the paragraph.

The space bar inserts an invisible character into the text, just like typing one of the letter, number, or punctuation characters. The space is invisible, but it is a real character, like any other. The Tab key also causes an invisible character to be placed in the document at the point where the Tab key was pressed.

Using Show ¶ is a good way to see if you accidentally typed extra spaces between words, and it lets you see how many blank lines you are creating each time you press the Return key. You can tell how text is formatted by using Show ¶—for example, did a tab cause a particular indentation or was it set using the first-line indent setting of the ruler? Show ¶ also gives you the ability to see and select certain characters in your document that would otherwise be hidden.

⌘-Y ➡ To see the hidden formatting characters in the text you've just typed, choose **Show ¶** from the Edit menu.

Your screen now shows characters that you probably didn't realize you had typed. Figure 7-9 shows an explanation of each character.

This symbol represents where the Tab key was pressed.

A dot is used to represent where the space bar was pressed. It is similar to a period but is slightly above the period on the line.

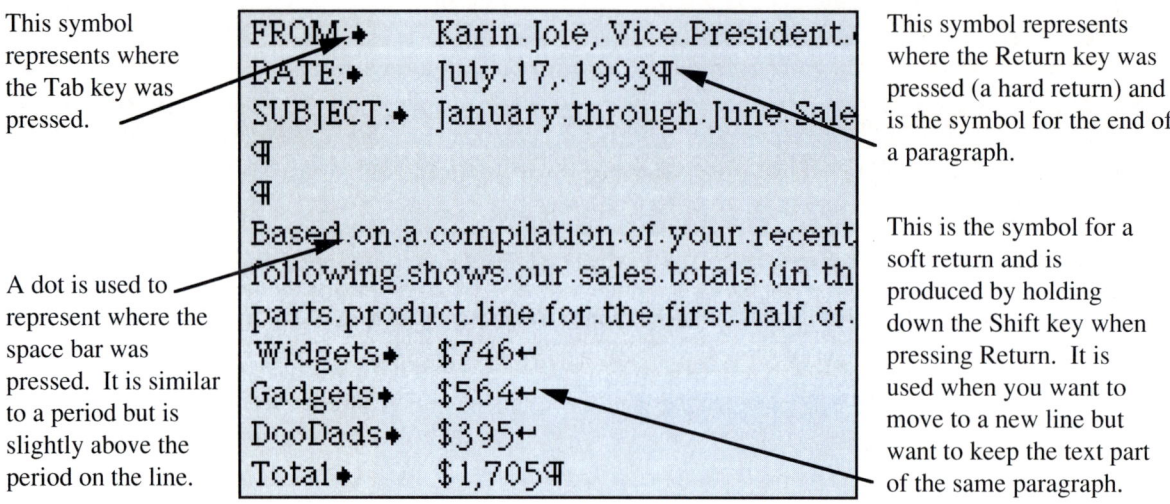

This symbol represents where the Return key was pressed (a hard return) and is the symbol for the end of a paragraph.

This is the symbol for a soft return and is produced by holding down the Shift key when pressing Return. It is used when you want to move to a new line but want to keep the text part of the same paragraph.

Figure 7-9   Viewing hidden formatting marks using Show ¶

Many people choose to work with Show ¶ on whenever they work in Microsoft Word. Throughout this project and the others in this chapter, you'll use this option to enable you to see the different formatting characters as you insert them and to make selecting those characters easier when editing and formatting your document. These special characters are visible on the screen only; they will not print when you print your document.

To change back to the normal view, you choose **Hide ¶** from the Edit menu. The Show ¶ command is one of the menu commands that toggles on and off. What appears on the menu is the opposite of what is in effect—**Hide ¶** won't be showing on the menu unless Show ¶ is in effect. See Figure 7-10.

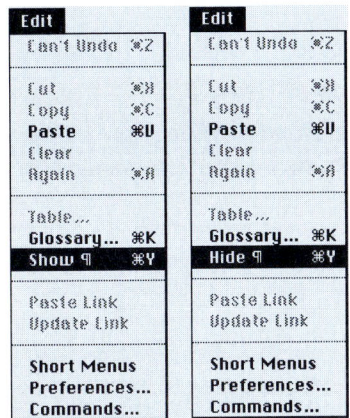

Figure 7-10   Show ¶ and Hide ¶ in the Edit menu

Selecting Text

Selecting a character, word, line, sentence, paragraph, or group of any of these elements points out to Microsoft Word the text you want to work with. There are several ways to select text in Microsoft Word:

- Click the I-beam pointer to the left of the character, word, or line you want to select, and then drag across the portion you want selected. *Selected text is highlighted.* (This is also called *wiping through text.*)

- To select an entire word, double-click on it.

- To select an entire sentence, hold down the Command key and click anywhere in the sentence.

- The *selection bar* provides a means of selecting large blocks of text. The selection bar is located at the far left of the document and appears to be a margin about 1/8-inch wide. When you move the I-beam pointer into the selection bar, the I-beam changes to an arrow that is pointing to the right.   Figure 7-11 shows the pointer when it is in the selection bar.

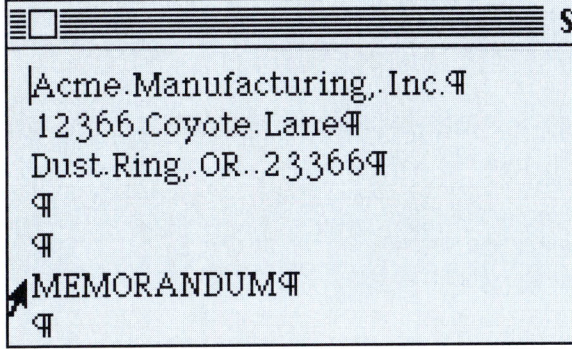

Figure 7-11   The pointer in the selection bar

- To select an entire line using the selection bar, position the pointer in the selection bar to the left of the line you want to select and click the mouse button.

- To select an entire paragraph using the selection bar, double-click in the area to the left of the paragraph. The entire paragraph becomes selected.

- To select any number of lines, click and drag up or down in the selection bar.

- To select a larger portion of the document, click to indicate the beginning of a selection, and then Shift-click to indicate the end of the selection. The portion of the document that you marked for selection will be highlighted.

⌘-Option-M
- To select an entire document, hold down the Command key and click once in the selection bar (the arrow must be pointing in toward the text).

Moving Text

The ability to move text or graphics from one place in a document to another, or between documents, is convenient and time saving. To move text, you must first select it using any of the methods described above. By selecting, you indicate what text you want to move. After it is selected, you cut the selected text from the document and copy it to the Clipboard using the Cut command from the Edit menu. The *Clipboard* is an area in computer memory that stores the most recently copied or cut item.

Once the text is in the Clipboard, position your insertion point in the document at the location the text should be moved to. Then the Paste command places the text from the Clipboard into the document at the insertion point.

⌘-C
Copying works the same way as Cut, except you use the Copy command from the Edit menu. Copy does not remove the text from the document like the Cut command does, it just places a copy of the selected text in the Clipboard for you to paste elsewhere in your document.

You'll move a paragraph in the Sales Report document now.

➡ Select the paragraph beginning "As you can see from the figures", which is near the middle of the Sales Report, by double-clicking in the selection bar to the left of the paragraph, as shown in Figure 7-12.

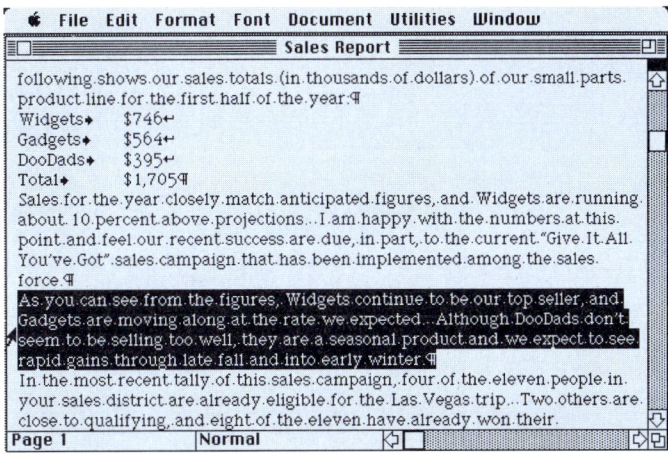

Figure 7-12 Selecting the paragraph to be moved

⌘-X ➟ With the paragraph selected, choose **Cut** from the Edit menu.

The selected paragraph is removed from the document and placed in the Clipboard.

➟ Click to the left of the first word in the paragraph beginning "Sales for the year" to set the insertion point in front of that paragraph. Your screen should look like the one in Figure 7-13.

When you set the insertion point in front of the paragraph, the pointer should not be in the selection bar, because that would cause the whole line to be selected. You can tell if you're in the selection bar—the I-beam will change to an arrow if you are.

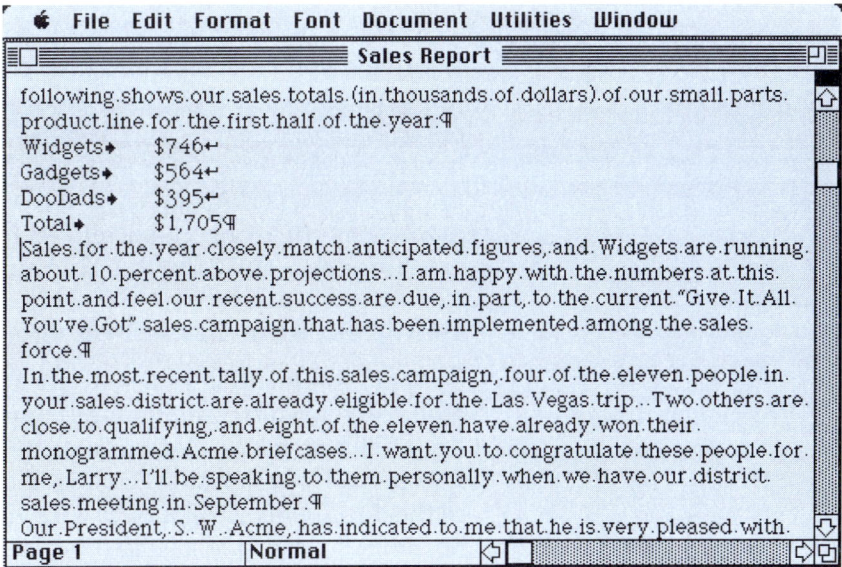

Figure 7-13 Setting the insertion point before moving the text

Setting the insertion point indicates to Microsoft Word where you want the text that you cut from the document to be pasted.

⌘-V   ➡   Choose **Paste** from the Edit menu.

The paragraph that you cut should now be pasted above where you had the insertion point, as shown in Figure 7-14.

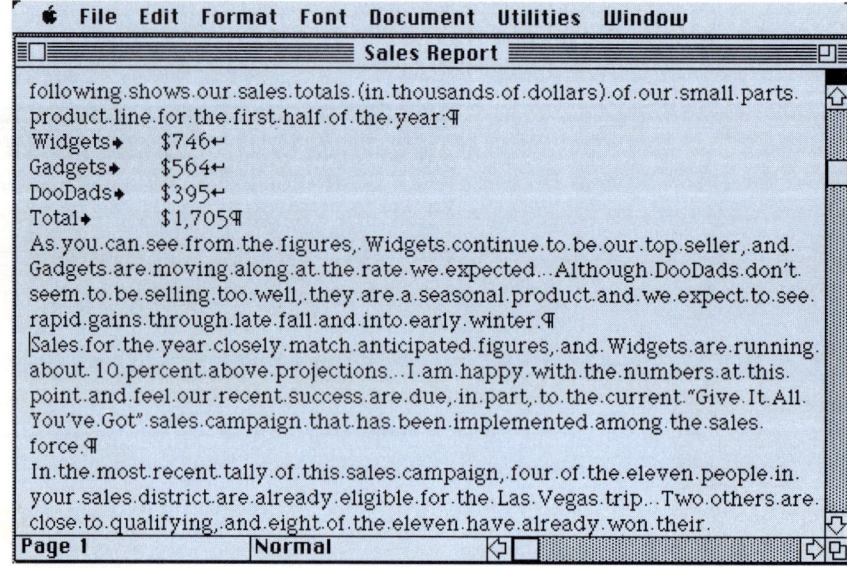

Figure 7-14   The paragraph after the move

⌘-S   ➡   Choose **Save** from the File menu to save these changes.

Searching and Replacing

There may be times when you want to replace every occurrence of a word with a different word. If your document is very long, this search and replace process could be a time-consuming task. Or maybe you'd just like to see each occurrence of the word to see if you've overused it, or you want to see each time it begins with a capital letter so you'll know how many sentences begin with that word. Microsoft Word gives you the ability to find characters, words, groups of words, punctuation marks, or formatting characters and to change them to just about anything you want, using the Find and Change commands.

Using the Find Command

The Find command is used to locate every occurrence of a character or group of characters. Both the Find command and the Change command begin the search at the insertion point. If you want to search the whole document, it's easiest to set the insertion point in front of the first word in the document. If you don't, when the search reaches the end of the document, a dialog box will ask you if you want to continue searching from the beginning of the document.

⌘-F   ➡   Click to the left of the first word in the document, "Acme", to set the insertion point there.

        ➡   Choose **Find** from the Utilities menu.

The dialog box that results is shown in Figure 7-15.

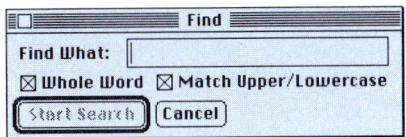

Figure 7-15   The Find dialog box

The Find What box is where you type the characters or words you want to find. Let's see if the word "our" has been used too often in this letter.

➡ Type **our** in the Find What box.

Two options in this dialog box help you narrow the specific words to find: the Whole Word and Match Upper/Lowercase options.

When you select the **Whole Word** option, Microsoft Word finds only words that stand on their own, those that are preceded and followed by a space. For example, if you told Word to find every occurrence of the word "the" without selecting the Whole Word option, it would find any words that had "the" anywhere in them—other, leather, theater, and so on. When you're looking for a specific word, use the Whole Word option. The Whole Word option is the default setting for the Find dialog box; yours should have an "x" in the box to the left of Whole Word. For the search you're about to make you want the **Whole Word** option selected.

The **Match Upper/Lowercase** option allows you to specify that you are looking for words that are capitalized (or not) in a certain way. Capitalizing the first letter of the word in the Find What box and using the Match Upper/Lowercase option will help you find words that begin sentences, for example. The Match Upper/Lowercase option is the default setting for the Find dialog box. For the search that you are about to make you want to find all occurrences of the word "our", so you do not want the **Match Upper/Lowercase** option selected.

➡ Click **Match Upper/Lowercase** to deselect that option (remove the "x" from the box to its left).

Return or Enter   ➡ Click the **Start Search** button.

If a match is found, Microsoft Word highlights the word in the document and stops.

The first occurrence of "our" is in the first paragraph, as shown in Figure 7-16.

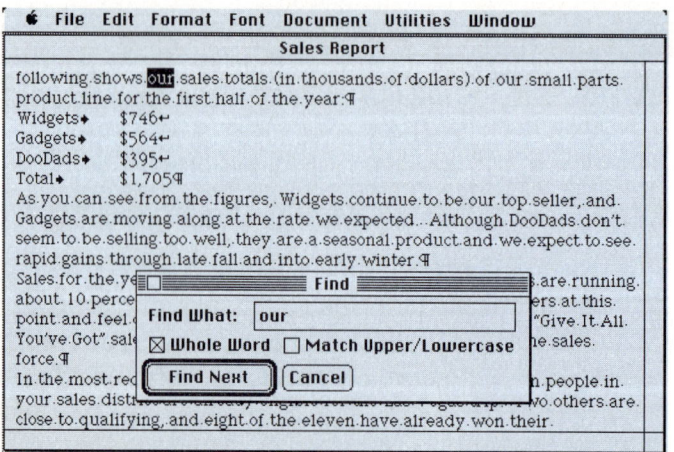

Figure 7-16   Finding the first occurrence of "our"

Return or Enter   ➟   Click the **Find Next** button to find the next occurrence of "our."

➟   Continue to click the **Find Next** button after each occurrence of "our" is found.

➟   When the "End of document reached" message is shown, click **OK** to that box, and then click the **Cancel** button in the Find dialog box.

There were many (11, to be exact) occurrences of "our" in the document, and it would sound better if some of them were changed to "the". You'll use the Change command for that operation. Using the Find command to count each occurrence of a word to determine if the word is overused is a good habit. Now that this exercise has given you the opportunity to see how the Find command works, you'll be able to see more clearly how the Find command differs from the Change command.

Using the Change Command

The Change command is similar to the Find command. You specify the group of characters you want changed, and then you specify what you want them changed to.

➟   Since you want the search to start at the beginning of the document, click to the left of the first word in the document to set the insertion point there.

⌘-H   ➟   Choose **Change** from the Utilities menu.

The dialog box that results is shown in Figure 7-17. Notice that in the Find What box is the word "our", which you were searching for in the Find operation. The Find and Change dialog boxes share the Find What box, so that when you search for a word in a Find operation you don't have to retype it in a subsequent Change operation.

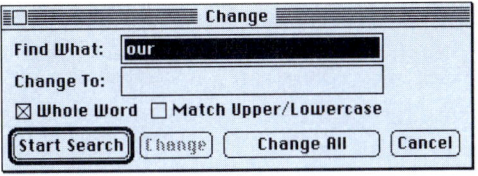

Figure 7-17   The Change dialog box

You'll recognize the Whole Word and Match Upper/Lowercase options from the Find dialog box. These options work the same as they did in the Find dialog box, and their settings also carry over from the Find dialog box to the Change dialog box.

➠   Click in the **Change To** box, and type **the**.

There are three buttons at the bottom of the dialog box. The Start Search button causes the search to begin, and you determine what action to take when each occurrence of the group of characters is found. You verify whether a group of characters is to be changed.

The Change All button changes all occurrences of the characters without having you verify each occurrence. Use this button instead of the Start Search button if you are sure you want all occurrences changed and don't need to verify each change.

The Cancel button cancels the Change operation.

Return or Enter   ➠   Click the **Start Search** button.

The first occurrence of the word "our" is found in the first paragraph. The Change dialog box looks like the one shown in Figure 7-18.

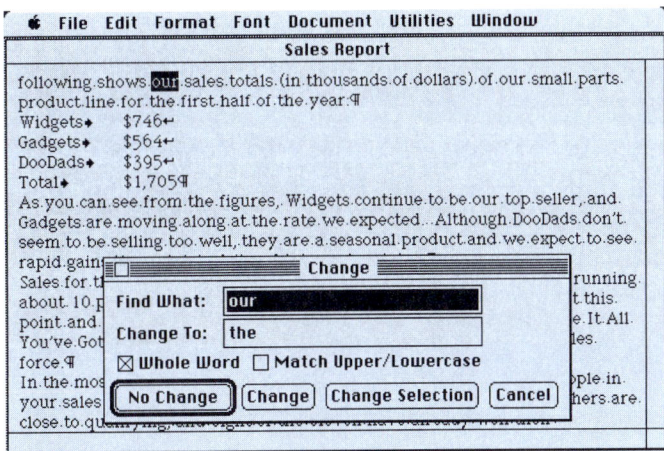

Figure 7-18   Changing the first occurrence of "our"

You click the **Change** button to replace the selected characters with the characters in the Change To box, or you click the **No Change** button to leave the selected characters unchanged. Whether you click **Change** or **No Change**, the search continues to the next occurrence of the characters in the document. The Change Selection button allows you to change just the selected text, and the Change dialog box stays on the screen. You can then enter a new Find What or Change To group of characters and start another search.

➠ Click the **Change** button so that the first occurrence of "our" is changed to "the" in the first paragraph.

➠ Click the **No Change** button so the second occurrence of "our" in the first paragraph is left unchanged.

➠ Click the **No Change** button to each occurrence of "our" in the second and third paragraphs.

➠ In the fourth paragraph, click the **Change** button to change the word "our" in the last sentence so that it reads "I'll be speaking to them personally when we have the district sales meeting in September."

➠ Click the **No Change** button for each occurrence of "our" in all but the last paragraph of the document.

➠ In the last paragraph, click the **No Change** button to the first occurrence of the word "our" in the second sentence.

➠ Click the **Change** button so that the second occurrence of "our" in the second sentence is changed to "the". The sentence should now read: "We can plan our television and magazine advertising strategies during the sales projection meeting early next week."

➠ When you get the "End of document reached" message, click the **OK** button, and then click the **Cancel** button in the Change dialog box to end the operation.

You should have made a total of three changes in that operation.

⌘-S ➠ Save your work by choosing **Save** from the File menu.

You can also use the Find and Change utilities to locate special formatting characters, such as paragraph marks and tabs. When you are searching for these characters, the caret (^) precedes the letter that represents the character. For example, to search for a tab mark you would enter **^t** in the Find What box. You can search for a paragraph mark using **^p**. For a list of special formatting characters that you can search for, see *Reference to Microsoft Word*.

You learned how to find and change specific words in your document using the Find and Change utilities. Next you'll learn to use the spelling checker to find and change words that you don't usually realize are in your document.

Using the Spelling Checker

Microsoft Word's *spelling checker* is an invaluable tool for editing your document, because it helps you locate and correct misspelled words, including those with typographical errors.

When using the spelling checker, Microsoft Word begins checking your document at the insertion point. To check the entire document without interruption, you must set the insertion point before the first word in the document. If you don't do this, Microsoft Word will check from the insertion point to the end of the file and then ask you if you'd like to continue checking from the beginning of the document.

If you already have a word selected and then you run a spelling check, Microsoft Word only checks the selected word. This is handy if you've already checked the entire document and just have an added word or paragraph to check. In that case, you select the word or paragraph before running the spelling check and the selection is the only portion of the document checked.

➡ Use the scroll bar to scroll backward in the document to the first line and click to the left of the line beginning with "Acme Manufacturing".

⌘-L ➡ Choose **Spelling** from the Utilities menu.

The dialog box shown in Figure 7-19 will result.

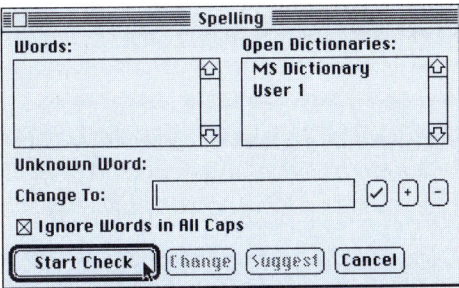

Figure 7-19   The Spelling dialog box

The Ignore Words in All Caps option allows you to bypass any words written in all capital letters. This is helpful if your document contains many acronyms, which are formed from the first letters of several words—for example, AM, PM, IRS. Spelling checker dictionaries do not usually contain acronyms. The default setting for this option is on, as you can see by the "x" in the box to its left. Leave this option selected when checking the Sales Report document.

Return or Enter ➡ To begin the spelling check, click **Start Check**, or press Return (because Start Check is the default choice).

The first unknown word the spelling checker finds is "Cassella," as shown in Figure 7-20. Notice that this word is highlighted in the document. Although this word is not misspelled, it is common for spelling checker dictionaries to omit proper names.

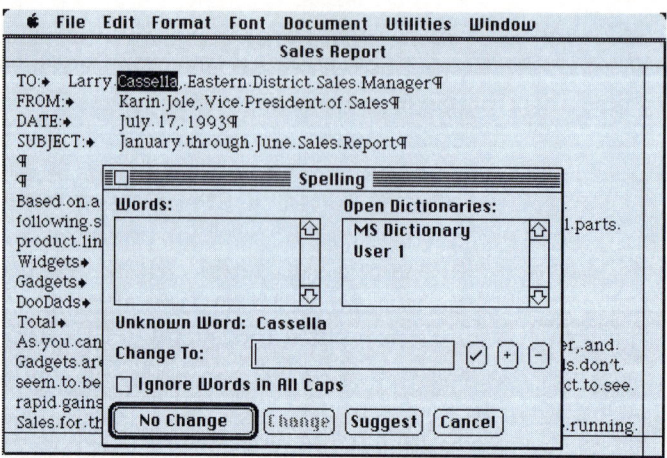

Figure 7-20   An unknown word found in the document

Several options are available when Microsoft Word finds an unknown word (one that is not in its dictionary): You can type the word that you'd like the highlighted word in your document to be changed to in the Change To box and then click the **Change** button. This will replace the highlighted word in your document with the word you typed.

Another choice is that you can click the **No Change** button, which indicates to Microsoft Word that you want to leave the word in question unchanged and move on.

You can click the **Suggest** button. This indicates that you'd like Microsoft Word to search through its dictionary and present one or more words that you may be trying to spell. If the spell checker is able to suggest any alternatives, a list of those words will appear in the Words portion of the dialog box, and the first word on the list will appear in the Change To field, as shown in Figure 7-21.

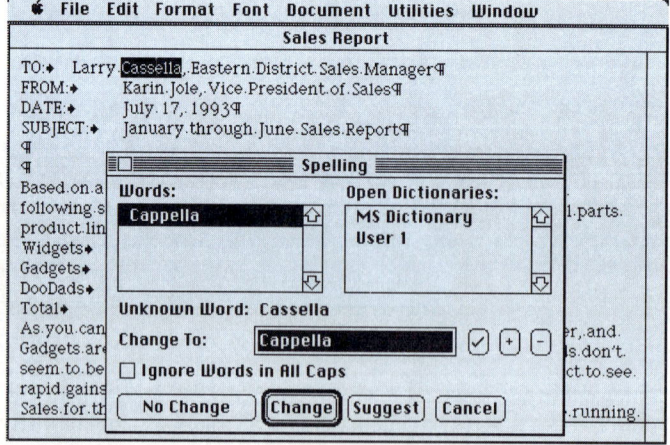

Figure 7-21   List of suggested words

You can scroll through the list of suggested words and select a word you'd like by clicking on that word and then clicking the **Change** button or pressing Return. The selected alternative word will replace the word in your document that the spell checker identified as unknown. If none of the words that were suggested will fit the word in question, as in this case, click the **No Change** button.

You could also add this unique word to the User 1 dictionary by clicking the plus button. Word will then consider it a correct spelling in the future.

➡ Click the **No Change** button.

Microsoft Word continues checking the document and presents each unknown word. This allows you to verify each word as it is located. When the entire document is checked, a dialog box will appear to indicate the end of the document was reached. Click **OK** in this box to end the spelling session.

➡ Finish checking your document for unknown words, making changes where appropriate.

➡ When the "End of document reached" message is shown on your screen, click **OK**, which cancels the spelling session.

⌘-S ➡ Save your document when you are finished using the spelling checker.

Remember to proofread for incorrectly placed words and other grammar problems that a spelling checker cannot catch.

FORMATTING TEXT

Now that your document is spell-checked and says what you want it to say, the next step is to make it look good on the page.

Changing Character and Paragraph Formatting

The basic formatting units used in Microsoft Word are the *character* and the *paragraph*.

The character is the smallest unit in Microsoft Word. Formatting characters can involve changing the *font*, or typeface, and *point size*. You can also change the character attributes to bold, italic, underline, and more. The position of the character on the baseline, where the bottom edge of the characters in that font normally line up, can be changed to create superscript and subscript characters. You can also stretch or shrink the space between characters.

These are some examples of character formatting:

This is Times 10 point size.

This is Times 12 point size.

This is **bold**, *italic*, underlined, shadow.

This is superscript, this is subscript.

This is condensed, this is expanded.

To change the formatting of a character or any group of characters, up to and including the entire document, you must first select the characters you want to change. Then you choose the attribute you wish to change to. You can also set the character formatting before typing. If no text is selected when you choose a character format, then whatever you type at the insertion point will have the formatting characteristics you chose.

Character formats are changed using the Character command, which is on the Format menu, although some more commonly used formats can be accessed directly from the Format menu. Fonts and font sizes can be accessed either from the Font menu or by using the Character command.

Some other formatting options apply only to paragraphs. A paragraph is a collection of characters that precede a paragraph mark or hard return, which you get when you press the Return key. A paragraph can consist of one character, one word, many sentences, or even a blank line. You can apply character formats to entire paragraphs (as long as the paragraph is selected), but you cannot apply paragraph formats to characters within a paragraph—paragraph formatting will affect the entire paragraph and not just the selected characters.

Some formatting options that apply only to paragraphs are indents, tabs, line spacing, borders, and alignment. To apply formatting to a paragraph, you do not need to select the paragraph so that it is highlighted, as you do when applying character formats. Placing the insertion point in a paragraph indicates the paragraph that the formatting will affect. The ruler also reflects the current settings for the paragraph that contains the insertion point. If the paragraph formatting is to affect more than one paragraph, you must select (highlight) all paragraphs you wish to format. Paragraph formatting can apply to the entire document, just as character formatting can, but the entire document must be selected first.

You'll do most of the character formatting first, and then you'll change the paragraph formatting.

➠ Scroll to the beginning of the document and select the first line by clicking in the selection bar to the left of that line, as shown in Figure 7-22.

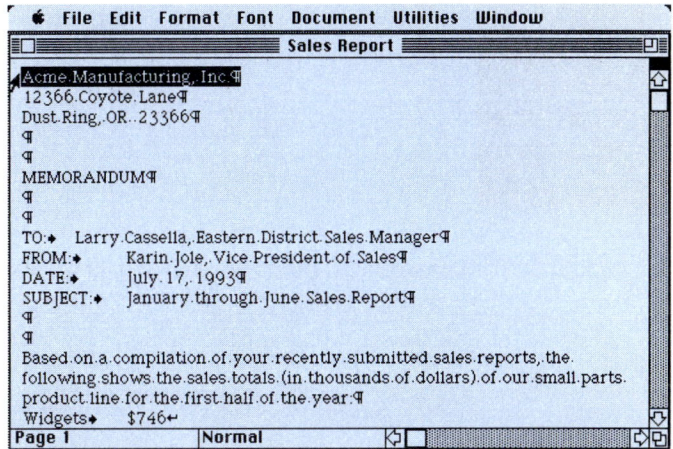

Figure 7-22   Selecting the first line in the document

⌘-D   ➡   Choose **Character** from the Format menu.

The Character dialog box has additional character formats that aren't available on the Format menu. This dialog box also allows you to set many characteristics at the same time rather than each one separately. If you click and hold down the mouse button in the arrow to the right of any of the drop-down fields, a list of available formats is shown. Figure 7-23 shows the available underline formats.

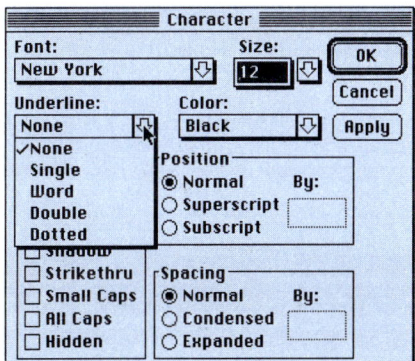

Figure 7-23   Available underline formats

➡   In the Character dialog box Style section, click **Bold** and **Italic**, as shown in Figure 7-24.

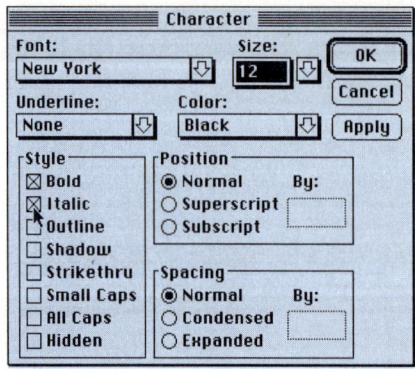

Figure 7-24   Setting bold and italic character formats

Return or Enter   ➡ Click **OK**.

The first line of the document is now bold and italic. Next you'll make that line have a larger point size than the rest of the document.

Although you could have changed the point size in the Character dialog box, you probably won't use that method as often as simply selecting the desired size from the Font menu, as you'll do now.

➡ With the same line still selected, choose **18 point** from the Font menu.

If you don't have that particular point size installed in your system, use any size larger than 12 point.

The first line of your document should look similar to the one shown in Figure 7-25.

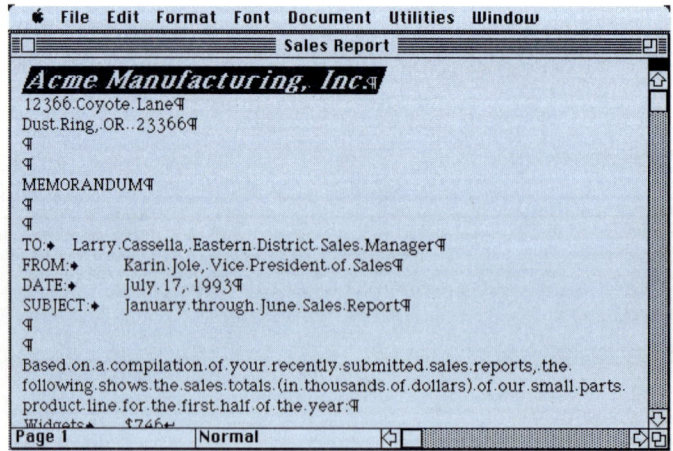

Figure 7-25   The first line—bold, italic, and 18 point

The next two lines of the address will be formatted bold. You'll use the Bold command in the Format menu to do this.

➤ Select the two address lines at the top of the document. Be sure that you don't include the first line, which you already formatted.

⌘-Shift-B ➤ Choose **Bold** from the Format menu.

Next you'll use the ruler to change alignment of these lines.

⌘-R ➤ Choose **Show Ruler** from the Format menu.

Using the Ruler

One of the most important parts of the Microsoft Word window is the *ruler*, which is located at the top of the window, just below the title bar. The default setting in Microsoft Word opens the window without the ruler showing. To show the ruler on the screen, choose **Show Ruler** from the Format menu. This is another menu item that toggles—if you do not need to view the ruler, choose **Hide Ruler** from the Format menu.

The ruler contains controls that allow you to change much of the paragraph formatting of your document. It allows you to easily set *text alignment, line spacing, tab stops,* and *margins*. With Microsoft Word you can format each paragraph using different ruler settings.

Figure 7-26 shows the ruler, and the following sections describe some of the controls and what they do.

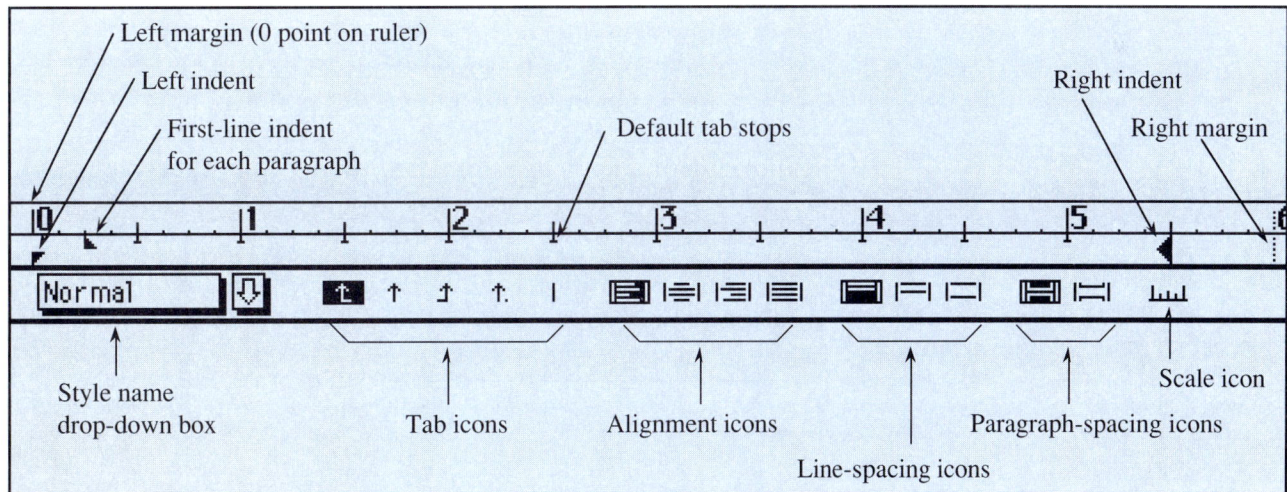

Figure 7-26 The Microsoft Word ruler

Let's discuss each of these controls and, where appropriate, you'll see samples of how the settings affect the text.

Alignment Controls

These four controls provide simple ways to set the *alignment* of an entire text block, whether it is a paragraph or an entire document. Alignment refers to the way the lines of text are placed between the left and right margins. *Justification* means that the text is aligned with both the left and right margins. In justified text, Microsoft Word places spaces between the words in a line to help the text line up evenly at the left and right margins. Notice that the text in each of the following definitions mimics the result you will get with that setting.

≡ This setting makes the text left-aligned and
    ragged on the right. This is also called *flush
    left*. All of the block will be aligned on its left
    side but will not be justified on the right.

≡   This setting aligns the text block by centering
        each line between the margins. The left
        and right sides will be uneven, unless the
            lines are exactly the same length.

≡   This setting aligns the text block at the
            right margin. This alignment is also called
                    flush right. As each line fills up, the text
            moves to the left while you type. When a
        word can't fit, it is dropped to the next line
                    on the far right side of the line.

≡ This setting is for justified text. Both the left and
    the right sides of the text are even. Justified text
    often has wide spaces between words, but
    hyphenating can minimize this problem.

The three lines that you just formatted, along with the Memorandum line, need to be centered on the page. You'll use the center-alignment setting on the ruler to accomplish this.

➠ Select the lines down through the line containing the word "Memorandum," as shown in Figure 7-27.

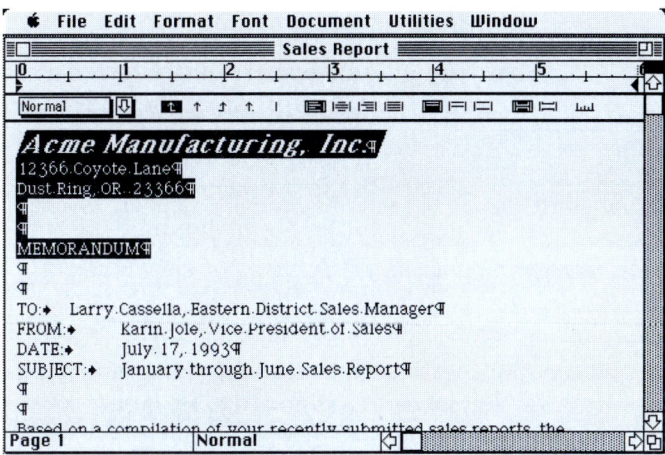

Figure 7-27   Selecting the lines to be centered

⌘-Shift-C    ➡   Click the center-alignment icon on the ruler.

All the lines that were selected automatically become centered between the margins on the page.

Line Spacing

These controls affect the *vertical spacing* between lines of text. Notice that the text for each definition mimics the result you will get.

|⚊| This control sets single-spacing. 12-point text is spaced at 6 lines per inch.

|⚊| This control sets 1-1/2-line spacing. 12-point

text is spaced as if it were 18-point text, resulting

in 4 lines per inch. An extra half line-space is

placed between each line of text.

|⚊| This sets double-spacing. 12-point text is spaced

as if it were 24 points high, resulting in 3 lines

per inch. An extra full line-space is placed

between each line of text.

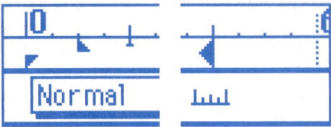

Indent Controls

There are three *indentation controls*: first line, left, and right. They control the widths and positions of lines of text.

- ▶ The *first-line indent* controls the beginning position of the first line of text. In the picture to the left, the first line of each paragraph is indented 1/4 inch from the left margin, which is represented by the lower left triangle. In Microsoft Word, you use the indent controls instead of spaces or tabs for first-line paragraph indents.

- ▶ The *left indent* controls where the text (other than the first line of a paragraph) is positioned with respect to the left margin.

- ◀ The *right indent* controls the location of text with respect to the right margin. This control affects all lines of the paragraph, even the first.

The paragraph that consists of four lines with the sales total for each product needs to be indented by 1/2 inch from the left margin. You'll use the indent controls on the ruler to do that now.

➡ Click anywhere within the line that reads "Widgets $746."

When typing these four lines you did not press Return at the end of each line, but instead you used the Shift-Return key combination to go to a new line. This kept you typing within the same paragraph, but on a different line within that paragraph. When you click within any of the four lines of this paragraph, the formatting changes you make with the ruler will affect the entire paragraph—all four lines. You'll see how this works now.

➡ Place the point of the arrow on the left indent marker on the ruler and drag to the 1/2-inch mark on the ruler. The first-line indent marker moves with the left indent marker, as shown in Figure 7-28.

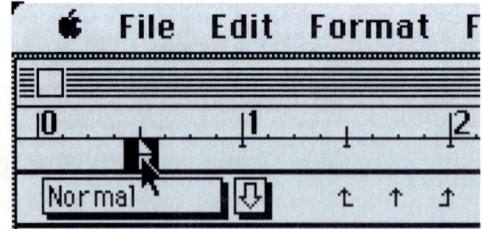

Figure 7-28   Moving the left indent marker

➡ When the marker is positioned on the ruler, release the mouse button.

All four lines in the selected paragraph are now indented 1/2 inch from the left margin, as shown in Figure 7-29.

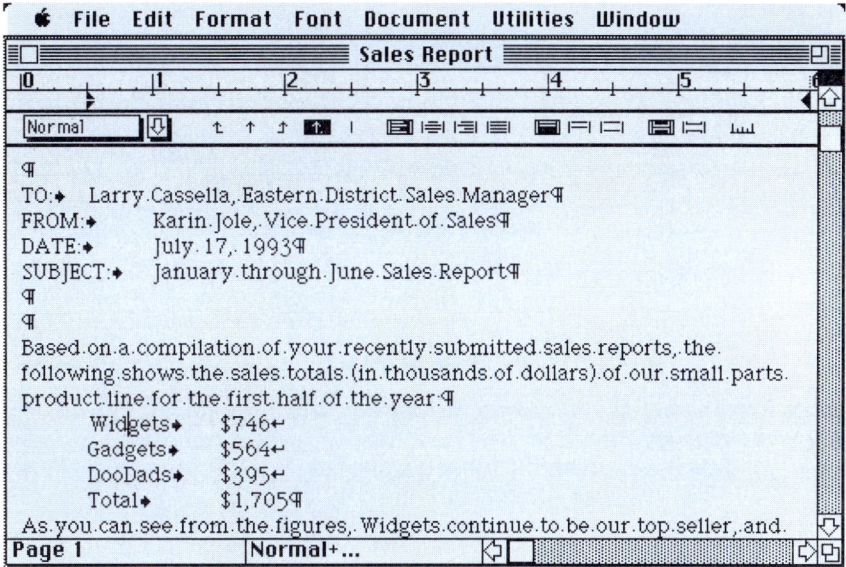

Figure 7-29   The lines indented 1/2 inch from the left margin

Tab Settings

Tab settings control how a column of information will align in present and succeeding rows. Each paragraph in Microsoft Word can have a different ruler. When you set the tab stops they control the current line and all succeeding lines, until you change or remove tab settings.

   A *left-aligned tab* means that the information in the column below this tab aligns with the left end of the first word in the column.

   A *center tab* centers items in the column below it.

   A *right-aligned tab* means that the information in the column below the tab will align with the right end of the last word in the column

   A *decimal-aligned tab* formats the column below it so that all items line up at the decimal point. You can then enter a column of numbers and have all the decimal points properly aligned, even when no decimal is actually typed.

   This is not really a tab control, but a *drawing tool* that enables you to place a vertical line in your document corresponding to the tool's position on the ruler. The vertical line continues down the page through each paragraph that is formatted with the vertical-line tool on its ruler. You do not have to press the Tab key or any other character to create the line. This is one way to create column separators in tabbed columns.

These tab settings have the following effects on text (see Figure 7-30):

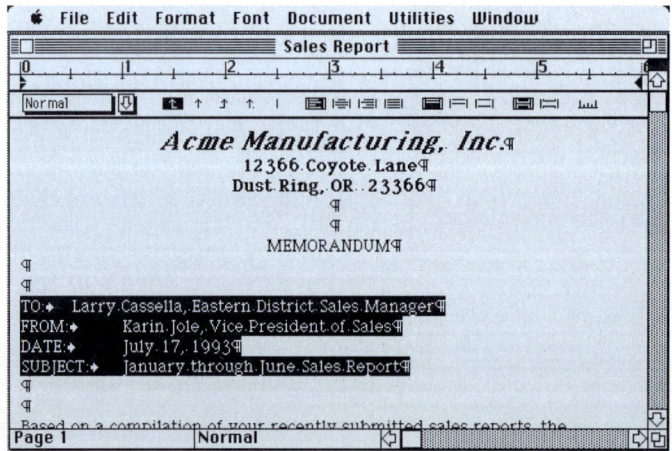

Figure 7-30 Samples of different types of tab stops

When you typed your document you pressed the Tab key to separate the "To," "From," "Subject," and "Date" from the text that followed those words. Now you'll use the tab settings to set a tab stop for those lines.

⟹ Select the four lines in the memo head, as shown in Figure 7-31.

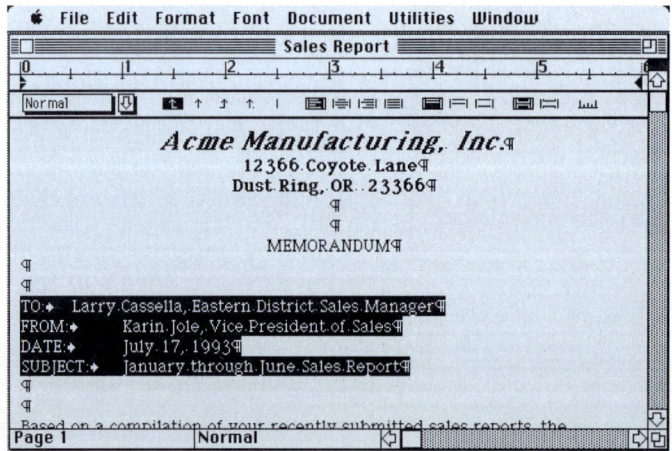

Figure 7-31 Selecting the memo heads

↑   ⟹ Click on the left-aligned tab marker on the ruler, and then click just below the 1-1/4-inch mark on the ruler. See Figure 7-32.

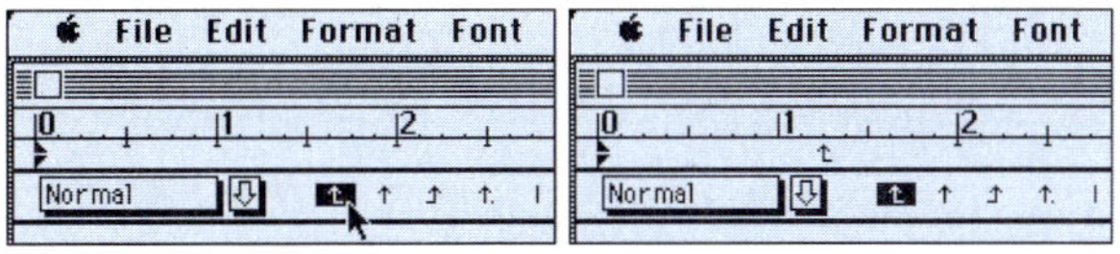

Figure 7-32   Selecting and positioning the tab on the ruler

This causes a tab stop to be placed in that position on the ruler for the selected paragraphs. A tab stop controls the position of the text that was typed after the Tab key was pressed.

Notice that the text to the right of the tab mark in the line is now aligned at 1-1/4-inch on the ruler in all four lines that were selected. You can also drag the tab to where you want it on the ruler if you want to make adjustments later.

Using the tab settings is the only way to align columns of text or numbers. Merely spacing the same number of times between columns, as is sometimes done on a typewriter, will not work, even though on the screen the text looks aligned. When printed, the columns will be jagged and will not align with one another.

There's a good reason for this—most Macintosh fonts are *proportional fonts*. This means that the wider characters, such as the uppercase M, take up more space on a line than the narrower characters, such as the lowercase i. *Monospace fonts*, however, consist of characters that are evenly spaced on the screen and when printed. Most typewriters use monospace fonts, which is why you can sometimes get away with spacing the same number of times between columns to line up text. But it just doesn't work that way on a Macintosh, unless you are using a monospace font such as Monaco or Courier.

In the second paragraph of the body of the memo you also used tabs to separate columns. You already changed the left indentation of this paragraph, and now you'll set up a decimal tab stop to align the column of numbers.

➡ Click anywhere within the line that reads "Widgets $746."

➡ Click on the decimal tab marker on the ruler, and then click just below the 2-1/2-inch mark on the ruler. See Figure 7-33.

Figure 7-33   Setting a decimal tab stop

The numbers should align on the tab stop, as shown in Figure 7-34.

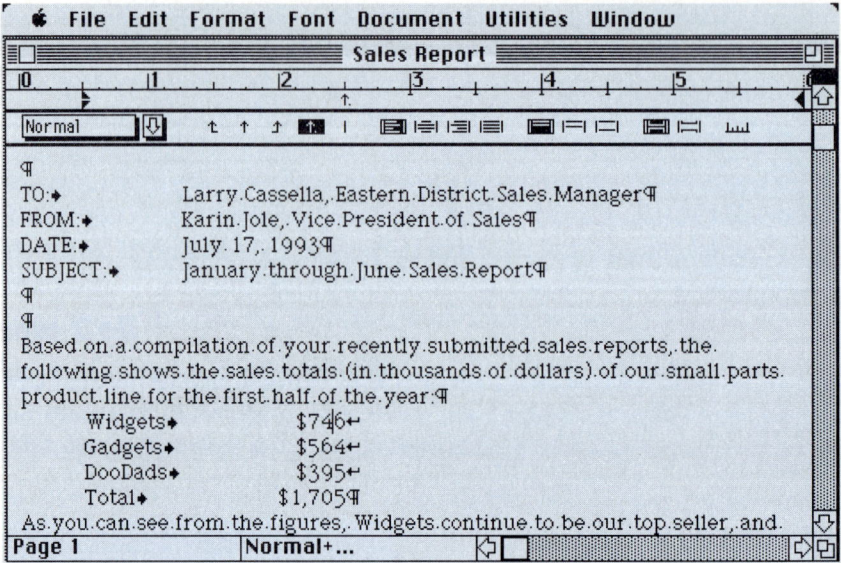

Figure 7-34   The document formatted with tab stops

⌘-S ➡ Save these changes by choosing **Save** from the File menu.

The next formatting you'll change in the document is the spacing between paragraphs.

Paragraph Spacing

Paragraph-spacing settings control the amount of space between paragraphs.

  ⊞   This setting causes paragraphs to be separated by the same amount of space as that between lines in the paragraph.

  ⊟   This setting places 12 points of extra space between paragraphs.

The body of the memo needs to have spaces between paragraphs. You'll select those paragraphs and then use the paragraph-spacing icon to place the space between paragraphs.

➡ Click to the left of the line beginning "Based on a compilation", the first paragraph below the memo heads, to set the insertion point to the left of the "B".

➡ Use the vertical scroll bar to position the last paragraph of the document on the screen.

➡ Hold down the Shift key while clicking after the last character in the document.

The body of the document, below the memo heads, should now be selected. This Shift-click method of selecting is useful when you are selecting large blocks of text.

⌘-Shift-O ⊟ ➡ With the text still selected, click on the space-between-paragraphs icon on the ruler.

Now the body of the memo has extra space after each paragraph, as shown in Figure 7-35.

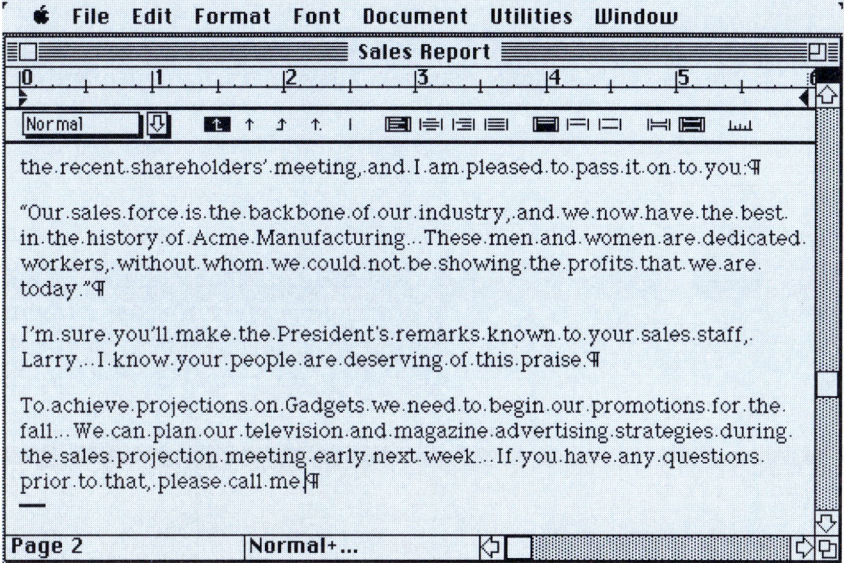

Figure 7-35   Placing extra space between paragraphs

Style Name Box

The style name box on the ruler shows the *style name* of the currently selected paragraph. A *style* is a set of formatting characteristics that defines the appearance of text. Applying a style to selected text causes the entire paragraph to take on those characteristics. Holding down the mouse button on the arrow to the right of the style name produces a *drop-down list* of the styles used in the document. You'll be learning more about styles in Project 2 of this chapter.

Scale Tool

The *scale tool* is used to toggle between the three different ruler scales available in Microsoft Word. The one you've seen up to this point is the *normal scale*, and it is the one you'll use primarily throughout this chapter.

The *page scale* is another ruler scale available, and it can be used to modify page margins, column widths, and spacing between columns. You'll learn more about adjusting page margins with it in just a moment. In Project 4 you'll learn more about columns.

The third type of ruler scale is the *table scale*, and it appears only when the currently selected text is a table. It can be used to change the width of cells in a table. You'll learn more about tables in Project 3 when you create a table.

Margins

Clicking on the scale icon on the ruler toggles it to the page scale. Clicking on the icon again toggles it back to the normal scale. When your ruler is in the page scale you can modify the margins of your entire document. The 0 point of the ruler represents where the left edge of the paper is, and you can drag the margin brackets relative to the edge of the paper. When using this method to change the margins (you'll learn some other methods in this chapter also), remember that the change affects the entire document, not just the paragraph that contains the insertion point.

You will be using many of these ruler formatting features when you work through the next four assignments in this chapter. You may need to refresh your memory by referring back to these explanations of the various tools until you become familiar with their uses.

For the purposes of this project you did the typing first and formatted the text later. Another way is to format as you go along, paragraph by paragraph. Either way is perfectly acceptable—it is a matter of personal preference.

Formatting settings made in the ruler affect the areas of text that you selected before you set the ruler formatting. If you set the ruler without selecting any text, the ruler settings will apply to subsequent paragraphs that you type. This is the way you format your paragraphs before typing them—set the ruler with the formatting characteristics that you want the paragraph to have, and then type the paragraph. The ruler settings stay in effect for each subsequent paragraph until you change them.

From this point on, the projects you'll be working through in this chapter require that the ruler be showing at the top of the document window. The ruler does not print, nor does it reduce the amount of print area available on the paper. Once you get used to having your formatting controls visible, you'll probably choose to view all of your documents with the ruler showing.

Before you move on to document formatting, you need to change the character and paragraph formatting of the president's quotation. To make the quotation look different from the rest of the letter, you will italicize it, reduce the point size, indent it on both sides, and remove the quotation marks. This is called a *block quote*.

First you need to remove the quotation marks, since they are not used with a block quote.

➡ Locate the paragraph beginning "Our sales force is the backbone", the third paragraph from the end of the document.

➡ Select the quotation mark at the beginning of the paragraph and press the Backspace key (the Delete key on some keyboards).

This deletes the first quotation mark.

➡ Delete the quotation mark at the end of the quote in the same manner.

Normally, when you quote something like this, you indent the left and right margins about 1/2-inch as a visual cue indicating a content change. You'll do that now.

➡ If the insertion point is not in the paragraph where you just removed the quotation marks, click anywhere in that paragraph to set the insertion point.

➡ To change the left indent of the selected paragraph, move the left indent and first-line indent markers together by clicking in the bottom marker and dragging both to the 1/2-inch mark on the ruler. See Figure 7-36.

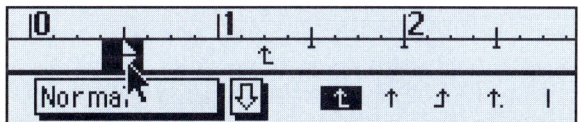

Figure 7-36   Dragging both indent markers

Next you'll change the right margin of this paragraph so that it is indented more than the rest of the document.

➡ Drag the right indent marker to the 5-1/2-inch mark on the ruler, as shown in Figure 7-37.

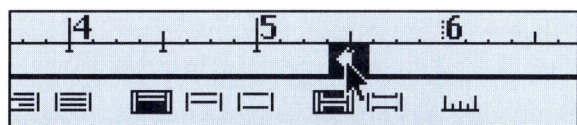

Figure 7-37   Changing the right indentation

Now that you've adjusted the margins of this paragraph to set it off as a block quote, the next step is to change the text of the quote to a smaller size and to italicize it. To change the character formatting for the quotation, you must select the entire quotation.

➡ Move the mouse pointer into the selection bar to the left of the paragraph and double-click.

This selects the entire paragraph, as shown in Figure 7-38.

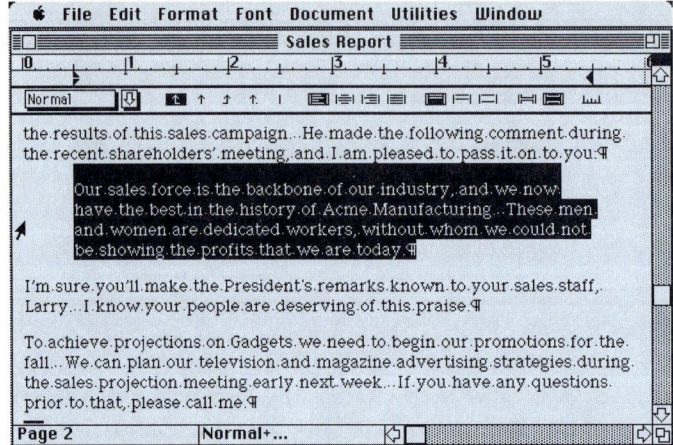

Figure 7-38   Selecting the paragraph using the selection bar

⟹   If you are using New York font, choose **10 point** from the Font menu. If you are using Times font, choose **12 point**.

⌘-Shift-I   ⟹   Choose **Italic** from the Format menu.

The block quote does not have to be italicized, since it is already differentiated from the other paragraphs by size and indent, but the italics makes it look even better.

Now you'll change the alignment of this paragraph to justified, which will make it even on both sides.

⌘-Shift-J ▤   ⟹   Click on the justified-alignment icon on the ruler, as shown in Figure 7-39.

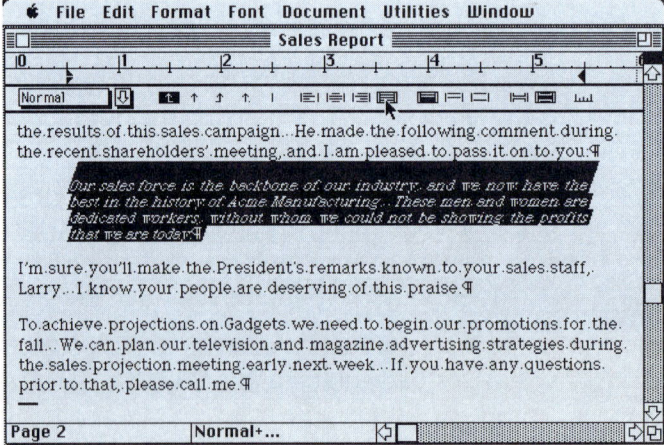

Figure 7-39   Using the justified-alignment icon

The previous steps have demonstrated how easy it is to apply different paragraph and character formats to blocks of text.

By now you should be getting used to saving your work whenever you make a significant change to your document.

⌘-S ➡ Save your work now.

FORMATTING THE DOCUMENT

Up to this point in this project you have worked with character and paragraph formatting, both of which affect the selected text. Now you'll learn about document formatting, which controls the look of the entire document.

Using the Document Command

Many of the document's formatting characteristics can be set using the Document dialog box. This dialog box appears when you choose **Document** from the Format menu.

➡ Choose **Document** from the Format menu.

The Document dialog box is shown in Figure 7-40.

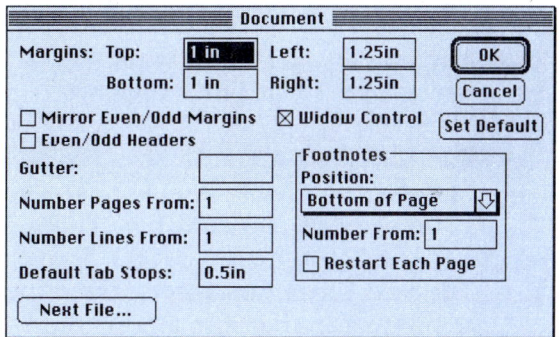

Figure 7-40 The Document dialog box

One way the margins of your document can be changed is through the Document dialog box. The default margin settings are 1 inch top and bottom and 1-1/4 inches left and right. To change these settings, you type in the box to the right of the margin you want to change.

➡ Double-click in the box to the right of Left and type **1**.

This changes the left margin to 1 inch.

➡ Double-click in the box to the right of Right and type **1**.

This changes the right margin to 1 inch.

Remember in the discussion of the ruler you read about changing page margins using the scale icon to toggle to the page scale. That is another way you can change page margins. You'll also learn about a third way to change page margins when you get to Project 4 in this chapter.

The Mirror Even/Odd Margins option is used when you're printing on both sides of the paper and putting the pages together in book form.

The Even/Odd Headers option is used to create separate headers and footers for the even and odd pages.

The Gutter box allows you to enter the amount of space you want to leave on the inside edge of the paper for binding the document.

The Widow Control option is the default setting for a document. It prevents a *widow*, the first line of a paragraph, from appearing by itself at the bottom of a page. When this option is set it also prevents *orphans*. An orphan is the last line of a paragraph appearing by itself at the top of a page.

The Number Pages From box allows you to begin numbering the pages of the document at a number other than 1. Normally you would leave this field blank, since usually you want the page numbers to begin with 1.

The Number Lines From box works like the Number Pages From box, except it refers to the starting line number for numbered paragraphs.

The Default Tab Stops box allows you to change the default tab stops, which are set at 1/2-inch intervals.

The Footnotes option allows you to determine the position of the footnotes on the printed page. The options in the drop-down list are Bottom of Page, Beneath Text, End of Section, and End of Document.

The Next File button allows you to specify a file that you always want to print when the current file is finished printing.

The only changes you needed to make to the document in this dialog box were to the left and right margins.

➡ Click **OK**.

Numbering Pages

In this chapter you'll learn three ways to number pages. You'll number the pages in this document using the Print Preview command, discussed in just a moment.

Another way to number pages is to use the automatic page numbering icon found in the header and footer windows. You'll learn about headers and footers and the page numbering icon in Project 4 of this chapter. Also in Project 4 you'll learn about page numbering using the Sections command.

Using Print Preview

Now that you've worked hard on this letter, you are probably eager to see what it looks like printed. You don't have to print your document to get an overall view of its layout. Microsoft Word allows you to preview it first by using the Print Preview feature, which is one of four available views in Microsoft Word.

The view you have been working in so far is called *Galley View*, Word's normal view. Unless you tell it otherwise, Microsoft Word opens any document in Galley View. Galley View allows you to write, edit, and format your document in the fastest working environment. However, as you'll learn in Project 4, all formats in Galley View don't always display the way they will look when printed.

Page View is another view available in Microsoft Word. This view allows you to see your document on the screen in approximately the same way it will look when it is printed. You can write, edit, and format your document in Page View also, although it is a much slower process than in Galley View. You'll use Page View in Project 4 of this chapter.

Outline View lets you look at your document as an outline and alter the structure of it using the features available in this view. Outlining is a topic not within the scope of this book.

Print Preview is the fourth view available in Microsoft Word. In Print Preview you can view the layout of whole pages of your document. Although this view allows only limited formatting, and you cannot access text directly from this view, it contains some time-saving shortcuts that allow you to see the document formatting changes immediately. You'll use this view several times when working through the projects in this chapter.

⌘-I ➡ Choose **Print Preview** from the File menu.

You view a scaled-down version of your document in Print Preview—it is just like it will look on the printed page. You can't edit a document in this view, nor can you access any of the menu commands. But you can make some changes to your document using the four icons on the left side of the window.

 The first is the page numbering icon, and it is one of the ways Microsoft Word enables you to number the pages of your document and position the page numbers. This is the method you'll use to number the pages of this memorandum.

Numbering Pages in Print Preview

➡ Click on the page number icon, the first one of the four.

Notice that the pointer changes to a "1" with arrows on both sides.

➡ Position the insertion point in the center of the bottom of the first page, and then click to tell Microsoft Word that this is where you want the page number to appear on all pages of the document. See Figure 7-41.

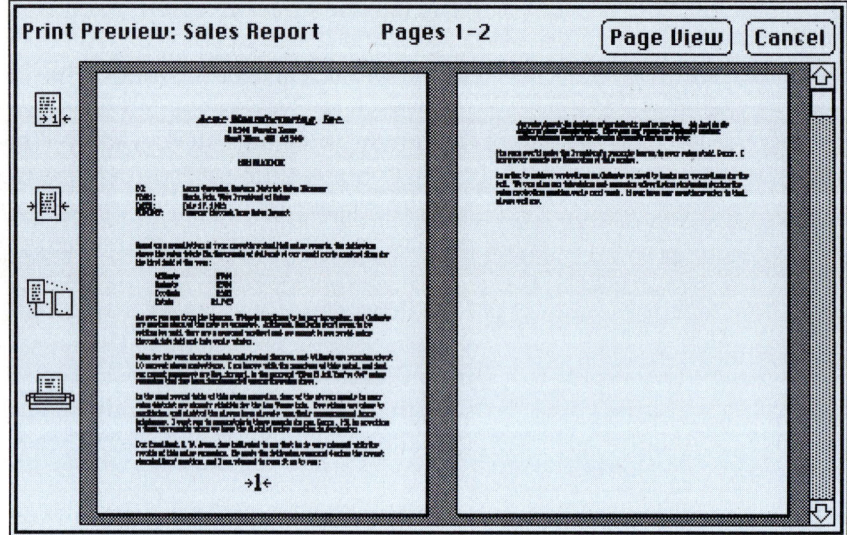

Figure 7-41   Numbering the pages

Microsoft Word will consecutively number each page of your document automatically. You do not have to manually type in each page number. The page numbers that are placed in your document in Print Preview are only visible when you are in either Print Preview or Page View or when you actually print the document. You cannot change the formatting of the page numbers with this method of page numbering. You get a default font and size for the numbers.

 The second icon on the Print Preview screen is the margins icon. If you click on it, it displays dotted lines around the edges of the page to indicate the boundaries of your margins, headers, and footers. There will be more detail about that icon in Project 4 of this chapter.

 The third icon down allows you to switch from two-page viewing to one-page viewing in Print Preview.

 The last icon allows you to print from this view. It works the same as if you had selected **Print** from the File menu and it presents the Print dialog box.

➡ Click the **Cancel** button in the top right corner of this window to return to the regular view of the document, Galley View.

➡ Scroll back through your document until you're before the block quote.

Controlling Page Breaks

Notice there is now a dotted line running across the document above the block quote, as shown in Figure 7-42. This line is what Microsoft Word uses to represent an *automatic page break*. Viewing your document in Print Preview caused the document to be *paginated*, which is the process of dividing the document into pages based on the document's margins, length, and paper size.

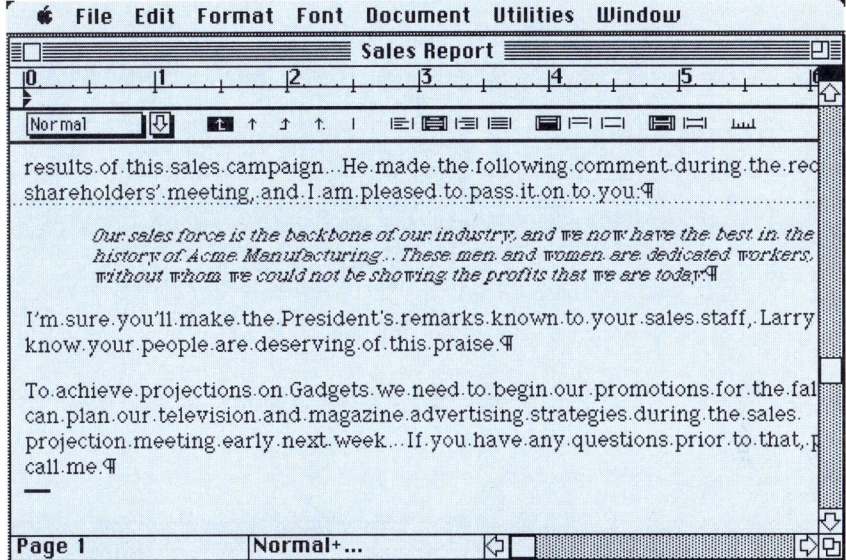

Figure 7-42   The automatic page break symbol

The other type of page break available in Microsoft Word is the *manual page break*. This is used when you want the page to break at a particular place, other than where an automatic page break would occur. A manual page break is entered by choosing **Insert Page Break** from the Document menu or by pressing Shift-Enter.

An automatic page break and a manual page break look different on the screen. Figure 7-43 shows both.

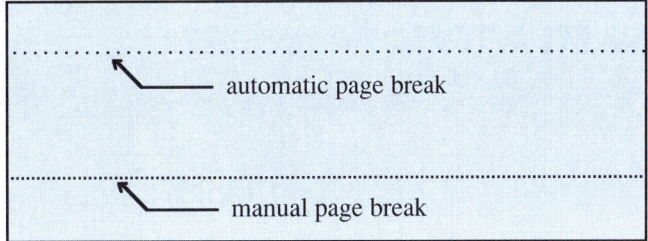

Figure 7-43   Automatic and manual page breaks

To delete a manual page break, select it and press the Backspace (or Delete) key.

Finally, now you're ready to print your document. Always save your work before printing.

⌘-S   ➡   Choose **Save** from the File menu.

PRINTING THE DOCUMENT

⌘-P ➡ Choose **Print** from the File menu.

If you are printing to an ImageWriter, your Print dialog box will look like the one shown in Figure 7-44.

Figure 7-44   The ImageWriter Print dialog box

If you are printing to a LaserWriter, your Print dialog box will look like the one shown in Figure 7-45.

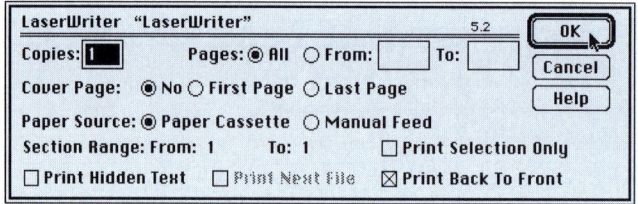

Figure 7-45   The LaserWriter Print dialog box

➡ Accept the default settings by clicking **OK**.

After your document prints, compare it to the finished document at the beginning of this project and make any necessary changes.

QUITTING MICROSOFT WORD

As in most Macintosh applications, the command to quit Microsoft Word is in the File menu.

⌘-Q ➡ Choose **Quit** from the File menu to exit Microsoft Word and return to the desktop. If you want to continue with the next project in this chapter, close this document by clicking in its close box.

If you try to quit Microsoft Word or close a document without saving your work since making any changes, Microsoft Word will ask if you want to save changes before closing. You can choose **Yes** (you do want to save changes before closing), **No** (you do not want to save changes before closing), or **Cancel** (you do not want to close the document).

Project 2: Creating a Document with Graphics

In this project you'll learn to insert a graphic into a document. Microsoft Word gives you the ability to easily combine graphics and text; you just have to open the application the graphic is in, copy the graphic to the Clipboard, and then paste it into your Microsoft Word document.

You can create illustrations in most Macintosh graphics applications, such as MacPaint and MacDraw II, and then copy them into your text document. You can also import charts from Microsoft Excel, and you can copy graphics from other Microsoft Word files. In addition, you can purchase commercial *clip art*—artwork that is usually copyrighted and distributed on disk from software suppliers—and incorporate it into your Microsoft Word document.

In addition to learning about moving graphics into your Microsoft Word document in this project, you'll learn to use styles, one of Microsoft Word's most powerful features. A *style* is a particular group of paragraph and character formatting characteristics to which you've assigned a name.

Giving a name to a set of paragraph and character formatting characteristics in Microsoft Word enables you to apply those characteristics repeatedly and consistently to different paragraphs in a document, without having to format each element separately.

If you don't assign a style explicitly in Microsoft Word, the default style, Normal, is assigned to any text you type. You've been using styles all along and probably didn't realize it.

To define a style, you indicate which formatting characteristics that style should contain, and then you attach a name to that style. A style definition can include tab settings, fonts, margin settings, line spacing, formatting such as underline or italic, and any other command that can be applied from the ruler or that can apply to a character or paragraph. To apply a style to a paragraph, you specify a previously defined style that you want to use for that paragraph, and the characteristics are applied to the text immediately.

If you want to modify a particular style, you change its format settings, and Microsoft Word instantly changes every paragraph that was assigned that style definition. This is certainly faster than selecting and changing the format for each paragraph separately.

A group of styles attached to a document is called a *style sheet*. You can transfer a style sheet to another document, so that the styles you created are available to be used in any document. That way different documents can have a consistent appearance.

In this project you'll learn to define and apply several different styles. You'll also learn to use *borders*, create special *indentation* effects, and create *tab leaders*.

When completed, the assignment that you turn in should look like the one shown in Figure 7-46.

WELCOME TO
Geno's
Deli

Our famous sandwiches and specialty items are served from 11:00 AM to 4:00 PM, Monday through Saturday. Closed Sunday.

Sandwiches
DELUXE REUBEN—a full 1/4-pound of corned beef, topped with baby swiss cheese, sauerkraut, and russian dressing, served grilled on pumpernickel bread.. 3.95
HAWAIIAN CHICKEN CLUB—sliced chicken, ham, lettuce, tomato, and pineapple slices, piled high on our toasted sunflower-seed bread 3.75
BACON AND ASPARAGUS SUPREME—crispy bacon, tender asparagus, and mushrooms, topped with melted cheddar cheese and served hot on an onion kaiser roll................................. 3.95

Side Orders
Curly Fries...................... 1.10   Bermuda Onion Rings.......... 1.10
German Potato Salad....... 1.25   Smoked Baked Beans .... .95

Desserts
HOT FUDGE SUNDAE—two scoops of mint ice cream, smothered with creamy hot fudge and topped with nuts and whipped cream 1.75
GENO'S CHEESECAKE—rich and creamy, with blueberry topping, and large enough to share..................................... 2.25

Beverages
Iced tea............................... .65   Milk... .75
Cola, Orange, Root Beer.... .75

CARRY-OUT AVAILABLE ON ALL MENU ITEMS

Figure 7-46   Final output of Project 2

In this project you will create a restaurant menu. It is intended that you create it using a partially completed document, entitled "Geno's Menu Unformatted," that is included on the *Macintosh Journey Projects* disk. The artwork for the menu is also on that disk and is entitled "Menu

Artwork." If you are using this book in a classroom environment, check with the instructor to ensure that "Geno's Menu Unformatted" and "Menu Artwork" are available. For information about ordering the *Macintosh Journey Projects* disk, see the last page of this book. A printed version of the unformatted menu is shown in Figure 7-47.

Our famous sandwiches and specialty items are served from 11:00 AM to 4:00 PM, Monday through Saturday. Closed Sunday.
Sandwiches
DELUXE REUBEN—a full 1/4-pound of corned beef, topped with baby swiss cheese, sauerkraut, and russian dressing, served grilled on pumpernickel bread
HAWAIIAN CHICKEN CLUB—sliced chicken, ham, lettuce, tomato, and pineapple slices, piled high on our toasted sunflower-seed bread
BACON AND ASPARAGUS SUPREME—crispy bacon, tender asparagus, and mushrooms, topped with melted cheddar cheese and served hot on an onion kaiser roll
Side Orders
Curly Fries 1.10   Bermuda Onion Rings   1.10
German Potato Salad   1.25   Smoked Baked Beans   .95
Desserts
HOT FUDGE SUNDAE—two scoops of mint ice cream, smothered with creamy hot fudge and topped with nuts and whipped cream
GENO'S CHEESECAKE—rich and creamy, with blueberry topping, and large enough to share
Beverages
Iced tea   .65   Milk .75
Cola, Orange, Root Beer .75

CARRY-OUT AVAILABLE ON ALL MENU ITEMS

Figure 7-47   Unformatted Geno's Menu

Geno's Menu Unformatted

One way to begin this project is to locate the document entitled "Geno's Menu Unformatted" and double-click on its icon. This will start Microsoft Word and open that document.

Another way to begin is to double-click on the Microsoft Word icon to launch the application, and then choose **Open** from the File menu. Locate the Geno's Menu Unformatted document (click the **Drive** button if necessary), and double-click on it to open it.

⌘-O   If you did not quit Microsoft Word after the last project, choose **Open** from the File menu and double-click on **Geno's Menu Unformatted** to open it.

Regardless of which method you chose, the document Geno's Menu Unformatted should be opened on your screen. It should now look like Figure 7-48.

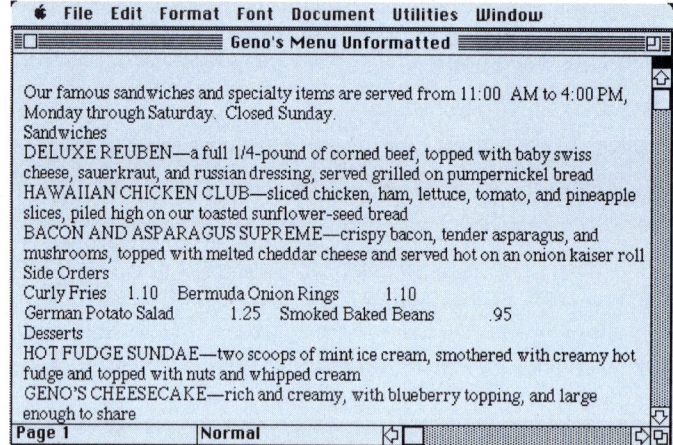

Figure 7-48   Geno's Menu Unformatted

Let's make a copy of this document, so you can leave the original intact.

➡ Choose **Save As** from the File menu.

➡ Click the **Drive** button, if necessary, to be sure you are saving the document on your disk.

➡ Replace the name "Geno's Menu Unformatted" with **Geno's Menu** by typing that name in the Save Current Document as box, as shown in Figure 7-49.

Return or Enter   ➡ Click the **Save** button.

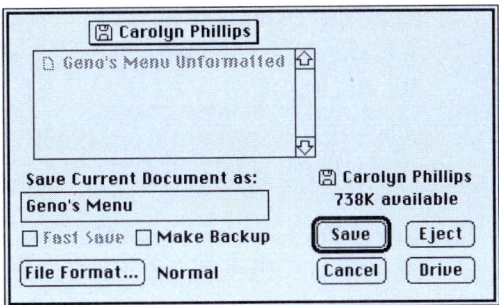

Figure 7-49   Saving the formatted menu

PLACING THE GRAPHIC

The artwork for the menu is in a document entitled "Menu Artwork" on the *Macintosh Journey Projects* disk which accompanies this book. You'll open that document now.

Opening Multiple Documents

Microsoft Word allows you to have more than one document open at a time. When you have multiple documents open, only one is considered active. The *active window* is the frontmost one showing on your screen. If your document windows are sized and arranged so that you can view more than one at a time on the screen, you can easily spot the active one because it has scroll bars and horizontal lines on either side of the title in the title bar. To make a different open document active, select it from the Window menu, and Microsoft Word activates it and places it in front of the others. You can also click anywhere in a window to make it active.

⌘-O   ➡   Choose **Open** from the File menu.

You are presented with a dialog box that lists the Microsoft Word documents available to be opened. See Figure 7-50.

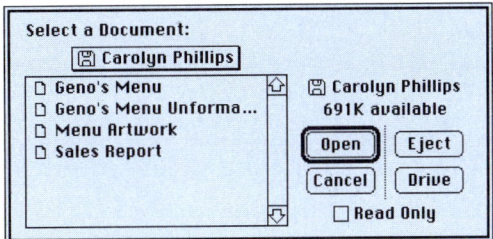

Figure 7-50   The Open dialog box

➥ Click the **Drive** button, if necessary, and scroll through the list of documents in the Open dialog box until you see the Menu Artwork document.

➥ Select that document from the list by clicking on it, and then click the **Open** button.

A shortcut for this procedure is to double-click **Menu Artwork** in the dialog box. Another is to click once on **Menu Artwork** and then press Return, because the **Open** button is the default. Whichever method you use, the document Menu Artwork should now be active on your screen.

➥ Click within the Welcome to Geno's Deli graphic to select it.

When you select a graphic, small black squares appear in the center bottom and on the right side of the drawing. The border around the drawing darkens, as shown in Figure 7-51.

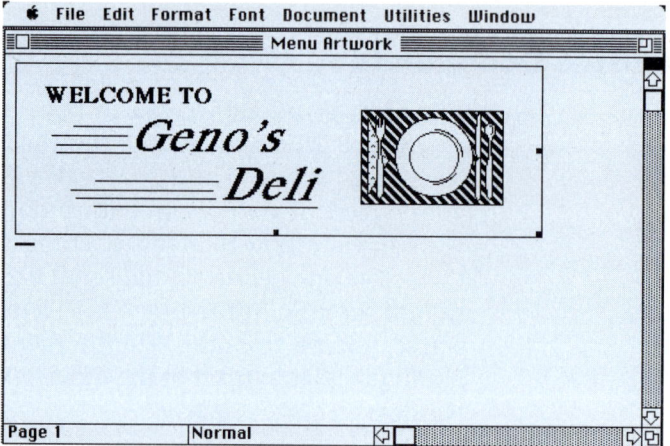

Figure 7-51   Selecting the graphic

Copying and Pasting

⌘-C ➥ Choose **Copy** from the Edit menu to copy the graphic to the Clipboard.

➥ Click in the close box in the upper left corner of the Menu Artwork document to close it.

Now you'll place the Menu Artwork into Geno's Menu.

⌘-V ➥ Click in the first line of **Geno's Menu** to set the insertion point there, and then choose **Paste** from the Edit menu.

Now you have pasted the Menu Artwork into Geno's Menu. Your screen should look similar to the one shown in Figure 7-52.

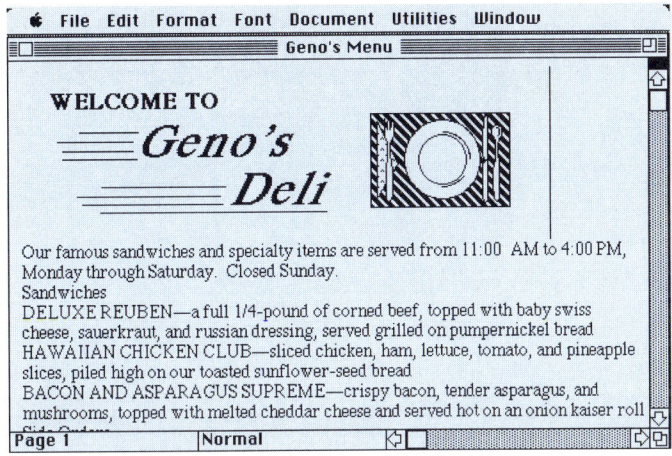

Figure 7-52   Placing the graphic in the document

⌘-S   ➡ Save your work now by choosing **Save** from the File menu.

You'll use Show ¶ and the ruler to help you format and see the effects of your formatting throughout this project, so you should activate them now.

⌘-Y   ➡ Choose **Show ¶** from the Edit menu.

⌘-R   ➡ Choose **Show Ruler** from the Format menu.

FORMATTING THE GRAPHIC

Centering the graphic and placing a border around it will make it stand out on the menu, so let's do that now.

Centering the Graphic

⌘-Shift-C |≡| ➡ To center the graphic, click on the graphic to select it, and then click on the center-alignment icon on the ruler.

⌘-M   ➡ With the graphic still selected, choose **Paragraph** from the Format menu.

If necessary, drag the Paragraph dialog box by its title bar to move it lower on the screen so that you can see the graphic.

Adding Borders

➡ Click the **Borders** button at the bottom of the Paragraph dialog box.

➡ In the resulting Paragraph Borders dialog box, click on the second line thickness down along the left side of the dialog box to select the thicker single line. Then click **Plain Box**. See Figure 7-53.

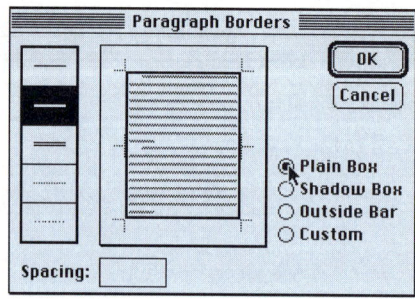

Figure 7-53   The Paragraph Borders dialog box

Notice that a box is drawn around the schematic diagram to represent the effects of your selection.

Applying Paragraph Borders

➡ Click **OK** in the Paragraph Borders dialog box, and then click **OK** in the Paragraph dialog box.

Now your menu graphic should have a border around it like the one shown in Figure 7-54.

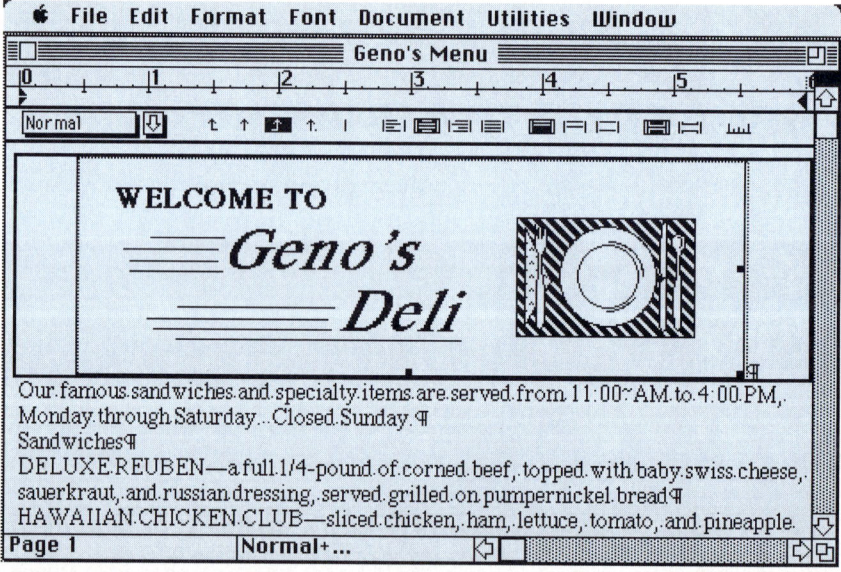

Figure 7-54   The border around the graphic

The left and right margins on the ruler control the relative width of the border you place around your text and graphics. Notice that the border extends about 1/2 inch to the left and right of the graphic in Figure 7-54. That is because the left and right margins of the ruler extend that far to either side of the graphic.

⌘-S   ➡ Save your work.

FORMATTING THE TEXT

Now you'll put a double line beneath the first paragraph and change the indentation so the paragraph is set apart from the rest of the menu.

⌘-M ➧ Click anywhere in the first line of the paragraph beginning "Our famous", and then choose **Paragraph** from the Format menu.

⌘-Shift-O ▯▯ ➧ Click on the paragraph spacing icon on the ruler to create a space before this paragraph.

➧ Hold down the Shift key, select the left indent marker, and drag it to the 1/2-inch mark on the ruler. See Figure 7-55.

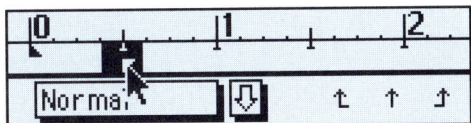

Figure 7-55   Setting a ¹/₂-inch indent

If you do not use the Shift key, the first-line indent marker and left indent marker move together.

This ruler change causes the second line only of that paragraph to be indented ¹/₂-inch from the left margin of that paragraph.

➧ Click the **Borders** button in the Paragraph dialog box.

➧ In the resulting Paragraph Borders dialog box, click on the third box down the left side to select the double line. Then click in the bottom part of the schematic diagram to place a double line there. See Figure 7-56.

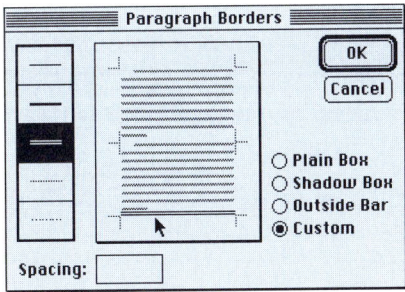

Figure 7-56   Placing a double line beneath the paragraph

➧ Click **OK** in this dialog box and again in the Paragraph dialog box.

Your paragraph should now be formatted like the one shown in Figure 7-57.

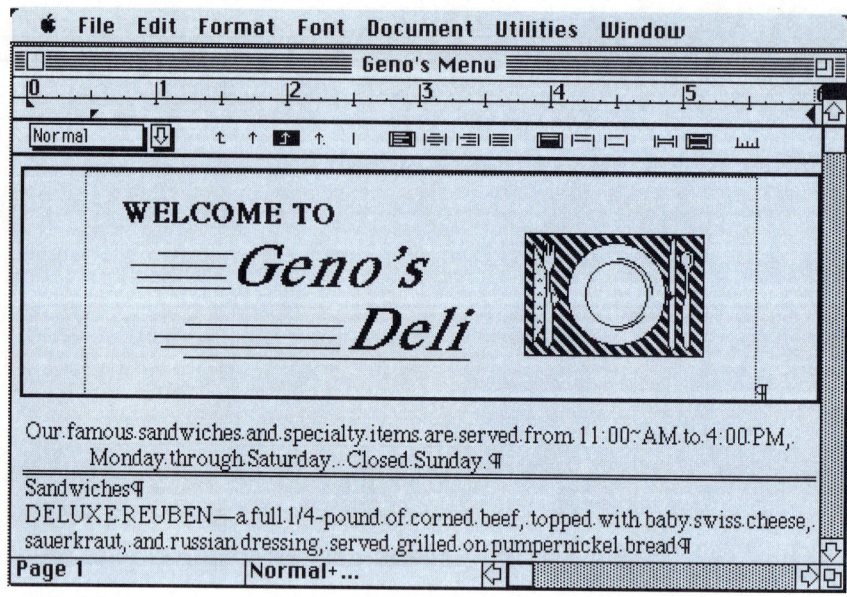

Figure 7-57   The formatted first paragraph

⌘-S ➡ Now is a good time to save your work.

Defining Styles

Let's create some styles that you can apply to the rest of your menu.

➡ Click in the line containing the word "Sandwiches", below the double line you just created.

⌘-T ➡ Choose **Define Styles** from the Format menu.

The resulting dialog box is displayed in Figure 7-58.

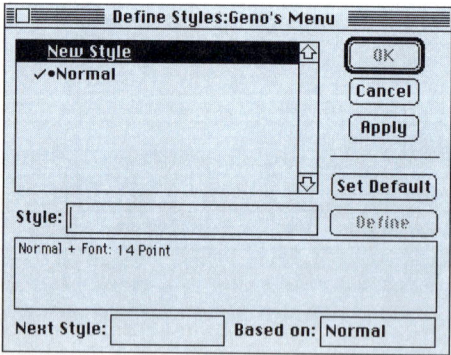

Figure 7-58   The Define Styles dialog box

Notice at the top of the dialog box that New Style is highlighted; Microsoft Word is expecting you to create a new style. The insertion point is waiting for you to type in a style name. The other style in the list is preceded by a bullet. This indicates that it is one of Microsoft Word's *automatic styles*. The checkmark to the left of the style Normal indicates that it is the style that the currently selected paragraph is formatted in.

The insertion point is in the field to the right of Style, ready for you to type in the name of the new style you're about to create.

In the bottom right corner of the dialog box the Based on box contains the word "Normal." This means that the style that you are about to create will contain the characteristics of the already existing style Normal, plus whatever modifications you choose.

Now you'll create a style that you can use to format text as bold and with a 12-point blank line in front of it.

➡ Type **Food Class** for the name of your new style, as shown in Figure 7-59.

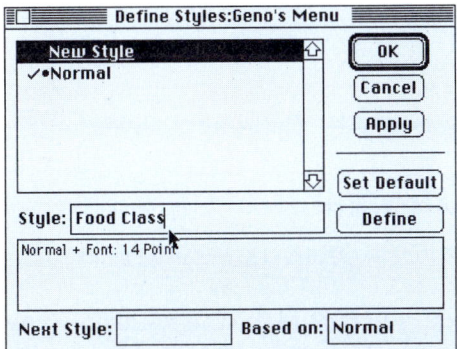

Figure 7-59   Typing the new style name

➡ With this dialog box still open, choose **Bold** from the Format menu.

Notice that Bold becomes part of the description of the style in the box beneath "Food Class."

➡ With this dialog box still open, choose **Paragraph** from the Format menu.

➡ In the Paragraph dialog box, type **12** in the Before box, as shown in Figure 7-60, and then click **OK**.

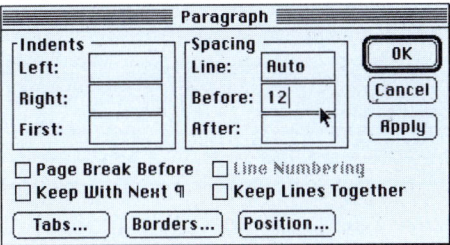

Figure 7-60   Placing a 12-point line before the paragraph

This last action created a 12-point blank line in front of the paragraph, similar to the way clicking on the paragraph-spacing icon would.

➡   In the Define Styles dialog box, click the **Define** button, as shown in Figure 7-61.

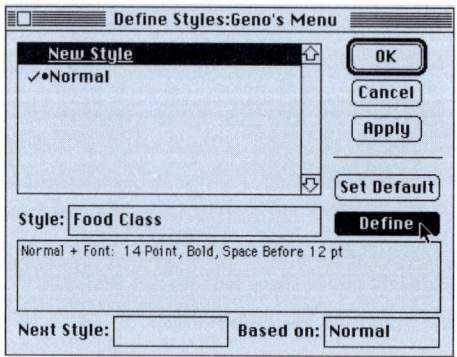

Figure 7-61   Defining the style

The new style, Food Class, that you created is added to the list of styles.

➡   Click **OK** in the Define Styles dialog box.

Now you should see the results of applying that style to the paragraph that contains the word "Sandwiches." See Figure 7-62.

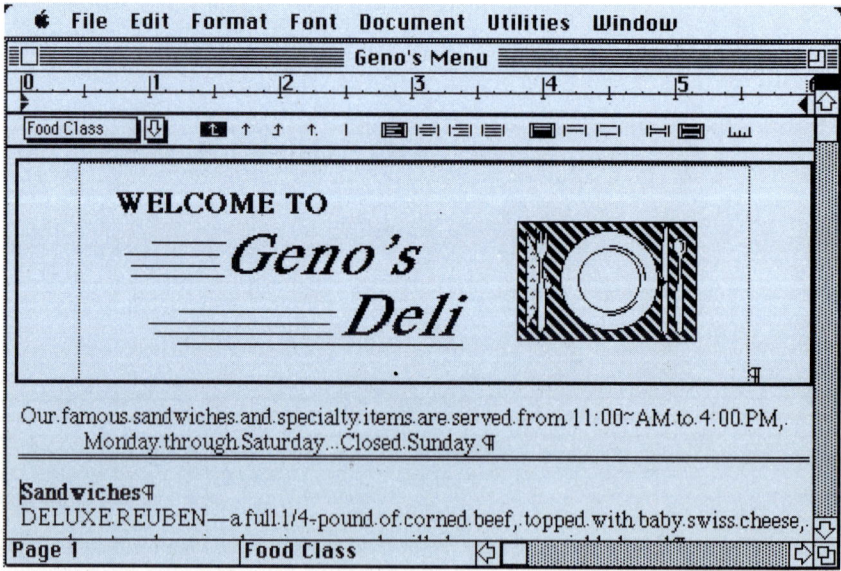

Figure 7-62   The first style applied

The name of the style that you created is now showing in the styles drop-down list on the ruler. If you click on the arrow to the right of this style name and hold down the mouse button, the list of styles used in this document are shown. A checkmark is beside the style name of the paragraph that currently contains the insertion point. See Figure 7-63.

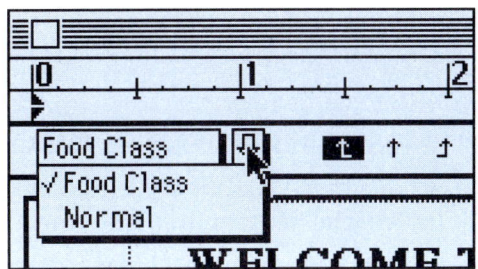

Figure 7-63   The styles drop-down field

⌘-S   ⟹   Save the changes you've made to your document.

Now you'll see how simple it is to apply this style to other paragraphs in your document.

⟹   Click in the paragraph containing the words "Side Orders," in the middle of the document.

⟹   Click on the arrow to the right of the styles drop-down list on the ruler and, holding down the mouse button, drag to the Food Class style so it is highlighted, as shown in Figure 7-64.

Be sure you click on the arrow to the right of the styles drop-down list, not on the name.

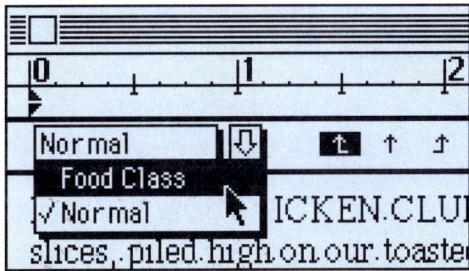

Figure 7-64   Selecting a style

⟹   Release the mouse button.

The selected paragraph should now have the same formatting characteristics as the Sandwiches paragraph.

⟹   Using the same method, apply the Food Class style to the paragraph containing the word "Desserts" and to the one containing the word "Beverages".

Now you'll create a different style to use to format the menu items. This style will have different left and first-line indentations and will have tabs set with *dot leaders*. A dot leader is one of several tab leaders that Microsoft Word uses to fill blank spaces before a tab stop. When you press the Tab key to move to a tab stop that has a leader, the blank space up to the tab stop is filled with your choice of dots, dashes, or underlines. You've probably seen dot leaders in tables of contents or between columns of figures.

You'll learn a different method for creating this style than you used previously. This time you'll format the paragraph and then assign the style definition by example.

➤ Click in the paragraph beginning with "Deluxe Reuben".

➤ Hold down the Shift key, and click on the left indent marker on the ruler (the bottom triangle) and drag it to the 1-inch mark on the ruler.

➤ With the Shift key still down, drag the first-line indent to the ½-inch mark on the ruler, so that your ruler now looks like the one shown in Figure 7-65.

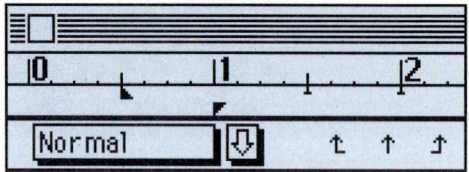

Figure 7-65   Changing the first-line indent

Changing the left and first-line indent markers in this manner will result in a *hanging indent* for the selected paragraph. A hanging indent is when the first line of the paragraph starts to the left of the left margin.

↑. ➤ To set the decimal tab, click on the decimal tab marker on the ruler. Then click on the ruler at the 5-5/8-inch mark to position the tab there.

⌘-M ➤ Choose **Paragraph** from the Format menu.

In the resulting Paragraph dialog box, notice the settings in the Indents section, as shown in Figure 7-66. Instead of dragging the left and first-line indents to their desired positions on the ruler, you could have typed the amounts into the appropriate boxes in this dialog box. Both methods work the same way.

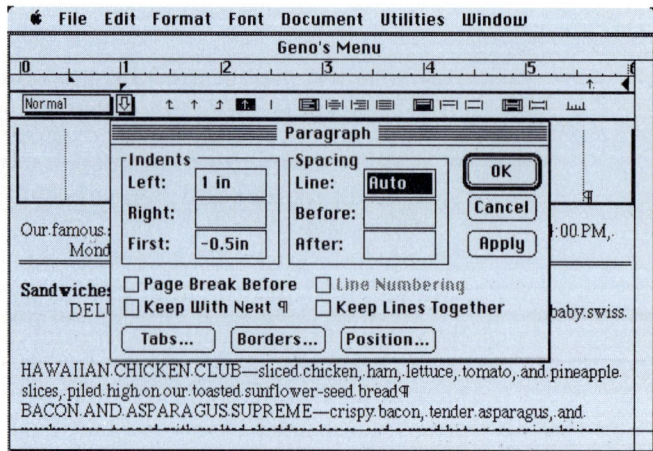

Figure 7-66   The Paragraph dialog box

The indents and tab setting on your ruler and in your Paragraph dialog box should match those shown in Figure 7-66.

Setting Tab Leaders

➥ Click the **Tabs** button in the Paragraph dialog box.

➥ Click on the decimal tab marker that you placed at the 5-5/8-inch mark on the ruler.

➥ In the Tabs dialog box, click the second button down in the Leader section. This is the one with the dots to the right of it, as shown in Figure 7-67.

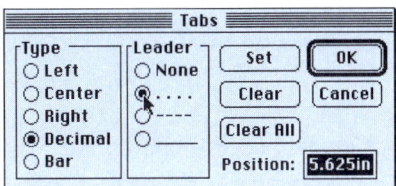

Figure 7-67   Selecting the dot leader

This will attach a dot leader to that tab. You'll see how a tab leader works in just a minute.

➥ Click **OK** in the Tabs dialog box, and then click **OK** in the Paragraph dialog box.

☝ Notice that the tab marker on your ruler now has a small dot to the left of it. This indicates that a leader has been applied to that tab stop.

Now that your paragraph is formatted, you'll define a style based on that formatting.

➥ To assign a style name to the paragraph you just formatted, make sure the insertion point is somewhere within that paragraph and then click the style name box on the ruler to select it.

➥ Type **Menu Item** into that box as shown in Figure 7-68.

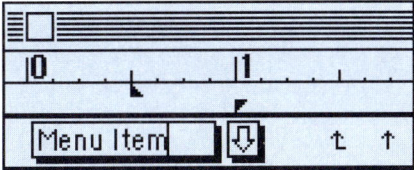

Figure 7-68   Typing in the style name

➥ Press Return.

When you press Return, a prompt will verify that you would like to define a style based on your current selection, as shown in Figure 7-69.

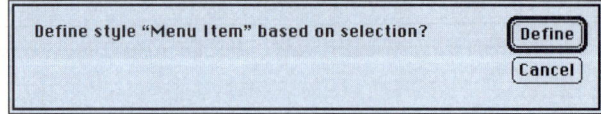

Figure 7-69   Define styles prompt

Return or Enter   ➡   Click **Define**.

You just went through the steps for defining a style based on an example. You now have a new style called Menu Item.

To complete the Deluxe Reuben menu item, you need to type in the price.

➡   Click after "pumpernickel bread" at the end of that paragraph and press the Tab key. Then type the price, **3.95**, as shown in Figure 7-70.

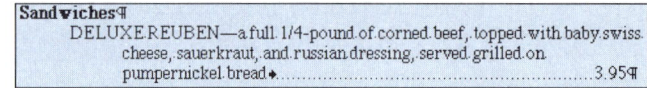

Figure 7-70   Adding the price to the menu item

The dot leader that you applied to the tab causes dots to lead up to the tab position, which makes the information easier for the eye to follow.

⌘-S   ➡   Save the changes that you've made to your document.

Now let's apply the Menu Item style to "Hawaiian Chicken Club".

➡   Click anywhere within that paragraph, and then select **Menu Item** from the style drop-down list on the ruler.

Add the price to this menu item.

➡   Click after "sunflower-seed bread" in that item, press the Tab key, and then type the price, **3.75**.

➡   Follow the same procedure for applying the style to the Bacon and Asparagus Supreme, Hot Fudge Sundae, and Geno's Cheesecake.

➡   Be sure to type in the prices for these items, which are **3.95**, **1.75**, and **2.25**, respectively.

There is one more style to be created for this document, "Side Orders and Beverages". This style will be indented 1/2 inch from the left margin and will contain three tab stops.

➡   Click in the line containing "Curly Fries".

➠ Drag the left indent and first-line indent markers to the 1/2-inch mark on the ruler.

↑. ➠ Click on the decimal tab marker on the ruler, and then click at the 2-5/8-inch mark and at the 5-5/8-inch mark on the ruler to place decimal tab stops there.

↥ ➠ Click on the left-aligned tab marker on the ruler, and then click at the 3-1/4-inch mark on the ruler to place a left-aligned tab stop there.

Your ruler should look like the one shown in Figure 7-71.

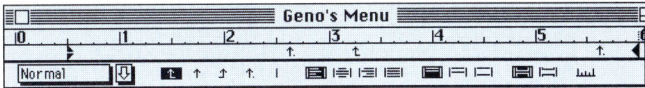

Figure 7-71   The left alignment and tab stops on the ruler

➠ Double-click on the first decimal tab (at 2-5/8 inches) on the ruler.

This brings up the Tabs dialog box. Be careful that you don't accidentally move the tab marker when you double-click on it.

➠ In the Tabs dialog box, click the button next to the dot leader in the Leader section. See Figure 7-72.

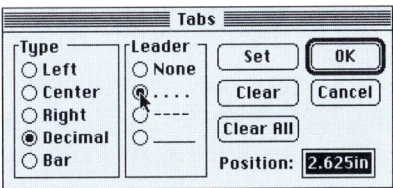

Figure 7-72   Setting a dot leader for the 2-5/8-inch tab

➠ Click the **Set** button.

That sets up the tab leader for the first tab marker on the ruler.

➠ Now click on the third tab marker on the ruler, which is set at 5-5/8 inches. Click the dot leader button for this tab marker also.

➠ Click **OK** in the Tabs dialog box.

You have already defined the style attributes by setting the indentation, tabs, and leaders. Now you need to name that definition. You'll use the Define Styles dialog box to define this style.

⌘-T ➠ Choose **Define Styles** from the Format menu.

➠ Type **Side Order/Beverage** for the style name.

Notice that all the attributes about the style are listed in the box below the style name, as shown in Figure 7-73. This is helpful if you need to verify a particular formatting characteristic. If you need to change a formatting characteristic, you can do so with the dialog box open, and the style description will reflect the changes.

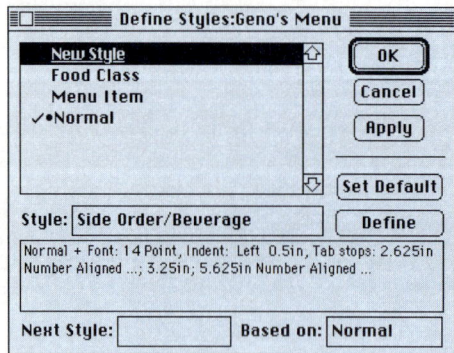

Figure 7-73   The Side Order/Beverage style

➡   Click **Define** in the Define Styles dialog box, and then click **OK**.

This Side Order/Beverage style needs to be applied to German Potato Salad, Iced Tea, and Cola, Orange, Root Beer.

➡   Follow the previous instructions to apply styles to these lines.

⌘-S   ➡   Save your changes.

The last formatting changes you need to make to this menu are to the Carry-Out Available line.

➡   Click in the selection bar to the left of the Carry-Out line at the bottom of the page to select the entire line.

➡   Click on the center-alignment icon on the ruler to center that line.

⌘-Shift-B   ⌘-Shift-I   ➡   Choose **Bold** from the Format menu, and then choose **Italic** from the Format menu.

The last line of the menu is now centered, bold, and italicized.

Now that you've made all these formatting changes, you should save and then print your completed document.

⌘-S   ➡   Choose **Save** from the File menu.

⌘-P   ➡   Choose **Print** from the File menu, and then click **OK**.

Compare your printed document to the finished menu at the beginning of this project, and make sure they look similar.

⌘-Q   ➡   To exit Microsoft Word, choose **Quit** from the File menu or just close the document and be ready for the next lesson.

Project 3: Creating a Table

In this project you'll learn how to use the *tables feature*, which is new with Microsoft Word 4. Using the tables feature is a straightforward way to arrange text in rows and columns. The intersection of a row and a column is referred to as a *cell*. You can put just about anything you'd like into a cell—numbers, words, paragraphs, groups of paragraphs, or graphics. You can format the contents of each cell with character and paragraph formats. You can also use any number of line and border combinations to format individual cells or the entire table.

Each cell has many of the properties of a small document, with its own top, bottom, left, and right margins and its own selection bar. Text word-wraps within a cell just as it does in a document.

In this project you will create an empty table and then fill it with data. However, tables can also be created by selecting existing paragraphs and converting them to a filled cell table using the Insert Table command. This project does not detail this type of paragraph-to-table conversion procedure, but additional information is available in *Reference to Microsoft Word*.

This project produces a food value table. You'll create this table by inserting an empty table grid and then filling each cell with the appropriate data. You'll use the ruler to center and left-align the contents of individual cells and to set decimal tabs within several cells at once. You'll use cell borders to create vertical lines between columns of cells and to create borders around groups of cells and the entire table.

Microsoft Word provides three commands for working with tables: Insert Table on the Document menu, Cells on the Format menu, and Table on the Edit menu. You'll work with each of these commands in this project.

The final output of this project is the table shown in Figure 7-74.

The following is a table showing the fat and cholesterol content of certain foods of interest to this particular study group. See Table 7.

Table 7. Fat and Cholesterol Content of Selected Foods Common to Diets of Elderly Nursing Home Patients				
Food Item	Portion Size	Total Fat	Saturated Fat	Cholesterol
		(grams)		(milligrams)
Lean ground beef	3 oz.	14	6.0	80
Tuna salad	1/2 cup	10	2.0	40
Peanut butter	2 Tbsp.	16	2.0	0
Whole milk	1 cup	8	5.0	33
Skim milk	1 cup	1	0.2	5
Butter	1 Tbsp.	11	7.0	31
Vanilla ice cream	1/2 cup	7	4.0	30
Source: USDA, Human Nutrition Information Service.				

Figure 7-74 Final output of Project 3

Microsoft Word

⮕ To begin the assignment, double-click on the Microsoft Word icon. If you did not exit Word since the previous project, choose **New** from the File menu.

Your screen will show a new document called "Untitled1".

⌘-R ⮕ Choose **Show Ruler** from the Format menu.

⌘-Y ⮕ Choose **Show ¶** from the Edit menu.

⮕ Select the paragraph mark (¶) in the first line. From the Font menu choose **Helvetica 12 point** if you'll be printing to a LaserWriter or **Geneva 12 point** if you'll be using an ImageWriter.

Selecting the paragraph mark before choosing the font is an example of setting the character format before you begin typing. The character format will remain in effect until you change it to something else.

The example in this project uses Helvetica font.

This time, let's save and name the document before going on with the rest of the project.

⌘-S ⮕ Choose **Save** from the File menu, and save the document as Food Value Table. Be sure you are saving this document on *your* data disk.

⮕ Type the following:

The following is a table showing the fat and cholesterol content of certain foods of interest to this particular study group. See Table 7.

⮕ Press Return twice to create a blank line.

WORKING WITH CELLS

As mentioned earlier, a cell occurs at the intersection of a row and column in a table. A row refers to the horizontal placement of cells, and a column refers to the vertical placement of cells. In a table consisting of four rows and three columns, each row consists of three cells horizontally and each column consists of four cells vertically, as shown in Figure 7-75.

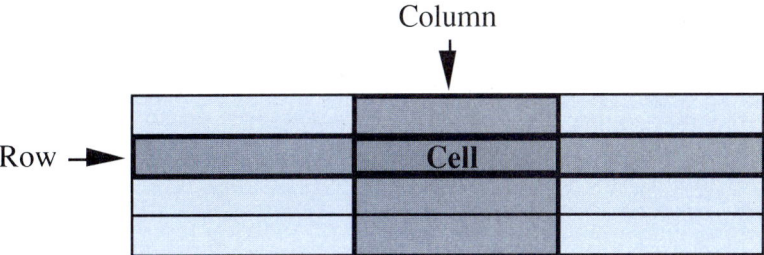

Figure 7-75   Relationship between rows, columns, and cells

A table can consist of just one cell, one row, one column, or any combination of groups of cells.

A cell works like a small document that is contained within the border of the cell. You can apply character and paragraph formatting to the contents of a cell, and you can wrap text within a cell.

The appearance of tables can be enhanced using borders and lines. Borders can apply to individual cells, groups of cells, or the entire table. Lines can improve the readability of tables by separating columns of data and by setting headings apart from the body of the table.

Creating a Single-Column Cell

➡ Choose **Insert Table** from the Document menu.

The dialog box that results is shown in Figure 7-76.

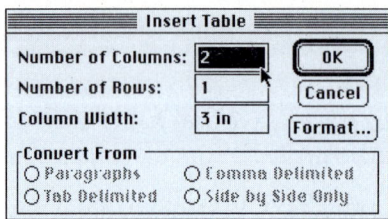

Figure 7-76   The Insert Table dialog box

➡ Type **1** to replace the highlighted 2 in the Number of Columns box.

Notice that the column width changed from 3 in to 6 in when you changed the number of columns. This is because Microsoft Word divides the text column width of your document (the distance between the left and right margins of the page) by the number of columns in the table, so that each column of cells is the same width. Since the column width of this document is 6 inches, the column width of your one-cell table is 6 inches also.

➡ Accept the rest of the settings in the dialog box (shown in Figure 7-77) by clicking **OK**.

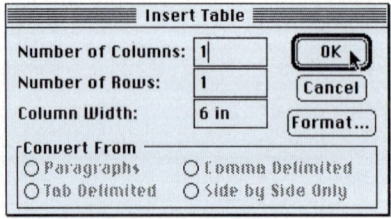

Figure 7-77   Dialog box set for one 6-inch-wide column

Now you see a dotted cell grid that consists of one row and one column and, therefore, one cell. The insertion point is inside the cell just to the left of the *end-of-cell marker*, which is represented by a black dot about the size of a lowercase "o". The cell also has an *end-of-row marker*, just outside and to the right of the cell grid. See Figure 7-78.

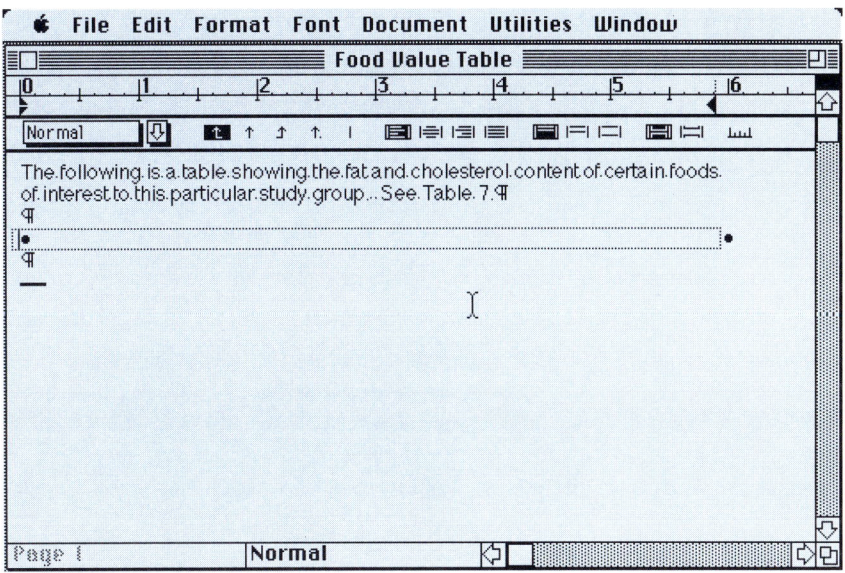

Figure 7-78   The first table

➡ Type the following into this cell without pressing Return:

Table 7. Fat and Cholesterol Content of Selected Foods Common to Diets of Elderly Nursing Home Patients

Notice how word wrap enables the text to flow to a new line in the cell without you having to control the placement of the lines. Although this is a single-column cell, you can create as many lines as needed and still remain within the same cell.

Your screen should look like the one shown in Figure 7-79.

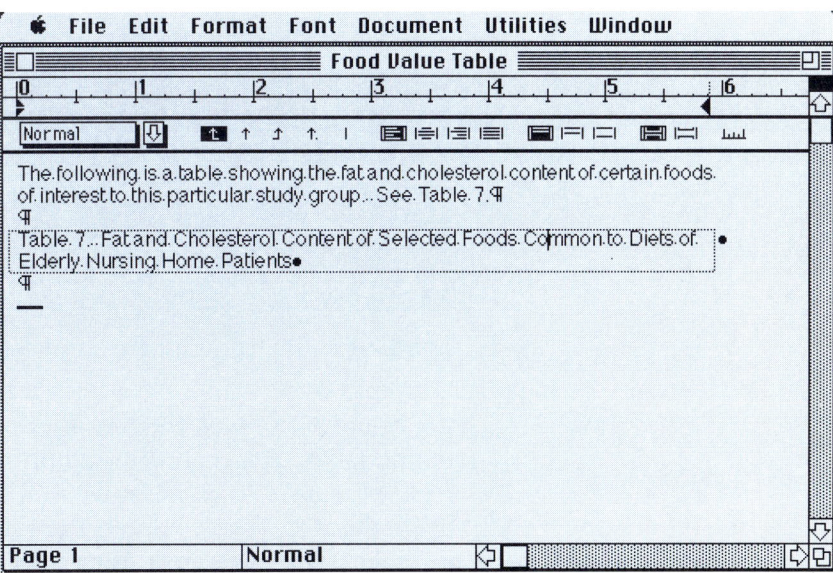

Figure 7-79   Cell contents of first table

⌘-S   ➡   Choose **Save** from the File menu.

Next you'll create a new 5-column, 10-row table.

Creating Multiple-Column and Multiple-Cell Tables

➡ Click to the left of the paragraph mark on the last line of your document, beneath the table above it.

➡ Choose **Insert Table** from the Document menu.

➡ In the resulting dialog box, change the Number of Columns to **5** and the Number of Rows to **10** and accept the rest of the settings by clicking **OK**. See Figure 7-80.

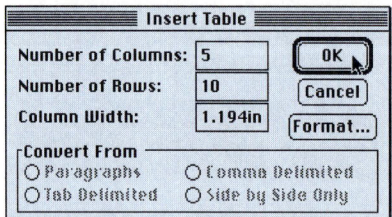

Figure 7-80   Setting up a 5-column, 10-row table

Now you have a grid on your screen that looks like the one shown in Figure 7-81.

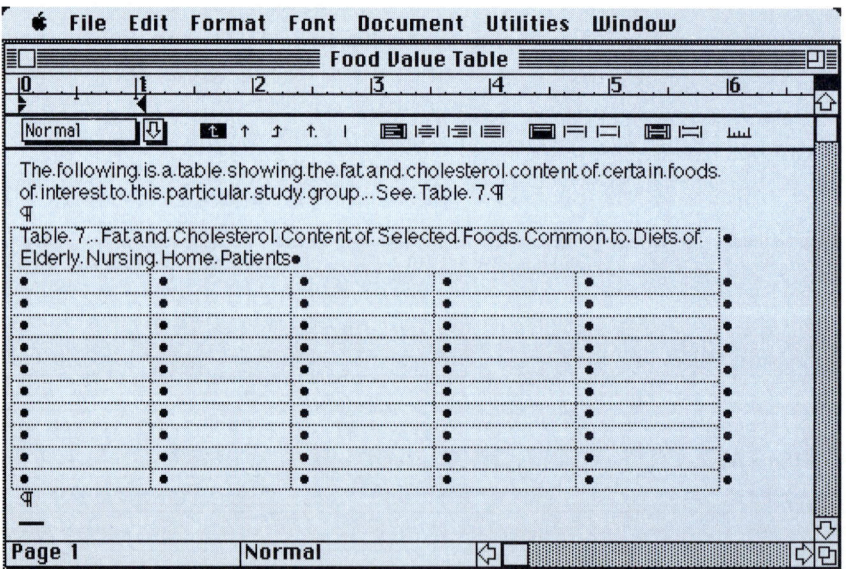

Figure 7-81   The grid for the multicolumn table

Now you need to type the headings in the first row of cells in the 5-column table. When you press Return or Shift-Return while typing in a cell, Microsoft Word advances you to the next line, but keeps you within the same cell. You press the Tab key to advance to a new cell in the table. When you are in the last cell of a row, pressing the Tab key advances you to the first cell in the next row.

Rather than creating a predetermined number of rows in a table, you can also create new rows as you need them. Pressing the Tab key when you reach the last row in a table creates a new row with the same characteristics as the one you just left, and that row is placed directly beneath the previous row. This is a handy feature, because it means you don't have to determine ahead of time how many rows you'll need in your table. It also allows you to format the first row of cells, and all new rows you create will be formatted the same as the original row.

In this project first you are creating the table grid and typing in the data. Then you are going to change the formatting of parts of the table once you've seen the layout of the text in the cells. Once you've gotten the hang of working with tables, feel free to format first and type later. As with any document you create, it is a matter of personal preference, and no one way is better than another.

➡ Type the column headings as shown in Figure 7-82.

These are shown with Show ¶ on, so you can see where the *new-line command*, or soft return (Shift-Return), was used to advance to a new line in the same cell.

To move to the next cell to the right, press the Tab key. To move back to a cell to the left, press Shift-Tab. Or click in any cell to begin typing there.

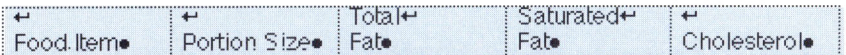

Figure 7-82   The column headings in the table

➡ After you've typed the heading in the last cell, press the Tab key to advance to the next row.

➡ Press the Tab key twice to advance to the third cell within this row, and type **(grams)**.

➡ Press the Tab key twice more to advance to the last cell, and type **(milligrams)**. See Figure 7-83.

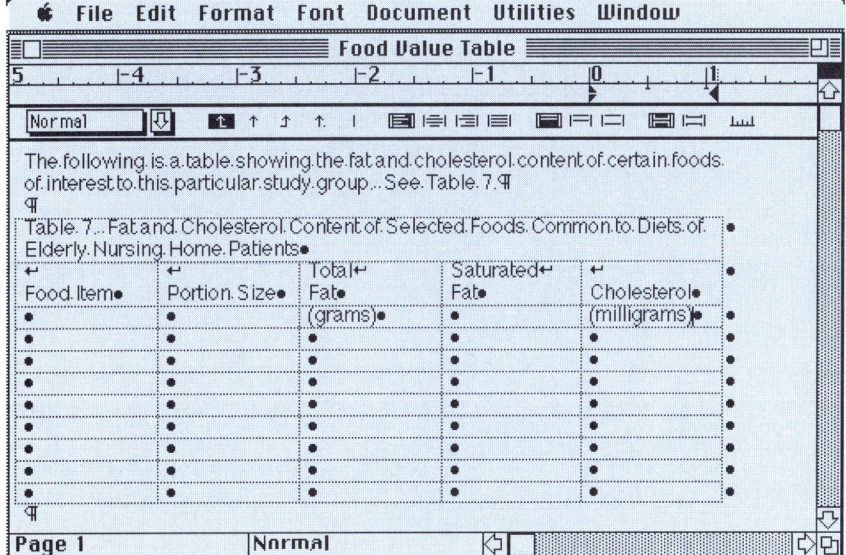

Figure 7-83   The second row of headings

➡ Press the Tab key to advance to the next row.

➡ Now type the rest of the data in the columns, pressing the Tab key to move between cells and also to advance to the next row of cells when you have finished typing a row. See Figure 7-84.

Table 7. Fat and Cholesterol Content of Selected Foods Common to Diets of Elderly Nursing Home Patients•				
↵ Food Item•	↵ Portion Size•	Total↵ Fat• (grams)•	Saturated↵ Fat• •	↵ Cholesterol• (milligrams)•
Lean ground beef•	3 oz.•	14•	6.0•	80•
Tuna salad•	1/2 cup•	10•	2.0•	40•
Peanut butter•	2 Tbsp.•	16•	2.0•	0•
Whole milk•	1 cup•	8•	5.0•	33•
Skim milk•	1 cup•	1•	0.2•	5•
Butter•	1 Tbsp.•	11•	7.0•	31•
Vanilla ice cream•	1/2 cup•	7•	4.0•	30•
•	•	•	•	•

Figure 7-84   Completing the table

⌘-S ➡ Save your work.

Don't worry about the unused row in the table—you'll get rid of it later.

Now you need to create a single-cell table at the bottom of the table you just completed. This will contain your source information.

➡ Click to the left of the paragraph mark (¶) in the last line of the document to set the insertion point there.

➡ Choose **Insert Table** from the Document menu.

➡ Type **1** to replace the highlighted 2 in the Number of Columns box.

➡ Accept the rest of the settings in the dialog box by clicking **OK.** See Figure 7-85.

Figure 7-85   Dialog box set for one 6-inch-wide column

Now you have another one-cell table beneath the multicolumn one.

➡ In that new one-cell table, type the following source information:

Source: USDA, Human Nutrition Information Service.

⌘-S ➡ Save your work.

FORMATTING CELLS

Now that all the information has been entered, you can change the look of the table.

Each cell has its own "selection bar" that you can use to select the contents of the cell. The selection bar is to the left of the cell marker if there is no data in the cell. If the cell does contain text, the selection bar is to the left of the text.

The title information in the first one-cell table should be bold. You'll select that text now.

➡ To select the contents of the one-cell table that contains the title information, click in the selection bar to the left of the text in that cell. See Figure 7-86.

The cell contents become highlighted.

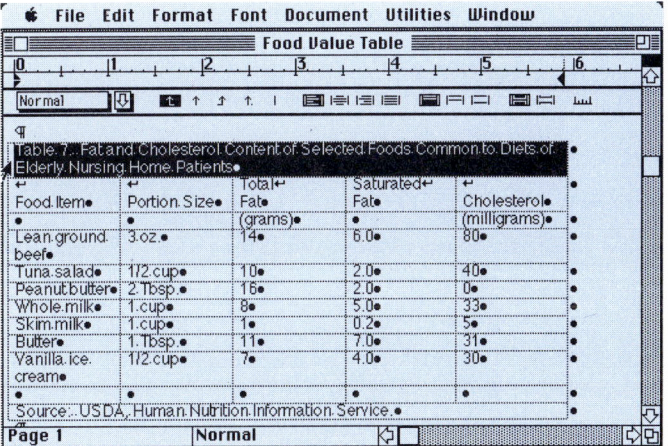

Figure 7-86 Using the cell selection bar

⌘-Shift-B ➡ Choose **Bold** from the Format menu.

This formatting affected only one cell. You are not limited, however, to formatting one cell at a time—you can format entire rows, columns, and tables by first selecting the block of cells to be formatted. Next you'll format many cells at one time.

Changing Cell and Column Widths

The first two columns of the multicolumn table should be larger than the other three, so let's change their width to 1-1/2 inches.

➡ Beginning in the cell containing the words "Food Item," click and drag through the selection bar of the first column, and continue dragging through the last cell of the second column.

This will highlight both columns, as shown in Figure 7-87.

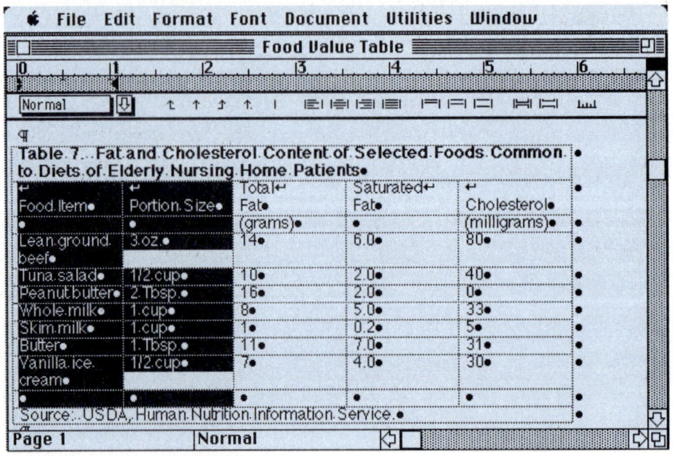

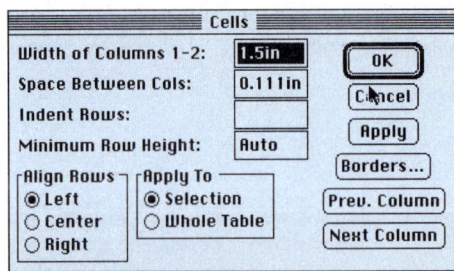

Figure 7-87   Selecting two columns

➡ Choose **Cells** from the Format menu.

➡ In the resulting dialog box, next to Width of Columns, change that box to read 1.5 in, as shown in Figure 7-88. Then click **OK**.

Figure 7-88   Dialog box showing changed width of columns

The result of widening the columns is shown in Figure 7-89.

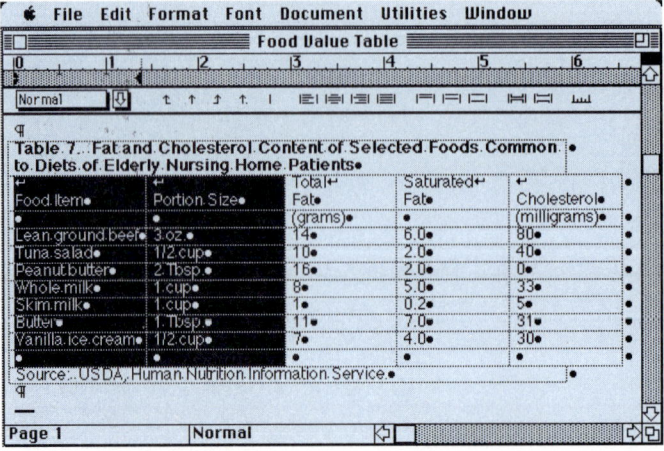

Figure 7-89   The wider first two columns

The changes you made to the column width in the Cells dialog box affected the columns you had selected. If you had selected only one column, one cell, or one or more rows, the change would have affected only whatever you had selected.

The width of these two columns has increased, and the three columns that weren't selected have remained the same. Each of these last three columns needs to be only 1 inch wide, so you can change them in the same manner.

➠ Drag through those three columns to highlight them, and then choose **Cells** from the Format menu.

➠ In the Cells dialog box, change the Width of Columns box to 1 in, and then click **OK**.

Notice that the total width of the 5-column table is now the same width as the 1-column table above it.

⌘-S ➠ Save your work now.

A shortcut for changing cell or column widths is to use the scale icon on the ruler. If you click on this icon while the insertion point is in a table, the scale switches to the *table scale*. This table scale shows "thumbtacks" placed along the ruler where cell margins are. You can drag to change the width of a cell in the row that contains the insertion point. The table scale is shown in Figure 7-90.

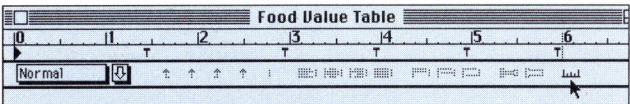

Figure 7-91   The table scale on the ruler

To change the width of an entire column using the table scale, you must first select the column. Otherwise, the change will affect only the row that contains the insertion point.

To toggle back to the normal ruler scale, click on the scale icon. Clicking on the scale icon while the ruler is in the table scale takes you to the page scale, which has brackets to represent where the page margins are. Clicking on the scale icon again returns you to the normal ruler scale. Notice that the alignment and spacing icons on the ruler are dimmed when you are in table scale or page scale. You must be in the normal ruler scale to access these settings.

Changing Cell Alignment

Now that the cells are the size they need to be for the data in the table, the alignment for each cell needs to be set.

The title information in the first 1-cell table should be centered.

⌘-Shift-C ⇒ Click anywhere in the first 1-cell table, and then click on the center-alignment icon on the ruler.

The text in the first column in the 5-column table should be left aligned. If you click in a cell in that column, you'll see that the ruler highlights the left-alignment icon, since left alignment is the default setting.

The text in the next column should be centered; you'll change the format to center alignment.

⇒ Hold down the Option key.

Notice that the pointer changes into a downward pointing arrow.

⇒ With the Option key held down, click on the cell in the second column that contains the words "Portion Size."

The second column becomes highlighted. Option-click selects an entire column.

⌘-Shift-C ⇒ Click on the center-alignment icon on the ruler. See Figure 7-91.

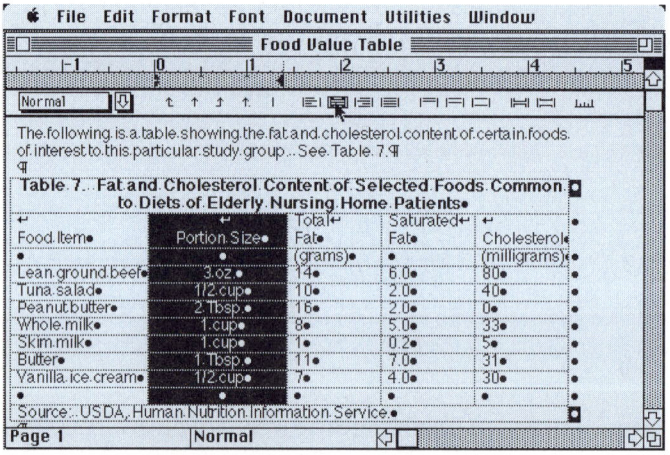

Figure 7-91   Centering the second column

Now the data in the second column is centered within the column.

Notice that the ruler becomes dimmed when more than one cell is selected. This indicates that each cell has different margins or other formats, and only the margins of the first cell selected are displayed.

The headings in the next three columns should be centered also.

⇒ Click and drag through the six heading cells in the last three columns, as shown in Figure 7-92.

⌘-Shift-C ⇒ Click on the center-alignment icon on the ruler.

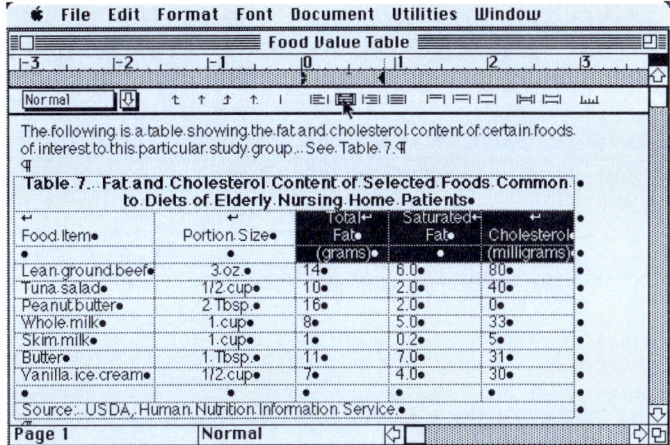

Figure 7-92   Selecting and centering the heading cells

The data in the last three columns of the rest of the table is numeric and should be decimal aligned. To do this you need to set a decimal tab for aligning the numbers.

➠   Click and drag through the last 3 columns in the 5-column table so that just those 3 columns are highlighted.

➠   Click on the decimal tab icon, and then click on the ruler so that the tab marker is approximately in the center of the Total Fat column, as shown in Figure 7-93.

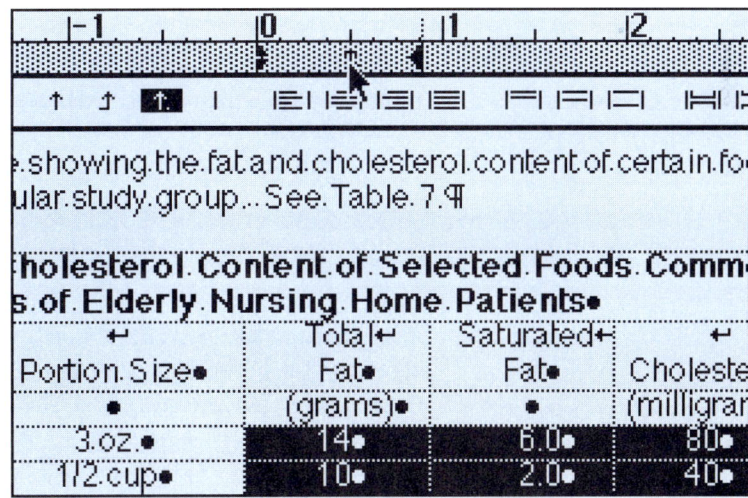

Figure 7-93   Setting a decimal tab for three columns

This will cause a decimal tab to be set at approximately the center of each of the three columns. When a decimal tab stop is placed in a cell, pressing the Tab key to advance to that cell automatically advances you to the decimal tab position within the cell. For any tab stop other than the decimal tab, you must use Option-Tab to move over to the stop.

⌘-S   ➠   Choose **Save** from the File menu.

Now that you've made all these formatting changes, your screen should look like the one shown in Figure 7-94.

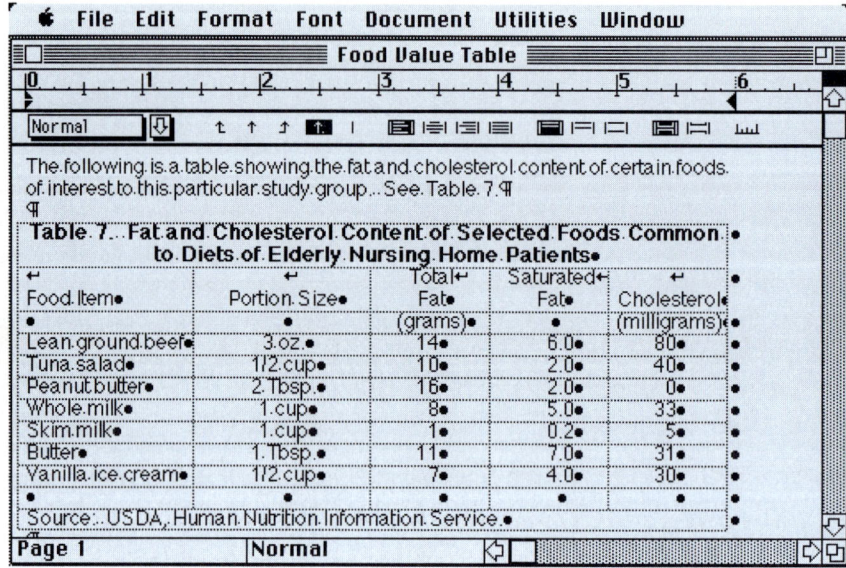

Figure 7-94   The formatted table

Borders and column separators will make this table easier to read. You'll learn how to add them next.

Adding Borders and Column Separators

➡ Select the entire table by holding down the Option key while double-clicking anywhere within the table.

The entire table becomes highlighted.

➡ Choose **Cells** from the Format menu, and click the **Borders** button in that dialog box.

➡ Select the double line from the five icons running down the left side of the dialog box, and then click on the top, bottom, left, and right edges of the schematic diagram to produce a border around the whole table. Your dialog box should look like the one shown in Figure 7-95.

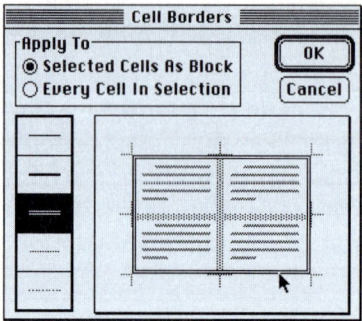

Figure 7-95   Applying the border to the block of cells

➡ Click **OK** in that dialog box, and then click **OK** in the Cells dialog box to get back to the table.

➡ Click anywhere outside the table to deselect it so you can see the border you just created.

Next you'll place a line above and below the column headings to set them off from the data in the columns.

➡ Double-click in the selection bar to the left of the Food Item column heading to select the whole row of column headings. See Figure 7-96.

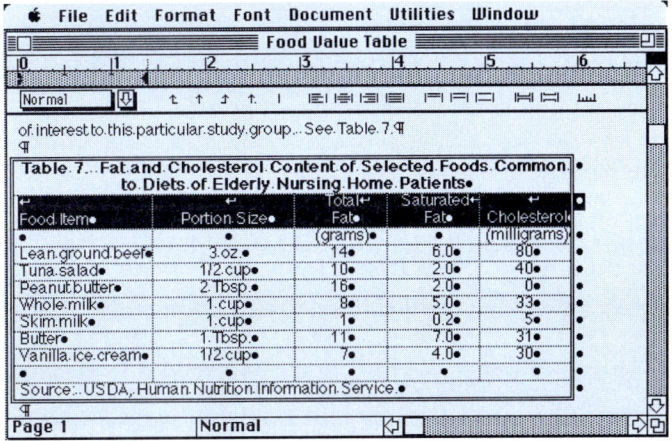

Figure 7-96   Selecting a row using the selection bar

➡ Choose **Cells** from the Format menu, and then click the **Borders** button.

➡ Select the single thin line, and then click at the top and bottom of the borders schematic to place a line above and below the selected block of cells. Leave the double lines on the left and right of the schematic. See Figure 7-97.

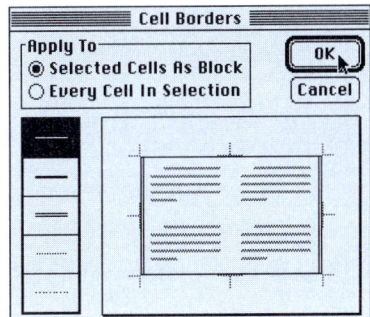

Figure 7-97   Adding borders to the headings

➡ Click **OK** in that dialog box and again in the Cells dialog box.

➡ To place a vertical line between the columns, select the three central columns of the table, as shown in Figure 7-98.

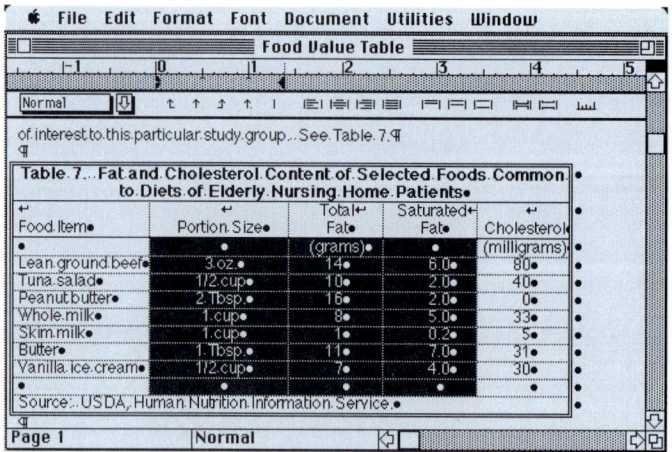

Figure 7-98 Selecting the central columns

➡ Choose **Cells** from the Format menu, and then click the **Borders** button.

➡ In the Cell Borders dialog box, click **Every Cell In Selection**.

This indicates that you want the borders applied to each cell in the selected area and not to the block of cells as a whole.

➡ Click on the left and right sides of the borders schematic diagram to place a line on each side of each cell in the selected block, as shown in Figure 7-99.

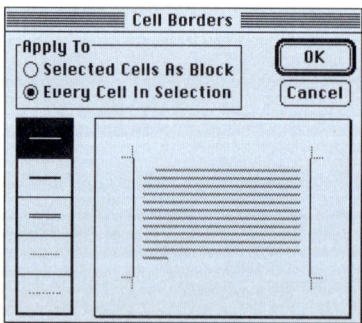

Figure 7-99 Adding column separators to the selected cells

➡ Click **OK** in the Cell Borders dialog box and again in the Cells dialog box.

➡ Finally, select the last cell in the table, the one containing the source information, as shown in Figure 7-100.

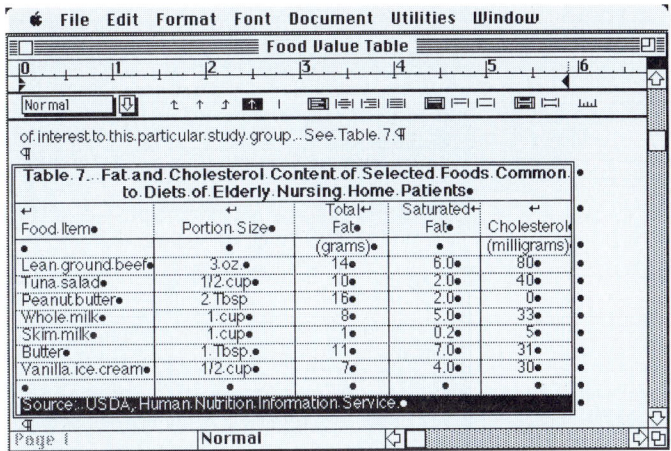

Figure 7-100   Selecting the last cell in the table

➡ Choose **Cells** from the Format menu, and then click the **Borders** button.

➡ Select the single thin line, and then click at the top of the borders schematic to place a line above the selected cell. Leave the double lines on the left, right, and bottom of the schematic. See Figure 7-101.

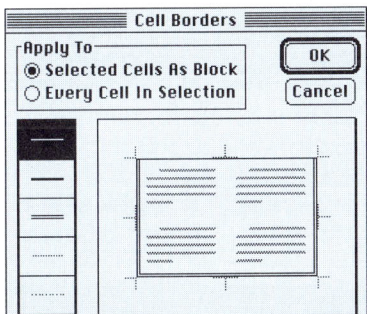

Figure 7-101   Adding borders to the last cell

➡ Click **OK** in that dialog box and again in the Cells dialog box.

⌘-S   ➡ Save your work.

Let's take a look at the table now that you've added the borders and column separators.

⌘-Y   ➡ Choose **Hide ¶** from the Edit menu.

Your table should look like the one in Figure 7-102.

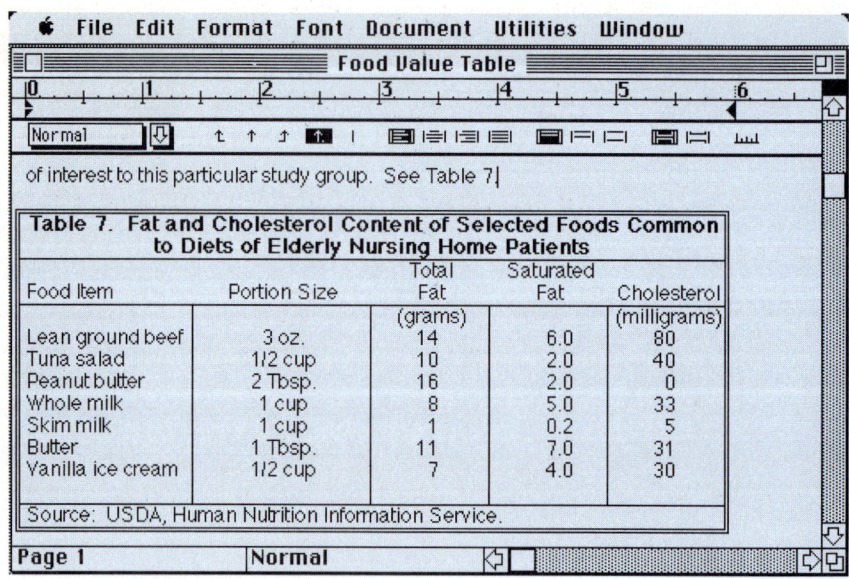

Figure 7-102   The table with the borders and column separators

Adding more white space in the table will keep it from looking so cramped. You'll do that now.

⌘-Y   ➡️   Choose **Show ¶** from the Edit menu.

Changing Spacing Between Rows

The contents of cells can be formatted using most of the commands for character and paragraph formatting. You'll use the Paragraph command to add space to some of the cells and rows.

⌘-M   ➡️   Click anywhere within the title cell of the table, and then choose **Paragraph** from the Format menu.

➡️   In the Paragraph dialog box, in the Spacing section, type **12** in the Before box and in the After box, as shown in Figure 7-103.

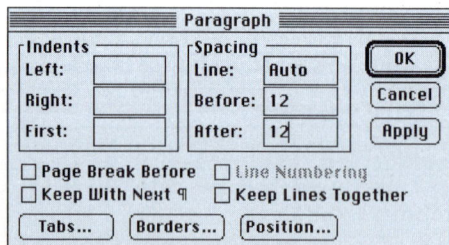

Figure 7-103   Placing a 12-point space before and after the text

➡️   Click **OK**.

The text in that cell now has a 12-point space above and below it.

➡️   Double-click in the selection bar to the left of the cell with the Food Item column heading to select the entire row. See Figure 7-104.

➠   Click on the space-before icon on the ruler.

This places a space above the text in the cells in the selected row, as shown in Figure 7-104.

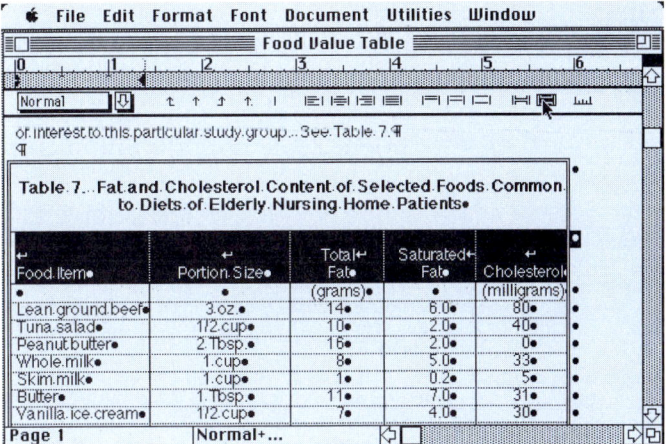

Figure 7-104   Placing a space above the row of column headings

➠   Click in the last cell in the table, the one containing the source information.

⌘-M   ➠   Choose **Paragraph** from the Format menu.

➠   In the Paragraph dialog box, in the Spacing section, type **12** in the Before box and in the After box, as shown in Figure 7-105.

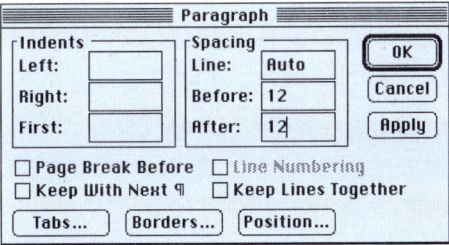

Figure 7-105   The space Before and After settings

➠   Click **OK**.

The text in the source information cell now has a 12-point space above and below it.

⌘-S   ➠   Save your work.

Now the table looks good, except for a few final touches. You'll do some final editing to fine-tune the appearance of the table.

EDITING THE TABLE

The empty row in the 5-column table needs to be deleted. You'll delete that row now.

Deleting Cells

➡ Double-click in the selection bar to the left of the empty cells at the end of the 5-column table to select the entire row.

➡ Choose **Table** from the Edit menu.

The dialog box that results is shown in Figure 7-106.

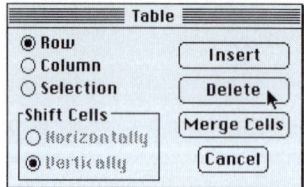

Figure 7-106   Deleting the selection

➡ Click the **Delete** button to delete the selected row.

Merging Cells

The word "(grams)" under the heading in the Total Fat column needs to be centered under both that column and the Saturated Fat column. To do this, you'll merge two cells. When you merge two cells, you create one cell that contains the contents of both.

➡ To merge the cell containing the word "(grams)" with the empty cell to its right, select both cells by dragging through them. See Figure 7-107.

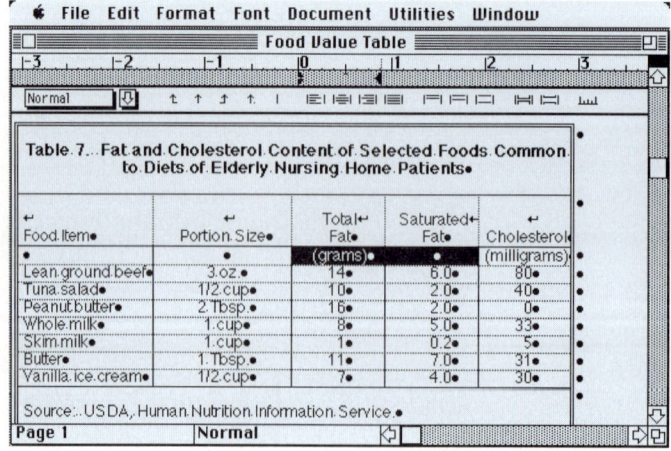

Figure 7-107   Selecting the two cells to be merged

➡ Choose **Table** from the Edit menu, and click **Merge Cells**, as shown in the dialog box in Figure 7-108.

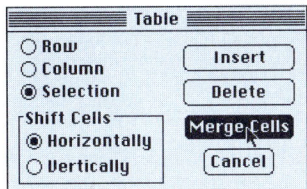

Figure 7-108   Merging the cells

➡ Select and delete the paragraph mark (¶) that was placed after "(grams)" in the merged cells so that the cell consists of only one line.

⌘-S ➡ Save your work.

➡ Scroll to the beginning of the document.

If you look closely at the document you'll see that the double border around the table extends beyond the left of the text in the first two lines of the document. In order for the text in a table to align with the text in the rest of the document, Microsoft Word places the border of the table slightly to the left of the left margin. In this case it will look better if the border aligns with the text in the first two lines. You'll adjust that now.

Adjusting Margins

➡ Hold down the Option key and double-click somewhere in the table.

This selects the whole table.

➡ Click on the scale icon on the ruler to display the table scale.

The ruler will be dimmed, and a "thumbtack" will appear under the 6-inch mark.

➡ Click and drag the left indent marker 1/8 inch to the right, as shown in Figure 7-109.

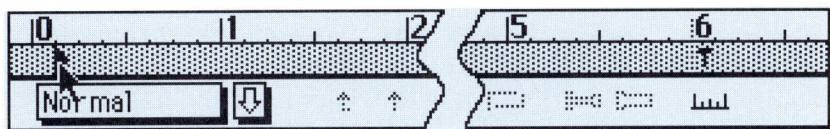

Figure 7-109   Moving the left indent for the table

The entire table will shift 1/8 inch to the right, and the left border of the table will line up with the text in the first two lines of the document.

⌘-R ⌘-Y ➠ Choose **Hide Ruler** from the Format menu and **Hide ¶** from the
Edit menu.

You should be able to see your entire finished document on the screen,
as shown in Figure 7-110.

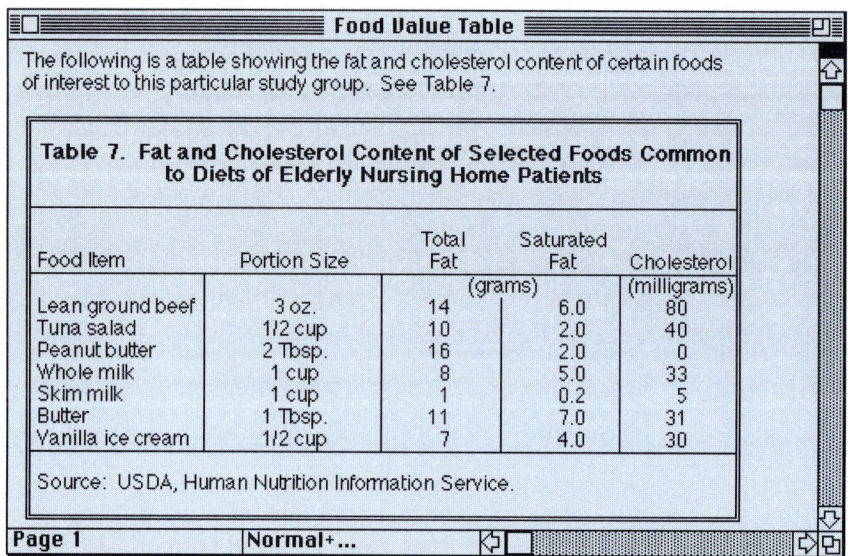

Figure 7-110   The finished Food Value Table

Changing Borders

Placing the borders around the cells can be somewhat tricky. If you did
not get the effect you wanted, you can follow these steps for removing
the borders from the cells or group of cells:

➠ Select the cell or block of cells that you want to remove the borders
from.

➠ Choose **Cells** from the Format menu, and then click the **Borders**
button.

➠ In the Borders dialog box, click on each line in the borders schematic
diagram that you want to remove. This will remove the line from
the schematic.

➠ Click **OK** in the Cell Borders dialog box and again in the Cells dialog
box.

⌘-S ⌘-P ➠ Save your work, and then print your document.

Compare your printed document to the one at the beginning of this
project and make any necessary corrections.

➠ Choose **Quit** from the File menu to exit Microsoft Word. Or, if you
are continuing with the next project right away, choose **Close** from
the File menu.

Project 4: Creating a Newsletter

Desktop publishing is a term heard often today. It refers to using a computer and one or more applications to create quality presentation documents, such as magazines, newsletters, annual reports, and brochures.

There are many page layout programs on the market that help the desktop publisher with design and production. These programs usually specialize in one area of desktop publishing and are used in combination with other programs to pull together the total project.

In this project, you'll learn to use features in Microsoft Word to create a newsletter worthy of the term "desktop publishing." Microsoft Word's page layout properties enable you to design the page without having to incorporate your work into another program. Microsoft Word also allows you to add graphics and documents from other programs to a Microsoft Word document.

This project introduces you to the *section* in Microsoft Word. A section is any part of your document that you designate as separate from another part. You can compare a section to a chapter in a book. A chapter is a part of the whole book, but it is also separate from other chapters.

You can divide a document into one or more sections and then format each section differently from other sections in the same document. You can even have several sections on one page, each formatted differently.

The formatting characteristics applied to a section are controlled through the section's dialog box. If you do not divide your document into sections, Microsoft Word treats the entire document as one section, and the settings in the Section dialog box will apply to the whole document.

You'll create four sections in a document in this project, and each section will be formatted differently. You'll also learn how to adjust margins using the Print Preview margins tool, and you'll be introduced to *Page View*.

A finished version of the *Traveling Times* newsletter is shown on the next page in Figure 7-111, and a printed version of the unformatted document that is used in this project is shown in Figure 7-112 on the page after that.

February Issue, Volume 14

MOUNTAIN RACING

On any given Saturday night from April to October, the roar of car engines can be heard throughout the Peachtown area of Murley, North Carolina.

Peachtown Raceway, located on old 46 just west of Peachtown, is a dirt track that features five classes of race cars from the Enduro class (the least expensive cars) to the Sportsman class (some of these cars range up to $30,000!).

Racers come from many surrounding areas of North Carolina, Georgia, and Tennessee. Although the monetary prizes are not very large, the fun and excitement for these drivers and their families are obvious.

All evening in the pits there is an air of frivolity as the drivers banter back and forth while waiting for their turn on the track. The more participants there are in each class, the more competition, challenge, and excitement. Amazingly, even on a cold or drizzly night the stands are full of spectators urging on their particular hero, and they don't even seem to mind when they are splattered with flying chunks of mud.

Attending Peachtown Raceway is always a fun evening for all, participants or spectators, and a good way to entertain kids. Be sure to put this on your list of things to do when visiting the mountains of western North Carolina.

Traveling Times

Bringing the world to you!

THE CAYMANS

On my recent travels to the island of Grand Cayman I survived an interesting experience. While I slept comfortably in an exclusive resort hotel, an incredible storm was tearing the island apart. A "norwester," as the islanders call it, had hit the main town of Georgetown and had done extensive damage. The public beach was completely washed away, and debris was scattered everywhere. Several shops in town were underwater, and a couple of homes had been transported from their original dwelling spots to new locations.

Grand Cayman is the largest of three islands just south of Cuba. Originally discovered by Christopher Columbus on his fourth voyage to North America, it was eventually settled by pirates and escaped slaves. In a treaty with Spain in 1670, the islands were transferred to England, and they have remained a British Crown Colony.

The island was an important food source for many generations, since it was inhabited with thousands of turtles and marine crocodiles called Caymanas (which is where the islands got their name). After depleting the turtle population over the years, the islanders now have a large turtle farm where they hope to manage the species and prevent it from becoming extinct. Turtle soup and other specialty dishes are still favorites on the island and are served in most restaurants. Unfortunately, most of the turtles at the farm escaped during the storm.

Another interesting aspect of the Caymans is the blending of races into a comfortable, integrated society. Being from different parts of the world and having several different ethnic backgrounds, these people have created their own unique culture. There is a native quality from Jamaica and many other Caribbean islands, along with an aristocratic air from the English

and Welsh influences. The language of the Caymans is English, but they do have their own melodic version of it that they use in everyday conversation with each other. It is a joy to hear, even when you have no idea what they are talking about.

The Cayman Islands are a paradise for divers and beachcombers. Three sides of Grand Cayman are surrounded by a reef that is perfect for snorkeling, while the fourth side has miles of white sand on its shoreline and is appropriately named Seven Mile Beach. There are also hundreds of shipwrecks within minutes of shore, where divers can search for buried treasure to their heart's content.

At the north end of the island is a tiny town called Hell. You can imagine the remarks that come from that place! At least I can say I made it to Hell and back!

—M. Swan

Figure 7-111   Final output of Project 4

On any given Saturday night from April to October, the roar of car engines can be heard throughout the Peachtown area of Murley, North Carolina.

Peachtown Raceway, located on old 46 just west of Peachtown, is a dirt track that features five classes of race cars from the Enduro class (the least expensive cars) to the Sportsman class (some of these cars range up to $30,000!).

Racers come from many surrounding areas of North Carolina, Georgia, and Tennessee. Although the monetary prizes are not very large, the fun and excitement for these drivers and their families are obvious.

All evening in the pits there is an air of frivolity as the drivers banter back and forth while waiting for their turn on the track. The more participants there are in each class, the more competition, challenge, and excitement. Amazingly, even on a cold or drizzly night the stands are full of spectators urging on their particular hero, and they don't even seem to mind when they are splattered with flying chunks of mud.

Attending Peachtown Raceway is always a fun evening for all, participants or spectators, and a good way to entertain kids. Be sure to put this on your list of things to do when visiting the mountains of western North Carolina.

On my recent travels to the island of Grand Cayman I survived an interesting experience. While I slept comfortably in an exclusive resort hotel, an incredible storm was tearing the island apart. A "norwester," as the islanders call it, had hit the main town of Georgetown and had done extensive damage. The public beach was completely washed away, and debris was scattered everywhere. Several shops in town were underwater, and a couple of homes had been transported from their original dwelling spots to new locations.

Grand Cayman is the largest of three islands just south of Cuba. Originally discovered by Christopher Columbus on his fourth voyage to North America, it was eventually settled by pirates and escaped slaves. In a treaty with Spain in 1670, the islands were transferred to England, and they have remained a British Crown Colony.

The island was an important food source for many generations, since it was inhabited with thousands of turtles and marine crocodiles called Caymanas (which is where the islands got their name). After depleting the turtle population over the years, the islanders now have a large turtle farm where they hope to manage the species and prevent it from becoming extinct. Turtle soup and other specialty dishes are still favorites on the island and are served in most restaurants. Unfortunately, most of the turtles at the farm escaped during the storm.

Another interesting aspect of the Caymans is the blending of races into a comfortable, integrated society. Being from different parts of the world and having several different ethnic backgrounds, these people have created their own unique culture. There is a native quality from Jamaica and many other Caribbean islands, along with an aristocratic air from the English and Welsh influences. The language of the Caymans is English, but they do have their own melodic version of it that they use in everyday conversation with each other. It is a joy to hear, even when you have no idea what they are talking about.

The Cayman Islands are a paradise for divers and beachcombers. Three sides of Grand Cayman are surrounded by a reef that is perfect for snorkeling, while the fourth side has miles of white sand on its shoreline and is appropriately named Seven Mile Beach. There are also hundreds of shipwrecks within minutes of shore, where divers can search for buried treasure to their heart's content.

At the north end of the island is a tiny town called Hell. You can imagine the remarks that come from that place! At least I can say I made it to Hell and back!

—**M. Swan**

Figure 7-112   Unformatted Traveling Times newsletter

Since the object of this project is not to focus on your typing skills, an unformatted document is used. This document is supplied on the *Macintosh Journey Projects* disk, which accompanies this book. Artwork for the newsletter is also supplied on the same disk.

RETRIEVING THE UNFORMATTED DOCUMENT

Traveling Times Unformatted

There are a couple of ways to begin this project. The most straightforward way is to locate the document entitled "Traveling Times Unformatted" and double-click on its icon. This will start Microsoft Word and open that document.

Another way is to double-click on the Microsoft Word icon to launch the application, and then choose **Open** from the File menu. Locate the Traveling Times Unformatted document (click the **Drive** button if necessary), and double-click on it to open it.

⌘-O   If you did not quit Microsoft Word after the last project, choose **Open** from the File menu and double-click on Traveling Times Unformatted to open it.

Whichever of the above methods you chose, the document Traveling Times Unformatted should be on your screen.

Since you do not want to alter the original document, the first thing you need to do is make a copy of this document to work with.

➧ Choose **Save As** from the File menu and change the document's name to **Traveling Times**. Verify that you are saving this document on your data disk, and then click **Save**. See Figure 7-113.

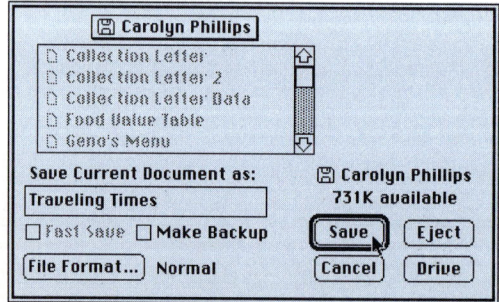

Figure 7-113   Saving the document as Traveling Times

FORMATTING THE DOCUMENT

A couple of formatting changes need to be made to this document before you divide it into sections.

⌘-R   ⌘-Y   ➡   Choose **Show Ruler** from the Format menu and **Show ¶** from the Edit menu.

➡   Select the entire document by holding down the Command key and clicking anywhere in the selection bar of the document, as shown in Figure 7-114.

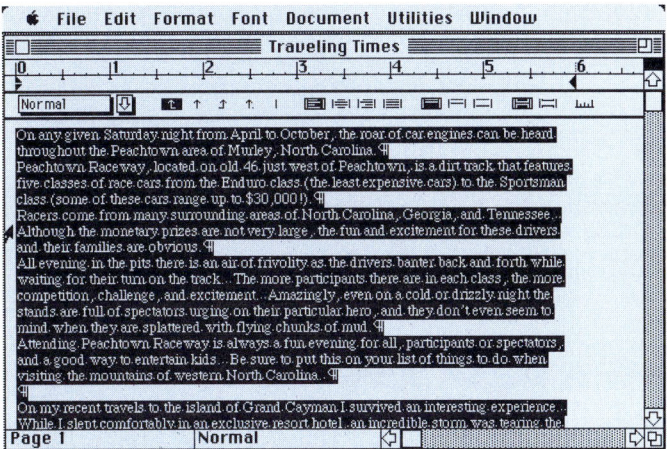

Figure 7-114   Selecting the entire document

➡   With the document selected, move the first-line indent marker on the ruler (the top triangle) to the 1/4-inch mark on the ruler to indent the first line of each paragraph.

⌘-Shift-J   ➡   Click on the justified-alignment icon on the ruler to justify the text between the margins. See Figure 7-115.

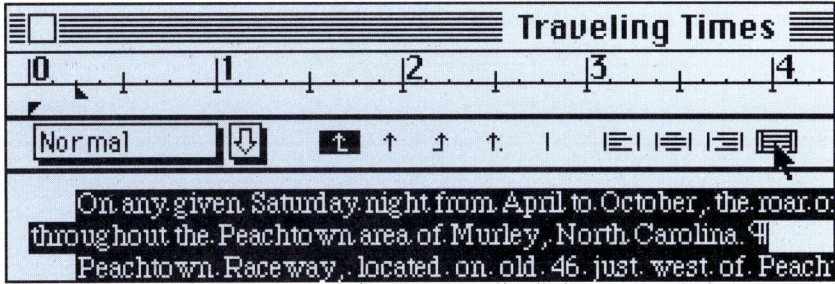

Figure 7-115   The ruler with 1/4 inch first-line indent

⌘-Shift-R   ➡   Scroll down to the last line in the document, "—M. Swan", and click anywhere in that line. Right-align that paragraph by clicking on the right-alignment icon on the ruler.

➡   Insert a blank line at the top of the document, and click to set the insertion point in that line.

⌘-Shift-B   ⌘-Shift-C   ➡   Choose **Bold** from the Format menu, and then type **MOUNTAIN RACING** in all caps. Click on the center-alignment icon on the ruler to center that line.

➡ Scroll to the middle of the document, where a Return marker separates the two newsletter articles.

➡ Insert another blank line in front of the line beginning with the words "On my recent travels" and click in that new line to set the insertion point.

⌘-Shift-B   ⌘-Shift-C   ➡ Choose **Bold** from the Format menu, and then type **THE CAYMANS** in all caps. Center it using the center-alignment icon on the ruler.

⌘-S   ➡ Save these changes to your document.

During the rest of the instructions for this project, you won't be prompted to save your work. That doesn't mean you shouldn't do so, it just means you should be thinking of that step on your own by now.

Now let's divide this document into four sections.

CREATING A NEW SECTION

➡ To set the insertion point, click in front of the Return marker separating the two articles.

➡ Hold down the Command key and press the Enter key (on the numeric key pad) to insert a *section break marker*.

Be careful to press the Enter key just once. If you keep holding it down, a series of section breaks will be created. If you had a heavy hand on this key, select the extra section markers by dragging through them, and then press Backspace to delete them.

Your screen should have a double dotted line running across it. This is the section break marker. See Figure 7-116.

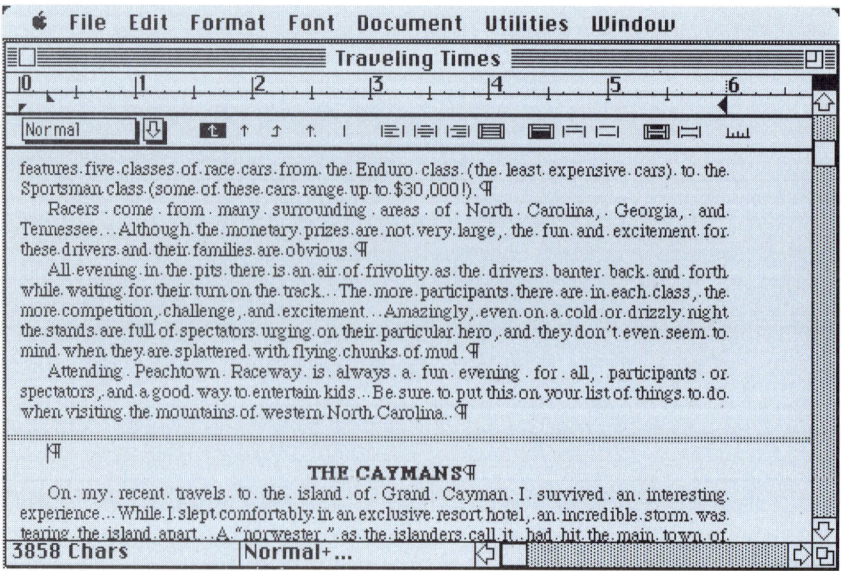

Figure 7-116   The section break marker

⟹ To create the next section, click to the left of the title line, "THE CAYMANS," that you typed a few steps back.

The insertion point should be to the left of the "T" in that line.

⟹ Use the Command-Enter key sequence to insert a section marker at that point, as shown in Figure 7-117.

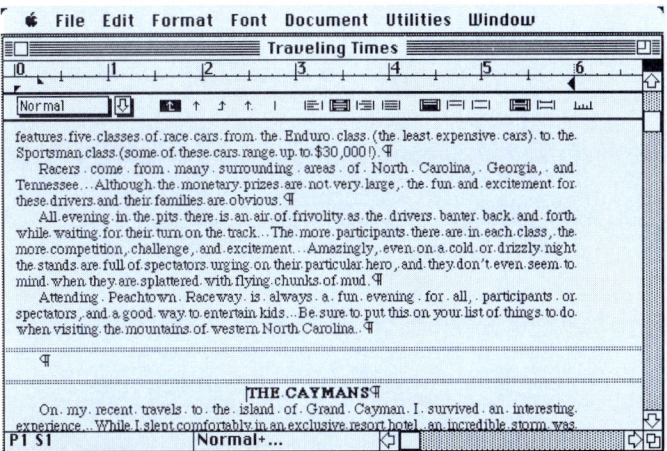

Figure 7-117 Inserting the second section break

Now let's create the last section at the end of the document.

⟹ Scroll to the end of the document and click after the last line in the document, "—M. Swan".

The insertion point should be to the right of the "n" in that line, at the end of "Swan".

⟹ Use the Command-Enter key sequence to insert a section marker there, as shown in Figure 7-118.

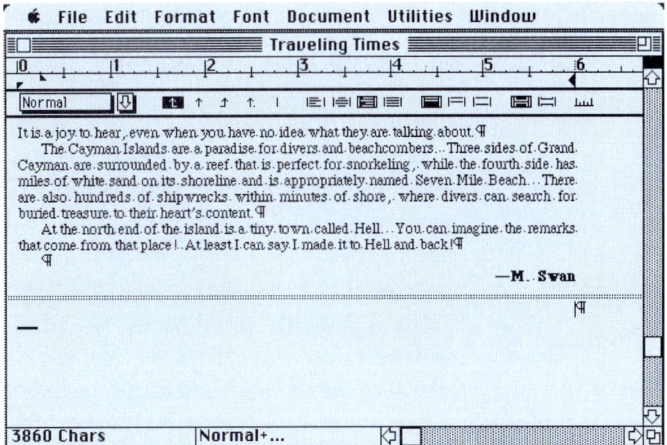

Figure 7-118 Inserting the third section break

Now the document is divided into four sections. The first section will be formatted in a two-column layout.

➡   Click anywhere in the first section, above the double lines.

This tells Microsoft Word which section you want to apply the changes to.

➡   Choose **Section** from the Format menu.

The resulting dialog box is shown in Figure 7-119.

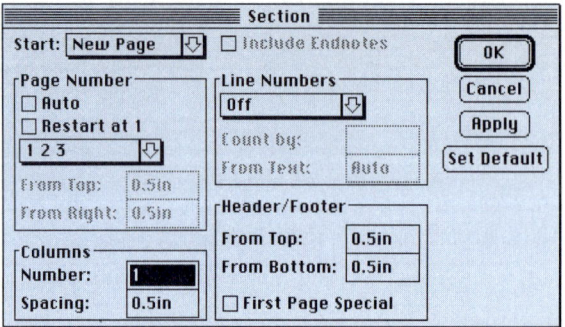

Figure 7-119   The Section dialog box

Since the options in this dialog box can be applied to your whole document if it consists of only one section (and most documents do consist of only one section), you need to understand what some of these options can do.

The Start portion of this dialog box consists of a drop-down list from which you choose where you'd like the section to start. The default is New Page, which causes the text in a section to begin on a new page. Other options are No Break, New Column, Even Page, and Odd Page. You'll be using the New Page and No Break options in your newsletter.

The Page Number portion allows you to number the pages of the section (or document) automatically. The drop-down list in this field gives you several number formats to choose from. To number pages from the Section dialog box, click **Auto**. The From Top and From Right boxes become activated, and the page number is positioned on the page using those fields. The newsletter you are creating in this project will not have page numbers.

In the Columns portion of the dialog box, Number indicates the number of columns that section should contain, and the Spacing box tells how much space should be between columns. The documents you've worked with in this chapter have all consisted of one column. In this project you'll combine two-column, one-column, and three-column layouts all on one page.

The Header/Footer portion allows you to change the vertical position of the headers and footers. (Headers and footers will be discussed in more detail later in this project.) The First Page Special option enables you to create a header and footer for the first page of the section (or document) that can be different from the standard header and footer. This is especially useful when you are creating a document that requires a title page, since the header and page number should not print on the title page. You would create a blank First Page Special header and footer and put the page number and other heading data in the standard header or footer, which applies to each subsequent page in a section.

Now you'll use the Columns portion in this dialog box to change the first section in the document to two-column format.

CHANGING THE NUMBER OF COLUMNS

➡ Change the number of columns to **2** in the Section dialog box, as shown in Figure 7-120, and then click **OK**.

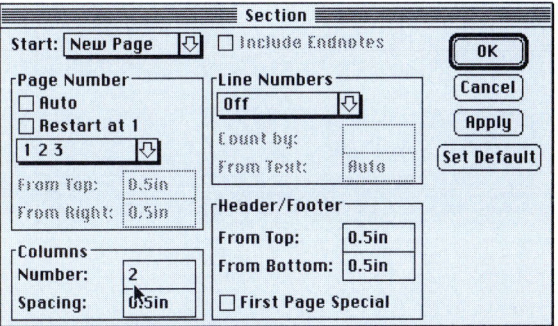

Figure 7-120   Changing the number of columns to 2

Your text is now shown in one column running down the left side of the screen. In *Galley View*, which is Microsoft Word's regular view, you can't view both columns at once, but *Page View* and *Print Preview* allow you to view the columns arranged next to one another on the page. After you set up the layout of your other three sections you'll use Page View and Print Preview to view the document.

➡ Scroll down to the second section of the document, the one that consists of one Return marker with a section break both above and below it.

➡ Click in the line between the section markers, and then choose **Section** from the Format menu.

➡ In that dialog box, click on the arrow to the right of New Page in the Start portion, and drag down to select **No Break**, as shown in Figure 7-121. Then click **OK** or press Return.

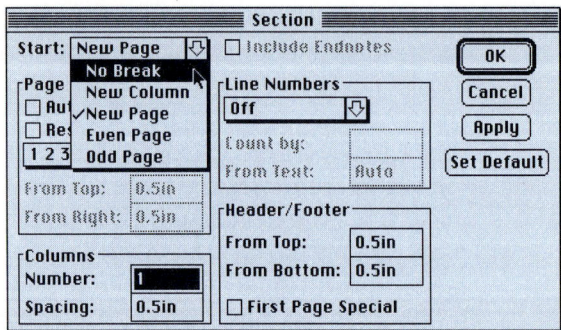

Figure 7-121   Changing the start to No Break

The No Break option tells Microsoft Word that this section will start where the previous section left off and will not begin on a new page or a new column.

Now let's work with the layout of the third section.

➠   Click on the same line that contains the title "THE CAYMANS", and choose **Section** from the Format menu.

➠   In the Section dialog box, change the Start to **No Break**, the number of columns to **3**, and the Spacing to **.25 in** as shown in Figure 7-122. Then click **OK**.

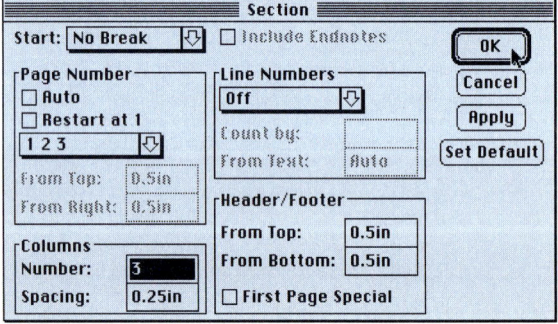

Figure 7-122   Settings for the three-column section

Now this section has a narrow column of text going down the left side of the page.

The fourth section of the document was created so that Microsoft Word will balance the length of the text in the columns above it. Inserting a section that has the No Break format at the end of a document causes Microsoft Word to adjust the lengths of the columns in the section that precedes it until they are approximately equal.

⇒ Scroll to the last section in the document, and click on the line below the last section marker in the document.

⇒ Choose **Section** from the Format menu, and in the Section dialog box change the Start to **No Break**. Click **OK**.

ADDING AND FORMATTING A GRAPHIC

Now you'll paste the Traveling Times logo into the newsletter.

On the *Projects* disk is a document called "Traveling Times Logo."

⌘-O ⇒ Choose **Open** from the File menu, and double-click on **Traveling Times Logo**.

⌘-C ⇒ Click on the graphic to select it, and then choose **Copy** from the Edit menu to copy it to the Clipboard.

⌘-W ⇒ Close that document by clicking in its close box.

⌘-V ⇒ Be sure the insertion point is in the blank line in the second section of the document. Choose **Paste** from the Edit menu to paste the graphic into that section.

Next you'll make some formatting changes to this section.

⇒ Select the lines between the section marks, but do not include the section marks. See Figure 7-123.

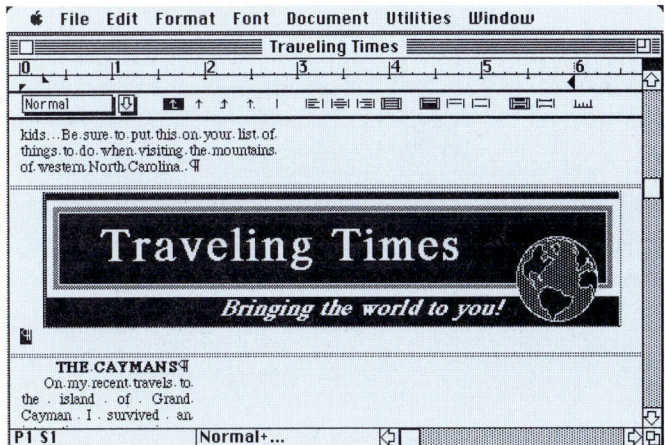

Figure 7-123   Selecting the area between section marks

⇒ On the ruler, move the first-line indent marker back to 0.

⌘-Shift-C ⇒ Drag the right indent marker to the 6-1/2-inch mark, and then click on the center-alignment icon on the ruler to center that section. See Figure 7-124.

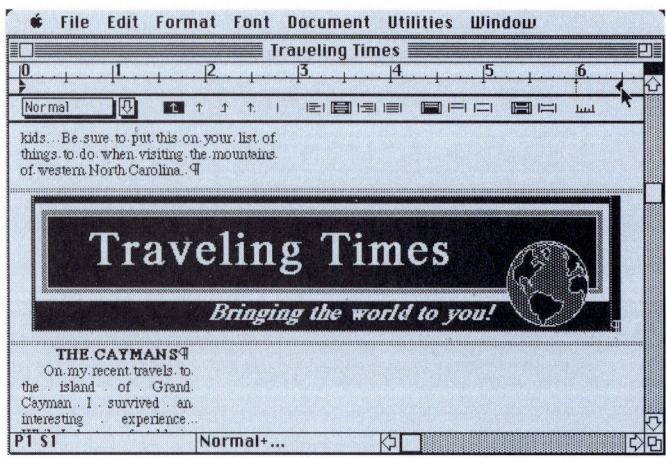

Figure 7-124   Formatting the second section with the ruler

Now you'll put a border around this logo and add some space above and below it.

⌘-M   ➡ Choose **Paragraph** from the Format menu, and click the **Borders** button in the Paragraph dialog box.

➡ In the Paragraph Borders dialog box select the double line, and then click at the top and bottom of the schematic diagram to place a double line above and below the selected graphic, as shown in Figure 7-125.

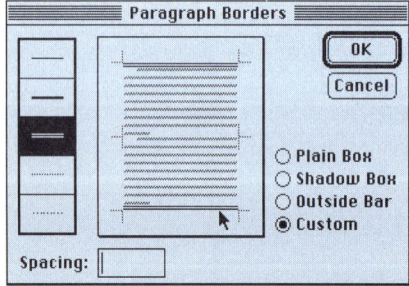

Figure 7-125   Placing a double line above and below the graphic

➡ Click **OK** in the Paragraph Borders dialog box.

That will take you back to the Paragraph dialog box. You'll change the paragraph spacing in the Paragraph dialog box.

In the Paragraph dialog box, you'll tell Microsoft Word to place a 6-point space above and below the selected paragraph or, in this case, the selected graphic. This will place a small space above and below the logo to set it off slightly from the text.

Setting the spacing from the Paragraph dialog box is similar to using the paragraph-spacing icons on the ruler, like you did in Project 1. However, using this option in the Paragraph dialog box allows you to specify the exact amount of space you want placed before or after the selected paragraph. To remove spacing before or after a paragraph in this dialog box, type **0** in the appropriate field.

➡ In the Spacing portion of the Paragraph dialog box, click in the box next to Before and type **6**. Press the Tab key to move to the box next to After, and also type **6** there, as shown in Figure 7-126. Then click **OK**.

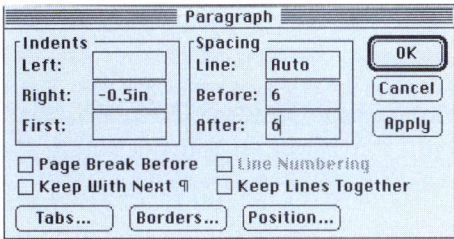

Figure 7-126   Changing the Before and After paragraph spacing

When you return to your document, your logo will have a double line and a 6-point space above and below it, as shown in Figure 7-127.

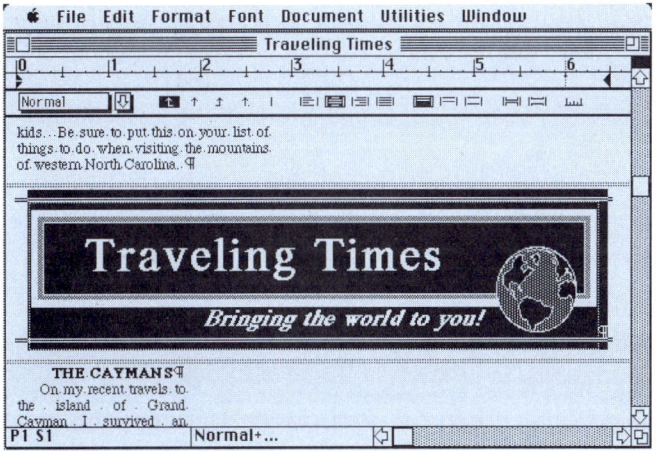

Figure 7-127   The logo with the borders and spaces

CREATING A HEADER

Next you'll create a header for the newsletter.

A *header* is text and/or graphics that appear at the top of every page, above the body of the document. A *footer* can also be text and/or graphics, but it appears at the bottom of every page, beneath the body of the document.

In Project 1 of this chapter you created a letterhead at the top of the memorandum, but it was actually placed in the document itself and printed only on the page on which you had typed it. It was done in this way so that it would print on the first page of the memorandum only.

In this project you'll make use of the header window. You'll also learn about the footer window since, except for their placement on the printed page, they are very similar. You won't use a footer in this project, but all that you'll learn about headers can be applied to footers as well.

A header or footer prints on every page of a document, unless the document has multiple sections and each of those sections has a header or footer. The First Page Special header was mentioned earlier in reference to the Section dialog box. For additional information on headers and footers see *Reference to Microsoft Word*.

The newsletter you are creating in this project consists of only one printed page, yet the instructions for creating headers are just as applicable for multipage documents.

➡ Scroll to the beginning of the newsletter, and click anywhere in the first section of the document.

Since each section can have a separate header and footer, you must indicate the section for which you want the header opened. If you recall from when you were setting up each section, the first section of this document is the only one that will begin on a new page. Therefore, this is the only section that will need a header.

➡ Choose **Open Header** from the Document menu.

An open window entitled "Traveling Times:Header (S1)" appears at the bottom of the screen. See Figure 7-128.

"(S1)" in your header title indicates the section this header applies to.

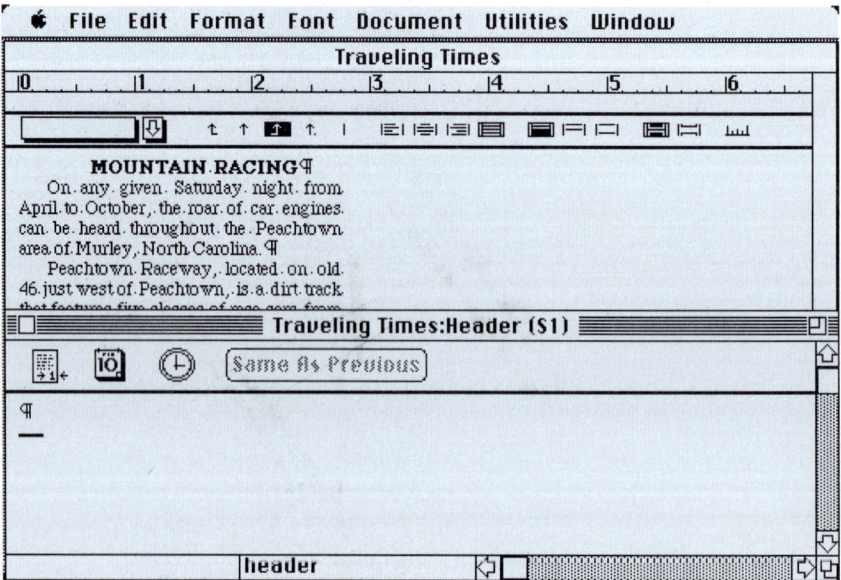

Figure 7-128   The header window

Using the Header Window Icons

Notice the three icons below the title bar in the left corner of the header window shown in Figure 7-128.

 The leftmost icon is the page numbering icon. If you click on that icon, it places a page number in the window at the insertion point. Using this icon tells Microsoft Word to place the correct page number in every page of the document, much as it does when you place a page number in a document while in Print Preview, like you did in Project 1 of this chapter. However, using this icon in a header or a footer allows you to adorn the page number with dashes on either side, the word "Page" in front of the number, or any special formatting such as font and size, which you cannot do with the Print Preview method.

 The middle icon is the automatic date icon. It places the current date at the insertion point in the header or footer. This date changes to the current date whenever you open or print the document. The date comes from the computer's system clock, the settings of which you can check or change in the Control Panel from the Apple menu.

 The rightmost icon is the automatic time icon. It works like the date icon, except that it places the current time at the insertion point in the header or footer. It also changes to the current time when the document is opened or printed. The time comes from the computer's system clock as well.

These icons are also found in the footer window and work in the same manner.

If you experimented with the date, time, or page number, make sure you have deleted them from the header window. To delete any of these entries, select the item and press the Backspace key.

You format the header with a ruler in the same way that you format the document. The header window uses a separate ruler from the one that is used for the rest of the document, however. You'll use the header's ruler to format your header.

⌘-R ➠ Choose **Show Ruler** from the Format menu.

⌘-Shift-B ➠ Choose **Bold** from the Format menu, and then type **February Issue, Volume 14** in the header window, as shown in Figure 7-129.

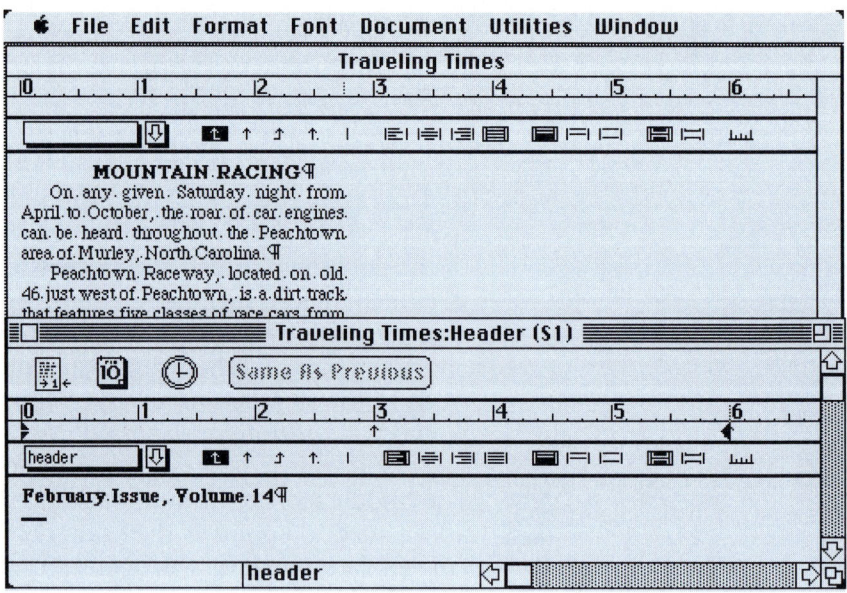

Figure 7-129   Typing text in the header window

⌘ -Shift-R ⊨≣| ➡ Click on the right alignment icon on the ruler in the header window
                     to align the text with the right margin of the page.

Now you'll place a border beneath the text in the header and a space
beneath the header line.

➡ Double-click in the top portion of the ruler in the header window,
   next to one of the numbers on the ruler.

This is a shortcut to choosing **Paragraph** from the Format menu. It
brings up the Paragraph dialog box.

➡ Click the **Borders** button in the Paragraph dialog box.

➡ In the Paragraph Borders dialog box select the thick single line, and
   then click in the bottom of the diagram to place a thick line below
   the paragraph, as shown in Figure 7-130.

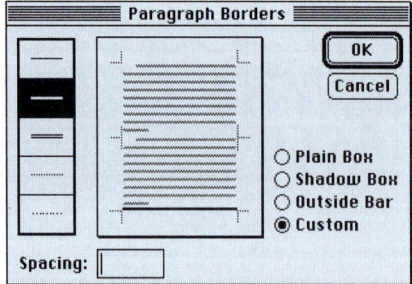

Figure 7-130   The Paragraph Borders dialog box

➡ Click **OK** to return to the Paragraph dialog box.

➡ In the Paragraph dialog box, type **12** in the box to the right of After
   in the Spacing section, as shown in Figure 7-131. Then click **OK**.

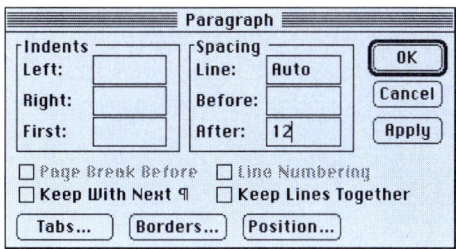

Figure 7-131 The space-after setting

Your header should look like the one shown in Figure 7-132.

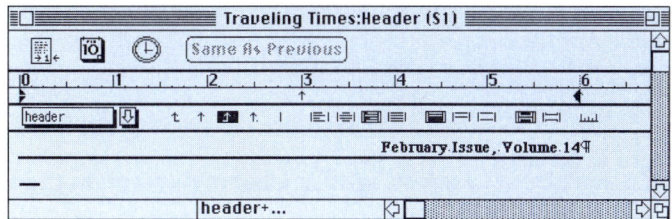

Figure 7-132 The completed header

➠ Once you have established that your header is correct, click in the close box of the header window to close the window.

The contents of the header and footer are visible only in Print Preview or Page View or when the document is actually printed.

You're probably curious to see the effects of all the formatting changes you've made to your document. You'll do that now using Print Preview.

Have you saved your work lately?

ADJUSTING THE MARGINS

⌘-I ➠ Choose **Print Preview** from the File menu.

It looks good, except that the newsletter has gone to a second page. You'll adjust that now.

The margins icon in Print Preview allows you to manually adjust the margins and then immediately see the results of the change. You'll adjust the margins until the entire document fits on one page.

 ➠ Click on the second icon down the left side of the screen. This is the margins icon.

When you do, dotted margin lines appear on the right-hand page.

➠ Click on the first page to select it. The margin markers appear there.

Now you'll adjust the margins by dragging the margin markers to different locations.

➠ Click on the bottom left handle of the margin marker that runs up the left side of the page, as shown in Figure 7-133.

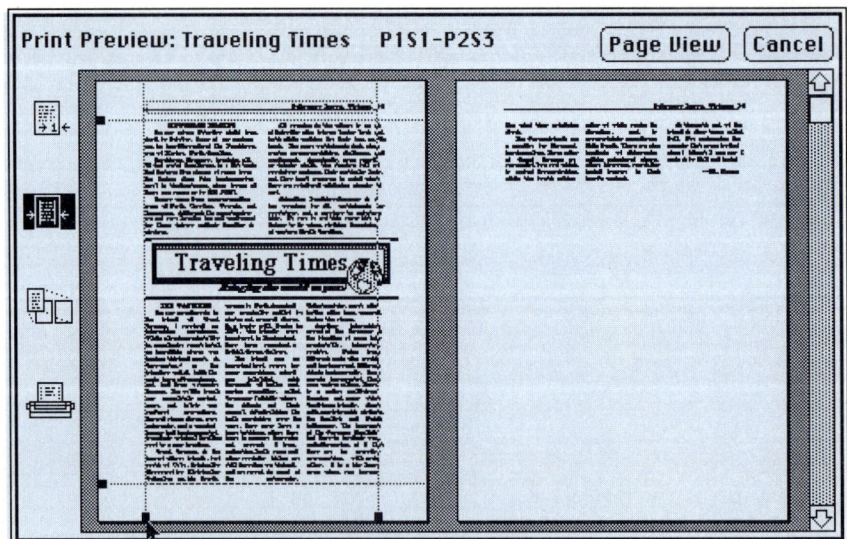

Figure 7-133   Clicking on the margin marker handle

➡ Hold down the mouse button and drag to the left so that the number showing at the top of the page, after the words "Print Preview: Traveling Times," changes to 0.75 in, as shown in Figure 7-134. Release the mouse button.

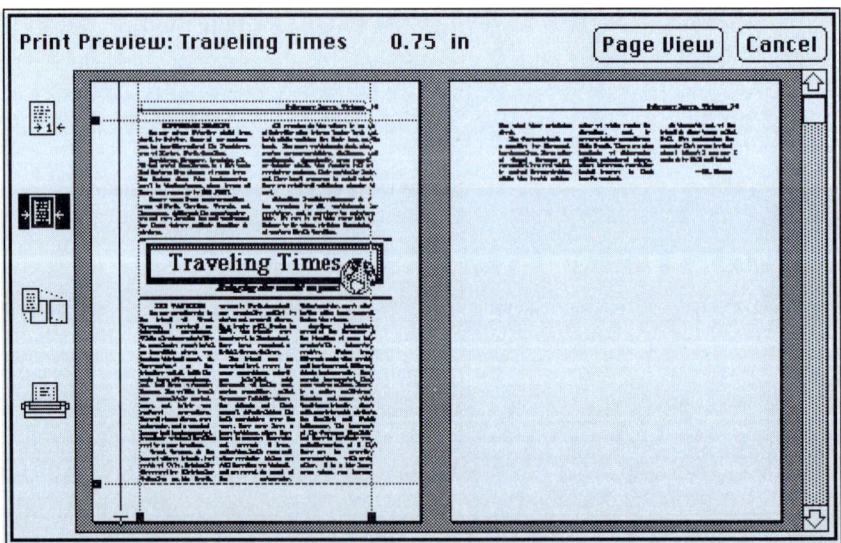

Figure 7-134   Changing the left margin

➡ Do the same with the right margin marker, dragging it so the margin width changes to 0.75 in for that side also.

 ➡ Click on the margins icon (or double-click on the page) to tell Microsoft Word to recalculate the margins and place this text between the new margins.

Notice how adjusting the margins made more text fit on the first page, as shown in Figure 7-135.

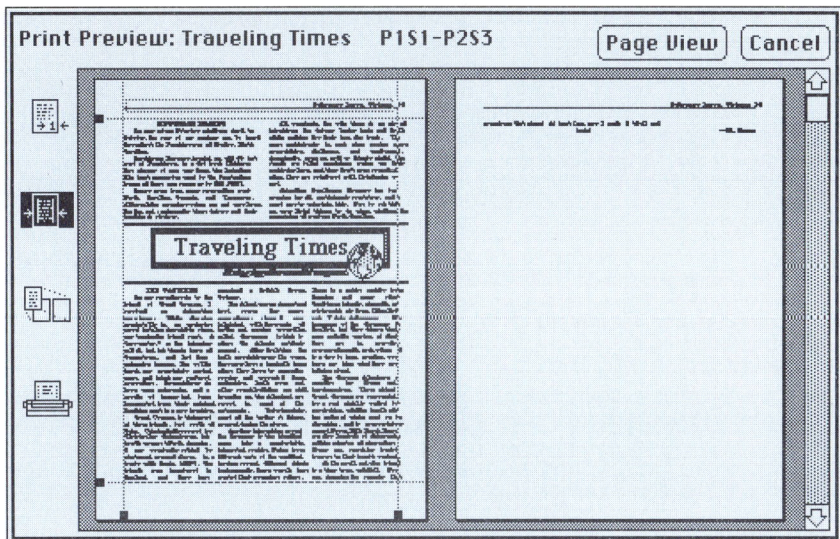

Figure 7-135   Adjusting margins to fit the text

Now let's adjust the top and bottom margins.

➠   Drag the handle for the top margin, which is at the top left of the page, so that the new dimension is 0.75 in.

➠   Drag the handle for the bottom margin, which is at the bottom left of the page, so that the new dimension is 0.50 in.

 ➠   Click on the margins icon to see the effects of these changes.

Your entire document should fit on one page now, like the one shown in Figure 7-136. If it doesn't, keep adjusting the margins in this manner until all the text fits on one page and the page on the right side in Print Preview is completely blank.

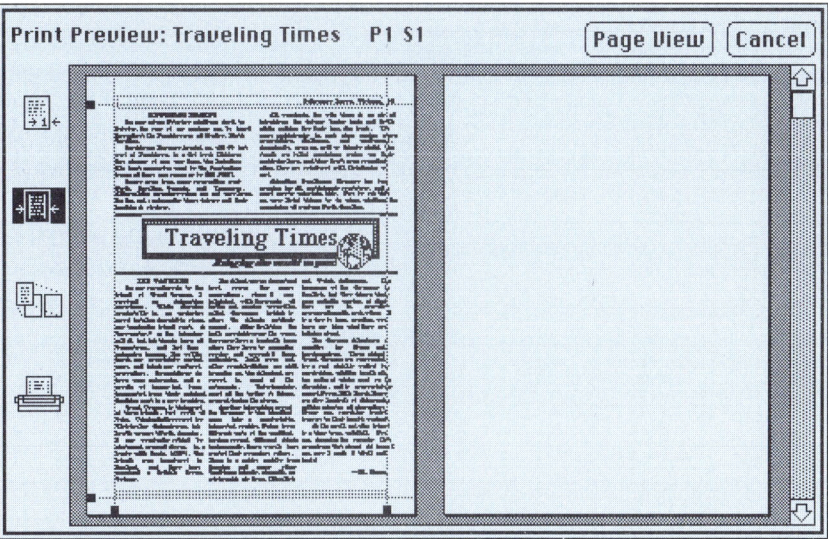

Figure 7-136   The document on one page

➠ Click **Cancel** when you are finished.

Although Print Preview offers limited document changes, it can help you determine how a document will look when it is printed.

When you use Page View you can see a full-scale version of your document showing exactly how it will look when printed. And, unlike in Print Preview, you can edit and format text while in this view.

⌘-Y   ⌘-B   ➠ Choose **Hide ¶** from the Edit menu, and then choose **Page View** from the Document menu.

➠ Scroll through your document to see a full-size view of how it will look when printed.

⌘-B   ➠ When you are finished, choose **Page View** again from the Document menu.

Galley View is not located on any menu. If you are in Page View, a checkmark will be to the left of Page View in the Document menu. To get back to Galley View, choose **Page View** again, which removes the checkmark beside Page View and returns you to Galley View.

⌘-S/⌘-P   ➠ Save and print the completed newsletter.

Compare it to the finished newsletter at the beginning of the project, and use the procedures that you learned in this project if changes are needed to make it resemble the sample newsletter.

⌘-Q   ➠ When you are finished, choose **Quit** from the File menu, or close the newsletter document and choose **New** from the File menu to begin the next project.

Project 5: Creating Merge Documents

This project introduces you to one of the best time-saving features of Microsoft Word—*print merge*. You'll create a print merge main document and data document that allow you to create multiple customized letters without having to type each one as a separate letter.

Figure 7-137 on the following page shows the four collection letters you will create in this project. As you create the different components of this print merge project, you'll be shown the final document at that point in the project.

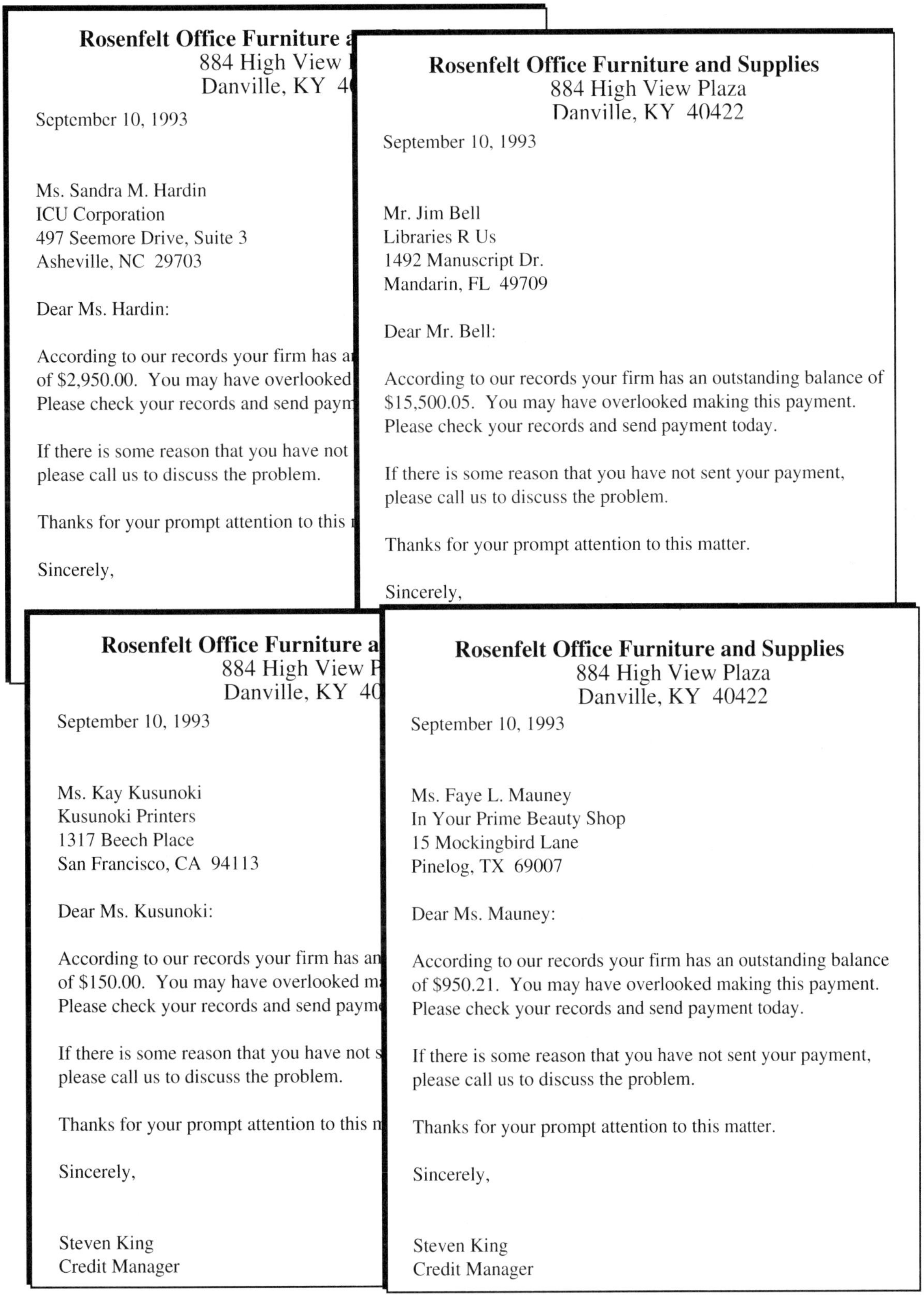

Rosenfelt Office Furniture a
884 High View I
Danville, KY 4(

September 10, 1993

Ms. Sandra M. Hardin
ICU Corporation
497 Seemore Drive, Suite 3
Asheville, NC 29703

Dear Ms. Hardin:

According to our records your firm has a
of $2,950.00. You may have overlooked
Please check your records and send paym

If there is some reason that you have not
please call us to discuss the problem.

Thanks for your prompt attention to this

Sincerely,

Rosenfelt Office Furniture and Supplies
884 High View Plaza
Danville, KY 40422

September 10, 1993

Mr. Jim Bell
Libraries R Us
1492 Manuscript Dr.
Mandarin, FL 49709

Dear Mr. Bell:

According to our records your firm has an outstanding balance of
$15,500.05. You may have overlooked making this payment.
Please check your records and send payment today.

If there is some reason that you have not sent your payment,
please call us to discuss the problem.

Thanks for your prompt attention to this matter.

Sincerely,

Rosenfelt Office Furniture a
884 High View P
Danville, KY 40

September 10, 1993

Ms. Kay Kusunoki
Kusunoki Printers
1317 Beech Place
San Francisco, CA 94113

Dear Ms. Kusunoki:

According to our records your firm has an
of $150.00. You may have overlooked ma
Please check your records and send payme

If there is some reason that you have not s
please call us to discuss the problem.

Thanks for your prompt attention to this n

Sincerely,

Steven King
Credit Manager

Rosenfelt Office Furniture and Supplies
884 High View Plaza
Danville, KY 40422

September 10, 1993

Ms. Faye L. Mauney
In Your Prime Beauty Shop
15 Mockingbird Lane
Pinelog, TX 69007

Dear Ms. Mauney:

According to our records your firm has an outstanding balance
of $950.21. You may have overlooked making this payment.
Please check your records and send payment today.

If there is some reason that you have not sent your payment,
please call us to discuss the problem.

Thanks for your prompt attention to this matter.

Sincerely,

Steven King
Credit Manager

Figure 7-137   The customized form letters

CREATING A COLLECTION LETTER

Microsoft Word

➡ To begin the assignment, double-click on the Microsoft Word icon. If you are already in Word with no file open, choose **New** from the File menu.

Your screen will show a new document called "Untitled1".

➡ From the Font menu choose **Times 12 point** if you'll be printing to a LaserWriter or **New York 12 point** if you'll be using an ImageWriter.

⌘-R ➡ Choose **Show Ruler** from the Format menu.

You'll begin the letter by typing the letterhead information on the first three lines.

➡ Type **Rosenfelt Office Furniture and Supplies** on the first line, and then press Return.

➡ Type **884 High View Plaza** on the second line, and then press Return.

➡ Type **Danville, KY 40422** on the third line, and then press Return three times to place two blank lines after the letterhead.

The letterhead should be centered and bold, and the first line will have a larger point size. You'll make those formatting changes now.

➡ Select the three lines you just typed by dragging down the selection bar to the left of the text, as shown in Figure 7-138.

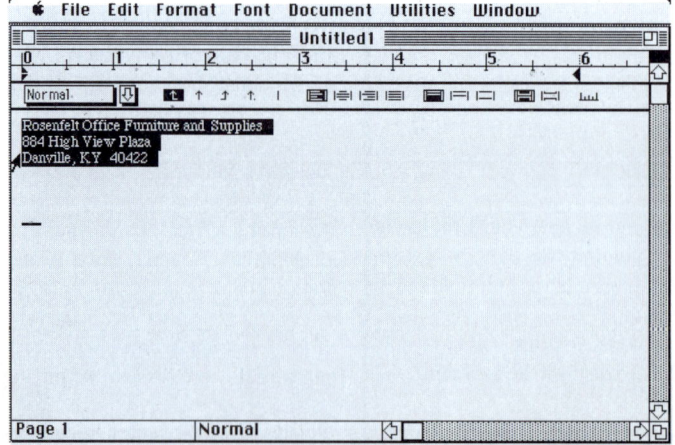

Figure 7-138   Selecting the text in the letterhead

⌘ -Shift-C ➡ Click on the center alignment icon on the ruler to center the selected lines.

⌘ -Shift-B   ➠   Choose **Bold** from the Format menu to bold face the selected lines.

            ➠   Select the first line of the letterhead, and choose **14 point** from the Font menu.

This makes the first line of the letterhead larger than the address lines.

After you've made these formatting changes, your letterhead should look like the one shown in Figure 7-139, which was typed using Times.

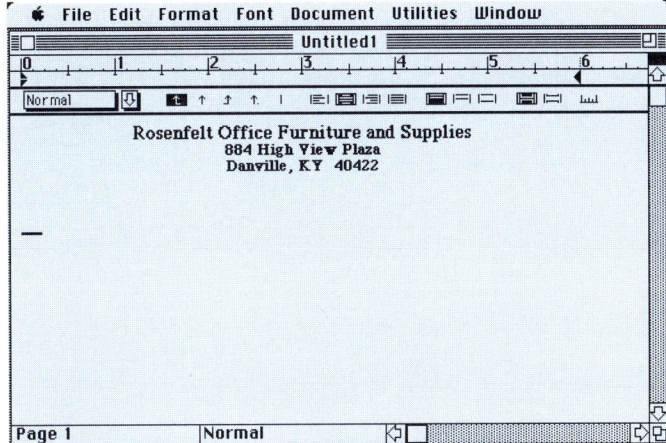

Figure 7-139   The formatted letterhead lines

Now you will save this document and name it.

⌘ -S   ➠   Choose **Save** from the File menu.

      ➠   In the resulting Save dialog box, click the **Drive** button, if necessary, to ensure that the document is saved on your data disk. Name this document **Main Collection Letter**, and then click the **Save** button.

⌘ -Y   ➠   Before continuing with the rest of the letter, choose **Show ¶** from the Edit menu.

The formatting characters shown in Show ¶ will allow you to keep track of the number of blank lines between several of the paragraphs and will be of use throughout the rest of the project.

      ➠   Click to the left of the last paragraph mark in the document to set the insertion point there, and then type today's date.

      ➠   Press Return four times after typing the date to place three blank lines after it, as shown in Figure 7-140.

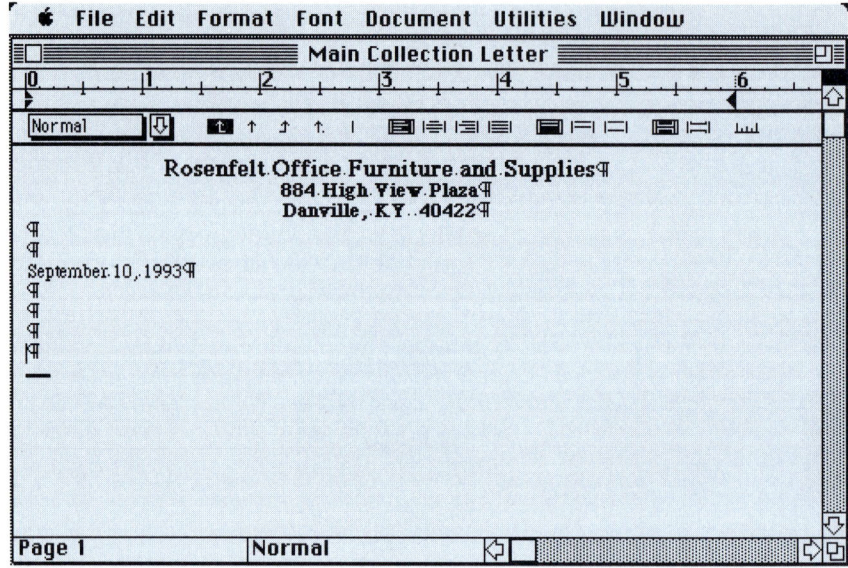

Figure 7-140   The date and three blank lines after it

➡ Next type the first line of the address at the insertion point:

Ms. Vicki Fitzgerald

➡ Press Return after that line, and then type the remaining lines of the address, pressing Return after each line:

IXI Corporation
3211 Dow Street, E.
DuPont, MI 53022

➡ After typing the Zip code, press Return twice to get a blank line, and then type:

Dear Ms. Fitzgerald:

➡ Press Return twice to get a blank line after the salutation.

In various projects in this chapter you used the space-after-paragraph icon on the ruler to place spaces between paragraphs. Sometimes it is just as easy to press the Return key to place a blank line after a paragraph, especially when some paragraphs will be followed by more than one blank line.

➡ Type the first paragraph of the letter:

According to our records your firm has an outstanding balance of $1,722.00. You may have overlooked making this payment. Please check your records and send payment today.

Continue typing the rest of the letter. Press the Return key twice at the end of each paragraph to leave a blank line between paragraphs. After typing **Sincerely**, press Return four times to leave three blank lines before typing **Steven King**.

➡ Type the following to finish the letter:

If there is some reason that you have not sent your payment, please call us to discuss the problem.

Thanks for your prompt attention to this matter.

Sincerely,

Steven King
Credit Manager

Now is a good time to save your work.

➡ Choose **Save** from the File menu.

The rest of your document should look like the one shown in Figure 7-141.

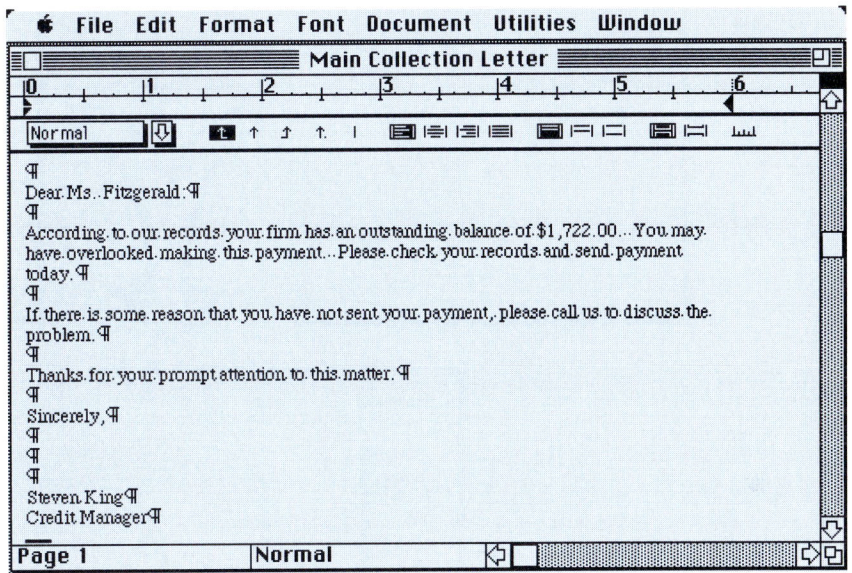

Figure 7-141   The rest of the document

You just created a collection letter that you could use as a template to then change and send to many people. To send it to a different company, you would first use the Save As command to save this letter under a different name, so you do not alter the original. You could then modify the letter by typing in a new company name, address, salutation, and amount due. You would follow this procedure for each letter you had to send and print each letter separately.

The above procedure would not be too tedious or time consuming if you had only a few letters to mail. But what if you had to do this with 75 letters on a monthly basis? Would you want to volunteer for the job of modifying each letter manually? Not only would the project take quite a bit of time, but also the letters would take up a lot of disk storage space. Fortunately, Microsoft Word allows you to create customized letters using its print merge feature.

The concept of print merge is simple: You create a *main document* that contains the body of your letter, and you use special *fields* to mark the parts that will change with each letter. You also create a *data document* that contains the information you want placed in the special fields in the main document. When you issue the Print Merge command, the information from the data file is merged with the main document to create customized form letters. This concept is illustrated in Figure 7-142.

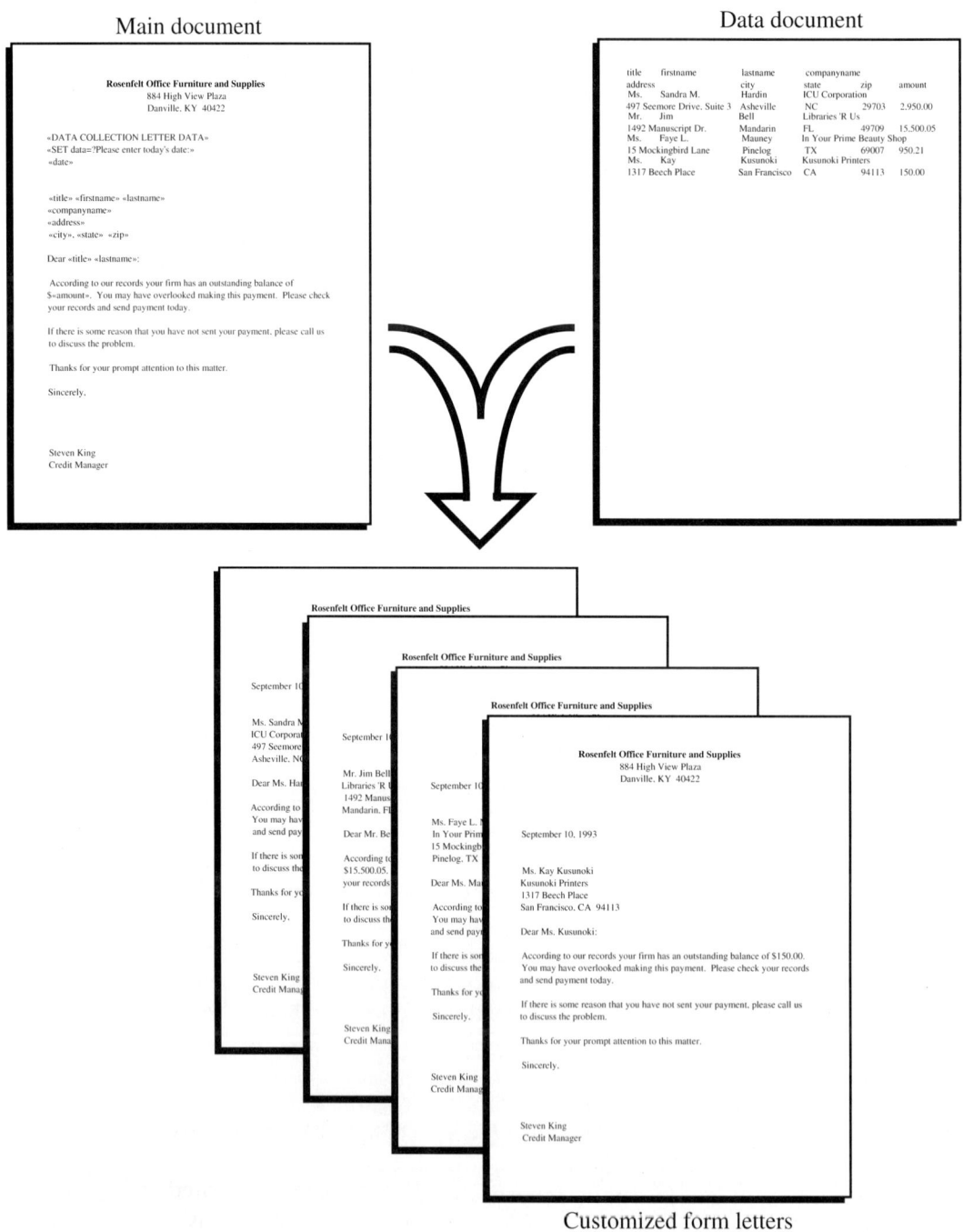

Figure 7-142   The print merge concept

PLANNING THE MERGE PROJECT

A print merge project requires some planning before you can actually create the documents. Let's discuss some of those considerations.

Defining the Steps

There are two key parts to every merge project: the main document and the data document. The main document contains the body of the form letter. The data document contains the names, addresses, and other data that will be merged with the main document to create the customized form letters.

The Data Document

The concept of a data file is basic to all computer applications. A file consists of related *records*. In the file illustrated in Figure 7-143, the records are related because each record contains data about student grades. The file consists of student grade records.

A record consists of related *fields*, or items. The fields shown in Figure 7-143 are related because they each contain information, or data, pertaining to one particular student. The individual fields that make up the student records are the name, course, and grade.

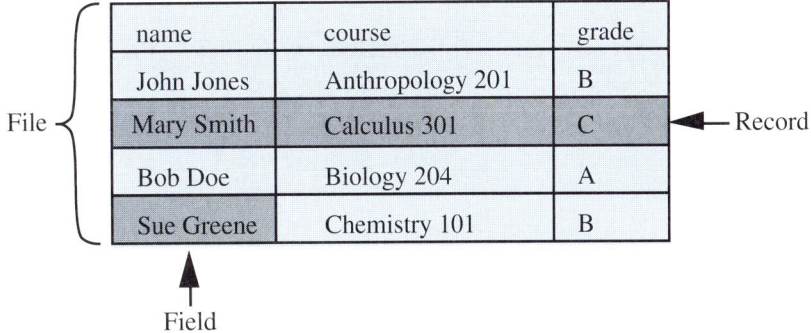

Figure 7-143   The file/record/field relationship

The group of fields to be used in one letter is referred to as a record. Your data document contains a record for each letter to be sent; therefore, if you're sending 20 customized letters, your data document will contain 20 records.

In this project you will create a data document in Microsoft Word. In some print merge projects you may use an existing data file for your data document, in which case you will not have to create one. Data documents, or databases, can be created in Excel, Microsoft Word, FileMaker, and many other applications.

If the data file does not already exist, you do not have to create it before you create the main document. However, creating the data document first can be helpful, because you will already have established the field names in the data file, and you'll know to use those same field names in the main document.

The Main Document

The main document, at the very least, contains the following:

- The text and layout of the form letter that will not change from one letter to the next

- The merge fields, the contents of which will change from letter to letter

- The statement that tells Microsoft Word the name of the data document to use when merging with the main document

In addition to the above parts of the main document, you can have many commands and instructions embedded in the main document. You'll learn more about these later in this project.

In this project you will be modifying the collection letter that you just created to use as the main document for the print merge. You won't have to retype the parts of the letter that will not change from one letter to the next.

The Print Merge Command

After the data document and the main document are completed, you issue the Print Merge command by choosing **Print Merge** from the File menu.

This command tells Microsoft Word to duplicate the text of the main document and to sequentially insert data from each record in the data document in the special merge fields in the main document. A separate letter is created for each record in the data document.

Defining Fields

When you create the documents for the print merge, you need to consider the field names to be used. The field names in the file illustrated in Figure 7-143 are name, course, and grade. The field names are representative of the actual data in each field—the name field contains the student's name, the course field contains the name of the course, and the grade field contains the student's grade. It is always a good idea to define a field with a meaningful name that accurately represents the field's contents. The field names "field1" and "55" do not accurately define the contents of a field.

With that in mind, keep the names as short and simple as possible. Use either all uppercase or all lowercase letters so you don't have to worry about whether you capitalized one and not another. If you use a field name that consists of two or more words, do not put spaces between the words. This is especially important if you are using a program other than Microsoft Word to create the data file, because many applications do not allow spaces embedded in field names.

You can determine the field names first and then use them consistently in both the main document and the data document. Since you have already typed the main collection letter, you probably have an idea about which parts will change from one letter to the next and which parts will not change.

The parts of the letter that will change are called *merge fields*. A merge field acts as a placeholder in the main document—it marks the slot where the contents of a field from the data document will be inserted. The contents of the merge fields will change with each new letter that is created in the print merge process.

Let's define the field names you'll be using in this project before you use them in both the main document and the data document.

⟹ Look at the main collection letter you just typed, the first part of which is shown in Figure 7-144.

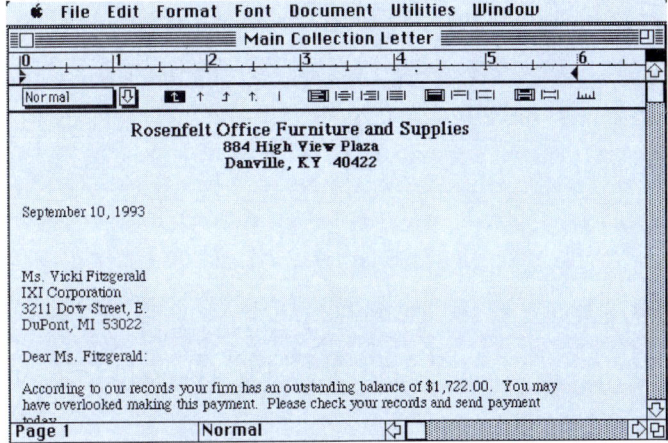

Figure 7-144   The first part of the main collection letter

It is likely that the date will change if you send these collection letters out each month, so that will be the first field to name. Let's call it "date".

The customer name is sure to change also. Although you may be tempted to group the entire name under one field name, notice that the letter uses just the title and last name in the greeting, "Dear Ms. Fitzgerald:". In such a case, you need to be able to use each part of the name as a separate field. Let's call the fields in the name "title", "firstname", and "lastname".

The name of the company will be different for each letter also. Let's call that field "companyname".

Since the address will change from letter to letter, let's call the address field "address". In some cases, you may have an address that requires two lines, such as a street address on one line and a post office box on another. In that case, you would break the address name field into two parts, such as "address1" and "address2". For this project, the address will require only one line, so "address" is sufficient.

You should also break the city, state, and Zip code into separate field names, since most mailings will probably be sorted by one of those fields before being taken to the post office. Even though the data document that you create for the purposes of this project will be small, it will show you the correct procedure to follow for any size mailing. Let's name those fields "city", "state", and "zip".

In the greeting you'll print the same "title" and "lastname" fields that you use in the address portion of the letter. You do not have to give another occurrence of those fields a different name.

The first sentence of the body of the letter states a specific amount owed. This will also change from letter to letter, so let's call that field "amount". The rest of the letter will not change from one letter to the next in the print merge process.

You just determined the field names you'll be using in the print merge documents. They are:

date

title

firstname

lastname

companyname

address

city

state

zip

amount

You'll use them in a minute when you create the main document. The completed main document will look like the one shown in Figure 7-145 on the next page.

Rosenfelt Office Furniture and Supplies
884 High View Plaza
Danville, KY 40422

«DATA COLLECTION LETTER DATA»
«SET date=?Please enter today's date:»
«date»

«title» «firstname» «lastname»
«companyname»
«address»
«city», «state» «zip»

Dear «title» «lastname»:

According to our records your firm has an outstanding balance of $«amount». You may
have overlooked making this payment. Please check your records and send payment
today.

If there is some reason that you have not sent your payment, please call us to discuss the
problem.

Thanks for your prompt attention to this matter.

Sincerely,

Steven King
Credit Manager

Figure 7-145   The print merge main document

CREATING THE MAIN DOCUMENT

In addition to adding merge fields to the main document, you will be using two sets of instructions in this project to tell Microsoft Word to do something other than just merge data. Merge fields and special instructions must be enclosed within special characters to have Word recognize them. These special characters, called *chevrons*, are « and ». These are not sets of two less-than and greater-than signs, but characters that you type using a particular sequence of keys.

Option-\ • To type the «, hold down the Option key and type a backslash (\).

Shift-Option-\ • To type the », hold down the Shift and Option keys and type a backslash (\).

The DATA Instruction

The first instruction to be placed in this letter is the DATA instruction. The DATA instruction tells Word the name of the data document to be merged with the main document to create the customized letters. The DATA instruction must come before any other instruction or merge field in the main document, and it is usually the first line of the form letter. You'll insert the DATA instruction now.

Option-\ ➥ Click to the left of the date and press Return to create a blank line above the date. Click on that blank line, and then hold down the Option key and type a backslash (\) to create the « character.

Shift-Option-\ ➥ Type **DATA COLLECTION LETTER DATA** (be sure to use all caps), and then press Shift-Option-backslash (\) to create the » character. See Figure 7-146.

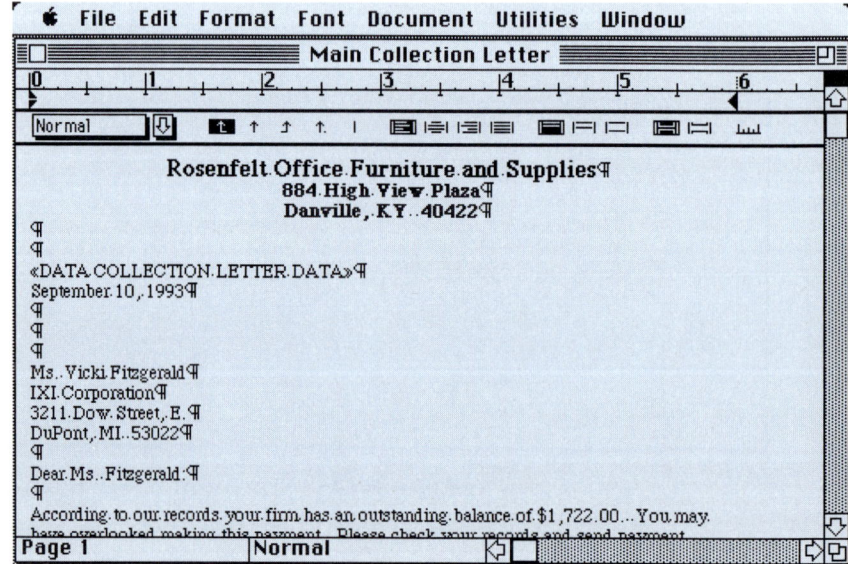

Figure 7-146   The DATA instruction

The DATA statement that you just typed tells Microsoft Word that the data document to merge with this main document is called COLLECTION LETTER DATA. See Figure 7-147.

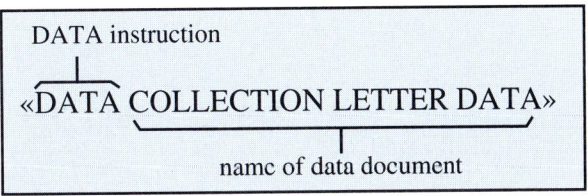

Figure 7-147   The parts of the DATA instruction

The SET Instruction

The next instruction to be placed in this letter is the SET instruction. This allows you to enter the value of a field interactively for each page. The SET instruction is used when the data in the field is likely to change each time you print merge the document.

You'll use the SET instruction instead of typing the date in the main document. The SET instruction must include the word "SET" followed by the name of the field you would like to set. Following the field name, you type an equal sign (=) and either a value to be assigned to the field or a prompt for Microsoft Word to use when asking you what value to assign to the field. If typing a prompt, you precede it with a question mark (?) to indicate that it is a prompt.

➡ Click in the selection bar to the left of the date to select that line.

You'll replace this line with the SET instruction for the date.

Option-\   ➡ Press the Option-backslash (\) to get the special character «, and then type the following:

SET date=?Please enter today's date:

Shift-Option-\   ➡ Follow that with the » character, which you get by pressing Shift-Option-backslash (\).

The SET instruction that you just typed tells Microsoft Word to prompt you for the data to be inserted into the date field each time you execute the print merge. The prompt "Please enter today's date:" will appear on the screen after you issue the Print Merge command. The date that you type at that prompt will be placed in the date field and will print wherever the merge field "date" appears in the main document. See Figure 7-148.

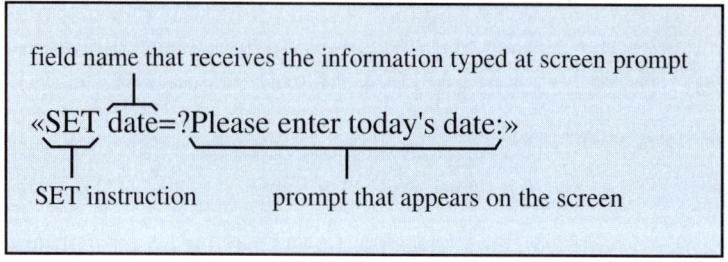

Figure 7-148   The parts of the SET instruction

Option-\   Shift-Option-\   ➡ Press Return to go to the next line, and then on that line type the "date" field name, enclosed between the special characters: «**date**»

Your screen should now look like the one shown in Figure 7-149.

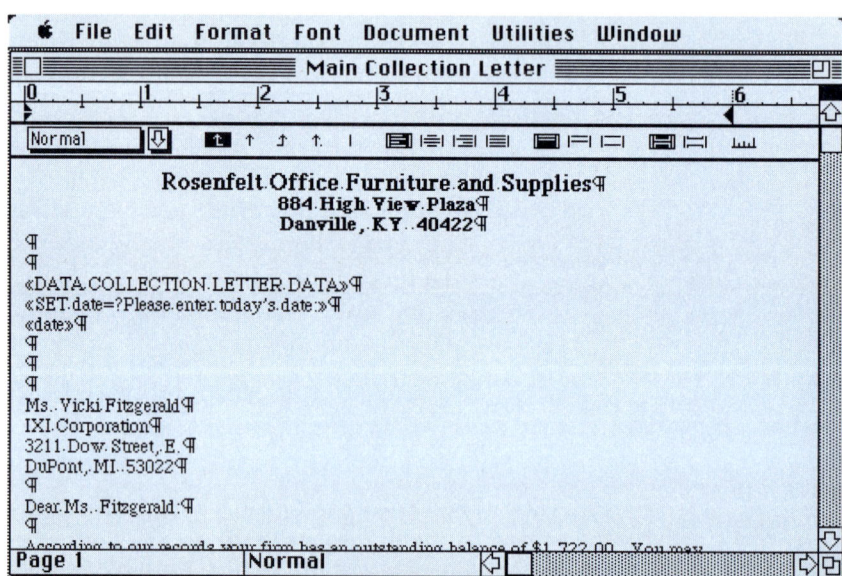

Figure 7-149   The SET instruction

⌘-S   Now is a good time to save your work.

➡ Choose **Save** from the File menu.

The DATA and SET instructions are just two of several instructions that Microsoft Word makes available in a print merge environment. The IF...ELSE...ENDIF instruction allows you to use *conditional printing*, which is the process of printing a field based on the contents of a particular field. The ASK instruction is similar to the SET instruction. It allows you to enter a value at a particular point in the document in response to a screen prompt. The NEXT instruction allows you to either skip a record in a data document or print more than one record on one merge document. The INCLUDE instruction enables you to include the entire contents of another document in the form letter. For more information on these advanced features, refer to *Reference to Microsoft Word*.

Enclosing the Field Names

Now you're ready to replace the name and address lines, the greeting, and the amount field in your letter with the merge fields.

➠ Click in the selection bar to the left of the first line to select **Ms. Vicki Fitzgerald**.

Option-\ Shift-Option-\ ➠ Type the following, using Option-backslash (\) to create « and Shift-Option-backslash (\) to create » :

«title» «firstname» «lastname»

Remember that the merge fields you are typing in the main document will be replaced with data from the data document. Be sure to use the appropriate spaces and punctuation between these merge fields, as though you were typing in the actual information. Using Show ¶ helps you verify that you have left a space between the fields, as shown in Figure 7-150.

«title».«firstname».«lastname»¶
IXI.Corporation¶

Figure 7-150   Leaving spaces between merge fields

➠ Select the line **IXI Corporation** and replace it with «**companyname**».

➠ Select the line **3211 Dow Street, E.** and replace it with «**address**».

➠ Select **DuPont** (but not the comma next to it) in the next line and replace it with «**city**».

➠ Select **MI** in the same line and replace it with «**state**».

➠ Select the Zip code **53022** in the same line and replace it with «**zip**».

⌘-S ➠ Choose **Save** from the File menu.

Your document should look like the one in Figure 7-151 when you're finished with the above instructions. Notice the spaces between field names and the comma after «city» are still intact.

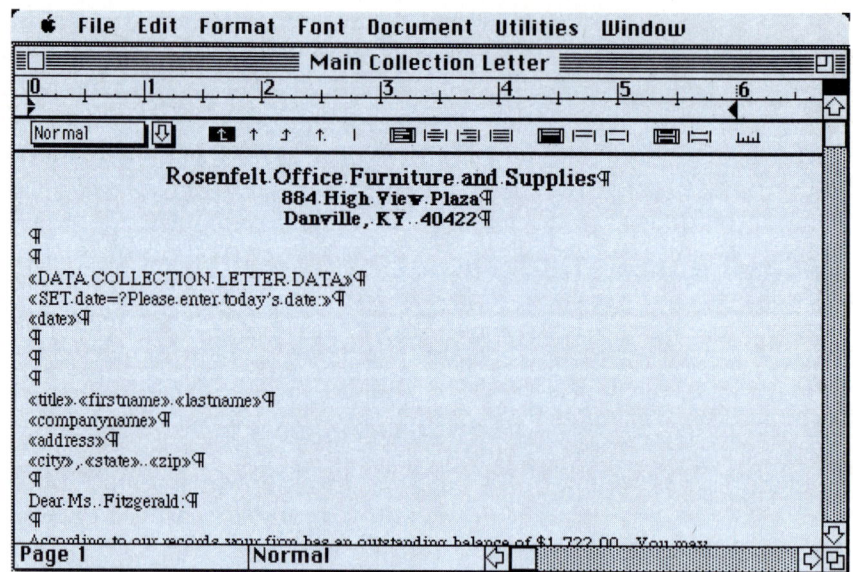

Figure 7-151   The merge fields in the address lines

Now you can see the main document taking shape and how the merge fields will be laid out on the page.

The greeting line will contain the "title" and "lastname" fields that you used in the address line. The same merge field may be referred to as many times as you want in a form letter. It is important, however, to be consistent when typing a field name that you are using more than once in your document. Each time the field name is used it must be typed *exactly* the same way, including uppercase and lowercase letters and spaces, commas, and other special characters. Copying and pasting a field name that you've used before rather than retyping it helps prevent errors.

➡ Click on and drag through **«title»** in the first line of the address to select it. Be sure to include the chevrons.

Double-clicking on a word selects a word, but it does not select the chevrons on either side of a merge field or the punctuation marks before or after a word.

⌘-C ➡ Choose **Copy** from the Edit menu to copy the selected text to the Clipboard.

⌘-V ➡ Click on and drag through **Ms.** (including the period) in the greeting line to select it, and then choose **Paste** from the Edit menu to paste the contents of the Clipboard over the selected text.

⌘-C ➡ Copy the «lastname» field from the first line of the address by selecting it and choosing **Copy** from the Edit menu.

⌘-V ➡ Select **Fitzgerald** in the greeting line (but not the colon after it) and choose **Paste** from the Edit menu to replace it with **«lastname»**.

The last merge field to change is the amount field.

➠ Select the **1,722.00** (but not the dollar sign before it and not the period after it) in the first paragraph of the letter and replace it with «**amount**». See Figure 7-152.

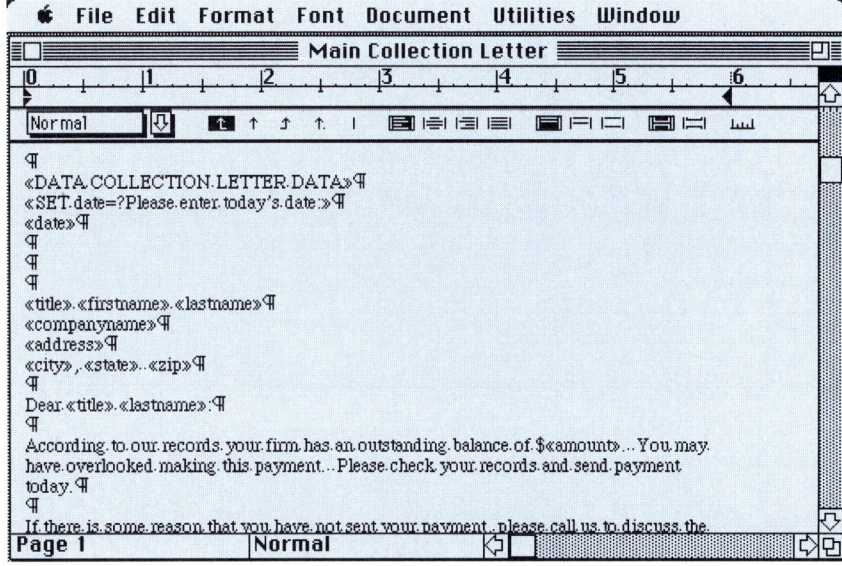

Figure 7-152   The "amount" merge field

Text Formatting

The text formats in the letter in this project will not vary from one field to another. You can emphasize the contents of a particular merge field, however, by having it print bold or italic, in a larger font, or with some other characteristic. If you want to do this, the merge field in the main document must be formatted the way you want the information to look when printed.

For example, suppose you wanted the amount to print in bold italics each time. You would select the merge field «**amount**» and choose **Bold** and **Italic** from the Format menu. The merge field itself would carry the formatting so that any information from the data document that prints in place of the "amount" field on the page will also be bold and italic.

The main document now contains all the merge fields and instructions needed to create the form letters.

⌘-S   ➠ Save this completed document now.

The next step is to create the data document. Your completed data document will look like the one shown in Figure 7-153 on the following page.

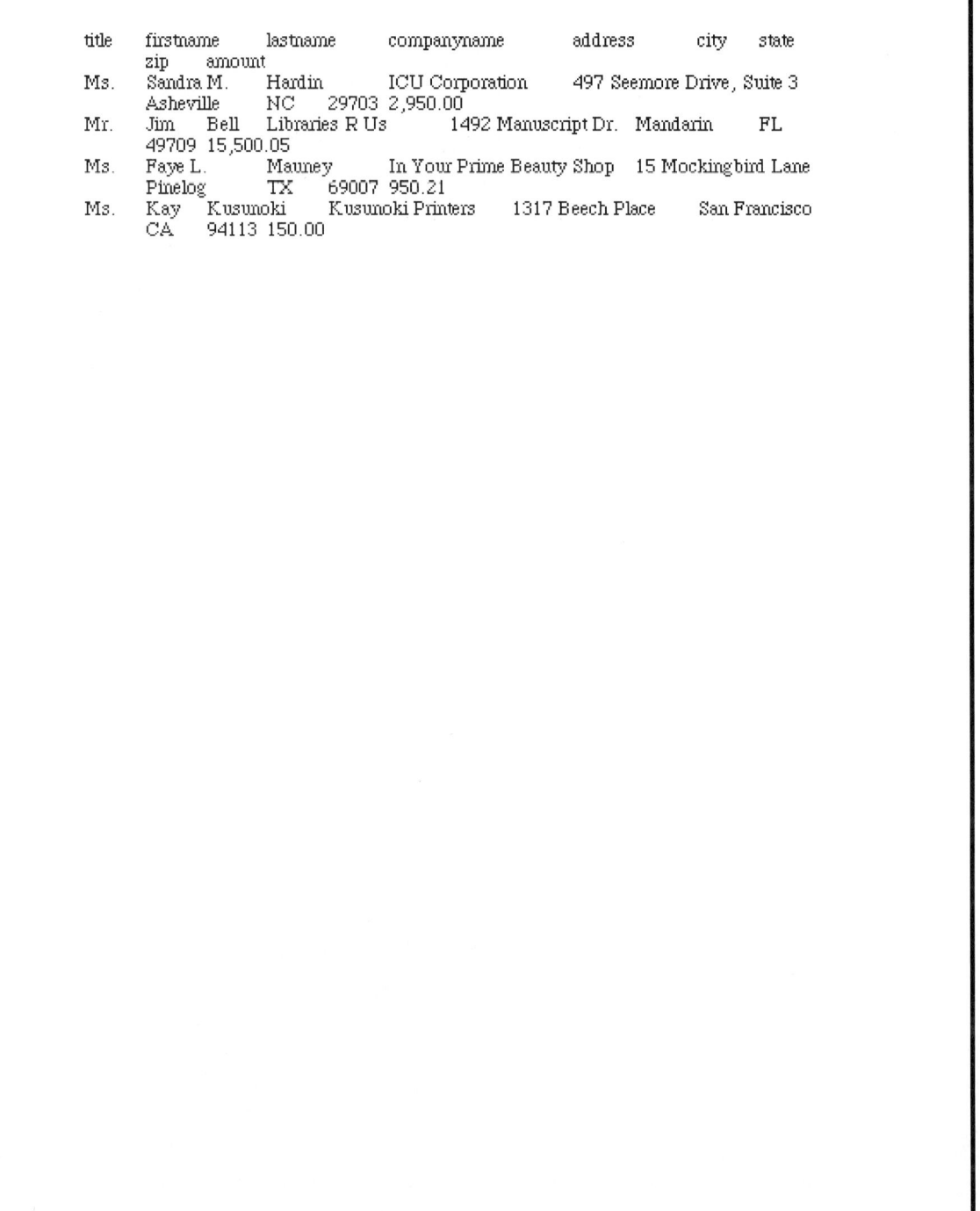

Figure 7-153   The print merge data document

CREATING THE DATA DOCUMENT

You'll need to open a new document that you'll use to create the data document, the one that Microsoft Word will use to get the information it needs to create each of the customized form letters.

⌘-N ➡ Choose **New** from the File menu to open a new, untitled document.

➡ From the Font menu choose **Times 12 point** if you're using a LaserWriter or **New York 12 point** if you're using an ImageWriter.

The data document consists of data records, which hold the text that is placed in each of the customized form letters. In this case, you will have one data record for each form letter you want to print.

Each data record is separated by a Return. It is important when typing each data record not to press Return until the entire record is entered.

Typing in the Header Record

The first record in the data document is the *header record*. This special record lists the fields in the order in which they appear in the other records, using the exact field names you used in the main document. Each of the field names in the header record can be separated with a comma or a tab character. The comma or tab character acts as a field *delimiter*, which indicates where one field ends and the next begins. The other records following the header record contain the data, and each of those fields within each record are also separated with either a comma or a tab character, the same as was used to separate the fields in the header record. If you use commas to separate the fields, fields that contain commas in the data must be surrounded by quotation marks.

Let's enter the header record now.

➡ In the new untitled document that you just opened, type the following field names. Press the Tab key where indicated.

title (press Tab) **firstname** (press Tab) **lastname** (press Tab) **companyname** (press Tab) **address** (press Tab) **city** (press Tab) **state** (press Tab) **zip** (press Tab) **amount**

➡ Do not press Return until after you have finished typing the word **amount**.

The header record you just typed contains the same field names as in the main document, spelled exactly the same way. Your header record should look like the one shown in Figure 7-154.

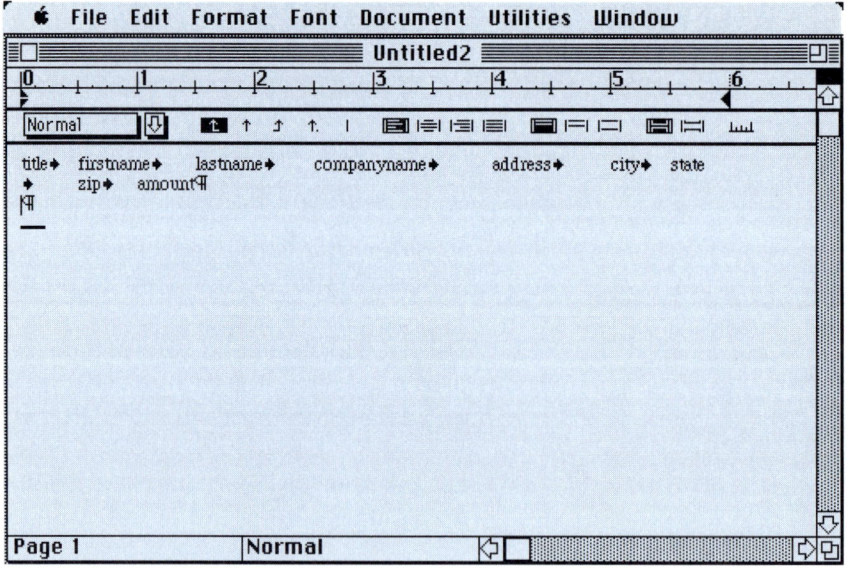

Figure 7-154   The header record

When you pressed the Return key after the word "amount" in your header record, that indicated to Microsoft Word that those were all the fields in the header record, and it placed the insertion point on the next line. That is where you'll begin your first data record.

Before you enter the data records, you need to save this document. It is important that it be saved under the same name as you told Microsoft Word in your DATA instruction in the main document. Figure 7-155 shows the DATA statement used in the main collection letter.

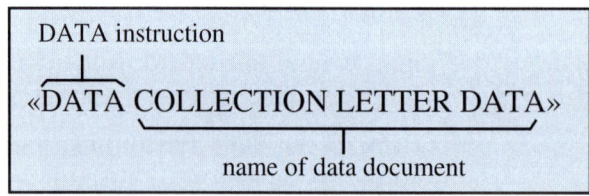

Figure 7-155   The data document name in the DATA statement

⌘-S   ➡   Choose **Save** from the File menu.

➡   In the dialog box that appears, verify that you are saving this document on your data disk. Beneath Save Current Document as, type in the name exactly as you had it in the DATA statement in the main document, in this case **COLLECTION LETTER DATA** (in all caps). See Figure 7-156.

Be sure you don't type any leading or trailing spaces when you type the filename.

➡   Click **Save** to save the file to your disk.

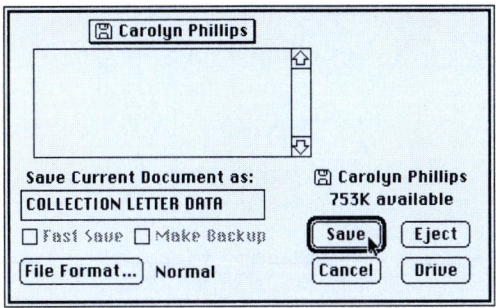

Figure 7-156 Saving the data file

Entering the Data Records

➡ Type the following, pressing the Tab key where indicated by (Tab). Press Return only after you have typed the entire data record (after the number 2,950):

Ms. (Tab) Sandra M. (Tab) Hardin (Tab)
ICU Corporation (Tab)
497 Seemore Drive, Suite 3 (Tab)
Asheville (Tab) NC (Tab) 29703 (Tab)
2,950.00

Your screen should look like the one shown in Figure 7-157.

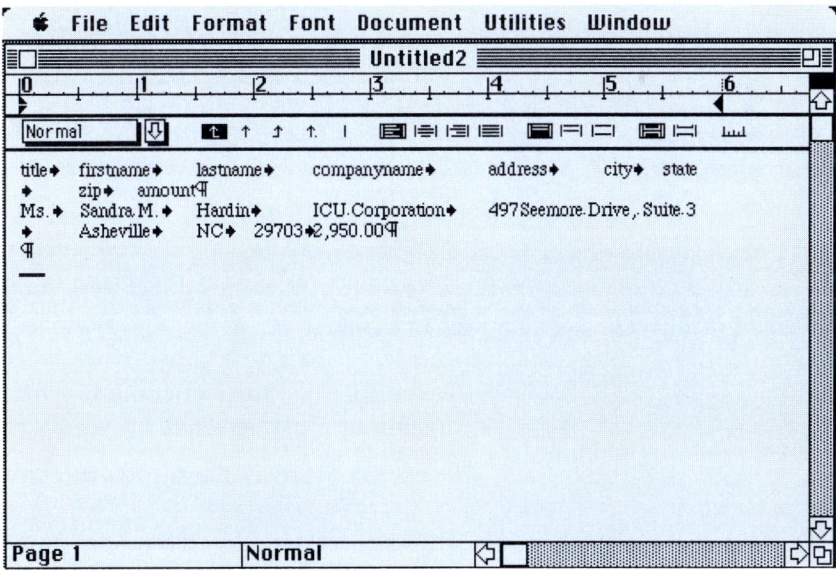

Figure 7-157 The first data record

➡ Now type in the next three data records, pressing the Tab key where indicated by (Tab). Press Return *only* where indicated:

Mr. (Tab) Jim (Tab) Bell (Tab) Libraries R Us (Tab)
1492 Manuscript Dr. (Tab) Mandarin (Tab) FL (Tab) 49709
(Tab)15,500.05 (press Return)

Ms. (Tab) Faye L. (Tab) Mauney (Tab)
In Your Prime Beauty Shop (Tab)
15 Mockingbird Lane (Tab) Pinelog (Tab) TX (Tab) 69007
(Tab) 950.21 (press Return)

Ms. (Tab) Kay (Tab) Kusunoki (Tab) Kusunoki Printers (Tab)
1317 Beech Place (Tab) San Francisco (Tab) CA (Tab) 94113 (Tab)
150.00

Figure 7-158 shows the completed data file.

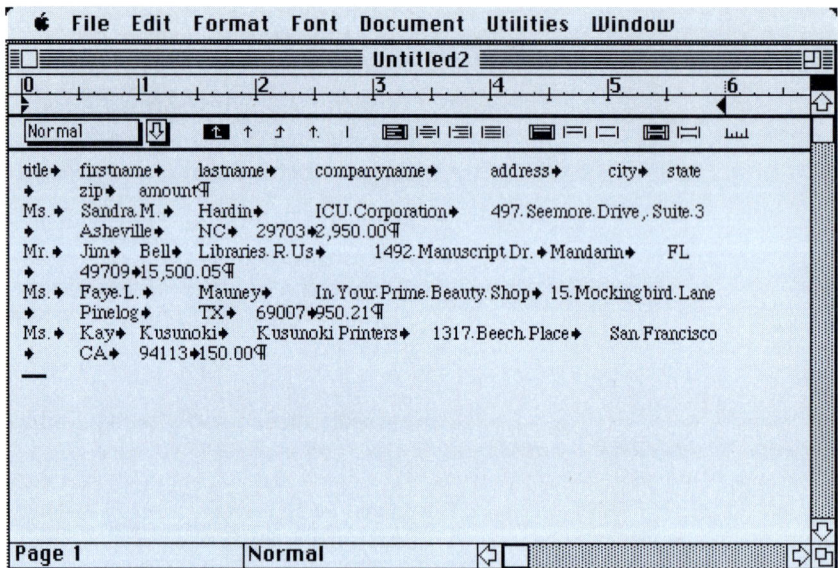

Figure 7-158   Data file after entering all data records

⌘-S ➡ Choose **Save** from the File menu to save the completed data
document.

RUNNING THE MERGE

To merge the main document with the data document, the main
document must be active on your screen.

➡ Select **Main Collection Letter** from the Window menu.

This will activate that document and bring it to the front.

The main document is the only one that must be open when you issue
the Print Merge command. The data document that you just created is
still open, however. Leave it open in case you need to make any changes
to it.

➡ Choose **Print Merge** from the File menu.

The dialog box that results gives you a choice of printing the resulting
documents immediately or merging them to create a new document on

your disk. If you choose **New Document**, you can view and modify the letters before sending them to the printer. This is probably the best choice, especially when merging a large number of records to create a large number of letters, but you must have enough free space on the disk to hold the new document.

CAUTION   When you're printing on an AppleTalk network, if you merge to the printer instead of to a new document, other print jobs can come between your letters because each letter is viewed as a different print job. Merging to a new document creates only one print job when you print the form letters.

➡ Click **New Document** in the Print Merge dialog box, as shown in Figure 7-159.

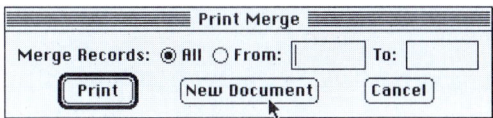

Figure 7-159   Print Merge dialog box

You should now see a prompt asking you to enter today's date, like the one shown in Figure 7-160.

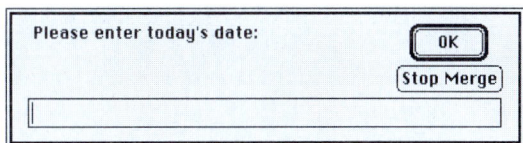

Figure 7-160   The date prompt

This prompt is the result of the SET instruction that you placed in the main document.

➡ Type in today's date, and then click **OK**, as shown in Figure 7-161.

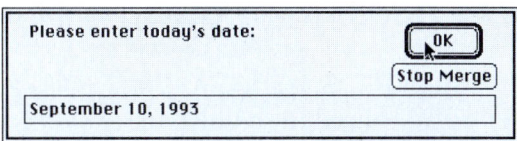

Figure 7-161   The date entered in the date dialog box

When you told Microsoft Word to create a new document, it created your merge letters and named them Form Letters1. This is what you'll be viewing after the merge completes. See Figure 7-162 (which shows the screen with Show ¶ off).

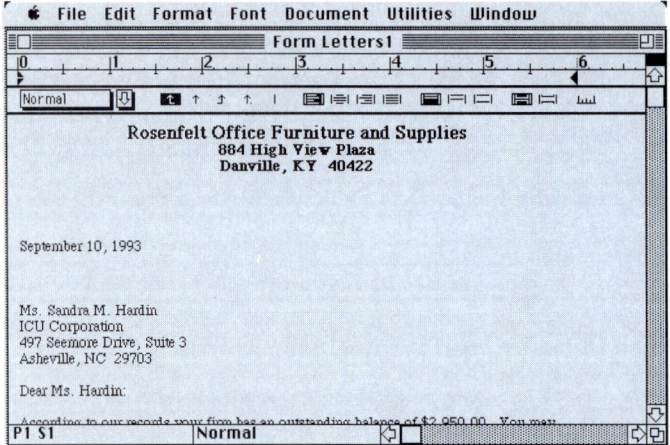

Figure 7-162   The merged documents

All the form letters are created in one file. As you scroll through the document, you'll see each letter separated by a section marker. In this case there are 4 letters in the document called Form Letters1, because you had 4 records in the data document. If you create a data document with 100 records, you would have 100 form letters in your Form Letters1 document.

➠ Scroll through the letters to be sure there are no errors.

⌘-S ➠ Since it is always a good idea to save your work before printing, save your form letters after you verify that they are correct.

⌘-P ➠ Choose **Print** from the File menu to print all the customized collection letters.

Troubleshooting

If your letters did not merge properly, you can probably track down the reason. The following are some potential error messages and their causes. Each time you correct an error and re-run the print merge, Microsoft Word names the resulting form letters document sequentially. The first time you run the print merge, the letters are called Form Letters1. If you run the merge again, the resulting document will be called Form Letters2, and so on. After you correct the errors, close the corresponding Form Letters document without saving it before running the print merge again. This will keep you from accumulating and becoming confused by different versions of the form letters.

If you get an error message that says "Missing comma or tab in data record":

• You may have pressed Return while still in the middle of a data record when you entered the data in your data document (which you saved as COLLECTION LETTER DATA). You will have the option to click either **OK** or **Help** to this error message. Click either option and, when finished, the COLLECTION LETTER DATA containing your merge records will be shown on the screen with the record in question highlighted. Turn on Show ¶, if necessary, to proofread this document for extra spaces, hard returns, or missing field delimiters (commas or tabs). Correct any mistakes and try to merge the documents again.

There is an easy way to verify that the records in your data document have the correct number of fields, are followed by a hard return, and contain delimiters in the proper positions. You select the whole document (Command-Option-M) and then place left-aligned tab stops on the ruler to format the data in neat columns and rows. You'll probably have to extend the right margin on the ruler to 10 or 11 inches to allow one complete record to fit on one line, but you won't be printing the data document anyway. Having the data in columns with the fields in the header record forming the column names lets you see at a glance if you have a problem in the data.

If you get an error message that says "Data record too long":

- You may have one quote missing, or you may have failed to enclose within quotation marks data that contained a comma in your merge document. This is a problem only if you used commas instead of tabs as field delimiters in your data records. You will have the option to click either **OK** or **Help** to this error message. The COLLECTION LETTER DATA containing your merge records will be shown on the screen, and the record in question will be highlighted. Correct the error in the record and try again.

- You specified in your header record that you would have nine data fields, and these were separated by eight tabs. You should always have one delimiter less than the number of fields. Extra delimiters will result in a "Data record too long" error message, and you will have the option to click either **OK** or **Help**. Whichever option you choose, eventually the COLLECTION LETTER DATA containing your merge records will be shown on the screen, and the record in question will be highlighted. Correct the record so it has the right number of delimiters (tabs or commas) and try again.

If you get an error message that says "Unknown field name":

- A field name that you used in your main document was not spelled the same way (this includes punctuation, spacing, and uppercase and lowercase characters) as in the header record in your data document. The field name in question will be highlighted on your Main Collection Letter document, and you'll be presented with a dialog box giving you the option to continue, stop merge, or get help. Regardless of the option you choose, you will need to correct the highlighted field name in the main document so it is exactly like the field in the header record in the COLLECTION LETTER DATA document. Then try again.

If you get a dialog box asking you to locate a particular document name:

- Microsoft Word cannot locate the document you have specified in your DATA statement. This generally means that you did not create your data document using the same name as you indicated in the DATA statement or that the document is in a different folder and/ or a different drive. *This document name must be exactly the same, including leading and trailing spaces.*

The printed output of this project consists of four letters. Be sure to compare them with the completed versions in Figure 7-137 at the beginning of the project and make any necessary changes.

⌘-Q ➡ Choose **Quit** from the File menu to exit Microsoft Word and return to the desktop. If you intend to continue with the additional projects, close the current files but don't quit Word.

SUMMARY

- Microsoft Word uses five formatting domains: the character, paragraph, table, section, and document. The character and the paragraph are the basic formatting units in Microsoft Word.

- The character, the smallest unit in a Word document, includes letters of the alphabet, punctuation marks, numbers, and symbols. Font type and size, underlining, character styles such as bold and italics, and spacing between characters are examples of different character formats. Different characters within a single paragraph can have different character formatting attributes.

- A paragraph is a collection of characters that is followed by a hard return. Paragraph formatting, such as line spacing, tab settings, text alignment, indentations, paragraph spacing, and paragraph borders, affect the entire paragraph that contains the insertion point. The ruler is used to format paragraphs, and ruler settings can be different for each paragraph.

- A table consists of rows and columns of cells, and each cell can contain characters and paragraphs that have different formatting characteristics.

- A section consists of one or more paragraphs and is followed by a section marker. Each section in a document can be formatted differently, and each document contains at least one section. Section formatting is controlled by the Section command, which controls the number of columns in a section, where the section should start, the page number the section should begin with, and whether each section should have a different header and footer.

- The document itself is the largest formatting unit in Microsoft Word. Some examples of document formatting are page margins and printing preparation. If multiple documents are open at the same time, only one can be active at a time.

- Graphics can be created in a graphics application and incorporated into a Microsoft Word document. Text and graphics can be selected and then moved, copied, or deleted from a document.

- A style is a set of formatting characteristics to which a name has been assigned. Once a style is defined, it can be applied to a paragraph or a series of paragraphs to quickly and consistently change the appearance of the text. A group of styles attached to a document is called a style sheet.

- A header is text and/or graphics that appear at the top of every page of a document. A footer is similar to a header, except that it prints at the bottom of every page of a document. A header or footer can also contain an automatic date and time stamp and a page number.

- The print merge feature of Microsoft Word allows you to create customized form letters by merging records from a data document with the unchanging body text of a main document.

KEY TERMS

active window
automatic page break
automatic styles

block quote
borders

cell
center tab
character
chevrons
clip art
Clipboard
conditional printing

data document
decimal-aligned tab
delimiters
desktop publishing
document
dot leaders
drawing tool
drop-down list

end-of-cell marker
end-of-row marker
extended keyboard

field
first-line indent
First Page Special
flush left
flush right
font
footer

Galley View

hanging indent
header
header record

I-beam pointer
indentation controls
insertion point

justification, justified text

left-aligned tab
left indent
line spacing, vertical spacing

main document
manual page break
merge fields
monospace fonts

new-line command

orphan

page scale
Page View
paginate
paragraph
paragraph-spacing settings
point size
print merge
Print Preview
proportional fonts

record   style name, style
right-aligned tab   style sheet
right indent
ruler   tab leaders
                                                tab settings, tab stops
scale tool   table
section   table scale
section break marker, section   tables feature
  marker, section break   text alignment, alignment
select
selection bar   widow
soft return   wiping through text
spelling checker

MICROSOFT WORD COMMAND KEYS AND SHORTCUTS

File Menu

New	⌘ -N
Open	⌘ -O
Close	⌘ -W
Save	⌘ -S
Print Preview	⌘ -I
Print	⌘ -P
Quit	⌘ -Q

Edit Menu

Undo	⌘ -Z
Cut	⌘ -X
Copy	⌘ -C
Paste	⌘ -V
Show/Hide ¶	⌘ -Y

Format Menu

Show/Hide Ruler	⌘ -R
Character	⌘ -D
Paragraph	⌘ -M
Define Styles	⌘ -T
Bold	⌘ -Shift-B
Italics	⌘ -Shift-I

Font Menu

Smaller point size	⌘ -Shift-<
Larger point size	⌘ -Shift->

Document Menu

Page View	⌘ -B
Insert Page Break	Shift-Enter
Insert Section Break	⌘-Enter

Utilities Menu

Find	⌘ -F
Change	⌘ -H
Spelling	⌘ -L

  In Speller:

Suggest Word	⌘ -S
No Change	⌘ -N

Ruler Commands

Left-align text	⌘ -Shift-L
Center text	⌘ -Shift-C
Justify text	⌘ -Shift-J
Right-align text	⌘ -Shift-R
Space After ¶	⌘ -Shift-O

General Commands

Cancel printing	⌘ -.
types «	Option-\
types »	Shift-Option-\
Select entire document	⌘ -Option-M
Accept the default, or the more heavily outlined button in a dialog box	Return or Enter

ADDITIONAL PROJECTS

The following projects are accompanied by briefer instructions than those you have previously completed in this chapter. If necessary, refer to the previous projects in this chapter for information and step-by-step instructions for any command that you don't remember how to use. Also, Microsoft Word's Help text contains valuable and easily accessed information. You will not be reminded to save your work—by now you should be thinking of that without having to be reminded.

Project 6: Creating a Report with Footnotes

In this project you'll create a report that has a different header for the first page than for the rest of the document. Project 4 of this chapter introduced you to headers and footers. You'll also learn about adding footnotes to your document. The final output of Project 6 is shown on the next two pages in Figures 7-163 and 7-164.

Kenyon Chekelele
Art101
February 7, 1993

The Classical Ideal in Greek Sculpture and Architecture

The classical period of Greek architecture and sculpture began around 480 B.C. The artwork of this period reflected the Greek infatuation with the concept of perfection and wholeness, that of the *ideal.* This classical ideal was represented by a striving toward internal consistency and organic unity as a means to bring form out of the chaos of nature. Balance and grace were the results.

Architecture

The temples of this period were designed as idealized dwelling places for perfect beings and were built using the Doric, Ionic, and Corinthian architectural orders. The Parthenon, a perfect example of the classical period of Greek architecture, was erected to serve both as a shrine to Athena and as the treasury of the Delian League. For that reason it had an east cella and a west cella. There were 17 columns on each of its 228-foot long sides and 8 columns on the 104-foot wide front and back. There were 6 additional columns on both the east and west ends that formed the inner porticos.

The technical skill and workmanship of the Parthenon are astonishing. No mortar was used anywhere. The stones were cut so that when they were fitted together they formed a single smooth surface. The columns were constructed of sections called drums, which were fitted and held tightly by square plugs in the center so that the joinings were hardly visible. The design of the Parthenon was based on the mathematical principle of the golden section. This flexible system of dividing lines into extreme and mean ratios was used to ensure harmonious proportions and allowed much latitude in actual practice.

Close examination of the Parthenon shows that what seems to be straight and correct is really a complex series of harmonious concave and convex curves. The architects Ictinus and Callicrates used aesthetics rather than mathematics to correct certain optical illusions and to create the illusion of flexibility.[1] Even the fluting of the columns was used not only to maintain a rounded appearance, but also to create graceful curves to please the eye. The Parthenon is a work of art, not merely an example of skillful engineering.

The organization of horizontals and verticals, the relationship of length and breadth to height, and the ratio of the solid masses to the openings between the columns all were according to the tradition of the Doric order of architecture. A unit of measure

---

[1] Olive Dilgores, *Art, Man and History.* New York: Gabriel Charles Press, 1972, p. 130.

Figure 7-163   Final output for page 1 of Project 6

know as the *module* was used to assure the proper ratio of parts to whole. The modules were flexible units of measure, such as the diameter and radius of a column, not fixed units like yards and feet. The module varied among structures, in keeping with the Greek ideal of structural integrity of single buildings.

Sculpture

The statues created during the classical Greek period concentrated on typical or general qualities rather than on unique or particular ones. This was done in order to seek a concept closer to perfection. The most beautiful details of several models were combined to achieve the ideal.

The *Doryphorus* (Spear Bearer) by Polyclitus puts into play his rational theory for ideal proportions for the human figure. Just as the Parthenon had its module derived from a unit of the building, Polyclitus took his module from a part of the body. The whole and all parts of the statue were expressed in multiples or fractions of the module. As with the optical refinements of the Parthenon, Polyclitus' canon also allowed for some flexibility to ensure harmonious grace.

The sculptor avoided representing the human being in infancy or old age, since these extremes implied incompleteness or imperfection. The majority were fashioned to represent gods who, if portrayed as humans, must have bodies of perfection. In the bronze statue of Poseidon (or Zeus) recovered from the sea off the coast of Greece,

The sculptings, or metopes, in the Doric frieze of the Parthenon were done in high relief to take full advantage of the bright sunlight. The *Lapith and Centaur* metope attributed to Phidias, uses the spreading folds of the mantle to form a backdrop for the idealistic human figure and makes a striking contrast with the grotesque centaur.[2] Phidias' *Athena Lemnia*, which stood on the Athenian Acropolis, was often referred to as "the beautiful" and approached the Greek ideal of chaste classical beauty.

The *Dying Warrior* from the east pediment of the temple at Aegina is and idealistic model of simplicity and restraint. Dignity and grace are embodied in its portrayal of the death of the lean and muscular warrior. The harmonious proportions of the *Kritios Boy* are represented by its enhanced lifelike expression and its *contrapposto* stance. In both cases the essential, ideal qualities of the subjects are captured.

---

[2]Wyman Colla, *The Philosophy of Art and Learning* Chicago: Nantahala Publishing Company, 1980, p. 241.

Figure 7-164   Final output for page 2 of Project 6

The margins for The Classical Ideal report are 1 inch top and bottom and .75 inch left and right.

➡ Choose **Document** from the Format menu to set the margins.

The font used in this project is Times 14 point.

The easiest way to create this report is to type the report first, and then go back and add the headers and footnotes.

➡ Refer to Figures 7-163 and 7-164 and type the body of the report. Do not type any of the header information (name, class number, date, and page number). Do not type the footnote reference marks (1 and 2) in the body text or the footnote text at the bottom of each page.

➡ Format the title of the report bold and centered and the Architecture and Sculpture headings bold and left-aligned. Italicize the words that require it.

➡ Use the spelling checker to check for misspellings.

Now that all the grunt work is done, you can add the headers.

➡ Choose **Section** from the Format menu and click the **First Page Special** box in the Header/Footer portion of the Section dialog box, as shown in Figure 7-165. Click **OK** when done.

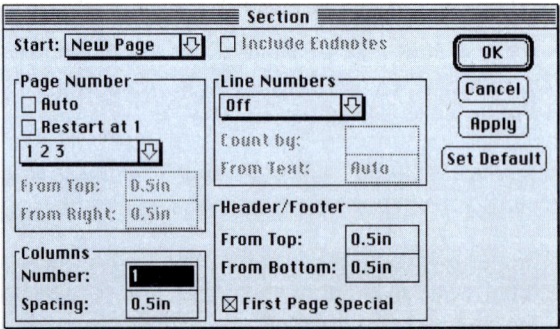

Figure 7-165   Choosing the First Page Special header option

When you open the Document menu, you now have two different headers and footers to choose from.

➡ Choose **Open First Header** from the Document menu.

The header window that results will contain the text that prints on the first page of your document only.

➠ Type your name on the first line of the header, the class number on the next line, and the date on the last line, as shown in the completed document in Figure 7-163. Press Return to create a blank line after the date. Format these lines right-aligned.

⌘-M ➠ Click in the line that contains the date, and choose **Paragraph** from the Format menu.

➠ In the Paragraph dialog box, click the **Borders** button, and then click in the bottom of the borders schematic to create an underline border effect. Click **OK** twice to get back to your document.

➠ Close the First Header window and then open the header window from the Document menu.

The contents of the header window will print on every page but the first.

➠ In the header window, type the word **Page**, press the space bar, and then click on the page number icon in the header window to place the automatic page number in the header. Press Return to place a blank line after the page-number line.

➠ Format the page-number line right-aligned, and then place an underline border beneath it like you did in the First Header window. Close the header window when finished.

➠ Use Page View or Print Preview to see the different headers on each page, and then return to Galley View.

Next you'll add the footnotes.

➠ Click to set the insertion point after the period that ends the second sentence in the fourth paragraph of the report—the paragraph beginning with "Close examination".

This is where the footnote reference mark will go. The other part of the footnote, the footnote text, will go at the end of the page.

⌘-E ➠ Choose **Footnote** from the Document menu.

The Footnote dialog box is shown in Figure 7-166.

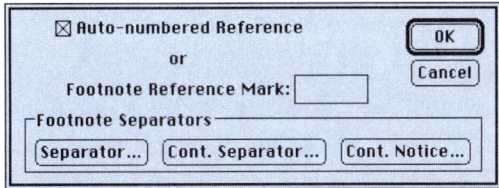

Figure 7-166 The Footnote dialog box

Notice that Auto-numbered Reference is already selected. This option allows Microsoft Word to number the footnotes automatically as you go along, beginning with number 1. If you wanted to use a footnote reference mark other than auto-numbered, you would type the character to use for the reference mark in the box to the right of Footnote Reference Mark.

The other options in the Footnote dialog box concern the footnote separator, which is a mark that separates the footnote text from the main text of the document. The default footnote separator is a line two inches long, which is standard for most documents.

➡ Since you want Word to insert an auto-numbered reference mark where the insertion point is, click **OK** to accept the settings in the Footnote dialog box.

The reference mark is inserted in your document at the insertion point, and the footnote window opens at the bottom of the screen. If Show ¶ is on, you'll see that the footnote reference marks are boxed with a dotted line. Notice that the same footnote reference mark is also placed in the footnote window at the bottom of the screen, and the insertion point automatically moves there for you to enter your footnote text.

➡ In the footnote window, type the footnote text that is shown at the bottom of the first page of the completed document in Figure 7-163. All character and formatting options are available in the footnote window just as they are in the document window.

You can use the scrollbars to scroll around in the footnote window. To close the footnote window, double-click in the split bar, as shown in Figure 7-167.

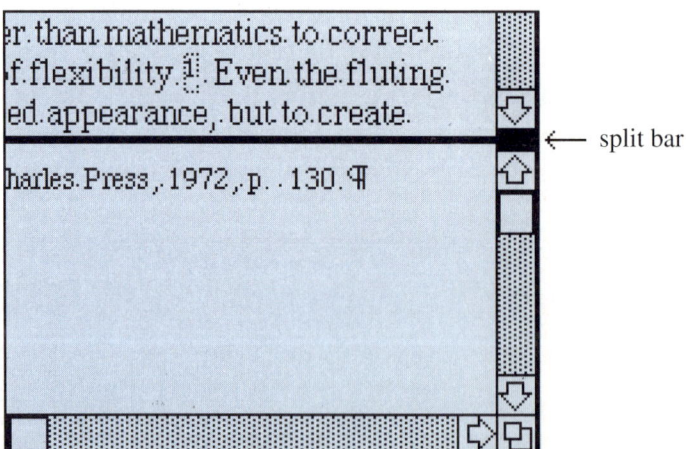

Figure 7-167   The split bar

➡ Now move to the second to the last paragraph of your document to insert the second footnote.

➡ Click after the second sentence in that paragraph, and insert the second footnote in the same mannter as you did the first one. Type the footnote text from the finished document shown in Figure 7-164.

If you close the footnote window and would like to do some editing to the footnote text, double-click on the footnote reference mark in the document to reopen the footnote window.

To delete a footnote, you select the footnote reference mark in the document and press the Backspace key. Not only does this delete the reference mark in the document, but it also deletes the footnote text in the footnote window and automatically renumbers any subsequent footnotes that were auto-numbered.

For more information about the footnote features, refer to *Reference to Microsoft Word*.

➡ Your report should now be complete. Compare it to the finished documents shown in Figures 7-163 and 7-164, and make changes as needed.

Project 7: Creating a Form

In this project you'll use the tables feature and cell borders to create a form. For additional help, refer to Project 3 in this chapter, which covers the tables feature. The final output of Project 7 is shown in Figure 7-168.

Student Grade Averaging Form

Course Name: _____

Date	Item	Grade
_____	_____	_____
_____	_____	_____
_____	_____	_____
_____	_____	_____
_____	_____	_____

Average _____

Course Name: _____

Date	Item	Grade
_____	_____	_____
_____	_____	_____
_____	_____	_____
_____	_____	_____
_____	_____	_____

Average _____

Course Name: _____

Date	Item	Grade
_____	_____	_____
_____	_____	_____
_____	_____	_____
_____	_____	_____
_____	_____	_____

Average _____

Figure 7-168   Final output for Project 7

The margins for the Student Grade Averaging Form are 1 inch top and bottom and .75 inch left and right.

➧ Use the Document command from the Format menu to set these margins.

The font used in this project is Helvetica 12 point.

You'll need to work with Show ¶ on and with the ruler showing.

➧ Begin by typing the title, **Student Grade Averaging Form**, and then press Return three times to create two blank lines after the title.

The title should be centered and formatted bold.

➧ Click to set the insertion point on the last blank line, and then choose **Insert Table** from the Document menu.

➧ The Insert Table dialog box should show settings for 2 columns, 1 row, and 3.5 inch column width. Accept those settings.

Now you should change the width of the first column in that table.

➧ Use the scale icon on the ruler to toggle to the table scale, and then drag the thumbtack column markers on the ruler so that the first column ends at 1-1/2 inches, and the second ends at 4-1/2 inches, as in the ruler shown in Figure 7-169.

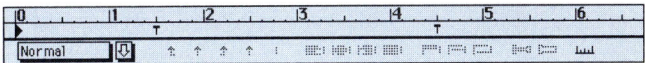

Figure 7-169   The column markers for the first table

➧ Click on the blank line below the table you just created, choose **Insert Table** from the Document menu, and insert a table that has 5 columns and 9 rows. Accept whatever column width is shown, since you'll be changing the column width anyway.

➧ Select all of the new 5-column, 9-row table, and then click the scale icon on the ruler to toggle to the table scale.

➧ Move the thumbtack column markers so that the first column of the 9-row table is 1-1/2 inches wide, the second column is 1/4 inch wide, the third is 1-1/2 inches wide, the fourth is 1/4 inch wide, and the fifth is 1-1/2 inches wide. Your ruler should look like the one shown in Figure 7-170.

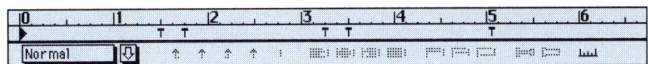

Figure 7-170   The column markers for the second table

Now you'll add an extra cell to the last row in the table.

➡️ Click to the left of the end-of-row marker in that row and choose **Table** from the Edit menu. In the resulting dialog box, click to insert the selection horizontally.

Now that the grid for the table is set up, type the text in the appropriate cells as shown in Figure 7-171.

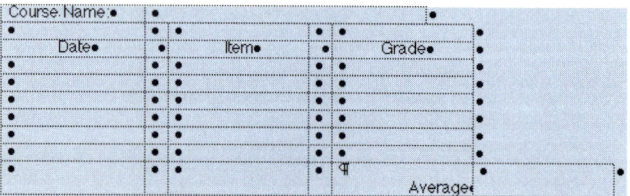

Figure 7-171 The text in the cells

Note that Course Name is left-aligned; Date, Item, and Grade are centered; and Average is right-aligned.

Finally, add the borders in this table to create the lines of the form.

➡️ The cell to the right of Course Name should be underlined, so click in that cell to set the insertion point.

➡️ Choose **Cells** from the Format menu, and then click the **Borders** button. Click at the bottom of the borders schematic to place a single line at the bottom of the cell, and then click **OK** in both dialog boxes to return to the document.

Place an underline in all but the last cell in the Date column beginning with the cell below the Date heading. Do the same with the Item column and the Grade column. The cell to the right of Average should have an underline border also. Refer to the completed form in Figure 7-168. Turning off Show ¶ lets you view the results of the underlining more clearly.

Rather than repeating the process of creating each of the other two tables needed in this document, you'll duplicate the table you just created.

➡️ Select the two blank lines after the Student Grade Averaging Form heading as well as the entire table.

➡️ Copy the table to the Clipboard, and then click in front of the blank line at the end of the document. Paste the table there.

Paste another copy of the table after the one you just pasted so that you have three identical tables in the document, each separated by two blank lines.

Compare your finished table with the completed document shown in Figure 7-168.

Part IV: Spreadsheets

Part IV: Spreadsheets introduces you to using the Macintosh to work with numerical problems.

Chapter 8 presents the basic concepts involved in using a Mac with spreadsheet applications.

Chapter 9 introduces you to using Microsoft Excel. This program is the most widely used electronic spreadsheet application on the Macintosh. It has powerful equation-solving capabilities and produces presentation-quality graphics. You will learn to create a number of spreadsheets, link spreadsheets, and produce line charts, pie charts, and bar and column charts.

Chapter 8: Spreadsheet Concepts

What You Will Learn in This Chapter

After reading this chapter, you should be able to:

- Understand the basic concepts of electronic spreadsheets and their use in numerical calculations

- Explain the organization of worksheets: rows, columns, and cells

- Recognize a cell's address

- Recognize a range

- Know what can be contained in a cell: text, numbers, and formulas

- Recognize and know how to interpret the three most common types of business graphics: pie charts, column charts, and line charts

WHAT IS A SPREADSHEET?

Ever since someone discovered how to keep track of business transactions there has been a need to organize, calculate, and present information about those transactions.

Manual Spreadsheets

At some point, the manual worksheet (also known as a spreadsheet) was created. A manual worksheet helps a person to organize and present information.

Small manual worksheets are easy to create and modify. As worksheets get larger and more complex, it takes more time and effort to create, use, and modify them. Complex spreadsheets, even those with simple calculations, are very time-consuming to use. As a worksheet gets larger, its potential for errors also increases.

Problems arise with spreadsheets when changes have to be made to correct errors or adjust to new business procedures. A manual spreadsheet must be recalculated, a process that is both time-consuming and error-prone. Manual recalculation of a large spreadsheet can take hours or days to complete and verify.

Electronic Spreadsheets

An *electronic spreadsheet* is a computerized version of the manual worksheet. It's like a sheet of paper with the pencil, eraser, and calculator built in.

An electronic spreadsheet allows you to enter, format, calculate, print, and edit your information. In addition, it will calculate and draw charts, which then may be printed. It can also be used to keep track of lists of information, sort that information into a different order, and present summaries about what is in the list.

Spreadsheets can be used whenever you have information that can be organized into rows and columns. They are specifically useful when you have numerical data that you intend to perform mathematical operations on. Once you have the information entered into the worksheet, you can analyze alternative possibilities, a process that is commonly called *what if... analysis or modeling.*

Spreadsheet Users

Spreadsheets are commonly used in business for accounting and management reports. However, business people are not the only ones who benefit from learning to use these applications. Anybody who performs large groups of calculations or complex calculations will benefit from using a spreadsheet. Spreadsheets are also useful for scientists, engineers, statisticians, medical practitioners, and anyone else who performs complex, time-consuming calculations on numerical data.

It generally takes a little longer to create a worksheet electronically than it does manually. The process may be faster or slower depending upon your familiarity with the software, your typing speed, and how comfortable you are with a particular method. Once the worksheet is created, however, the manual system cannot compete with the electronic version. If you change a value in an electronic worksheet, the worksheet is recalculated with the speed of a computer and often is completely recalculated before you could even find your calculator to start recalculating a manual worksheet.

A spreadsheet can display information on the screen, and if you specify a formula for it to use, it can perform numerous calculations in a very short period of time. After these calculations are performed, the display is automatically updated to show the results of the calculations. If you change any of the data, the calculations are again performed and the display is updated. This rapid feedback is what makes a spreadsheet so valuable.

With the knowledge of a little algebra and the use of the many built-in functions provided by a spreadsheet, you can perform intensive and sophisticated mathematical analyses of problems in the fields of business, finance, statistics, science, engineering, and others that involve numerical processing.

SPREADSHEET TERMINOLOGY

Spreadsheets are organized around the use of a worksheet that is divided into a table composed of *rows* and *columns* (see Figure 8-1).

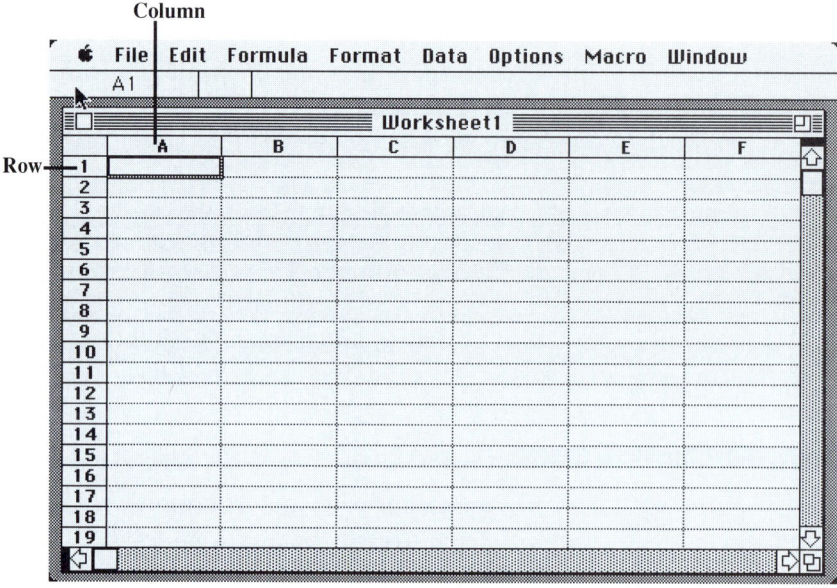

Figure 8-1   A spreadsheet's rows, columns, and cells

As you can see in Figure 8-1, each row is assigned a number, and the columns are designated by letters of the alphabet. Although you can see only 19 rows and 6 columns, a spreadsheet is much larger than that. Spreadsheet programs can create worksheets that are hundreds of columns wide and thousands of rows long. Most spreadsheets, however, are likely to be no larger than a couple of dozen columns wide and a hundred or so rows long, and many are much smaller than that.

Cells and Addresses

Each row of a spreadsheet intersects each column, and this intersection is known as a *cell*. A cell is the basic storage component of a spreadsheet. Cells have an *address* that is composed of the letter of the column and the number of the row. The top left cell is in column A and row 1, so it is known as cell A1.

A cell must be selected before anything can be entered into it. When the cell is selected, it becomes the *active cell*, and it can be recognized because it is highlighted. Cell A1 in Figure 8-1 is the active cell; it is surrounded by a heavier border than the other cells.

Information can be entered into the active cell. This information can be one of three types of data: text, numbers, or formulas.

Text is any combination of words or letters in a cell. It can be descriptive information to identify the contents of other cells, or it can be data, such as customers' names and addresses.

A cell can contain a number, also known as a *value*. This value can be any real number, such as 1, 3.14159, 363.34, -17, and so on. If needed, a very large or very small number can be entered using a spreadsheet's variation of scientific notation.

Formulas

Electronic spreadsheets are mainly used to perform numerical calculations. These calculations are described to the spreadsheet by entering an algebraic expression, or *formula*, into the cell. Formulas are composed of combinations of cell addresses, numeric constants, and mathematical operators. The mathematical operators are a plus sign (+) for addition, a minus sign (–) for subtraction, an asterisk (*) for multiplication, and a slash (/) for division.

There is a difference between storing a number or a formula in a cell. You could manually add the contents of the two cells A1 and A2 and enter the total into cell A3. If you then changed cell A1 or A2, you would manually have to add them again and replace the contents of A3 with the new result.

Instead, a cell might have a formula telling it to add the contents of cells A1 and A2. If this formula were in cell A3, it would be written as **=A1+A2**. (The equals sign (=) tells Excel that a formula—not a value—is about to be entered.) The spreadsheet would then add the values of cell A1 and cell A2 and display the result in cell A3. If you change the value in either of the other two cells, the spreadsheet would automatically recalculate and display the new result in cell A3. No matter how many times you change either or both of the first two cells, the program automatically updates the result displayed in cell A3.

Functions

In addition to allowing you to create simple formulas, spreadsheets provide a set of pre-programmed formulas called built-in *functions*. They are convenient shorthand for a series of arithmetic formulas you could enter instead.

A function lets you perform complicated calculations with less work on your part. One of the most common functions is SUM(), which adds a group of numbers that are listed as a cell range within the parentheses. Each list of numbers or cells is known as an *argument* of the function. Another common function is AVERAGE(), which computes the average of the numbers in its argument list. It does this by calculating the sum of the numbers and then dividing the result by the total number of items in the argument list. Other functions are more complicated. For example, the SQRT() function calculates the square root of the values listed within the parentheses.

An example of a simple business spreadsheet that uses the SUM() function is shown in Figure 8-2. This spreadsheet is used to calculate the profit or loss resulting from toy sales for the first three months of the year.

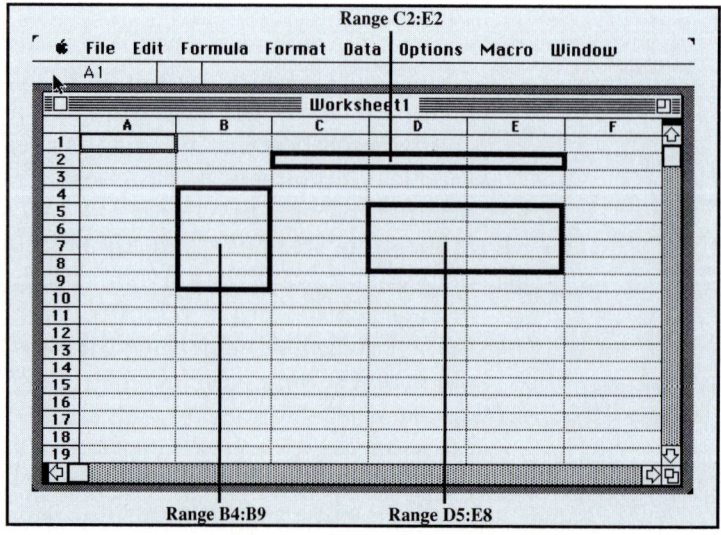

Figure 8-2   A simple profit or loss worksheet

Cell Ranges

Many formulas require you to refer to multiple cells. A range of cells is a group of contiguous cells that is treated as a unit.

The address of a range of cells is composed of the address of the top left cell, a colon (:), and the address of the bottom right cell in the group. For example, the range of cells that includes C2, D2, and E2 is referred to as C2:E2.

Examples of ranges and their addresses are shown in Figure 8-3. A range may consist of several cells in a single row (C2:E2), several cells in one column (B4:B9), or a group of cells in multiple rows and columns (D5:E8).

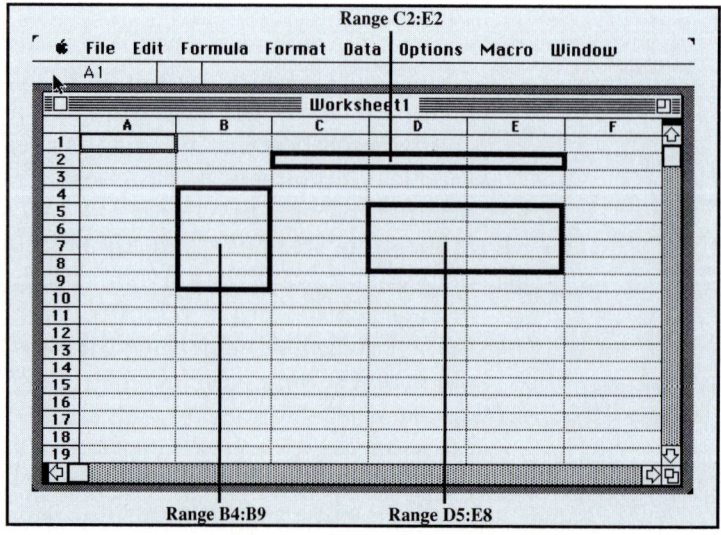

Figure 8-3   Examples of cell and range names

The largest group of cells in Figure 8-3 consists of four cells in column D and four cells in column E. This range of cells is named D5:E8. Let's say you want the total of the values in cells D5:E8, and you want this total stored in cell D10. You could enter a formula such as =D5 + D6 + D7 + D8 + E5 + E6 + E7 + E8 into cell D10, but that gets cumbersome very quickly. Using functions and cell ranges within a formula is more efficient. The formula =SUM(D5:E8) can be read as "Equals the sum of cells D5 through E8."

BUSINESS GRAPHICS

A worksheet provides a detailed numerical view of a problem. It is difficult to summarize this information when presented as a spreadsheet, however, because people have difficulty assimilating and understanding large collections of numbers.

Graphical representations are absorbed and interpreted much more quickly than numerical data. Just as pictures, drawings, and other graphical elements can make a book more interesting, business graphics can make a presentation more interesting and more informative. *Business graphics* provide a visual, easily understood overview of the data stored in the worksheet.

Many electronic spreadsheets provide the ability to easily create presentation quality business graphics. All you have to do is indicate the data to be graphed and the style of chart to be produced, and then the computer does the work.

In addition to helping you get your point across, high quality presentation graphics also create a positive impression of your presentation.

Types of Business Graphics

Two types of business graphics have evolved since the development of the electronic spreadsheet: analytical and presentation graphics.

Analytical graphics are designed to help you interpret data. *Presentation graphics* illustrate data for presentations to higher management, clients, and other presentations in which image and quality are important.

Many spreadsheet programs have the capabilities to produce high quality graphics, although specialized presentation applications typically offer more features. For many presentations, the combination of programs such as Microsoft Excel and Claris MacDraw allows you to create very high quality graphics. Other programs, such as Microsoft PowerPoint and Aldus Persuasion, will accept graphics from spreadsheets, and they include professionally designed formats to help you create high quality presentations.

Most presentation graphics programs allow you to edit and enhance the graphs and charts you produce. In many cases, they allow you to create drawings, diagrams, speaker's notes, audience handouts, and slides. An advantage of using spreadsheet programs on the Macintosh is its interchangeability of graphics between programs. All charts and graphs produced in Macintosh spreadsheet programs may be incorporated easily into presentation programs.

Even though the computer and spreadsheet do much of the work, you will still need a certain amount of skill to create a presentation using the correct charts. These programs provide tools, but they will not substitute for a person's skill and knowledge.

Types of Charts

Many types of charts are used to present numerical data. In this chapter you are introduced to the three most common: pie charts, bar or column charts, and line charts.

Several charts are shown in this section as samples of these three types. Each chart represents a portion of the data contained in the business worksheet presented previously, which is repeated in Figure 8-4 for easy reference.

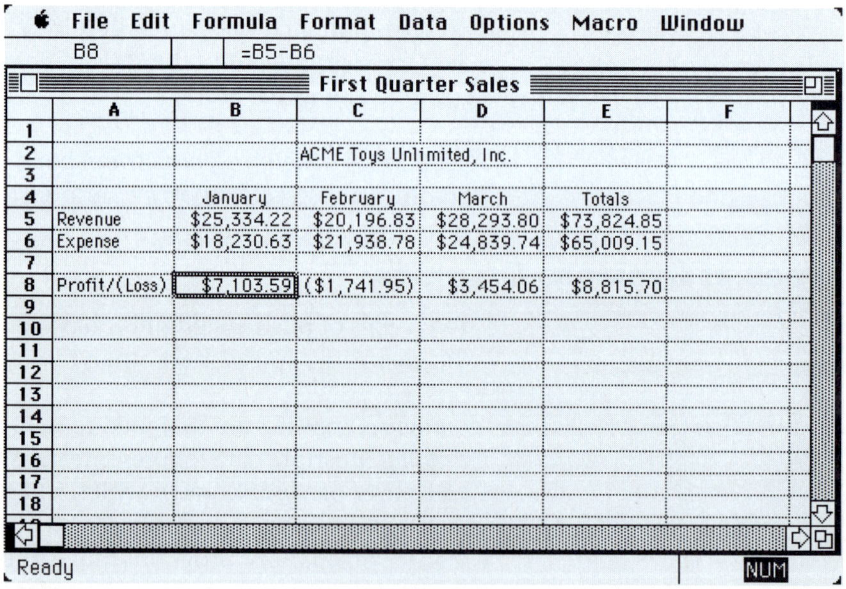

Figure 8-4   A simple profit or loss worksheet

Pie Charts

A *pie chart* shows how several amounts make up a whole. Only one *variable*, or data series, may be shown using a pie chart.

Figure 8-5 shows a pie chart illustrating revenue (the data series). The revenue for each month is compared to the total revenue for the entire period. The slices of the pie, and the percentage of the total revenue represented by each month's amount, are calculated and displayed.

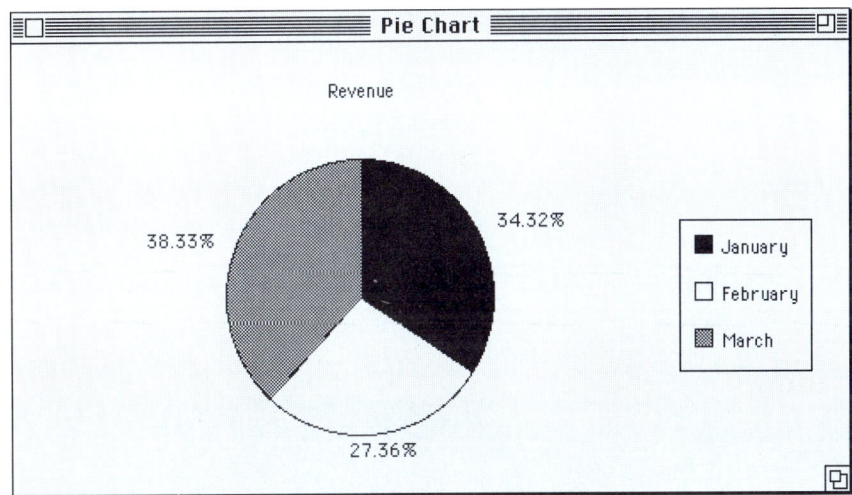

Figure 8-5   Pie chart of revenue for three months

Sometimes it is useful to draw attention to one of the values in a pie chart. In these cases, an *exploded pie chart* is used. This means that one slice is pulled away from the others to emphasize it.

In Figure 8-6, the slice representing March has been exploded.

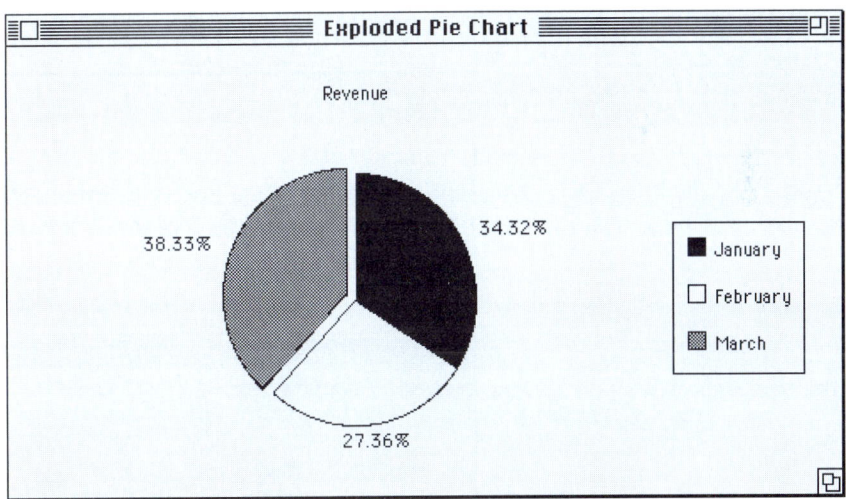

Figure 8-6   Exploded pie chart

Pie charts have the advantage of being understood by nearly everyone. However, they can only show the proportional relation of several values within a single data series.

Column and Bar Charts

Column charts and *bar charts* are used to illustrate discrete quantities and compare them to different quantities of the same variable.

Both types of charts are essentially the same; they differ only in the orientation of the rectangles used to graph the data. Column charts are oriented so that the rectangles are taller than they are wide, whereas bar charts are rotated 90°, so the bars are wider than they are tall. Values are graphed vertically in column charts and horizontally in bar charts.

Figure 8-7 shows revenue amounts for January, February, and March. This chart represents three values within the revenue data series. It is clear that February had the lowest revenue and that March had the highest.

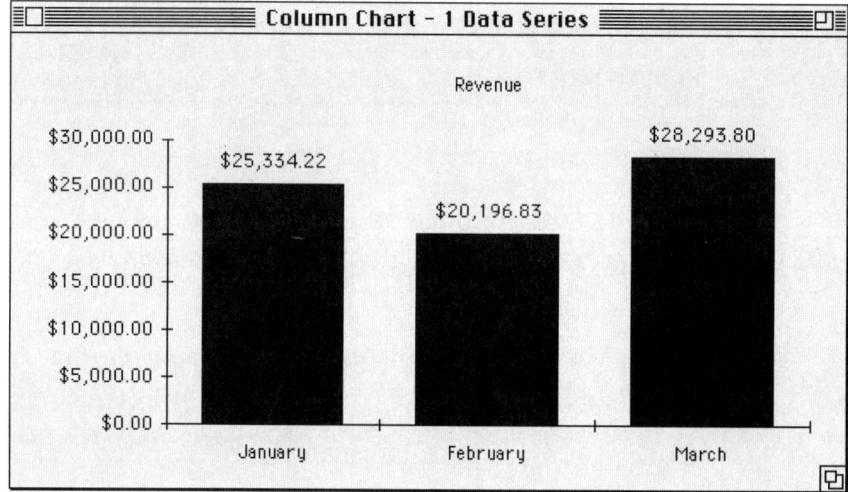

Figure 8-7   Column chart showing three values of one variable

Unlike pie charts, bar and column charts can also show the relationship between multiple data series. Figure 8-8 shows a column chart representing three data series.

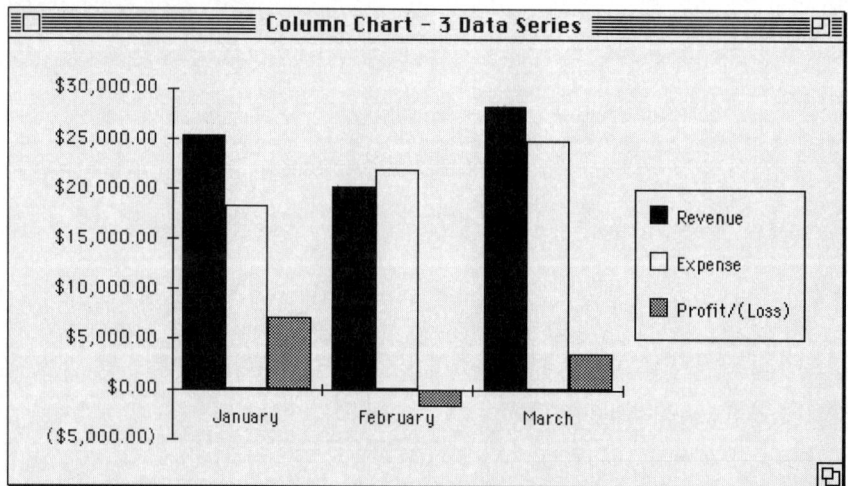

Figure 8-8   Column chart showing three instances of three variables

This chart compares the relation between revenue, expense, and profit or loss over three months. It is useful for spotting trends that may be important. For instance, while revenue is fluctuating over the three month period, expenses seem to be steadily increasing. Should this trend continue, it may have serious consequences, and it should be carefully watched for the next several months.

Line Charts

If you want to present information to analyze longer trends and cycles that can be spotted more easily, you can choose a *line chart.*

Like column charts, line charts allow the presentation of multiple occurrences, or *data points,* of several variables. Its advantage over column or bar charts is that it allows more data points to be graphed in a given space than can be shown clearly in a column chart.

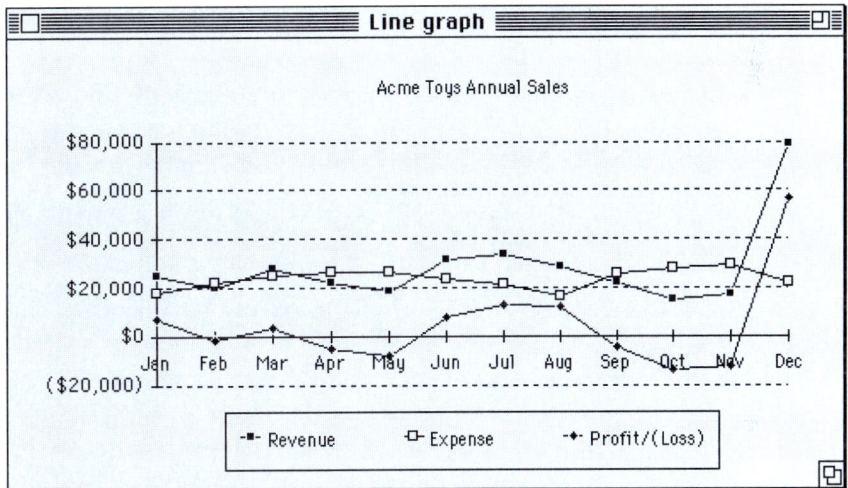

Figure 8-9   Twelve-month line chart of sales information

Figure 8-9 shows a continuation of the data presented in Figure 8-8 over a 12-month period. As you can see, the rising expenses noted above did not really signal a trend. This view, which shows a longer period of time, offers a glimpse into the cyclic nature of sales for this particular toy company. Another line chart showing the last ten years of sales history might provide useful insights for predicting next year's sales.

Chapter 8 has introduced you to general spreadsheet and business graphics concepts and terminology. Chapter 9 introduces you to Excel, a powerful spreadsheet program. With this program, you can increase your ability to analyze data and create presentation graphics.

In Chapter 9 you have the opportunity to learn to create worksheets and produce the three types of charts discussed in this chapter.

CHAPTER SUMMARY

- Spreadsheets, or worksheets, are forms used to organize data into rows and columns.

- Electronic spreadsheets are computerized versions of manual worksheets and feature faster analysis and fewer computational errors than manual methods.

- Cells are formed from the intersection of rows and columns. A cell is the storage unit used in a worksheet. There is one active cell in a worksheet, and that is where information will be entered or modifications will be made. Any cell can be made the active cell by selecting it.

- A cell can contain either text, a number, or a formula. Formulas may be composed of a combination of arithmetic expressions created by the user and built-in, pre-programmed formulas known as functions.

- A cell has an address composed of the letter representing its column and the number representing its row. Thus, a cell defined by the intersection of column D and row 14 is named D14. Multiple cells, in rectangular blocks, can be treated as a single unit by defining a range of cells.

- Business graphics provide clear, visual, easy to understand presentations of the data contained in a worksheet. Analytical graphics are used to interpret the information in the worksheet, and presentation graphics are higher quality visual aids used to illustrate the information in the worksheet.

- Three types of charts are used commonly to graph data visually: pie, column or bar, and line charts.

KEY TERMS

active cell	line chart
analytical graphics	
argument of a function	modeling
bar chart	number
business graphics	
	pie chart
cell	presentation graphics
cell address	
column	range
column chart	row
data points	spreadsheet
data series	
	text
electronic spreadsheet	
exploded pie chart	value
	variable
formula	
function	what if... analysis

Chapter 9: Microsoft Excel 2.2

What You Will Learn in This Chapter

After reading this chapter and completing the projects in it, you should be able to:

- Enter data into a worksheet

- Change the width and format of a cell

- Select ranges of cells

- Insert and delete rows and columns

- Create formulas

- Apply functions

- Save and print worksheets

- Create, format, and print charts

- Link data from one worksheet into another

- Learn shortcuts to replicate data and formulas

- Use absolute and relative cell referencing

E xcel is the most widely used and one of the best spreadsheets available on the Macintosh. It combines spreadsheet, presentation graphics, and limited database functions into one powerful, integrated package.

STARTING EXCEL

Microsoft Excel

The first step in learning to use Excel is to start the program.

➡ Locate Excel's icon on your computer's desktop. Double-click on the icon to start Excel.

When Excel starts, it automatically opens a blank worksheet and names it "Worksheet1". Figure 9-1 shows this screen and identifies its parts. (The cancel box and enter box are not visible until you enter or modify a formula.)

Parts of a Worksheet

Each part of the worksheet screen is explained next, but neither Figure 9-1 nor the definitions cover the standard parts of a Macintosh window, only the objects specific to Excel.

Active cell: This cell's contents will be affected if you enter any text, numbers, or formulas or if you make any formatting changes.

Reference area: There is only one active cell at a time, and this area of the screen shows the address of that cell.

Cancel box: This is visible only when the formula bar is active; it allows you to cancel any changes you have made to the contents of the active cell.

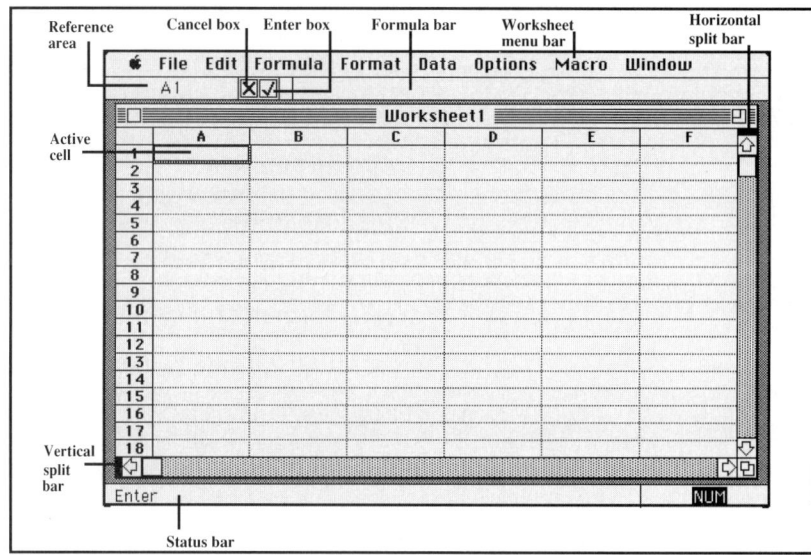

Figure 9-1   Some of Excel's controls and indicators

Enter box: This is visible only when the formula bar is active; it allows you to accept any changes you have made to the contents of the active cell. This is the same as pressing Enter on the keyboard.

Formula bar: This area displays the actual contents of the active cell. If the active cell contains a formula, you will see the full formula in this area and not the results of calculating that formula.

Split bars: These controls are used to divide the Excel window into two or four panes. If you press on the *vertical split bar*, you can drag a dividing line to the right that will split the window into two vertical windows. You would do this, for example, to see titles in column A and totals farther to the right. (You will do this in Project 4.)

                      The *horizontal split bar* allows you to split the window into two horizontal panes, one above the other. This would allow you to see the top and bottom of a column of values that is too long to fit on the screen.

                      By using both horizontal and vertical split bars, you can split the window into four independently scrolling panes, allowing you to see four sections of a large worksheet at the same time.

To remove a split bar, drag it back to its original position and release it.

Status bar: This area displays very brief information about the current state of Excel (Ready, Calculating, and so on) or information about the currently selected command.

Rows and Columns

Excel, like other spreadsheets, is organized around the use of a window divided into a table composed of *rows* and *columns.*

As you can see in Figure 9-2, each row is assigned a number, and the columns are designated by letters of the alphabet. Although you can see only 19 rows and 6 columns, the spreadsheet is much larger than that.

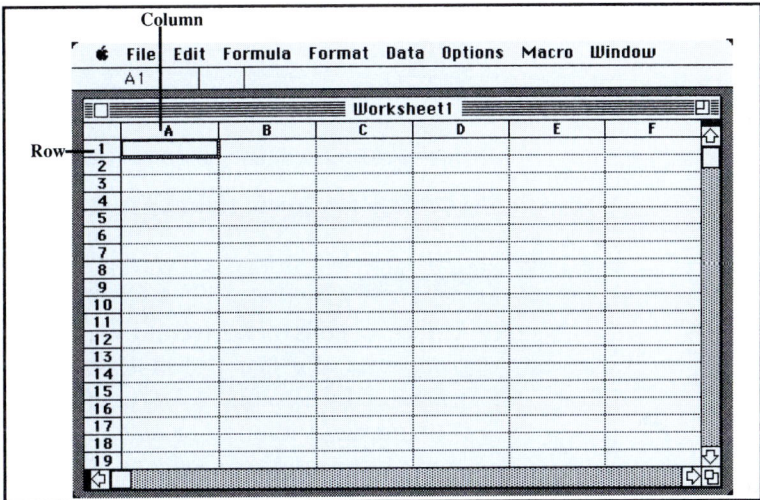

Figure 9-2   Upper left corner of blank worksheet

You can think of this worksheet as a huge sheet of paper that you are looking at through a window. By clicking on the scroll bars, you cause the sheet to move behind the window, allowing you to see other parts of the sheet.

Cells

The intersection of a row and a column is called a *cell.* A cell is named by combining its column letter and row number.

You can see if Figure 9-3 that there are 16,384 rows and 256 columns. The columns are lettered A...Z, but then the alphabet ends, so the next columns are AA...AZ, then BA...BZ, and so on, up through IV. If you multiply the number of rows (16,384) by the number of columns (256), you find that there is a total of 4,194,304 cells in an Excel spreadsheet. The top left cell of the worksheet (see Figure 9-2) is named A1, and the lower right cell of the worksheet (see Figure 9-3) is named IV16384.

Although this many cells technically are available in the spreadsheet, your computer probably does not have enough memory to use all of them. The average spreadsheet usually has no more than a few hundred rows and fewer than 100 columns, and many spreadsheets are much smaller.

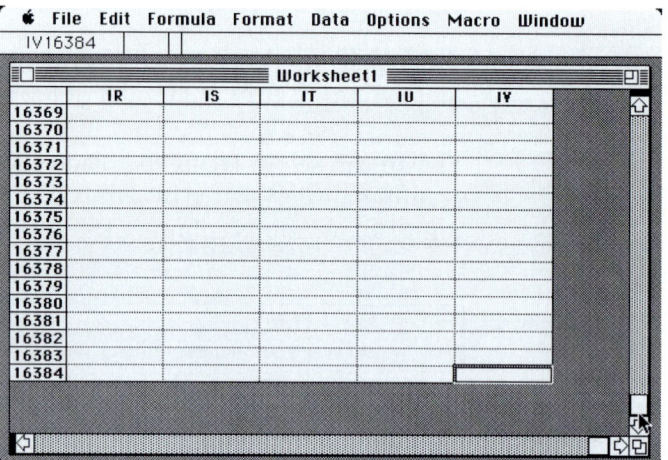

Figure 9-3   Lower right corner of blank worksheet

Ranges

A group of cells is referred to by specifying the first (upper left) cell in the group and the last (lower right) cell. These two cell references are separated by a colon (:). For example, a group of cells consisting of C2, D2, and E2 is referred to as C2:E2 (see Figure 9-4). You might find it useful to pronounce C2:E2 as "C2 through E2".

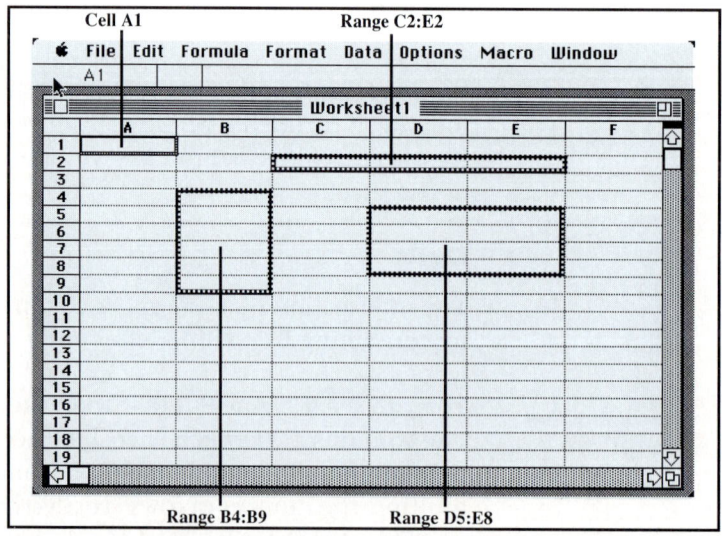

Figure 9-4   Examples of cell and range names

A *range* may consist of more than one cell in a single row (C2:E2), several cells in one column (B4:B9), or a group of cells in multiple rows and columns (D5:E8).

Cell Contents and Attributes

Cells may contain text, a number, or a formula. Regardless of information type, a cell's contents is limited to a maximum of 255 characters.

In addition to the actual contents, a cell may also contain certain attributes that determine how the contents will be displayed. These attributes include text and numerical formats, border lines or shades, and alignment choices. A cell, even an empty one, may have these attributes associated with it.

Unlike older electronic spreadsheet programs, Excel is designed to take advantage of many of the graphics features of the Macintosh. By specifying different fonts, sizes, and styles, as well as other formats that may be applicable, you can produce a report that not only is informative, but also is visually appealing.

Depending on the contents of a cell and its attributes, Excel may display something on the screen that is different from what the cell actually contains.

Figure 9-5 shows a simple worksheet that contains several kinds of data.

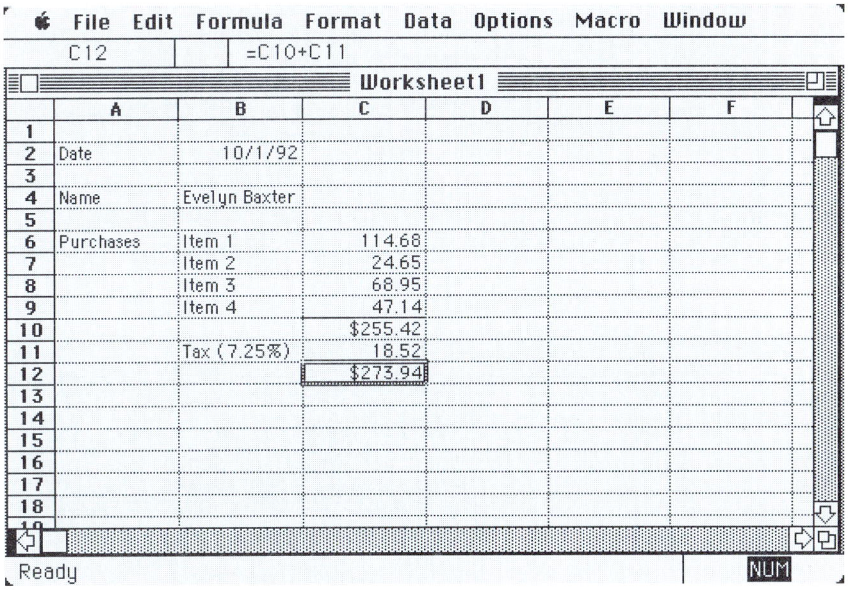

Figure 9-5   A simple worksheet

Text

Cells A2, A4, and A6 (and others) in Figure 9-5 contain text. Any text can be typed into a cell. Text typed into a cell is treated as a constant; it will not be changed by Excel. You, however, can modify it any time you want, by selecting the cell and typing new text.

Most worksheets contain groups of numbers, and those numbers are identified by typing text into adjacent cells. This worksheet contains text used as labels (Date, Item 1, and so on). It also contains text used to represent data (Evelyn Baxter). This spreadsheet could be expanded to include the customer's address, credit information, shipping address, and other such textual data if desired.

None of the text cells in Figure 9-5 has any special formatting attributes, so they all show the text in the same font, size, and style.

Numbers

Cells B2 and C6:C9 contain numbers. Numbers are the basic data used in a worksheet to produce useful results. A number, like text, is a constant value. Once you type a number into a cell it will not change. You are free to go back later and change the number any time you wish.

The number in B2 is formatted to represent a date, and all of the cells in column C are formatted to show all values rounded to two decimal places.

Cells C9 and C11 have been formatted to show a solid border on the bottom of the cell, to represent a line indicating an arithmetic sum.

Cells C10 and C12 are formatted as currency, so a dollar sign is added in front of the number. This dollar sign is inserted by Excel, not by the person creating the worksheet. It is not a part of the value in the cell; it is an attribute that affects how the value is displayed.

Formulas

Cells C10, C11, and C12 contain formulas. The main purpose of a spreadsheet program is to perform numeric calculations and present the results, and cells containing formulas are the basic mechanism used to do this. In this worksheet, there are only three formulas. You can tell Excel to show the formulas in a worksheet, instead of the values calculated by the formulas, by choosing **Display** from the Options menu, and then selecting **Formulas**. You would then see the worksheet as shown in Figure 9-6.

	File	Edit	Formula	Format	Data	Options	Macro	Window

C12		=C10+C11	

Worksheet1

	A	B	C
1			
2	Date	32416	
3			
4	Name	Evelyn Baxter	
5			
6	Purchases	Item 1	114.68
7		Item 2	24.65
8		Item 3	68.95
9		Item 4	47.14
10			=SUM(C6:C9)
11		Tax (7.25%)	=7.25%*C10
12			=C10+C11
13			
14			
15			
16			
17			
18			

Ready   NUM

Figure 9-6   Displaying formulas in the worksheet

A *formula* must start with the equals character (=). The formula in cell C10 is **=SUM(C6:C9)**. This uses the built-in SUM() function, which tells Excel to calculate the sum of the numbers in those cells. When the sum is calculated, it is displayed in the cell containing the formula.

Cell C11 says to multiply the results of the sum calculation by 7.25% and display the results. Finally, C12 has a formula to add the total of the purchases and the calculated sales tax and show the resulting value.

Figures 9-5 and 9-6 represent the same worksheet: the first shows the display as it would normally be seen, and the second shows the optional view of the formulas instead of their calculated results.

You may be wondering why the date in cell B2 was replaced by the number "32416". The date was entered by typing **10/1/92**. Excel recognized this as a valid date and automatically converted it into the serial number representing the number of days since Excel's base date of January 1, 1904.

Excel calculates a formula and displays the results, not the formula itself, on the screen This is one of the main features that make a spreadsheet so powerful and easy to use. If you change a formula, or the numbers or formulas in cells it refers to, Excel recalculates and displays the new value automatically.

Cell Addressing in Formulas

Two types of cell addressing can be used when you are creating formulas in Excel: relative and absolute.

In the sample worksheet just presented there was a formula used to calculate the sum of four numbers. The formula in cell C10, **=SUM(C6:C9)**, tells Excel to add the numbers found in the four cells just above C10. As long as you do not copy this formula and paste it somewhere else in the spreadsheet or tell Excel to duplicate the formula for you, you don't have to be aware of how Excel addresses the cells in the formula.

Excel has a powerful, time-saving feature that lets it automatically duplicate formulas accross a row or down a column when you tell it to do so. It is when you make use of this feature that you must be aware of the differences in relative and absolute addressing.

Relative Addressing

Most formulas used in Excel are based on *relative addressing*. Relative addressing is like giving directions to somebody who is trying to find something nearby. You might tell him to go to the second red light, turn left, and go three blocks. This is a relative method of giving directions. If you were standing in a location two blocks away, the same directions would cause the other person to arrive at a different destination.

Unless you tell it otherwise, Excel uses relative addressing in interpreting formulas.

Let's assume that you want to add another column of numbers, located in cells D6:D9. Instead of having to retype the same formula in cell D10, you can tell Excel to *fill* the formula one cell to the right. When Excel copies the formula into the next cell, it automatically adjusts the formula so that it reads =SUM(D6:D9). This is because Excel thinks you still want to add the four cells above the new formula's location (which is now cell D10).

In this case, and most similar cases, this assumption and modification would be correct.

Absolute Addressing

In some cases, however, you will encounter situations when the cell address in the formula should be interpreted as an *absolute address*.

For example, you might want the formula in cell D10 to show the sum of the cells C6:C9, just as it does in cell C10. There is a simple way to tell Excel not to adjust the cell references in the formula. To make a cell address absolute rather than relative, you change the formula to read =SUM($C$6:$C$9). Absolute addresses (with the dollar signs) will not be adjusted when Excel duplicates the formula.

You will encounter situations in Projects 3 and 4 in this chapter when it will be necessary to use absolute addressing to produce the correct results. The reasons for using absolute rather than relative addressing will be explained whenever the situation arises in those projects.

Charts

In addition to its worksheet features, Excel has a wide range of charting functions for displaying numeric data in graphic form. The charting aspects of Excel also make wide use of the Macintosh's graphics capabilities and allow you to create presentation-quality charts, which can be printed directly to your ImageWriter or LaserWriter.

Excel offers a wide variety of chart types such as pie charts and bar charts. You will learn about charting in Project 2.

In the first four projects in this chapter you will learn to create, modify, save, and print worksheets and charts.

GETTING HELP

Like most top-quality Macintosh programs, Excel offers extensive online help. Three main types of help are available. (This assumes that you copied the Excel help file from the distribution disk onto your work disk when you originally installed the program.)

The first way to get help is to choose **Help** from the Window menu. This offers a variety of help information through which you can browse. When you open the Help window, you will see that the terms have solid underlines (see Figure 9-7).

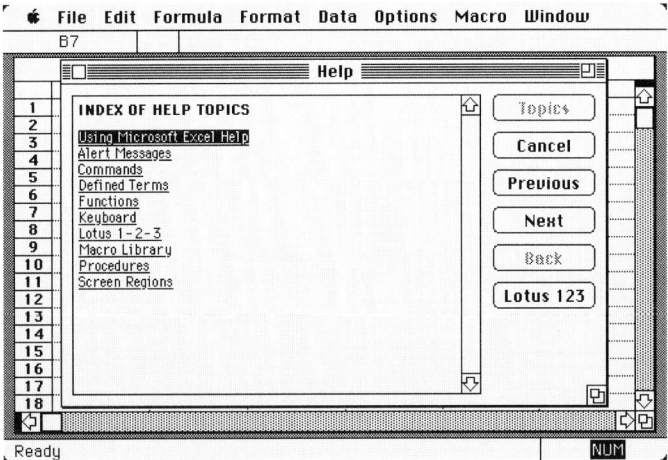

Figure 9-7   Excel's opening Help screen

A term with a solid underline is known as a *jump term*. When you point to this type of term and click the mouse button, Help will find the information associated with that term and take you to it. By clicking on these *linked terms*, you can jump from one topic to another and follow a thread of interrelated topics.

If you click on the underlined phrase **Defined Terms**, you then jump to its screen (see Figure 9-8). Whenever you click on a jump term, you descend one level deeper in the help system. To return to the level from which you just jumped, click the **Back** button.

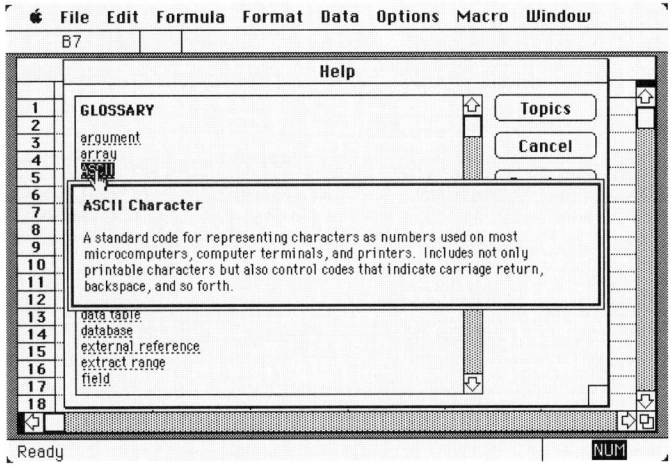

Figure 9-8   Defined Terms help screen showing definition of ASCII character

Each dotted underlined term is called a *defined term*. If you point to this term and then press and hold down the mouse button, a box appears containing a brief description of the term. When you release the mouse button, the box disappears.

Clicking the **Next** button moves you to the next screen about that topic. The Previous button takes you to the previous screen.

If you are familiar with Lotus 1-2-3, you can click the **Lotus 1-2-3** button to retrieve information about the Excel equivalents of Lotus 1-2-3 commands.

The second way to get help while in Excel is in the form of its *context-sensitive help*. If you are using Excel and want help on the current context, press Command-/ (Command-slash). For example, if you are working in a dialog box and want help, pressing Command-/ will provide information about the dialog box and any options or responses you may select.

The third way to get information, when you want to specify the context, is to press Command-? (Command-question mark, or Command-Shift-slash). The pointer will turn into a question mark. You can then click on an object or choose a command. Instead of the click causing an action to occur, Excel will give you information about the object or command you selected.

For example, suppose you are working in a worksheet, and you want more information about the formula bar. You could choose Help and then find the information associated with the formula bar, but there is an easier way.

If you type Command-?, the pointer changes to a question mark. You can then move the pointer into the formula bar area (see Figure 9-9).

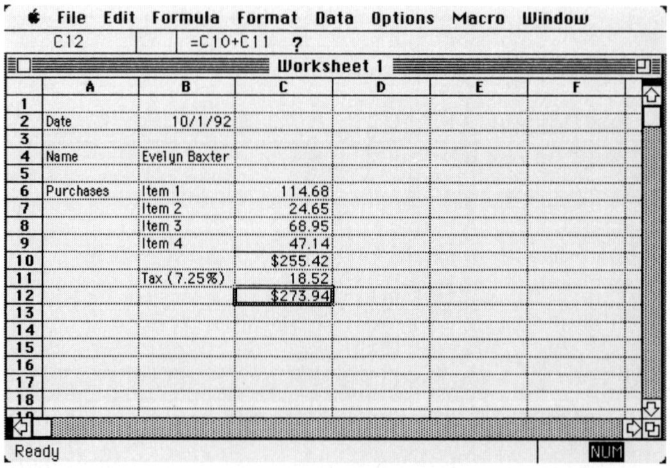

Figure 9-9   Getting help by typing Command-?

Clicking the mouse button while the question mark pointer is in the formula bar will show its Help screen (see Figure 9-10). If you had clicked while the pointer was in the worksheet area, you would have been presented with general information about the worksheet.

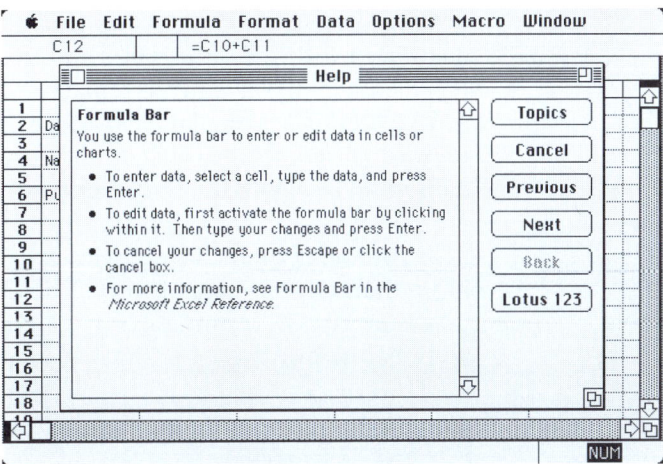

Figure 9-10   Help screen for the formula bar

If you are in a dialog box when you type Command-?, it will work the same as typing Command-/. The dialog box is the current context, so you will be presented with the Help screen for that dialog box.

Any time you are working in Excel, this help feature is available, and it is usually easier than looking up a topic in the manual. Remember, however, that the manual contains more in-depth information about the topics than Help does.

SAVING YOUR WORK

The first time you save your document, Excel asks you, by way of the dialog box shown in Figure 9-11, where you want your document saved and what you want it to be named.

Clicking the **Drive** button toggles between one or more floppy drives and hard drives, depending on the hardware you are using. The Save dialog box shows the name of the floppy disk or hard drive as that drive is selected. You are saving your document on the selected disk or hard drive with the name showing in the Save dialog box. In the dialog box shown in Figure 9-11, the name of the disk, Miguel Garcia Data, is shown in two places. Always be aware of where you are saving your work.

After you have saved the first time, the next time you choose **Save** Excel assumes you want your document to be saved in the same place and under the same name. You should be careful about saving your document in the correct place the first time you save it, so you can find it later. The Save process is much quicker the second and subsequent times, because you are not prompted for any additional information.

The Save As command is similar to the Save command, except that it gives you the option to give your document a different name and save it in a different location. Every time you choose **Save As** from the File menu you are prompted with the dialog box shown in Figure 9-11. This is the same dialog box you see the first time you save your document.

When you use the Save As command and you attempt to save the document with the same name and in the same location as before, you will be asked if you want to replace the old document. This is because no two files in a particular location can have the same name. If you want to save different versions of the same document use the Save As command and give the document a different name.

Save your work often. Save at least every ten minutes, so you never lose more than ten minutes of work. The Command-key equivalent of the Save command, Command-S, is a helpful shortcut. Always save your work before printing.

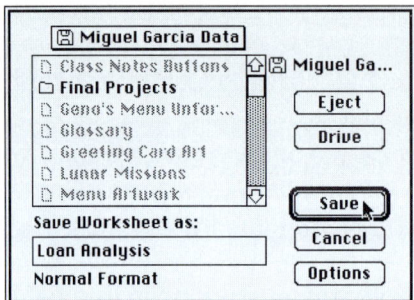

Figure 9-11   The Save dialog box

Be aware that you can save a document before you actually type anything into it and that many people do it this way. However, you will be given explicit instructions for saving your work at appropriate times throughout the project.

Project 1: Creating a Worksheet

In this project you will learn to add text, numbers, and formulas to create a worksheet. Then you will save three different copies of the worksheet to be used in Projects 2, 3, and 4. In Project 1, you will create a worksheet and calculate three different loans: a student loan, a car loan, and a house loan.

All loans are not the same; the amount it costs to pay back a loan depends on how much was borrowed (principal), the periodic interest rate (annual and monthly rates in these cases), and the length of time before the loan is repaid (term of the loan).

From these figures you can calculate the amount of the monthly payment, the total amount to be repaid to the lender, and the amount of interest incurred.

The final output of Project 1 is shown in Figure 9-12.

Loan Analysis   **Miguel Garcia**

Loan Type   Student Loan

Total Amount $2,500.00
Down Payment $0.00
Term of Loan   5 years
Annual Interest Rate   8.500 percent

Amount Financed $2,500.00
Term of Loan   60 months

Monthly Payment $51.29

Total Amount to be Repaid $3,077.48
Total Interest $577.48

6/2/90   10:29 AM

Figure 9-12   Final output of Project 1

ORGANIZING A WORKSHEET

To perform a basic loan analysis, you need enter only four values: total amount, down payment, number of periodic payments, and annual interest rate. The worksheet will then use several formulas to calculate the loan information and very quickly will display the results of those calculations on the screen.

You will informally divide the worksheet into two areas: data entry (input) and results of the calculations (output).

You can use this worksheet to calculate any amortized loan (assuming the loan is repaid monthly). There are many situations where all the formulas and formatting in a worksheet may be used in solving more than one problem. In these cases it makes sense to develop a standard worksheet, and then copy that worksheet and change only the text and numbers necessary to solve each problem.

A worksheet used in this manner is known as a *template*. A template contains all the formulas, labels, formatting, and constant text for solving the problem. Whenever you want to solve a problem that has been defined in a template, you should copy the template, and then make changes and enter appropriate data into the copy. This way you won't risk damaging or losing the original.

In Project 1, you will create a general purpose loan analysis template. Then you will make three copies of this template, change only the information that is different, and produce three specific loan worksheets.

ADDING TEXT TO A WORKSHEET

In this worksheet you must enter text, numbers, and formulas. It is often easiest to enter all text, then all numbers, and then all formulas. You can enter them in any order, and it is not necessary to enter them as groups. Some people prefer to complete one part of the worksheet before going on to the next. Whenever you create worksheets, feel free to enter the contents of the cells whichever way you prefer.

In this project you will begin by entering the text.

Of the millions of possible cells in a worksheet, only one is active at a time. The active cell has a border around it, and its address is listed in the reference area of the screen.

➡ Click cell **A1** to make it the active cell if it is not already active. Type **Loan Type** and press the Return key.

This will enter the text into cell A1 and accept it. When you accept a cell's contents by typing the Return key, Excel will make the next cell below that one the active cell. This allows you to quickly type information into a column of cells without having to select each cell and make it active before typing its contents.

You can also have a cell's text accepted by clicking the enter box or pressing the Enter key. If you do this, Excel accepts the text and leaves A1 as the active cell.

A number of keystrokes can be used to select a different active cell. When a new cell becomes active, the border around the formerly active cell is removed and the new active cell is highlighted. The active cell does not move; Excel makes another cell active, but it looks like the active cell moves around the screen as each cell is highlighted in turn. Speaking loosely, many people refer to this process as moving the active cell.

The keys shown in Table 9-1 perform the indicated operations in Excel.

Key	Action
Enter	Accepts formula but does not move active cell
Return	Accepts formula and moves active cell down
Shift-Return	Accepts formula and moves active cell up
Tab	Accepts formula and moves active cell right
Shift-Tab	Accepts formula and moves active cell left
Right arrow	Moves active cell right. If an arrow key is used while a formula is being entered or modified, it will change the formula and not make a different cell active.
Left arrow	Moves active cell left
Up arrow	Moves active cell up
Down arrow	Moves active cell down

Table 9-1   Keys that affect active cell and formulas in Excel

Since you want to continue entering text in column A, you accepted the text by pressing the Return key, which caused Excel to accept the text into cell A1 and make the cell below A1 the new active cell. As you can see now, cell A2 is outlined and the reference area shows A2 is active.

Return ➡ There is no text to enter in cell A2, so press the Return key again to make A3 the active cell.

➡ Refer to Table 9-2, and enter the appropriate text into each of the listed cells. Note that the last three entries go into column C instead of column A.

Cell address	Text to be entered
A1	Loan Type
A3	Total Amount
A4	Down Payment
A5	Term of Loan
A6	Annual Interest Rate
A8	Amount Financed
A9	Term of Loan
A11	Monthly Payment
A13	Total Amount to be Repaid
A14	Total Interest
C5	years
C6	percent
C9	months

Table 9-2   Text to be entered into the worksheet

When you finish, your screen should look like the one shown in Figure 9-13.

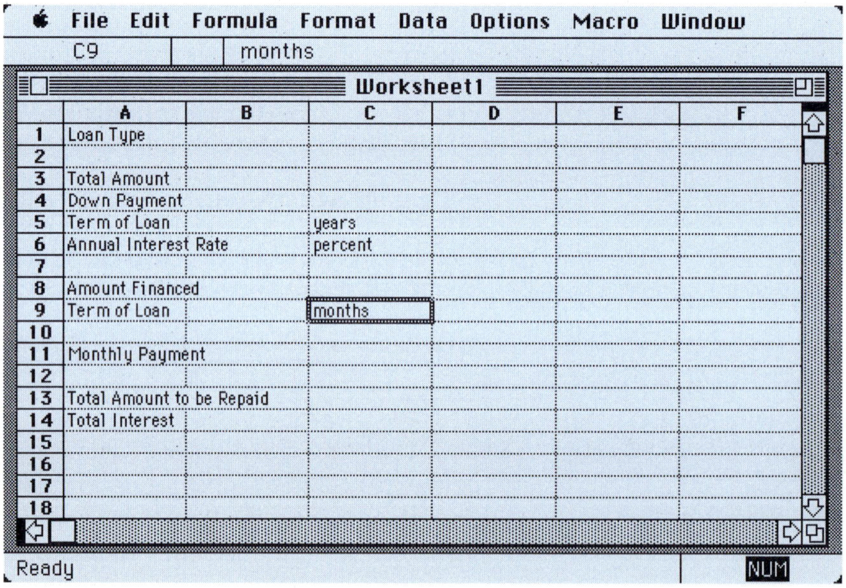

Figure 9-13   Worksheet with all text entered

CHANGING COLUMN WIDTHS

You will be entering numbers and formulas into column B, but you will encounter a problem, because some of the text in column A does not fit and it continues into column B. For instance, note how the label "Annual Interest Rate" in Figure 9-13 extends into column B.

Excel allows up to 255 characters to be entered into a cell. This means you easily can enter more text than will fit into a column. If the cell to the right is blank, Excel allows the text to "spill over" into the blank cell. In fact, text can continue into several empty cells.

If the cell to the right is not empty, Excel will truncate the text and will only display whatever text will fit into the current column width. This does not mean that any of the text is lost. If you click on the cell and make it active, you will see the entire contents of that cell in the formula bar.

In a couple of minutes you will be adding numbers and formulas into column B, and this will cause any text that overflows from column A to be truncated. You want to be able to see all the text in column A, so you will make the column wider.

⟹ Move the pointer to the right border of column A between the A and B at the top of the column.

The pointer changes into a vertical bar with arrows pointing left and right, as shown at left. While you see this pointer and you continue pressing the mouse button, you can make column A narrower or wider by moving the mouse to the left or to the right.

⟹ Press the mouse button and move the mouse to the right until all the text in column A fits into the column; then release the button.

Figure 9-14 shows how the screen looks during (left screen) and after (right screen) this operation. The left screen shows that cell A's right border has been "grabbed" and moved past the longest text in column A. (It looks like column B is being adjusted, but that is because the right border of column A has been dragged almost to the right border of column B.) In the screen on the right, the mouse button has been released, and Excel has resized column A and has moved the left side of column B to where the pointer was when the mouse button was released.

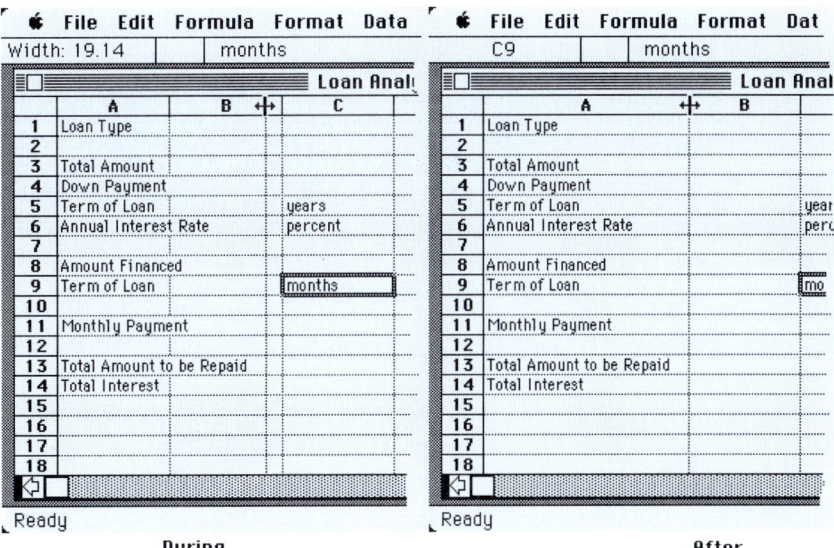

During   After

Figure 9-14   Changing the width of column A

Now that all the text fits into column A, none will be truncated.

SAVING THE WORKSHEET

Be careful about saving your document in the correct place the first time you save it, so you can find it later. The Save process is much quicker the second and subsequent times, because you are not prompted for any additional information.

Save your work often. Save at least every ten minutes, so you never lose more than ten minutes of work. The Command-key equivalent of the Save command, Command-S, is a convenient shortcut.

⌘-S ➠ Choose **Save** from the File menu.

➠ Click the **Drive** button, if necessary, to switch drives until the name of your data disk is showing above the Eject button, where "Miguel Garcia" is in Figure 9-15.

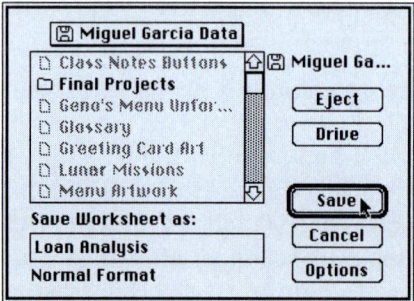

Figure 9-15 The Save dialog box

➠ Type **Loan Analysis** as the name of your document, and then click the **Save** button.

ENTERING NUMBERS

If you are currently attending college, or have been to college, you might be familiar with student loans. We will use this worksheet to analyze a loan for $2,500 for 5 years at 8.5% interest. (Of course, there are a wide variety of terms and conditions for student loans. At the end of this project you will be given the opportunity to analyze several loans and compare them.)

There are only four numbers to enter into this worksheet.

➠ Refer to Table 9-3 below and enter the appropriate numbers into each of the listed cells.

Cell address	Number to be entered
B3	2500
B4	0
B5	5
B6	8.5

Table 9-3   Numbers to be entered into Loan Analysis worksheet

You learned earlier that Excel allows up to 255 characters to be contained in a cell and that text can spill over into blank cells to the right.

The 255-character limit applies to cells containing numbers, but the ability to "spill over" does not apply. If a cell is not wide enough to show the entire number contained in the cell (according to any formatting you have chosen), Excel will always show number signs (#) across the cell. This is an error message to alert you to change the format of the cell or to make the column wider.

FORMATTING NUMBERS

Excel provides many predefined formats for displaying numbers, as well as the ability to create your own custom formats.

Most of the values to be displayed in column B will be dollar amounts. Some of the other values will be percentages or integers. Since most will represent currency, let's tell Excel to display all the numbers in column B as currency. Then let's select individual cells and assign them a different format.

Any time you reassign the format for a cell, it overrides any previous formatting.

To format all of column B, you must select a range of cells. Previously you have worked with only a single cell at a time. Excel allows you to select a range of cells upon which to operate, but even when a range of cells is selected, there still is only one active cell.

The distinction between a cell's contents and its formatting attributes is important. There is only one active cell, and it is the only cell in which you can enter text, numbers, or formulas. In Figure 9-16, all of column B is selected, but only cell B1 is active. You can see this by looking into the reference area, where it shows B1.

You can modify the format of any selection of cells all at one time. This will not affect the contents of the cells, but only how they will be displayed.

➠   Select column B by clicking on the letter **B** at the top of the column.

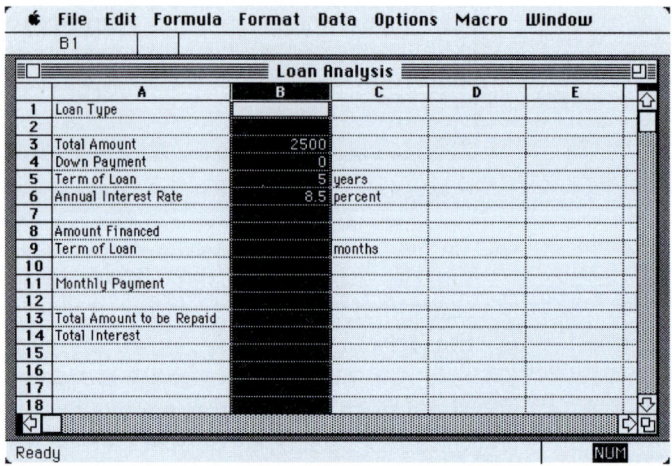

Figure 9-16   Selecting an entire column

Notice that all of column B is highlighted, but cell B1 is outlined and shown in white, and the reference area shows that B1 is the active cell (see Figure 9-16).

➡ Select **Number** from the Format menu. Select the format shown in Figure 9-17 by clicking on it, and then click **OK**.

A shortcut for selecting a format from the list is to double-click on it.

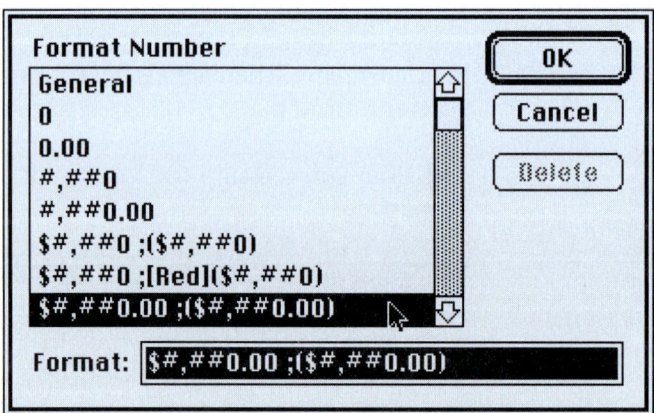

Figure 9-17   Choosing a currency number format

All the cells in column B now display their number values as currency with two decimal places. Let's select a different format for three of the cells that will not contain currency values.

In this case, the first and last cells contain numbers representing currency. The cells with other formatting are interspersed inside this group, so it is faster to format the whole group as currency first and then go back and deal with the exceptions.

When you encounter a situation where there is no clear majority of cells with the same format, it is probably better to format each cell with its particular format. But, whenever you can format a range of cells it is faster, even if you have to go in a change a few.

The term of the loan will be entered in years. Sometimes it will be an integer value, such as 3 or 5, but other times it might be 2.5 or 1.25 years. Since most loans are for whole years, this was the easiest way to organize the worksheet. We could have opted to let you enter the number of months, which might be useful if loans are made for terms like 30 months. With a little more work, the worksheet could let you enter years and months, such as 2 years and 6 months. It is up to the person who designs a worksheet to determine the most useful form for entering data into a worksheet.

You want the value to be displayed using the fewest number of digits to the right of the decimal point. The format that will do this is the General format. Assume that you will be the one using this worksheet and that you will not enter some value such as 3.912767349 for the term of the loan.

⇒   Select B5, where the term of the loan in years was entered, by clicking in the cell. Choose **Number** from the Format menu. Double-click **General** to select and apply it.

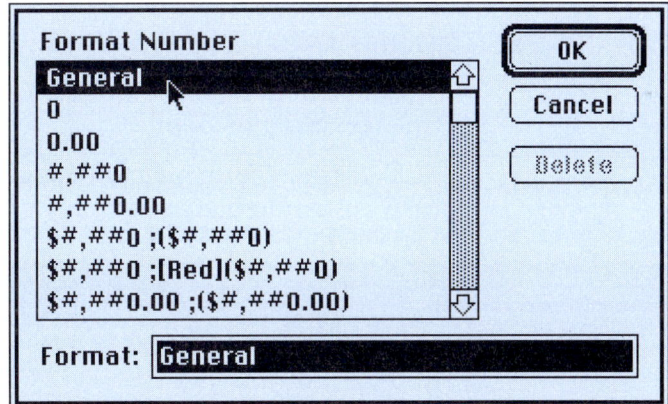

Figure 9-18   Choosing a general number format

Cell B9 will contain the term of the loan in months. You want this value to be displayed as an integer, so let's tell Excel to format cell B9 to show no digits to the right of the decimal point.

⇒   Double-click on **0** to set the format of cell B9.

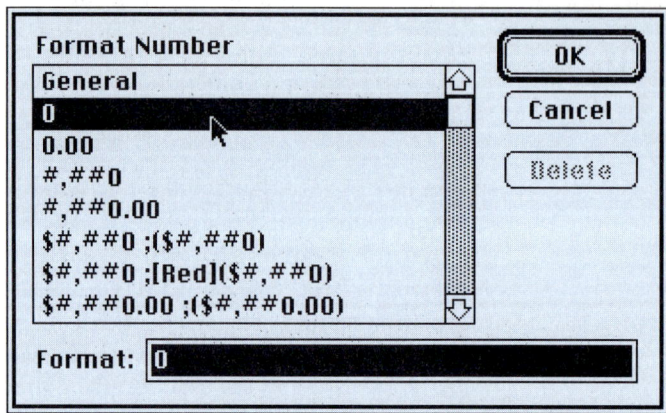

Figure 9-19   Choosing an integer number format

Cell B6 contains the value for the annual interest rate. Since these interest rates frequently have been designated in eighths of a percent, you need to allow the display of three digits to the right of the decimal point. Excel does not have a predefined format for this, so let's create a custom format.

➟ Tell Excel that you want to format the number in cell B6 (use the techniques you have used for the previous cells). When you get to the dialog box shown in Figure 9-20, click (do not double-click) on **0.00**.

This format will now appear in the box at the bottom, labeled "Format:".

➟ Position the pointer to the right of the last zero and click to position the text insertion point.

➟ Add another **0** by typing (see Figure 9-20). Click **OK** to accept your new custom format.

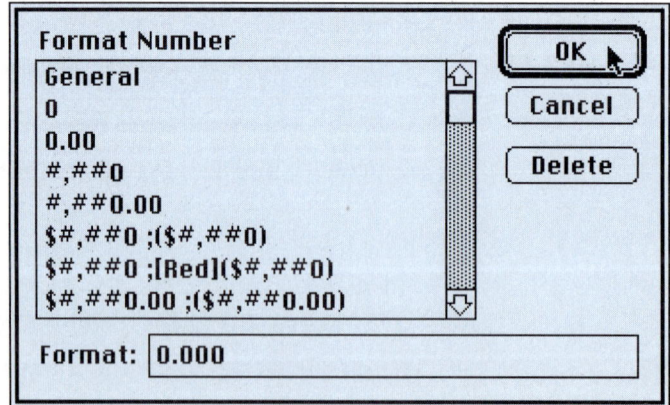

Figure 9-20   Creating a custom number format

At this point, you have entered all the text and numbers needed for this worksheet, and you have formatted the numbers as you need them to appear.

⌘-S   Now is a good time to save your worksheet.

FORMATTING CELLS

Another formatting option is to change how data is aligned: either to the right, left, or centered. Alignment is a purely aesthetic consideration and has no effect on calculations or sorting. Text is automatically aligned left, and numbers are aligned right.

Excel offers the normal style options that can be applied to individual cells or cell ranges, such as bold, italic, or underline. Because of its grid orientation, it also provides the capability of drawing complete or partial borders around cells. Examples would be placing a box around a key number or emphasizing the column header range by making those cells bold and outlined.

CREATING FORMULAS

A paper spreadsheet can display text and numbers as well as an electronic spreadsheet can. If all you want to do is to present information, you can do it manually or with other programs such as word processors.

The real power of an electronic spreadsheet comes from its ability to store a formula in a cell, automatically recalculate all formulas when something changes, and then display the current results on the screen.

Using Excel's Built-in Functions

Excel has a total of 131 built-in worksheet functions that you can use to create formulas. These functions are organized into 11 categories: Database, Date and Time, Financial, Information, Logical, Lookup, Mathematical, Matrix, Statistical, Text, and Trigonometric.

Excel's Help has information available on each of these functions and groups of related functions. One of the most used functions is the SUM() function, which totals the contents of a range of cells.

Let's see what Help has to say about the SUM() function.

➥   Choose **Help** from the Window menu.

➥   Click on **Functions**.

➥   Scroll down the list of functions until you find SUM(), and then click on it.

Excel presents a brief explanation for the function and some examples of its use (see Figure 9-21).

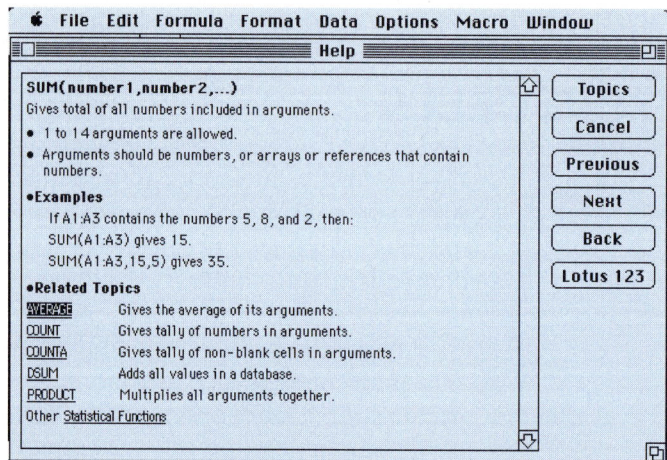

Figure 9-21   Sum() function Help screen

If you want to use any of these built-in functions, you have two choices for entering them into your formula: (1) you can type the formula into the formula bar, or (2) you can choose **Paste Function** from the Formula menu. If you decide to use the Paste Function command, you have a choice of whether to have Excel show a list of *arguments* in the formula or not.

An argument is one of the values or cell addresses that will appear inside the parentheses of the function. For example, if you want to add all the values in cells A1, A2, A3, and A4, you have two choices: (1) you can enter the formula:

$$=A1+A2+A3+A4$$

Or (2) you can use the SUM() function:

$$=SUM(A1:A4)$$

In the first case the formula tells Excel to add the value in cell A1 to the value in A2 to the value in A3 to the value in A4 and then to store the results in the current cell. In the second case, the formula tells Excel to calculate the sum of the values stored in the range of cells from A1 to A4. (The range "A1:A4" is the argument for the SUM() function in this case.)

Both formulas will result in the same value appearing in the current cell. The only difference is how much effort it might take you to enter the formulas. If you needed the sum of only two or three cells, the first formula might be the easiest. If, instead of two or three cells, you needed the sum of 100 cells, the second alternative would be a much better choice. Both methods work; you can choose the one that is most convenient for you.

Entering Formulas

To enter a formula into a cell, you must begin by typing an equals sign. This equals sign is the signal that tells Excel that you are entering a formula rather than text or a number. Remember, Excel displays text just as you entered it, but it must calculate the results of a formula and display the results in the cell that contains the formula.

You can always see the entire formula whenever the cell is the active cell. The formula will be shown in the formula bar, located just below the menu bar at the top of the screen. You can also edit a formula in the formula bar.

The formula you will enter into cell B8 is =**B3-B4**, but don't enter it yet. This formula tells Excel to subtract the value displayed in cell B4 from the value displayed in cell B3 and to show the results of this calculation in cell B8. (Remember, this is a formula using relative addressing. It really tells Excel to subtract the value in the cell that is located four cells above B8 from the value in the cell five cells above B8 and then display the results in B8.)

Refer back to cells B3 and B4. Cell B3 represents the total amount of a purchase or prospective loan, and B4 represents the down payment amount. Cell B8 represents the amount you will actually borrow. Therefore, this formula tells Excel to subtract the amount of the down payment from the total amount, giving the amount to be financed. Since you have previously formatted this column to show values with dollar signs and commas, your result will be displayed automatically as currency.

There are two ways to enter the formula into Excel. You can type the formula, or you can use the mouse to point to cells or ranges of cells to be placed into the formula.

You will now enter the formula into cell B8 using each method.

➠ Select cell **B8** by clicking in it.

➠ Type the = key, and then type **B3-B4**.

➠ Press the Enter key to tell Excel to accept the formula, calculate it, display the results, and keep cell B8 active.

When you pressed the Enter key, Excel rapidly calculated the results, and you now see $2,500.00 displayed in cell B8 (as shown in Figure 9-22).

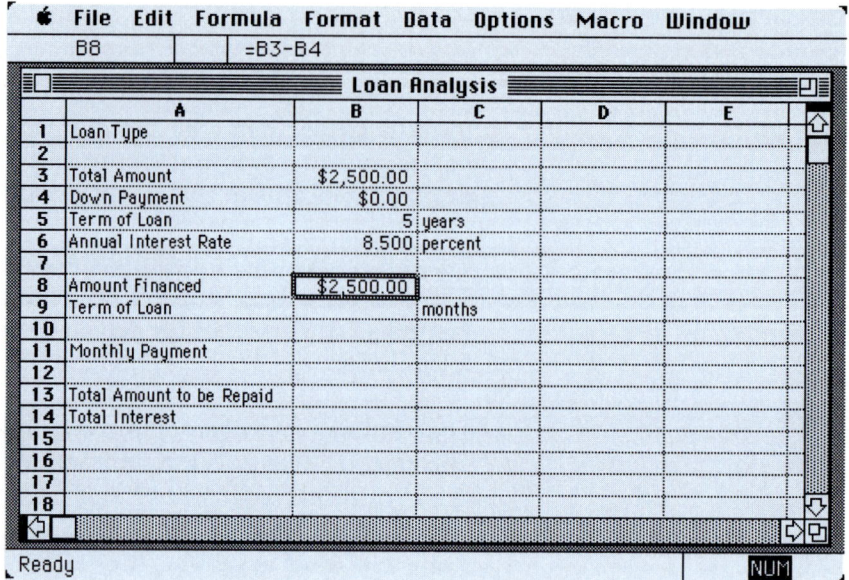

Figure 9-22 Entering formula to calculate Amount Financed

With such a simple formula, typing is probably the easiest way to enter it. An alternative method for entering the formula allows you to specify cells or ranges of cells using the mouse. Enter the formula again using this method.

➡ Select cell **B8**, and type the = key.

 This tells Excel that you are entering a formula into this cell. As soon as you do this, the equals sign is shown in the formula bar, and two new boxes appear as shown to the left.

The box with the X is the cancel box. If you click in this box any time you are entering or editing something in the formula bar, the edit will be cancelled, and the cell and its contents will be left as they were before you began the current edit.

The box with the checkmark is the accept box. Clicking in this box is the same as pressing the Enter key. The current contents of the formula bar will be accepted into the cell.

➡ Select cell **B3**.

An effect often called "marching ants" surrounds the cell, and B3 is added to the formula in the formula bar.

This marching ants selection shows that you have selected only one cell to be added to the formula. The marching ants are there as a visual confirmation of the cell(s) you have selected to be added to the formula.

➡ Type a minus sign.

The marching ants disappear from cell B3, to show it is no longer selected. Any math operator will cause the marching ants to go away, and the operator will be added to the formula. Excel's operators are shown in Table 9-4.

Operator	Represents	Example	Meaning
^	Exponentiation	=2^3	2 cubed
*	Multiplication	=2*3	2 times 3
/	Division	=2/3	2 divided by 3
+	Addition	=2+3	2 plus 3
-	Subtraction	=2-3	2 minus 3

Table 9-4   Common math operators used in Excel

➠   Select cell **B4**.

B4 is surrounded by the marching ants, and its address is added to the formula. The formula bar now shows **=B3-B4**.

➠   Now press the Enter key, or click on the accept box.

As soon as you do this, the marching ants will disappear from cell B4, and the cancel and accept boxes go away. The formula is accepted into the cell, and Excel quickly calculates the formula and shows the result in cell B8.

This method seems like a lot of work compared with the previous method, and on such an easy formula it may be. However, it has the benefit of being more intuitive. Instead of having to concentrate on the addresses of the cells and type them in, pointing and clicking allows you to think something like, "In this formula take this cell and subtract that cell from it". Whenever you think of "this cell" or "that cell" all you have to do is point and click.

This method of using the mouse to select cells is even easier when you need to specify a range of cells. In that case, you click on a corner of the range, hold down the mouse button, and drag to the diagonally opposite corner. As you drag the mouse, a rectangle will become highlighted as you select the range of cells inside the rectangle. The entire range is surrounded by the marching ants and the address of the range is entered into the formula bar.

As an example, suppose you wanted to enter =SUM(B3:D9) into cell B12 of a new worksheet. You could type **=SUM()** into the formula bar. Then click between the parentheses to position the insertion point. This tells Excel you want to insert something between the parentheses. You could type **B3:D9** directly into the formula bar if you prefer. Or, you could drag from cell B3 to D9. As you do this the marching ants will surround the range you are selecting. You don't even have to look at the cell addresses; just drag and select the ones you want, and Excel will enter their addresses into the formula bar (see Figure 9-23).

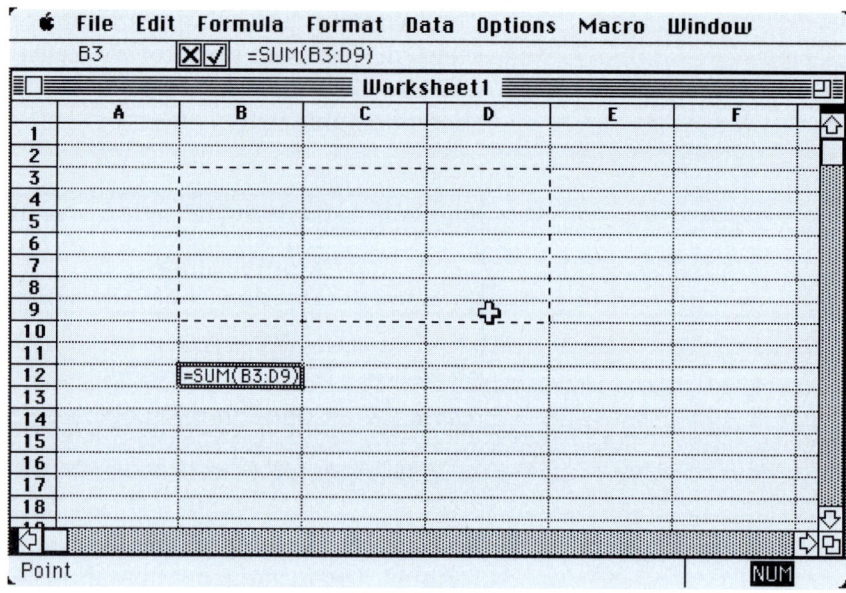

Figure 9-23   Entering a range into a formula by dragging with the
pointer

Using Paste Function

You will now enter the formula into cell B9 to calculate the term of the
loan in months, based on the term of the loan in years, which you
previously entered in cell B5.

This formula will multiply the value in cell B5 by 12.

Let's tell Excel to force the value in cell B9 to be an integer. This may be
done by using the function INT(). The formula you will enter into cell
B9 is **=INT(B5*12)**. As before, you can type this into the cell, or you can
type part of it and select cell B5 to add it to the formula. You will use the
second method, with the addition of using Paste Function from the
Formula menu.

➡ Select cell **B9** and type =.

➡ Choose **Paste Function** from the Formula menu.

➡ Scroll down in the list until you see INT(), and then double-click on
    it to select it. (See Figure 9-24.) You can also enter the first letter of
    any function to jump to that section of the alphabetized list.

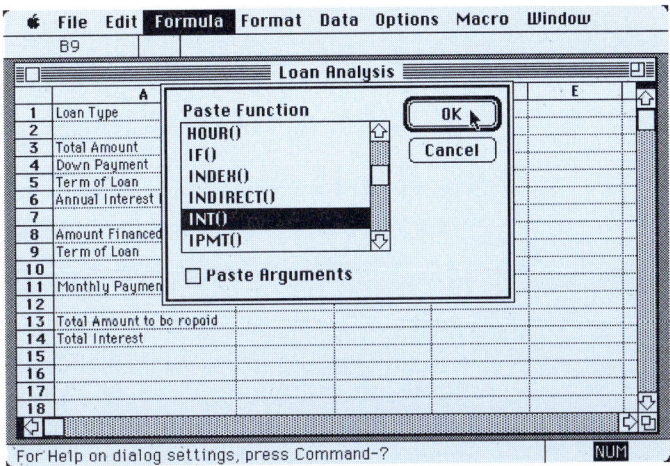

Figure 9-24   Pasting the integer function into a formula

Look at the screen on your computer. Notice that the formula bar now contains =**INT()**, and the insertion point is inside the parentheses.

➡ Select cell **B5**, and then type ***12** and accept the formula (see Figure 9-25).

	A	B	C	D	E
1	Loan Type				
2					
3	Total Amount	$2,500.00			
4	Down Payment	$0.00			
5	Term of Loan	5	years		
6	Annual Interest Rate	8.500	percent		
7					
8	Amount Financed	$2,500.00			
9	Term of Loan	60	months		
10					
11	Monthly Payment				
12					
13	Total Amount to be Repaid				
14	Total Interest				
15					
16					
17					
18					

B9   =INT(B5*12)

Figure 9-25   Completed formula using built-in integer function

Your worksheet should show 60 as the term of the loan in months.

Now it is time to calculate one of the most important parts of a loan analysis—the monthly payment. To do this, you will make use of two of Excel's built-in formulas: PMT() and ABS(). PMT() means "payment" and ABS() stands for "absolute value".

The PMT() function is a multipurpose financial function. You will be using it to calculate the periodic payment to repay an amortized loan.

This means that you will be making a regular (monthly) payment, which will be applied to the loan in two ways. First, your payment will be applied to the interest on the remaining balance of the loan for the month, then anything left will be applied to reduce the amount you owe. If you pay more than the regular payment amount, more will be applied to reducing the balance.

This worksheet assumes that you will pay exactly the monthly payment each month.

One of the features of amortized loans that usually comes as a surprise to first-time borrowers is the ratio of payment to interest versus the payment to reduce the principal (outstanding balance). If you borrow money to buy a house and the loan is for 30 years, you will be paying only a few dollars to reduce the loan and hundreds of dollars in interest. If the loan is for fewer years, the proportion of interest to principal will be smaller—you will be paying less for interest and more toward principal—but your monthly payments will be higher.

Before the widespread use of electronic spreadsheets it was difficult for consumers to compare different loan packages, but with this worksheet, you will be able to enter just four values and almost immediately see the monthly payment, total payback amount, and the total interest over the term of the loan.

The other function, ABS(), is the Absolute Value function. Since you are repaying a loan, the PMT() function will calculate your monthly payment as a negative value. The payment amount on this worksheet should be shown as a positive amount, so the ABS() function is used to make it so. The absolute value function will make a negative number positive and will not affect zero values or positive numbers.

To begin the formula in cell B11 you will start with the absolute value function.

➡ Select cell **B11**, choose **Paste Function**, select the **ABS()** function from the list, and accept it.

➡ Now, again choose **Paste Function**, scroll down and select **PMT()** from the list (do not double-click).

➡ Check **Paste Arguments** (see Figure 9-26). Click **OK**.

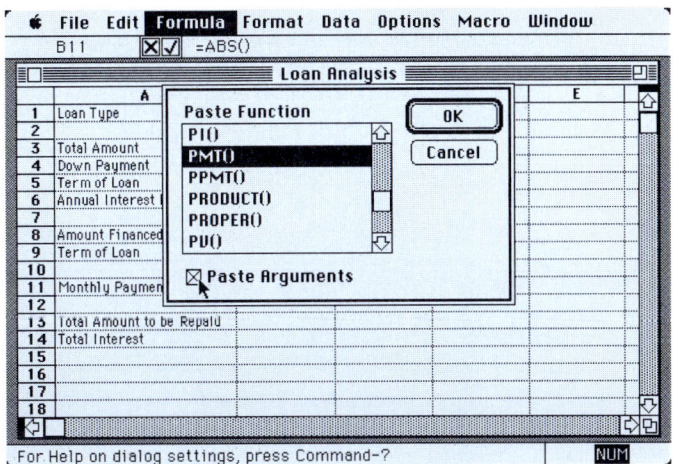

Figure 9-26   Pasting the payment function and its arguments into a
                 formula

The formula bar will now have the ABS() function and the PMT()
function pasted into the formula bar. By choosing **Paste Arguments**, you
told Excel to add a list of dummy arguments to indicate what needs to
be within the parentheses for the PMT() function to calculate the
monthly payment on your loan.

A *dummy argument* is a group of letters that represent what the function
expects to find inside the parentheses. They are called "dummy"
arguments because they are only placeholders and must be replaced
with actual parameters.

There are five arguments for the PMT() function: rate, nper, pv, fv, and
type. Their meanings are shown in Table 9-5.

Argument	Meaning
rate	the periodic interest rate, in this case, monthly
nper	the number of periods in the term of the loan; in this case, it represents months
pv	present value (amount to be financed)
fv	future value (this is not applicable to this project)
type	indicates whether payment is made at the beginning or end of the period (defaults to beginning) and can make a big difference when payments are made quarterly or annually

Table 9-5   Arguments necessary for PMT() function

To calculate the monthly payment, you will need to supply values only
for the rate, number of periods, and present value.

➡ To specify the rate, move the pointer to the formula bar and double-
    click on the word "rate."

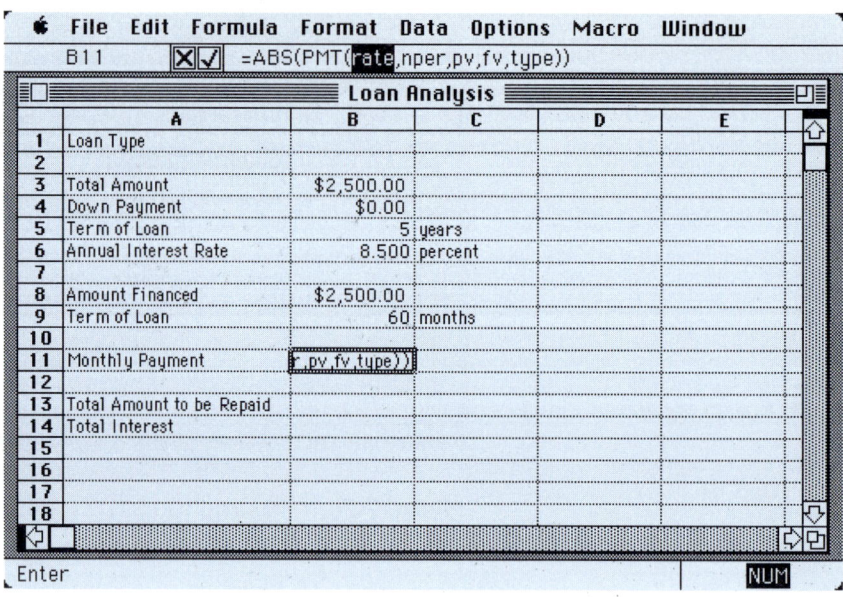

Figure 9-27   Replacing the rate argument with its associated value

➡ The annual interest rate is in cell B6, so click on **B6** to replace the
    word "rate" with the cell address **B6**.

This will tell Excel that the periodic rate is 8.5. However, this would not
be correct, since Excel would interpret this to mean that the monthly
interest rate is 850%, and that clearly is not correct. To convert the 8.5
to percent form, you must divide it by 100 to get 8.5%, which is the
annual rate, and then divide that by 12 to get the monthly interest rate.
The easiest way is to tell Excel to divide the contents of cell B6 by 1200
to convert it directly to the monthly interest rate as a percentage.

➡ The insertion point is directly after B6, so type **/1200** to tell Excel to
    divide the amount in cell B6 by 1200.

The next step is to replace the dummy argument "nper" with the
location of the cell that contains the term of the loan in months.

➡ Double-click on **nper** to select it, then select cell **B9**.

➡ Now tell Excel the present value, **pv**, is in cell **B8**.

Since you don't need the last two arguments, "fv" and "type", you can
delete them from the formula bar (see Figure 9-28).

➡ Select **,fv,type** and press Delete (or Backspace). Be sure to include the
    leading comma, and do not delete either of the trailing parentheses.
    Press the Enter key or click the accept box to accept the formula.

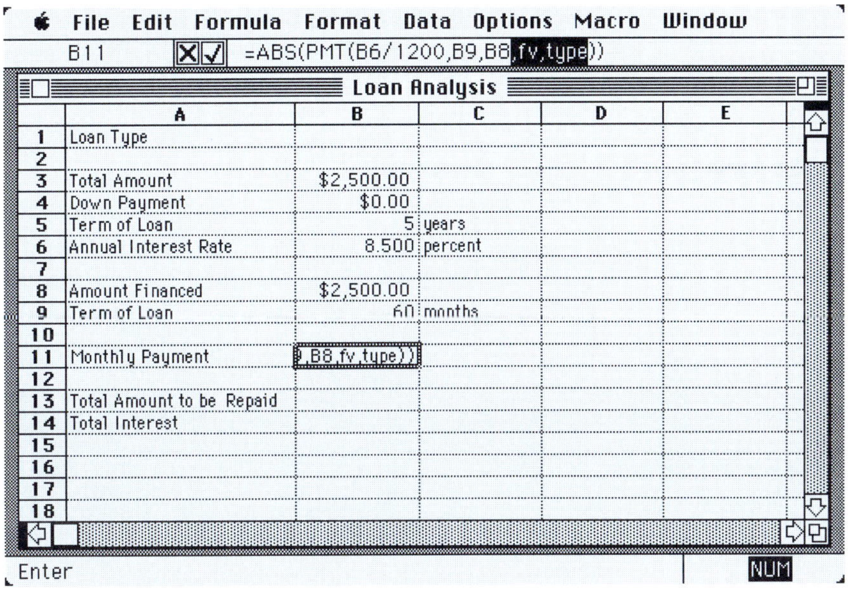

Figure 9-28 Deleting unnecessary arguments from the formula

The payment formula has now been entered, and your display should show the monthly payment (see Figure 9-29).

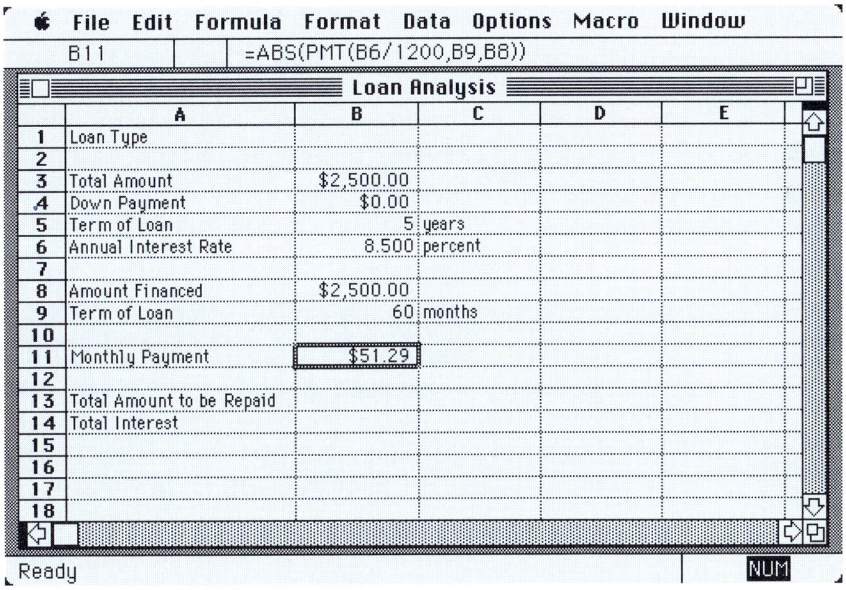

Figure 9-29 The completed monthly payment formula

All that is left is to add the formulas to calculate the total amount to be repaid and the total interest. The total amount to be repaid is calculated by multiplying the number of payments by the payment amount. The total interest is the total amount to be repaid minus the amount financed.

➡ Enter the formula =B11*B9 into cell B13, and =B13-B8 into cell B14. Now, in cell B1, type **Student Loan**.

⌘-S   You have completed the worksheet for Project 1. The next thing you will do is print the worksheet you just completed. It is always a good idea to save a document before printing it. Save your work now.

PRINTING

Printing from Excel involves defining how you want the worksheet to appear and then issuing the Print command. You can indicate how you want the output to appear by using the Page Setup command. When you have finished setting up the page's appearance, you tell Excel to print the document.

Page Setup

Excel allows you to print headers and footers when you print your worksheet and gives you the option of printing the row and column headings and gridlines shown on the screen. These options are available in the Page Setup dialog box, which is selected by choosing **Page Setup** from the File menu.

Before you print your worksheet, you will modify the headers and footers and choose not to print gridlines and row and column headings.

Header and Footer Formatting

➥   Choose **Page Setup** from the File menu.

The first thing you will do in this dialog box is change the headers and footers. A *header* is text that appears in the top margin, and a *footer* appears in the bottom margin, of every page. In this book, the page number and chapter title appear in the header at the top of each page.

Unless you tell Excel otherwise, it has a set of default values that will be printed in the header and footer. The filename of the document (what you named it when you saved it) will be displayed in the header, and the word "Page" and the page number will appear in the footer.

A default value is there for your convenience. In many instances, you might want these things printed on your output so you can identify it and keep the pages in order. A default value may easily be changed if you want something else, or nothing at all, in the header or footer.

In this project, let's change the header so that the filename is at the left margin and your name is at the right margin of the page. The output will be only one page long, so let's change the footer to show the date and time.

Before you can change what will appear in the header and footer, you need to know the available options. To learn more about this, you can use Excel's Help.

⌘-?   ➥   Press Command-Shift-/ (Command-?).

Excel opens its Help window and selects the File Page Setup screen:

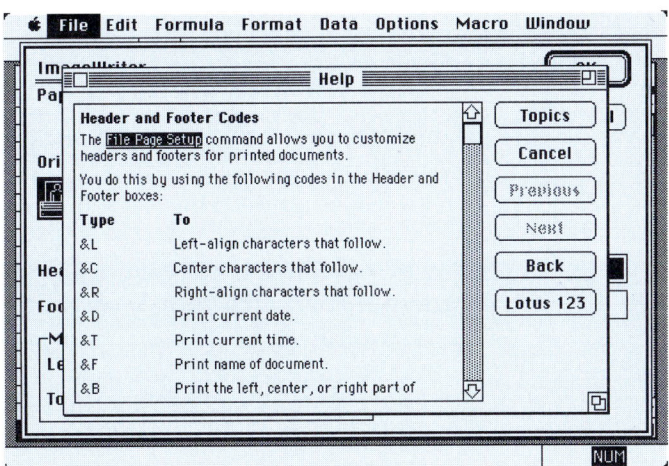

Figure 9-30 Help screen for Page Setup dialog box

➠ Move the pointer to the underlined words "header and footer codes." The arrow pointer will change to a pointing hand (see Figure 9-30). Click the mouse button.

This tells Excel to show the screen that describes these codes.

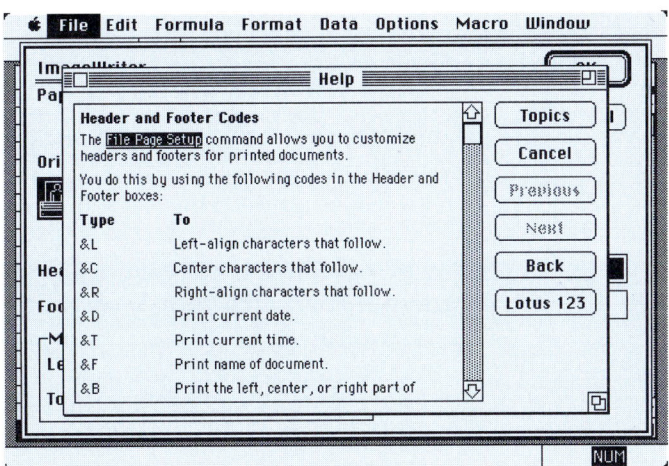

Figure 9-31 Header and footer codes for Page Setup

➠ When you are finished reading this screen, click the **Cancel** button.

Let's change the header first. Later, when you are printing other worksheets, you can choose what you want to have appear in the headers and footers. For now, enter the following commands (substituting your name in place of the words "Your Name"):

➠ Header: **&LLoan Analysis&R&B***Your Name*

➠ Footer: **&C&D   &T**

(Insert five spaces after the "D" in the footer so the date and time will be separated by five spaces instead of running together.)

This header format tells Excel to print the words "Loan Analysis" against the left margin of the paper and to print your name in bold characters against the right margin.

The footer format says that you want to center the current date, five spaces, and the current time at the bottom of the page.

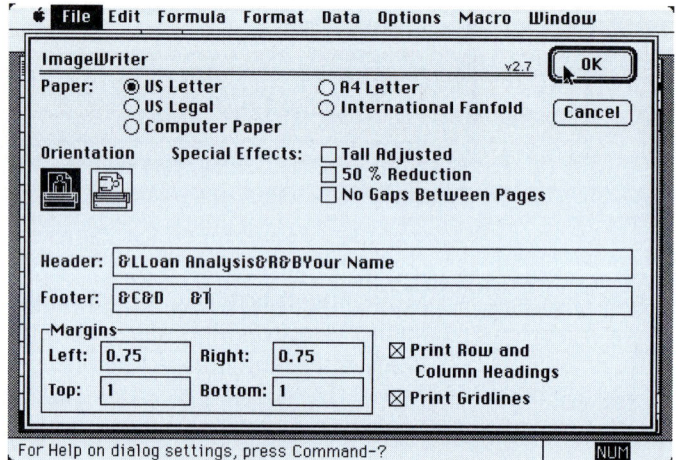

Figure 9-32   Changing the header and footer codes

Turning Off Gridlines and Row and Column Headings

Figure 9-32 shows that the *gridlines* and the row and column headings will be printed. You can tell that because there is an "X" in the check box next to each option. This is the default.

If Print Gridlines is selected, each cell will be shown on the page surrounded by dotted lines, as you see them on the screen when working in the worksheet.

Row and column headings are the alphabetic headings that appear at the tops of the columns and the numeric headings that appear on the left of the rows. These headings are used to determine cell addresses.

The output from this loan analysis worksheet does not need either of these features to be printed, so you can tell Excel not to print them.

➡ To turn off these features, click the appropriate check boxes in the Page Setup dialog box so the "X" disappears in each one, and then click **OK**.

Page Preview

Excel allows you to preview your document before you print.

⌘-P ➡ Choose **Print** from the File menu, and then click **Page Preview** in the Print dialog box. Click **OK** or press Return.

You will see a reduced view of the worksheet, including the headers and footers you just changed (see Figure 9-33).

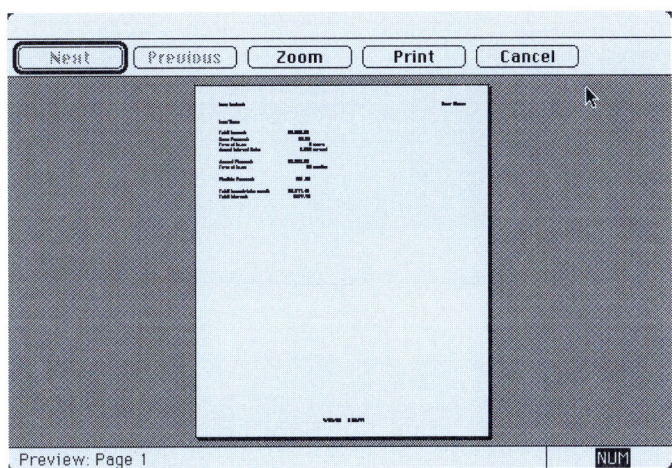

Figure 9-33   Reduced Page Preview screen

 Although this display is too small to read, it gives you an overall view of the worksheet. There are two ways to get a closer view of it. You can click the **Zoom** button, or you can move the pointer (now in the shape of a magnifying glass, as shown at left) over the part of the page you want to see magnified and click the mouse button.

➡ Use one of these methods to zoom into the previewed page and make it larger.

You now have several choices. There are five buttons at the top of the screen (see Figure 9-34). Next will take you to the next page, if there is one, and let you preview it. Previous moves you back to the previous page. Either, or both, of these buttons will be dimmed if there is no page available in that direction. In this case, the document is only one page long, so both buttons are dimmed.

You know what Zoom does. Print tells Excel to quit previewing and print the document, and Cancel tells Excel to close the screen and not print. You remain in preview mode until you deselect Page Preview in the Print dialog box.

Now that you have made the suggested changes, it is time to print your document.

➡ Click the **Print** button to print your worksheet.

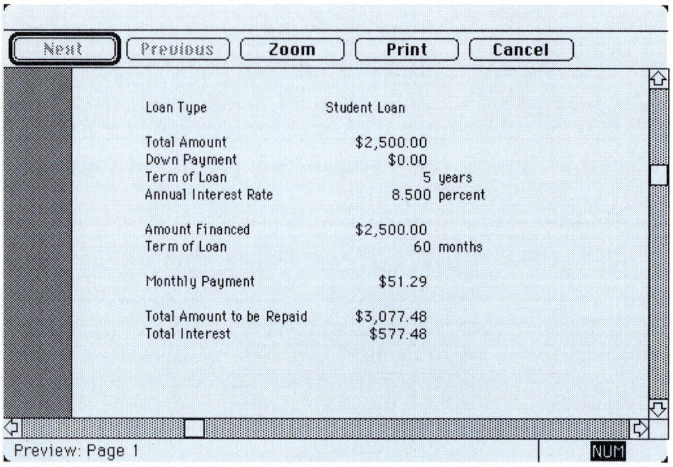

Figure 9-34   Enlarged Page Preview

WHAT IF... EXERCISES

As previously discussed, one of the most powerful features of electronic spreadsheets is their ability to automatically recalculate all formulas and update the display whenever any changes are made.

In this last section of Project 1, you will calculate several student loans, car loans, and house loans, and then save the last one of each of these to your disk to use in Projects 2, 3, and 4.

Note: When analyzing some of the following loans, you may see a string of number signs (#) in one or more of the cells. This is an error message, and it means that the value in that cell is too wide to fit. You can remedy this by increasing the width of the column containing these symbols.

These exercises are presented so you can experience the speed of Excel and the power of *"what if"* analysis. As you work through these exercises, you will learn how easy it is to use a worksheet for loan analysis.

If you intend to work through Projects 3 and 4, you must work through these what if... exercises. The spreadsheets you will save in steps 5, 10, and 15 will be used in those projects.

Calculating Student Loans

You have already entered all the data to evaluate a student loan into the template you created, so let's save a copy of it.

➡ Choose **Save As** from the File menu. Save a copy of this worksheet onto your disk and name it Student Loan.

What if...

1. The interest rate rose to 9.25%? How much would the monthly payment increase? How much would the total interest repaid increase?

    *Hint: Select the cell that contains the annual interest rate. Type **9.25** and accept it.*

2. What if the interest remained at 8.5% and the term increased to 7 years? How would that affect the monthly payment and total interest?

    *Hint: Select the cell that contains the annual interest rate. Type **8.5** and accept it. Select the cell that contains the term of loan, and enter **7** into it.*

3. What if the interest remained at 8.5% and the term decreased to 3 years? How would that affect the loan?

4. What if the interest rose to 11% and the term increased to 7 years? How would that affect the loan?

5. What if the amount is $5,000, the rate is 9%, and the term is 5 years?

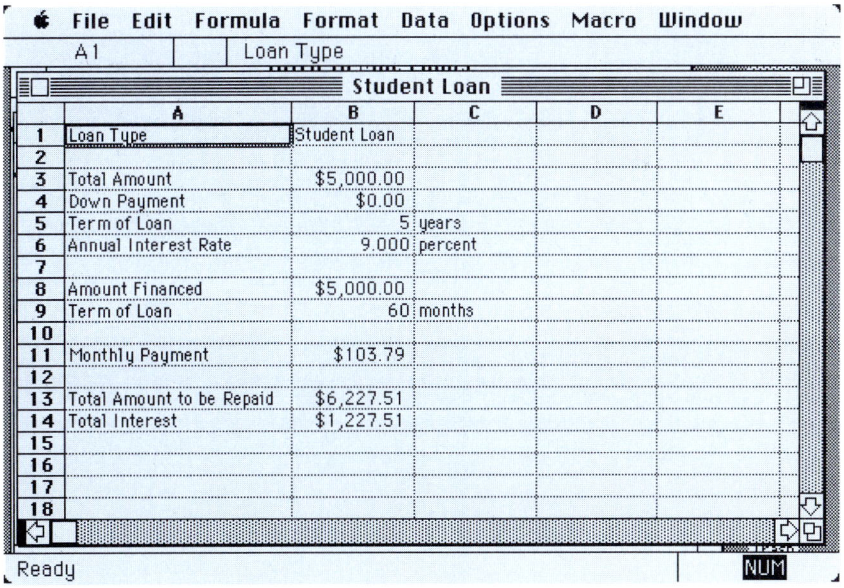

Figure 9-35   Final version of Student Loan worksheet

➠ Save this worksheet with the amounts in step 5 for use with Projects 3 and 4.

Calculating Car Loans

You are ready to evaluate a car loan, so save a copy of this worksheet.

➠ Enter **Car Loan** in cell B1. Choose **Save As** from the File menu. Save a copy of this worksheet onto your disk and name it Car Loan.

What if...

6. The car you want to purchase costs $17,995.37 and the interest rate is 12% for 5 years? You will put down a down payment of $2,000. What is the amount of the monthly payment? How much total interest would you have to repay?

7. What if the interest remains at 12% and the term decreases to 4 years? How would that affect the monthly payment and total interest?

8. What if the dealer offered either an interest rate of 3.9% or $1,000 back? The term of the loan is 5 years. If you take the lower interest rate your down payment remains at $2,000. If you take the cash back, your interest rate is 12%, and you add the extra $1,000 to your down payment, for a total of $3,000. Which is the best deal? Why?

9. What if the interest was 10%, the down payment was $2,000, and the term of the loan was 6 years? How would that affect the loan?

10. What if you decide to buy a different car, which costs $9,996.77, and you can finance it for $1,500 down at 8.9% for 5 years? What would your monthly payments and total interest be?

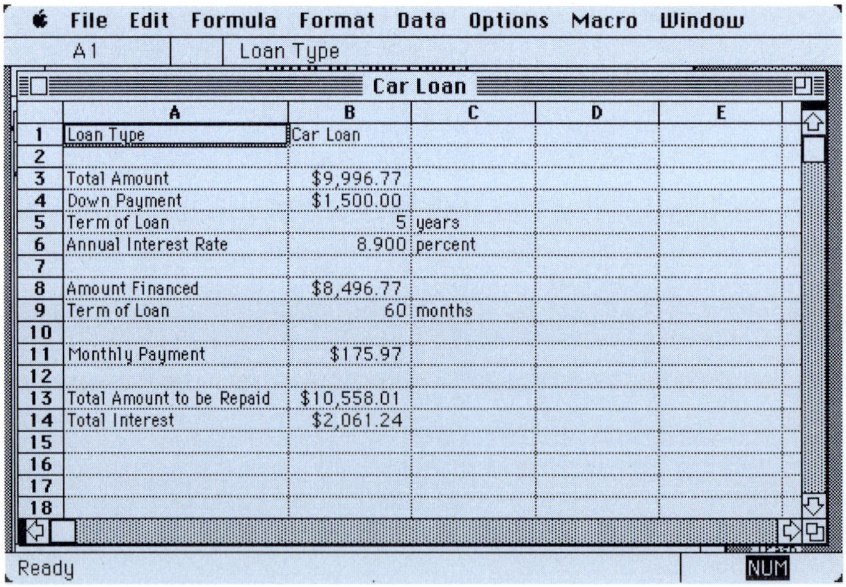

	A	B	C	D	E
1	Loan Type	Car Loan			
2					
3	Total Amount	$9,996.77			
4	Down Payment	$1,500.00			
5	Term of Loan	5	years		
6	Annual Interest Rate	8.900	percent		
7					
8	Amount Financed	$8,496.77			
9	Term of Loan	60	months		
10					
11	Monthly Payment	$175.97			
12					
13	Total Amount to be Repaid	$10,558.01			
14	Total Interest	$2,061.24			
15					
16					
17					
18					

Figure 9-36 Final version of Car Loan worksheet

⌘-S ➡ Save this worksheet with the amounts in step 10 for use with Projects 3 and 4.

Calculating House Loans

You are ready to evaluate a house loan, so save a copy of this worksheet.

➡ Label this loan as a House Loan (in cell B1). Choose **Save As** from the File menu. Save a copy of this worksheet onto your disk and name it House Loan.

What if...

11. The house costs $45,000 with 15% down, and it can be financed for 30 years at 11.875%? What would be the monthly payment, total amount repaid, and total interest? (Hint: Don't calculate the down payment and then enter an amount. Enter a formula multiplying the total amount by .15. After all, this *is* a spreadsheet program!)

12. What if you put down 25% and financed it for 10.9%? How would that affect the monthly payment and total interest?

13. What if you had the same terms as in #1, but you financed it for only 20 years? How would that affect the loan?

14. What if the interest rose to 14% and the term stayed at 20 years? How would that affect the loan?

15. Evaluate the loan for a house costing $51,500 that you can buy with 20% down. You can get fixed-rate financing at 10.5%. What are the monthly payments and total interest repaid for this loan if the term is 10, 15, 20, 30, or 40 years.

```
 File   Edit   Formula   Format   Data   Options   Macro   Window

     A1                 Loan Type

                         House Loan
            A                 B             C         D         E
 1   Loan Type         House Loan
 2
 3   Total Amount          $51,500.00
 4   Down Payment          $10,300.00
 5   Term of Loan                30 years
 6   Annual Interest Rate    10.500 percent
 7
 8   Amount Financed       $41,200.00
 9   Term of Loan               360 months
10
11   Monthly Payment          $376.87
12
13   Total Amount to be Repaid  $135,674.13
14   Total Interest         $94,474.13
15
16
17
18

 Ready                                                      NUM
```

Figure 9-37   Final version of House Loan worksheet

⌘-S   ➡ Change the term of the loan back to 30 years and save the worksheet with the amounts in step 15 for use with Projects 3 and 4.

This completes Project 1.

⌘-W   ➡   Close the active worksheet now.

You have saved the original Loan Analysis, as well as three additional worksheets: Student Loan, Car Loan, and House Loan.

The Loan Analysis worksheet will be used in Project 2, where you will learn to use some of Excel's charting features.

The other three worksheets will be used in Project 3, where you will create a monthly budget, and in Project 4, where you will expand that monthly budget into an annual budget.

Project 2: Creating Charts

In this project you will learn to create charts, modify their formats, and print them. You will use the Loan Analysis worksheet from Project 1 to create a column chart that compares the amount borrowed to the total amount of interest for a loan. You will add a title and a legend to the chart, modify the patterns used in the chart, change the format, and print the chart. Then you will modify the worksheet, produce a pie chart, and print it.

Many people have difficulty comparing numbers that are printed in a list, but when those numbers are presented in a chart, they are often easier to grasp.

To begin this project, you should have completed Project 1 first, since you will be using the Loan Analysis worksheet that you developed there as the basis for starting this project.

➡   If you have quit Excel since completing Project 1, insert your data disk into the drive, find the Loan Analysis document, and double-click on its icon.

➡   If you have not quit Excel since completing Project 1, close all open worksheets, and open the Loan Analysis worksheet that you created in Project 1.

The final output of Project 2 is shown in Figure 9-38.

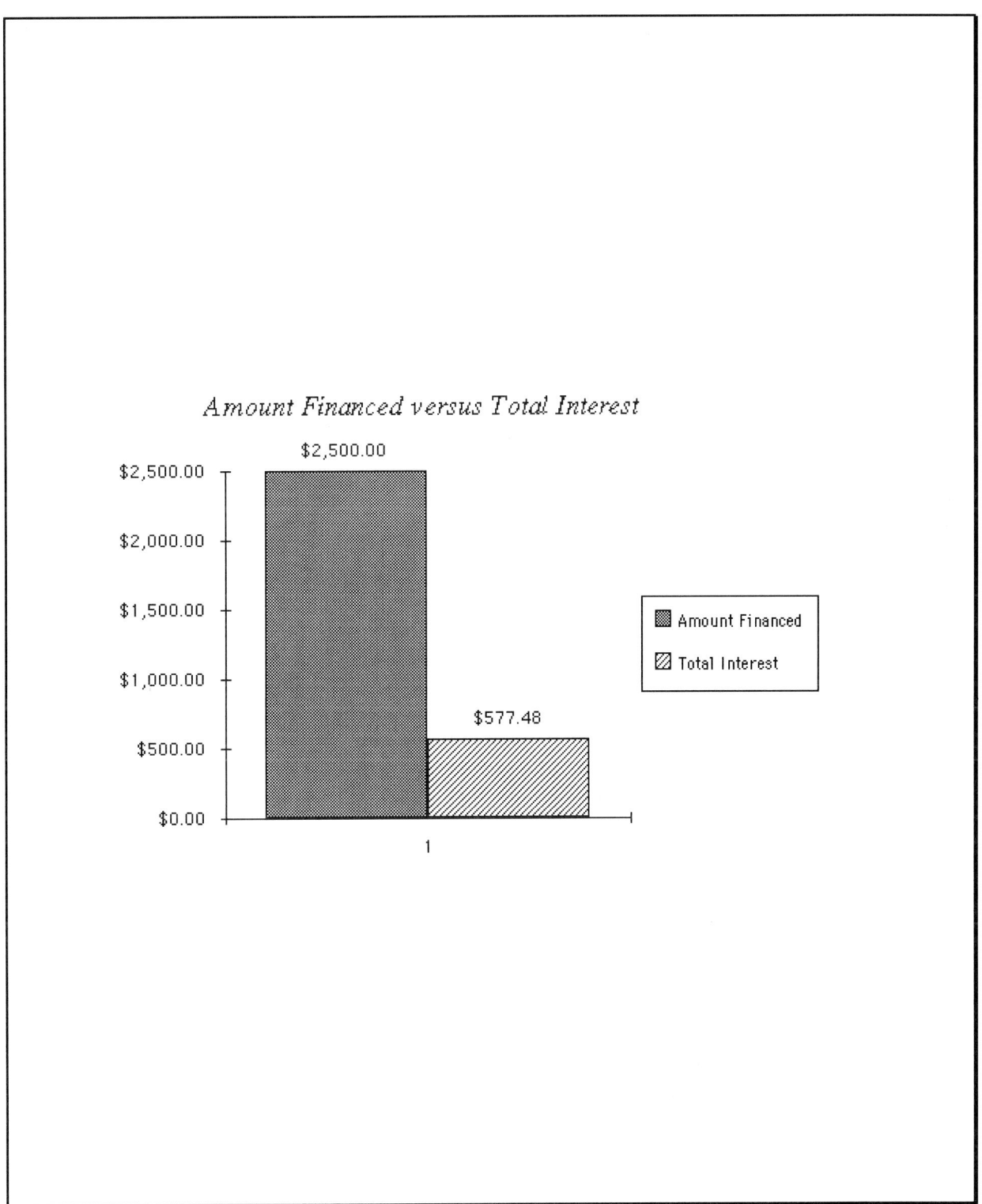

Figure 9-38   Final output of Project 2

TYPES OF CHARTS

Excel offers a wide variety of chart types, several of which are discussed next.

A *column chart* (see Figure 9-39) offers comparisons between two or more groups of data, known as *data series*. (For example, you can chart income amounts for several months and also expense amounts for the same months. This would be two data series. Each month would contain two columns, one for each data series.) Excel has eight column chart variations available.

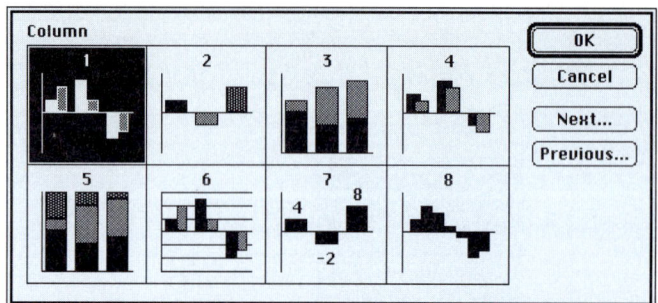

Figure 9-39   Excel's column chart options

A *line chart* (see Figure 9-40) is used to show changes that occur over a period of time. They are also useful for spotting trends, because they emphasize the rate of change over time. Excel offers eight types of line charts. Line charts can also show more than one data series.

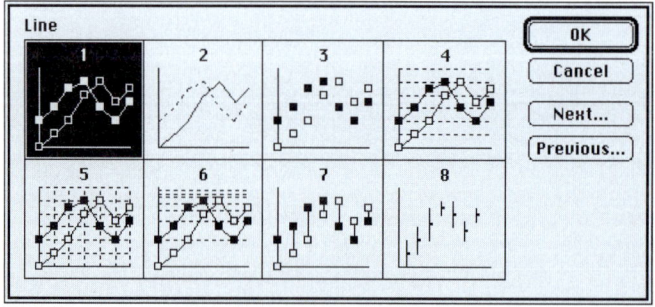

Figure 9-40   Excel's line chart options

A *pie chart* (see Figure 9-41) shows a whole composed of a group of items. All items shown in a pie chart must be a part of one single whole. *This means that only one data series may be shown using a pie chart.*

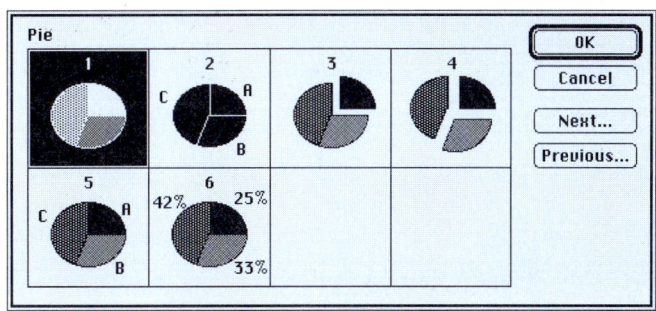

Figure 9-41   Excel's pie chart options

Excel also provides *area, bar, scatter,* and *combination* charts. When you chart your data, you can easily change the type of chart, or one of the styles for a chart, by choosing the one you want from the Gallery menu. In fact, you might decide to display the same data using different charts to emphasize different aspects of the data in each chart.

PARTS OF A CHART

The various parts of a chart are shown in Figure 9-42 and described below.

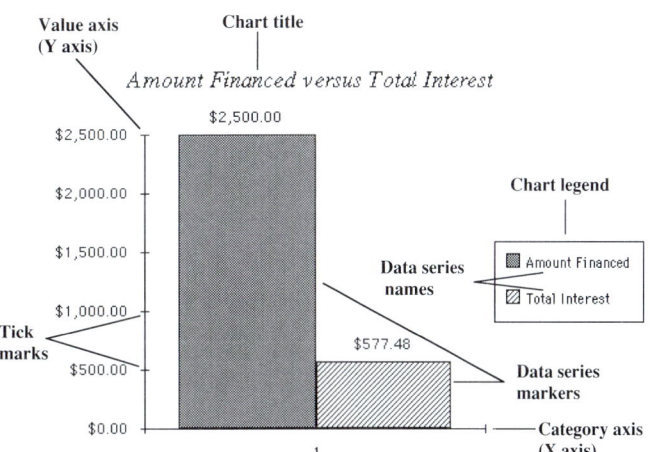

Figure 9-42   Major parts of a chart

Chart title	The text used for the title of the chart. There may also be subtitles present.
Category axis	The horizontal axis (or X axis) commonly used to show the data classifications, or categories. A pie chart has no category axis.

Data series markers	This is the indicator used on a chart to represent each group of data items. A column chart or bar chart uses rectangles for markers, and a line chart uses small symbols such as circles, rectangles, triangles, and so on.
Chart legend	The symbols and text used to identify the different groups of data items shown in the chart.
Tick marks	The short lines that intersect the axes and are used to represent divisions on the category axis and the scale on the value axis.
Value axis	The vertical axis (or Y axis) that is used to plot the quantity or unit of measure for the data items. A pie chart has no value axis.

CREATING A COLUMN CHART

Excel makes it easy to create a column chart from the worksheet. Some electronic spreadsheets make you specify many values before you can see a chart. With Excel, you just select a group of cells, and Excel opens a new chart that automatically contains the data you selected on the worksheet.

Selecting the Cells

To produce this chart, you will need to select the cells containing the amount financed and the total interest.

It would seem natural to select just those two cells, but if you chart just those cells, you will find it harder to add a legend to indicate what the cells represent. For that reason, you should also select the titles to the left of the cells, as shown in Figure 9-43.

➡ Select cells **A8** and **B8** by pressing the mouse button on A8 and dragging over to B8; then release the button.

Selecting a range of cells using this method works just fine if all the cells are contiguous (next to each other without any gaps between them). Sometimes, as in this case, you need to select groups that are not contiguous. If you were to press and drag from A14 to B14 now, you would select the new range, but the process would deselect the first two cells.

Excel gives you an easy way to make noncontiguous multiple selections. If you select one or more cells, and then hold down the Command key, Excel will allow you to add additional cells or ranges to the current selection. That is what you will do now to select the cells in row 14.

➡ Hold down the Command key, and select cells **A14:B14**.

Now that you have selected the cells you want to chart (see Figure 9-43), you need to tell Excel to open a new chart.

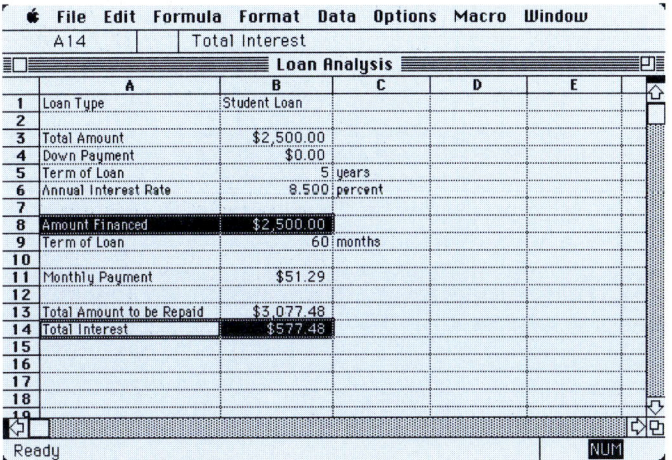

Figure 9-43   Making a multiple-cell selection using the Command key

Creating a New Chart

When you create a new file, Excel gives you a choice of opening one of three types of files: Worksheet, Chart, or Macro Sheet (see Figure 9-44).

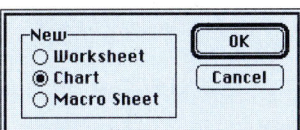

Figure 9-44   New File dialog box

You have already completed a worksheet, and in this project you will create a chart. A chart is used to display the information contained in a worksheet in the form of a graphic.

A macro sheet is used to contain a series of Excel commands that are used to automate specific tasks. Macros are useful if you perform a task or series of tasks on a regular basis. However, macros are beyond the scope of this book.

⌘-N ➡ Choose **New** from the File menu. Since you want to create a new chart, select **Chart** and click **OK**.

(You could optionally choose to double-click **Chart** as a shortcut.)

In a few seconds, a new window appears on the screen showing your data in a column chart (see Figure 9-45).

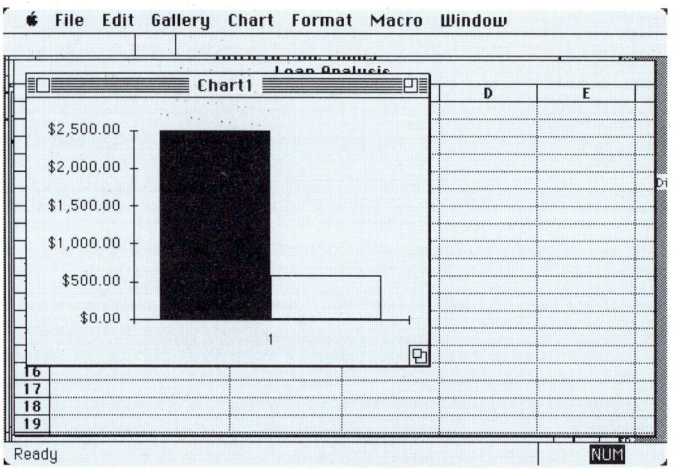

Figure 9-45   Creating a new column chart

The left column represents the amount of the loan, and the right column represents the total interest.

Excel offers an easy way of labeling this chart so that each column's meaning would be readily apparent to anyone. This label is known as a legend.

Adding a Legend

Whenever you create a chart showing more than one series of data, it is a good idea to add a legend. A *legend* is an area on the chart that shows the pattern of each column and tells what that column represents.

Since you previously chose a title to the left of each value in the worksheet before you created the chart, adding a legend is only a matter of issuing the command.

➡ Choose **Add Legend** from the Chart menu. Click the **Zoom box** to enlarge the chart.

Excel adds a box to the right of the chart, showing a rectangle labeled "Amount Financed" and another rectangle labeled "Total Interest."

It is difficult to tell exactly what amount each of the columns represents, but you can tell Excel to show the amount represented at the top of each column. To do this, you will select a different style of column chart from the Gallery menu.

➡ Select **Column** from the Gallery menu.

This will produce a dialog box showing eight different types of column charts. The one you want is shown in box number 7.

➡ Click on column chart style number 7, and then click **OK**.

Excel quickly redraws the chart, and now each column has the value from the worksheet shown at the top of the column (see Figure 9-46).

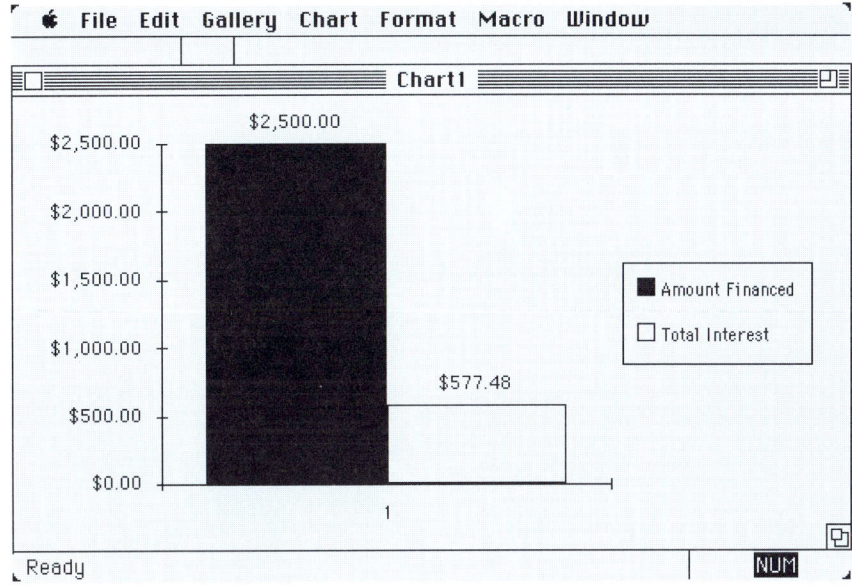

Figure 9-46   Changing to column chart style 7

That's how easy it is to create a chart in Excel. Now that you have a good start on this chart, it is a good time to save it.

The first new chart you create in a session is named "Chart1" by default. When you choose **Save** from the File menu, or type Command-S, Excel recognizes this as a default name and puts up the Save As dialog box so you can name the chart and specify where it is to be saved.

⌘-S ➡ Save the chart to your data disk, and name it Loan Column Chart.

Adding a Title

The chart now shows two amounts, both graphically and numerically, and indicates in the legend what they represent. Most charts also contain some type of title that indicates what the whole chart represents.

Adding a title to your chart consists of telling Excel to place text in the title element, typing that text, and defining the font, size, and style you desire.

➡ Choose **Attach Text** from the Chart menu.

Figure 9-47 shows that you can attach text to several elements of a chart, including the title, value axis, category axis, and series and data points.

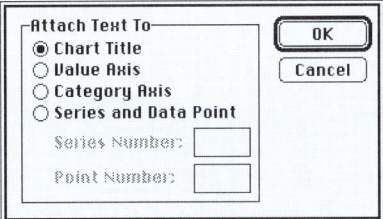

Figure 9-47   Attach Text dialog box

➡ Select **Chart Title** if it is not selected, and then click **OK**. (You can double-click **Chart Title** if you prefer.)

Excel will create a text block, attach it to the chart (surrounded by eight selection squares), and put the word "Title" in the formula bar as shown in Figure 9-48.

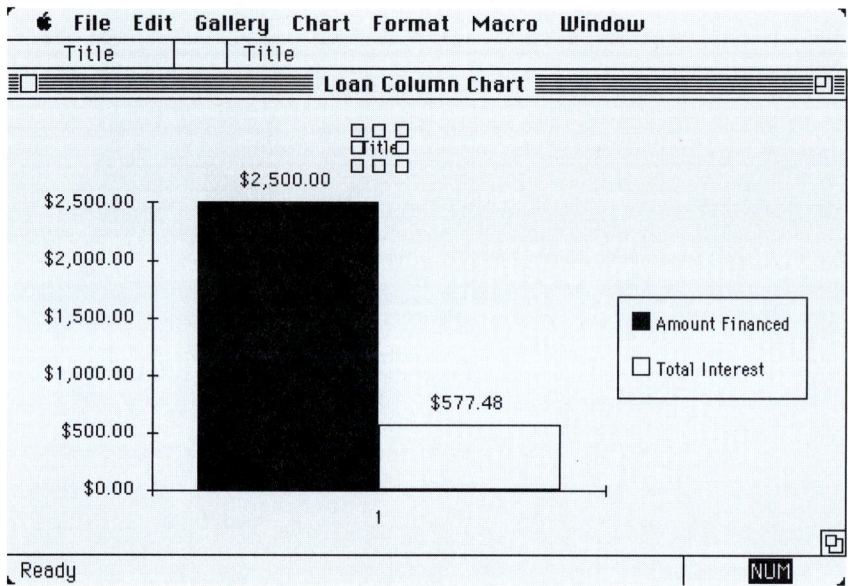

Figure 9-48   Attaching text to the chart title

Using Selection Squares

Text objects (such as titles) are surrounded by eight *selection squares* when they are selected. These selection squares may be black or white, depending upon what type of object is currently selected.

Text surrounded by black squares may be resized and moved, but text with white selection squares is sized and placed by Excel, and you can not change this placement. The title will be surrounded by white squares, which indicates that Excel will automatically size and place the text, based on its length, size, style, and font.

You can move or size a text element that is surrounded by black selection squares by clicking on one of the squares and dragging it.

Chart Formatting Options

Many formatting options are provided for changing the appearance of a chart in Excel.

This project suggests that you change the format of three elements: the text in the title, the patterns in the columns, and the placement of the legend. By making these changes, you will learn how to modify the chart to suit your preferences. The methods you use here will apply to any Excel chart you create or modify in the future.

Formatting Text

The first formatting you will do is to change the font, size, and style of the title.

⇒ While the title is selected, type **Amount Financed versus Total Interest**, and then press Return.

You will see the title change in the formula bar as you type. Unlike text in cells, text elements in Excel, such as the title, can be only one font, size, and style.

Notice that the title is still surrounded by selection squares. To deselect the title, you can click anywhere in the chart window outside the chart area. This is a little difficult to do, because clicking anywhere on the chart will select the entire chart. The easiest way to deselect an element is to click between the top of the chart window and the top selection squares for the title.

⇒ Click in the chart window to deselect the title.

Now that you have entered the title, you might notice that the default size and style are a little too small for the title. You can make the title larger and more distinctive by modifying it.

⇒ Select the title by clicking on it, and then choose **Font** from the Format menu. Choose **Times** font, **18-point**, and **italic** (see Figure 9-49). If these choices are not available on your computer, make a comparable choice from what is available.

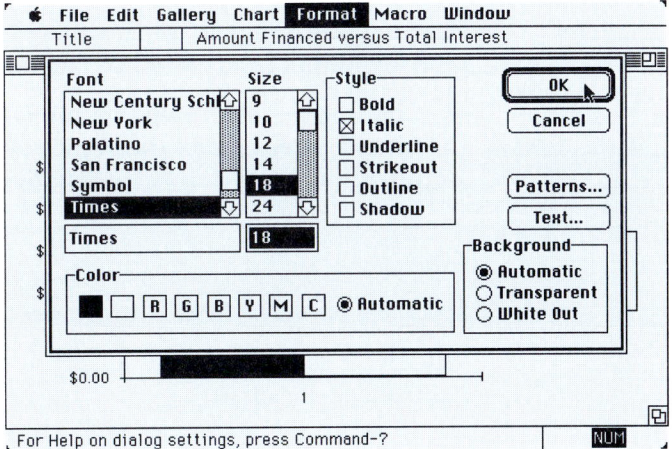

Figure 9-49 Changing the font, size, and style for the title text

Changing Patterns

There is nothing wrong with the black and white columns on this chart (if you have a color monitor they may be green and red), but there may be times in the future when you want to select a different pattern for one or more columns.

Selecting a different pattern is a matter of double-clicking on the column you want to change and then selecting which pattern you want it to have. For this project, you will change the Amount Financed column to medium gray and the Total Interest column to a light diagonal stripe.

➡ Click on the Amount Financed column to select it. Choose **Patterns** from the Format menu. Select the medium gray pattern (second from the left) inside the Area rectangle (see Figure 9-50).

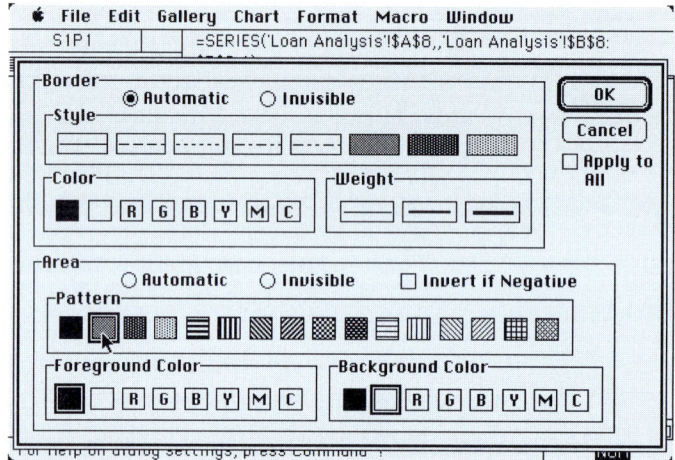

Figure 9-50   Changing the column pattern

(As a shortcut, you could have double-clicked on the Amount Financed column to change the pattern assigned to it. You can use this shortcut to format any element in the chart window. Double-clicking on an element automatically selects it and brings up the Patterns dialog box.)

➡ Change the Total Interest column to the medium diagonal striped pattern (third from the right) by double-clicking on the Total Interest column and then clicking on the appropriate pattern.

Any item in a chart that has a pattern can be changed using this method.

Moving the Legend

When you tell Excel to add a legend, the default placement is on the right side of the chart.

Sometimes the legend would look better if it were moved to another location. If you click on the legend, you will see that it is surrounded by white selection squares, which indicate that you cannot just drag it to another location.

If you want to move the legend, you can select it and then choose **Legend** from the Format menu. The legend can occupy one of four locations: Bottom, Corner, Top, or Vertical.

➡ Select the legend, and use the Legend command in the Format menu to move it to the bottom of the chart.

When the legend was on the right side, the title seemed to be off center. However, when you moved the legend to the bottom, the columns got wider, and now they look too wide for their height. Excel lets you move the legend to any of these four locations so you can see how the chart will appear and choose the one you like best.

➡ Try moving the legend to the other locations, and then put it back where it started by selecting **Vertical**.

⌘-S ➡ Now is a good time to save your work.

After you've made these formatting changes, your chart should look like the one shown in Figure 9-51.

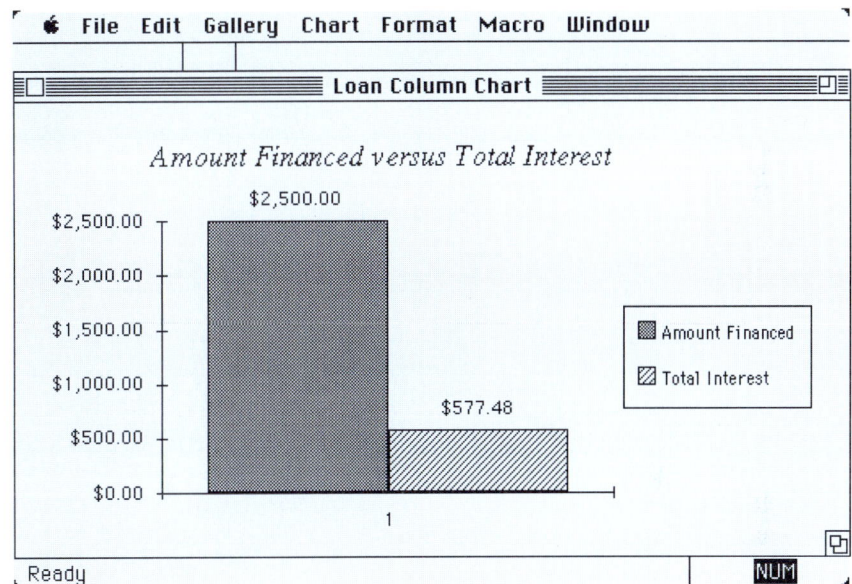

Figure 9-51 Column chart after formatting changes

Updating the Chart

You have created a chart that will graph whatever values are contained in the Loan Analysis worksheet.

You can resize and move both the worksheet and chart so they are both visible. If you modify any of the values in the worksheet, the chart will be redrawn to reflect that change.

Depending upon the size of your monitor, you can choose to either slide the window to the right or resize it. The purpose is to be able to see the chart and column B of the Loan Analysis worksheet at the same time. If you have a large monitor, you can place both windows where they are visible, and size them to suit yourself.

Be advised, however, that how the chart is printed is directly related to how you dimension the chart window.

➡ Move the Loan Column Chart window to the right until the legend disappears from the right side of the screen (if you have a regular-size Mac screen).

➡ Use the size box of the Loan Analysis worksheet to resize its window. Move the windows around until they are both visible (see Figure 9-52).

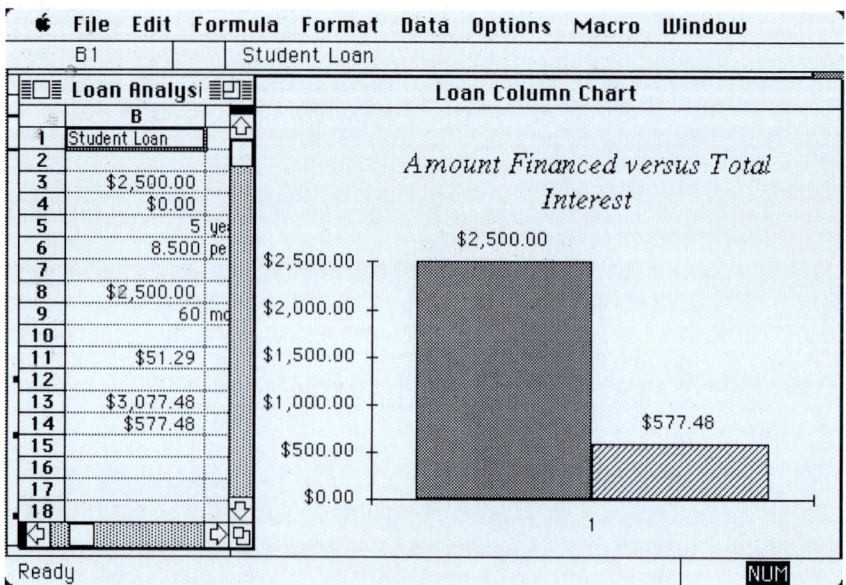

Figure 9-52   Resizing the windows to display both the chart and the worksheet

Figure 9-52 shows the chart you should see if you saved this worksheet and used Save As to create a duplicate worksheet before entering the student loan figures in the what if... scenarios in Project 1.

WARNING   **Do not save the changes** you make to the worksheet in the next three action steps.

Refer back to the what if... steps numbered 5, 10, and 15 in Project 1.

➡ Enter the final values in step 5 into the worksheet and watch the chart change to reflect the new values.

➡ Enter the final values in step 10 into the worksheet and notice how the chart changes (see Figure 9-53).

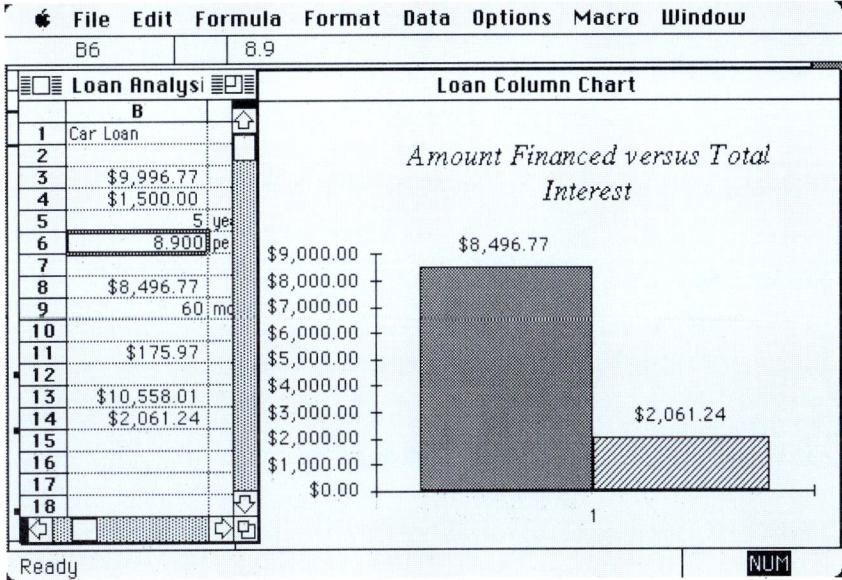

Figure 9-53   The car loan amounts from step 10 in Project 1

➡ Enter the final values in step 15 into the worksheet and watch the chart change again.

Notice that this chart (Figure 9-54), unlike the other two, shows that the total interest is larger than the amount financed. Why is this?

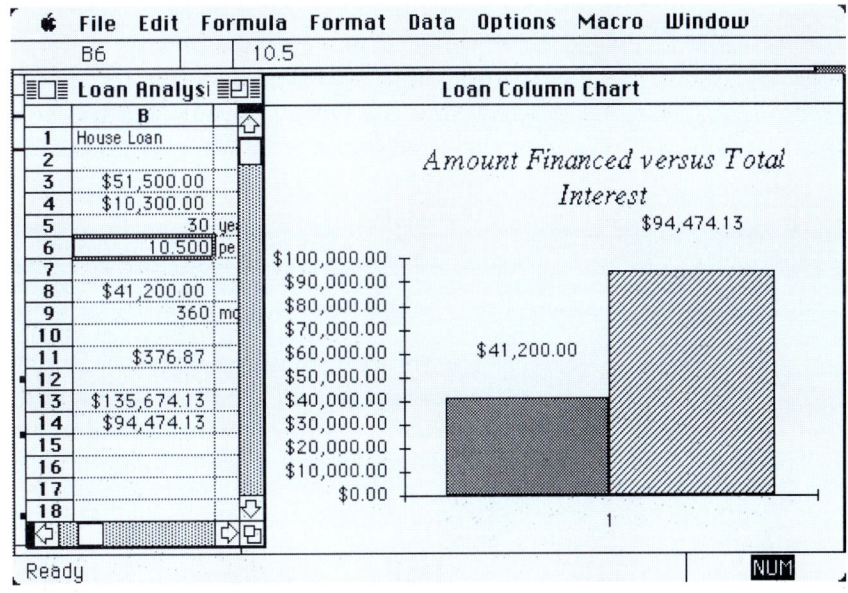

Figure 9-54   Chart of the house loan from step 15 in Project 1

When a loan is amortized, the loan is calculated so that the sum of the payments over a period of time will exactly equal the sum of the interest and the amount financed. As the length of the loan increases, the payments decrease, but the total interest increases because you are paying less toward reducing the debt with each payment.

A house loan financed for 25 years will have a higher monthly payment, but the total interest will be less than a loan financed for 30 years. In fact, for the house loan you just calculated, if you increase the term of the loan to 107 years or more, the monthly payment will not decrease any further. Adding more years to the term of the loan will only increase total interest.

➠ Close the Loan Column Chart (without saving the changes).

You might find it an interesting exercise to vary nothing but the term of the loan and watch the interaction between total interest and the monthly payment.

CREATING A PIE CHART

The amount financed plus the total interest adds up to the total amount of all the payments. This means that the two components make up a whole. There is a better chart than the column chart for comparing more than one item that adds up to a whole. The type of chart that is most useful for this type of comparison is the pie chart.

In the next several steps of this project, you will make some of the most common mistakes that new spreadsheet users encounter. Then you will learn how to set up your worksheet properly to keep from making these kinds of mistakes.

WARNING Sometimes saving your work frequently is not enough of a safeguard against losing your work. Since you have been advised that you will be making a few mistakes along the way, you probably don't want to risk losing the work you put into the Loan Analysis worksheet. A good method to use when there is potential for damaging a worksheet is to make a backup copy of the current (correct) version, and then work from that copy.

➠ Choose **Save As** from the File menu. Name the worksheet Loan Analysis 2.

You will now modify the Loan Analysis 2 worksheet so you can generate a pie chart to compare the amount financed and total interest amounts. You will be working with the house loan figures in step number 15 of the what if... scenario of Project 1.

Modifying the Worksheet

You will start this chart the same way you started the column chart.

➠ Select the four cells (**A8:B8** and **A14:B14**) the same way you did before.

➠ Create a new chart.

➠ Add a legend and move it to the bottom.

➠ Select pie chart style **6**.

What happened to the total interest amount (see Figure 9-55)? Why is there only one patterned rectangle and a number 1 in the legend?

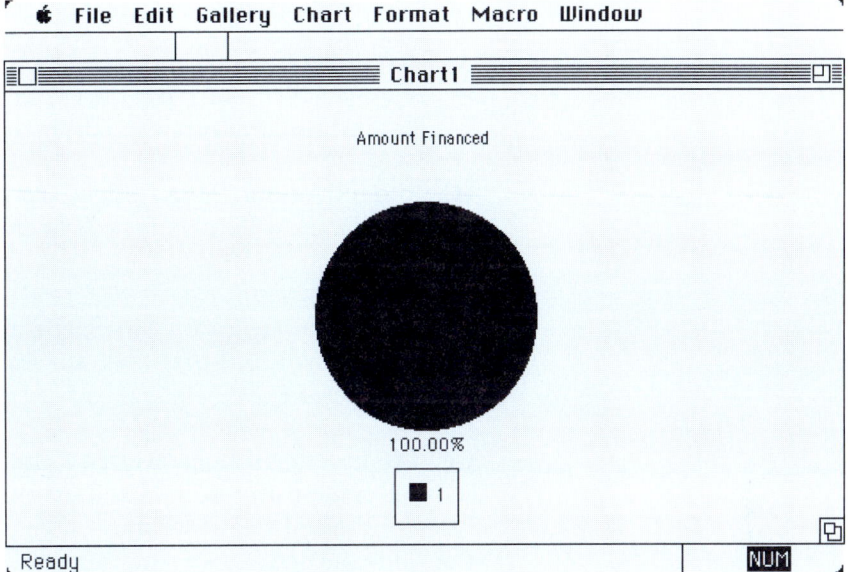

Figure 9-55 Creating a pie chart that doesn't do exactly what you want

The answer to these questions lies in the differences between column charts and pie charts. Column charts allow the comparison of multiple values that do not necessarily comprise a whole amount. Pie charts, on the other hand, only allow the comparison of multiple values that do comprise a whole. (If you present information to other people using charts, you would be well advised to find a good book on charting techniques and study it to learn the differences between chart types and their advantages and disadvantages for the types of data you present.)

When you selected a noncontiguous group of cells, Excel assumed this to represent more than one data series. To create the pie chart for this project, you have to rearrange the worksheet so that the two amounts are next to each other (contiguous).

Adding New Formulas

You need to make a copy of the four cells and paste them on two adjacent rows. Since you are becoming an experienced Macintosh user, you probably have already started hatching a plan to accomplish this. Maybe it goes something like this: "All I have to do is copy the first two cells and paste them below the last row of the worksheet. Then I can copy the other two cells and paste them right below that."

Maybe you are even more creative and have decided that you only have to copy the amount financed cells and paste them directly below the total interest amount.

This sounds like a good plan, but it will not work.

⌘-W ➡ Click in the close box to close the new pie chart without saving it. (You can also choose **Close** from the File menu, or type Command-W.)

⌘-C ➡ Select cells **A8:B8** and copy them. (You can use the Copy command from the Edit menu, or type Command-C.)

⌘-V ➡ Select cell **A16**, and paste the two cells into **A16:B16**. (Use either the Paste command from the Edit menu or type Command-V.)

How did the Amount Financed on row 16 become $376.87? The answer to this lies in how Excel helps you in creating large and/or complicated worksheets.

If you examine the formula in cell B8 and compare it with the formula in B16, you will find that they are similar, but Excel has made some changes for you.

Cell B16 has the formula =B11-B12, but cell B8 has the formula =B3-B4. In both cases, using relative addressing, they tell Excel to subtract the value of the cell four rows above the cell containing the formula from the value of the cell five rows higher.

Look at the value displayed in cell B16. If you move up five rows you will find the value $376.87. The cell four rows above B16 is empty. When Excel tries to subtract the empty cell from the cell with $376.87, it produces the result $376.87, just as if the value of the empty cell were a zero.

To correct this problem, you will modify two of the formulas using absolute addressing. There are at least two ways to accomplish your objective. You could easily type the new formulas into cells B16 and B17, using the exact formulas in B8 and B14. This is a valid way to solve this problem, but it would not help you learn about using absolute addressing in creating formulas. Therefore, let's modify the formulas in B8 and B14, and then copy and paste them into rows 16 and 17.

Modifying the Formulas

Before you make the modifications to the two formulas, why don't you erase what you already copied into row 16? There are several ways to do this.

Since you haven't done anything since pasting the values into row 16, the easiest way to remove them is to choose **Undo** from the Edit menu, or type Command-Z. This will always undo the last thing you did.

If you want to clear some cells and it was not the last thing you did, you can click on a cell, press the Backspace or Delete key, accept the new empty value, and do the same to any other cells you want to clear. Whenever you are erasing one or only a few cells, this is often the fastest and most convenient method.

Excel provides a third method that is more useful if you want to erase a larger group of cells. It also provides a selective way to delete only the formula or format of the cell, a note attached to the cell, or all of these attributes. This is performed using the Clear command from the Edit menu. Let's try this method here.

⇒ Select cells **A16:B16**.

⌘-B ⇒ Choose **Clear** from the Edit menu.

⇒ Select **All**, and accept it by clicking **OK**.

Now that you have erased the incorrect information, modifying the formula in cell B8 to produce correct results is a straightforward process.

⇒ Click in cell **B8**. Change the formula to =**$B$3-$B$4** by either retyping the whole formula or inserting the dollar signs in the formula bar.

The dollar signs are the means by which you inform Excel that you want to refer to exactly cells B3 and B4 (absolute addressing), not the cell five rows higher and the cell below that (relative addressing).

Four ways to use absolute and relative addressing are shown in Table 9-6.

B4	Relative column and relative row (the default)
$B4	Absolute column and relative row
B$4	Relative column and absolute row
$B$4	Absolute column and absolute row

Table 9-6   Four possibilities for absolute and relative addressing

Depending upon the circumstances, you might use any of these four methods of addressing. The most common methods, by far, are the first and last ones shown in the table. The two middle forms are for special circumstances, and you should be careful in their use.

⌘-C ⌘-V ⇒ Now that the formula has been adjusted using absolute addressing, copy cells A8:B8 and paste into cell A16.

⌘-C ⌘-V ⇒ Modify the formula in cell B14 so that it also uses absolute addressing, copy A14:B14, and paste into A17.

⌘-S ⇒ Save your worksheet again.

You have adjusted the formulas so that they will produce the correct values when they are copied and pasted, and they have been moved so that they are contiguous. It is time to once again try to create a pie chart.

Creating a New Chart

      ⇒ Select cells **A16:B17**.

⌘-N ⇒ Choose **New** from the File menu, and create a new chart.

      ⇒ Select pie chart style 6.

      ⇒ Add a legend, and move it to the bottom.

This will produce the chart shown in Figure 9-56.

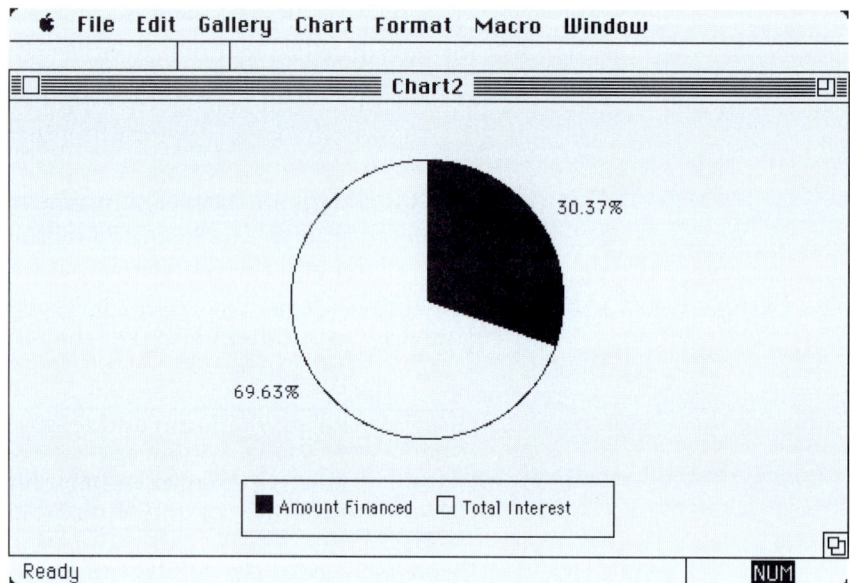

Figure 9-56 Pie chart comparing Amount Financed and Total Interest

      ⇒ Choose **Save As** from the File menu, name the chart, and save it onto your data disk.

Printing the Chart

Now add a title of your choice, change any patterns you wish, save the chart, and print it. Remember that the dimensions of printed versions are a result of how the chart appears on your display.

If you decide to come back later and recalculate a loan and want to see this pie chart, you will have to use the worksheet you saved as Loan Analysis 2, because it is the one linked to the pie chart you just created.

If you are going to do the what if... exercise below, do not close the Loan Analysis 2 worksheet or the pie chart.

WHAT IF... EXERCISES

To complete this exercise, change the amount in the Term of Loan cell in the Loan Analysis 2 worksheet, and the chart will be redrawn. Click on the chart to make it active, and print it. Click on the worksheet to make it active again and make the next change. You do not need to create a new chart each time.

1. Using the loan conditions in step 15 of the house loan in Project 1, modify the worksheet to produce the charts necessary to compare the different loan options. (The cost is $51,500, with 20% down, at 10.5% per year.) Print a chart for the loan at 15, 20, and 40 years. Compare the changes in monthly payments and the amount of interest you will pay to the lender. Compare the percentage composition of the loan by comparing the pie charts showing amount financed and total interest.

This completes Project 2.

Project 3: Creating Linked Worksheets

In this project you will create a new worksheet representing a monthly budget. It will be composed of three main sections: income, expenses, and surplus/deficit. You will learn to format date values and change the font, size, and style of values displayed in a cell.

You also will learn to link values from one worksheet to another. This is a very powerful and useful feature of Excel.

As an example, in this project you will link the monthly payment values calculated in the student, car, and house loans from Project 1. If you were to look at a different loan package, it would automatically recalculate the loan, and if this budget worksheet were also open it would be updated as well. That way you could see the impact on the rest of your budget caused by that particular loan package.

You will also create two charts in this project. A pie chart will show the breakdown of all your expenses, and a column chart will show the comparisons of total income, total expenses, and any surplus or deficit.

Figures 9-57, 9-58, and 9-59 show the final output of Project 3.

```
Monthly Budget                                          Miguel Garcia


Budget
                    Jan 1994
Income
     Income #1      $1,400.00
     Income #2        $735.00
Total Income        $2,135.00

Expenses
     House            $376.87
     Car              $175.97
     Education        $103.79
     Food             $250.00
     Clothes           $75.00
     Insurance        $150.00
     Utilities        $185.00
     Entertainment    $200.00
Total Expenses      $1,516.63

Surplus/Deficit       $618.37
```

Figure 9-57   Final output of Project 3 worksheet

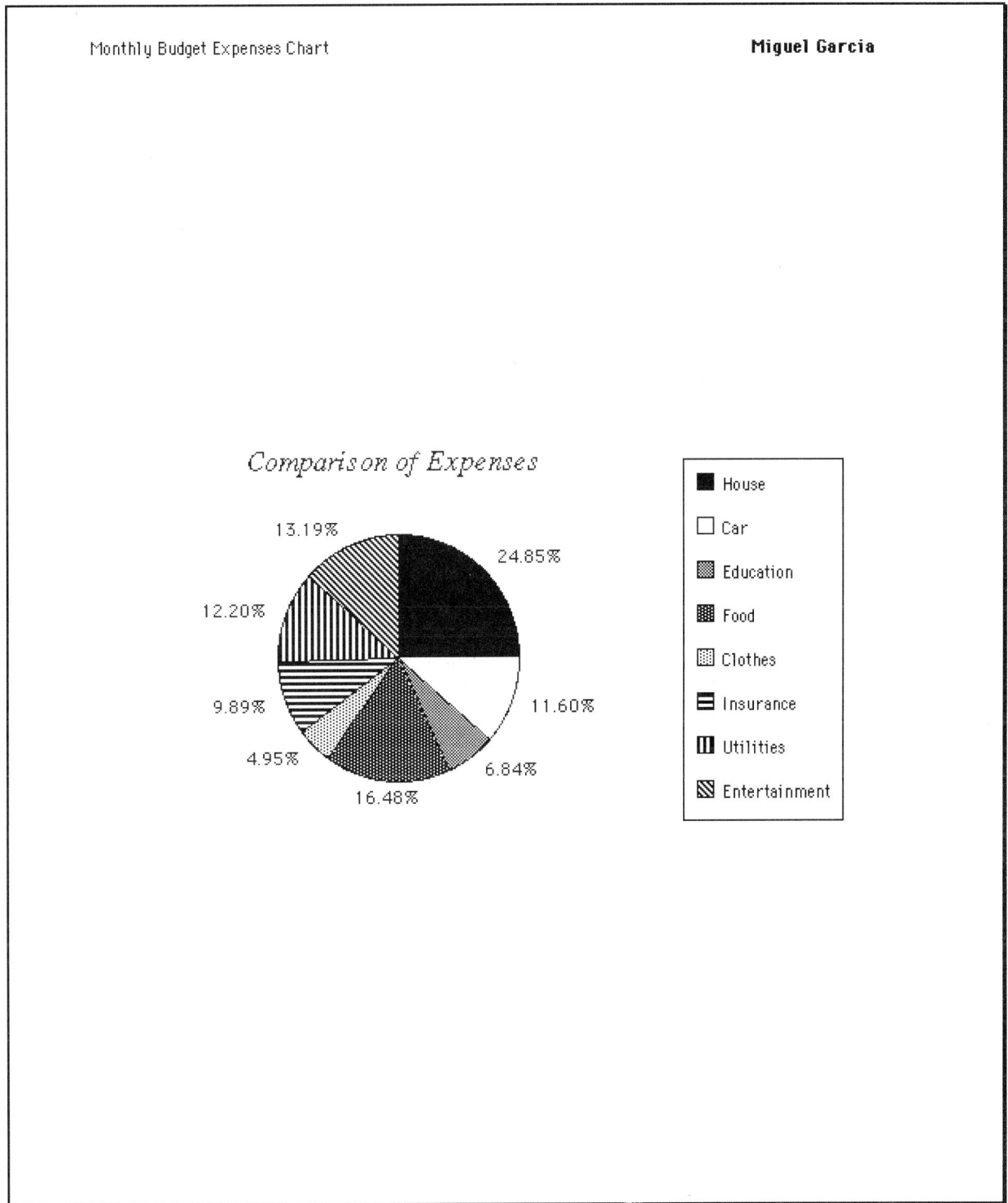

Figure 9-58 Final output of Project 3 pie chart

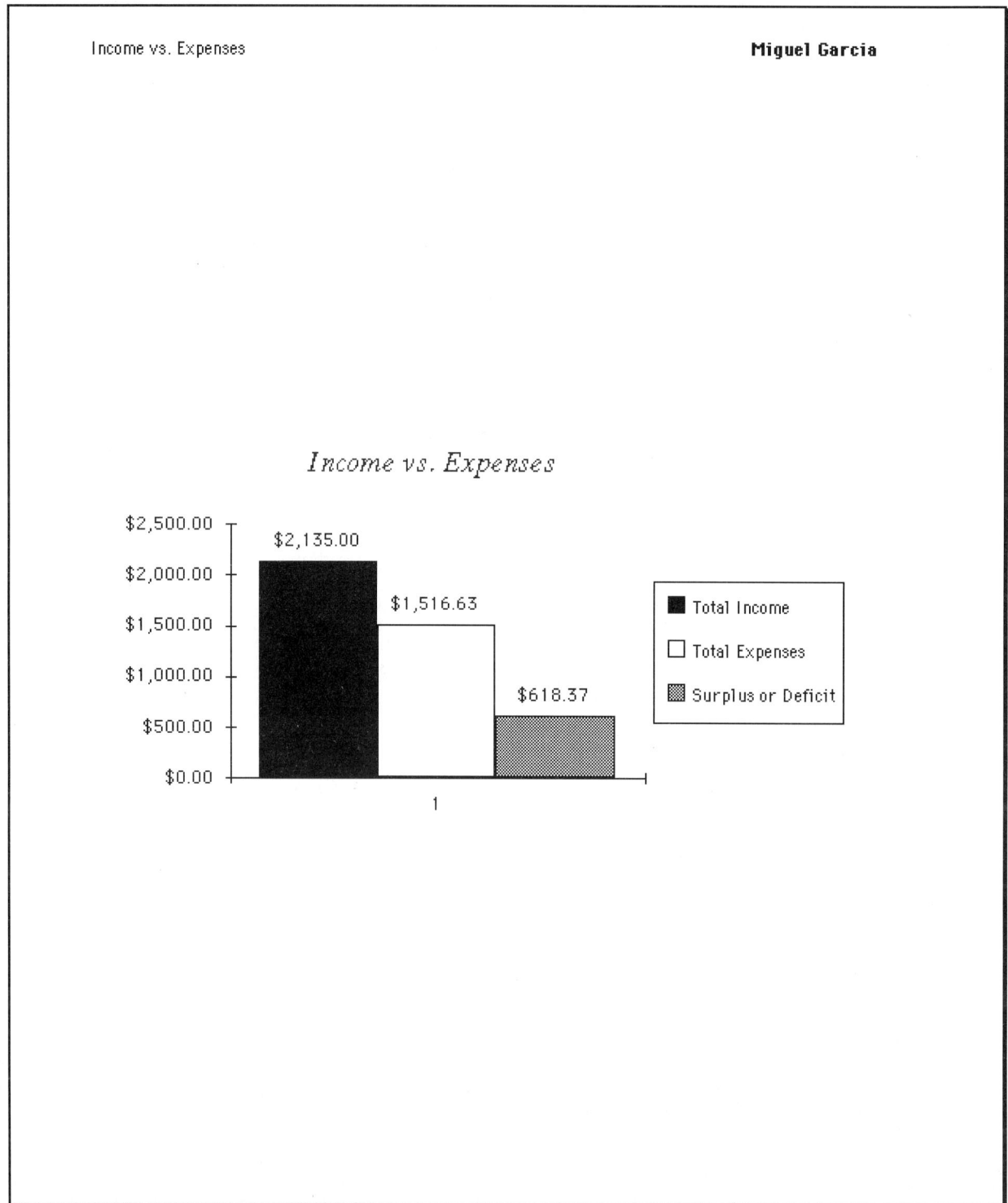

Figure 9-59 Final output of Project 3 column chart

To begin this project, you must have completed Project 1 first. You will be using the three worksheets that you developed in the what if... exercises in that project as important components of this project.

⇒ If you have quit Excel, restart it by double-clicking on its icon.

⇒ If you have not quit Excel, close all open files.

⌘-N ⇒ Create a new worksheet by choosing **New** from the File menu.

ENTERING TEXT AND NUMBERS

⇒ Enter the text shown in Table 9-7 in the indicated cells.

Cell address	Text to be entered
A1	Budget
A3	Income
A6	Total Income
A8	Expenses
A17	Total Expenses
A19	Surplus/Deficit

Table 9-7   Text to be entered into new worksheet in column A

These cells are used to represent titles and total lines.

⇒ Continue adding the text shown in Table 9-8 into column B.

Cell address	Text to be entered
B4	Income #1
B5	Income #2
B9	House
B10	Car
B11	Education
B12	Food
B13	Clothes
B14	Insurance
B15	Utilities
B16	Entertainment

Table 9-8   Text to be entered in column B

⇒ Resize column A so that your worksheet looks like the one shown in Figure 9-60.

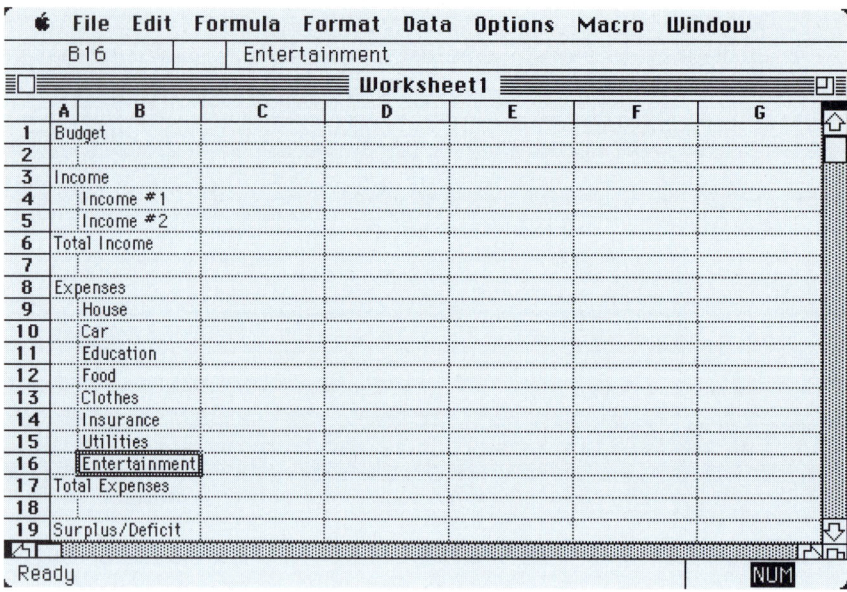

Figure 9-60   Resizing column A to simulate indented category titles

By resizing column A so that it is only about two characters wide, you make the categories look like they are indented between the group titles and the total lines. In a word processor you would have done this by pressing the Tab key. Since Excel does not let you tab in a cell and typing two or three leading spaces results in uneven alignment, this is the easiest way to make your category titles and names appear to be indented and aligned.

⇒ Name this worksheet Monthly Budget, and save it onto your data disk.

FORMATTING DATES

A monthly budget should be labeled with the month and year it represents. Excel allows you to enter dates using more than one method. Excel allows you to use the DATE() function, but it also allows you to type the date directly, such as in 1/1/94.

If you use the second method (1/1/94), Excel will assign the date format m/d/yy to the cell. In this worksheet it is necessary to show only the month and year, so let's tell Excel to use a different format.

⇒ Enter **1/1/94** in cell C2. Choose **Number** from the Format menu, and scroll down to the date formats.

Excel offers four standard formats for dates. These formats, and how they would show 1/1/94, are listed in Table 9-9.

Date format	Displayed as
m/d/yy	1/1/94
d-mmm-yy	1-Jan-94
d-mmm	1-Jan
mmm-yy	Jan-94

Table 9-9 Excel's four standard date formats

When you design a date format, you can specify how Excel will display the month, day, and year, how many characters for each, the order in which they will be displayed, and what punctuation you want, if any. The codes for creating these formats are shown in Table 9-10.

Date format	Meaning	Displayed
d	day as number	1-31
dd	number with leading zero	01-31
ddd	day as abbreviation	Mon
dddd	day as full name	Monday
m	month as number	1-12
mm	number with leading zero	01-12
mmm	abbreviated name	Jan
mmmm	full name	January
yy	last two digits of year	00-99
yyyy	year as four-digit number	1904-2040

Table 9-10 Codes used to create new date formats in Excel

This worksheet will show the date using the abbreviated name of the month and the year as four digits. It will not show the day, because the amounts in each column apply to the whole month. When you entered the date, you specified the first day of the month, but you don't need to show it here.

➠ To create the custom format, click in the Format box, and type **mmm yyyy** (see Figure 9-61).

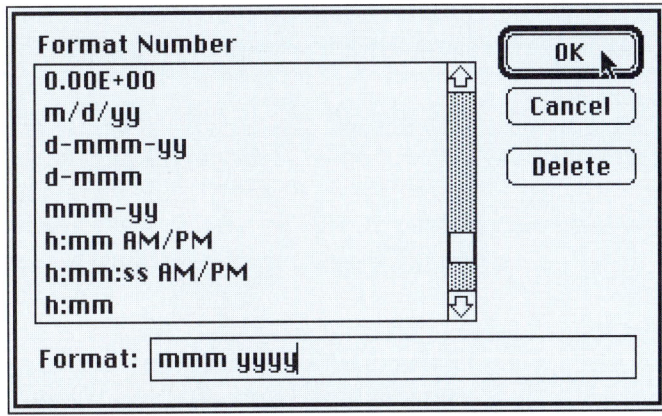

Figure 9-61 Entering a custom date format

The ability to create custom formats makes Excel very flexible and allows you to make your spreadsheet look as you want it to look. You can create custom formats for time and numbers as well. Excel even allows you to have different formats for positive, negative, and zero values. If you are using a color monitor and printer, you can have positive numbers displayed in black and negative numbers in red. You can even add text in a format by enclosing it in quotation marks.

Although these types of formats are beyond the scope of this book, you can learn all about them by looking up "Format Number" in the *Microsoft Excel Reference*.

NAMING CELLS AND RANGES

In Project 2 you learned about absolute and relative cell addressing and how they were used in composing formulas. Excel offers another way to create formulas: by naming cells or groups of cells and then using those names in the formulas instead of their addresses.

Table 9-11 contains a list of five cell ranges. When you entered formulas into the worksheet in Project 1, you entered the address of the cell. In this project, you will learn to name a cell or range of cells and then use the name you defined in the formula. This makes a formula more understandable and easier to read.

Cell range	Name
C4:C5	Income
C6	Total_Income
C9:C16	Expenses
C17	Total_Expenses
C19	Surplus

Table 9-11   Naming cells and ranges of cells

Notice that Total_Income and Total_Expenses have underline characters instead of spaces separating the words (see Table 9-11). Excel does not allow cell names to have any spaces in them. You have the option of jamming the words together, but that reduces the legibility of the names. The underline character (created by typing Shift-hyphen) separates the words without using spaces.

Let's name these five ranges and enter the formulas referring to them in the worksheet.

➡ Select cells **C4:C5**, and then choose **Define Name** from the Formula menu.

Notice that Excel has entered the range of cells in the "Refers to:" box using absolute addressing (see Figure 9-62).

➡ Name this range Income and click **OK**.

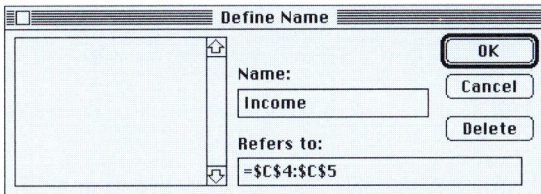

Figure 9-62   Name cells C4:C5 as Income.

➡ Define the Expenses, Surplus, Total_Income, and Total_Expenses names in the same manner.

As you define each of these named ranges, you will see the previously defined names in the scrolling list on the left side of the Define Name dialog box.

ENTERING FORMULAS

Now that you have defined the names of these ranges, you can use them to create formulas that are more understandable. For example, the formula =Total_Income – Total_Expenses is much more meaningful than =C6-C17.

You can enter formulas using the Paste Name command in the Formula menu, or you can type the formula instead. If you choose to type the names yourself, you must be careful that you make no mistakes when typing. The name must be entered *exactly* the same as it was defined. Using Paste Name instead of typing the names will prevent making any mistakes due to typographical errors or not remembering the exact name you defined.

The Paste Name command works similarly to the Paste Function command you have already learned to use. In fact, in creating many formulas, both of these commands are used.

You will enter only three formulas in this worksheet. They will be used to calculate the sum of the income amounts, the sum of all the expenses, and the surplus or deficit (which, you may remember, is calculated by subtracting the total expenses from the total income).

Try using the Paste Name method first to enter the formula for calculating the total of the income sources. If you were told to add all the incomes, you would have no trouble doing that, because you would recognize that the income amounts were in cells C4 and C5. You would then determine the sum of these amounts. You might use a formula like total income = C4+C5 or total income = SUM(C4:C5). That's all there is to calculating the sum of the incomes. Let's tell Excel to do this for you.

➡ Start the first formula by clicking on cell **C6**.

➡ Type = and then use Paste Function to enter the SUM() function into the formula bar.

You've told Excel that you want it to calculate the sum of something, so now tell it which something you want it to add.

➡ Choose **Paste Name**, select **Income**, and then click **OK** or press Enter or Return (see Figure 9-63).

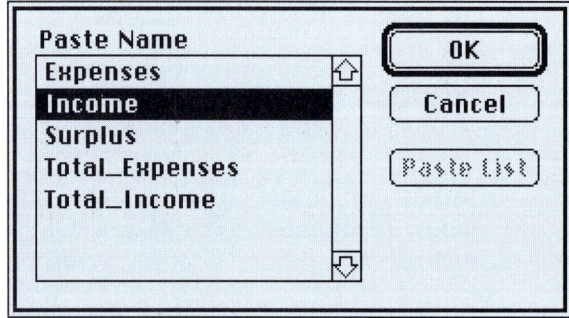

Figure 9-63 Pasting a named group of cells into a formula

➡ To enter the other two formulas, enter the expressions shown in Table 9-12 into the proper cells.

Cell	Formula
C17	=SUM(Expenses)
C19	=Total_Income - Total_Expenses

Table 9-12 The two remaining formulas for this worksheet

These are all the formulas you need for this worksheet.

➡ Format all the cells that will contain numbers as currency, and then enter the numbers shown in Table 9-13 into the appropriate cells (in column C).

Category	Cell	Number
Income #1	C4	1400
Income #2	C5	735
Food	C12	250
Clothes	C13	75
Insurance	C14	150
Utilities	C15	185
Entertainment	C16	200

Table 9-13 Amounts to be entered into column C

Notice that you did not enter a number or formula into the House, Car, and Education categories. That is because you will now link the calculated monthly payments from the worksheets you created in Project 1 into the appropriate cells in this worksheet.

PASTING AND LINKING VALUES

Excel has the ability to link a value in one worksheet to a cell in another worksheet. Once the link has been established, any changes made in the first worksheet would be reflected automatically in the second worksheet.

If both worksheets are open, the change would immediately take place. If only one worksheet was open when the change was made, and the changes were saved to disk, the second worksheet would be updated whenever it was next opened.

When you open a worksheet that depends on values located in a different worksheet, Excel will ask if you want to update the references to that unopened worksheet (see Figure 9-64).

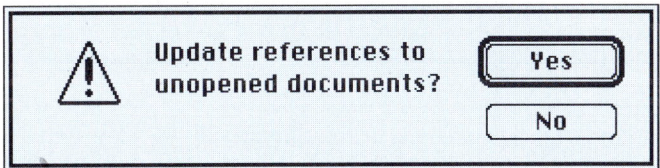

Figure 9-64   "Update references to unopened documents?" dialog box

If you answer "Yes," Excel will read the needed values and will then recalculate the worksheet that is open to reflect any changes made to the other one. Sometimes, though, you might want to print the last version of the worksheet and do not want to update the document to reflect any changes made since the last time it was saved. In that case, you can answer "No" and Excel will open the worksheet just as you last saved it.

This ability to link worksheets is especially valuable if you have to create reports on a periodic basis that depend on values stored in multiple spreadsheets. If you link the worksheets, the summary or report document you must complete can be automatically updated to reflect any changes you may have made in the other worksheets during the period since you last produced the report.

It is common for many families to have one or more loan payments that must be paid each month. Over a period of several years the amounts of these loans will change, and it would be convenient if the current amount of the loan(s) were automatically shown in the budget worksheet.

In this project, the budget shows a house payment, a car payment, and an education loan payment. If the monthly payment amount of each of these loans could be linked to the budget worksheet, then you would have a powerful tool for evaluating new purchase options not only by the monthly payment, but also by how they would affect your budget.

Therefore, let's link each of the three loans this family must repay (remember, you calculated and saved them in the what if... exercises in Project 1) to this budget worksheet.

Let's start with the Student Loan worksheet. To link this loan payment to the budget, you will copy the monthly payment amount from the Student Loan worksheet and then paste it into the appropriate cell in the Monthly Budget worksheet.

This means that you must have two worksheets open at the same time. If you have a large monitor, this is a simple thing to do: just move them to where they are both visible. On the smaller, standard Macintosh screen you don't have room to show two large windows. You have a choice of letting the windows overlap or of resizing them and placing them so you can see the appropriate parts of the worksheets at the same time.

Remember, only one window in an application is active at any time, so only one will have lines in the title bar, visible scroll bars, and other visible controls. If the window you need to use is not active, click anywhere in that window, and Excel will make it the active window.

You can also tell Excel which window you want to make active by choosing its name from the Window menu. All open worksheets, charts, and macro sheets will be listed by name in the Window menu. If you want to activate a window that can't be seen on the screen, just choose its name in the Window menu and it will be brought forward and made the active window.

➡ Open the Monthly Budget worksheet and then the Student Loan worksheet. Place them so you can see them at the same time (see Figure 9-65).

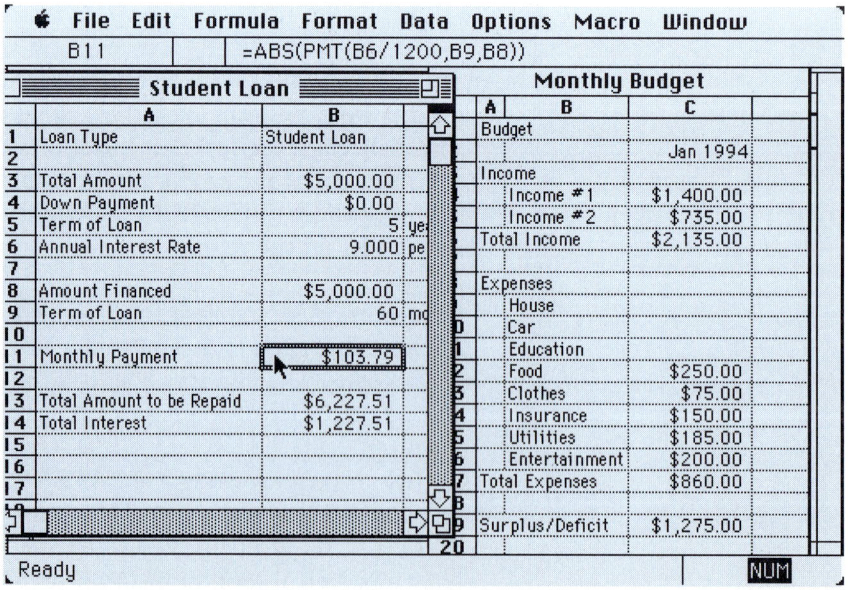

Figure 9-65   Arranging the worksheets on screen so both are visible at once

➡ If it is not already the active window, activate the Student Loan worksheet window.

➠ Select cell **B11** (the monthly payment amount) to make it the active cell.

⌘-C ➠ Copy the payment amount.

➠ Click in the Monthly Budget window to activate it (or choose it from the Window menu).

➠ Select the **Education** expense cell (**C11**).

➠ Choose **Paste Link** from the Edit menu.

Paste Link is a command that saves you a lot of work when linking worksheets. All you have to do is point to the cell from which you want to link and tell Excel to copy it. Then, by selecting the cell to which the first cell will be linked and choosing **Paste Link**, you tell Excel not only to remember the origination cell's address, but also the name of the worksheet, the disk on which it is located, and the pathway through the folders to find the worksheet.

Excel then pastes all this into the destination cell. If both worksheets are open and you make a change to the Student Loan worksheet, Excel will update the Student Loan worksheet, and then it will update the Monthly Budget.

Try this now, and watch as both worksheets change.

➠ Change the Annual Interest Rate in the Student Loan worksheet to 10%.

If you were not watching carefully, you may have missed seeing them change. After you make this change, your worksheets should contain the values shown in Figure 9-66.

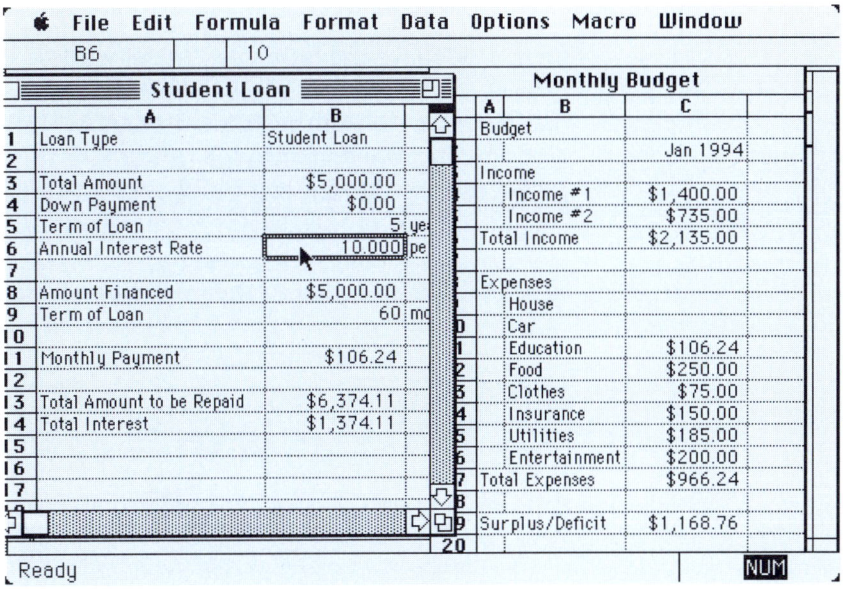

Figure 9-66 Changing the interest rate now modifies both worksheets.

➡ Try this again. Leave the interest rate at 10%, and change the Total Amount to $7,500.

You can see that the monthly payment amount rose, and in the Monthly Budget the total expenses increased and the surplus decreased (as shown in Figure 9-67).

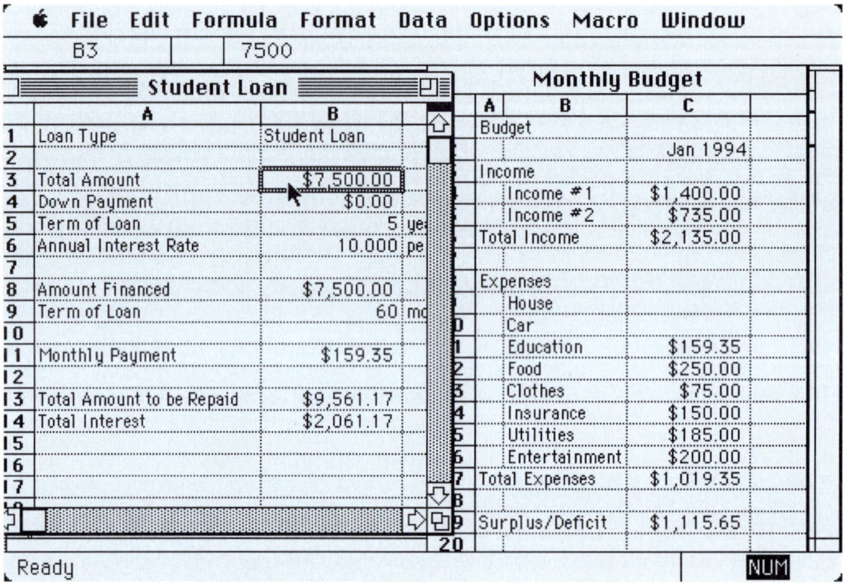

Figure 9-67   Changing Total Amount affects both worksheets

Now you are finished with the Student Loan worksheet.

➡ Close the Student Loan worksheet. When Excel asks if you want to save the changes, answer **No**, so you can leave it with the same amounts it had when you opened it.

⌘-S ➡ Save the Monthly Budget worksheet.

After closing the Student Loan worksheet, look at the formula in the Education expense cell of the Monthly Budget. The formula will have changed to show the names of the disk, folders, and worksheet and the address of the cell(s) that are linked to this cell. (Your formula should look similar to the one shown in Figure 9-68, but there may be some differences due to the way your disk is organized.)

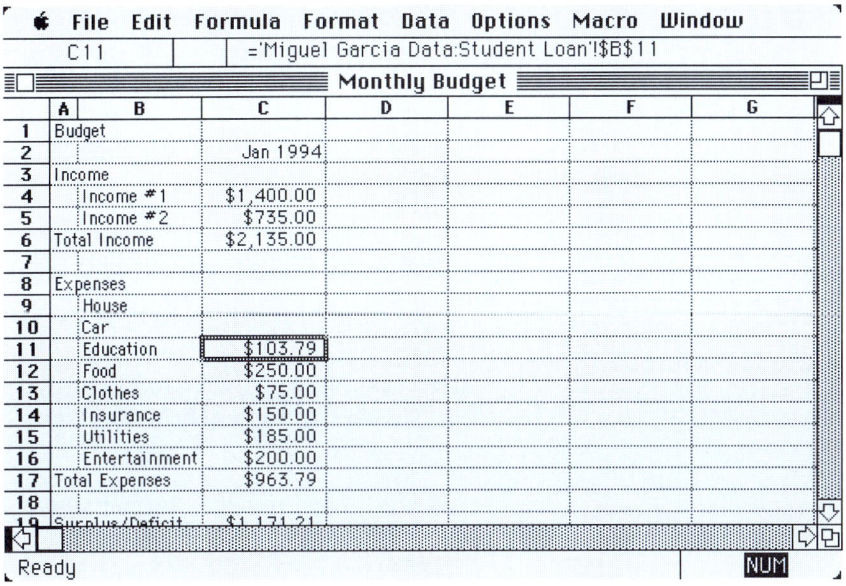

Figure 9-68   Formula showing link to cell B11 of the Student Loan
                  worksheet

In this case, the formula for cell C11 is ='**Miguel Garcia Data:Student
Loan'!$B$11**. In addition to showing the absolute address of the cell
that contains the information (after the exclamation point in the
formula), it also lists the disk and worksheet names. The address of the
worksheet (which contains the disk name, any folders that must be
opened, and the worksheet's name) is enclosed in single quotes. In this
case, it says "link this cell to the amount shown in cell B11 in the Student
Loan worksheet stored on a disk named Miguel Garcia Data".

If Miguel had stored this worksheet in the Final Projects folder on his
disk, the formula would have read ='**Miguel Garcia Data:Final
Projects:Student Loan'!$B$11**. The procedure for storing the worksheet's
location is to name the disk, then any folders that must be opened (Final
Projects), then the worksheet. Each of these items must be separated by
a colon (:). The entire location must be enclosed in single quotes, and
this must be followed by an exclamation point (!) before the cell or range
address is listed. Fortunately, Excel does all of this automatically when
you choose the Paste Link command.

Before linking a spreadsheet to another one, it is a good idea to save the
worksheet in case something goes wrong. If a problem occurs, you won't
lose any of your valuable work, and all you have to do is close the
worksheet (*without saving it*), and then open the version you saved
before the problem occurred.

➠ Using the procedure you just learned, open the House Loan and link its monthly payment to the Monthly Budget, and then close the House Loan.

You did remember to save the Monthly Budget before starting the next step, didn't you?

➠ Link the monthly payment from the Car Loan worksheet to the Monthly Budget, and close the Car Loan.

⌘-S ➠ Save the Monthly Budget worksheet.

After completing these steps, you should have a Monthly Budget containing the values shown in Figure 9-69.

🍎	File	Edit	Formula	Format	Data	Options	Macro	Window

C19	=Total_Income-Total_Expenses

Monthly Budget

	A	B	C	D	E	F	G
1	Budget						
2			Jan 1994				
3	Income						
4		Income #1	$1,400.00				
5		Income #2	$735.00				
6	Total Income		$2,135.00				
7							
8	Expenses						
9		House	$376.87				
10		Car	$175.97				
11		Education	$103.79				
12		Food	$250.00				
13		Clothes	$75.00				
14		Insurance	$150.00				
15		Utilities	$185.00				
16		Entertainment	$200.00				
17	Total Expenses		$1,516.63				
18							
19	Surplus/Deficit		$618.37				

Ready   NUM

Figure 9-69   The completed Monthly Budget

This project will be used again in Project 4, so the final version must be saved. (*Do you get the feeling that saving your work often is important?*)

The next time you open the Monthly Budget worksheet, Excel will ask you if you want to update references to unopened documents.

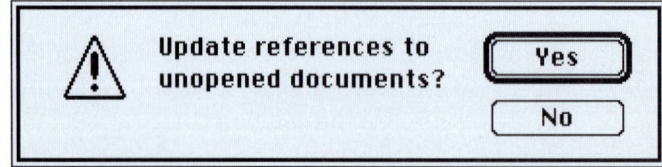

⚠ **Update references to unopened documents?**   ☐ Yes   ☐ No

Figure 9-70   The dialog box you will see whenever you open Monthly Budget

Excel is asking if you want it to read the three loan worksheets that are linked to the Monthly Budget and adjust the budget worksheet to reflect any changes you may have made to the loan worksheets since the last time the Monthly Budget was saved.

This is very handy. Even if your budget is not open and you make changes to one or more of the loan worksheets, Excel can automatically update the budget the next time you open it if you answer this question with Yes. If you answer the question with No, the Monthly Budget will be opened with the same figures it had the last time you saved it, even if you did modify one or more of the other three worksheets to which it is linked.

CREATING A PIE CHART

The next step in completing this project is to create a pie chart showing a comparison of the expenses. You will not have to move any cells, because this worksheet was designed to make this an easy task.

⇒ Select cells **B9:C16**, and then create a new pie chart, using pie chart number 6. Add a title and a legend, and make whatever format changes you prefer.

Your chart should look similar to the one shown in Figure 9-71.

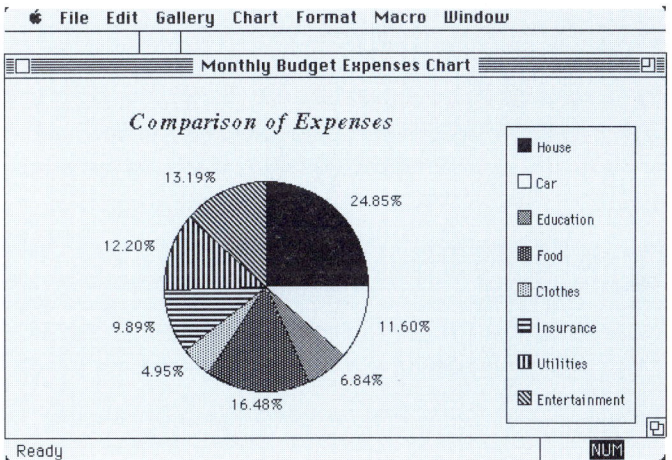

Figure 9-71 Pie chart comparing expense amounts

⌘-S ⇒ Save this pie chart as Monthly Budget Expenses Chart.

⌘-P ⇒ Print the pie chart.

CREATING A COLUMN CHART

The pie chart was easy to create. Now let's create a column chart comparing total income, total expenses, and surplus/deficit. You want to show the three numbers on the chart, and the legend should contain a name for the numbers represented by the columns in the chart.

To select noncontiguous cells or ranges of cells, use Command-click at the beginning of each range to tell Excel that you want to treat noncontiguous cells as a group.

➡ Select cells **A6:C6**, **A17:C17**, and **A19:C19** and create a column chart.

What's wrong with this chart? There is a space for a data series with no data. You chose a selection three columns wide, and Excel assumed that the first column had the title of the data series, and it does. Then Excel assumed that both columns B and C contained data associated with that series, but that is not correct. Because there is no information in column B in these rows, Excel plotted a column with a height of zero.

This is not what you want to do. If you moved the titles into column B, you could select the cells in B and C in each row, and Excel's assumptions about creating a new chart should work. It sure seems a shame to have to go in and rearrange your worksheet after getting this far. Luckily, you don't have to do that.

➡ Close the new chart without saving it. Using Command-click again, choose only cells **C6**, **C17**, and **C19**. Create a new column chart. Add a legend to the chart.

When you told Excel to add the legend, it put the legend on the right side of the box with three patterned rectangles, but there are no words associated with the patterns. This is because you chose only cells containing numbers, and Excel had nothing to use as names for those numbers.

There is an easy way to modify the data series you just charted so Excel will have a name associated with each one.

➡ Click on the column on the left (which represents income).

When you do, Excel shows a formula that starts with **=SERIES(,,** in the formula bar. The space between the opening parenthesis and the first comma is where the name of the series goes.

➡ Click between the opening parenthesis and the first comma, and enter "**Total Income**" (you must enter the quotation characters). Accept the formula.

Your chart should now look similar to the one shown in Figure 9-72.

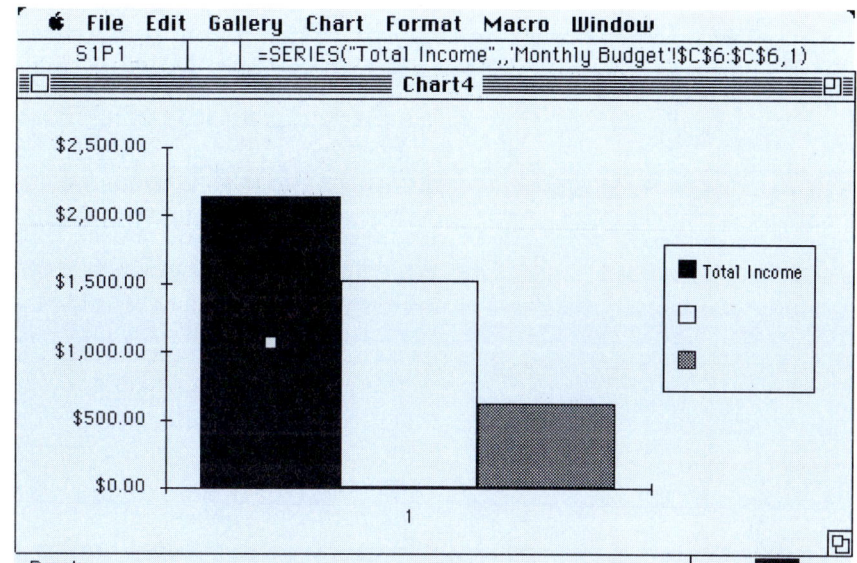

Figure 9-72   Naming the Total Income data series

➡ Select the center column and name it "**Total Expenses**", and then name the right column "**Surplus or Deficit**".

Your chart should have a complete legend. You can now add a title and make any formatting changes you desire.

⌘-S   ➡ Save this chart as Monthly Budget Column Chart.

You now have completed Project 3. Be sure to save a copy of the Monthly Budget worksheet for use in Project 4.

WHAT IF... EXERCISES

When you work through these what if... exercises, do not save any changes that you make to your worksheets, so you will have the proper values in the Monthly Budget for use in Project 4.

There are a number of things you can do now. A change to any of the three loan worksheets will affect the Monthly Budget worksheet as well as the two charts you just created.

For example:

1. What if you spend $1,000 this month to buy that new video camera you've been dying to own? This will make your expenses for the month greater than your income, and your surplus will turn into a deficit. *Hint: Try adding $1,000 to the Entertainment expense category.*

2. What if you bought that $20,000 car you've been wanting? How will that affect your budget? Could you afford it? *Hint: Modify the Car Loan worksheet and see how it affects your budget.*

3. What would happen if you got a 20-year house loan instead of 30 years? How much extra money would you have for something else by not having to make house payments for an extra ten years? (*Hint: Subtract the total amount to be repaid for the 20-year loan from the same value for the 30-year loan.*) How much would your monthly payment increase? Would it fit into your budget?

Project 4: Developing an Annual Budget

In this project you will modify the monthly budget you created in Project 3 and expand it into an annual budget. You will learn to use the split bars, create a sequential data series, and make extensive use of the Fill Down and Fill Right commands.

You will create two charts in this project. A pie chart will show the breakdown of all your expenses, and a line chart will show the comparisons of total income, total expenses, and any surplus or deficit over the 12-month period.

The final output of Project 4 is shown in Figures 9-73, 9-74, 9-75, and 9-76.

Budget	Jan 1994	Feb 1994	Mar 1994	Apr 1994	May 1994	Jun 1994	Jul 1994
Income							
Income #1	$1,400.00	$1,400.00	$1,400.00	$1,400.00	$1,400.00	$1,400.00	$1,400.00
Income #2	$735.00	$735.00	$735.00	$735.00	$735.00	$735.00	$735.00
Total Income	$2,135.00	$2,135.00	$2,135.00	$2,135.00	$2,135.00	$2,135.00	$2,135.00
Expenses							
House	$376.87	$376.87	$376.87	$376.87	$376.87	$376.87	$376.87
Car	$175.97	$175.97	$175.97	$175.97	$175.97	$175.97	$175.97
Education	$103.79	$103.79	$103.79	$103.79	$103.79	$103.79	$103.79
Food	$250.00	$250.00	$250.00	$250.00	$250.00	$250.00	$250.00
Clothes	$75.00	$75.00	$75.00	$75.00	$75.00	$75.00	$75.00
Insurance	$150.00			$600.00			$150.00
Utilities	$185.00	$185.00	$185.00	$140.00	$100.00	$65.00	$120.00
Savings	$213.50	$213.50	$213.50	$213.50	$213.50	$213.50	$213.50
Entertainment	$200.00	$200.00	$200.00	$200.00	$200.00	$200.00	$200.00
Total Expenses	$1,730.13	$1,580.13	$1,580.13	$2,135.13	$1,495.13	$1,460.13	$1,665.13
Surplus/Deficit	$404.87	$554.87	$554.87	($0.13)	$639.87	$674.87	$469.87

Figure 9-73   Final output of Project 4, budget page 1

Aug 1994	Sep 1994	Oct 1994	Nov 1994	Dec 1994	Totals	Percent of Total Income
$1,400.00	$1,400.00	$1,400.00	$1,400.00	$1,400.00	$16,800.00	65.57%
$735.00	$735.00	$735.00	$735.00	$735.00	$8,820.00	34.43%
$2,135.00	$2,135.00	$2,135.00	$2,135.00	$2,135.00	$25,620.00	100.00%
$376.87	$376.87	$376.87	$376.87	$376.87	$4,522.47	17.65%
$175.97	$175.97	$175.97	$175.97	$175.97	$2,111.63	8.24%
$103.79	$103.79	$103.79	$103.79	$103.79	$1,245.54	4.86%
$250.00	$250.00	$250.00	$250.00	$250.00	$3,000.00	11.71%
$75.00	$75.00	$75.00	$75.00	$75.00	$900.00	3.51%
					$900.00	3.51%
$120.00	$65.00	$65.00	$100.00	$170.00	$1,500.00	5.85%
$213.50	$213.50	$213.50	$213.50	$213.50	$2,562.00	10.00%
$200.00	$200.00	$200.00	$200.00	$200.00	$2,400.00	9.37%
$1,515.13	$1,460.13	$1,460.13	$1,495.13	$1,565.13	$19,141.57	74.71%
$619.87	$674.87	$674.87	$639.87	$569.87	$6,478.43	25.29%

Figure 9-74   Final output of Project 4, budget page 2

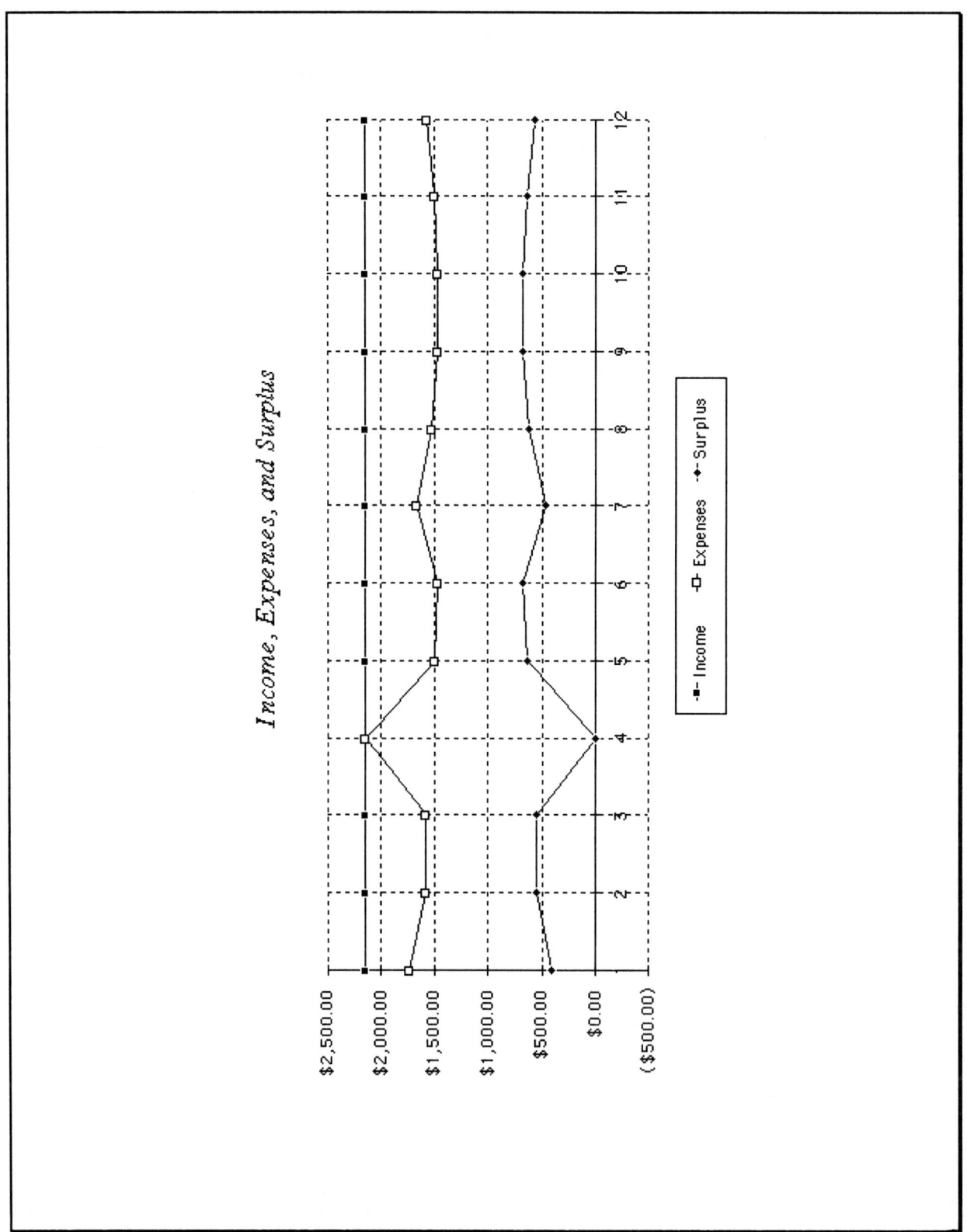

Figure 9-75   Final output of Project 4 line chart

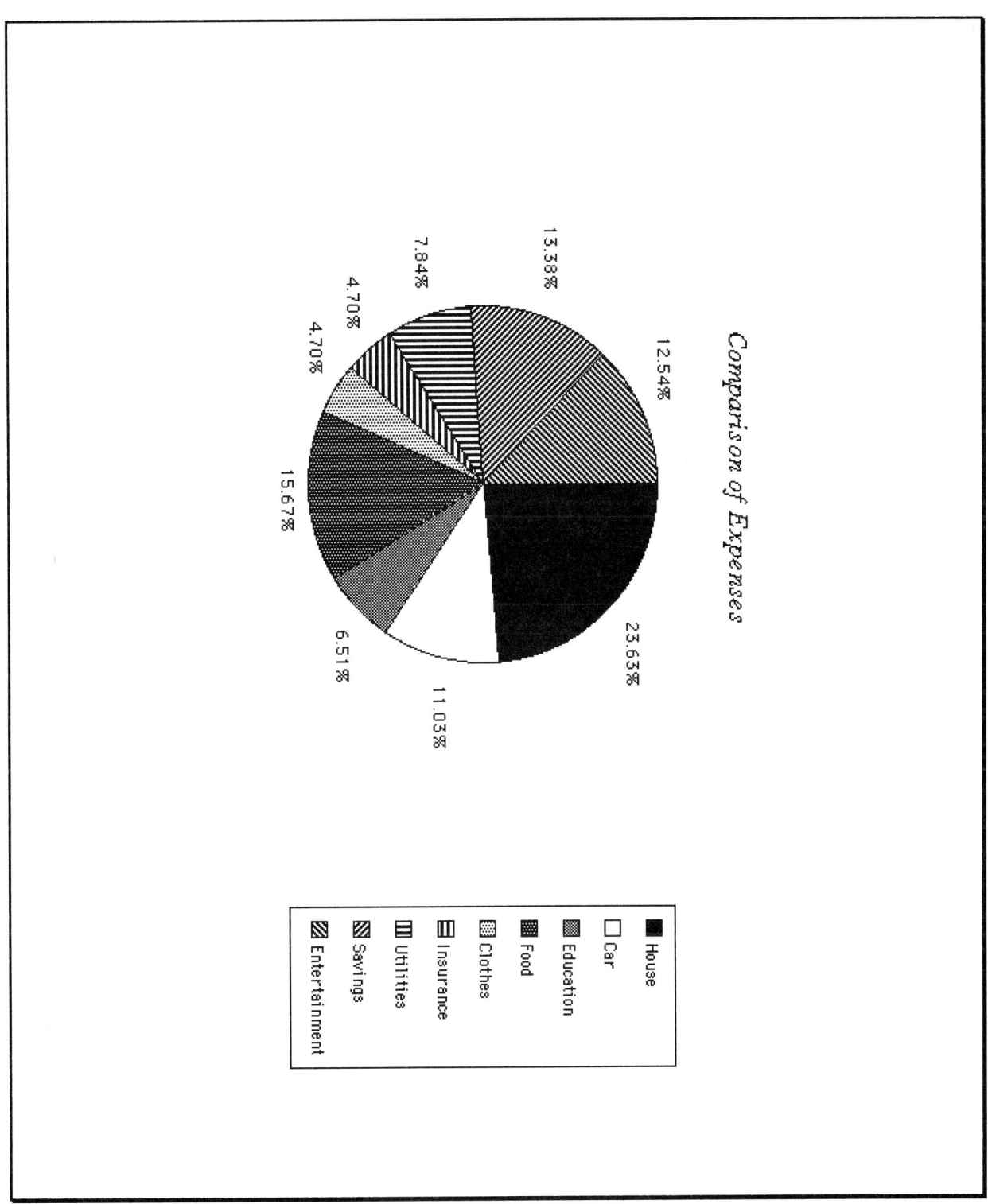

Figure 9-76 Final output of Project 4 pie chart

To begin this project, you should have completed Project 3 first, since you will be using the monthly budget you developed there as a starting point for this project.

➡ If you have quit Excel, restart it by double-clicking on the Monthly Budget icon. If not, open Monthly Budget.

➡ Save this worksheet as Annual Budget onto your data disk.

This will not change the monthly budget, but only makes a copy of it, names the copy Annual Budget, closes the original worksheet, and makes this new Annual Budget the active worksheet.

CREATING A DATA SERIES

An annual budget usually has a list of the 12 months across the top of the budget. Then, under each month's name, there is the amount for that month for each income and expense category.

To create the data series you need to select cells C2 through N2. You will make use of the automatic scrolling feature of Excel. If you press the mouse button in a cell and drag the pointer past the edge of the window, the window will scroll and extend the selection as it scrolls.

➡ Press the mouse button on cell C2 in the left pane, hold the mouse button down, and drag the pointer to the right side of the screen. Hold the mouse button down until you have scrolled through and selected all the cells in row 2 over to cell N2.

That may not have been an easy thing to control if you are new to automatic scrolling. This is a slow, and unnecessarily difficult, way to select large numbers of cells.

Now that you have some experience in automatic scrolling and selecting, let's learn a better way to do this.

➡ Scroll back to the left, using the scroll bar, so that column A is visible in the worksheet window.

You could add the month names now by typing them into cells D2 through N2, but Excel offers several easier ways to accomplish this. Let's add the month names in this worksheet by creating a data series.

The first thing you will notice is that you cannot show a whole year on a standard Macintosh monitor. Excel allows you to get around this problem by using the split bars. You will use the vertical split bar (located in the lower left corner of the worksheet window) to allow you to see the cells on the left and right sides of the worksheet. This means that you will not be able to see the cells in the middle of the worksheet.

➡ Point to the vertical split bar and drag it over the border between columns D and E.

This splits the window into two vertical panes, each having its own horizontal scroll bar, and they both share the vertical scroll bar. .

➡ Click on the right pane's scroll bar until column N is centered in the pane.

One handy method for selecting cells is to click on the first one and then Shift-click on the last one. This will be especially useful for this project since you will be making several wide selections.

To add the data series, you must first select cells C2:N2. As you have seen, you can click on **C2** and drag to **N2**, but it causes the window to scroll and is often difficult to control. An easier method is to click on the first cell and then Shift-click on the last.

➡ Click on cell **C2** in the left pane, and then Shift-click on cell **N2** in the right pane (see Figure 9-77).

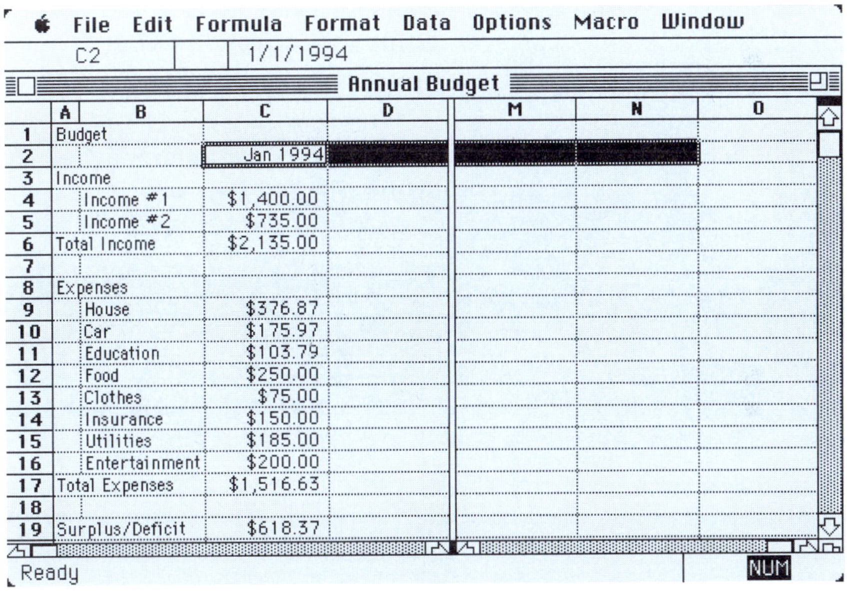

Figure 9-77   Making a wide selection using two vertical panes

This is a much faster and easier method to make selections across a number of columns. This method also works vertically, across multiple rows, if you split the screen using the horizontal split bar.

Notice that the first cell in the selection was formatted in Project 3 as a date. If you had not already formatted that cell as a date, you would have to do so now.

When you create a data series, the first cell in the selection must have a value in it. If the first cell is empty, the data series will be empty. Since cell C2 has a starting date, you can create a series of dates quickly using the Series command.

➧ Choose **Series** from the Data menu.

You will see the dialog box shown in Figure 9-78.

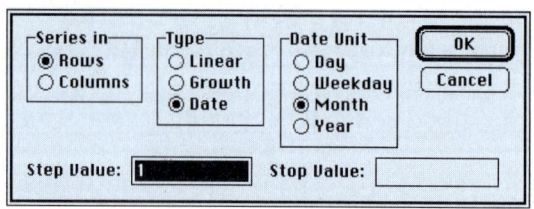

Figure 9-78   Creating a series of date values

The data series you will create will be on a single row and will be a date increasing by one month per column.

➧ Select **Month** under the Date Unit. You don't have to specify a stop value, because Excel will automatically stop when it reaches the last cell in the selection (N2).

Return ➧ Click **OK** or press Return.

You should now see the month names at the top of the columns as shown in Figure 9-79.

```
 🍎  File  Edit  Formula  Format  Data  Options  Macro  Window
       C2              1/1/1994
≡□▢══════════════════ Annual Budget ══════════════════▢◲
     A│   B        │    C     │    D     ║    M     │    N     │    O     │⇧
  1 │Budget        │          │          ║          │          │          │
  2 │              │ Jan 1994 │ Feb 1994 ║ Nov 1994 │ Dec 1994 │          │
  3 │Income        │          │          ║          │          │          │
  4 │  Income #1   │$1,400.00 │          ║          │          │          │
  5 │  Income #2   │  $735.00 │          ║          │          │          │
  6 │Total Income  │$2,135.00 │          ║          │          │          │
  7 │              │          │          ║          │          │          │
  8 │Expenses      │          │          ║          │          │          │
  9 │  House       │  $376.87 │          ║          │          │          │
 10 │  Car         │  $175.97 │          ║          │          │          │
 11 │  Education   │  $103.79 │          ║          │          │          │
 12 │  Food        │  $250.00 │          ║          │          │          │
 13 │  Clothes     │   $75.00 │          ║          │          │          │
 14 │  Insurance   │  $150.00 │          ║          │          │          │
 15 │  Utilities   │  $185.00 │          ║          │          │          │
 16 │  Entertainment│ $200.00 │          ║          │          │          │
 17 │Total Expenses│$1,516.63 │          ║          │          │          │
 18 │              │          │          ║          │          │          │
 19 │Surplus/Deficit│ $618.37 │          ║          │          │          │⇩
 Ready                                                              NUM
```

Figure 9-79   Filling a selection with a series of dates

⌘-S ➧ This is a good time to save your work.

ADDING FORMULAS

Now that you have set up the month names, it is time to use Excel's powerful replication features to quickly expand the monthly budget into an annual budget.

The first step is to tell Excel that February's amounts are the same as January's amounts. This will not be strictly true, but it allows you to rapidly expand the spreadsheet and then go back and make specific adjustments as necessary.

➡ Select cell **D4** and enter the formula =C4.

Excel will display 1400 as the Income #1 amount for February.

Notice that the format is not for currency. This is because you only set the cells in column C as currency format. Since most of the cells in this worksheet will contain currency amounts, the next step is to select the entire spreadsheet and choose the currency format.

➡ Select the entire worksheet by clicking in the top left rectangle to the left of Column A and above row 1.

The entire worksheet will be highlighted.

➡ Select the currency format from the Format menu.

Notice that the month headings on row 2 changed to currency also. You can correct this by selecting those cells again and formatting them with the special date format you previously created.

➡ Select row 2 by clicking the row number. Select the date format from the Format menu.

DUPLICATING FORMULAS AND NUMBERS

Now that you have set up the proper formats, you can duplicate the formula in cell D4 down the column so that each category's January amount will be displayed in February also.

⌘-D ➡ Select **D4:D19**, and choose **Fill Down** from the Edit menu.

Notice that all the cells between D4 and D19 momentarily show 1400 then recalculate almost immediately. Since cells C7, C8, and C18 were blank, Excel has put $0.00 into cells D7, D8, and D18. You want these cells to be blank, and the easiest way to do this is to select them and use the Clear command.

➠   Make a multiple selection of cells **D7:D8** and **D18**.

⌘-B ➠   Choose **Clear** from the Edit menu, and then click **All** in the dialog box. Click **OK**.

Your worksheet should look like the one shown in Figure 9-80.

	A	B	C	D	M	N	O
1	Budget						
2			Jan 1994	Feb 1994	Nov 1994	Dec 1994	
3	Income						
4		Income #1	$1,400.00	$1,400.00			
5		Income #2	$735.00	$735.00			
6	Total Income		$2,135.00	$2,135.00			
7							
8	Expenses						
9		House	$376.87	$376.87			
10		Car	$175.97	$175.97			
11		Education	$103.79	$103.79			
12		Food	$250.00	$250.00			
13		Clothes	$75.00	$75.00			
14		Insurance	$150.00	$150.00			
15		Utilities	$185.00	$185.00			
16		Entertainment	$200.00	$200.00			
17	Total Expenses		$1,516.63	$1,516.63			
18							
19	Surplus/Deficit		$618.37	$618.37			

Figure 9-80   Clearing empty cells

Now you are ready to fill in all the monthly budgets for March through December.

➠   Select cell **D4** in the left pane, and then Shift-click on cell **N19** in the right pane.

This allows you to select all the cells representing February through December. You must select the February amounts, because you are going to duplicate the formulas from these cells into all the months through December.

⌘-R ➠   Choose **Fill Right** from the Edit menu.

After you click in a cell to deselect the large selection, your worksheet should look like the one shown in Figure 9-81

	A	B	C	D	M	N	O
1	Budget						
2			Jan 1994	Feb 1994	Nov 1994	Dec 1994	
3	Income						
4		Income #1	$1,400.00	$1,400.00	$1,400.00	$1,400.00	
5		Income #2	$735.00	$735.00	$735.00	$735.00	
6	Total Income		$2,135.00	$2,135.00	$2,135.00	$2,135.00	
7							
8	Expenses						
9		House	$376.87	$376.87	$376.87	$376.87	
10		Car	$175.97	$175.97	$175.97	$175.97	
11		Education	$103.79	$103.79	$103.79	$103.79	
12		Food	$250.00	$250.00	$250.00	$250.00	
13		Clothes	$75.00	$75.00	$75.00	$75.00	
14		Insurance	$150.00	$150.00	$150.00	$150.00	
15		Utilities	$185.00	$185.00	$185.00	$185.00	
16		Entertainment	$200.00	$200.00	$200.00	$200.00	
17	Total Expenses		$1,516.63	$1,516.63	$1,516.63	$1,516.63	
18							
19	Surplus/Deficit		$618.37	$618.37	$618.37	$618.37	

Figure 9-81   Annual Budget after filling February values through December

In just a few easy steps you have told Excel to expand the monthly budget into a full 12-month annual budget.

ADDING MULTIPLE COLUMNS

Now you will add two more columns to the worksheet. Column O will contain the totals for each category for the year, and column P will contain formulas that calculate the total for each category as a percentage of total income.

You will add the titles for the columns and then create two formulas and use Fill Down to duplicate them.

➡ Select cell **O2** and enter **Totals**.

➡ Type **Percent of** in cell P1.

➡ Enter **Total Income** in cell P2.

➡ Select these three cells, choose **Alignment** from the Format menu, and in the dialog box click **Right** to have them align Right.

Return ➡ Click **OK** or press Return.

Before you add the formulas for these two columns you should change the format for the font displayed in cells O4:P19. If they are displayed the same as the other values, it will be hard to see where the monthly values end and these summary columns begin.

➠ Select cells **O4:P19**, then choose **Font** from the Format menu. Change the font to Bold and click **OK**.

You will now add the formulas for cells O4 and P4.

➠ Select **O4** and enter **=SUM(C4:N4)**, and in **P4** enter **=O4/$O$6**.

The formula in cell P4 needs a little explanation. It tells Excel to take the sum of all 12 monthly Income #1 amounts (calculated in O4) and divide it by the amount in O6 (which is the total annual income). You need to use relative addressing for O4, because you want Excel to use the sum of each respective category when you use Fill Down. You must use absolute addressing for cell O6, because you always want to divide the total for each category by the total annual income.

When you enter the formulas, Excel calculates the total in cell O4 but gives you an error message in P4, #DIV/0! (see Figure 9-82). This means that you are dividing by zero, which is an undefined mathematical operation. You receive this error message because you have not filled the formulas down yet, so there is no value in cell O6. This will be rectified in the next step.

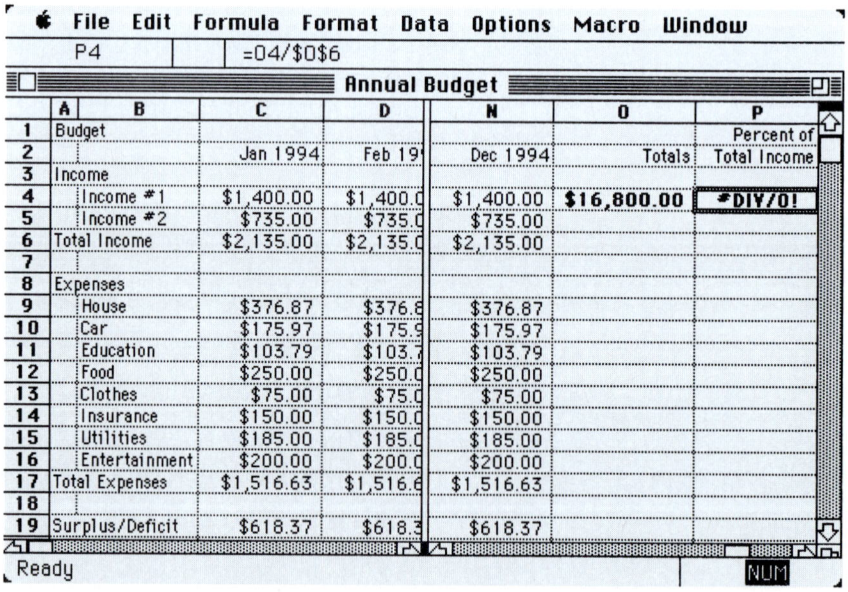

Figure 9-82   Division by zero error message

⌘-D ➠ Select cells **O4:P19** and choose **Fill Down** from the Edit menu.

⌘-B ➠ Clear the unnecessary formulas in cells O7:P8 and O18:P18.

➠ Select **P4:P19**, choose **Number** from the Format menu, and then choose **0%** from the scrolling list. Click **OK**.

The result is shown in Figure 9-83.

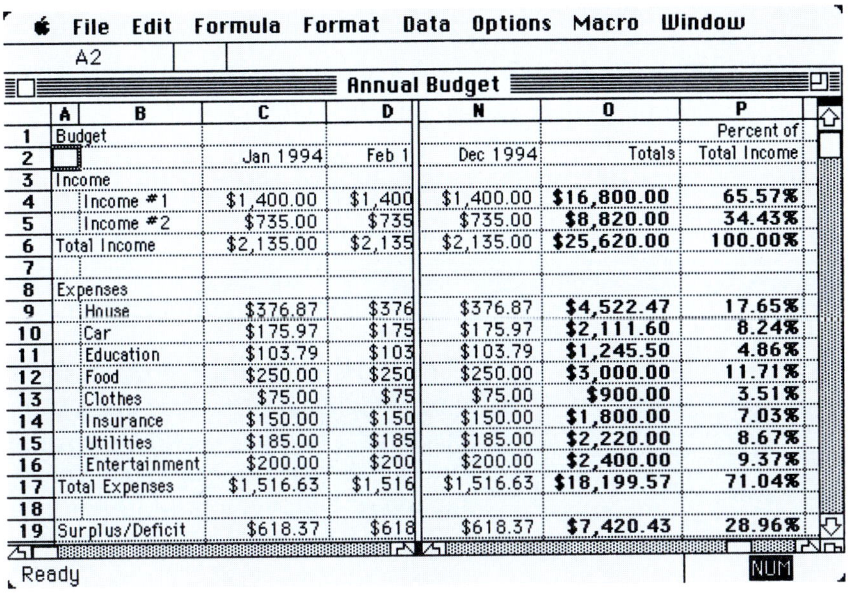

	A	B	C	D	N	O	P
1	Budget						Percent of
2			Jan 1994	Feb 1	Dec 1994	Totals	Total Income
3	Income						
4		Income #1	$1,400.00	$1,400	$1,400.00	**$16,800.00**	**65.57%**
5		Income #2	$735.00	$735	$735.00	**$8,820.00**	**34.43%**
6	Total Income		$2,135.00	$2,135	$2,135.00	**$25,620.00**	**100.00%**
7							
8	Expenses						
9		House	$376.87	$376	$376.87	**$4,522.47**	**17.65%**
10		Car	$175.97	$175	$175.97	**$2,111.60**	**8.24%**
11		Education	$103.79	$103	$103.79	**$1,245.50**	**4.86%**
12		Food	$250.00	$250	$250.00	**$3,000.00**	**11.71%**
13		Clothes	$75.00	$75	$75.00	**$900.00**	**3.51%**
14		Insurance	$150.00	$150	$150.00	**$1,800.00**	**7.03%**
15		Utilities	$185.00	$185	$185.00	**$2,220.00**	**8.67%**
16		Entertainment	$200.00	$200	$200.00	**$2,400.00**	**9.37%**
17	Total Expenses		$1,516.63	$1,516	$1,516.63	**$18,199.57**	**71.04%**
18							
19	Surplus/Deficit		$618.37	$618	$618.37	**$7,420.43**	**28.96%**

Figure 9-83 Budget after filling Totals and Percent of Total Income columns

This completes most of the steps necessary to create an annual budget. All that is left is to make a few refinements, correct three errors, and modify some of the amounts for insurance.

Additionally, you will insert a new row so you can add a Savings category, and you will create a pie chart and a line chart.

EDITING THE DATA

One of the most glaring problems with this worksheet is that almost nobody pays constant monthly payments for insurance. You will now modify this worksheet so that three insurance payments are made. While you are doing this, you can take advantage of Excel's ability to attach a note to a cell for an explanation about why something is being done.

The first step is to clear all the formulas in the Insurance category for February through December.

⌘-B ➡ Select **D14:N14** and clear only the formulas. If you don't remember how to clear formulas, refer back to the "Adding Formulas" section of this project.

Notice that the total for the Insurance category was changed, but there seems to be a problem with the formulas that calculate the monthly total expenses. This is because you started with a formula specifying a named range and then replicated formulas that told each month to use the same total as the month before.

You need to change the formulas for total income, total expenses, and surplus/deficit, and then fill them to the right.

➠ Click in cell **C6** and change the formula to =**SUM(C4:C5)**.

⌘-R ➠ Select cells **C6:N6** and choose **Fill Right** from the Edit menu. (*Do not fill into columns O and P.*)

⌘-R ➠ Enter =**SUM(C9:C16)** in cell **C17**, select cells **C17:N17**, and choose **Fill Right** from the Edit menu.

⌘-R ➠ Enter =**C6-C17** in cell **C19**, select cells **C19:N19**, and choose **Fill Right**.

This will correct the formula errors.

Many times when using a spreadsheet, you will encounter values for which origins and purpose are not immediately clear. Excel lets you attach notes to a cell to explain why the values are in the cell and where they came from. These notes are not visible on the screen, and they will not appear when you print unless you choose to see them.

This family, like most families, has insurance policies that cover the house and the car. The house insurance is paid annually in April, and the car insurance is paid twice per year, in January and again in July. The January payment insures the car from January through June, and the July payment covers the next six months.

Table 9-14 lists the insurance values that will be entered and the explanatory notes associated with the payment.

Month	Insurance amount
January	$150 for car insurance (Jan-Jun)
April	$600 for annual house insurance
July	$150 for car insurance (Jul-Dec)

Table 9-14   Insurance amounts for three months

You could enter the three payments into the appropriate cells, but without attaching a note, you would not have an explanation for the amounts.

Since you don't want to be confused later when you open the worksheet, enter the insurance amounts into their cells and attach the explanatory notes to those cells.

The easiest way to get to the cell for April's insurance is to scroll the right pane of the window to the left until April is visible. This will still leave the categories showing in the pane on the left (see Figure 9-84).

		A	B	C	D	E	F	G	
						Annual Budget			
1		Budget							
2				Jan 1994	Feb 1	Mar 1994	Apr 1994	May 1994	
3		Income							
4			Income #1	$1,400.00	$1,400	$1,400.00	$1,400.00	$1,400.00	$
5			Income #2	$735.00	$735	$735.00	$735.00	$735.00	$
6		Total Income		$2,135.00	$2,135	$2,135.00	$2,135.00	$2,135.00	$
7									
8		Expenses							
9			House	$376.87	$376	$376.87	$376.87	$376.87	
10			Car	$175.97	$175	$175.97	$175.97	$175.97	
11			Education	$103.79	$103	$103.79	$103.79	$103.79	
12			Food	$250.00	$250	$250.00	$250.00	$250.00	
13			Clothes	$75.00	$75	$75.00	$75.00	$75.00	
14			Insurance	$150.00			$600.00		
15			Utilities	$185.00	$185	$185.00	$185.00	$185.00	
16			Entertainment	$200.00	$200	$200.00	$200.00	$200.00	
17		Total Expenses		$1,516.63	$1,366	$1,366.63	$1,966.63	$1,366.63	$
18									
19		Surplus/Deficit		$618.37	$768	$768.37	$168.37	$768.37	

Figure 9-84   Entering April's insurance amount after scrolling the
right pane

➡ Enter **600** for April's insurance, and then choose **Note** from the
Formula menu. Type **House insurance**, **annual**, in the Cell
Note dialog box, click **Add**, and then click **OK** or press Return (see
Figure 9-85).

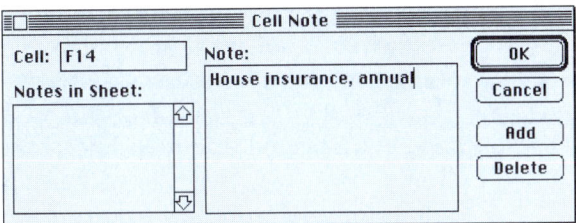

Figure 9-85   Add a note to April's insurance amount in cell F14.

If you want to see the notes for a worksheet, you can choose **Note** from
the Formula menu, and all attached notes will be listed in the scrolling
list on the left in the Cell Note dialog box. Select any cells listed, and the
associated note will appear in the box where you just entered the note
for the house insurance.

➡ Add the amount and note for the car insurance in July and for the
car insurance in January, as well. Refer back to Table 9-14 for the
information you need.

While you are making changes to expenses with fluctuating amounts,
it is a good time to modify the Utilities expense. For this budget you can
assume that winter heating bills will cause utilities to be higher than in
the spring and fall, and air conditioning in late summer will also be
higher.

➡ Enter the amounts shown in Table 9-15 into the specified month's utility expense (*do not clear* the existing formulas first).

Month	Amount
April	140
May	100
June	65
July	120
September	65
November	100
December	170

Table 9-15   Utility expenses

INSERTING ROWS

The budget shows that you are running a surplus every month, so before the money slips through your fingers, it might be a good idea to budget 10% of take-home pay to go into savings each month.

Although a savings category was not planned for, Excel will let you quickly add it.

⌘-I ➡ Select all of row **16** by clicking on the row number to the left of the row. Choose **Insert** from the Edit menu.

As a shortcut, you can also press Option-click on the row number to insert a row. If you want more than one row, use Option-click and drag to select the number of rows to insert.

Since you selected one row, Excel inserted one new row. If you had selected five rows, that's how many would have been inserted. This same command works for inserting columns if that is what is selected before issuing the command.

The Delete command works in a similar manner. Select the rows or columns you want to delete, and then issue the command.

The action performed by the Delete command is similar to that of Cut, but it is not an equivalent process. Cutting a selection moves it to the Clipboard, where it can be pasted into a new location. Delete removes the rows or columns from the spreadsheet and closes up the space they occupied. Deleting does not move the contents of these erased cells to the Clipboard.

➡ Name the category by entering **Savings** in cell **B16**. The formula for C16 is =C6*.1.

⌘-R ➡ Select **C16:N16** and choose **Fill Right** from the Edit menu.

You need to tell Excel to calculate the year-end summary amounts for the new row.

⌘-D ➡ Select **O15:P16** and choose **Fill Down** from the Edit menu.

Your worksheet should now look like the one in Figure 9-86.

	A	B	C	D	N	O	P
2			Jan 1994	Feb 1	Dec 1994	Totals	Total Income
3		Income					
4		Income #1	$1,400.00	$1,400	$1,400.00	$16,800.00	65.57%
5		Income #2	$735.00	$735	$735.00	$8,820.00	34.43%
6		Total Income	$2,135.00	$2,135	$2,135.00	$25,620.00	100.00%
7							
8		Expenses					
9		House	$376.87	$376	$376.87	$4,522.47	17.65%
10		Car	$175.97	$175	$175.97	$2,111.60	8.24%
11		Education	$103.79	$103	$103.79	$1,245.50	4.86%
12		Food	$250.00	$250	$250.00	$3,000.00	11.71%
13		Clothes	$75.00	$75	$75.00	$900.00	3.51%
14		Insurance	$150.00			$900.00	3.51%
15		Utilities	$185.00	$185	$170.00	$1,500.00	5.85%
16		Savings	$213.50	$213	$213.50	$2,562.00	10.00%
17		Entertainment	$200.00	$200	$200.00	$2,400.00	9.37%
18		Total Expenses	$1,730.13	$1,580	$1,565.13	$19,141.57	74.71%
19							
20		Surplus/Deficit	$404.87	$554	$569.87	$6,478.43	25.29%

Cell O15 = SUM(C15:N15)

Figure 9-86   Adjusting formulas to calculate summary values for new category

⌘-S ➡ Save your work to your data disk.

Now is a good time to print the worksheet. You can set the headers and footers and decide about printing gridlines and row and column headings.

The Annual Budget worksheet will be wider than it is tall, so change the page orientation to wide (also known as landscape).

➡ Choose **Page Setup** from the File menu. Change the orientation of the page to wide by clicking on the icon on the right under Orientation that shows the page turned sideways.

⌘-P ➡ Print the Annual Budget worksheet.

CREATING A LINE CHART

Creating this line chart will be fairly straightforward, since most of it is automatic. You can format the chart's title and place the legend as you desire. The only adjustment you will need to make to the chart is adding the data series' titles for the legend.

Select the monthly summaries for total income, total expenses, and surplus/deficit.

➡ Click on cell **C6**, and then Shift-click on cell **N6**.

➡ Now add the expenses to the selection by Command-clicking on **C18** and Shift-clicking on **N18**.

➡ Use the same method to add the surplus/deficit amounts to the selection (see Figure 9-87).

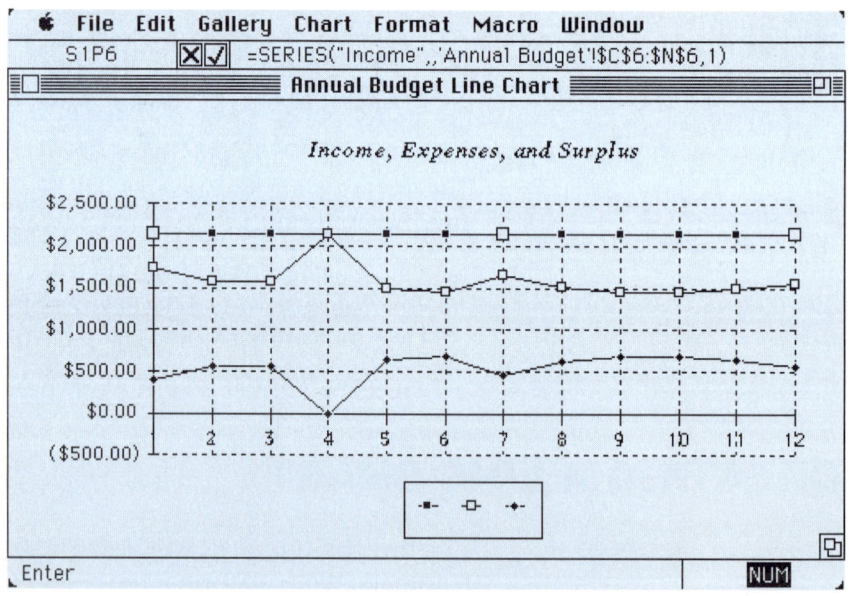

Annual Budget spreadsheet

	A	B	C	D	N	O	P
2			Jan 1994	Feb 1	Dec 1994	Totals	Total Income
3	Income						
4		Income #1	$1,400.00	$1,400	$1,400.00	$16,800.00	65.57%
5		Income #2	$735.00	$735	$735.00	$8,820.00	34.43%
6	Total Income		$2,135.00	$2,135	$2,135.00	$25,620.00	100.00%
7							
8	Expenses						
9		House	$376.87	$376	$376.87	$4,522.47	17.65%
10		Car	$175.97	$175	$175.97	$2,111.60	8.24%
11		Education	$103.79	$103	$103.79	$1,245.50	4.86%
12		Food	$250.00	$250	$250.00	$3,000.00	11.71%
13		Clothes	$75.00	$75	$75.00	$900.00	3.51%
14		Insurance	$150.00			$900.00	3.51%
15		Utilities	$185.00	$185	$170.00	$1,500.00	5.85%
16		Savings	$213.50	$213	$213.50	$2,562.00	10.00%
17		Entertainment	$200.00	$200	$200.00	$2,400.00	9.37%
18	Total Expenses		$1,730.13	$1,580	$1,565.13	$19,141.57	74.71%
19							
20	Surplus/Deficit		$404.87	$554	$569.87	$6,478.43	25.29%

C20 =C6-C18

File Edit Formula Format Data Options Macro Window

Ready   NUM

Figure 9-87   Making a multiple selection to create a new line chart

➡ Create a new line chart and add the legend and a title. Choose the line chart style from the Gallery menu that matches the one shown in Figure 9-88.

File Edit Gallery Chart Format Macro Window

S1P6   =SERIES("Income",,'Annual Budget'!$C$6:$N$6,1)

Annual Budget Line Chart

Income, Expenses, and Surplus

Enter   NUM

Figure 9-88   New line chart showing Annual Budget amounts

➡ Add the names for the data series, as shown in the formula bar in Figure 9-88 and explained in Project 3.

➡ Use the Page Setup command from the File menu to choose a wide orientation for printing.

⌘-S ➡ When you have entered all the names for the data series, save the chart as Annual Budget Line Chart.

⌘-P ➡ Print the chart.

Your chart should look like the one shown in Figure 9-89.

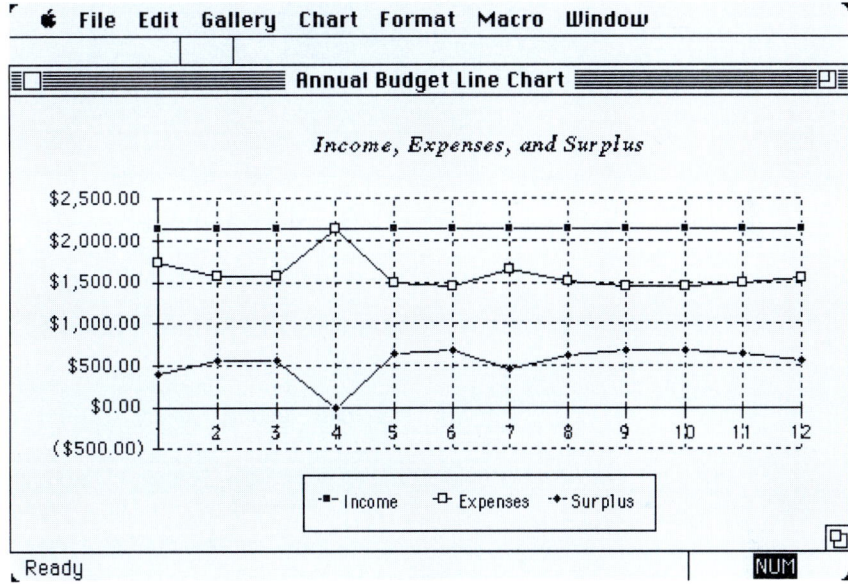

Figure 9-89 Line chart after naming data series for legend

This chart will be used in the what if... exercises in this project.

CREATING A PIE CHART

This next chart will be even easier to create than the line chart. All you have to do is select the cells showing year-end totals for the expense categories. To keep from having to manually add all the names, you can select them before creating the new chart.

➡ Select the cells, as shown in Figure 9-90, and create a new pie chart.

File   Edit   Formula   Format   Data   Options   Macro   Window

	O9		=SUM(C9:N9)			

Annual Budget

	A	B	C	D	N	O	P
2			Jan 1994	Feb 1	Dec 1994	Totals	Total Income
3	Income						
4		Income #1	$1,400.00	$1,400	$1,400.00	$16,800.00	65.57%
5		Income #2	$735.00	$735	$735.00	$8,820.00	34.43%
6	Total Income		$2,135.00	$2,135	$2,135.00	$25,620.00	100.00%
7							
8	Expenses						
9		House	$376.87	$376	$376.87	$4,522.47	17.65%
10		Car	$175.97	$175	$175.97	$2,111.60	8.24%
11		Education	$103.79	$103	$103.79	$1,245.50	4.86%
12		Food	$250.00	$250	$250.00	$3,000.00	11.71%
13		Clothes	$75.00	$75	$75.00	$900.00	3.51%
14		Insurance	$150.00			$900.00	3.51%
15		Utilities	$185.00	$185	$170.00	$1,500.00	5.85%
16		Savings	$213.50	$213	$213.50	$2,562.00	10.00%
17		Entertainment	$200.00	$200	$200.00	$2,400.00	9.37%
18	Total Expenses		$1,730.13	$1,580	$1,565.13	$19,141.57	74.71%
19							
20	Surplus/Deficit		$404.87	$554	$569.87	$6,478.43	25.29%

Ready   NUM

Figure 9-90   Make a multiple selection to create new pie chart

➡   Make the page orientation wide, and add a title and a legend.

⌘-S ➡   Save this chart as Annual Budget Expenses Pie.

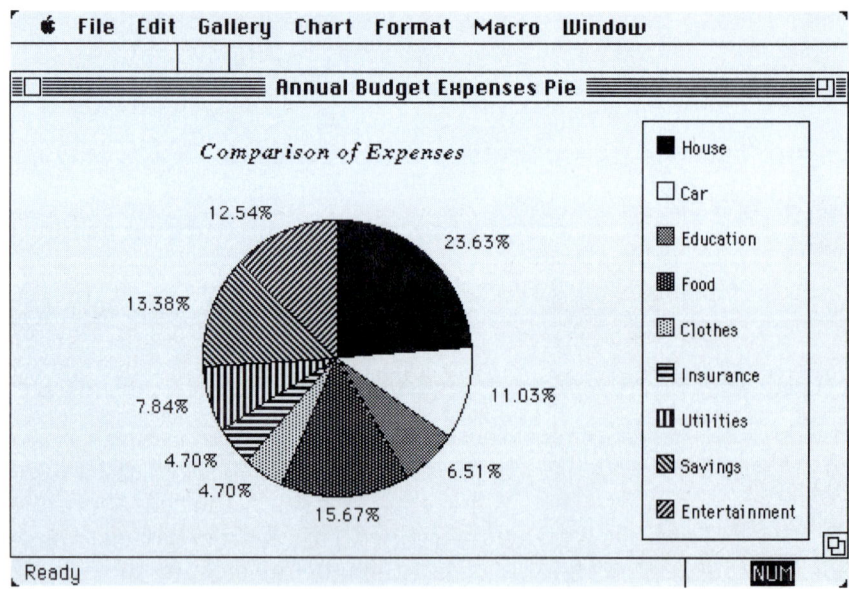

Figure 9-91   Annual Budget pie chart comparing expenses

You will be using this chart and the line chart in the what if... exercises in this chapter. Now is a good time to save and print this chart.

WHAT IF... EXERCISES

When you work through these exercises, be sure to save your Annual Budget worksheet first, and then do not save the changes you make in this section. As a reminder, you might remember that you can always use the Save As command to create a backup with a different name. You then can make any changes to that document without affecting the original. This is a handy way to make a backup of an important document before making any major changes, or before trying any new procedures. It is easier to make backup copies than it is to replace lost information.

1. What if the employer of the person earning Income #1 offered to send this person back to school in September for some specific courses and offered to pay half salary during the semester and reimburse educational expenses when the semester is over?

2. If this person decides to accept the offer, the employer guarantees a $100 per month raise (in net, or take-home, pay) starting in December. The employee will incur $1,000 in additional educational expenses in September.

3. You will need to adjust Income #1 to $700 for September, October, and November. December income will be $100 more than in August, plus the reimbursement of the $1,000 expenses.

4. Make these changes and print the worksheet. Open each of the two charts that you just created, and print them. Compare these printouts with what you previously printed.

5. For what month(s) will this family have to dip into savings because their expenses exceeded their income?

Do not save these changes to your Annual Budget worksheet.

CHAPTER SUMMARY

- Excel is an electronic spreadsheet program that incorporates and integrates worksheets, charts, macros, and databases.

- Worksheets are central to data analysis in Excel.

- Worksheets are organized in columns and rows. The intersection of a row and a column is a cell. A cell is located by its address. Columns are named by letters and rows by numbers. A cell will have an address designated by a letter-number combination, e.g., A9.

- A cell can contain text, a number, or a formula.

- Formulas refer to values and the contents of other cells. When referring to the contents of other cells, formulas can use relative addressing or absolute addressing.

- When the contents of a cell referred to by a formula changes, all cells dependent on that cell change automatically.

- Excel allows you to change the width of a column and the format of a cell.

- The values shown in a worksheet can be charted into area, bar, column, combination, pie, and scatter charts.

- Worksheets can be created, saved, opened, modified, printed, and linked.

- Excel facilitates rapid spreadsheet construction using data series and the Fill Right and Fill Down commands.

KEY TERMS

absolute addressing
active cell
area chart
arguments

bar chart

cancel box
cell
column
column chart
combination chart
context-sensitive help

data series
defined term
dummy argument

enter box

fill
footer
formula bar
formula

gridlines

header
horizontal split bar

jump term

legend
line chart
linked terms

pie chart

range
reference area
relative addressing
row

scatter chart
selection squares
status bar

template

vertical split bar

what if... analysis

COMMAND KEYS AND SHORTCUTS

Activity	Command-key equivalent
Activate next window	⌘-M
Activate previous window	Shift-⌘-M
Calculate Now	⌘-=
Cancel	⌘-. (period)
Clear	⌘-B
Close Window	⌘-W
Copy	⌘-C
Cut	⌘-X
Define Name	⌘-L
Delete	⌘-K
Fill Down	⌘-D
Fill Left	Shift-⌘-R
Fill Right	⌘-R
Fill Up	Shift-⌘-D
Formula Find (displays dialog box)	⌘-J
Formula Find next	⌘-H
Formula Find previous	Shift-⌘-H
Goto	⌘-G
Help	⌘-/ or ⌘-?
Insert	⌘-I
New	⌘-N
Note	Shift-⌘-N
Open	⌘-O
Paste	⌘-V
Print	⌘-P
Quit	⌘-Q
Save	⌘-S
Save As	Shift-⌘-S
Select All Cells	⌘-A
Select Chart	⌘-A
Undo	⌘-Z

Editing in the Formula Bar

Activity	Command-key equivalent
Activate formula bar	⌘-U
Cancel entry	⌘-. (period)

Choosing Dialog Box Options

Activity	Command-key equivalent
Format Border (Outline)	⌘-Option-0 (zero)
Format Border (Left)	⌘-Option-Left Arrow
Format Border (Right)	⌘-Option-Right Arrow
Format Border (Top)	⌘-Option-Up Arrow
Format Border (Bottom)	⌘-Option-Down Arrow
Format Number (General format)	⌘-Option-~
Format Number (0.00 format)	⌘-Option-!
Format Number (h:mm AM/PM format)	⌘-Option-@
Format Number (d-mmm-yy format)	⌘-Option-#
Format Number ($#,##0.00;($#,##0.00) format)	⌘-Option—$
Format Number (0% format)	⌘-Option-%
Format Number (0.00E + 00 format)	⌘-Option-^
Formula Select Special (Notes option)	⌘-Shift-O (letter O)
Formula Select Special (Current Region option)	⌘ -*
Formula Select Special (Row Differences option)	⌘ -\
Formula Select Special (Column Differences option)	⌘-Shift-\
Formula Select Special (Precedents: Direct Only option)	⌘ -[
Formula Select Special (Precedents: All Levels option)	⌘-Shift-[
Formula Select Special (Dependents: Direct Only option)	⌘ -]
Formula Select Special (Dependents: All Levels option)	⌘-Shift-]
Options Display Formulas (toggles between formulas and values)	⌘ -' (backquote)

Additional Projects

The following project is accompanied by briefer instructions than those you have previously completed in this chapter. It requires that you apply what you learned in the first four projects. If necessary, refer back to the preceding four projects for information and instructions for any procedures that you aren't familiar with.

You will not be reminded to save your work—you should be thinking of that on your own by now.

Project 5: Bar Chart

This project is easy to complete. It requires you to create a worksheet and then produce a bar chart. The worksheet has no formulas or calculations; it is there just to hold the data for the chart.

The final output of Project 5 is shown in Figure 9-92.

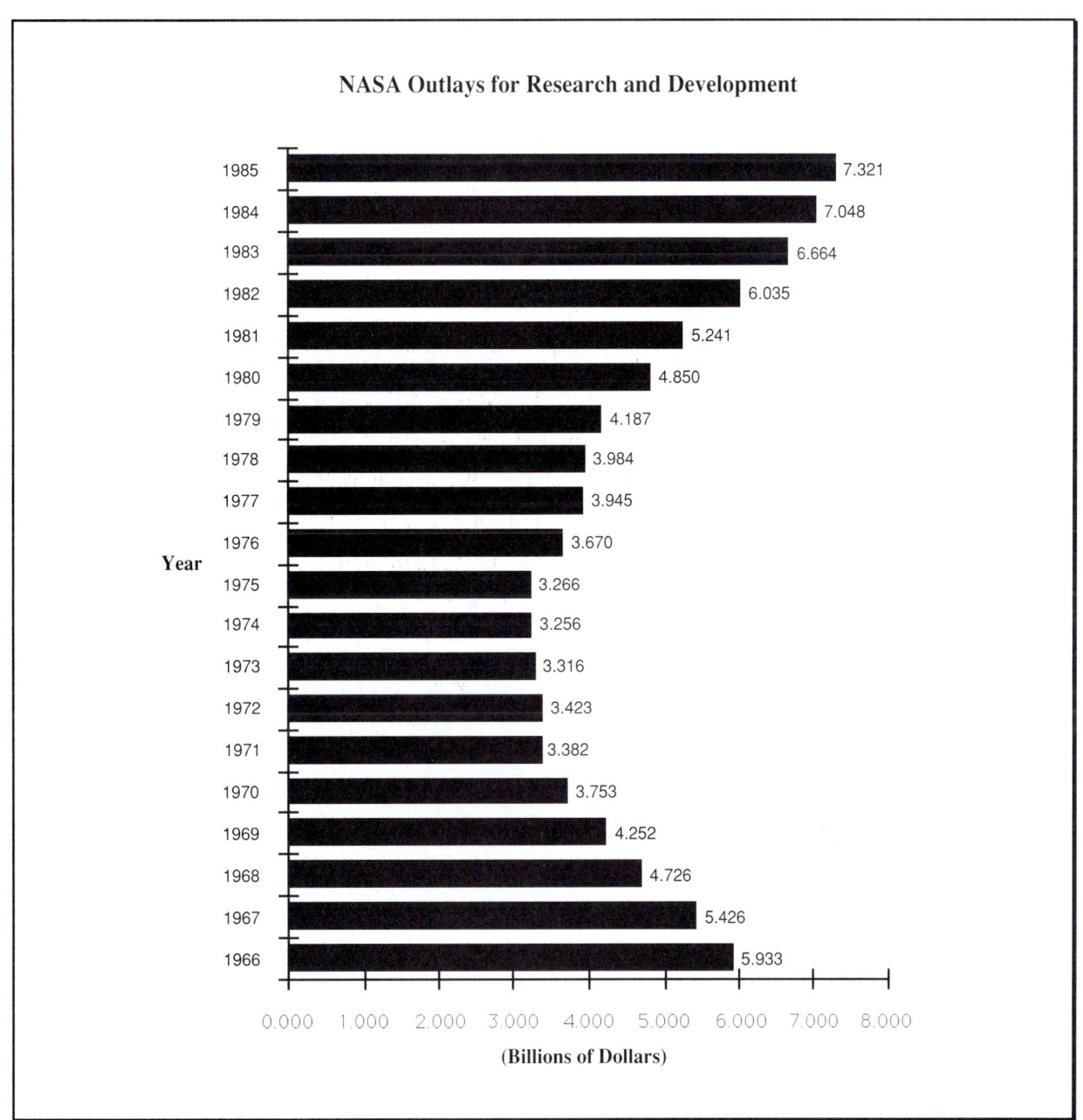

Figure 9-92 Final bar chart output of Project 5

It is up to you how you set up your worksheet as far as formatting, titles, and other features are concerned. You may want to model the worksheet after the one in shown in Figure 9-93. The only data you actually have to enter are the years and the amounts spent in those years. Excel has certain defaults for determining category and data series names from data entered into a worksheet. If the selection is wider than it is tall, Excel expects to find the category names in the first row of the selection and the data series names in the first column. If the selection is taller than it is wide, Excel will look for the data series names in the first row and the category names in the first column.

In either case, the top left cell in the selection should be blank.

➡ One method of approaching this task is to create a data series in row 6 (starting in B6), beginning with 1966 and advancing one year with an ending date of 1985.

➡ You might want to put a title for row 7 in cell A7, one such as Total Outlays. Enter the values for each year starting with 1966 by placing the outlay amount in the cell below the year. For example, you could put 1966 in cell B6 and then 5.933 in cell B7.

➡ If you have the dates in row 6, the data series title in cell A7, and the data series values in the rest of row 7, Excel will know how to label each bar with the correct year. Leave cell A6 blank. Since the worksheet will be wider than it is tall, Excel will assume that row 6 represents the categories and row 7 holds the data (see Figure 9-93).

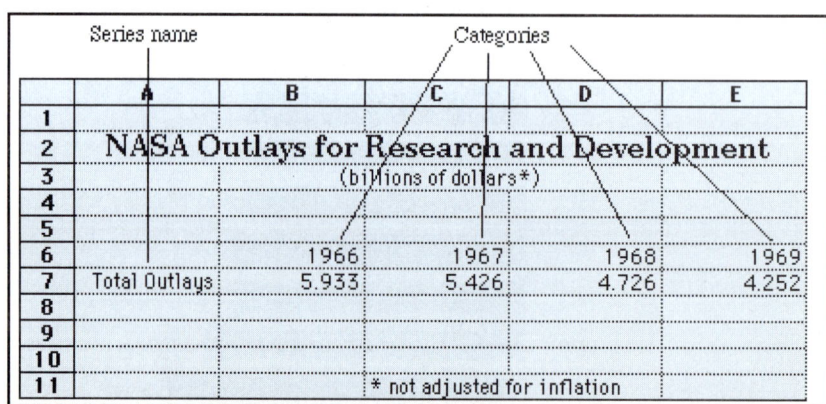

Figure 9-93   Excel defaults for category and series names in wide worksheets

The amounts in Table 9-16, in billions of dollars, are not adjusted for inflation.

Year	Amount
1966	5.933
1967	5.426
1968	4.726
1969	4.252
1970	3.753
1971	3.382
1972	3.423
1973	3.316
1974	3.256
1975	3.266
1976	3.670
1977	3.945
1978	3.984
1979	4.187
1980	4.850
1981	5.241
1982	6.035
1983	6.664
1984	7.048
1985	7.321

Table 9-16   Amounts spent by NASA (billions of dollars) for R & D

➠ Select all necessary cells from A6 through the dollar amount for 1985, create a new chart, and select the bar chart that shows dollar amounts at the end of each bar.

➠ Assign text to the title, category axis, and value axis to match what is shown in Figure 9-92.

➠ Choose **Page Setup**, and select **Full Page** size. This makes the chart taller when it is printed.

This completes Project 5.

Part V: Information Management

Part V introduces you to managing lists of information on the Macintosh. You don't have to use a computer to manage small amounts of information or information that rarely changes, but if you have information that changes frequently, or if a large amount needs to be managed, you will probably find that using a computer is an indispensable part of getting the job done.

Chapter 10: Information Management Concepts introduces you to the organization and manipulation of information.

Chapter 11: FileMaker II shows you how to use one of the most popular information management applications available for the Macintosh. It is not the most powerful application and would not be suitable for large corporations to manage their information, but for personal management, small businesses, and departments in larger organizations, FileMaker provides enough power and flexibility to manage information.

Chapter 12: HyperCard 1.2 teaches you how to access information provided by others and how to create your own stacks and use them. You will learn to print reports and customize the stack so that it suits your purpose.

Chapter 10: Information Management Concepts

What You Will Learn in This Chapter

After reading this chapter, you will understand:

- The difference between data and information

- How to organize information into databases, files, records, and fields

- Information management's standard operations

- Common terminology associated with information management

Almost everybody has to keep track of some type of list. This can be a to-do list or a simple list of names and addresses. On the other hand, it can be something as complicated as a list of a company's financial transactions for a year or complete lists of the resources, materials, and suppliers needed to build a skyscraper office building.

PERSONAL INFORMATION MANAGEMENT

For personal use, it is often convenient to store a list in a book or on something like 3x5 cards. These methods are okay if the lists are relatively short or if you are a very organized person.

Most likely, you already manage various lists in your daily life, such as a shopping list, a list of things to do, or appointments on a calendar. These types of lists are discarded when they are no longer useful. Other types of information must be updated. Examples of the latter include address books, business card files, credit card numbers, insurance policies, and investments.

Like many of us, you may find that it is difficult to remember to keep this information up to date. You might organize information in piles (on your desk, floor, and bookshelves), or you might be the type of person who organizes your audio library alphabetically by performer and keeps each type of music separated by category. Most people fall somewhere between these two groups. Regardless of your personality and preferences, you probably don't have to manage large amounts of personal information.

Let's say you keep a list of information concerning your friends. This list probably contains their names, addresses, birthdays, and so on. A convenient way to keep track of this information is to store it on a collection of 3x5 cards. Each card contains information about one person, and the cards are stored in a box, in alphabetical order.

This collection of cards can be called a *file,* and each card is a *record* of information about one person. More than one piece of information about the person is on a card. Each individual piece of information (name, address, and so on) can be called a *field* or *item.*

If you meet a new person and become friends, you can fill out a new card and add it to the file. If someone moves, you can change the information or replace the old card with a new one with correct information. If you no longer want to keep information about a person, you can remove the card and discard it.

For many personal needs, this type of a filing system is sufficient. On the other hand, businesses, even small ones, must manage much more information than most individuals.

BUSINESS INFORMATION MANAGEMENT

A business can use a file of 3x5 cards, but the situation quickly becomes complex. Let's say you work for a small business and keep track of a list of contacts at other businesses. These contacts can be clients, customers, suppliers, people to whom you refer business, professional and trade acquaintances, and others with whom you do business.

You've decided to store the information on one card for each contact person. When the file is small, it is easily managed. There are only a few names to remember. Then, things begin to change. People move, change companies, change jobs in a company, change occupations, and do all the other things that people do, including dying. Sometimes you will know about these changes, and other times you will learn only when you try to contact someone.

You may find that some companies have several people whom you regularly contact, so you start another file. This file is organized by company name and lists each contact person at that company on the company's card.

Over time, some people are listed in the contact person file, others are listed in the company file, and some are listed in both. If a person changes jobs, you must remember to change the information on each card that lists the person. Of course, you don't always remember to do this.

Sometimes, however, you may have difficulty remembering how you stored a card with the name and address you need. Did you store it alphabetically by the company's name, or did you store it by the last name of the person you need to call? Do you also have information on this company stored on other cards by other persons' last names? What happens if you can only remember that the person you need to contact is named Piya, and you can't remember her last name or the company for which she works.

In a small card system, this usually is not a critical problem, but what happens if you work in a company that has 1,000, 10,000, or 1,000,000 or more items of information that need to be managed? Would you want to be the person who had to maintain an accurate card file on thousands of people? Of course not. Even if you did want to do this, there would be a point at which the collection of information would grow so large or it would change so often that you could not perform your duties.

For centuries, business managers have had to manage three major resources: money, materials, and people. In this century, a new resource has been added to this list: information. Computerization has made it possible to manage large amounts of information, and, at the same time, it has accelerated the rate at which information changes. To remain competitive in a rapidly changing world, all businesses must now manage their four major resources better.

Effective and efficient management of large amounts of changeable information has been one of the major goals of the computing industry since the early 1950s. As the industry has progressed and new hardware, software, and procedures have been developed, the systems used to accomplish this goal have changed.

Let's briefly explore the systems that have been designed to manage business information. What types of information are managed in a business, and who needs access to which information? The answers to these questions are as varied as the number of organizations, but let's look at a "typical" organization.

A traditionally organized business has a hierarchical management structure (see Figure 10-1).

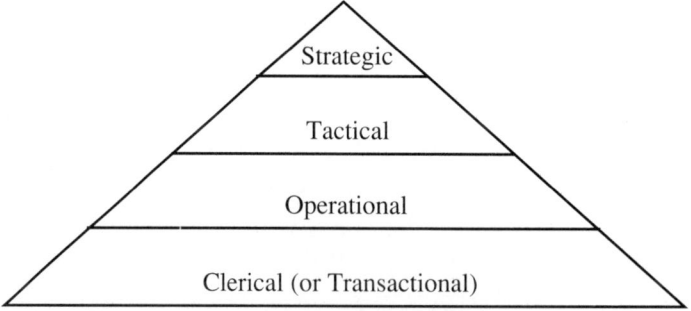

Figure 10-1   The management hierarchy

The majority of clerical and lower-level management personnel are located in the clerical, or transactional, level. Of all management personnel, their duties are most defined, their daily activities are most structured, and their decision-making authority is most restricted. They are involved with repetitive tasks and are primarily concerned with processing various business transactions. Their information needs typically involve data entry, error correction, transaction tracking, and producing periodic reports for higher management.

As you travel up the management hierarchy, there are fewer people on each level. Their daily activities are less structured, they have more latitude and authority in their decision making, and the type of interactions they have with the organization's information changes.

Personnel at the operational level are responsible for completing well-defined tasks that are usually short-term in nature. They also are responsible for implementing and achieving goals set at the tactical level. Information needs at this level typically involve operational feedback, in the form of detail reports, summary reports, and exception reports. Using a retail department store as an example, a *detail report* might show every item carried in inventory, and a *summary report* might show sales totals for the week organized by department. An *exception report* might list only the best-selling (or worst-selling) items sold by the store or any departments that did not meet their sales projections for the week.

Tactical level managers typically are responsible for setting and meeting goals designed to achieve strategic objectives determined at the highest level of the company. These managers usually are concerned with budgetary and operational matters. They also are responsible for setting relatively short-term goals and for planning how to achieve those goals. Much of their information needs revolve around periodic reports, but occasionally they will seek "what if..." analyses to help them make decisions.

A what if... analysis is used to answer a question such as, "What if we sell only 75 percent of the gizmos we are projecting next year?" This is the type of question that must be considered when planning company goals and budgets.

Relatively few managers and officers are at the strategic level. Their daily activities are least structured and their decisions are least programmed and restricted. They are most concerned with long-range planning and setting organizational objectives. Their information needs typically are one-time reports on trends affecting the company, what if... analyses, and projections.

The computing industry's approach to managing business information has paralleled this short journey through the management hierarchy.

File Management

In the 1950s and 1960s this process was called *electronic data processing* (EDP). Data processing involves converting raw facts, or *data*, into *information*. Data becomes information when it is organized, collated, and sorted so that it becomes accessible and useful. During this stage of development, the primary goal of business automation was to reduce clerical costs by automating clerical tasks. Each department and division had its own set of independent computerized systems. A large amount of the information management effort was duplicated on separate machines. On a given machine, the information might be duplicated for use by different programs.

Most information at that stage was stored in separate files. A file might contain information used to produce a particular report. Business had hundreds of these files and developed computerized systems to manage them. A file might contain information on employees, customers, accounts payable, accounts receivable, inventory, payroll, work in progress, shipping, receiving, or any other type of information used to produce a management report or account for a transaction. Programs, or groups of programs, were written to manage each of these files, and information management systems based on this method of data processing were known as *file management systems*.

The process of keeping files up-to-date, complete, and correct is known as *file maintenance*. Many problems are associated with maintaining multiple, separate files. For example, much of the information in one group of files may be repeated in other files. This repetition is known as *redundancy*. Systems that had to maintain hundreds of separate files ran into the same problems encountered by an individual maintaining a 3x5 card file. When information changed, all the files containing that information had to be individually updated, a process that was time-consuming, expensive, and prone to error. Unfortunately, the problems associated with updating redundant data can result in an item of information existing as different versions in the same system.

These types of information management systems did automate the transactional and operational aspects of a company's information resources, but they did little to help higher management. Each department or division maintained its own records, and company-wide management systems were not available. Management wanted a way to tie these systems together into a *management information system* (MIS).

At the time, however, several problems prevented this from happening. First, the information on the computers was stored on reel-to-reel magnetic tape. A large file might be stored on several tapes, and finding a particular item of data to change might not be accomplished easily and quickly. Second, the information was redundant, so it might take mounting and modifying several tapes to accomplish a change. Third, the information was stored in locations that might be widely separated, and data communication over phone lines was slower, more expensive, and less reliable than it is today.

Hardware, software, and procedures changed in the 1970s. The first problem, data storage, was solved when the price of disk drives declined dramatically. Not only did the price decline, but also the reliability of disks and the amount of data that could be stored on a disk increased. In a few years, most computer systems were using disk drives as their main method of data storage.

Tapes store information sequentially; that is, one item after another. To reach an item, all the preceding tape must pass through the system, like finding a particular song on an audiocassette. This method is known as *sequential access*. Disk drives can access information sequentially, but they can also locate information directly, a process known as *direct access* (or *random access*).

Databases

The ability to access information directly led to the solution of the second problem, redundant information. Methods were devised to organize information so it could be accessed and processed more efficiently. The organizational method chosen for storing information in related files was the *database*. Three major types of databases are currently in use: hierarchical, network, and relational. Of these, the relational model is used popularly in microcomputer database systems. Therefore, it is the only one that will be explored here.

Relational Databases

A *relational database* can be composed of one or more related files. Each of these files is organized into a tabular structure consisting of rows that represent *records* (also known as tuples) and columns that represent *fields* (also known as attributes or *items*).

One of the major advantages of a relational database over a file management system is the reduction of data redundancy. As an example, schools must manage a lot of information about courses offered, instructors, students, which courses students have taken, when courses were taken, and grades received in the courses.

In a file management system, you might include a student's name, address, phone number, and other pertinent information every time she or he takes a course; if the student takes 40 courses, the system would contain 40 occurrences of all this information. What do you do when the student's address changes? You have to find and change all 40 occurrences and make sure they all match.

Using a relational database system, information can be divided into multiple files, each of which is designed for efficient data storage. For example, you can store all the basic student information in the student file, which would consist of name, address, phone number, financial aid status, scholarship status, any disciplinary action taken, and other pertinent information. The student is assigned a unique identifying number (usually his or her Social Security Number), and this number is used to relate information in one file with information in another file. A field used to relate information in more than one file is known as a *key field*.

An example of a partial student file is shown in Figure 10-2.

Student Number	Last Name	First Name	Phone
111-22-3333	Godfrey	Geneva	555-6848
123-45-6789	Adams	Rebecca	555-7452
321-54-9876	Prather	Lillie	555-1597
666-88-7777	Avary	Arch	555-7486
987-45-1236	Borreson	Lori	555-3287
999-99-1111	Cavalier	Jamie	555-5874

Figure 10-2   Example of a student file

One way to look at the contents of this file is to think of it as a table of information. There are multiple rows and columns (like a spreadsheet) in the file. All the information on a particular student will be located on the same row. Each row represents one record in the file (see Figure 10-3).

Student Number	Last Name	First Name	Phone
111-22-3333	Godfrey	Geneva	555-6848
123-45-6789	Adams	Rebecca	555-7452
321-54-9876	Prather	Lillie	555-1597
666-88-7777	Avary	Arch	555-7486
987-45-1236	Borreson	Lori	555-3287
999-99-1111	Cavalier	Jamie	555-5874

Figure 10-3   A student record in the student file

Each column in the table represents a single field. Figure 10-4 shows the field that represents the students' last names.

Student Number	Last Name	First Name	Phone
111-22-3333	Godfrey	Geneva	555-6848
123-45-6789	Adams	Rebecca	555-7452
321-54-9876	Prather	Lillie	555-1597
666-88-7777	Avary	Arch	555-7486
987-45-1236	Borreson	Lori	555-3287
999-99-1111	Cavalier	Jamie	555-5874

Figure 10-4   The Last Name field in the student file

Class names and the instructors assigned to teach the class could be stored in a class file. Of course, like the student file, more information would have to be in this file than what is shown. Each class is assigned a class number, usually consisting of an abbreviation for the department teaching the course followed by a unique identifying number for the course within that department. Other information such as credit hours, class hours, lab hours, and prerequisites would probably be in the file as well. Figure 10-5 shows a partial example of a class file.

Class Number	Class Name	Instructor
ACC 103	Cost Accounting	Nichols
ART 101	Art Appreciation	Dockery
BUS 211	Office Machines	Hughes
EDP 150	Pascal I	Dillard
EDP 641	Compiler Design	Young
PHY 453	Thermodynamics I	Erker

Figure 10-5   A class file

A record of all courses taken by all students could be maintained in a completed courses file (see Figure 10-6). This file would contain two key fields. The Student Number field is used to relate to information in the student file, and the Class Number field relates to information in the class file.

Student Number	Class Number	Qtr Taken	Grade
111-22-3333	ACC 103	92-3	A
123-45-6789	EDP 150	91-4	B
321-54-9876	BUS 211	91-2	A
666-88-7777	ART 101	92-4	B
987-45-1236	PHY 453	90-1	B
999-99-1111	EDP 641	91-3	A

Figure 10-6   The completed courses file

When a student requests a transcript, the registrar enters the student number assigned to that student (or former student). The database program sorts the completed classes file by the Qtr Taken field (if the file is not already stored in that order), finds every occurrence of the student number in the file, and then prints a transcript. Of course, additional processing is necessary to group the courses by quarter (or semester), calculate the quality points earned (based on credit hours and grade received), and calculate the student's grade point average for each period and the cumulative grade point average. Additional information may be added to the transcript based on information stored in other files for honors earned and extracurricular activities that may be noted.

A database system using multiple, specialized files reduces redundancy to the point where data is duplicated in the key fields only. Specifying that the information in the key fields must not be modified eliminates the problem of updating multiple occurrences of an item. If a student moves, any information that needs to be changed can be found in one place.

Each file is simple in design and easy to update. Associating, or relating, information in different files leads to less wasted space on the disk and a reduced possibility of information being partially updated. Unforeseen information can be added to reports by creating and relating new files, modifying the program to look up information in the new files, and adding this information to the report as needed.

Network Databases

The third problem that had to be overcome before management information systems became widely useful was communication between distant systems. In the 1970s data communication became cheaper, faster, and much more reliable. This led to formation of wide area networks. A *wide area network* is formed when several computer systems communicate with each other by sending information over a *common carrier*, such as the phone system.

Digital signals used in computers are not compatible with the analog signals used in phone systems. Therefore, to send and receive computer information over the phone lines, a conversion device is used. This device, known as a *modem,* modulates a computer's digital signals into sound (analog signals) at one end of the phone system, and a compatible modem demodulates the sound back into electronic digital signals at the other end for the other computer. The term "modem" derives from the process of *mo*dulating and *dem*odulating.

Today, hundreds of databases are available worldwide on computer networks. Anyone with an account and a password can use these systems to access many types of information and to send and receive messages (a process known as electronic mail).

With computers communicating over the phone lines, information could be accessed directly, and transactions could be processed as they were made instead of being entered into the system at a later time. This was known as transaction processing. The 1970s brought a big increase in transactional processing systems.

In the 1980s information management systems became widely available. With the introduction and widespread availability of microcomputers, information management systems went through similar stages of evolution as were seen in mainframes and minicomputers in the 1960s and 1970s. First, file management systems became available, and these were quickly followed by more powerful database systems.

Recently, information management systems, which were formerly described using traditional terms ("file management systems" and "database systems"), have begun to blur the distinctions between the two traditional system types. In the world of microcomputers, most people refer to any information management system as a database system, regardless of whether it meets the technical definition. Bowing to popular usage, this book will refer to programs such as FileMaker as databases.

Microcomputers brought another difference to computing. It is very likely that a company will have many microcomputers located in the same building. This situation is not as likely with minicomputers and mainframes. As communications became more important during the 1980s, a new method of connecting computers was developed and became known as a local area network. A *local area network* (LAN), technically, is a connection of communicating computers that do not use any lines or equipment belonging to a common carrier. By popular usage, a group of microcomputers that send and receive information to and from each other is called a LAN.

Just as minicomputers and mainframes developed database systems that operate over a wide area network, microcomputers now have databases that work over a local area network. This allows multiple users to modify information on a common database from any computer having access to the LAN. Once again, departments in large companies have their own local database management facilities. But, for the first time, small companies have access to computing power similar to that relegated to only the world's largest companies a few years ago.

USES OF INFORMATION MANAGEMENT SYSTEMS

Some of the activities and terminology associated with managing information have already been presented, along with some of the pitfalls of manual methods. Computerized information management systems are designed to automate many tasks. Specifically, these programs will help you do the following:

- Organize your information

- Store that information

- Perform mathematical calculations

- Add new records

- Delete existing records

- Edit the contents of selected records

- Retrieve individual records or groups of records that match specific criteria

- Sort the information into a different order

- Print reports in different formats

Each of these functions is discussed below.

Organizing Information

Several types of information management programs exist, but all of them are designed primarily to help you organize information, store it on the computer, retrieve information, modify it, and produce reports. Information can be organized into databases, files, records, and fields.

Storing Information

When you have determined the organization of the information, you describe it to the computer by creating a new file. At this time, the program requires you to specify each field to be used and what type of information will be contained in that field (date, number, text, graphics, formula, and so on). In most information management programs, only one type of information may be contained in each field.

Once the organization is described to the computer, you may then add information to the file. This is usually done by creating a new record and then filling in each of the fields for that record. For a customer, this might involve entering name, address, phone number, credit rating, credit limit, and other information that describes that particular customer.

Performing Calculations

Not all information is directly typed into a file. Whenever calculations are required, it is frequently easier (and more accurate) to let the computer do them for you.

For example, if you were a real estate agent and wanted to add a new house listing to your file, you could have fields set up for, among other things, the length and width of the house. Then when you enter this information, the program could multiply the contents of these two fields and store the square footage of the house in the appropriate field. You could even have the cost per square foot calculated automatically.

Adding Records

When you first defined the contents of the file, you might have entered the information you had available at that time. Information management programs also allow you to enter new information at any time after the file is created.

If you are running a business, you (hopefully) will have a steady stream of new customers discovering your store and purchasing the items you sell. Therefore, the information management program must allow you to add new customers.

Deleting Records

Not only does new information present itself and old information change, but also eventually some information becomes obsolete. Suppose you have a list of insured household items, and one of the items listed is a top-quality 35mm camera. The camera was very expensive when you bought it, but even with proper care and attention it finally wore out. When you discard the camera, it is also appropriate to discard the information in the insured items file.

Editing Records

The information in each record will be as correct as it was when you entered it, but, as we all know, things change.

Suppose you maintain a list of the names and addresses of your friends. Over a period of several years, chances are that many of them will have different addresses from the ones you entered originally.

Information management programs allow you to retrieve the record containing the information on a particular friend, and then you can edit any information stored in that record. For example, if a friend has moved to a different state, the street address, city, state, Zip code, and telephone number will have to be changed.

There is another reason that the ability to modify information contained in a file is important. When the information was originally entered, there is always the possibility that it was typed incorrectly. The program has to allow you to correct mistakes easily.

Retrieving Records

Information that has been entered into the computer is of little value if you can't retrieve it at a later time. If you have a list of customers and want to send a special mailing to all who live in a particular city or town, you can have the computer search through the list and select only those whose city matches the one in which you are interested. In this way you can select subsets of the entire customer file. In this case, the subset is the group of customers who live in a particular city.

You can also find a single record. Suppose you have a file that contains information on improvements that you have made to your house. At a later time, you want to find the total cost of adding the deck. If the improvement was entered as "deck", you can tell the program to find the record containing "deck" and it would very quickly find the record and show it to you on the screen.

You might also need to find information on a person, but you can only remember part of that person's name. In manual systems, you would be forced to look through each card until you found what you were looking for, but in a computerized system, you can tell the computer to find all names that match the portion you remember. The computer will do this many times faster than you can.

Sorting Records

An information management system can quickly sort an entire file, or subset of the file, to display information in any order you want.

The records in a file are sorted into order by the contents of a chosen field, known as the *sort field*, or the field on which the sort order will be based. Common sort field selections include the name fields for alphabetic sorts, Zip code field for printing mailing labels, amount-sold-this-year field to find the best customers, and so on.

For instance, if you have a name and address file, and you want to group the people by city, you could sort first by city, then by last name, then by first name, and the information would be sorted accordingly. If you had the following list of names and cities:

Wesley	Myers-Smith	New York
June	Kelong	Boston
Don	Herring	Atlanta
Dena	Taylor	Boston
Diane	Herring	Atlanta
Luke	Kelong	Boston

The city, last name, first name sort command would give the following list:

Diane	Herring	Atlanta
Don	Herring	Atlanta
June	Kelong	Boston
Luke	Kelong	Boston
Dena	Taylor	Boston
Wesley	Myers-Smith	New York

Note that the people living in a particular city are grouped, and the cities are presented in alphabetical order. Then, within each city group, the people are sorted alphabetically by last name. If more than one person has the same last name, they are further sorted by first name.

Sorting does not change the placement of the fields in the report, it just modifies the order in which each record is displayed or printed.

Creating Reports

Historically, the main use for an information management system was to organize information so that reports could be produced. The information was entered into the computer, and the computer sorted and selected the records that met the specified criteria. Then, the information was output in the form of a printed report.

Since those early days, a different type of use has evolved. Minicomputers and microcomputers led to an interactive form of information management. Interactive use of an information management system provides timely information on a specific subject almost immediately.

There still are times, however, when printed reports are more useful than interactive access. For instance, your bank maintains all of the transactions affecting your checking account in its database, but at the end of the month it sends you a printed statement so you can verify both your set of records and the bank's. Any financial accounting system must maintain a paper trail, or series of printed reports, for auditing purposes.

In the next two chapters you will be introduced to two popular information management systems for the Macintosh: FileMaker II and HyperCard.

CHAPTER SUMMARY

- Each piece of information is called a field or item. Several related items that describe one person, place, or thing are called a record. Multiple related records may be grouped together into a file. A database is composed of several related files.

- Data is raw information. When data has been organized (processed) so that it becomes accessible and useful, it is known as information.

- Businesses manage four major resources: money, materials, people, and information.

- Information must be correct and up-to-date to be useful. There is a time value associated with information, because old information is not as valuable as current information.

- Different people in a business organization have different information needs. Information management systems provide both interactive access and printed reports. Common reports include detail, summary, and exception reports. In some cases, particularly financial accounting systems, printed reports are necessary to provide an audit trail.

- What if... analyses are used to answer questions about future possibilities. For users trying to develop accurate projections, computers allow the examination of multiple scenarios such as, "What if the inflation rate is 3 percent?" or "What if the inflation rate is 6 percent?".

- Early information management systems were known as file management systems because information was stored in separate files that were not associated with each other. Later, database management systems were designed to allow the information in several files to be associated (or related), to reduce redundancy, and to allow easier updating of information.

- Information in a database is stored on disk drives, so the information can be directly accessed and updated. Many computer systems communicate with other computer systems over networks. Microcomputers are often connected over a local area network to allow for sharing of information between computers and to allow interactive access to a centralized database.

KEY TERMS

common carrier

data
database
detail report
direct access

electronic data processing (EDP)
exception report

field
file
file maintenance
file management system

information
item

key field

local area network (LAN)

management information system (MIS)
modem

random access
record
redundancy
relational database

sequential access
sort field

Chapter 11: FileMaker II

What You Will Learn in This Chapter

After reading this chapter and completing the projects in it, you should be able to:

- Create a new file and enter data into it

- Modify data in a file

- Delete records

- Find specific records and records that match one or more criteria

- Create a new layout

- Create calculation fields

- Create detailed reports

- Print reports

- Link files together using lookup fields

FileMaker is one of the best-selling information management programs for the Macintosh. It will do all the standard tasks found in a program that manages information on a personal computer. Unlike similar programs on most other computer systems, however, FileMaker is designed for use on the Macintosh, and it takes advantage of the Mac's graphics capabilities to help you create reports with visual impact and style.

STARTING FILEMAKER

FileMaker II

To start working with FileMaker, you need to have the FileMaker II application and the Inventory data file loaded into your computer. The Inventory file is included on the *Macintosh Journey Projects* disk that is available for use with this book. *(Project 1 in Chapter 1 tells you how to copy all the files on the* Projects *disk onto your data disk.)*

This Inventory file will be used later in Project 3. Let's open it now and take a look at it.

➠ Double-click on the Inventory data file icon, as shown in Figure 11-1.

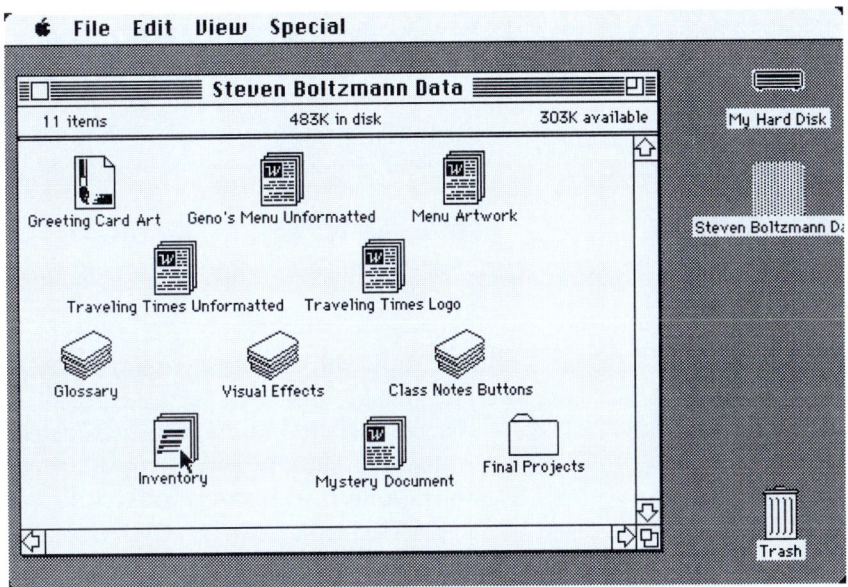

Figure 11-1   Opening Inventory file from the desktop

In a few seconds the Inventory file will open and you will see a screen like the one shown in Figure 11-2 (without the arrows and labels).

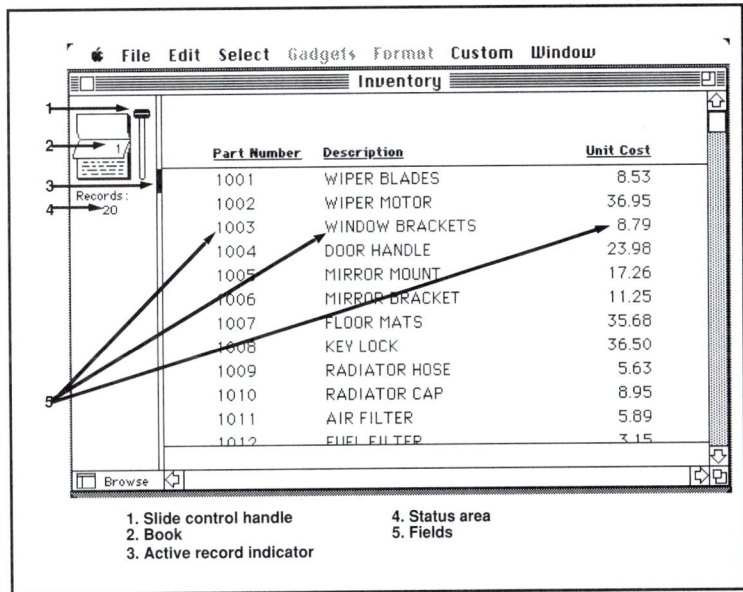

Figure 11-2   What's what on the FileMaker screen

The opening screen tells you a lot about the Inventory file. The *status area* shows there are 20 records in the file, and the first record is active. The active record can be determined in two ways: the center page of the *book* has the number 1 displayed, and the *active record indicator* (the small black area between the two vertical lines) is next to the first record.

BROWSING THROUGH THE FILE

At this point you should see the first 12 records in the Inventory file on your screen. This means that 8 more records are not currently visible. You can see them by scrolling through the file.

There are two ways to scroll through the records. The first is to use the *slide control handle*, and the second is to click on the bottom page of the book.

The slide control handle method (see Figure 11-3) will let you smoothly and quickly slide to a particular record if you know the record number. As you pull up or down on the slide control handle, the current record number is displayed on the middle page of the book. When you release the handle, the display scrolls to the record indicated in the middle book page. This is particularly efficient when you want to go to the first or last record in the file.

Figure 11-3   Changing active record with slide control handle

Notice that the top page of the book is blank when the first record is active, and the bottom page is blank when the last record is active. A page with simulated text on it shows that there are additional records in that direction.

The second scrolling method, clicking on the bottom page, will take you one record closer to the bottom of the file (see Figure 11-4). You can also click on the top page to move closer to the first record in the file.

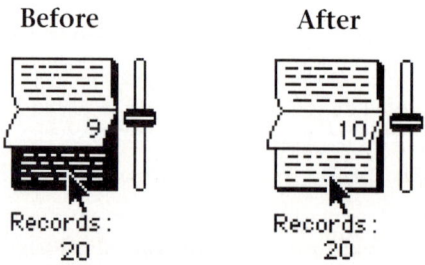

Figure 11-4   Changing the active record by clicking on the book

GETTING HELP

Whenever you are using a program such as FileMaker, there are times when you haven't learned, or can't remember, the proper procedures or commands to perform. FileMaker II includes online help so you won't have to stop what you are doing and find the information in the reference manual.

⌘-/ ➡ Choose **Help** from the Apple menu (see Figure 11-5).

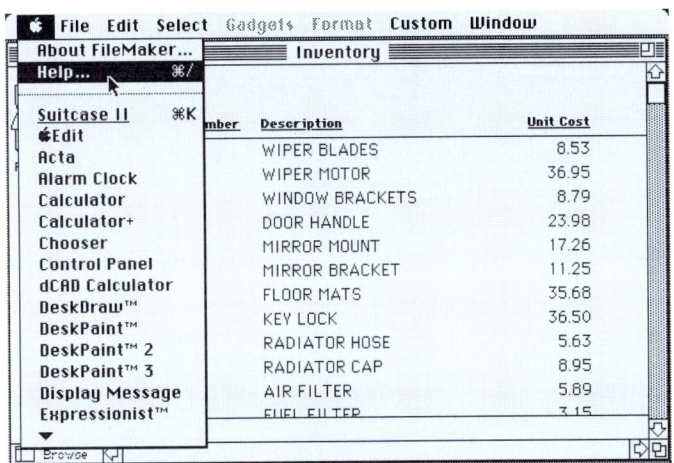

Figure 11-5   Getting FileMaker help

This brings up the opening screen for the help facility, offers some information on using FileMaker, and allows you to open the Help file (see Figure 11-6).

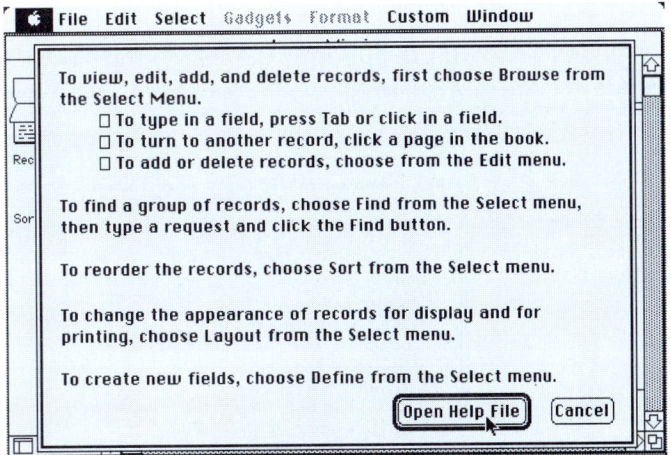

Figure 11-6   Opening the Help file

➡ Click **Open Help File**.

If the FileMaker Help file is not on your disk, you must quit FileMaker and then copy the Help file from the distribution disk into the folder on your hard disk that contains FileMaker. Then you can re-enter FileMaker and again try opening the Help file.

If you originally installed the Help file properly, or if you just went back and installed it, when you click the Open Help File button, you will see the screen shown in Figure 11-7.

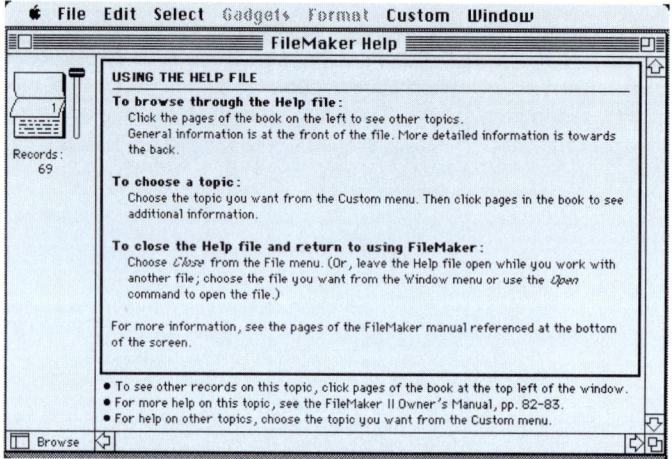

Figure 11-7   Using the Help file

⌘-1   ➠   If your screen does not look like the one shown in Figure 11-7, choose **Using the Help File** from the Custom menu.

The status area shows that there are a total of 69 records in the Help file.

If you want help on other topics, you can choose **Scripts** from the Custom menu (see Figure 11-8). Or, to make it even easier, you can choose one of the options available in the Custom menu.

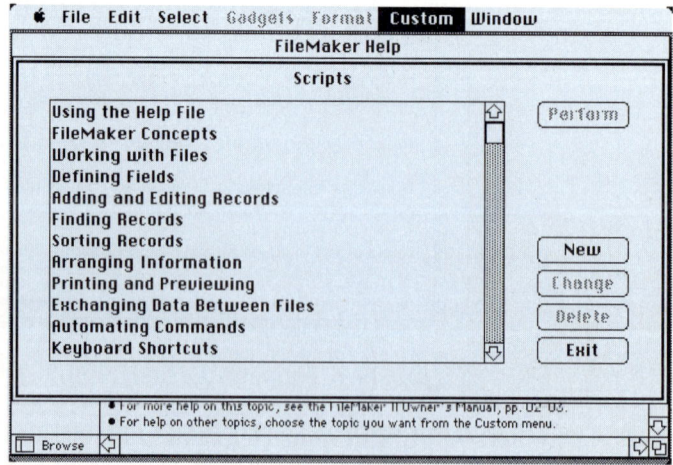

Figure 11-8   Scripts dialog box

For instance, if you want more information on understanding FileMaker concepts:

⌘-2 ➠ Choose **FileMaker Concepts** from the Custom menu.

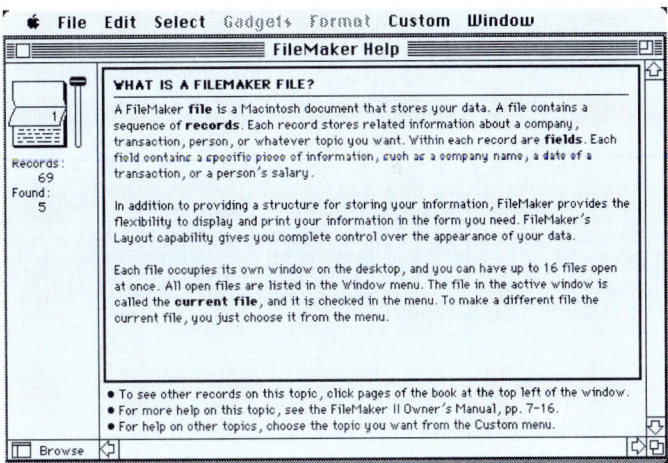

Figure 11-9 FileMaker Concepts help record

This shows the first of five records associated with this topic (look at the status area below the book). Notice, at the end of the next to last line on the screen, that you are told to see pages 7-16 in the FileMaker II Owner's Manual for further help. This field is updated for each record in the help file, and it will tell you where to look for more information on each of the 69 records.

If you can't find what you need listed in the Custom menu, choose **Find** in the Select menu and tell it what you want to find in the Help file.

⌘-F ➠ Choose **Find** from the Select menu.

This brings up the following screen (see Figure 11-10), where you can enter your *search criteria*.

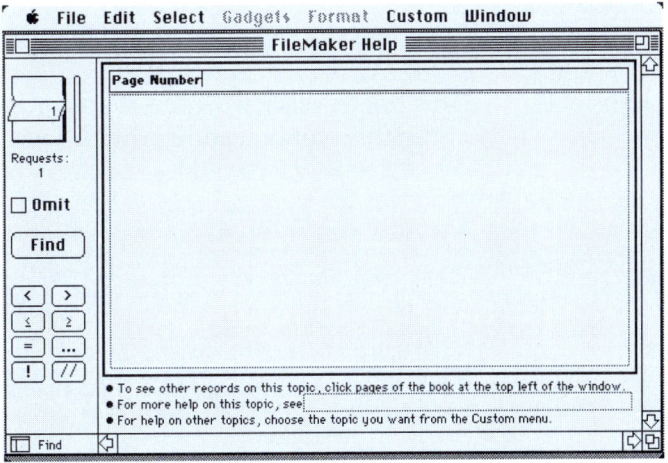

Figure 11-10 Finding information in the Help file

Now suppose that you want to find more information on how to add automatic page numbers to a report.

➡ Click in the field across the top of the FileMaker Help window, then type **Page Number** as shown at the top of the screen (see Figure 11-10), and then click the **Find** button.

This finds one record with the information on page numbers and tells you to see pages 184-186 in the reference manual (see Figure 11-11).

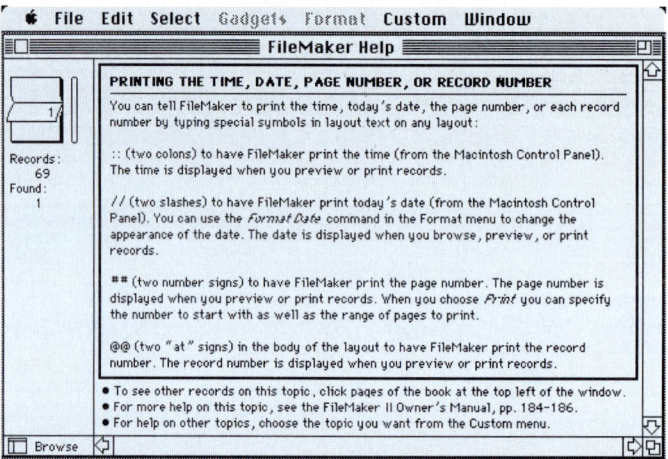

Figure 11-11   Page numbering help

Read this screen to learn about the codes used to add the current time, date, page number, and record number to any layout.

Take a few minutes now to look through the Help file and familiarize yourself with what is available and where you can find it.

When you are finished with the Help file, you can close the FileMaker Help window and go back to using the Inventory file. Whenever you close the Help file, you will be returned to whatever file was in use before you asked for help.

⌘-W ➡ Close the Help file by clicking in the close box.

This brief overview of the Help command should give you a start in using this handy feature provided with FileMaker.

SAVING YOUR WORK

Unlike other programs, information management applications such as FileMaker have no Save command. Since the application is designed to allow you to enter and update information, your work is saved automatically by the program.

When you create a new file, you are given the opportunity to specify the name of the file, the drive on which to store it, and the folder (if any) in which it will be saved. Then, as you work with the file, FileMaker will save it for you periodically.

This has some good features, as well as a couple of potential problems of which you need to be aware. When everything works correctly, you will not lose any information. That's good. However, when something goes wrong, it may damage a FileMaker data file. There are two ways to guard against serious problems with your data file: backing up the file and saving a copy of the file.

You must remember to make a backup copy of any file that contains important information when working in FileMaker.

The first reason for backing up is to make an insurance copy of the file in case of computer, disk, or power failure. If your equipment fails you can lose important information. Making backups is the *only* way to keep from losing information.

The second reason is important whenever you use a program that automatically saves your work for you, especially when every modification to a file is not saved when you make the change. FileMaker can tell when you are not working with the file. When you take a break or stop to talk to someone or to read something and you are not actively using FileMaker, it will take this time to save the file. It does not save every modification immediately after the change is made.

There are times (between when FileMaker last saved your file and you take the next short break) that the file on the disk does not match the work you have done. You might have made some important changes to the file since the last time it was saved. If the power goes out, there is the potential that your file might be damaged.

Another action that can damage a file is to stop working while FileMaker is running and just turn off the computer (before FileMaker has a chance to save your last modifications to the file). Many computer users develop this bad habit when working with other programs. For example, you could open MacPaint, create a painting, save it, print it, and just turn off the computer. Chances are you would not encounter any problems by doing this.

However, this is a very bad habit. When you are using a computer as sophisticated as the Macintosh, you must follow proper procedures to protect yourself from losing data. Always choose **Quit** *to close an application, and then choose* **Shut Down** *before turning off power to the computer.*

When using FileMaker, it is imperative that you quit the program properly. When you close a file, it is updated so that the copy on the disk matches what is in the computer's memory. When you choose **Quit**, FileMaker will update any open files.

If you do not follow these procedures, you are leaving yourself open for problems. The easiest way to avoid problems is to *backup your work* and *quit FileMaker properly.*

FileMaker also allows you to save a copy of the file at any time while you are working. (This is similar to the Save As command in other programs.) Saving a copy of the file you are using is a good habit to develop. In this chapter, you will be reminded to save a copy of a file when you have made major modifications to it, but you will not be reminded to make backup copies using the Finder.

Naming and deciding where to store a file will be covered when you create a customer file in Project 1. You will be introduced to saving a copy of a file after you enter data into that file.

This concludes the introduction to FileMaker. Before you continue with Project 1, you should close the Inventory file.

⌘-W ➡ Choose **Close** from the File menu.

Project 1: Creating a Database

Let's suppose that you are the owner of B & K Auto Parts, a store that sells to customers around the country. You publish a catalog and advertise in a number of large cities. Some of your customers are individuals, and others are businesses that use or resell the parts they purchase from you. You want to use FileMaker to keep track of customers and inventory and to automate the production of invoices when customers place orders.

In Project 1, you will create a Customers file. You will learn how to define the fields for each customer, enter data, format the fields for proper display, edit the data, and print the contents of the file.

In Project 2 you will learn to print detailed reports based on information in the Customers file. In Project 3 you will create the Sales Invoices file, and you will learn to interconnect files and create invoices using information looked up in the Customers and Inventory files.

In these three projects, you will learn the basics of using FileMaker.

PREFIX	Ms.
FIRST	Sandra
MI	M.
LAST	Hardin
TITLE	
COMPANY	
ADDRESS	497 Seemore Drive, Apt. 3.
CITY	Asheville
STATE	NC
ZIP	29702
COUNTRY	
AREA CODE	234
PHONE NUMBER	555-2922
ENTRY DATE	7/11/86
CUSTOMER NUMBER	1001
BUSINESS TYPE	
REGION	

PREFIX	Mr.
FIRST	George
MI	M.
LAST	Lapmont
TITLE	Manager
COMPANY	Bell Tires
ADDRESS	2354 78th Avenue
CITY	Bellvue
STATE	WA
ZIP	71356
COUNTRY	
AREA CODE	651
PHONE NUMBER	555-2654
ENTRY DATE	10/21/86
CUSTOMER NUMBER	1002
BUSINESS TYPE	Tire Dealer
REGION	

Figure 11-12   First page of Project 1

SELECTING WORK MODES

There are five work modes in FileMaker that allow you to do all of the standard information management tasks, as presented in Chapter 10. These modes are accessed by choosing one of them from the Select menu, and the currently selected mode is indicated with a checkmark (see Figure 11-13). A brief overview of these commands follows.

Figure 11-13   FileMaker's Select menu

Define

The *Define* command is used when creating a new file or when modifying the structure of an existing file. This lets you define what fields make up the records in the file and what types of information can be stored within those fields.

Browse

The *Browse* mode lets you view the information contained in a file. In addition to looking at the information, you can also add new data, delete records, and modify data.

Find

Find allows you to tell the computer what information you want to find, and the computer then searches all the records and selects only the ones that match the criteria you provided. You can optionally omit records that contain specified information as well.

Sort

If you want to access or present information in a specific order, you use the *Sort* command. This allows you to specify the fields that will be used to sort the file. You can sort alphabetically, numerically, or chronologically, in ascending or descending order. You can also specify more than one sort field.

Layout

If you want to look at the information in a different manner, you use the *Layout* mode to design a different view. You can't change the contents of a field in the layout view, but you can change the position and appearance of fields, graphics, and text. This new view then can be used for browsing through the information and for printing reports.

DEFINING FIELDS

As discussed in Chapter 10, a *field* is the lowest level of information storage in a *file*. You can design a *record* in FileMaker that consists of more than one field. Once all the fields have been defined (a process consisting of naming the field, specifying its type, and choosing any entry options), you then can enter information into the fields.

All records in the file have the same fields, but the contents of those fields in each record can be (and usually are) different. The data file is the collection of all the records that have been entered.

The process of creating a new data file consists of defining fields, formatting fields, and entering information into one or more records. Each record in the Customers file will contain information about one customer. After you define all the fields and exit the definition mode, you will automatically change to browse mode. FileMaker will create the first record, and you then can enter information about the first customer.

What types of information need to be stored for each customer? You need to enter the customer's name, address, and phone number, at least. It might also be useful to know when a customer was entered into the file, so you can determine how long that person has been a customer, and to assign a unique identifying number to each customer.

Field Types

Each field can hold only one type of information: text, number, date, picture, calculation, or summary. Each field type is explained below.

Text

Text is a versatile type of information. It can hold anywhere from one character to as many as you can show on your layout. When you enter text into a *text field*, FileMaker automatically wraps any word that doesn't fit onto the next line. If you wish, you can press the Return key to end a line or to create a blank line. This lets you organize your text into paragraphs.

FileMaker can sort text fields alphabetically in ascending or descending order based on the information at the beginning of the field.

FileMaker automatically creates an index of each word in a text field so you can find records containing any word you need to find in any text field of the file. Even though you can type up to about 32,000 characters in a text field, you will find that FileMaker will slow down when you access files with very large fields. For this reason it is best to keep text fields relatively short.

Number

A *number field* also can contain as much information as you care to enter, but it must be on only one line. Only the numeric portion of the information is indexed, and FileMaker lets you find a particular number or a number within a certain range that you specify.

Number fields may be sorted in increasing or decreasing order by value.

Number fields may be automatically formatted to include commas, dollar signs, and percent signs. You also can specify how many digits you want to appear to the right of the decimal point. Formatting number fields in FileMaker is similar to formatting cells in Excel.

In addition to specifying a format, you can tell FileMaker to treat a number field as representing a logical Yes or No. A value of zero represents No, and any nonzero value represents Yes.

Number fields can be used in calculations. By putting the name of the field in a calculation or summary formula, you can tell FileMaker to calculate other resulting values, such as how many items are on an invoice, the sales tax amount, and the total amount of the sale.

Any formatting that is in effect in a number field only affects the display. The unformatted value is used in any calculations or summaries and in any find or sort operations.

Date

You can enter a date by typing the numeric values for the month, day, and year. Dates may be entered in the form 7/4/92 or 7-4-92. These dates are then indexed so you can find any specific date or any date within a specified range of dates. *Date fields* may be sorted chronologically in normal (ascending) or reverse (descending) order.

Like number fields, date fields can be formatted in several different styles. The shortest format is "7/4/92" and the longest is "Saturday, July 4, 1992".

Date fields can be used in calculation and summary formulas. For example, to determine how long a customer has been a customer, you can subtract the date they were entered into your Customers file from today's date.

Any date entered into a date field *must* include the month, day, and year values. This restriction exists so that date calculations will return the correct results. If you want to store the month, year, day of the week, or any other subset of a date, you should enter it into a text or number field.

Picture

A *picture field* lets you store any graphics image you can cut or copy from any application or desk accessory. You cut or copy the picture and then paste it into the picture field.

Picture fields cannot be sorted, nor can you do a find on the information they contain.

If you need to find information contained in a picture field, you must add a separate text field, where you can enter a description of the picture field's contents. This separate text field can be used as an index for sorting or finding the contents of the picture field.

Calculation

Calculation fields let you enter a formula that will determine a value based on other fields within the same record. Formulas can result in text, number, or date results. These results can be formatted using the appropriate formats for the type of result the calculation produces (such as text, number, or date). You can also use the results of a calculation field in another formula in a different field.

Data cannot be directly entered into a calculation field. All calculations are automatically updated whenever a field containing a value that is used in the formula is modified.

All values resulting from formulas in calculation fields are automatically indexed in FileMaker, so you can use the Find command to locate specific information. You can also sort the file into alphabetical, numerical, or chronological order, based on the results displayed in a calculation field.

Summary

A *summary field* is different from the calculation field in a very important aspect. Calculation fields let you compute values using fields within the same record only. Summary fields let you compute values using the contents of one field spanning a group of records.

For example, you can use a calculation field to calculate the total amount of the sale for one invoice and a summary field to summarize the total amount of all sales for the group of records currently being browsed.

Unlike a calculation field, which can contain any formula you can construct, a summary field allows you to choose one summary formula from a predefined list consisting of average, count, fraction of total, maximum, minimum, standard deviation, or total.

The results shown in the summary field will change, depending on the group of records currently being browsed. If you are browsing the entire file, the summary applies to all records in the file. If you are browsing a subset of records as the result of a find command, the summary applies to only the records in that subset. Whenever you modify information in a field being summarized, or when you add or delete a record, the summary will be recalculated.

Summary fields are also different from calculation fields because the values they calculate cannot be used as input into other calculation formulas.

Files cannot be sorted and specific records cannot be found based on summary fields, because summary fields contain information that applies to groups of records and not to specific records.

Now that you know something about what can be put into each type of field, let's create the Customers file, define its fields, and enter the customer records.

The first step in this process is to tell FileMaker that you want to create a new file.

➡ Choose **New** from the File menu.

FileMaker presents a dialog box so you can name the new file and indicate where it is to be stored (see Figure 11-14).

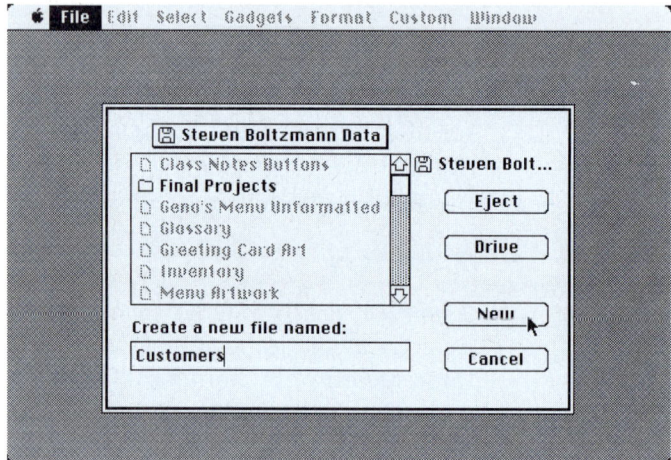

Figure 11-14   New file dialog box

➡ Name the file Customers, and make sure that it will be stored on your data disk. Click **New** to create the file.

FileMaker creates the new file and then opens the Field Definition dialog box (see Figure 11-15).

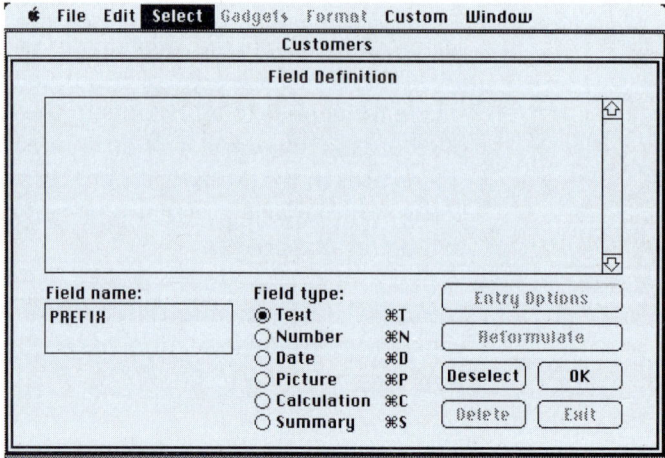

Figure 11-15   Field Definition dialog box

The first field that you enter is a text field that will be used to store the prefix to be attached to the customer's name. The field type defaults to Text, and that is what you want for the first several fields.

FileMaker has no rules about the way you capitalize field names. Some people prefer to capitalize all letters in a field name, others prefer to capitalize only the first letter in each word, and others prefer to use all lowercase letters. Unlike some other database programs, FileMaker lets you capitalize the names to suit yourself and also allows you to enter spaces between the words in the field names.

In Project 1, it is suggested that you use all capital letters in the field names to easily distinguish between field names and other information in the project. Project 2 adds three more (calculated) fields to the Customers file, and it is suggested that you capitalize the first letter of these field names, so you can easily distinguish between the fields that contain calculated results. The rest of the projects in the chapter suggest capitalizing the first letter of each word in the field name.

You can choose a style you like and name the fields to suit your preferences as you continue to use FileMaker in other projects after completing this chapter.

You start defining the fields by entering the name of the first field.

➠ Enter **PREFIX** in the "Field name" box. Click **OK**.

Depending upon the customer, this prefix can take such values as Mr., Ms., Mrs., Dr., Rev., and a number of others. Most of the common prefixes are in the list just mentioned.

Entry Options

In addition to providing six types of field contents, FileMaker provides a number of entry options for fields. This means that FileMaker automatically enters some values, provides lists from which you can choose others, and checks to see that the contents of a field meet certain criteria that you can specify.

Field Value List

In this case, you want FileMaker to display a list of name prefixes from which you can choose. This makes data entry faster and helps to avoid typographical and spelling errors. Let's tell FileMaker to display a list in the prefix field.

When you clicked the OK button, FileMaker placed the field name and type in the list at the top of the Field Definition dialog box. You can see PREFIX and Text in the upper box now.

➠ Click on **PREFIX** to select it, and then click **Entry Options**.

FileMaker displays the Entry Options dialog box for the PREFIX field (see Figure 11-16).

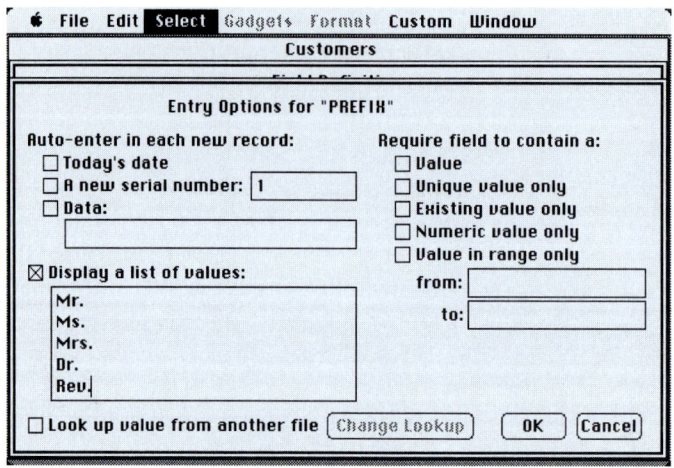

Figure 11-16   Entry options for the PREFIX field

➡ Click **Display a list of values:**.

An "X" appears in the check box to show that this option is active. Now add the list of titles to be displayed in the PREFIX field. You should enter one title per line, and press the Return key to go to the next line. Don't press Return after the last title.

➡ Enter **Mr.**, **Ms.**, **Mrs.**, **Dr.**, and **Rev.** in the list on separate lines (see Figure 11-16).

When you have entered these values and checked that they are entered correctly, you can accept this list and continue defining other fields.

➡ Click **OK**.

When you return to the Field Definition dialog box, the word "List" has been added on the right side of the line containing "PREFIX" and "Text".

You have now learned how to name a field, choose the type of contents for that field, and choose entry options for the field.

Now, you can continue defining the customer's name. Most customers have a first name, a middle initial, and a last name, but you might be tempted to enter the entire name into one field. You will find that it is easier to use a separate field whenever possible for each piece of information you might need to access. Separating the name into three fields allows you to easily access any portion of the name. For example, if you want to address somebody using their prefix title and last name, it is easier to do if these parts of the name are in separate fields. Later, in Project 2, you will add a calculation field to calculate the full name (except for middle initial) based on the information in the three name fields you will now define.

Let's start with the first name. Remember, the default field type is text, so you don't have to choose the style for these fields. You will not add any entry options to the first name or middle initial fields.

➡ Type **FIRST** in the "Field name" box and click **OK**.

Now define the middle initial field.

➡️ Type **MI** for the field name, and then click **OK**.

Field Requirements

The last name will be defined like these other fields, with one exception. You want to be sure that every customer has a name entered before the record is saved in the file. There may be times when you won't know the first name or middle initial, but you must enter at least the last name for a customer before adding a record to your data file.

This is not a restriction that FileMaker imposes; rather, it is added here to ensure the integrity of your data. You can tell FileMaker that the last name field must contain information before it is acceptable for saving in the file. If you mistakenly omit entering a last name, FileMaker will detect this mistake and tell you. Since this is an option for entering information into the field, you need to add an entry option for the last name field.

➡️ Enter **LAST** for this field's name (see Figure 11-17), and then click **OK**.

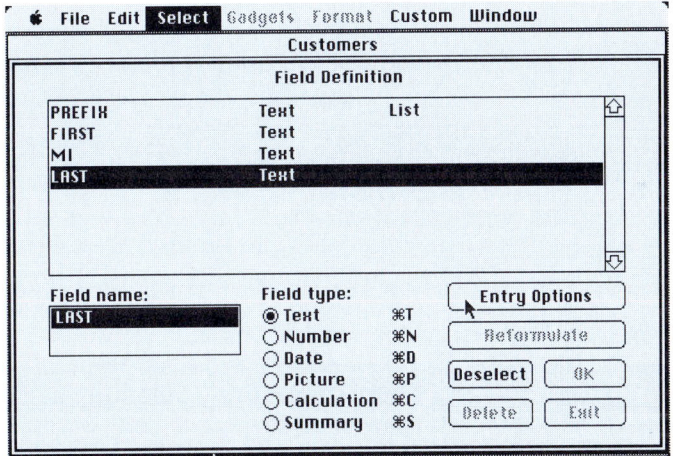

Figure 11-17   Defining the last name field

➡️ Select the last name field, and click **Entry Options** (See Figure 11-17).

In this case, all you want FileMaker to do is check that a value has been entered into the field. There is no way for FileMaker to know if the last name is a valid name, but it can check to see that something is in the field before accepting a record.

On the right side of the Entry Options dialog box is a list of check boxes, below the phrase "Require field to contain a:". The first item is "Value," and this is the one you want to select.

➡️ Click **Value** to select it, and then click **OK** (see Figure 11-18).

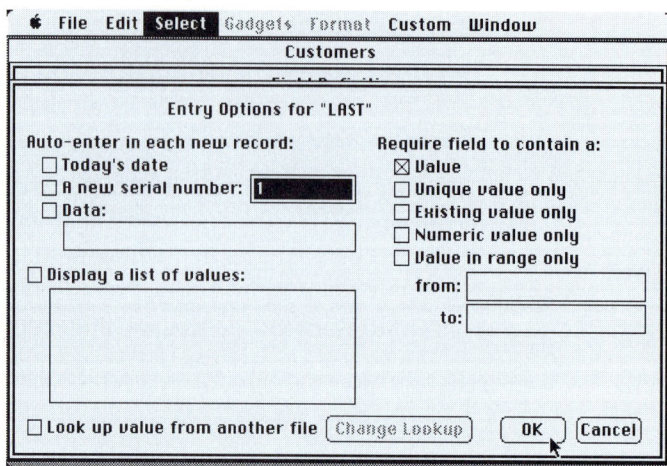

Figure 11-18   Requiring a value in the last name field

The next nine fields all contain text, and none have any special entry options.

➠   Define the following text fields: TITLE, COMPANY, ADDRESS, CITY, STATE, ZIP, COUNTRY, AREA CODE, and PHONE NUMBER.

You should see a list of fields in the upper box with the word "Text" next to them. It is important that the field names are spelled correctly as listed in the instructions. If you make a mistake, select the field, and correct the name.

Automatic Entry

The next field to be entered is a date field, and it will contain the date when the customer was entered into the Customers file. This date will be automatically entered by FileMaker through the use of an entry option.

➠   Click **Date**, and name the field ENTRY DATE. Click **OK** (see Figure 11-19).

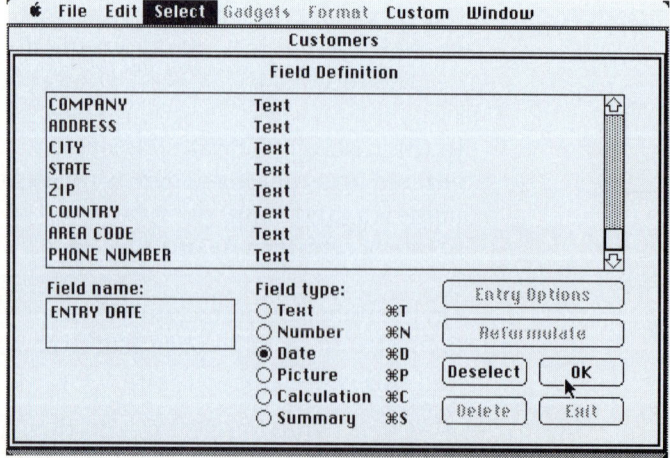

Figure 11-19   Defining the ENTRY DATE field

Now, let's add the entry option for the field.

➠ Select the field and click **Entry Options**.

You can choose to have FileMaker automatically enter values for you when a new record is added to the file. On the left side of the Entry Options dialog box are three options. Under the phrase "Auto-enter in each new record:" is a "Today's date" check box.

All Macintosh computers have a clock and a calendar that run all the time. (A battery supplies power when the computer is turned off or unplugged.) The current date and time can be set using the Control Panel desk accessory. FileMaker can check this calendar to determine the date. It is up to you to be sure the clock and calendar are set correctly, and don't forget to change the clock if you live in a state with Daylight Savings Time.

Choosing the Today's date option tells FileMaker to enter the date that it finds in the system's calendar into the ENTRY DATE field.

➠ Click **Today's date**, and then click **OK** (see Figure 11-20).

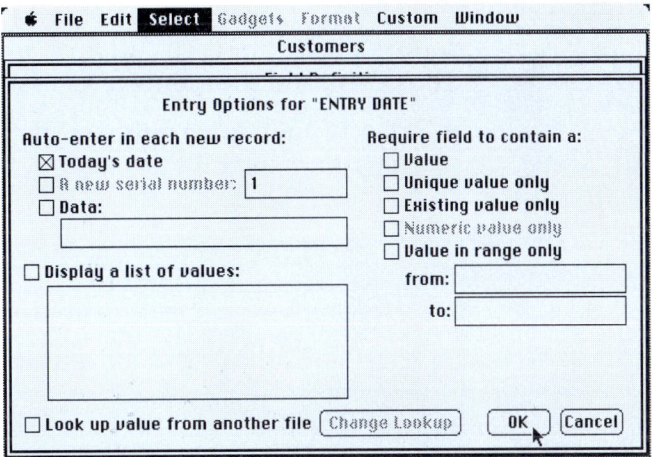

Figure 11-20   Choosing automatic entry of today's date

The next field is a number field where FileMaker will automatically enter a unique identifying number for each customer. Let's tell FileMaker to make the first customer number 1001 and then sequentially number each customer after that.

Start by telling FileMaker that this is a number field, and then enter the name.

➠ Click **Number**, name the field CUSTOMER NUMBER, and then click **OK**.

Now add the entry options.

➠ Select the CUSTOMER NUMBER field and click **Entry Options** (see Figure 11-21).

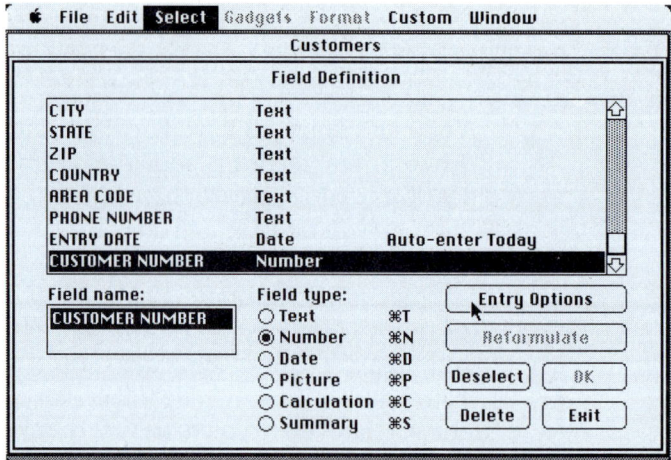

Figure 11-21 Adding entry options to the CUSTOMER NUMBER field

In the last field, ENTRY DATE, you told FileMaker to automatically enter the current date. In this field you will tell FileMaker to enter a new serial number, starting with 1001.

➡ Click **A new serial number:**, and enter **1001**.

You want to be sure each customer number is different, so you need to tell FileMaker to allow unique values only in this field.

➡ Click **Unique value only** (see Figure 11-22). Now click **OK** to accept these entry options.

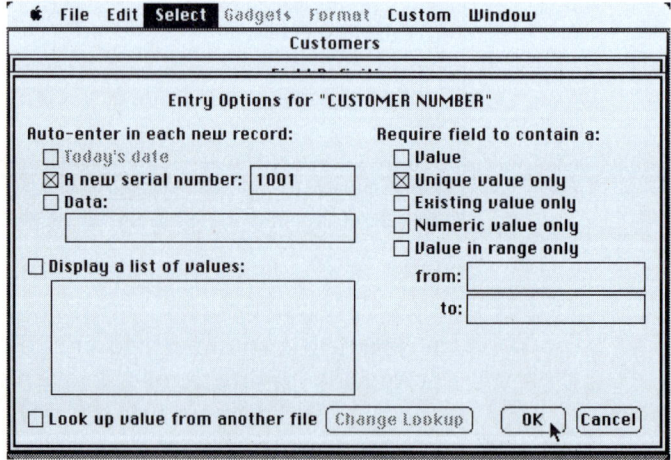

Figure 11-22 Choosing entry options for unique number

Many of your customers represent a business, so it is useful to enter the business type for each business customer. This is another case where a list of values is helpful.

➡ Create a new text field named BUSINESS TYPE, and open its Entry Options dialog box.

Now, enter the list of values available for this field.

⟹ Click **Display a list of values:**.

⟹ Enter the following items into the list: **Auto Body Repair**, **Auto Dealer**, **Car Wash**, **Glass Repair**, **Mechanic**, **Tire Dealer**, and **Welder** (see Figure 11-23). Click **OK**.

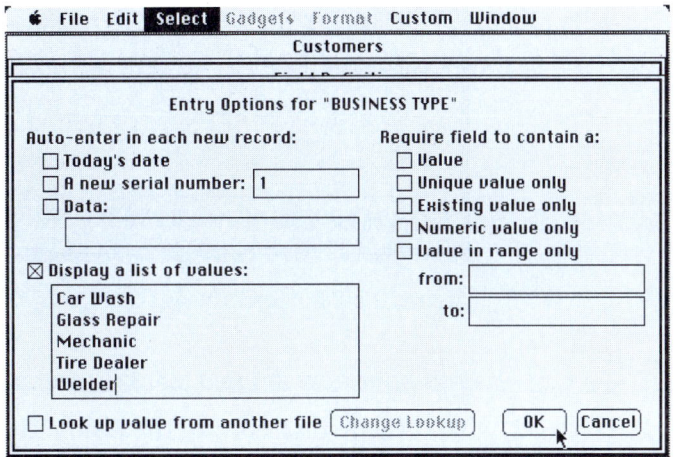

Figure 11-23   Specifying a list of items for BUSINESS TYPE

A major benefit of using a list for entering information into the field becomes obvious when you try to find all customers who represent a particular type of business. By choosing from a list, you know that the type of business is entered exactly the same each time. Then if you tell FileMaker to find all records where the business type is Tire Dealer you can be confident that it will find all occurrences and not miss any because of typographical errors or because some were entered as Auto Tire Dealer, for example.

If the business type is not in the list, you can still type an entry into the field. When you find that you have entered the same business type several times, you can choose to define fields, and add the new business type to the list.

The last field you will define for the Customers file is the REGION field.

You have not yet divided your service area into regions, but sometime in the near future you plan to do so. Let's set aside a field for later use. You plan to organize your customers into nine regions, numbered 1 through 9, and you want to store this number for each customer. Additionally, you want FileMaker to verify that the region number is in this specified range. This can be accomplished by requiring the field to contain a value in the range from 1 to 9 only.

⟹ Create a new number field named REGION.

⟹ In the Entry Options dialog box, click **Value in range only**, enter **1** in the "from:" box, and then enter **9** in the "to:" box (see Figure 11-24). Click **OK**.

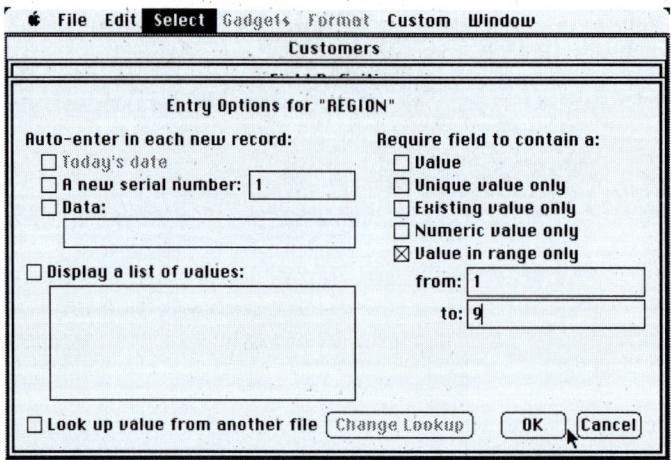

Figure 11-24   Specifying a range of values for the REGION field

You have now defined all of the fields for this file.

➥ When you return to the Field Definition dialog box, click **Exit**.

➥ Click anywhere on the bold field titles on the left to deselect the record.

FileMaker will ask if it is ok to allow the LAST field to remain empty. When you defined the fields, you told FileMaker to be sure a value existed in the last name field before accepting a record. In a few moments, you will enter information into this record, but, for now, tell FileMaker it is ok.

➥ Click **OK**.

FileMaker will create a default vertical layout showing the fields in the order they were entered, and will create the first record (see Figure 11-25). In Project 2 you will learn how to change the formats of the fields and create three new detailed layouts for use with this file. For the remainder of this project, you will use the default layout created for you by FileMaker.

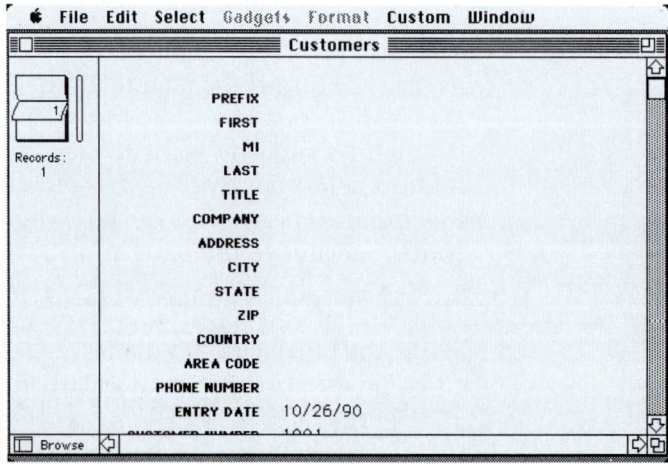

Figure 11-25   The first record after defining the fields

Notice that the entry date and customer number have already been entered by FileMaker. (Your date should be different from the one shown in the figure.)

You have done a significant amount of work now, so it is a good time to save a copy of this file.

➧   Choose **Save a Copy** from the File menu.

FileMaker gives you three choices for the copy: Copy of this file, Compressed copy, and Clone (see Figure 11-26).

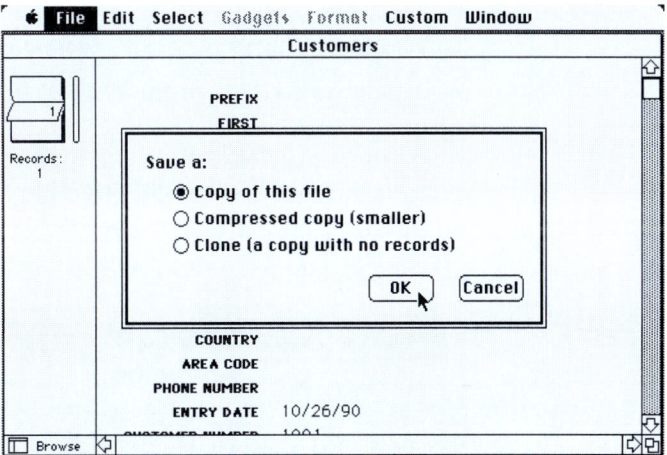

Figure 11-26   Three choices for saving a copy of the Customers file

The first option is the default, and it is the one you will choose this time.

➧   Click **OK**.

FileMaker will suggest naming this file Copy of Customers and will place it on the same drive and in the same folder with the Customers file (see Figure 11-27). This is what you want to do.

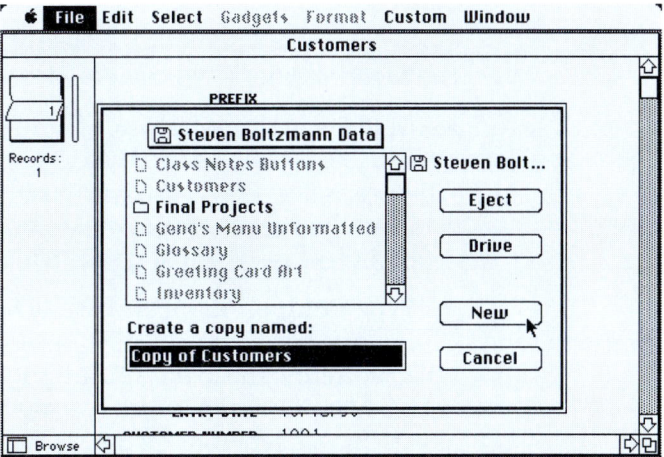

Figure 11-27   Saving a copy of the Customers file

⇒   Click **New** to create the new file.

ENTERING DATA

Now that you have defined all the fields that are necessary for this file, it is time to create new records and enter data. FileMaker created the first (mostly) blank record when you exited from initially defining the fields. It has already entered the current date and the customer number (1001).

The other fields are blank and will remain blank until you enter the data. Let's enter the name and address of your first customer.

To begin entering data, you have to activate the list in the PREFIX field.

⇒   Click to the right of the PREFIX field label.

Clicking in the area where the fields are located activates the record. When you click in the PREFIX field, all the fields in the record are outlined with dotted lines. The PREFIX field is a text field with an entry list, so the list becomes visible (see Figure 11-28).

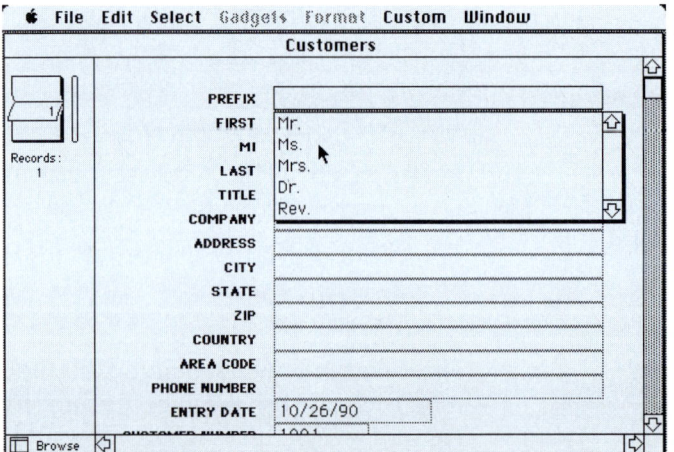

Figure 11-28   Entering the prefix data

The first customer is Ms. Sandra M. Hardin, so let's enter her name.

⇒   Double-click on **Ms.** to enter it into the PREFIX field.

When you select from a list, FileMaker enters what you selected into the field and then moves the insertion point to the beginning of the next field, in this case, the first name field.

⇒   Type **Sandra** into the first name field, and then press the Tab key.

When you enter the name, the insertion point remains at the end of the field. You can choose between two methods for moving to the next field. As with most operations on the Macintosh, you can click on a field with the mouse to activate the field and move the insertion point. In this case, there is a faster way, and that is to press the Tab key. Any time you press the Tab key, the contents of the current field are accepted and the next field in the record becomes the active field. In this case, pressing the Tab key moved the insertion point to the beginning of the middle initial field.

➠ Type **M.** in the middle initial field, and then type Tab.

Now the insertion point should be at the start of the last name field.

➠ Type **Hardin**, and then tab to the next field.

Ms. Hardin, as your customer, does not represent a company, so you won't enter a title or company. The next information is to be entered into the ADDRESS field.

➠ Press the Tab key until the insertion point is in the ADDRESS field.

Ms. Hardin's address is 497 Seemore Drive, Apt. 3, Asheville, NC 29702.

➠ In the ADDRESS field, type **497 Seemore Drive, Apt. 3**, and then tab to the CITY field.

➠ In the CITY field, type **Asheville**, and then tab to the STATE field.

➠ In the STATE field, type **NC**, and then tab to the ZIP field.

➠ In the ZIP field, type **29702**, and then tab to the next field.

Ms. Hardin lives in the United States so you don't have to enter anything in the COUNTRY field. Her phone number is (234) 555-2922.

➠ Tab to the AREA CODE field and enter **234**, then, after moving to the PHONE NUMBER field, enter **555-2922**.

FileMaker has already entered the entry date (yours will show the current date) and the customer number (1001). The first eight customers you will enter are old customers; some have been customers for several years. After entering those customers, you will enter a couple of new customers. In the case of a new customer, you will accept the entry date that is automatically entered. For someone who already is a customer, you can override the entered date and type in the correct one. Let's do that for Ms. Hardin.

➠ Tab to the ENTRY DATE field and press Backspace (or Delete) to erase the automatic entry.

➠ Type **7/11/86** for her entry date.

If you would like to see the rest of the record, you can click on the down arrow in the scroll bar. Click on the up arrow in the scroll bar to return to the top of the record.

Visually inspect the information you have entered, and compare it with the record shown in Figure 11-29. If you have made any mistakes, click in the field with the error and correct your mistake.

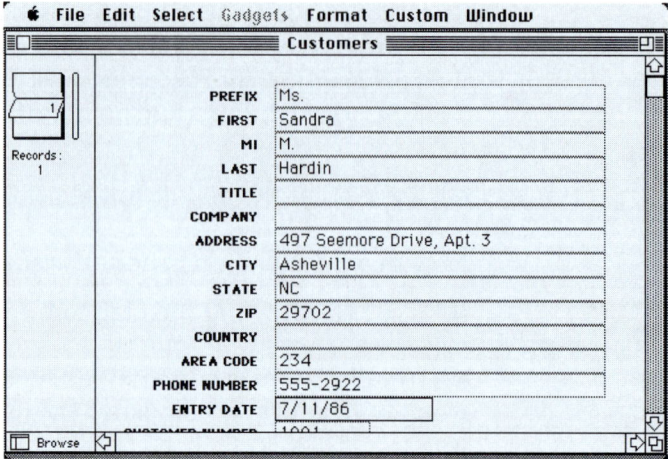

Figure 11-29   First record after entering data

New Record

When you are sure the information is correct, tell FileMaker to accept this customer and create a new record for the next customer.

⌘-N   ➠   Choose **New Record** from the Edit menu.

Ms. Hardin is now added to the file. FileMaker checks to see that there is something entered into the last name field and that the customer number is different from all other customer numbers in the file. It performs these checks because you told it to do so when you specified the entry options while defining the fields.

When record 2 is created, it becomes the active record, and the insertion point is positioned automatically in the first field of the record, which is the PREFIX field. Since the PREFIX field has a list, the list becomes visible and the computer waits for you to select one of the entries (see Figure 11-30). Remember, however, that you can type a prefix directly in the field if what you need to enter is not in the list.

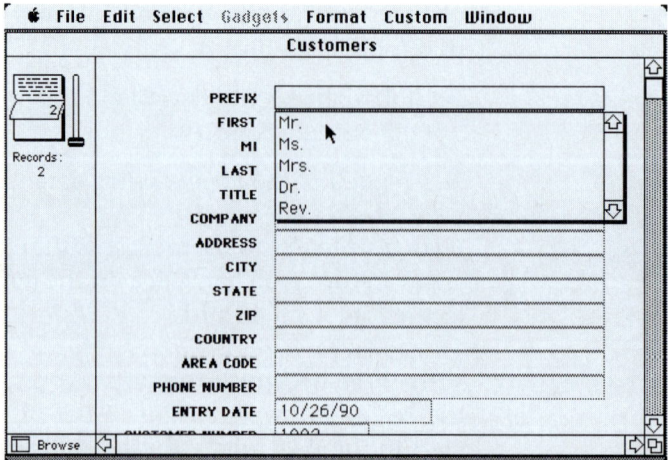

Figure 11-30   The newly created second record

The next customer is Mr. George M. Lapmont.

➡ Enter **Mr.** by double-clicking on it in the list, then enter the rest of his name in the appropriate fields. Don't forget to press the Tab key to move to the next field.

Mr. Lapmont is the manager of Bell Tires, which is a company that purchases from you regularly.

➡ Enter **Manager** in the TITLE field and **Bell Tires** in the COMPANY field.

Bell Tires is located at 2354 78th Avenue, Bellvue, WA 71356. Their phone number is (651) 555-2654.

➡ Enter **2354 78th Avenue** in the ADDRESS field, **Bellvue** in the CITY field, **WA** in the STATE field, and **71356** for the ZIP field.

➡ You don't need to enter a country, so skip that field by using the Tab key. Enter **651** in the AREA CODE field and **555-2654** in the PHONE NUMBER field.

FileMaker has already entered the entry date and customer number into the record, but you need to change the entry date.

➡ Replace the date entered by FileMaker with 10/21/86.

➡ Activate the BUSINESS TYPE field by moving to it using the Tab key or by clicking in the field with the mouse.

When the BUSINESS TYPE field becomes active, it shows the list you defined. Bell Tires is a tire dealer.

➡ Click on the down arrow in the business type list to scroll down until you can see Tire Dealer. Double-click on **Tire Dealer** to enter it into the field (see Figure 11-31).

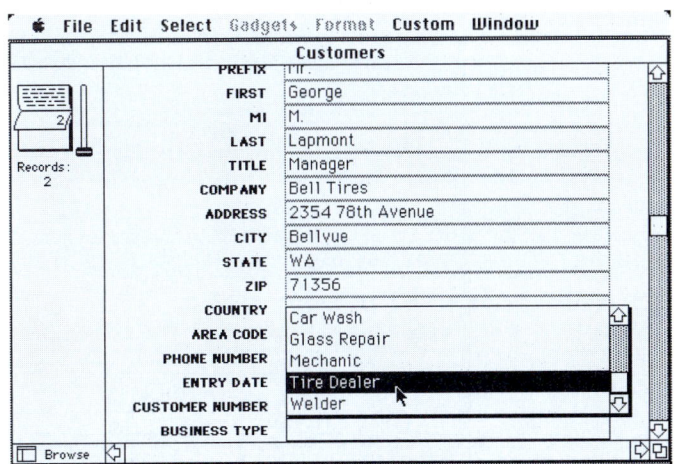

Figure 11-31   Entering the business type into a record

Now you can visually verify that the information on this customer is entered correctly (see Figure 11-32).

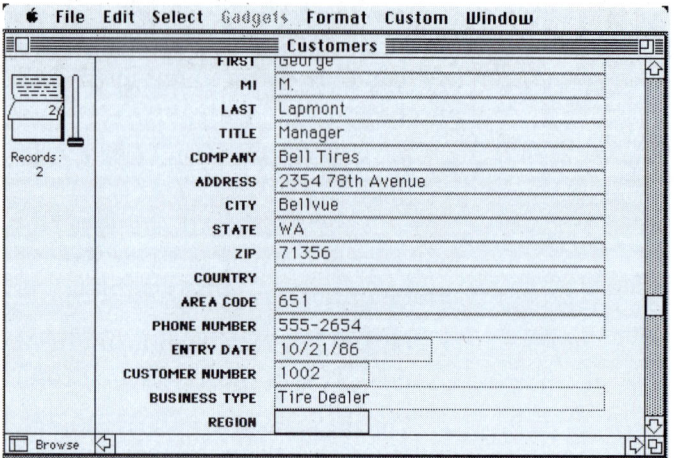

Figure 11-32   Completed second record

When you are sure the information is correct, accept this record and create a new one.

⌘-N   ➡   Choose **New Record** from the Edit menu.

The next customer to be entered is Mr. Jim Bell, who lives at 1492 Document Drive, Mandarin, FL 49709. His phone number is (203) 555-2731. His date for becoming a customer was 11/01/86.

➡   Enter the information for this customer into the proper fields.

When you have completed entering this data, check your entry against the record as shown in Figure 11-33.

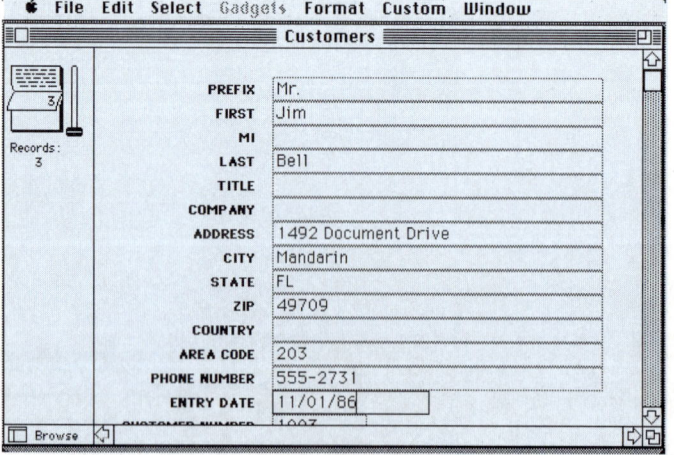

Figure 11-33   Completed entry for Jim Bell

When this information is correct, create a new record and enter the information for your West Coast attorney, Ms. Kay B. Kusunoki.

⌘-N   ➠   Choose **New Record** from the Edit menu.

➠   Type the attorney's name in the appropriate fields, and then type **Attorney** in the TITLE field.

Ms. Kusunoki's address is 7531 Second Street, San Francisco, CA 92846. Her phone number is (978) 555-2383. Her entry date should be 01/14/87.

➠   Enter the address and phone number into the proper fields.

Verify that you have entered this data correctly (see Figure 11-34).

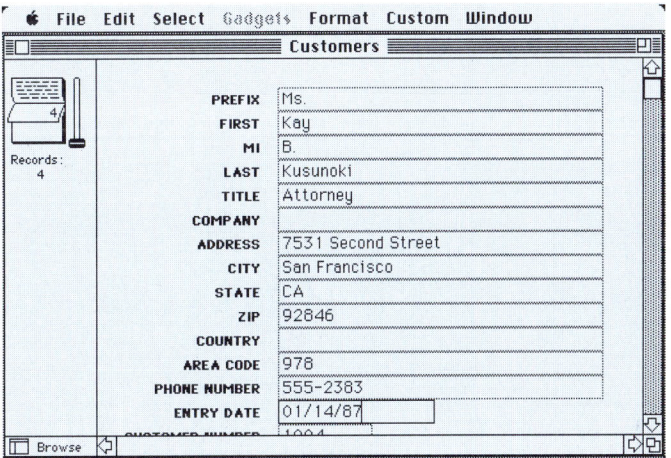

Figure 11-34   Completed record for Ms. Kusunoki

➠   Using what you have learned about entering new customers, enter the four customers listed below:

Ms. Faye Mauney
15 Mockingbird Lane
Pinelog, TX 69007
(833) 555-0927
10/19/87

Mrs. Mattie L. Dilbeccio
Owner
Grape Creek New and Used Cars
14709 Main Street
Grape Creek, NC 28087
(702) 555-1092
11/06/87
Auto Dealer

Dr. Jose S. deAngello
117 Third Street
Apache Junction, AZ 78273
(604) 555-7826
08/06/89

Mr. Gary H. Westmoreland
Owner
Western Carolina Welding
2741 Highway 141
Peachtree, NC 28915
(703) 555-1273
09/29/90
Welder

You should now see Mr. Westmoreland's information on the screen (see Figure 11-35).

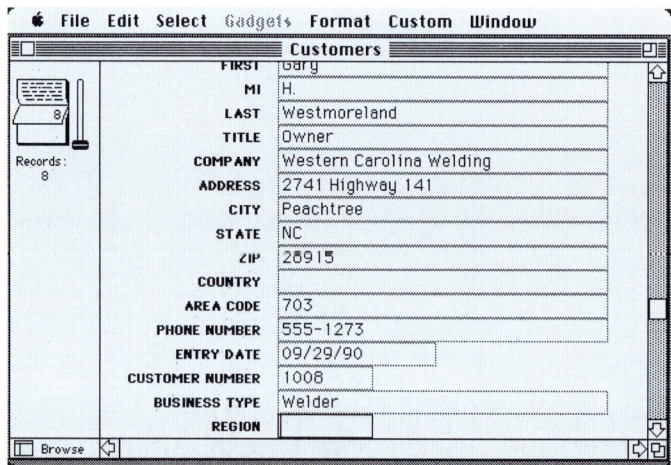

Figure 11-35   Completed record for Mr. Westmoreland

➡ Now, enter two more customers, using information of your choosing. Accept the entry date entered by the computer.

This demonstrates how FileMaker can enter the date for you automatically for convenience and accuracy but still offers the flexibility to enter other information in the field if needed.

➡ When you have completed entering these six names, click on the last record, anywhere to the left of the fields to deactivate the record.

When you click outside the area of the screen that contains the fields, the fields are no longer outlined (see Figure 11-36).

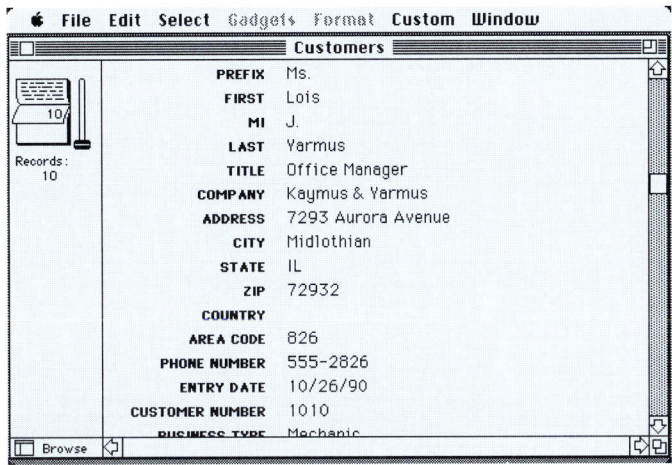

Figure 11-36   The last record has been entered.

⇒ This is a good time to save a copy of this file. Choose **Save a Copy** from the File menu, name it Copy 2 of Customers, and click **New** to create the new file on your data disk.

You now have the current Customers file and two backup copies on your data disk.

EDITING DATA

FileMaker lets you modify information in the file at any time. Standard Macintosh editing techniques are used to select, modify, and delete text in a field.

Since you can modify information in a field at any time, there are times when it is easier and faster to duplicate a record and then edit the information in some of the fields.

Duplicate Record

You have now entered ten customers. In this case, none of the customers that you were entering had similar data. Sometimes, however, you will enter a series of customers who have several fields containing the same information. When this situation arises, you can frequently save time by duplicating a record rather than creating an entirely new one.

Let's say that you need to add information on the following customer *(don't enter anything yet)*:

Mrs. June Brooks
Route 4, Box 199
Pinelog, TX 69007
(833) 555-0835

Finding a Record

Before you add the customer, you remember that you already have at least one customer in Pinelog, Texas, and some of the information in that customer's record will match this one. Let's find that customer.

⌘-F   ➧   Choose **Find** from the Select menu.

FileMaker presents you with the Find screen, which looks like a blank record (see Figure 11-37).

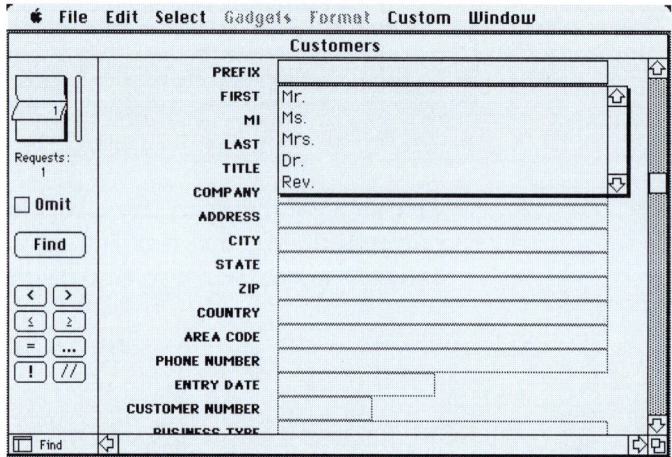

Figure 11-37   FileMaker's Find screen

The PREFIX field is showing its list, but you are not going to enter anything in that field. You want to find all customers who live in a city named Pinelog.

➧   Click in the CITY field and type **Pinelog**. Click **Find** (see Figure 11-38).

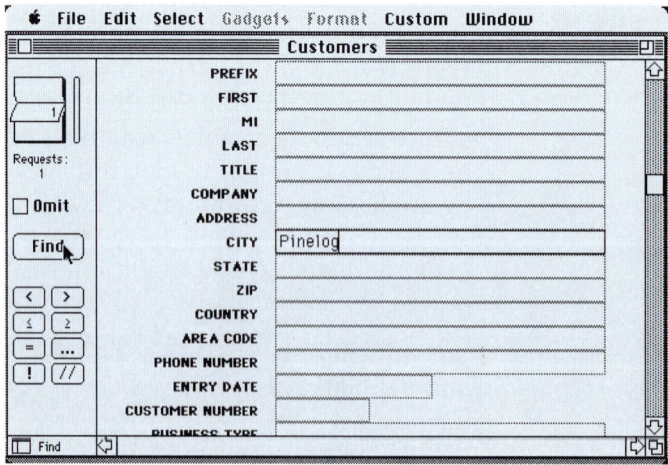

Figure 11-38   Entering the search criteria

By entering **Pinelog** in the CITY field, you tell FileMaker that you are only interested in any record with that name in that field. You can further restrict the search by entering information in other fields.

When you click the **Find** button, FileMaker finds all records containing Pinelog. It finds one customer who lives in a city named Pinelog: Ms. Mauney. This is the same city where Mrs. Brooks lives, and looking at both addresses tells you that, indeed, several fields will contain the same information. In this case, it makes sense to duplicate Ms. Mauney's record and modify it.

⌘-D   ➧   Choose **Duplicate Record** from the Edit menu.

Notice that this record looks just like Ms. Mauney's original record, except that FileMaker has given it a different customer number already. Now you have to edit the fields that contain different information.

The PREFIX field is already active and showing its list. You need to choose **Mrs.** from the list.

➧   Double-click **Mrs.** to enter it in the PREFIX field.

➧   Double-click on the first name field in the record and type **June** to enter it as the first name.

➧   Double-click on the existing last name and type **Brooks** to enter it in the last name field.

➧   Select the entire ADDRESS field by double-clicking on the first word in the address, holding down the mouse button, and dragging to the right until all the address is selected. Type **Route 4, Box 199** to enter the new address.

The information in the CITY, STATE, ZIP, and AREA CODE fields is the same for both customers so those fields don't need to be changed.

➧   Double-click on the phone number and type **555-0835**.

The current date and proper customer number are entered automatically when you duplicated the record.

Your screen should look like the one shown in Figure 11-39.

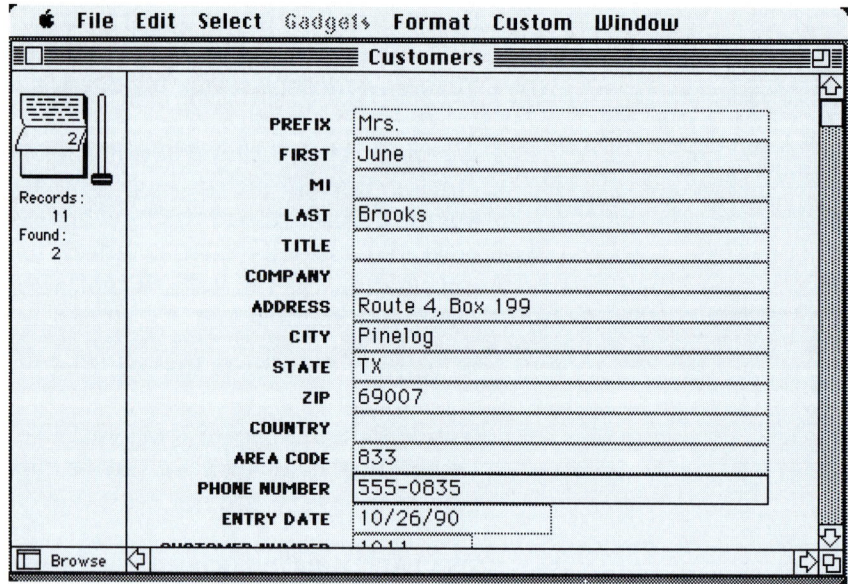

Figure 11-39   The duplicated record after editing the data

Look at the status area. It shows that there are now 11 records in the file and 2 are found. You told FileMaker to find the records that contain Pinelog in the CITY field, and now there are two records that match that criteria.

Let's tell FileMaker to find all records in the file.

⌘-G   ➠   Choose **Find All** from the Select menu.

       ➠   Now is a good time to save a copy of this file.

Assume that you are done entering information into the Customers file and want to quit.

⌘-Q   ➠   Choose **Quit** from the File menu.

Delete Record

At a later date, suppose you need to delete Mrs. Brooks' record from your file. To do this, you can open the Customers file, find the record you want to delete, and tell FileMaker to remove that record from the file.

➠   Find the icon of the Customers file on your data disk and double-click on it to start FileMaker and open that file.

Before you closed the Customers file, you were looking at the last record in the file, but now when you open the file again, the first record is on the screen. You need to find Mrs. Brooks' record.

⌘-F   ➠   Choose **Find** from the Select menu.

       ➠   Type **Brooks** in the last name field, and then click **Find**.

The record will appear on the screen in a moment. Deleting this record is fast and easy.

⌘-E   ➡   Choose **Delete Record** from the Edit menu.

You will be asked if you want to permanently delete this record (see Figure 11-40).

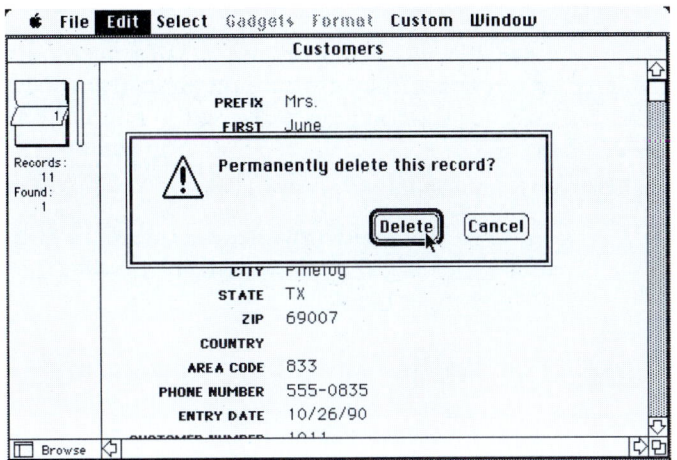

Figure 11-40   Dialog box to confirm deletion of a record

➡   Click **Delete**. The record is then removed from the Customers file.

You should now see the tenth record on the screen.

BROWSING

You have been working in Browse mode for most of this project. This mode lets you view records, add new records, duplicate records, change the information in a record, and delete records. This is the mode you will use most of the time when you are working in FileMaker, because it lets you work with the information contained in the file. Another mode, Layout, lets you modify the arrangement and appearance of fields, graphics, and text. You will learn to use Layout mode in Project 2.

Since you have not learned to create alternate layouts, you have been looking at the information in the Customers file using the default layout FileMaker created for you. FileMaker lets you create as many different layouts for a file as you want. You can browse through the information in the file using any of those layouts.

Before completing Project 1, let's practice moving through the file a little.

The top left corner of the window contains the book, slide control handle, and status area. You can use the book or the slide control handle to move through the file and view different records.

Using the Book

The book lets you go one record closer to the first or last record. You can click on the top page of the book (if it is not blank) to go one record closer to the first record. Clicking on the bottom page of the book takes you one record closer to the end of the file.

Record 10 is showing on the screen now. The bottom page is blank, and this indicates that you are currently viewing the last record in the file. If the top page were blank, you would be viewing the first record.

➡ Click the top page of the book.

You should now see record 9 on the screen. Now that you are not viewing the last record in the file, the bottom page of the book is no longer blank.

Another way to use the book is to click on the middle page, and then type the number of the record you want to see. Let's say you want to see customer number 1003. The customers were numbered starting with 1001, and this means that customer number 1001 is in the first record, number 1002 is in the second record, and so on. To see customer number 1003, all you have to do is view the third record.

➡ Click the middle page of the book, type **3**, and then type Return or Enter.

You should now be viewing the information for customer number 1003.

Using the Slide Control Handle

The slide control handle is useful for moving quickly to the first or last record in the file. Also, as your file becomes larger and deletions create holes in the record number sequence, you will no longer have as clear a relation between the book page number and the customer number. Then the slide control handle will allow you to move closer to where you think the record you want may be.

➡ Point to the slide control handle, press the mouse button and while holding the mouse button down, drag the handle to the bottom.

You are now looking at the last record in the file again. To view the first record you could drag the handle to the top. As you drag the handle, the number in the middle page of the book changes to represent the record you would see if you released the mouse button. Move to record number 3 again.

➡ Drag the slide control handle until the middle page of the book has a 3 showing. Release the mouse button.

➡ Now, use any of these methods to move to the first record.

PRINTING A FILE

You have now created a file, defined its fields, and entered data into the file.

It is handy to keep a paper copy of the file in case anything happens to the copies stored on the disk. (You did make several copies and a backup, didn't you?)

There are two reports you can print whenever you have created a file and entered data into it. Both reports are available by choosing the Print command.

⌘-P   ⟹   Choose **Print** from the File menu. When the dialog box for printing is displayed, accept the default values by clicking **OK**.

FileMaker will print a report containing all ten records and their contents. The report should take about six pages, and the first page should look like the one shown in Figure 11-12, at the beginning of this project.

The second report that is useful for documenting the field definitions of a file is also printed using the Print command.

⌘-P   ⟹   Choose **Print** from the File menu.

This time, you want to change one of the options in the dialog box that appears.

⟹   In the bottom line of the dialog box, click **Field Definitions**.

This tells FileMaker to print the definitions of the fields, rather than the contents of all the records.

⟹   Click **OK**.

FileMaker will print a report that should look like the one shown in Figure 11-41.

Field Name	Field Type	Formula / Entry Option
PREFIX	Text	List: Mr. Ms. Mrs. Dr. Rev.
FIRST	Text	
MI	Text	
LAST	Text	Required value
TITLE	Text	
COMPANY	Text	
ADDRESS	Text	
CITY	Text	
STATE	Text	
ZIP	Text	
COUNTRY	Text	
AREA CODE	Text	
PHONE NUMBER	Text	
ENTRY DATE	Date	Auto-enter today's date
CUSTOMER NUMBER	Number	Auto-enter serial number: 1012 Unique values only
BUSINESS TYPE	Text	List: Auto Body Repair Auto Dealer Car Wash Glass Repair Mechanic Tire Dealer Welder
REGION	Number	Value in range from " 1" to " 9"

Figure 11-41   Report showing field definitions of Customers file

This concludes Project 1.

You will continue to use the Customers file in the next two projects.

Project 2: Creating Detail Reports

In Project 2, you will learn to create two types of *detail reports* based on the information you entered into the Customers file in Project 1. You will create two *columnar reports* and a report that prints mailing labels. These reports will be created using FileMaker's preset styles for columnar and *label reports*.

A columnar report prints information in columns, and a label report prints information in a grid-like pattern consisting of several rows and columns.

These reports are called detail reports because they print something for each record that is currently selected. A *summary report* does not give details for each record, it just provides information about the current selection as a whole. Where a detail report might show how much you are owed by each customer, a summary report might show only the total amount you currently have in accounts receivable, the average amount for each customer, and the number of transactions in the file.

FileMaker also lets you create a new *blank report* and place fields, graphics, and text anywhere on the page. The flexibility provided by the blank report demands a cost in terms of time and effort, but it allows you to design a report that shows the information you want in exactly the way you want to present it. You will learn to create a report from a blank layout in Project 3.

The output of the three reports you'll create in Project 2 appears in Figures 11-42, 11-43, and 11-44.

October 27, 1991
7:33 PM

FIRST	**LAST**	**CUSTOMER NUMBER**
Sandra	Hardin	1001
George	Lapmont	1002
Jim	Bell	1003
Kay	Kusunoki	1004
Faye	Mauney	1005
Mattie	Dilbeccio	1006
Jose	deAngello	1007
Gary	Westmoreland	1008
Glenda	Rider	1009
Lois	Yarmus	1010

Page 1

Figure 11-42 Final output of Project 2, customer name and identification
number report

October 27, 1991
10:14 PM

FIRST	LAST	AREA CODE	PHONE NUMBER
Jim	Bell	203	555-2731
Jose	deAngello	604	555-7826
Mattie	Dilbeccio	702	555-1092
Sandra	Hardin	234	555-2922
Kay	Kusunoki	978	555-2383
George	Lapmont	651	555-2654
Faye	Mauney	833	555-0927
Glenda	Rider	827	555-2783
Gary	Westmoreland	703	555-1273
Lois	Yarmus	826	555-2826

Page 1

Figure 11-43   Final output of Project 2, customer name and phone number report

Mrs. Mattie L. Dilbeccio
Grape Creek New and Used Cars
14709 Main Street
Grape Creek, NC 28087

Mr. Gary H. Westmoreland
Western Carolina Welding
2741 Highway 141
Peachtree, NC 28915

Ms. Sandra M. Hardin
497 Seemore Drive, Apt. 3
Asheville, NC 29702

Mr. Jim Bell
1492 Document Drive
Mandarin, FL 49709

Ms. Faye Mauney
15 Mockingbird Lane
Pinelog, TX 69007

Mr. George M. Lapmont
Bell Tires
2354 78th Avenue
Bellvue, WA 71356

Ms. Lois J. Yarmus
Kaymus & Yarmus
7293 Aurora Avenue
Midlothian, IL 72932

Dr. Jose S. deAngello
117 Third Street
Apache Junction, AZ 78273

Ms. Glenda Rider
1294 Skyline Trail
Denver, CO 82742

Ms. Kay B. Kusunoki
7531 Second Street
San Francisco, CA 92846

Figure 11-44   Final output of Project 2, mailing labels report

CREATING CUSTOMER LISTS

FileMaker is capable of producing many different types of layouts, and you have a wide range of formatting features to customize these layouts to fit your particular needs. When you create a new layout, FileMaker offers you four choices: standard, columnar, label, or blank.

Project 1 introduced you to the standard layout. This project will guide you through completing columnar and label layouts. You will learn to create customized reports from a blank layout in Project 3.

FileMaker's columnar reports give you the tools to create *ad hoc* reports quickly and easily. If you want a list of a few items from a file, you can create that list by creating a new columnar report and specifying the fields that should be in the report. FileMaker will create a layout showing those fields in the order you specified. With a little practice, this process takes only a few seconds to complete.

The first columnar report you will create lists the customers' names (last name and then first name) and their customer numbers. In Project 3, you will create a sales invoice file, and that file will look up information about the customer's name and address from the Customers file. The key field that connects these two files will be the customer number. When a customer buys auto parts, you will enter the customer number into the proper field on the invoice.

It is easy to print a report that shows the customers' names and numbers, and that report can be used when entering customer information into the Sales Invoices file. If you know the customer's name, you can look in the list and find his or her number. (Of course, you can use the Find command in FileMaker to find this number even faster.)

There will be times, however, when you will know a customer's number, but not his or her name. In this situation, you want to have a report that is printed in numerical order based on the CUSTOMER NUMBER field.

FileMaker can quickly sort a file based on any field you specify. In this project, you will sort the customer name and number list in two ways: alphabetically by name and numerically by customer number. The mailing labels will be sorted by Zip code.

A report can be printed in alphabetical order by customer name, in numerical order based on the customer number, in chronological order based on the date of sale, or even in ascending or descending order based on the amount of the sale. Depending on the circumstances, the information you already have available, and what you are trying to find, all of these formats can be very useful.

Layout Mode

FileMaker allows you to create and use several different layouts with each data file. A layout determines how the information contained in the selected records is presented on the screen or on a printout.

You can place text (for labelling fields or showing explanatory information), graphics (lines, rectangles, ovals, or images copied from other graphics programs), and the fields used by the file. Each of these three elements is treated as an object by FileMaker. You can move, resize, and delete graphics. Text and fields can be modified by changing their size, position, font, style, alignment, and formatting attributes.

Standard Layout

The view you have been using is the default layout that FileMaker created, using the fields you defined in the order in which they were defined. This lists the name of the field on the left and then each of the fields from top to bottom aligned immediately to the right of the field name (see Figure 11-45).

This is not always the best way to display your information, so FileMaker allows you to change the default layout and/or create new ones.

For example, you can make a field in the standard layout longer or shorter. You can change the font, size, style, and alignment of the text in the fields or in the explanatory labels to the left of the fields.

If you want a more customized layout, however, the creation of a different layout is better than modifying the standard layout, in most cases.

Let's give it a try. If you quit FileMaker since completing Project 1, you should restart. The easiest way to open FileMaker and the Customers file is to find the Customers file icon and double-click on it.

If you haven't quit FileMaker, you need to open the Customers file.

➠   Open the Customers file, if it is not already open.

⌘-L   ➠   Choose **Layout** from the Select menu.

This will show you the standard layout that was created for you when you defined the fields in Project 1 (see Figure 11-45).

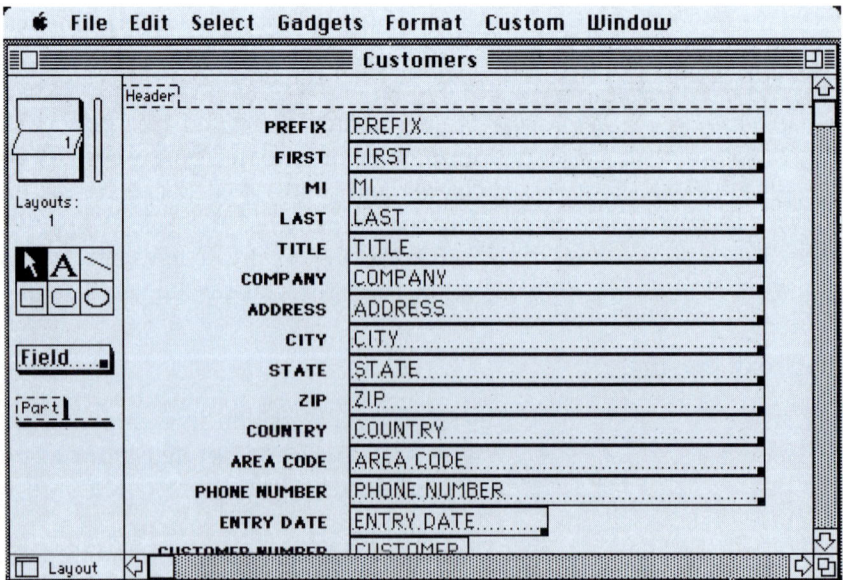

Figure 11-45   Default layout created by originally defining fields

In Project 1 all the fields were named using all uppercase characters. In this project, you will add three calculation fields, and they will be named using upper- and lowercase characters to help distinguish between them. FileMaker does not specify this style of naming fields, it is used in Project 2 only to help you differentiate between the fields you created in Project 1 and these you define here.

Adding a New Layout

Adding a new layout is a straightforward process in FileMaker. When Layout mode is chosen, the Edit menu changes. Command-N in Browse mode means create a new record. The same command in Layout mode means create a new layout.

Before you add a new layout to the Customers file, let's look at the tools available in Layout mode.

Palette Tools

FileMaker provides several tools that may be used to create new layouts. The icons representing these tools are shown in Figure 11-46, and the tools are then described individually.

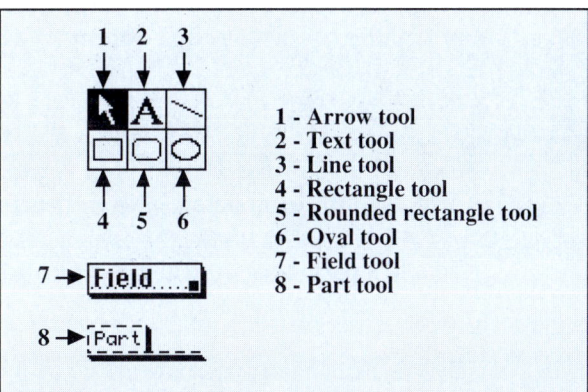

Figure 11-46   Tools used in Layout mode

 Arrow Tool - As you probably already know from using other Macintosh applications, the arrow tool lets you select, move, and reshape objects. The arrow tool also allows you to change the size of layout parts. This tool is the default tool.

 Text Tool - Clicking this tool somewhere on the layout anchors an insertion point where you can add text. If text already exists, you can edit that text by selecting parts of it and typing the replacement text.

 Line Tool - Move the mouse to where you want to anchor one end of a line, press the mouse button and hold it down, drag the line to where you want it, and then release the button to anchor the other end.

Rectangle Tool - Move the mouse to where you want one of the corners of the rectangle, press the mouse button and hold it down to anchor the first corner, then drag the outline to where you want the diagonally opposite corner. Release the mouse button to anchor the second corner and draw the rectangle.

Rounded Rectangle Tool - This works the same as the rectangle tool, except that the corners of the box will be rounded.

Oval Tool - As with the rectangle and rounded rectangle tools, select one corner, and then press the mouse button and drag to the diagonally opposite corner. This will define a rectangle, and the oval will then be drawn so that it is inset inside the rectangle you just defined.

 *Field Tool* - By clicking on the field tool and then dragging it onto the layout, you can add and position a field anywhere on the layout. FileMaker lets you choose from a list of all the fields, so you can designate which field you want. You can add new fields to a layout, add fields you previously removed, or even show the same field more than once on the same layout.

Once a field is placed, you may select it with the arrow tool and, by dragging the box on the lower right corner, you can resize the box larger or smaller to display the contents of the field as you want.

Part Tool - There are several parts to a FileMaker layout. The main ones are the header, body, and footer. You may also create title header, title footer, sub-summary, and grand summary parts. These parts will be discussed in more detail later in this project and the next one.

To add a part, click on the part tool and then drag the part to where you want it on the layout.

By selecting a part with the arrow tool, you can make the part longer or shorter. All parts extend completely across the layout horizontally.

These tools allow you to place fields wherever you want, to add text (which can be in any font or size available), and to use lines, ovals, and rectangles to group the different parts of the layout or to add graphic emphasis.

FileMaker also lets you import graphics from other programs (such as MacPaint and MacDraw) and use these graphics as the background for creating a new layout. You can draw a form in a graphics program, paste it into FileMaker, and then add the fields onto the drawing of the form. You can also use this capability to paste company logos and other graphic elements onto a layout.

Now that you are familiar with the tools available in Layout mode, let's create a new customer list report. This will be a columnar report that will list the customers' last names, first names, and customer numbers.

⌘-N ⇒ Choose **New Layout** from the Edit menu.

When you issue this command, FileMaker displays a dialog box asking for the type of new layout you want (see Figure 11-47).

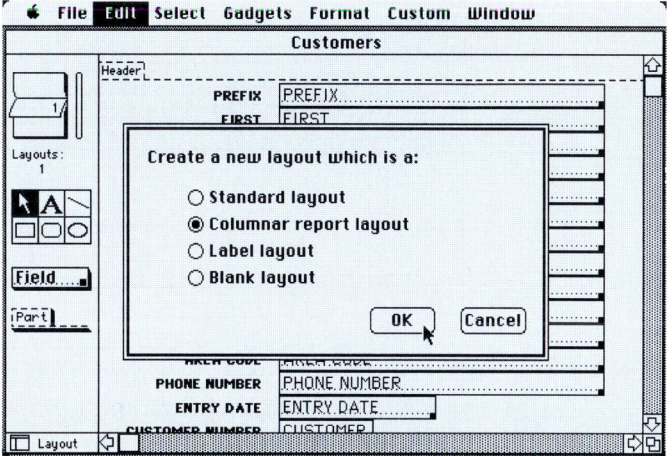

Figure 11-47   Dialog box for selecting type of new layout

⇒ Click **Columnar report layout**, and then click **OK**.

Columnar Layout

Now that you have told FileMaker that the new layout is a columnar report, it assumes that you want to display only a few of the fields instead of all of them. The next thing you see is a dialog box that will let you choose the fields you want listed in this layout.

In this case, you want to show the first name, last name, and customer number. Let's tell FileMaker to add the FIRST field to the report.

⇒ Click on **FIRST** in the scrolling field on the left.

This selects the first name field and activates the »Move» button. If you click the »**Move**» button, it tells FileMaker that you want the selected field to be the first field in the left column of the report.

⇒ This is what you want, so click »**Move**» (see Figure 11-48).

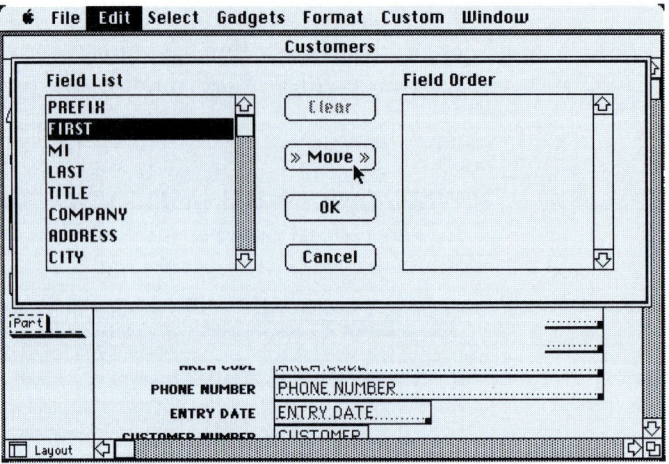

Figure 11-48   Moving the first name field into the report

Like most Macintosh commands, this is a process of selecting the object (first name field) and then specifying the action for the object (move it into the report). Many of these two-step commands have equivalent shortcut commands. When specifying a field to move into a report, you can double-click on the field you want, and it will be selected and moved into the field order list with one action.

➠ Double-click on **LAST** to move it into the field order list.

➠ Double-click on **CUSTOMER NUMBER** to move it into the field order list.

You have now specified the fields you want in this report, and the dialog box should contain these three fields in the order shown in Figure 11-49.

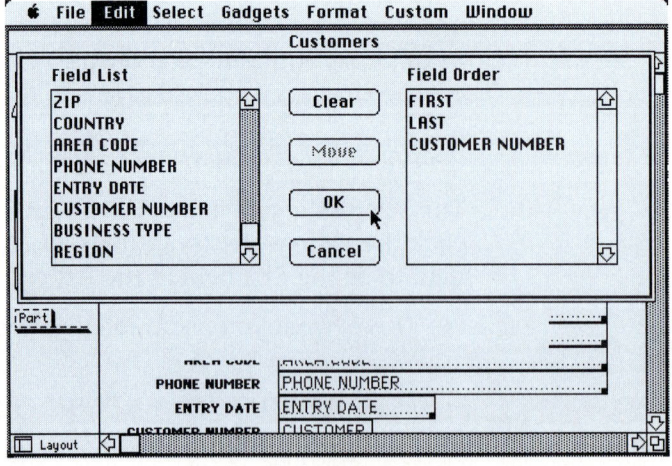

Figure 11-49   Specifying the three fields to show in this report

➠ When you have verified that the fields you have chosen are correct, click **OK**.

FileMaker now produces the column layout using the three fields you just chose (see Figure 11-50). Notice that the book has changed to show that there are now two layouts for this file.

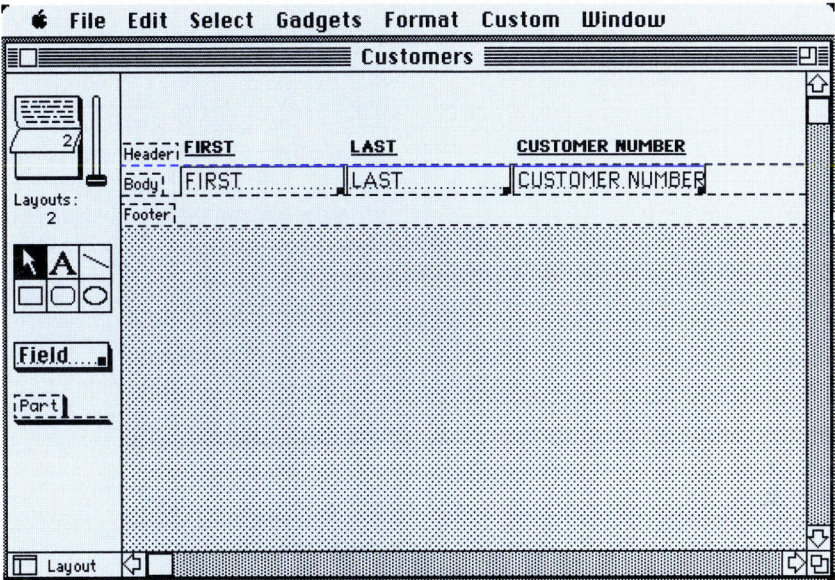

Figure 11-50   The layout for your customer list

As part of this process, FileMaker has selected the View as List option from the Gadgets menu. Let's look at the differences in how this layout works when View as List is not selected and then again when it is.

➠   Choose **View as List** from the Gadgets menu to deselect it.

⌘-B   ➠   Choose **Browse** from the Select menu.

When View as List is not selected, Browse will only show one record using the currently selected layout. Your customer list is not a list since you deselected this option (see Figure 11-51).

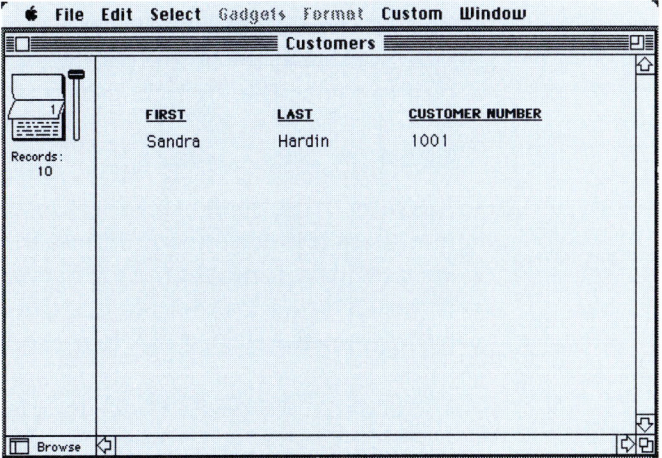

Figure 11-51   A columnar layout that is not a list

Since you really wanted this to be a list, let's go back to select View as List again. You can only choose commands from the Gadgets menu from within Layout mode.

⌘-L   ➡   Choose **Layout** from the Select menu.

      ➡   Choose **View as List** from the Gadgets menu.

Go back into Browse mode and compare the results.

⌘-B   ➡   Choose **Browse** from the Select menu.

You have now produced the customer list you wanted (see Figure 11-52).

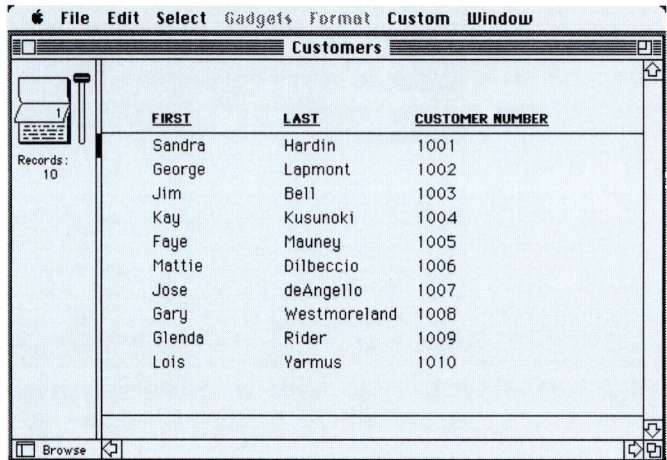

Figure 11-52   A columnar layout with View as List selected

This is a good time to save a copy of the file. When you save a copy of the file it also saves all the layouts that you have created.

Before you print the report, let's add page numbers. Because the value of information is directly related to how current it is, let's also add the date and time on the printout.

You only want these items to appear once on each page. You can put the page number at the bottom of the page in the footer, and the date and time can go at the top right corner of the page in the header.

Headers and Footers

A *header* is the margin at the top of the page where normal body information is not printed. Information placed in the header area of a layout will be printed at the top of every page and will appear at the top of the screen in Browse mode. You can delete the header from any layout by dragging the Header part to the top of the screen until it disappears.

The body area is printed once for every record. This is where the last name, first name, and customer number fields are located in this report (refer back to Figure 11-50).

A *footer* is the margin at the bottom of a page. Information placed in the footer is printed at the bottom of every page and is shown at the bottom of the screen in Browse mode. Like the header, the footer can be removed from a layout. To delete the footer, drag the Footer part up to the Body part until the Footer part disappears.

Two special parts, the title header and title footer, are used to replace the header and footer on just the first page.

You can use FileMaker to learn more about headers and footers and also about adding page numbers, the date, and the time to a layout. As you have already seen, FileMaker's Help file is valuable for learning to use the program. What can it tell you about layouts and page numbers?

Let's find out.

⌘-/   ➧   Choose **Help** from the Apple menu.

Now you can use one of the predefined scripts to find the layout information.

⌘-8   ➧   Choose **Arranging Information** from the Custom menu.

You are presented with the first of 15 records that are available for arranging information (see Figure 11-53).

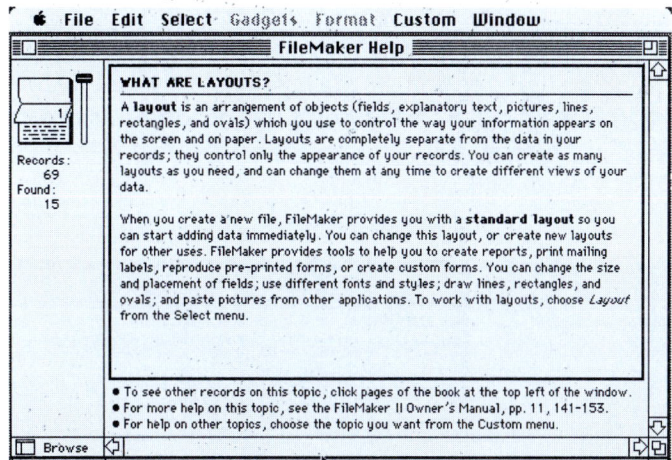

Figure 11-53   The first of 15 help records on layouts

It is worth your time and effort to at least skim the information in these 15 records. One in particular has the information you are looking for. You can have FileMaker find it for you.

⌘-F   ➧   Choose **Find** from the Select menu.

You are presented with the Find screen showing the three active fields in the Help file.

➧   Type **page number** in the top field (see Figure 11-54).

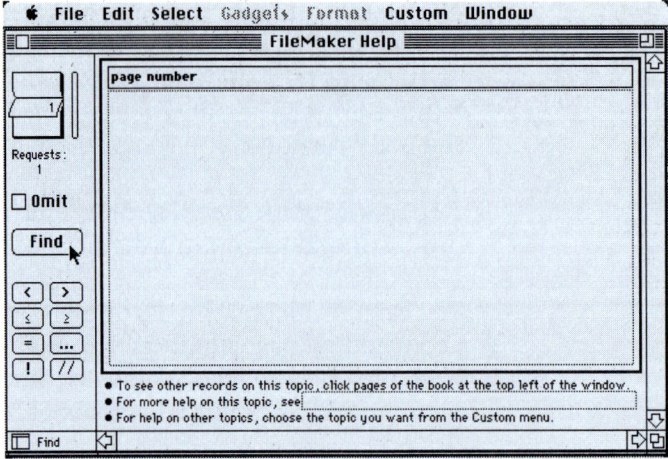

Figure 11-54   Finding help on page numbers

If this seems familiar to you, it may be because this is the example for using the Help file that was presented in the introductory part of this chapter.

If any of the records contain "page number" in the top field, FileMaker will quickly locate them. Note that capitalization is not important when you use Find to locate something in a file.

⇒   Click **Find.**

FileMaker now presents you with help on adding time, date, and page numbers to a layout (see Figure 11-55). It also mentions record numbers, but they won't be added to this report.

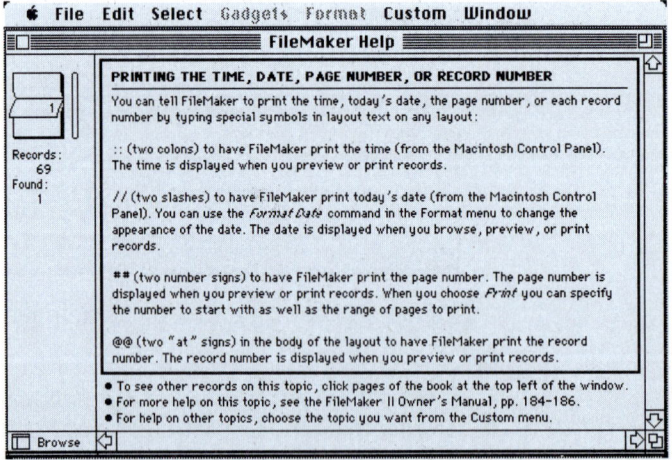

Figure 11-55   The help record for page numbers

Now that you know all about this subject, you can close the Help file and add these codes to your customer list layout.

⌘-W   ⇒   Close the Help file.

You will add the page number placeholder (##) in the footer area of the layout. To do this, you must be in Layout mode.

⌘-L ➥ Choose **Layout** from the Select menu.

You must use the text tool to add these placeholders.

➥ Click on the text tool in the tool palette.

➥ Click in the footer, under the last name field, and type **Page ##.**

➥ Now click in the header, at the top of the screen above the CUSTOMER NUMBER field, and type **//**. Type Return to go to the next line, and type **::** (see Figure 11-56).

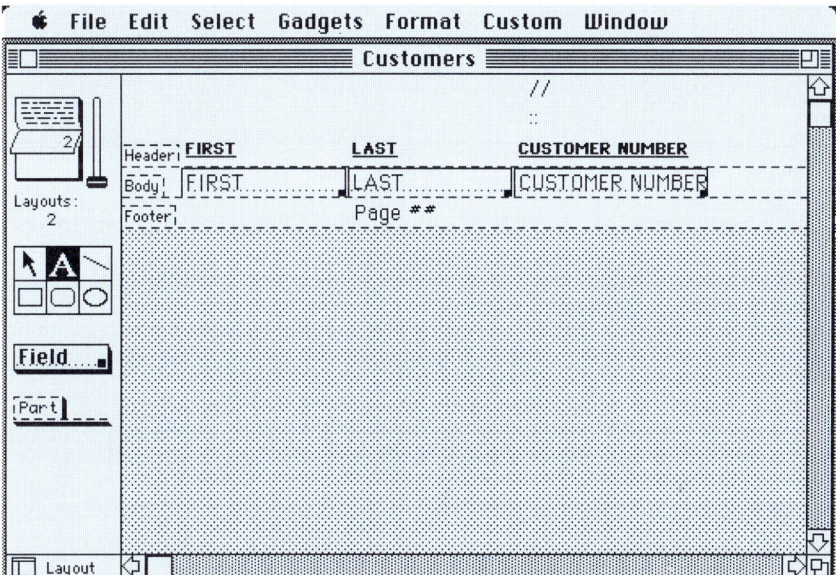

Figure 11-56   Adding text to the header and footer

⌘-B ➥ Choose **Browse** from the Select menu.

Notice that the date has replaced the first placeholder in the header section on the screen (see Figure 11-57).

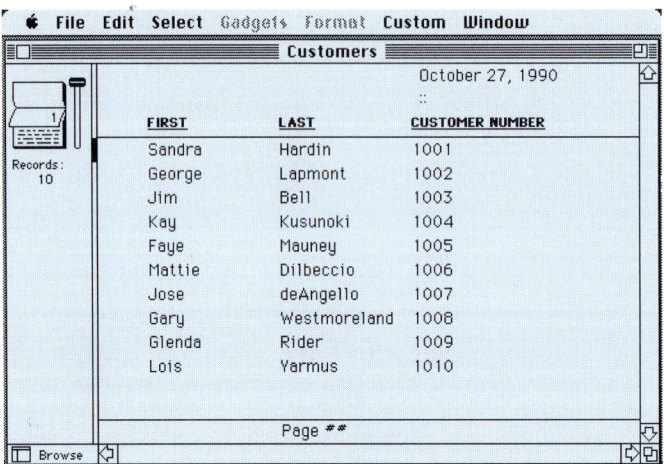

Figure 11-57 Browsing the report after modifying the header and footer

The page number and time placeholders, however, are just the way you entered them. These codes will be replaced with the actual page number and time when the report is previewed or printed. Let's preview the report and see.

Previewing a Report

Preview shows how the report will look when it is printed. There are two views: full size and reduced. Full size shows the information at a readable size, but, unless you have a large monitor, you can only see a portion of the page. The reduced view shows the entire page and how all the elements are placed, but it is too small for reading the information.

By switching between full size and reduced, you can see the details of what will be printed and also get an overview of the page as a whole.

⌘-U ➧   Choose **Preview** from the File menu.

You will see the top left corner of the report page. As you can see, the time is entered into the header (see Figure 11-58). If you were to scroll to the bottom of the page, you would find that the page number is showing in the footer.

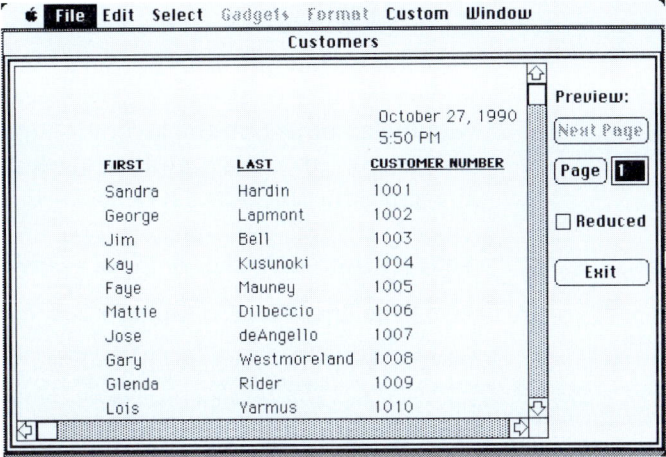

Figure 11-58   Previewing the customer list report

You can also choose to see the reduced view of the entire page.

➡ Click **Reduced**.

You are now presented with a reduced view of the page that shows the header, body, and footer information as it will appear on the page (see Figure 11-59).

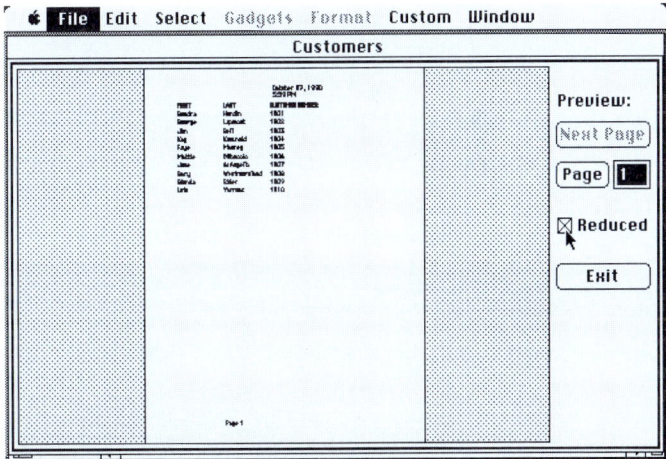

Figure 11-59   Reduced preview of the customer list

Notice that the report is not automatically centered on the page. Since this is an internal report (one that will not be shown outside the company) it is not a problem, but let's try moving the date and time to the upper right side of the page. Some reports that you might want to print at a later date might need to be centered to present a better appearance.

To modify the report's layout, you must exit from the preview and then change to Layout mode.

⇒ Click **Exit**.

⌘-L ⇒ Choose **Layout** from the Select menu.

Moving an object on the layout is a matter of selecting the arrow tool, clicking on an object, and, while holding down the mouse button, dragging the object to a new location.

Let's try moving the page number object.

⇒ If the arrow tool is not selected, click on it to select it.

⇒ Click on the page number object, and drag it to the left.

Don't be concerned about where to move it at this point. Notice that a horizontal dotted line extends from the object to the left and right when you move it (see Figure 11-60). This is an extension of the baseline of the text, and it helps you to align this text object with other text objects. If you drag the page number horizontally to the left, you will see that the baseline extension aligns exactly with the bottom of the page number placeholder (Page ##) that you originally entered in the footer.

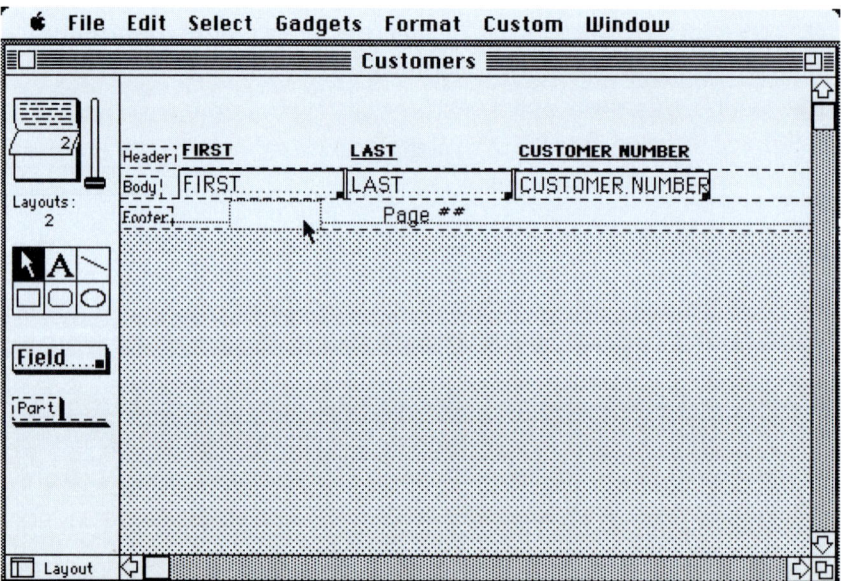

Figure 11-60   Dragging the page number object

⇒ Drag the page number object to the right, until its left edge aligns with the left edge of the CUSTOMER NUMBER field. Release the mouse button to place the page number.

You should be sure that the page number is entirely in the footer. If you later preview the page or print it and you see the page number overlaying the customer number in the body of the report, it means that you accidentally placed the page number object in the body part of the layout. This is an easy mistake to make. The solution is to move the page number object entirely into the footer.

You can adjust the date and time so that they print at the top right corner of the page.

➠ Click on the right scroll arrow until a vertical line appears.

This vertical line marks the right side of the page.

➠ Drag the date and time placeholders to the right until they are about an inch and a half from the right side of the page (see Figure 11-61).

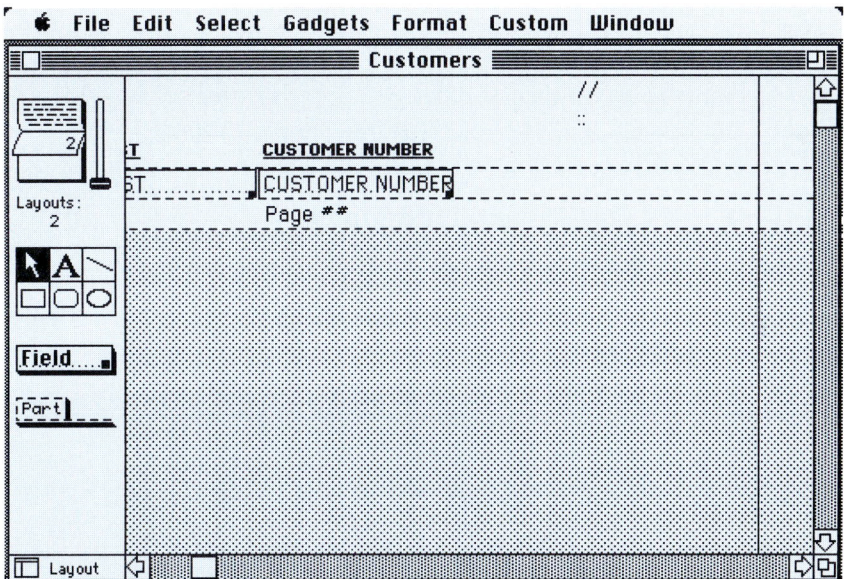

Figure 11-61   Layout after moving date and time placeholders

You can now preview the report to see if the date, time, and page number are where you want them.

⌘-U ⌘-L ➠ Alternating between the Preview and Layout modes, adjust the date, time, and page number placeholders until they are placed properly on the page.

Printing the Report

When you have the placeholders where you want them, it is time to print the report.

⌘-B ➠ Choose **Browse** from the Select menu.

⌘-P ➠ Choose **Print** from the File menu. Accept the defaults by clicking **OK**.

Compare the output of your report with the output shown in Figure 11-42.

This completes the customer list showing the customer numbers.

➠ This is a good time to save a copy of your Customers file.

Let's create another columnar report that lists the customer's first name, last name, area code, and phone number. It is created like the first report, by changing to Layout mode and telling FileMaker to create a new layout.

⌘-L ➡ Choose **Layout** from the Select menu.

⌘-N ➡ Choose **New Layout** from the Edit menu.

➡ When the dialog box appears, select **Columnar report layout**, and then click **OK.**

Next, FileMaker will present a dialog box that allows you to select the fields that will appear in the report.

➡ Double-click on **FIRST.**

➡ Continue by double-clicking on **LAST, AREA CODE,** and **PHONE NUMBER.**

You should now have four fields listed in the Field Order box on the right (see Figure 11-62).

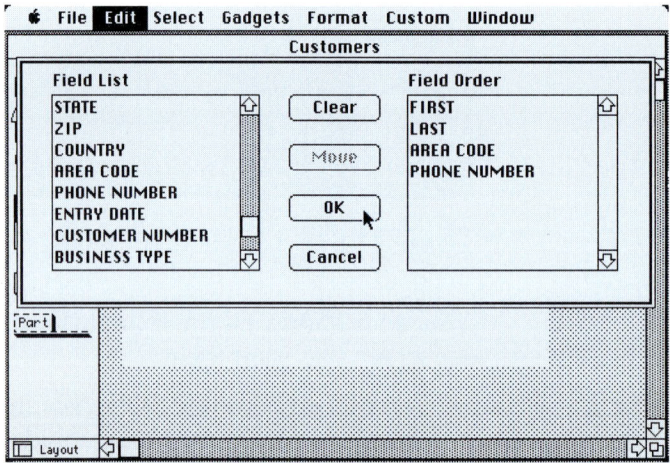

Figure 11-62   Selecting the fields for the second columnar report

➡ When you have verified that the fields are correct, click **OK.**

FileMaker quickly produces the layout you just specified. All you need to do to customize this report is to add the page number placeholder in the footer and the date and time placeholders in the header.

➡ Click on the text tool.

➡ Using the procedures you learned in the last few pages, add the date, time, and page number placeholders in their appropriate positions. You can align the left edge of the page number with the left edge of the AREA CODE field.

You should now have a layout that looks like the one shown in Figure 11-63.

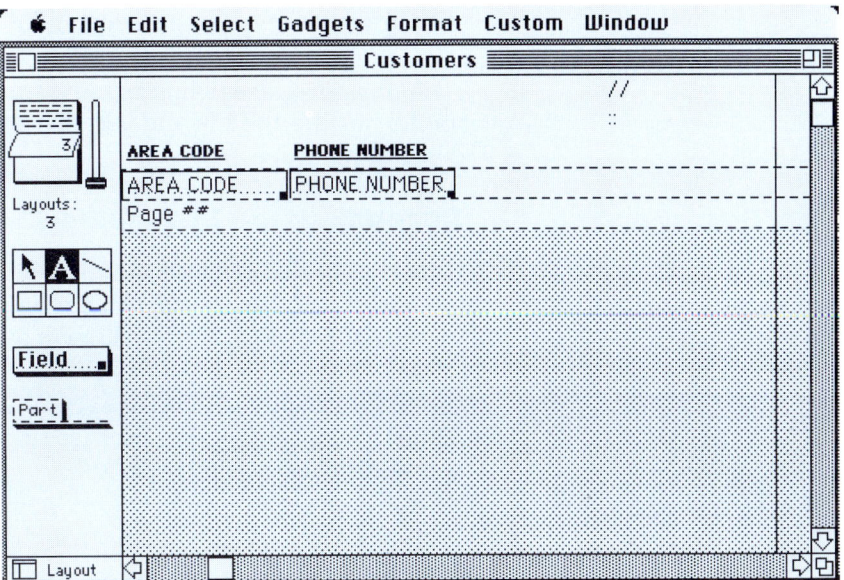

Figure 11-63 The layout for the customer phone number report

➡ Click on the arrow tool.

⌘-B ➡ Change to Browse mode.

The list appears on your screen showing the four fields you selected. Notice that the list is shown in the order in which you entered the records. Because the customer number was automatically entered as you added customers to the file, this results in the list being shown in customer number order.

This is not a convenient order for this report. Generally, when you want to find the customer's phone number you would look for the customer's name (just like using the phone book). Let's change the order of this report so that the names are listed in alphabetical order.

Sorting Records

FileMaker has the ability to sort information in every type of field except for picture fields and summary fields. Text fields can be sorted alphabetically, number fields can be sorted numerically, and date fields can be sorted chronologically.

The way the sort works depends on the type of field. If it is a calculation field, the result depends on the type of results you selected for the field.

Fortunately, FileMaker is smart enough to determine which sort is appropriate for each field. All you have to do is tell it which fields to use for the sort keys.

Sort Command

The Sort command is accessed by choosing **Sort** from the Select menu. If a file is already sorted, you can also choose the Unsort command, which returns the records to the order in which they were added to the file.

⌘-S ➧ Choose **Sort** from the Select menu.

FileMaker puts up a dialog box and waits for you to specify the fields to use for sorting the file and whether to sort each field in ascending or descending order.

Ascending and Descending

For a text field, *ascending* order means sorting the records of the file in order from A to Z based on one or more specified fields. *Descending* order sorts from Z to A and is also known as a reverse sort.

Number fields are sorted based on the numeric value of the specified field(s). Ascending order is the same as smallest to largest order. Descending order is the opposite.

Date fields are sorted based on the chronological order of the date. Ascending sorts arrange the records from earliest date to latest date. Using a descending date sort results in the most recent dates being listed first, followed by events that happened further in the past.

FileMaker uses a series of rectangles with each one getting larger to pictorially represent an ascending sort. A series of rectangles getting smaller represents a descending sort (see Figure 11-64).

▁▃▅ Ascending Order

▅▃▁ Descending Order

Figure 11-64 Symbols used to represent sort order

Sorting Levels

Files can be sorted by one or more fields. If only one *sort field* is specified then the records will be sorted based on the contents of that field only.

If more than one sort field is specified, the first field determines the most significant order of the file, and the second and subsequent fields are used only when duplicate entries exist in the earlier sorted fields.

For example, to sort a list of names in alphabetical order, you could specify the last name field for the sort. Then everyone would be sorted by last name. If two or more people had the same last name, they would not be sorted by first name, but would appear based on the order in which they were added to the file.

To be sure that the names are sorted properly—by last name first, and then by first name for people with the same last name—you must specify two sort fields. In this case, the last name field is the most important, so it is added to the Sort Order list first, and then the first name field is added to the list.

➧ Double-click on **LAST** in the Field List.

The default order for a field is ascending, as shown at the bottom of the dialog box. When you double-clicked on the last name field, it was moved to the Sort Order list, and the ascending order icon is shown next to it.

➧   Double-click on **FIRST** in the Field List.

In a similar manner, the first name field is added to the list, and the ascending order icon is displayed next to it as well (see Figure 11-65).

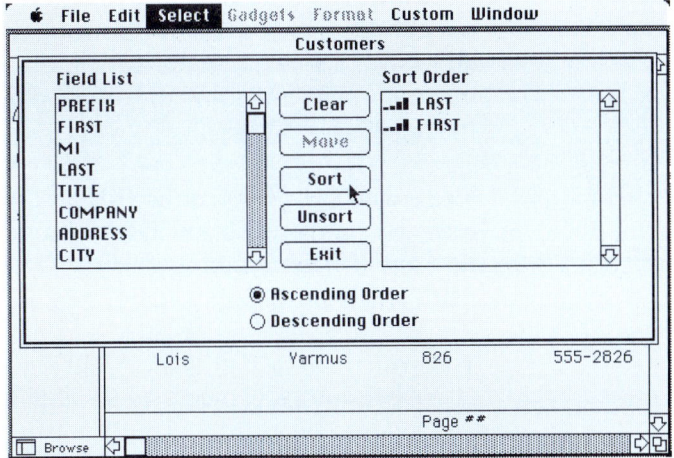

Figure 11-65   Choosing the sort order for the report

Now you are ready to sort the file.

➧   Click **Sort**.

Printing the Report

Change to Browse mode, and then print the report.

⌘-B   ➧   Choose **Browse** from the Select menu.

When you browse the file, you should see all the customers listed in alphabetical order.

⌘-P   ➧   Choose **Print** from the File menu. Accept the default values by clicking **OK**.

Compare the output of this report with the output of the report shown in Figure 11-43.

➧   This is a good time to save a copy of your file.

CREATING MAILING LABELS

Now that you have learned to create columnar lists and how to sort them into the order you want, it is time to create, sort, and print mailing labels for your customers.

Modifying the Customers File

Before you create the label format, it will make things easier if you add some new fields to the file.

Each label will have information on it that is stored in nine fields in the file: prefix, first name, middle initial, last name, company name, address, city, state, and Zip code.

Since there are only six lines of text available on the label, FileMaker will let you specify only six fields for automatic placement when you create the new label layout. Then you would have to resize the first four fields and move them up to the first line of the label. You would have to manually place and resize the other fields until you completed designing the labels.

There is an easy way around this problem that will also make Project 3 easier to complete. All you have to do is create new text calculation fields that *concatenate* (combine) the information from several fields into one field.

You will create a Full Name field that will concatenate the PREFIX, FIRST, MI, and LAST fields. Address2 will combine the CITY, STATE, and ZIP fields. The third field, Phone, will combine the AREA CODE (enclosed in parentheses) and the PHONE NUMBER.

Notice that the names for these new fields are composed of upper- and lowercase letters and that the fields already defined are all in uppercase. This technique is used to help you remember that these new fields are calculation fields that combine information already entered in the earlier fields. Again, this is just a matter of style and it is not required by FileMaker.

Let's add these three fields to the file.

Adding Text Calculation Fields

You will define these three fields in a moment. You can define a field from any mode by choosing the Define command, but since FileMaker automatically places new fields on whatever layout you are in before you choose **Define**, let's switch to Layout mode first.

⌘-L ➡ Choose **Layout** from the Select menu. Use the book or slide control handle to change to layout number 1.

Now you are ready to define the three text calculation fields.

➡ Choose **Define** from the Select menu.

⌘-C ➡ Click **Calculation** to indicate the type of this field, and then type its name, **Full Name**, into the field name box. Click **OK**.

When you click OK, FileMaker displays the formula dialog box for a calculation field. Figure 11-66 shows what your screen will look like when you enter the formula.

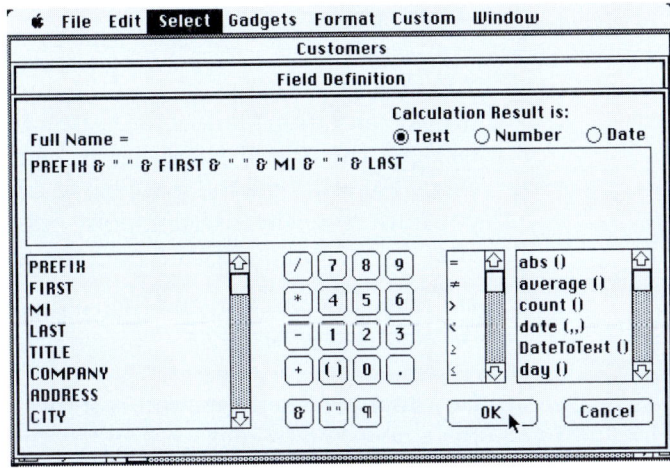

Figure 11-66   Calculation formula for the Full Name field

The calculation result should be designated as Text. Let's change how the result is displayed from the default Number.

➡ Click **Text** to designate the type of calculation result.

A formula that combines four existing fields has been entered next. In a text formula, each field or *string literal* (something inside quotation marks) must be combined using the concatenate operator, which is the ampersand (&) character in FileMaker.

The formula in Figure 11-66 says to display in the Full Name field a string of text composed of the prefix followed by a space, the first name, another space, the middle initial, another space, and the last name.

There are three scrolling lists and a keypad in this dialog box. The list on the left contains all the defined fields. The keypad is available so you can click on numbers, the decimal point, mathematical operators (+ – / *), parentheses, quotation marks, a paragraph marker (¶), and the string concatenation operator (&).

The next scrolling list contains a number of logical operators, and the last list contains built-in functions that you can use in creating formulas.

There are several ways to enter the formula in the formula box. You can choose to type the entire formula if you want, or you can use a combination of typing and clicking in the lists and on the keypad to enter the formula.

The first thing to do is enter the name of the first field.

➡ Click on **PREFIX** in the field names list.

This enters this word in the formula box. Now you need to tell FileMaker to concatenate a space character and another field to this one.

➡ Click on **&** in the keypad.

➟ Click on "" in the keypad.

You now have PREFIX & "" in the formula. There is no space between the two quotation marks, but the insertion point is automatically placed between them, and FileMaker is waiting for you to type something there. You will type the space bar to add one space character, and then you must move the insertion point outside the closing quote by clicking after the second quote or typing the right arrow key.

➟ Press the space bar, and then either click after the quote or press the right arrow key.

Now that the insertion point is at the end of the formula, you can type the ampersand or click on it in the keypad.

➟ Click on &.

Now you need to add the first name field.

➟ Click on **FIRST** in the field names list.

The calculation formula should now read PREFIX & " " & FIRST.

Refer to Figure 11-66 to see how the completed formula should look.

➟ Using the steps just described, add MI and LAST to the formula, separating each field with & " " &.

If you make any mistakes you can use Backspace or Delete to erase the part that is incorrect, and then continue entering the formula.

➟ When you have verified the accuracy of your formula, click **OK** to accept it.

You should now be back in the Field Definition dialog box, and the Full Name field should be visible at the bottom of the scrolling list. As much of the formula as fits is seen to the right of the field name.

Before you continue with the next two calculation fields, let's see what the Help file says about defining fields, calculation formulas, functions, and operators.

➟ Click **Exit** to leave the field definition dialog.

⌘ -/ ➟ Choose **Help** from the Apple menu, and then, when the opening screen appears, click **Open Help File**.

You want more information about defining fields, so...

⌘ -4 ➟ Choose **Defining Fields** from the Custom menu.

FileMaker will find a group of 16 records containing information on this topic. All 16 contain valuable information that you should look at.

Let's see what it says about text calculations.

➟ Scroll to record 5.

You will now see a screen like the one shown in Figure 11-67.

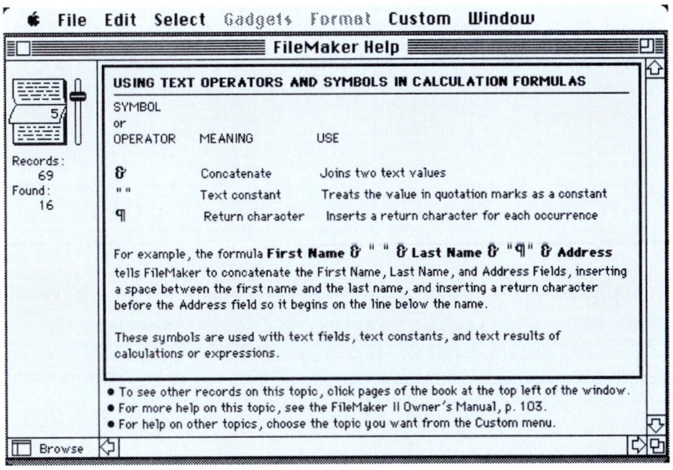

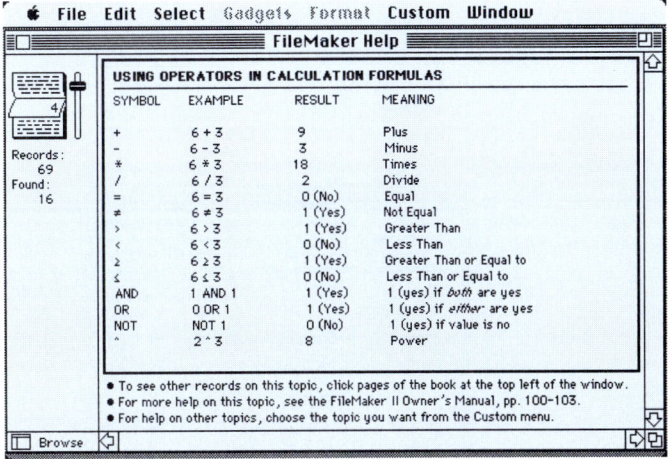

Figure 11-67   Text operators and symbols record in the Help file

This explains more about what you just did when you entered the formula in the Full Name field.

➧ Click the top page of the book to move to record 4.

A record appears that contains information about FileMaker's mathematical and logical operators that are used in calculating and comparing the contents of fields (see Figure 11-68).

Figure 11-68   Help for mathematical and logical operators

➧ Move to record 6.

Records 6 through 10 list information about FileMaker's built-in functions (see Figure 11-69).

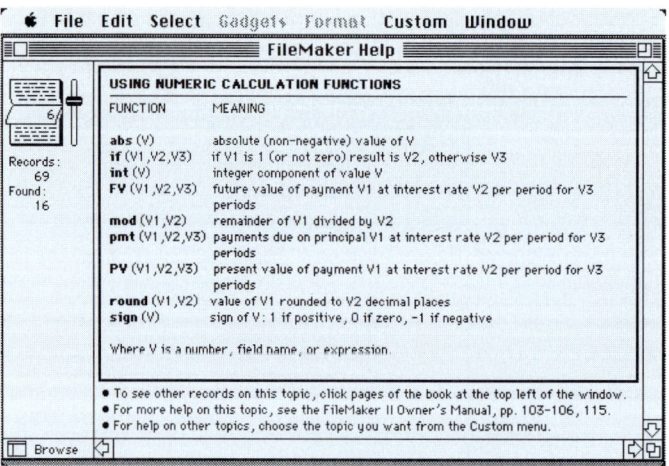

Figure 11-69   Help for built-in functions

➡ Skim the contents of records 6 through 10.

⌘-W ➡ When you have read the records, close the Help file.

Now that you know more about calculations, operators, and functions, let's define the Address2 and Phone fields.

➡ Choose **Layout** from the Select menu, go to layout number 1, and then choose **Define**.

The Address2 field's formula is similar to the one you entered in the Full Name field. This field concatenates the CITY, STATE, and ZIP fields. The only difference is a comma that should appear after the city.

After you enter the CITY field and the text concatenate operator into the formula box, you enter the quotation marks, with a comma and a space between them (see Figure 11-70).

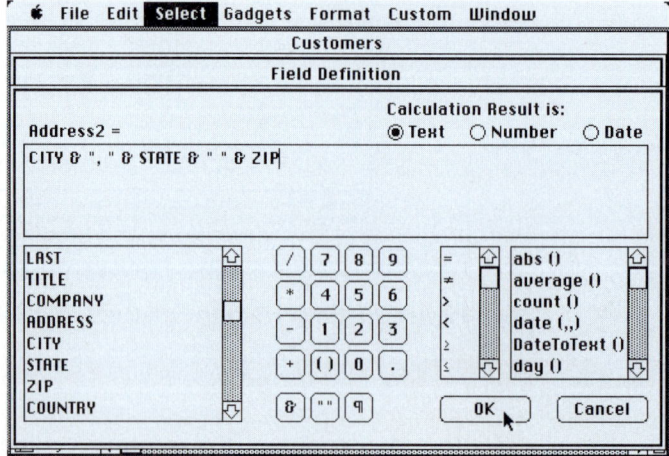

Figure 11-70   Calculation formula for the Address2 field

➠ Designate the calculation result by clicking **Text**.

➠ Enter this formula: **CITY & ", " & STATE & " " & ZIP**.

➠ When you have done this and verified the formula, click **OK**.

Now you are ready to define the Phone field.

This field will contain a text result and the following formula:

"(" & AREA CODE & ") " & PHONE NUMBER.

Notice that there is a space after the right parenthesis after the area code (see Figure 11-71).

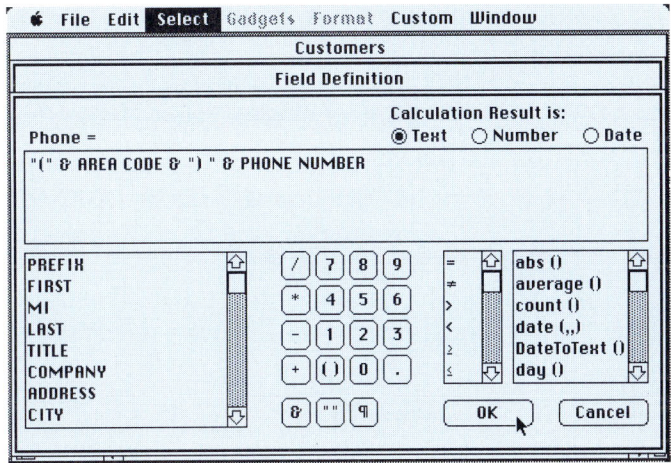

Figure 11-71   Calculation formula for the Phone field

➠ Enter the formula as shown, verify it for accuracy, and then click **OK** to accept it.

This returns you to the Field Definition dialog box. You don't want to define any more fields.

➠ Click **Exit**.

You can verify that the new fields work correctly by visually examining them in Browse mode.

⌘-B   ➠ Change to Browse mode.

➠ Scroll to the bottom of the record and look at the contents of the last three fields (see Figure 11-72).

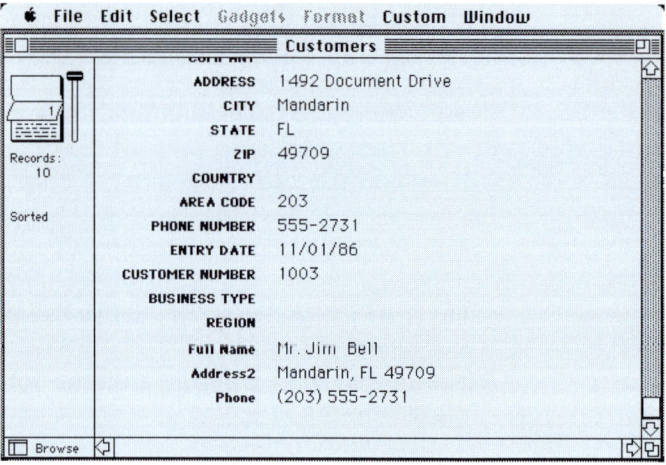

Figure 11-72   Browsing the records to check the new fields

➡ Click on the bottom page of the book to look at the next record, and
   continue checking all the records.

➡ If you have any mistakes, choose **Define** and redefine the fields that
   are not working correctly. To do this, click on the field's name, click
   Reformulate, and then re-enter the formula.

It is a good idea to print the field definitions report when you have
modified any of the fields in the file.

⌘-P ➡ Choose **Print** from the File menu, click **Field definitions**, and then
       click **OK**.

⌘-L ➡ When everything looks ok, choose **Layout** from the Select menu.

You have completed defining the new fields, so you are ready to create
the label layout.

Label Layout

Most labels are printed using one of two formats: 1-up or 3-up. These are
terms that describe how many labels are on each row. A *1-up* format has
only one label on each row, and *3-ups* have three on a row.

Other formats are available, but these are the most popular.

Label Dimensions

A standard letter-size sheet of paper is 8.5 inches wide and 11 inches tall.
Depending on the printer you are using, you can use more or less of the
page. An ImageWriter prints 8 inches horizontally, and a LaserWriter
prints a little less.

Mailing labels are made by a number of companies and are available for
continuous feed through a dot-matrix printer and on single sheets for
laser printers.

Most mailing labels are about 1 inch tall. Depending on the printer you have and the labels you buy, the labels may be 2.5, 3, or 3.5 inches wide. Since every printer will print 3-up labels that are 1 inch high and 2.5 inches wide, this is the format you will use for your labels. It is also the default size that FileMaker suggests.

This label size results in printing 33 labels per page (3 columns by 11 rows). Some laser printer labels are designed with a half-height label at the top and bottom, which results in 10 rows of usable labels (and 30 labels per page).

When you choose a label format of 1 inch high and 2.5 inches wide, FileMaker automatically sizes the text so that you can print up to six lines of text on each label.

You can design formats that will print on both the 33-labels-per-page format and the format that prints 30 labels per page. The vertical placement of the first row of labels can be adjusted by moving the Header part of the label layout up or down until the information is printed exactly on the labels.

Creating the Label Layout

Creating a new label layout is a quick and easy process.

⌘-N   ➟   Choose **New Layout** from the Edit menu, click **Label Layout** in the dialog box that appears, and then click **OK**.

A dialog box will appear asking for the number of labels you want across the page. The default is 3. The label size default is 2.5 inches wide and 1 inch tall.

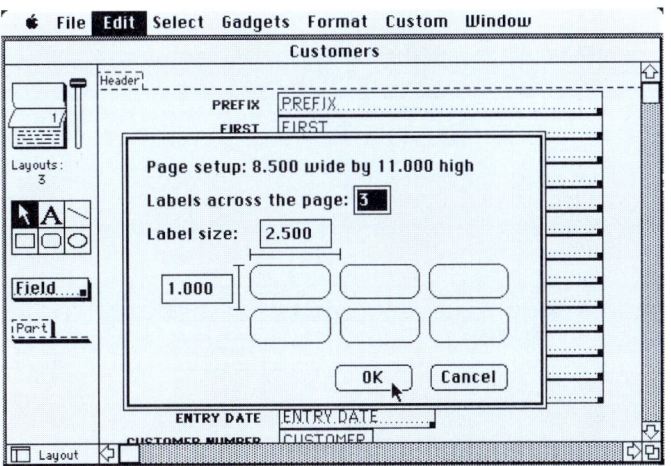

Figure 11-73   Defining the number of labels across and their size

➟   This is the format you want, so click **OK**.

Now you can select the fields that will appear in this layout: Full Name, COMPANY, ADDRESS, and Address2.

➡ Double-click on the appropriate fields, then click **OK** (see Figure 11-74).

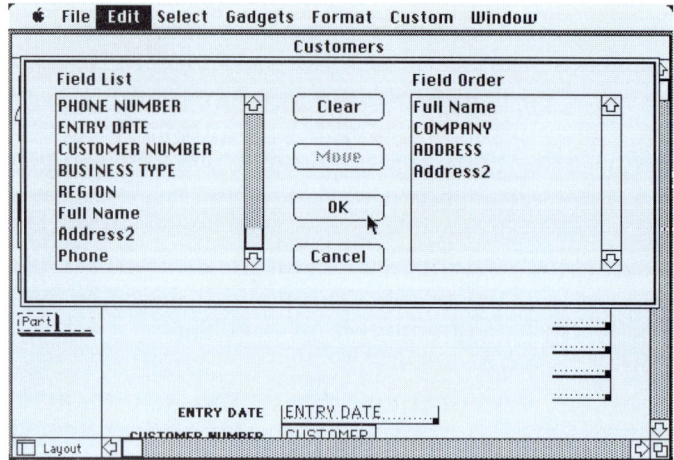

Figure 11-74   Selecting the fields to appear in the layout

FileMaker will then create a new label layout for you, as shown in Figure 11-75.

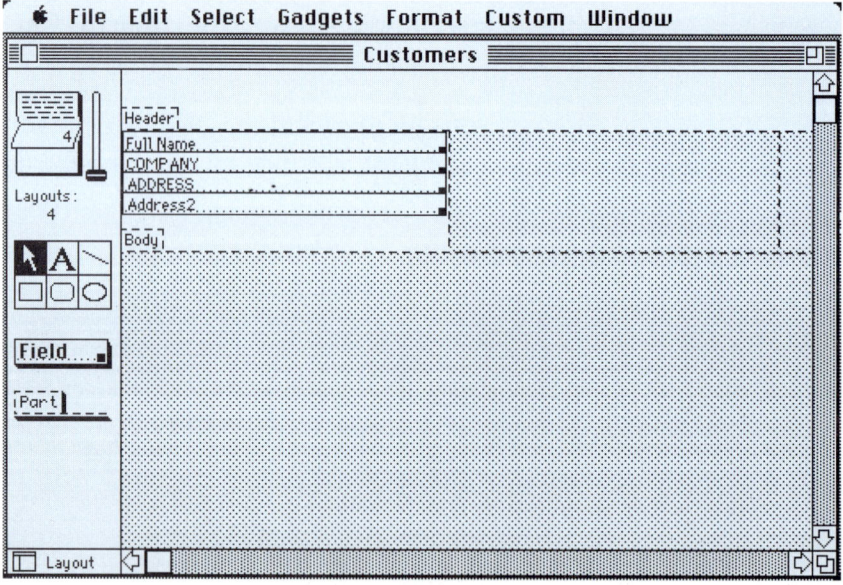

Figure 11-75   The new mailing label layout

Notice that the four lines of text are crowded against the top edge of the label. Let's center them vertically by selecting all four fields and dragging them down one line.

You already learned how to move a page number object left and right. Moving a field up and down works the same way. In fact, it will be easy to move these fields, because FileMaker has made each of the fields $\frac{1}{6}$ inch high and constrains their movement using an invisible grid with the same measurements. If you click on a field and drag it down, it will jump down to the next line.

You can move each of the fields individually or select all four fields and move them as a group. To select all four fields, click on one to select it, and then Shift-click on each of the other fields to add it to the selection.

Another way to select all four fields is to move the pointer above the fields, press and hold the mouse button down, drag the mouse diagonally down and to the side to create the dotted outline of a selection rectangle, and, when the rectangle touches all four fields, release the mouse button to select the fields (see Figure 11-76).

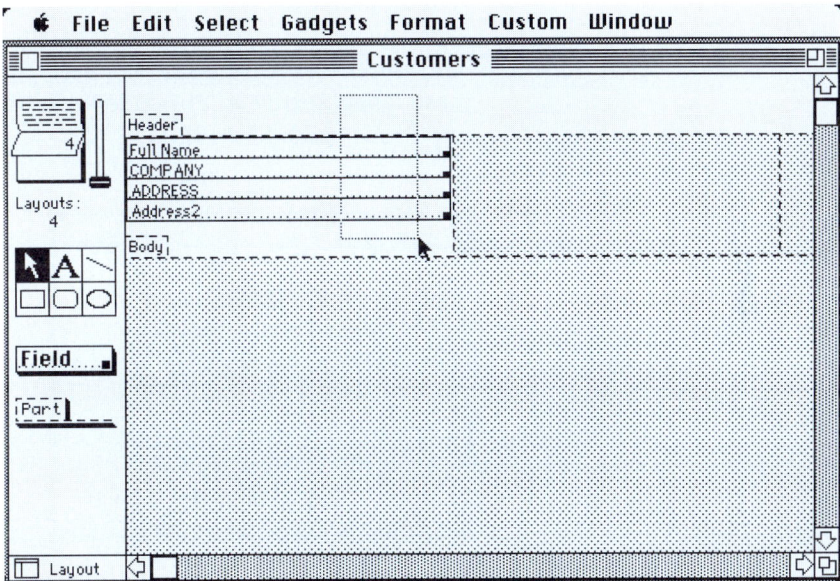

Figure 11-76   Selecting four fields with the selection rectangle

➠ Using either method, select the four fields and move them down one line so there is a blank line at the top and one at the bottom of the label.

Gadgets

You are nearly done with this layout. You are probably not aware, however, that FileMaker selected several options from the Gadgets menu when it created this layout for you.

Press the mouse button on the Gadgets menu title, and you will see that three options are checked to show that they are active (see Figure 11-77).

Figure 11-77   FileMaker has selected three options.

The invisible grid has been discussed (since it is selected the fields will jump one line when you move them down).

The other two options, Column Setup and Slide Objects, need some explanation.

In the Column Options dialog box, FileMaker has already selected three columns of labels and has specified the order to be across a row and then down to the first column in the next row (see Figure 11-78).

When you use these mailing labels, you would start at the top of the first page and remove the top left label, then you would remove the center one, and then the top right one before going to the next row. If you had these labels sorted in Zip code order, this printing order would be an important consideration.

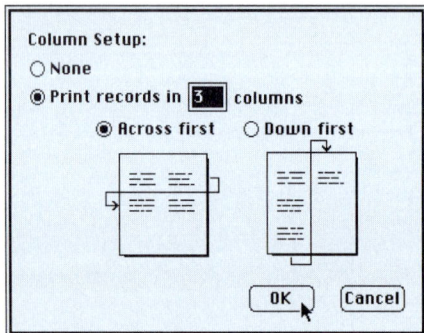

Figure 11-78   Column Setup options

Sliding Objects

Slide Objects is a little more complicated than Column Setup.

The Slide Objects dialog box is shown in Figure 11-79. It contains three options.

Figure 11-79   Slide Objects options

Sliding objects left is used when you want punctuation to closely follow the end of text in a preceding field or when another field follows on the same line. In this layout, you have already taken care of this potential problem by defining the Address2 field, which combines the CITY, STATE, and ZIP fields into one field.

Sliding objects up is used when a field is empty and you don't want a blank line to print on the report. In this mailing label layout, the COMPANY field is on the second line. Some customers represent a company and will have information entered in this field, and some don't represent a company and the field is empty. By telling FileMaker to slide objects up, you won't end up with blank second lines on the labels. Don't be surprised when you see blank company lines when you browse the layout. Sliding objects only applies to previewing and printing the report.

Sliding parts up is used to remove empty space when an object has been slid up. You do not want this checked on this layout, because all of the labels are 1 inch tall. The parts must not slide up in this case.

You can look at the label report by going into the Browse mode.

⌘-B ➠ Choose **Browse** from the Select menu.

You will now see the label for Mr. Bell. Notice that the labels are presented in sorted order, because they were sorted alphabetically when you created the layout.

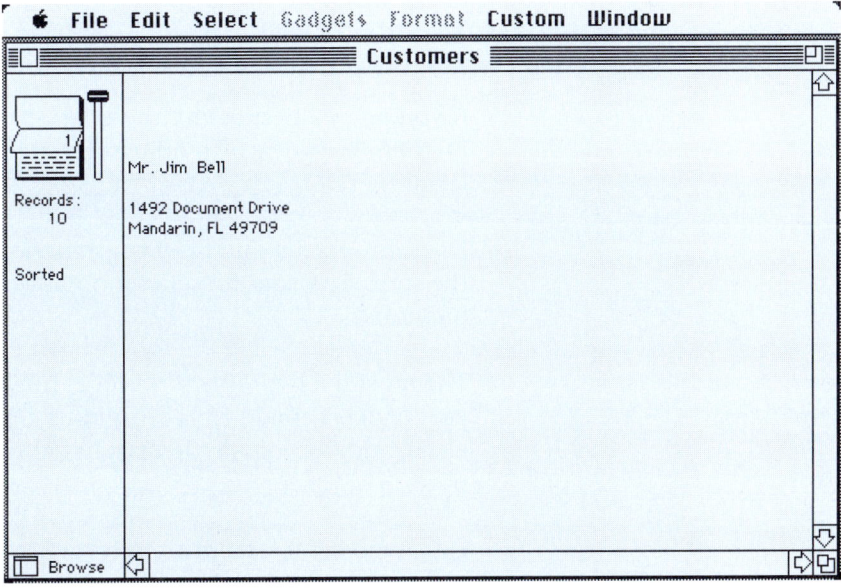

Figure 11-80 Browsing the mailing labels

You can see what the labels will look like when they are printed by previewing the report.

⌘-U ⇒ Choose **Preview** from the File menu. When the preview comes onto the screen, click the right scroll arrow so you can see that some records have three lines and others have four lines.

Figure 11-81 shows that the slide objects up option is working correctly.

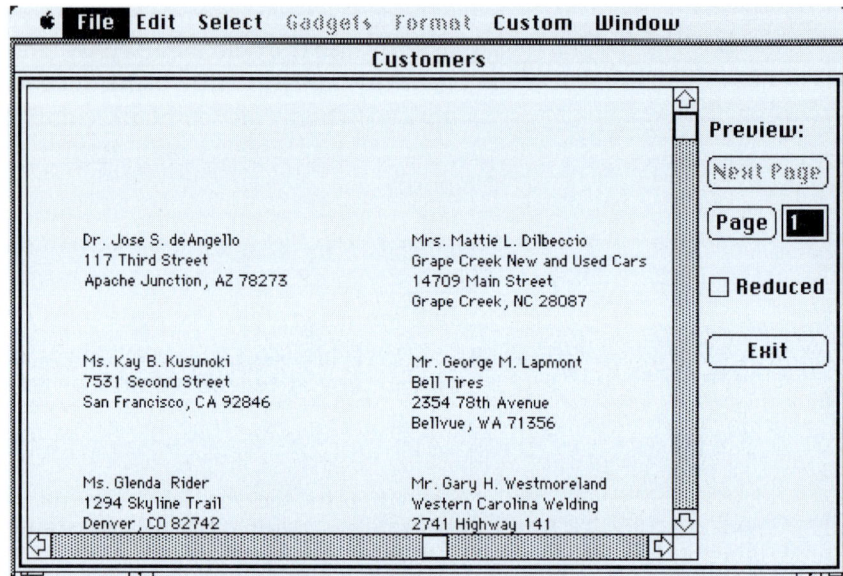

Figure 11-81   Previewing the mailing labels

Aligning Labels on a Page

If you are really printing these labels on pre-cut, gummed labels, you might have to do a little adjusting to be sure the text fits correctly on the labels.

Different printer and label combinations make it impossible to give all the steps involved for all combinations, but a general method can be presented.

The most likely problem involves how the labels are formatted on the page. Labels made for continuous feed through dot-matrix printers usually do not have a top margin—the first label starts at the top of the page.

Labels made for laser printers sometimes have a half-inch margin at the top and bottom of the page, because some laser printers cannot print on the top and bottom labels of a 33-labels-per-page format. These labels have a half label at the top and the bottom, resulting in 30 full labels on the page.

Adjusting the vertical placement of the labels involves making the header in the layout shorter or taller. This can be done by clicking on the Header part and dragging it up or down. In fact, if you need to, you can remove the header entirely, by dragging the Header part up to the top of the screen and releasing the mouse button.

If you print labels on both dot-matrix and laser printers, you can duplicate the layout you just created and adjust one version for the dot-matrix printer and the other for the laser printer.

⌘-B   ➠   Exit the preview, and go back to Browse mode.

Sorting Customers by Zip Code

The Customers file is presently sorted alphabetically, but for mailing labels you should sort by Zip code. If you mail enough letters, you can get a discount from the post office by sorting the letters into Zip code order.

⌘-S   ➠   Choose **Sort** from the Select menu.

➠   Specify the sort order by double-clicking on **ZIP** (see Figure 11-82).

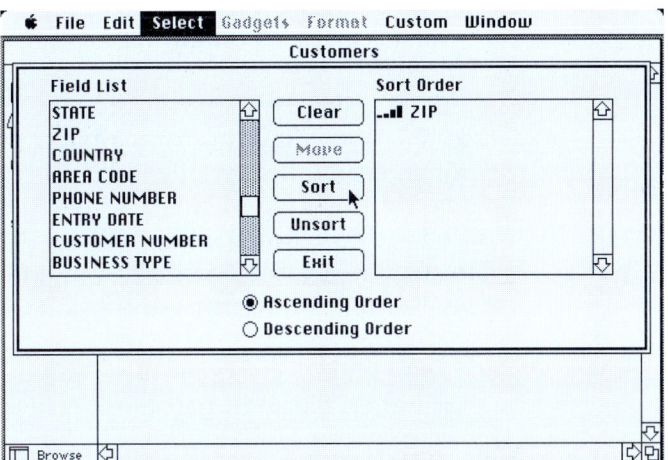

Figure 11-82   Specifying a Zip code sort order

➠   When you have done this, sort the file by clicking **Sort**.

Print Mailing Labels

You have completed creating the mailing labels, and now all that is left is to print them.

⌘-P ➠ Choose **Print** from the File menu, and accept the defaults by clicking **OK**.

Compare the mailing labels you printed with the output shown in Figure 11-44.

➠ Don't forget to save a copy of the Customers file.

This completes Project 2. You have learned a lot about creating reports using the preset formats available in FileMaker. Project 3 will lead you through creating a new file and a custom layout using the blank layout option.

In Project 1 you created a Customers file, and you produced reports from that file in Project 2. For Project 3 you will also use the Inventory file, which is included on the *Macintosh Journey Projects* disk.

In this project, you will create a new Sales Invoices file. You will create a new layout starting from a blank one, and you will learn how to interconnect this new file to the Customers and Inventory files.

You will learn how to place fields on the layout using the field tool, how to add graphics objects created in other applications, and how to add lines and boxes to enhance the appearance of a layout.

You will use a customer number field to link to information in the Customers file and a part number field to link to the Inventory file.

You will create fields that can look up information in other files. For example, the Name field can look up the customer number in the Customers file and copy the customer's name into the Sales Invoices file.

In completing this project, you will learn to use many of the tools, commands, and gadgets available in FileMaker. You will also learn how to format the information presented in a field.

INVOICE

1417 South Jonquil St.
Smyrna, GA 30829
(404) 555-7283

Fax: (404) 555-6284

INVOICE NUMBER
90005

CUST NO 1006
NAME Mrs. Mattie L. Dilbeccio
ADDRESS 14709 Main Street
Grape Creek, NC 28087

SALES DATE
Oct 29, 1990

PART NO	QTY	DESCRIPTION	UNIT COST	EXT. COST
1013	4	HEAD GASKET	$15.87	$63.48
1007	12	FLOOR MATS	$35.68	$428.16
1001	48	WIPER BLADES	$8.53	$409.44
1008	2	KEY LOCK	$36.50	$73.00
1010	4	RADIATOR CAP	$8.95	$35.80
1002	5	WIPER MOTOR	$36.95	$184.75

75   ITEM COUNT

SUB TOTAL $1,194.63
SALES TAX $65.70
SHIPPING COST $56.25

GRAND TOTAL $1,316.58

Figure 11-83 Final output of Project 3

BACKING UP CUSTOMERS AND INVENTORY FILES

If you were working in a real business and you were using FileMaker to manage the business's information, it would be vitally important that you make regular backups of the information in the files.

This does not involve just saving a copy of a file periodically. Making a *backup* implies that the copy is on a different disk. To protect yourself as much as possible, you should keep two or three generations of backups, and at least one copy should be stored in a different building. More than one business has been seriously hurt when someone broke into the building and stole their computer(s). The really bad part of the story was when the thieves stole the backups of all the data, because the backups were stored with the computers.

Theft, fire, or other catastrophic damage to your computer system, when it is used to manage all of the information for a business, can be a disaster. This damage can be lessened by getting into the habit of making daily backups of the information stored on the computer and storing at least one copy off site.

CREATING SALES INVOICES

If you quit FileMaker after completing Project 2, you need to restart it.

➡ Find the FileMaker icon and double-click on it to start.

➡ When the Open File dialog box appears, click **New** to create a new file.

➡ When the next dialog box appears, name the file Sales Invoices and then click **New** and save it onto your data disk.

Defining Field Types

You are once again presented with the Field Definition dialog box. You will define 16 fields for this file.

Number Fields

The first four fields you will define are number fields. They will be used to hold the invoice number, customer number, part number, and quantity ordered.

⌘-N ➡ Click **Number** to choose the type of field.

➡ Name the field Invoice Number, and then click **OK**.

You will now select the entry options for this field.

➡ Click on the field to select it, and then click **Entry Options**.

➡ Click **A new serial number:** and type **90001** into the box.

This number represents the invoices for the year 1990, starting with invoice number 001. This is a hint for creating invoice numbers. This file will have invoices for years other than 1990.

You want each invoice to have a unique number, so you need to tell FileMaker.

➠ Click **Unique value only**.

The Entry Options dialog box should look like the one shown in Figure 11-84.

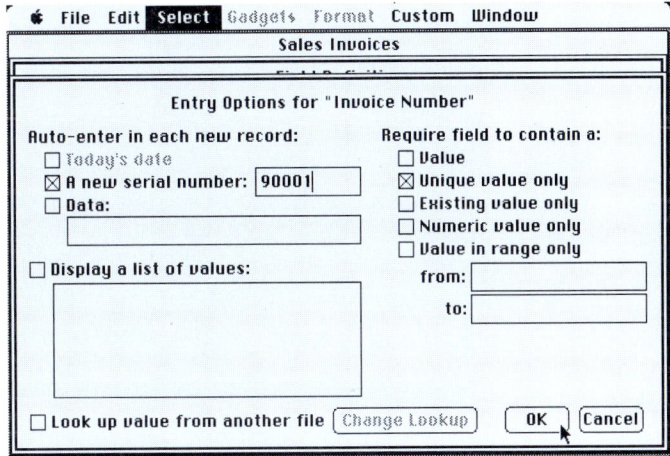

Figure 11-84 Entry options for Invoice Number field

➠ Click **OK** to accept the options.

The next field will hold the customer number.

➠ Name the new field Customer Number, and click **OK**.

Create another field to hold the part number.

➠ Name the next field Part Number, and click **OK**.

You must be able to store the quantity of each part that a customer wants to buy. This field will be named Qty, which is an abbreviation for quantity.

➠ Name the next field Qty, and click **OK**.

This completes defining the number fields.

Date Fields

There is one date field for this file: Sales Date.

You could define this field as an auto-enter field and have FileMaker enter the current date whenever the record is added. In this case, that option has not been chosen. If you accept orders over several days and then process them all on one day, you may elect to enter the date they were received as the sales date. If you always want the current date to appear on the invoice, you can select the entry option.

⌘-D   ➠ Click **Date** to choose the type of field.

➠ Name the date field Sales Date, and click **OK**.

You have now defined the first five fields, and the Field Definition dialog box should look like the one shown in Figure 11-85.

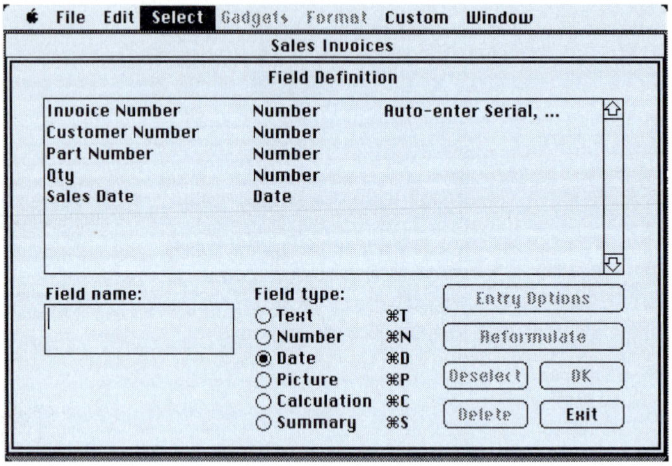

Figure 11-85   First five field definitions

Lookup Fields

The next five fields will be defined so they can look up information in the Customers file or the Inventory file.

You will use the Customer Number field to serve as a link to the Customers file, and the Part Number field will link to the Inventory file. Fields used for this purpose are known as *key fields* or *lookup fields*.

The first four of these lookup fields will store text, and the last one will store a number.

⌘-T   ⟹   Click **Text** to choose the type of field.

⟹   Name the new text field Name, and then click **OK**.

⟹   Select the field in the list, and then click **Entry Options**.

⟹   At the bottom of the Entry Options dialog box, click **Look up value from another file**, and then click **OK**.

You are presented with a standard open file dialog box.

⟹   Double-click on **Customers** to link to that file.

The Customers file is read from the disk, and in a few seconds another dialog box appears that contains three scrolling lists.

The top left corner of this dialog box shows the name of the field that will receive the value looked up in the Customers file. The top right list shows all the field names defined in the Customers file and allows you to select which one to copy into the field you are currently defining.

There are two scrolling lists in the middle of the dialog box. These lists allow you to select the key field in each file.

In this case, you want to copy the Full Name from the Customers file into this new Name field. You only want to do this when the Customer Number field in the Sales Invoices file matches a value stored in the CUSTOMER NUMBER field in the Customers file.

➦ Click on **Full Name** in the "from 'Customers':" list.

➦ In the "When what is typed in:" list, click on **Customer Number**.

➦ In the "matches a value in:" list, click on **CUSTOMER NUMBER**.

The dialog box should appear like the one shown in Figure 11-86.

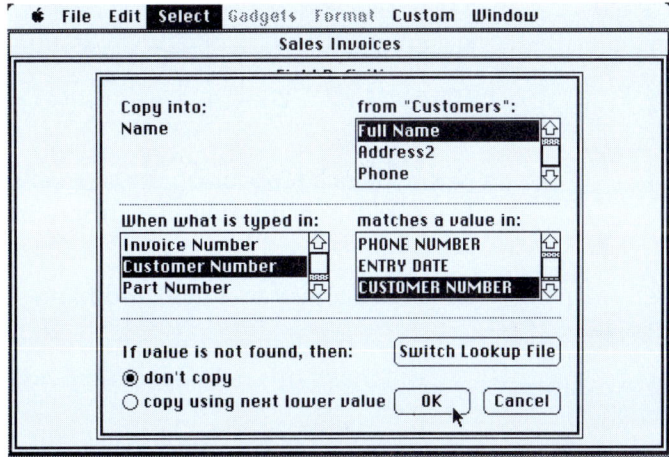

Figure 11-86   Dialog box for looking up Full Name

➦ If your dialog box matches the one shown in Figure 11-86, click **OK** to accept the link.

Now you can use the same procedure to look up the address of the customer in the Customers file.

➦ Create a new text field and name it Address. Click **OK**.

➦ In the Entry Options dialog box for this new field, click **Look up value from another file**. Click **OK**.

When you click **OK** this time, you will not see the open file dialog box because FileMaker expects you to continue looking up values in the Customers file. You can change the lookup file whenever you need to.

FileMaker remembers that you are using the Customer Number field in the Sales Invoices file to link to the CUSTOMER NUMBER field in the Customers file. All you need to specify this time is the name of the field in the Customers file that contains the address.

➦ Scroll to ADDRESS and click on it in the "from 'Customers':" list, and then click **OK** (see Figure 11-87).

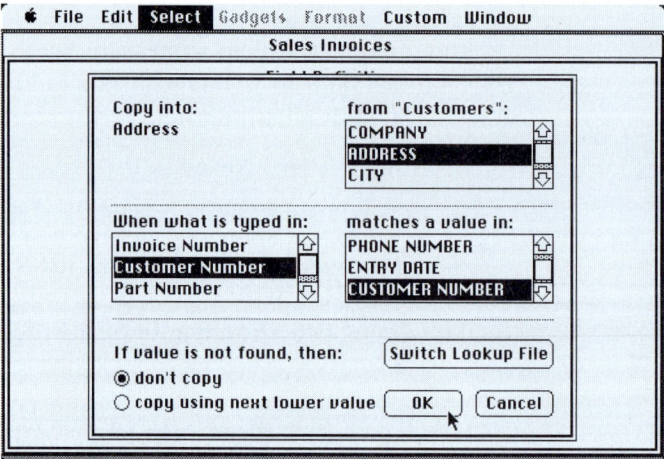

Figure 11-87   Looking up the customer's address

Next, you need to look up the city, state, and Zip code for the customer. You could use three fields for this in this file, but let's take advantage of the Address2 field you created in the Customers file in Project 2.

➧   Create a new text field and name it Address2. Then click **OK.**

➧   Select the Address2 field in the list, and then click **Entry Options** and make this field a lookup field.

➧   Tell FileMaker to copy the Address2 field from the Customers file into the Address2 field in the Sales Invoices file. Click **OK.**

When you were creating the number fields for the Sales Invoices file, you created a field named Part Number. Let's use that as a key field to look up the description and unit cost of a part in the Inventory file.

➧   Create a text field named Description, accept it, make it a lookup field in the entry options, and click **OK.**

This time you want to look up values in the Inventory file instead of the Customers file.

➧   Click **Switch Lookup File**, and then when the open file dialog box appears, double-click on **Inventory.**

In the lookup dialog box, the top right list says "from 'Inventory':" now.

You will link the Inventory file to the Sales Invoices file using the Part Number field in both files.

➧   Click on **Description** in the "from 'Inventory':" list.

➧   Click on **Part Number** in both middle lists.

Your dialog box should look like the one shown in Figure 11-88.

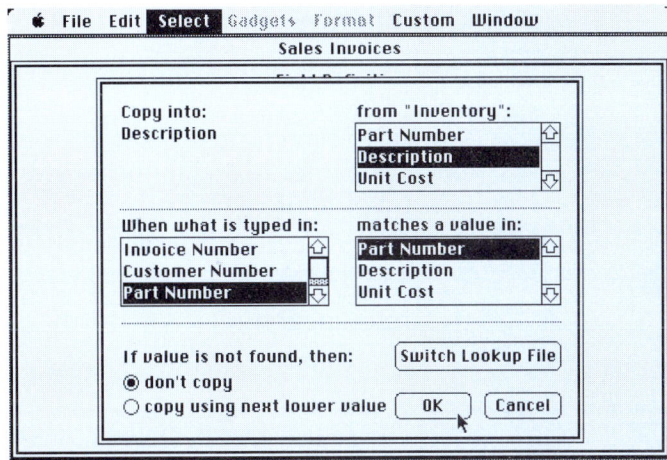

Figure 11-88   Settings to look up Description in the Inventory file

➠   If everything matches, click **OK**.

The last lookup field will store a number. The unit cost, or cost of one part, is stored in the Inventory file. You need to know the cost of one item so you can multiply it by the quantity ordered by the customer to determine the extended cost for that item.

⌘-N   ➠   Click **Number** to choose the type of field.

➠   Name the new field Unit Cost, and make it a lookup field.

The part number still links the Inventory and Sales Invoices files, so tell FileMaker to copy the value in Unit Cost in the Inventory file into the Unit Cost field in Sales Invoices.

➠   Click on **Unit Cost** in the "from 'Inventory':" list.

➠   If your screen looks like the one shown in Figure 11-89, click **OK**.

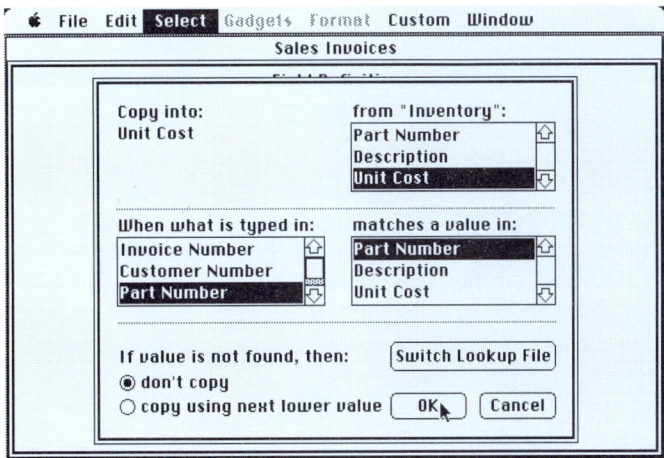

Figure 11-89   Settings to look up Unit Cost in the Inventory file

This completes defining the lookup fields for the Sales Invoices file.

Calculation Fields

The next fields that need to be defined are six calculation fields.

You learned to create text calculation fields in Project 2, and you are looking up information in those fields and copying it into fields in the Sales Invoices file.

In this project, you will create six simple calculation fields.

⌘-C   ➠   Click **Calculation** to choose the type of field.

➠   Name the new field Ext Cost, and then click **OK**.

When you click **OK**, FileMaker shows the same dialog box you used in Project 2 to enter a formula.

The formula for the extended cost field is the quantity (Qty) ordered multiplied by the cost of an individual item (Unit Cost).

➠   Enter the formula Qty * Unit Cost by clicking on **Qty** in the field list, then clicking on the asterisk (*), and finally clicking on **Unit Cost** in the field list (see Figure 11-90).

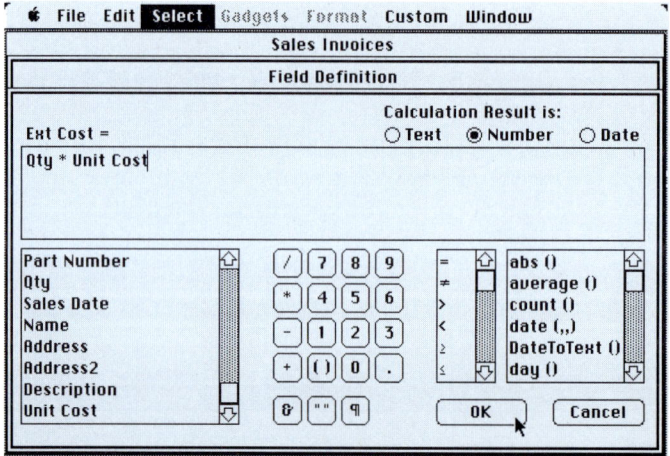

Figure 11-90   Entering a formula to calculate extended cost

➠   When the formula is correct, click **OK**.

At the bottom of the Qty field in the invoice, you want FileMaker to show the total number of items ordered. Through experience, you have determined that charging 75¢ per item will cover the shipping costs. To calculate the shipping costs, you first need to determine the total number of items ordered and then multiply that by $0.75. The first step is to create the Item Count field.

➠   Create a new number calculation field named Item Count, and then click **OK**.

The Qty field will be formatted as a *repeating field*. Repeating fields can hold more than one value. To get the number of items ordered, you must take the sum of all values entered in the Qty field. The formula for this is sum(Qty).

➠ Enter this formula by scrolling down the function list until you see sum(), and then click on it. This moves the function to the formula and leaves the insertion point between the parentheses. Now, click on **Qty** in the field list to enter it between the parentheses (see Figure 11-91).

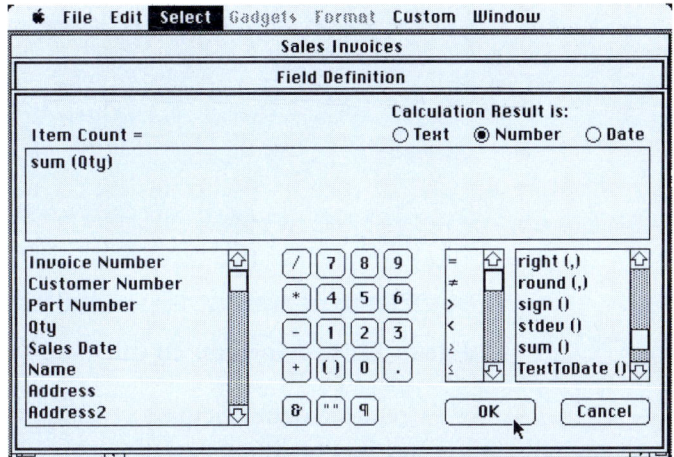

Figure 11-91   Entering the formula for the Item Count field

➠ When your formula looks like the one in Figure 11-91, click **OK**.

➠ Using the same technique, create a new calculation field named Sub Total, and enter the following formula: **sum(Ext Cost)**. Click **OK** to accept the field and its definition.

This tells FileMaker to calculate the sum of all values entered in the extended cost field and put the result in the Sub Total field.

The next field will calculate sales tax on the order, which is calculated by multiplying the Sub Total by 5.5 percent (or .055). When you multiply the Sub Total (containing a value with two digits to the right of the decimal point) by .055 (containing three digits right of the decimal point), you end up with a number with five digits to the right of the decimal point. You want to round this resulting value to two digits to the right of the decimal point.

The round(,) function will accomplish this. This function has a comma between the parentheses because it takes two arguments inside the parentheses. The first argument is the value to be rounded, and in this case that value is calculated by the formula **Sub Total * .055**. The second argument to the round function determines the number of digits to the right of the decimal point that will be preserved. Therefore, the full formula becomes **round(Sub Total * .055,2)**.

This formula is shown in Figure 11-92.

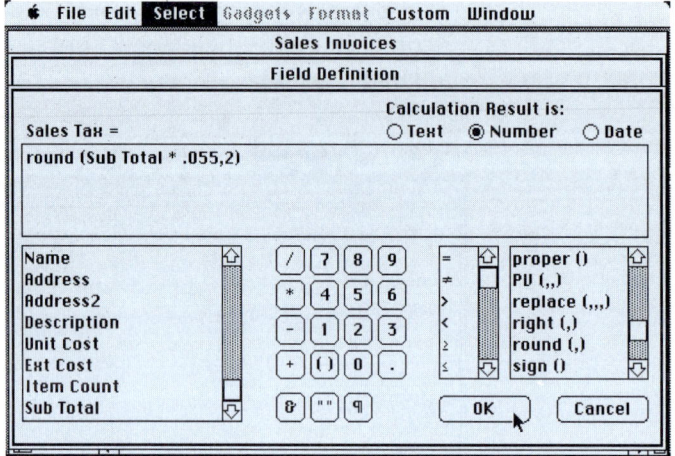

Figure 11-92   Formula to calculate sales tax

⟶ Create a new calculation field named Sales Tax, and enter the formula as shown in Figure 11-92. Click **OK** to accept it.

Had you only wanted to affect the number of decimal places displayed instead of the actual calculation, you could omit the round function and fix the number of digits with the Format Number command from the Format menu.

Now you must create a new shipping cost field.

⟶ Create a new calculation field named Shipping Cost, and enter the formula **Item Count * .75**. Click **OK** to accept it after you have verified that it is correct.

The last calculation field for the Sales Invoices file is the Grand Total field. This is the sum of the Sub Total, the Sales Tax, and the Shipping Cost.

⟶ Create a new calculation field named Grand Total, and enter the formula **Sub Total + Sales Tax + Shipping Cost**. Click **OK** to accept it.

Your Field Definition dialog box should look like the one shown in Figure 11-93.

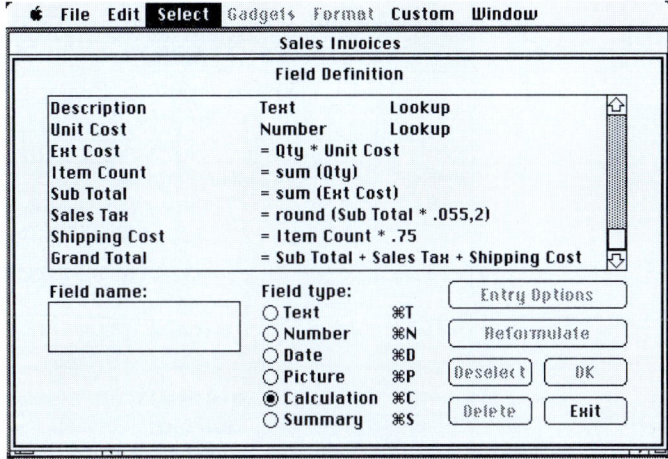

Figure 11-93 The formulas for the calculation fields

This completes the field definitions for the Sales Invoices file.

➡ Click **Exit** to leave the Field Definitions dialog box.

➡ This is a good time to save a copy of the file onto your data disk.

Entering Data

Now that you are in Browse mode, let's try entering a sales invoice into the standard vertical layout that FileMaker just created.

Suppose that Ms. Kay Kusunoki sends an order for 3 wiper motors. Her customer number is 1004, and the wiper motors have a part number of 1002.

➡ Click just to the right of the Customer Number label to activate the field.

➡ Type **1004** and then press Tab.

FileMaker looks up this customer number in the Customers file and copies the customer information into the fields you specified (Name, Address, and Address2).

Typing the Tab key accepts the information you entered into the Customer Number field and then activates the next field: Part Number.

➡ Type **1002** in the Part Number field, and then press Tab.

The unit cost and description are found and are copied into the appropriate fields. FileMaker then attempts to calculate the Ext Cost, Sub Total, Sales Tax, and Grand Total fields. At this point, they all contain zero values, because you have not entered anything into the Qty field.

➡ Type **3** in the Qty field, and then press Tab.

FileMaker recalculates the amounts in the fields (see Figure 11-94).

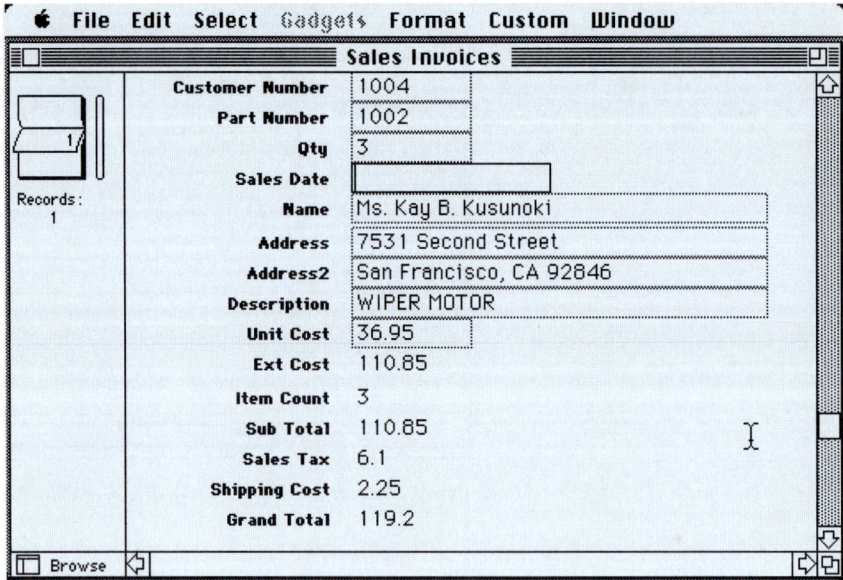

Figure 11-94   First invoice with looked up and calculated values

⇒ Enter 10/29/90 in the Sales Date field to complete the transaction.

As it stands now, this layout has several problems. You can enter only one item per invoice, and the dollar amounts are not formatted to look like dollar amounts.

Let's solve this problem by creating a new layout. This time you will begin with a blank layout and build it from there.

⌘-L ⇒ Change to Layout mode.

⌘-N ⇒ Choose **New Layout** from the Edit menu.

⇒ When the dialog box appears asking for the type of layout, click **Blank layout** (see Figure 11-95). Then click **OK**.

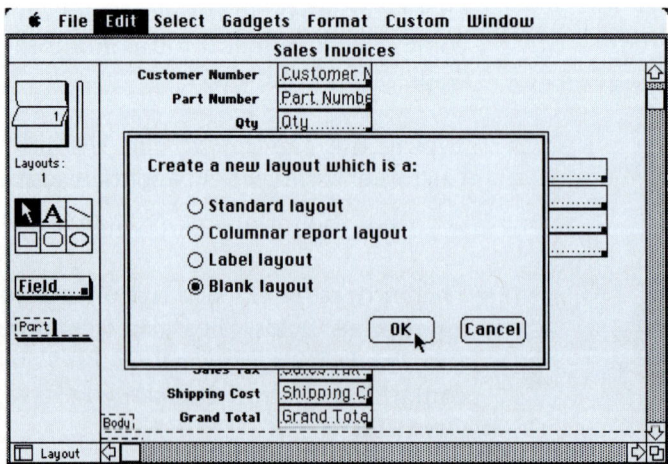

Figure 11-95   Creating a blank layout

The first thing you will do to create this new layout is to place a graphic object.

➠   Save a copy of this file, and then quit FileMaker.

Placing a Graphic

The B & K Auto Parts logo is included on the *Macintosh Journey Projects* disk. It is stored twice on the disk. Both a MacPaint and a MacDraw document are available. If you will be printing on an ImageWriter, it doesn't make much difference which you choose, but if you are printing on a LaserWriter, open and copy the MacDraw logo, because it will look better when printed.

➠   Using whichever application you prefer (or have available), open one of the logo files, select the logo, and copy it.

➠   Now that the logo is on the Clipboard, close the graphics application.

➠   Open FileMaker again by double-clicking on the Sales Invoices icon.

➠   Change to Layout mode.

You are back where you were before you quit, but now you can paste the logo onto the layout.

➠   Choose **Paste** from the Edit menu.

The logo will be placed onto the layout (see Figure 11-96).

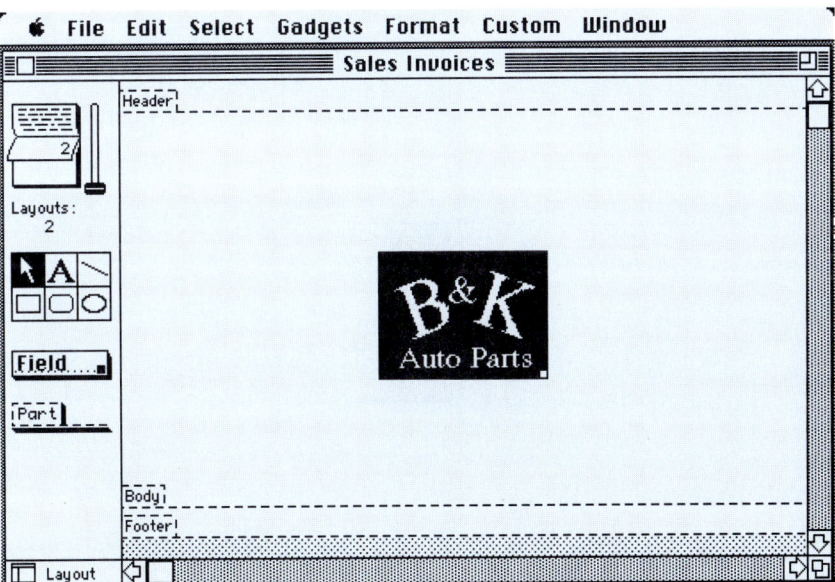

Figure 11-96   Pasting a graphic object from another application

➠   Drag the logo to the top of the screen, into the header area (see Figure 11-97).

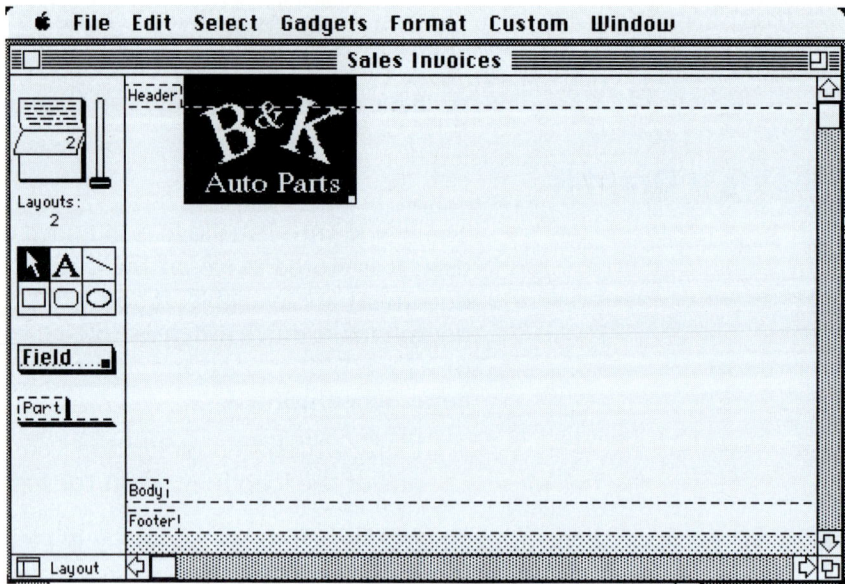

Figure 11-97   Moving the logo into the header

You must enlarge the header so that the logo is entirely enclosed. Placing the logo in the header area makes the logo appear on every page printed from this layout.

➡ Drag the Header part down below the logo (see Figure 11-98).

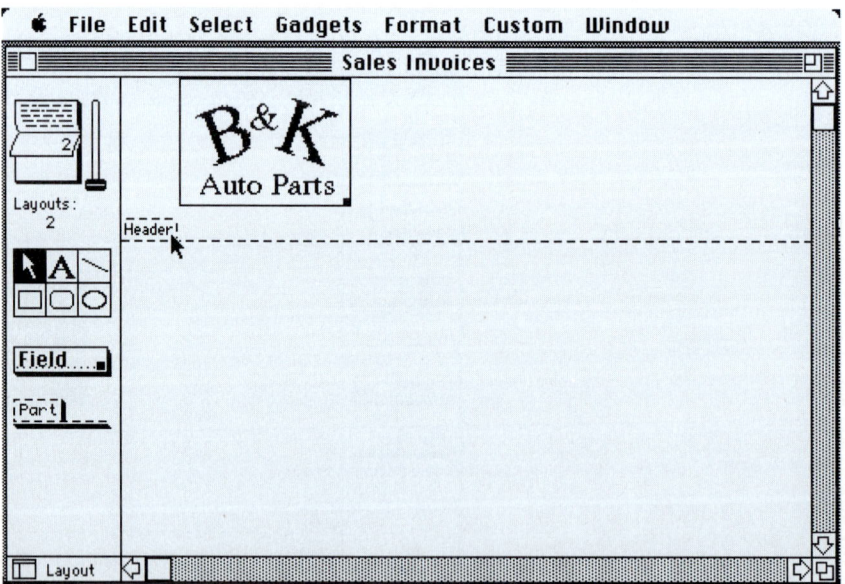

Figure 11-98   Dragging the Header part so it encloses the logo

➡ Now drag the logo to its final position in the top left corner of the layout (see Figure 11-99).

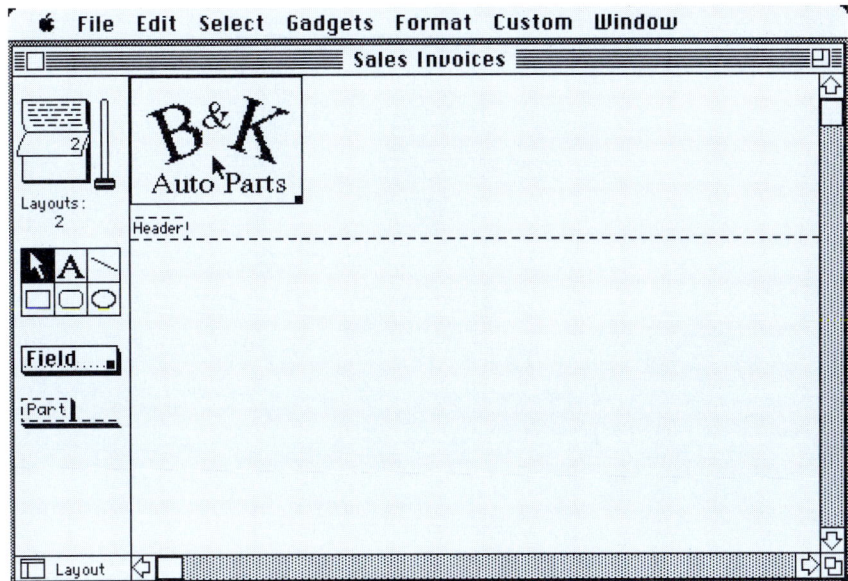

Figure 11-99 Placing the logo in its final position

Adding Text Labels

Now, let's add the address and phone numbers into the header of this layout. The default text is Geneva, 12 point, plain text, aligned left.

➡ Click on the **text** tool.

If you wanted, you could scroll to the right in the layout window until you could see the vertical line denoting the right side of the page. You could then enter the address and phone numbers in the top right corner of the page. If you were printing real invoices, you would want to do this.

Since this is an exercise, it is more convenient to place the address and phone numbers in the top right corner of the screen, rather than the top right corner of the page.

➡ Click a couple of inches from the right side of the screen, near the top of the header.

➡ Type the following text into the header of the layout as shown in Figure 11-100. (Press Return at the end of each line and again between the phone number and fax number to make a blank line.)

    1417 South Jonquil St.

    Smyrna, GA 30829

    (404) 555-7283

    Fax: (404) 555-6284

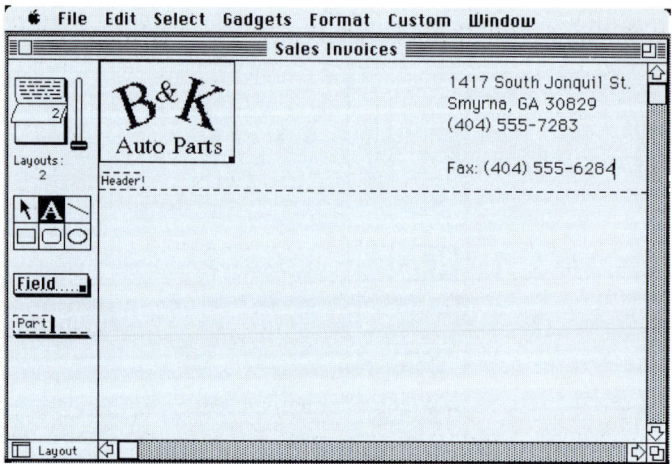

Figure 11-100   Adding text information to the header

Now you can add the word INVOICE in the header.

➥   Click about halfway between the logo and the address.

You can choose the font you want to use and how it will appear by making choices from the Format menu.

➥   Choose a large, easy-to-read font such as Helvetica or Geneva, 18 point, underlined and bold, aligned center.

➥   Type **INVOICE** (see Figure 11-101).

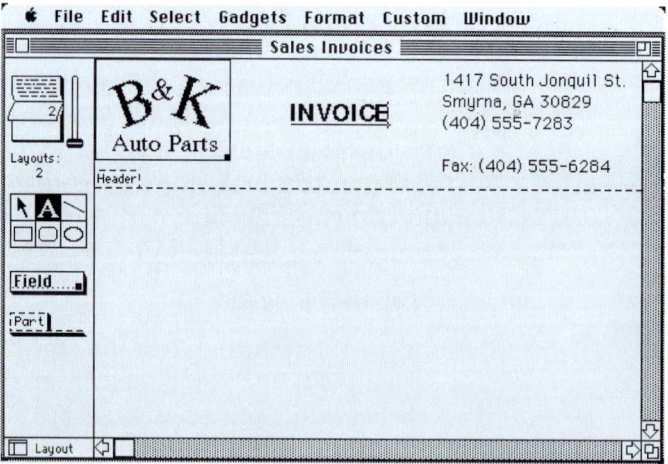

Figure 11-101   Entering more text in the header

➥   Drag the text elements around inside the header until you are satisfied with their placement.

You are now ready to enter some text labels into the body of the layout.

➥   Select **Geneva**, **9 point**, **bold**, and **align right** from the Format menu.

➥   Click in the body part of the layout, and then type **CUST NO**, **NAME**, and **ADDRESS** (see Figure 11-102).

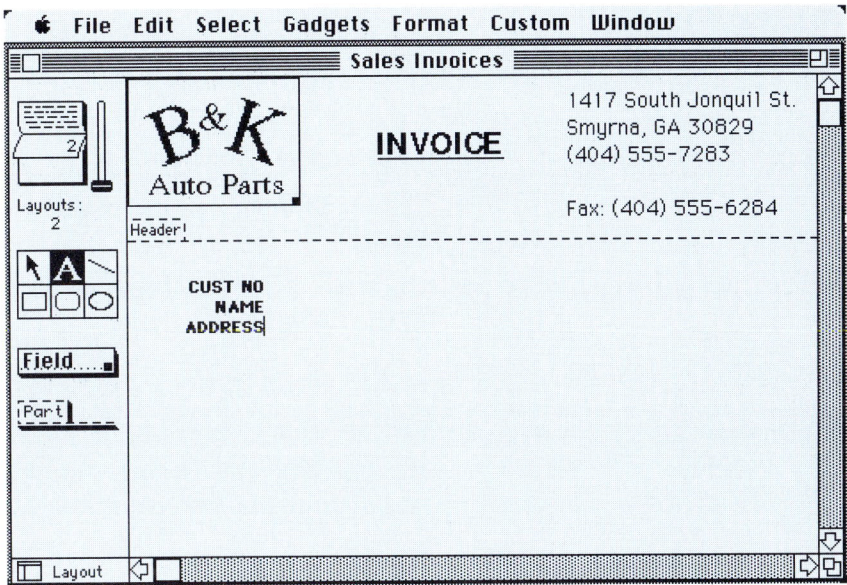

Figure 11-102   Entering text labels in the body of the layout

The next text to enter is the labels for invoice number and sales date (see Figure 11-103).

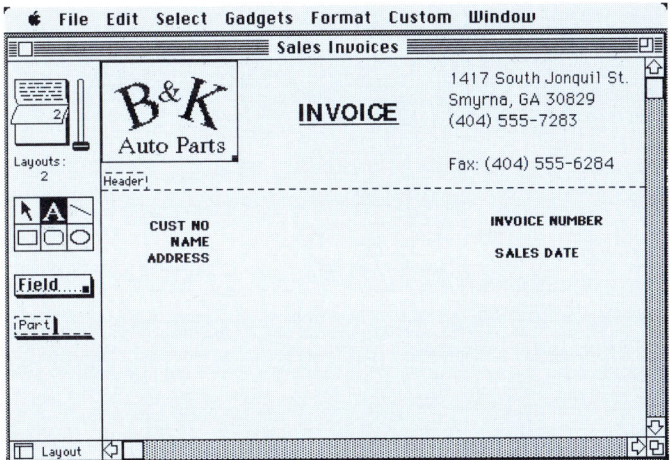

Figure 11-103   Adding text labels for fields

➡ Click to the right of CUST NO and below the fax number.

➡ Select **align left** from the Format menu.

➡ Type **INVOICE NUMBER**, and then press Return twice.

➡ Type **SALES DATE**.

Your screen should look like the one shown in Figure 11-103.

Adding Fields

It is time to drag some fields onto the layout, but first, you need to select the style for the text in the fields.

➡ Click on the arrow tool.

➡ Choose **Geneva**, **9 point**, **plain text**, and **align left** from the Format menu.

➡ Click on the field tool, and drag a field onto the layout to the right of the CUST NO text label.

A list will appear showing all the fields that are defined in the Sales Invoices file.

➡ Double-click on **Customer Number** so the new field will show the information you entered in the customer number.

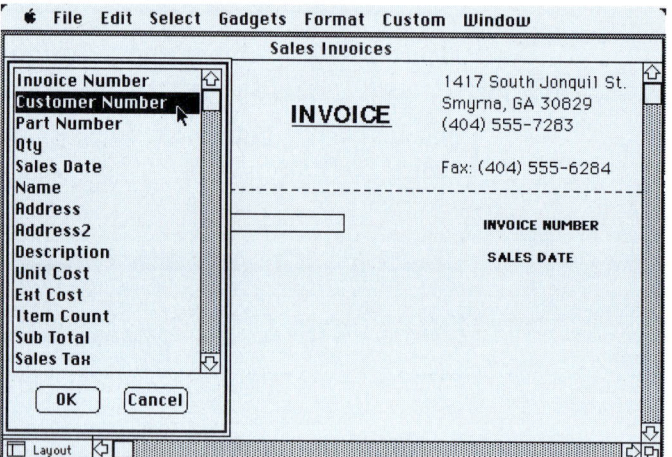

Figure 11-104   Adding the Customer Number field to the layout

➡ Drag another field onto the layout, right below the first one, and double-click on **Name** in the scrolling list.

➡ Drag the Address field below the Name field.

➡ Drag the Address2 field below the previous one.

Your screen should now look like the one shown in Figure 11-105.

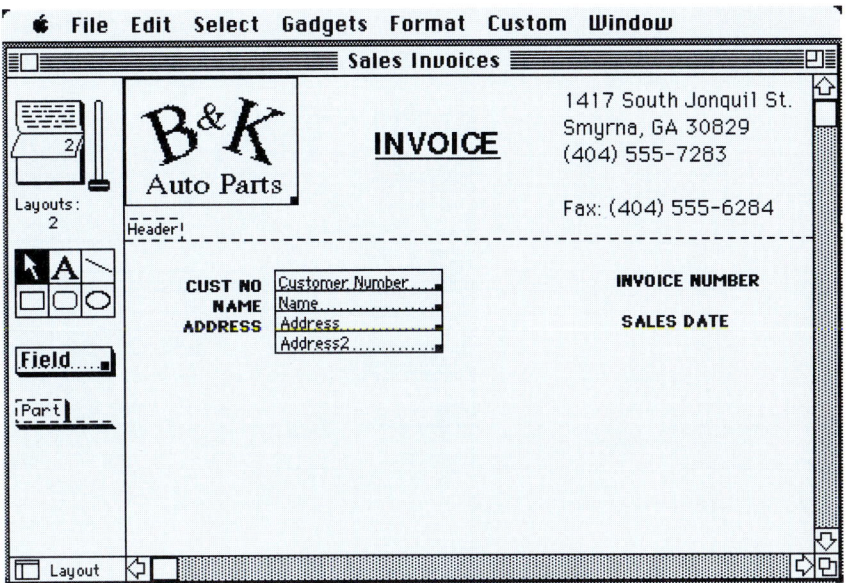

Figure 11-105   Entering the first four fields for this layout

The default length for the name and two address fields is not long enough for all values. You can increase the length of the fields quickly.

➧ Drag the black square in the lower right corner of the Name field to the right (see Figure 11-106).

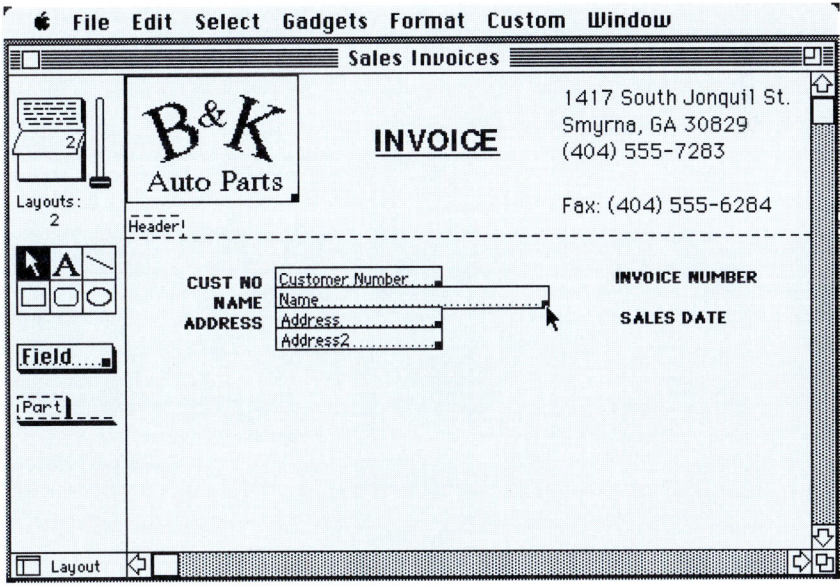

Figure 11-106   Making the Name field longer

➧ Now make the Address and Address2 the same length as the Name field (see Figure 11-107).

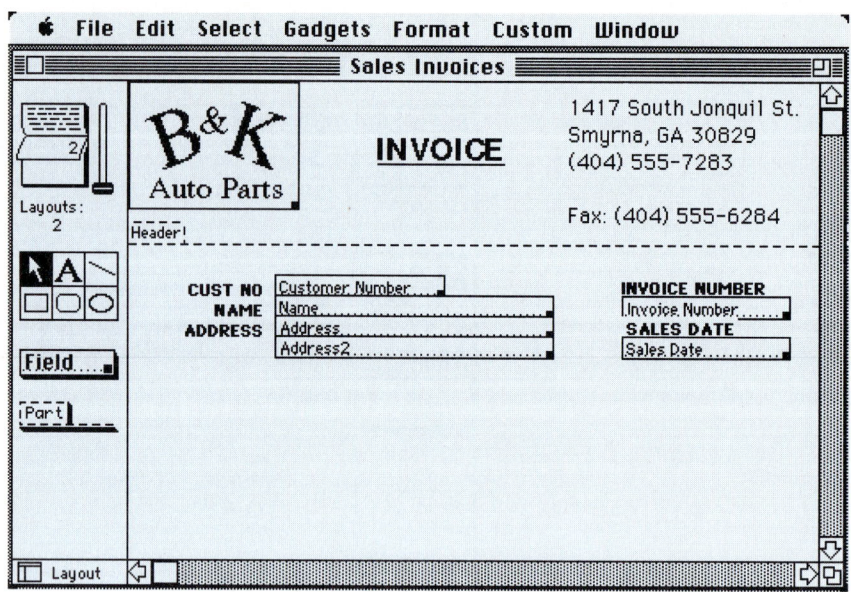

Figure 11-107   Extending the length of three fields

➡ Add the Invoice Number and Sales Date fields to the layout as shown in Figure 11-107.

Notice that the SALES DATE label obscures part of the bottom of the Invoice Number field. You can fix that by moving the Invoice Number field and label up higher on the layout.

➡ Select the Invoice Number field and text label, and then drag them up one line on the layout (see Figure 11-108).

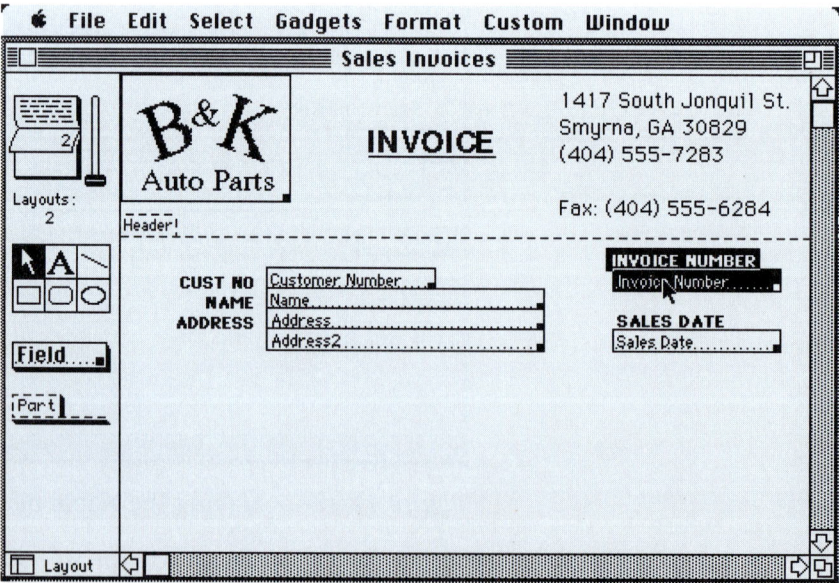

Figure 11-108   Moving the Invoice Number field and label

⇒ This is a good time to save a copy of this file.

The next thing to be done is to add five text labels horizontally across the layout (see Figure 11-109).

⇒ Click on the text tool, and then choose **Geneva**, **9 point**, **bold**, and **align left** from the Format menu.

⇒ Click below the address label, and then type **PART NO.**

⇒ Click a little to the right of that label, and then type **QTY.**

⇒ Continue clicking and typing in this manner until you have added the other three text labels: **DESCRIPTION**, **UNIT COST**, and **EXT. COST.**

You should now have five new text label objects (see Figure 11-109).

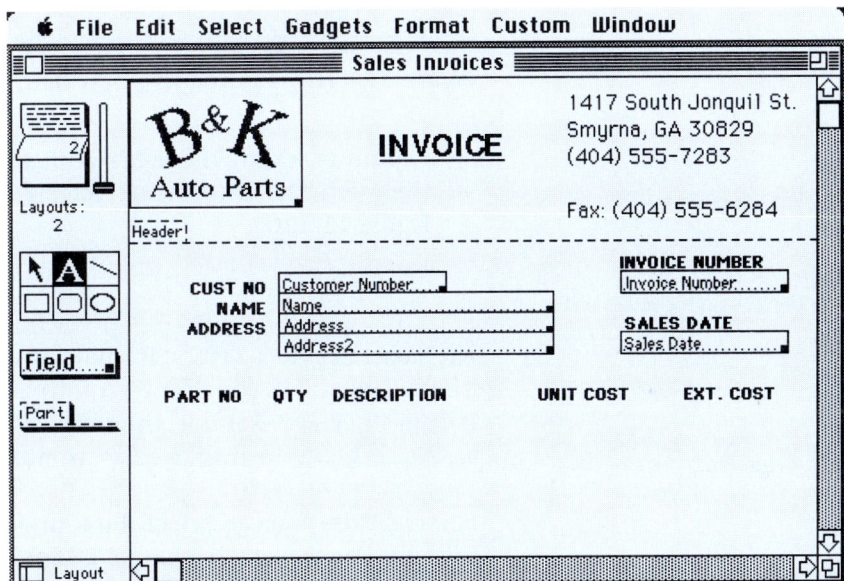

Figure 11-109   Entering five new text labels

You can now enter the five fields that correspond with the labels you just entered (see Figure 11-110).

⇒ Click on the arrow tool.

⇒ Choose **Geneva**, **9 point**, **plain text**, and **align left** from the Format menu.

⇒ Drag the Part Number field onto the layout.

⇒ Shorten the field as shown in Figure 11-110.

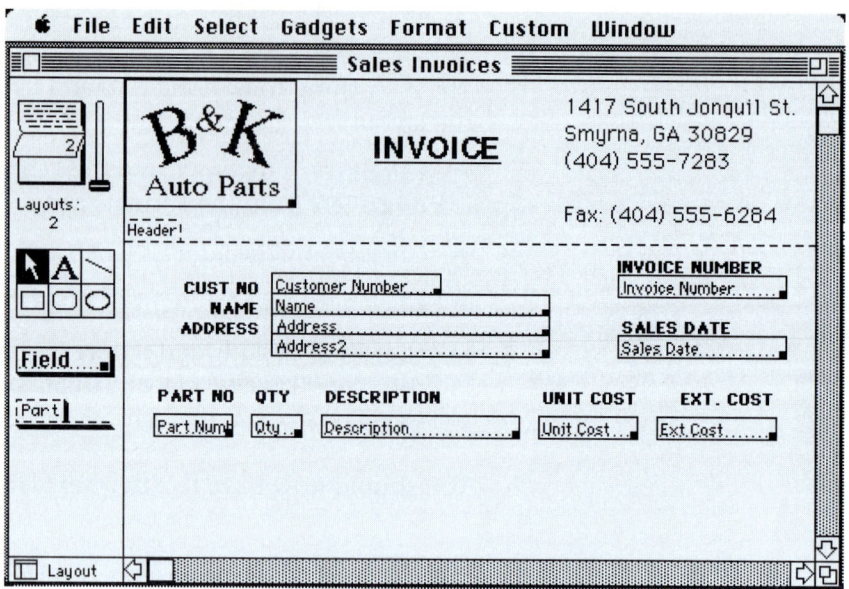

Figure 11-110 Adding five new fields to the layout

➠ Continue adding the fields, adjusting their position, and changing their lengths until your screen looks like the one shown in Figure 11-110.

Formatting Fields

FileMaker provides several formatting options that may be selected for a field. This allows you to enter information in one format and to display it in another. For example, the entry date might be entered by FileMaker as 10/22/90 but be displayed as Monday, October 22, 1990.

For all fields, you can select the font, size, style, and alignment of the information displayed in the field. FileMaker offers additional formatting options for text, number, and date fields. A fourth type of formatted field is the repeating field. These formatting options are presented below.

Text Fields

You have been formatting text fields in this project since you created the blank layout.

Font, size, style, and alignment can be set for every field or text object. All text within each field must be formatted the same, but all fields do not have to be formatted alike.

Number Fields

Number fields can be formatted, or they can be left unformatted.

If you choose to format a number field, you have several choices. You can choose to have FileMaker insert commas in fields that contain a value that is greater than or equal to 1,000.

You can choose to have FileMaker add notation characters to the contents of a field:

> If you choose dollar notation, the field will be displayed with a leading dollar sign and negative numbers will be enclosed in parentheses.

> If you choose percent notation, the number will be displayed as a value 100 times greater than what it really is and will be followed by a percent sign (%). For example, a sales tax of .055 would be displayed as 5.5%.

You can specify a fixed number of digits to be displayed to the right of the decimal point. A positive number of digits will round the number to that many digits to the right of the decimal point. If you specify a negative number of digits, the number will be displayed rounded that many digits *to the left of the decimal point.*

For example, a value of 456.789 that is in a field with 2 fixed digits would be displayed as 456.79. The same value in a field with 0 fixed digits would be displayed as 457. If you specified -2 fixed digits, the number would be rounded two digits to the left of the decimal point, and would be displayed as 500.

Number fields can also be formatted to display the contents as a logical Yes or No. If the field is empty, or if it contains non-numeric characters (other than Y, Yes, N, or No), it will be displayed as empty. If the field contains a value of 0 (zero), No, or N, it will be displayed as No. If the field contains any value except for 0 (zero), or if it contains Yes or Y, then it will be displayed as Yes.

The part number and quantity fields will contain integers (whole numbers) only, so you want to format them so they won't display any digits to the right of the decimal point.

➡ Select the **Part Number** and **Qty** fields and then choose **Format Number** from the Format menu.

➡ When the dialog box appears (see Figure 11-111), click **Fixed number of decimal digits:**, and enter **0** in the box. Click **OK**.

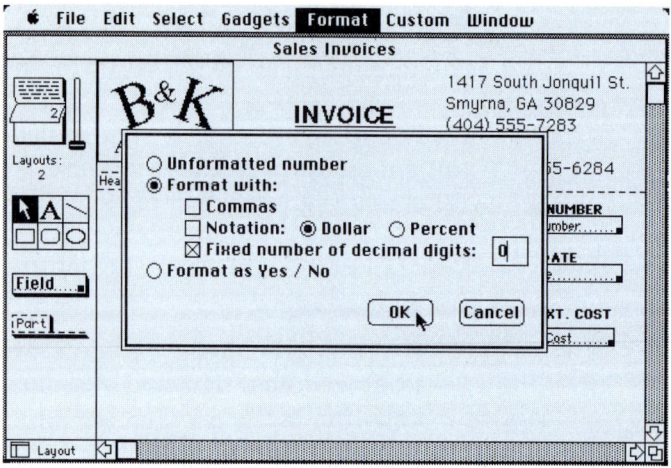

Figure 11-111   Formatting fields to contain integer values

The unit cost and extended cost fields will display dollar amounts, and should show dollars and cents. You should format these fields with commas, dollar notation, and 2 fixed decimal digits.

➡ Select the **Unit Cost** and **Ext Cost** fields and then choose **Format Number** from the Format menu.

➡ When the dialog box appears (see Figure 11-112), click **Commas**, **Notation: Dollar**, and **Fixed number of decimal digits:**, and then enter **2** in the box. Click **OK**.

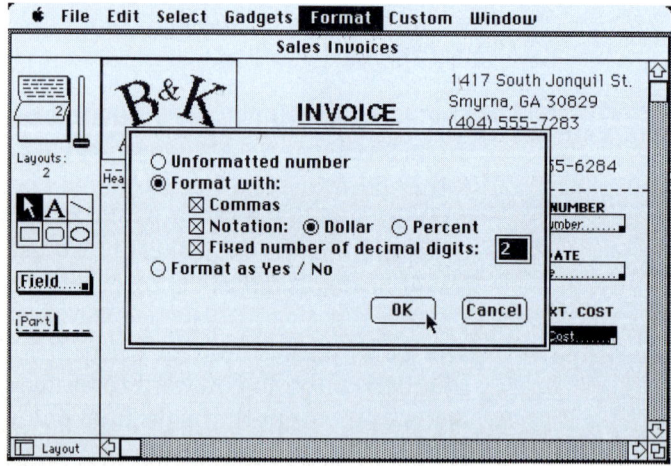

Figure 11-112   Formatting fields to contain dollar amounts

Date Fields

Date fields, calculation fields with date results, and date placeholders (//) can be formatted to display the date according to your preferences.

You can choose from five formats for date fields, plus one for unformatted dates.

Unformatted date fields will display the date just as you enter it.

Let's format the date so that it will display the three-letter abbreviation for the month, the day of the month, and then the four-digit value for the year. Using this format, 10/22/90 would be displayed as Oct 22, 1990.

➠ Select the **Sales Date** field and then choose **Format Date** from the Format menu.

➠ When the dialog box appears, click **Jul 22, 1988** (see Figure 11-113). Click **OK**.

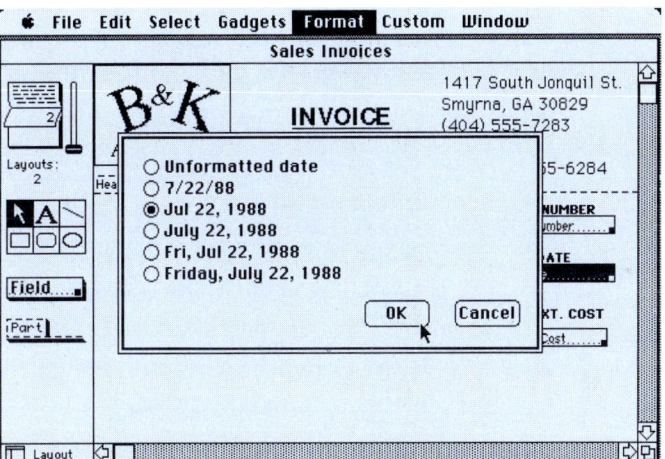

Figure 11-113   Formatting a date field

After all of the work you've done, you're probably wondering what the invoice looks like now. Let's find out.

⌘-B   ➠ Change to Browse mode.

The formats you specified have changed the presentation of the information shown in this layout (see Figure 11-114).

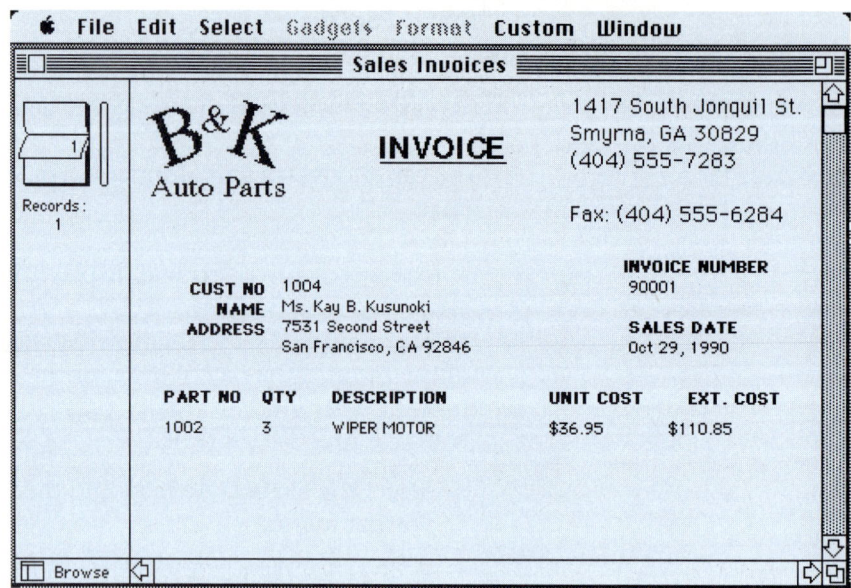

Figure 11-114   Viewing the format changes

Notice that the Part Number, Qty, Unit Cost, and Ext Cost fields should be aligned on the right, so the numbers will line up correctly.

⌘-L ➡ Go back to Layout mode.

➡ Select the **Part Number**, **Qty**, **Unit Cost**, and **Ext Cost** fields and then choose **align right** from the Format menu.

➡ Make sure the labels above these four fields are lined up with the right side of the fields. Drag any labels or fields that aren't aligned properly.

⌘-B ➡ Go back to Browse mode, and verify the alignment and format of the fields you just modified.

⌘-L ➡ Return to Layout mode.

➡ This is a good time to save a copy of the file.

Repeating Fields

Your customers usually order two to five different items with each order, but this layout only lets them order one item per invoice.

Let's make the bottom five fields *repeating fields* and allow for six entries in each one.

You can format any text, date, number, picture, or calculation field to show more than one value by formatting the field to repeat.

➡ Select the **Part Number, Qty, Description, Unit Cost,** and **Ext Cost** fields.

➡ Choose **Repeat** from the Format menu, enter **6** in the Values box when the dialog box appears (see Figure 11-115), and then click **OK**.

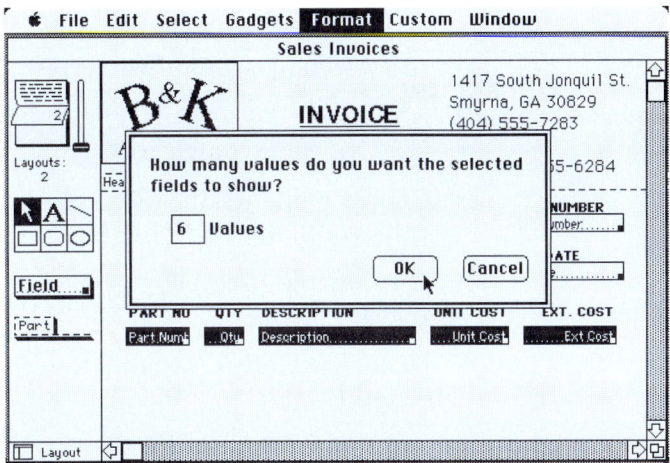

Figure 11-115   Formatting fields to repeat six times

Each of the fields has now extended downward for five more lines (see Figure 11-116).

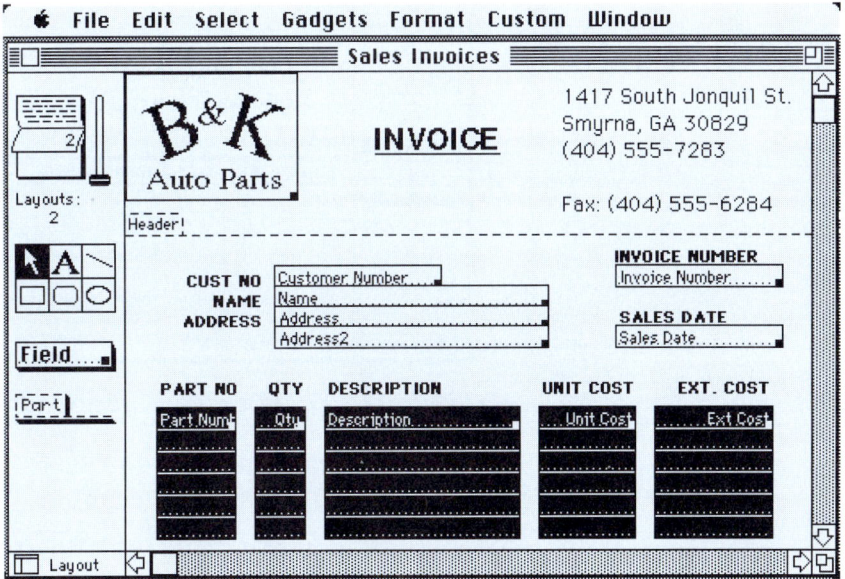

Figure 11-116   The newly formatted repeating fields

If you were to switch back to layout 1, you would only see the first item in each of these fields, because the fields are only formatted for repeating values in this layout. Any entries you made in this layout would still be there, but you could not see or modify them in layout 1.

Adding Lines and Boxes

FileMaker provides the tools for adding lines, rectangles, rounded rectangles, and ovals to a layout.

Let's draw rectangles around the repeating fields and their headings and then separate the columns with vertical lines.

➠ Click on the rectangle tool.

➠ Choose a line width of 2 pixels from the Format menu. (Choose the second line below hairline.)

⌘-Y ➠ Turn off the invisible grid by choosing **Invisible Grid** from the Gadgets menu.

➠ Draw a rectangle around the column headings as shown in Figure 11-117.

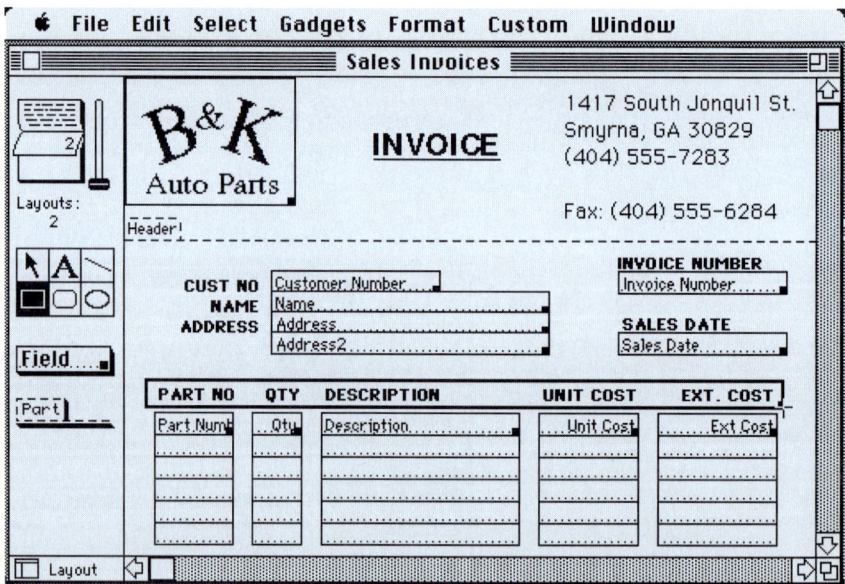

Figure 11-117   A rectangle surrounds the column headings.

➠ Change the line width to 1 pixel (by choosing the line below the hairline in the Format menu).

➠ Draw another rectangle, this time surrounding the repeating fields. Be careful to align it correctly with the rectangle you drew around the column headings (see Figure 11-118). Be sure that the rectangles you draw do not overlap other rectangles or the fields. They must completely enclose the fields without overlapping or touching them.

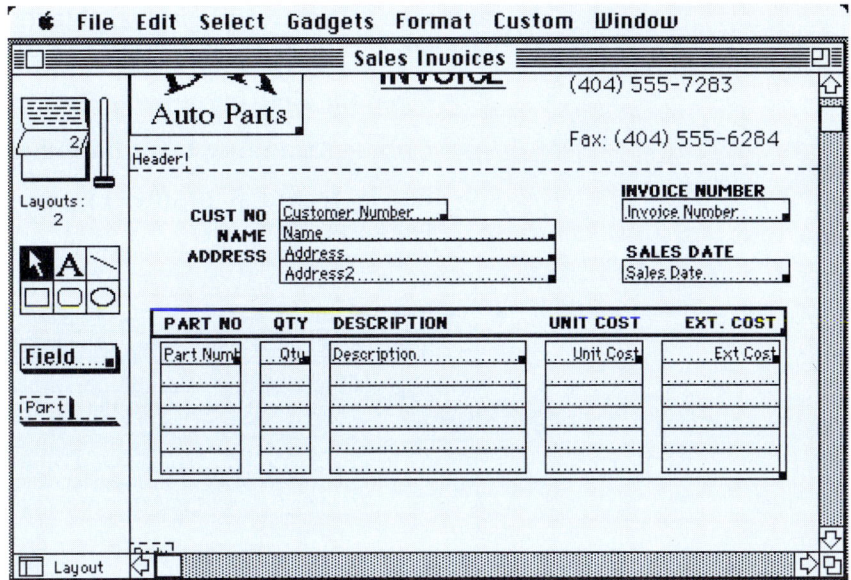

Figure 11-118   A second rectangle surrounds the repeating fields.

⌘-B   ➥   Choose **Browse** to see the results of the changes you have made.

Your screen should look like the one shown in Figure 11-119.

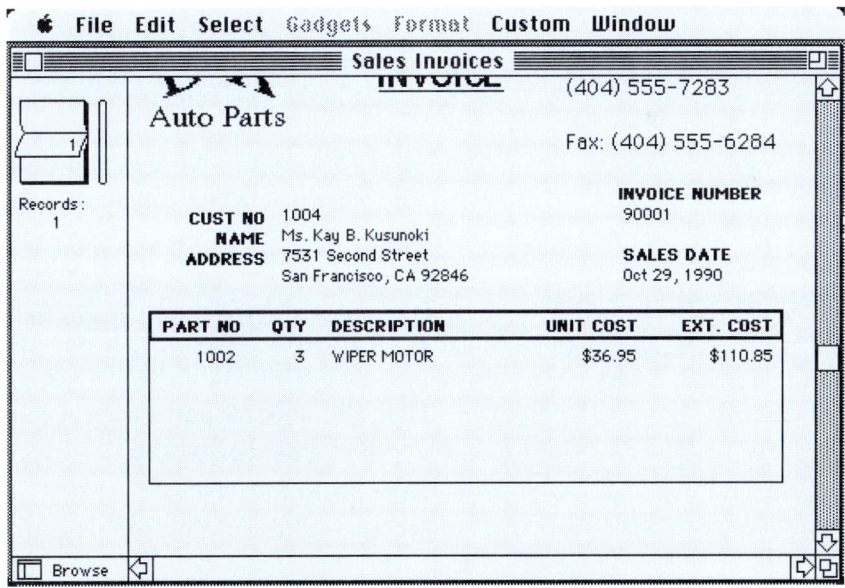

Figure 11-119   Viewing the changes made in the layout

⌘-L   ➥   Change back to Layout mode.

Now you are ready to add vertical lines to the layout to separate the columns. There is an easy way to ensure that the lines are perfectly vertical. FileMaker provides a gadget called *T-Squares* that will be useful for adding these lines.

Let's see if there is any help available concerning lining up objects in the layout.

⌘-/ ➡ Open the Help file.

⌘-8 ➡ Choose **Arranging Information** from the Custom menu.

➡ Go to record 5 of the 15 records found on this topic (see Figure 11-120).

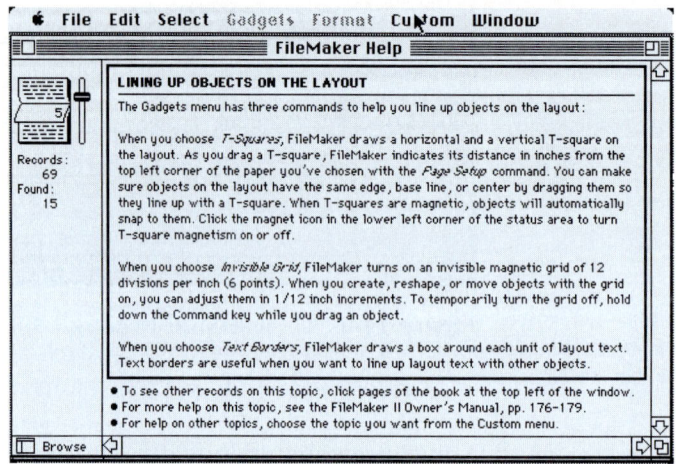

Figure 11-120   Helpful information on lining up objects

This screen contains information about invisible grids and T-squares. You should read this screen to learn more about using the T-squares.

The other 14 screens in this selection have valuable information that should make more sense now that you have some experience working with layouts.

⌘-W ➡ After you have read this screen, close the Help file.

Now, you can use the T-squares to help you draw the vertical lines.

⌘-T ➡ Choose **T-Squares** from the Gadgets menu.

➡ Drag the vertical part of the T-squares midway between the Part Number and Qty fields.

➡ Drag the horizontal part of the T-squares to the exact bottom of the rectangle surrounding the repeating fields (see Figure 11-121).

A magnet icon is showing below the part tool in the status and tool area. The T-square lines are magnetic (will attract the pointer and any objects it manipulates) when the magnet is black with lines emanating from it (as it is in Figure 11-121).

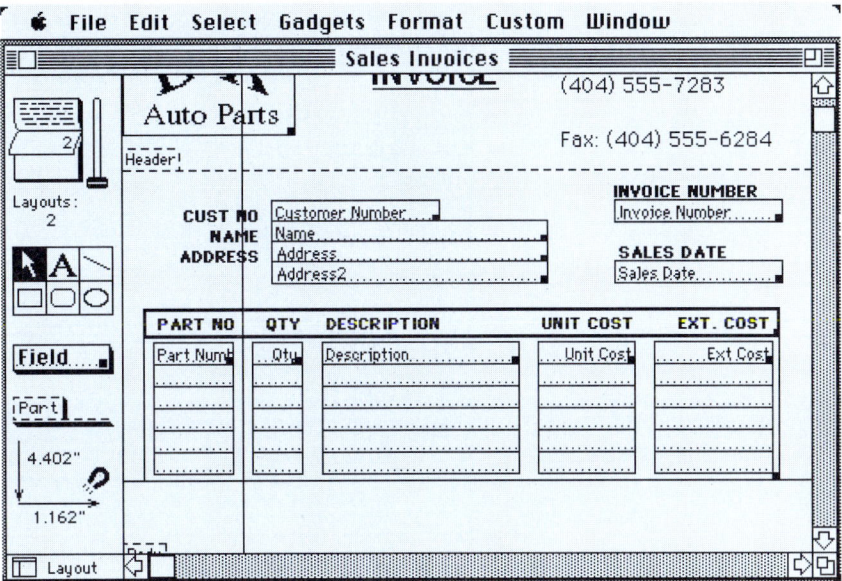

Figure 11-121   Positioning the T-squares for a vertical line

If the magnet is a hollow white outline (turned off), it means the T-squares will not magnetically attract the mouse pointer.

➡ If the magnet is turned off, click on it to turn it on.

➡ Choose the line tool and set the width to 1 pixel.

Now draw the vertical line between the Part Number and Qty fields.

➡ Starting at the top of the rectangle surrounding the column headings, carefully align the pointer on the vertical part of the T-squares and the top part of the rectangle.

➡ Draw a line downward to the intersection of the two parts of the T-square, and then release the mouse button.

The "magnetic" properties of the T-square constrained the line to be vertical and caused it to stop exactly at the bottom of the rectangle surrounding the repeating fields.

⌘-B ⌘-L ➡ Confirm that the line is correct by changing to Browse mode (see Figure 11-122), and then return to the layout.

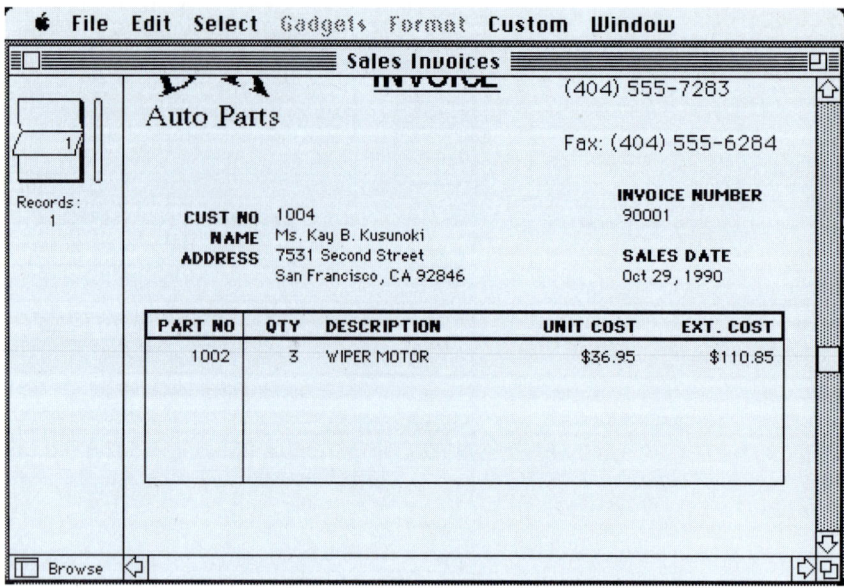

Figure 11-122   The layout after adding one vertical line

➠ Click on the arrow tool to select it.

➠ Drag the vertical part of the T-square to the right and place it between the Qty and Description fields.

➠ Select the line tool.

➠ Add a vertical line separating these two fields.

➠ Continue moving the T-square and adding lines until all the columns are separated.

⌘-B ⌘-L ➠ Confirm the placement of the lines by changing to Browse mode, and then return to the layout.

Now you can add a box below the quantity column that will hold the Item Count field.

⌘-T ➠ Remove the T-square by choosing **T-Squares** from the Gadgets menu.

➠ Use the rectangle tool to add a box under the Qty field. Make it about the size of the one shown in Figure 11-123. Do not overlap other objects.

➠ This is a good time to save a copy of the file.

Adding the Calculation Fields

You have added all of the objects to this layout except for the calculation fields and the text labels for those fields.

The first calculation field you will add to the layout is the Item Count field. Adding a calculation field is just like adding any of the other fields: drag a new field from the field tool, choose the name of the field, and adjust it for position, size, and font attributes.

➡ Select the arrow tool.

➡ Drag a field into the rectangle you drew under the quantity column, and, after releasing the field, double-click on **Item Count** in the scrolling list.

➡ Place the field as shown in Figure 11-123, and size it so it fits entirely inside the rectangle, without overlapping.

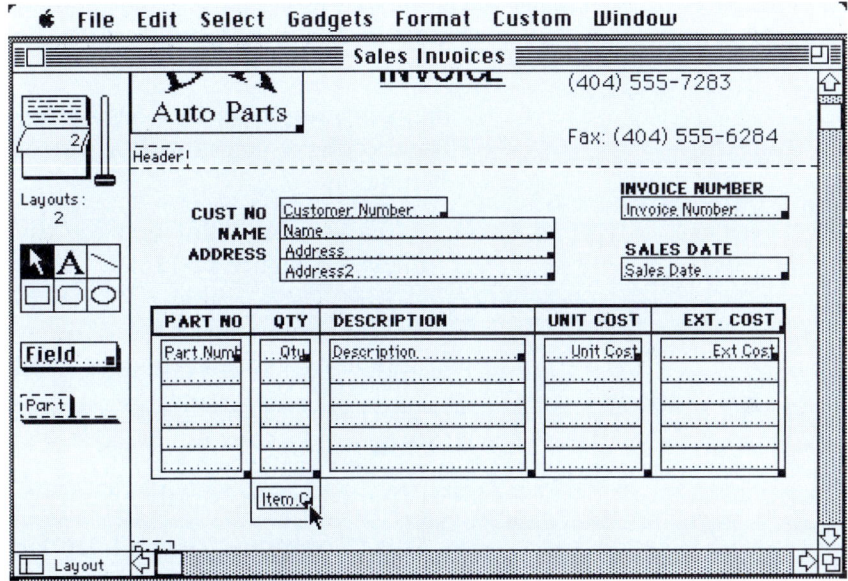

Figure 11-123   Adding the Item Count field

⌘-Y ➡ Choose **Invisible Grid** from the Gadgets menu to turn on the invisible grid.

➡ Choose **Geneva**, **9 point**, **bold**, and **align right** from the Format menu.

➡ Add the text labels shown in Figure 11-124 to the bottom of the layout.

➡ Choose **plain text** from the Format menu.

➡ Drag the **Sub Total**, **Sales Tax**, **Shipping Cost**, and **Grand Total** fields onto the layout (see Figure 11-124).

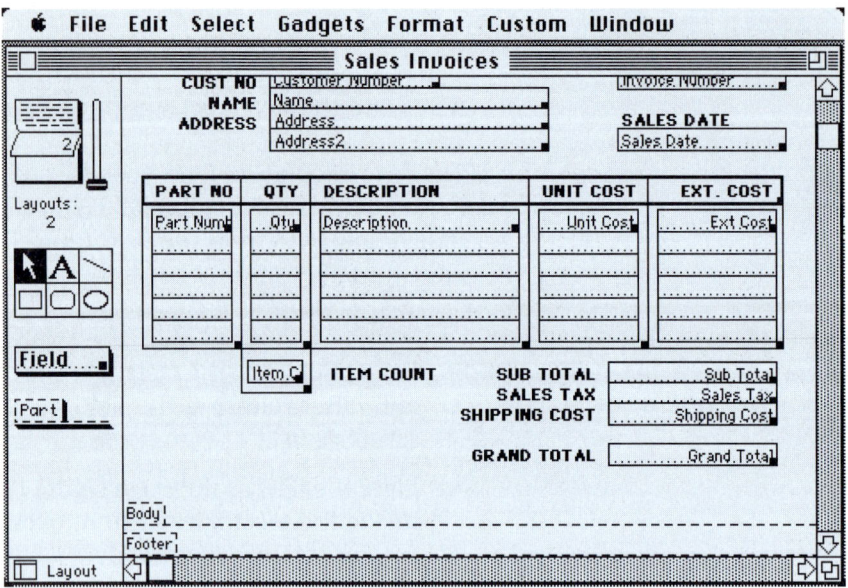

Figure 11-124   Layout #2 with all fields in place

A blank line was left between the Shipping Cost and Grand Total fields. This was done so you can add a horizontal line to indicate that addition is being done.

➠ Add a horizontal line between the Shipping Cost and Grand Total fields (see Figure 11-125).

The last four fields you added to the layout represent dollar amounts, so you should now format them as such.

➠ Select the last four fields you added by clicking on one and then Shift-clicking on the others.

➠ Choose **Format Number** from the Format menu.

➠ Select **Commas**, **Notation: Dollar**, and **Fixed number of decimal digits: 2**. Click **OK**.

Now you can make the grand total amount stand out by making it bold.

➠ Select the **Grand Total** field, and then choose **bold** from the Format menu.

Specifying Tab Order

You are almost done with this layout, but before you change to Browse mode and enter some transactions, you need to change the tab order of the fields.

In this type of layout, the top left field would be active first, and when you type the Tab key, the next field to the right would become active. If there were no more fields to the right, the next one down would become active.

You don't want to have to tab through the Name, Address, Address2, and other fields, because the only information you will type into this form will be in the Customer Number, Sales Date, Qty, and Part Number fields. You can change the tab order of the fields by selecting the fields you will use and creating a tab group.

➠ Select the Customer Number, Sales Date, Part Number, and Qty fields (see Figure 11-125).

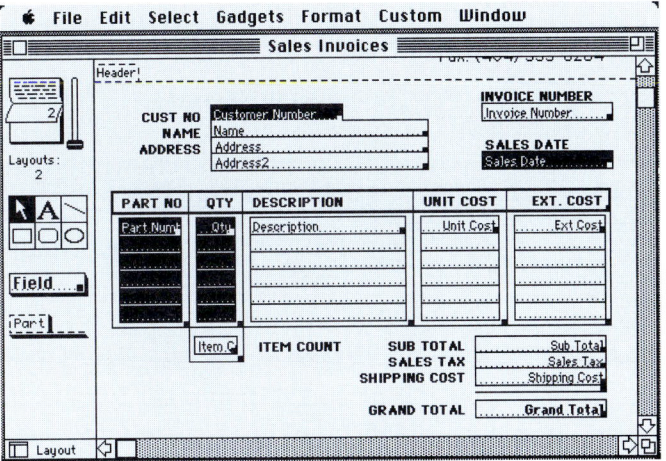

Figure 11-125   Selecting the fields to make a tab group

If you can't select individual fields, it is probably because your rectangles or fields overlap each other. Using the arrow tool and moving the objects so they don't overlap should correct the problem.

➠ Choose **Tab Order** from the Gadgets menu.

FileMaker displays a dialog box like the one shown in Figure 11-126.

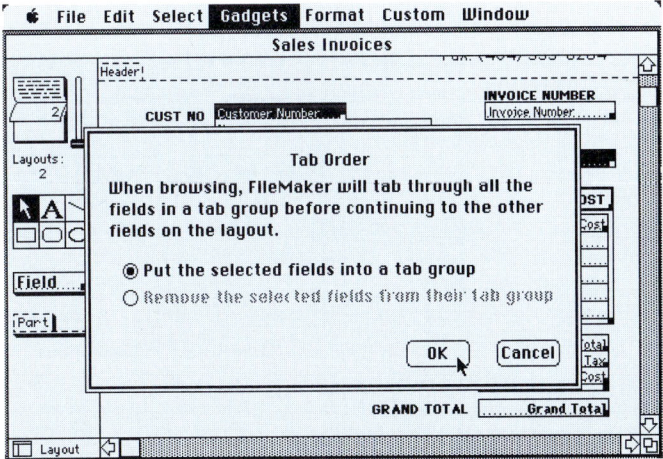

Figure 11-126   Dialog box for creating or removing tab groups

➠ Select **Put the selected fields into a tab group**, and then click **OK**.

➠ Click in a blank area of the layout to deselect the fields.

You have completed the creation of this layout.

➠ This is a good time to save a copy of your file.

Entering New Sales Invoices

Now that you have created this new layout, let's enter some transactions and see how it works.

⌘-B   ➭   Change to Browse mode.

Suppose one of your customers, Ms. Sandra Hardin (customer number 1001), ordered 1 radiator hose (part number 1009) and 1 radiator cap (part number 1010). Let's add a new record to process the transaction.

⌘-N   ➭   Choose **New Record** from the Edit menu.

You will enter the transaction information into this record and type the date into the Sales Date field.

➭   Type **1001** in the Customer Number field, and then type Tab.

The customer information is read from the Customers file and displayed on the screen.

➭   Type 10/29/90 into the Sales Date field, and then tab to the next field.

➭   Type **1009** into the Part Number field, and then tab to the next field.

The contents of the Description and Unit Cost fields are read from the Inventory file and displayed on the screen.

➭   Type **1** into the Qty field, as shown in Figure 11-127, and then press Tab to advance to the next field.

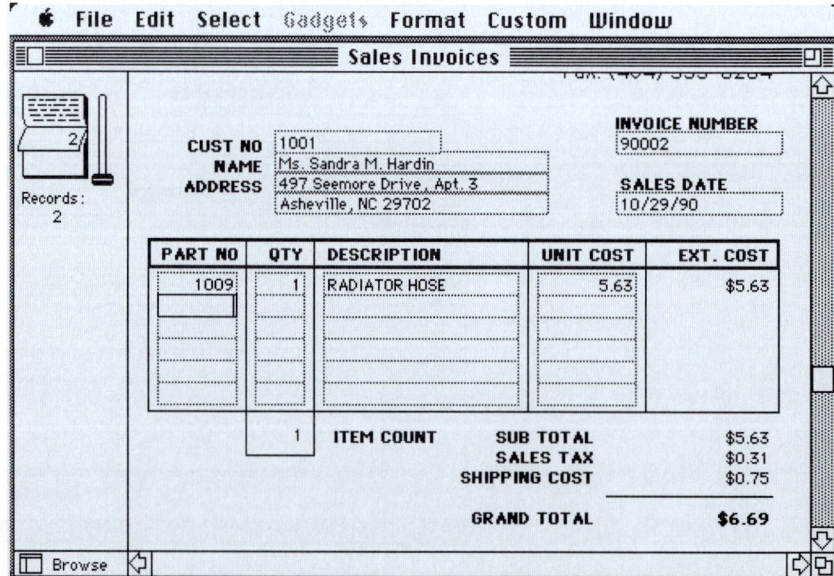

Figure 11-127   Ms. Hardin's partially completed transaction

➡ Complete the order by entering the proper information for 1 radiator cap.

The grand total for this order should be $16.88.

The next transaction, on 10/29/90, is from Mr. Gary Westmoreland (#1008), who wants 2 engine mounts (#1014), 1 package of wiper blades (#1001), and 1 door handle (#1004).

⌘-N ➡ Add a new record, and enter the information to complete this transaction. Enter the current date for the sales date.

Verify that your results match those shown in Figure 11-128.

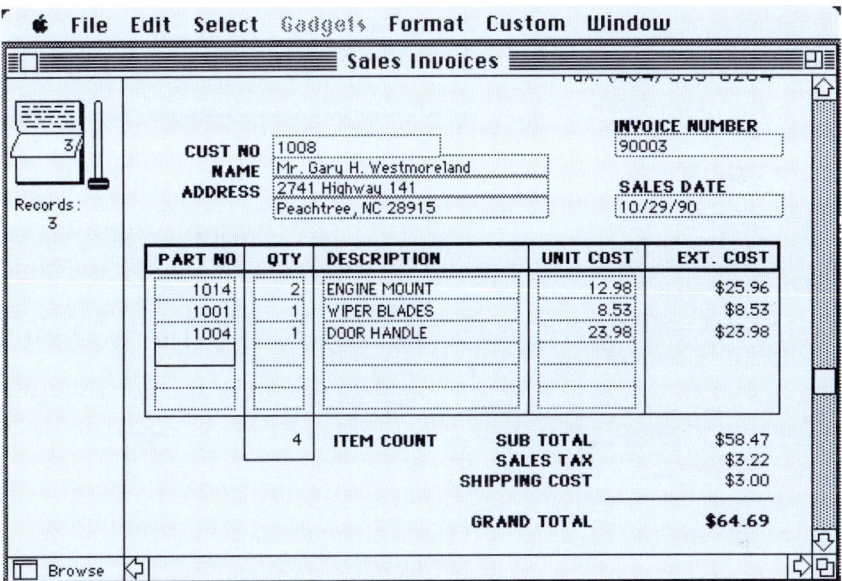

Figure 11-128   Mr. Westmoreland's order

Mr. Jim Bell (#1003) places an order next, and he wants to purchase 1 mirror mount (#1005) and 1 fuel filter (#1012).

⌘-N ➡ Add a new record, and enter the transaction.

Compare your sales invoice with the one shown in Figure 11-129.

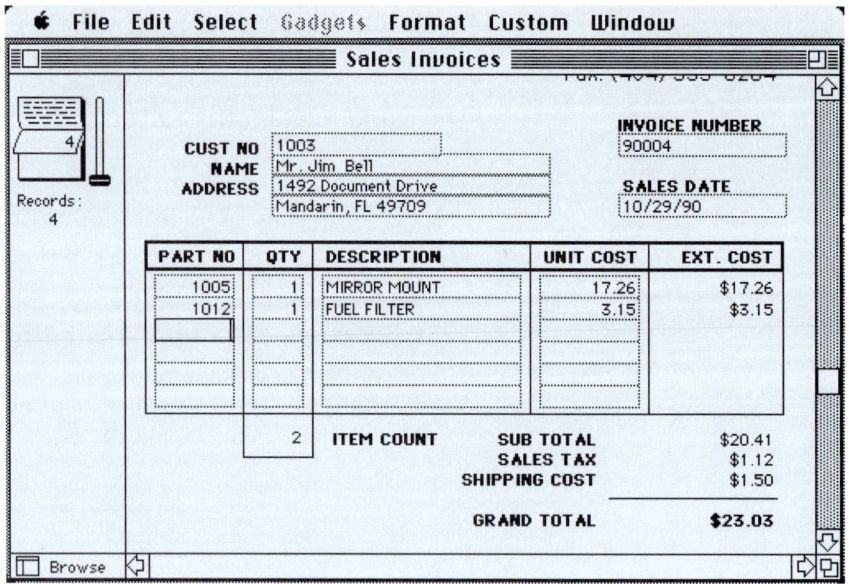

Figure 11-129   Mr. Bell's completed order

The next order comes from Mrs. Mattie Dilbeccio of Grape Creek New and Used Cars (#1006), and it is a large order. She wants to purchase 4 head gaskets (#1013), 12 floor mats (#1007), 48 wiper blades (#1001), 2 key locks (#1008), 4 radiator caps (#1010), and 5 wiper motors (#1002).

⌘-N   ➡   Add another record, and enter the transaction.

Compare your results with those shown in Figure 11-130.

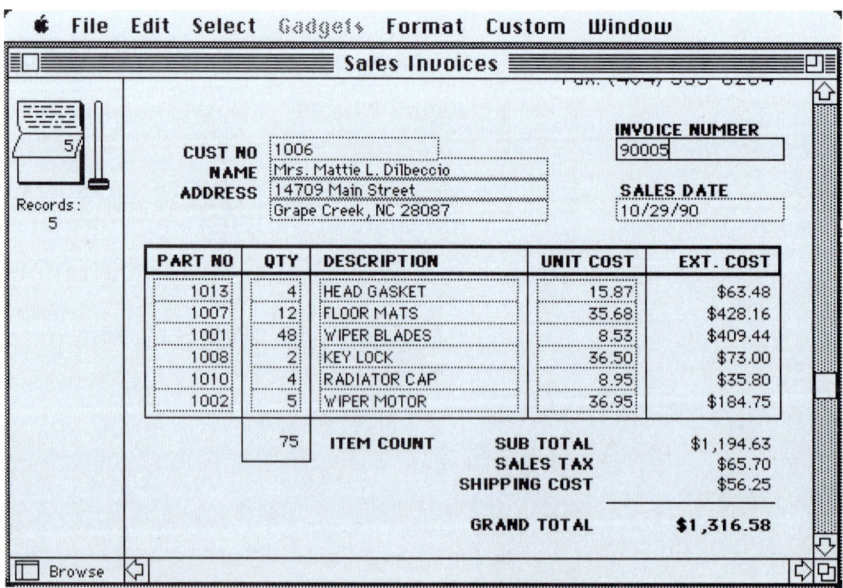

Figure 11-130   Mrs. Dilbeccio places a large order.

Next, you receive an order from Ms. Faye Mauney (#1005). She wants 1 package of window brackets (#1003) and 1 mirror mount (#1005).

⌘-N ➡ Enter the transaction, and compare your results with those shown in Figure 11-131.

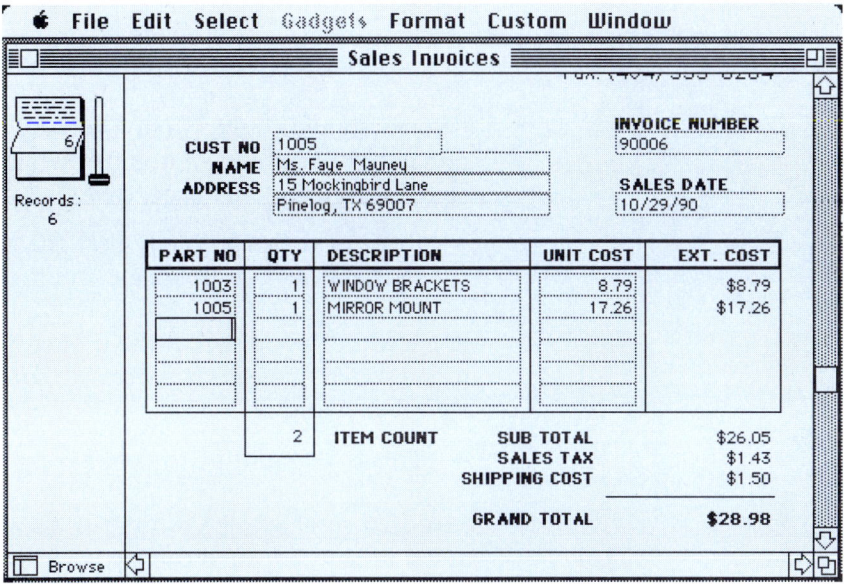

Figure 11-131   Ms. Mauney's order has been entered

The last order today is another order from Grape Creek New and Used Cars (#1006). This time, they order 24 radiator hoses (#1009), 12 fuel filters (#1012), 2 engine mounts (#1014), and 60 fan belts (#1015).

⌘-N ➡ Enter the order and compare it with the results shown in Figure 11-132.

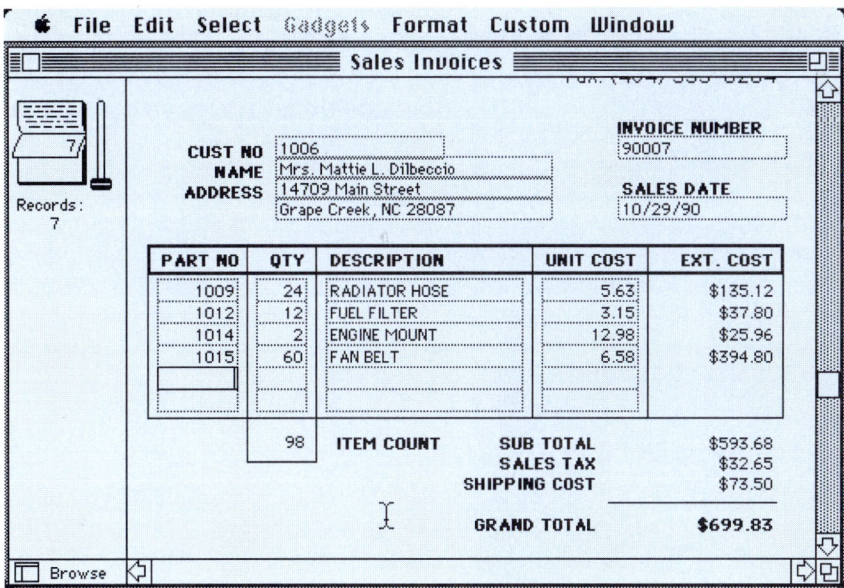

Figure 11-132   Grape Creek New and Used Cars' second order

This completes the data entry for today's orders.

PRINTING SALES INVOICES

Now, before printing the invoices, let's preview them to see how they will look.

➡ Choose **Preview** from the File menu. Click **Reduced**.

If you designed your form small enough, you will see two records on the previewed page, and that is not what you want. If you do have two records showing on a page, there is a simple solution.

➡ If you have this problem, change to Layout mode, drag the Body part farther down on the page, and then return to Browse mode.

Preview the page again. If the problem persists, change back to Layout mode and drag the Body part down some more until you only have one record showing on a page.

➡ This is a good time to save a copy of this file.

Now that you have entered all the information for today's transactions, and you have adjusted the layout to show only one record per page (if necessary), it is time to print all seven of the invoices.

➡ Choose **Print** from the File menu. Accept the defaults by clicking **OK** in the Print dialog box.

You have defined a number of fields in this file, so it is a good idea to print a field definition report and save it for documentation purposes.

➡ Choose **Print** from the File menu. Click **Field Definitions**, and then click **OK**.

Your field definitions report should look like the one shown in Figure 11-133.

Congratulations! You have completed Project 3.

Field Name	Field Type	Formula / Entry Option
Invoice Number	Number	Auto-enter serial number: 90008 Unique values only
Customer Number	Number	
Part Number	Number	
Qty	Number	
Sales Date	Date	
Name	Text	Lookup: "Full Name" in "Customers" when "Customer Number" matches "CUSTOMER NUMBER"
Address	Text	Lookup: "ADDRESS" in "Customers" when "Customer Number" matches "CUSTOMER NUMBER"
Address2	Text	Lookup: "Address2" in "Customers" when "Customer Number" matches "CUSTOMER NUMBER"
Description	Text	Lookup: "Description" in "Inventory" when "Part Number" matches "Part Number"
Unit Cost	Number	Lookup: "Unit Cost" in "Inventory" when "Part Number" matches "Part Number"
Ext Cost	Calculation (Number)	= Qty * Unit Cost
Item Count	Calculation (Number)	= sum (Qty)
Sub Total	Calculation (Number)	= sum (Ext Cost)
Sales Tax	Calculation (Number)	= round (Sub Total * .055,2)
Shipping Cost	Calculation (Number)	= Item Count * .75
Grand Total	Calculation (Number)	= Sub Total + Sales Tax + Shipping Cost

Figure 11-133   The printout of the Sales Invoices field definitions

SUMMARY

- FileMaker provides excellent online help.

- Even though FileMaker automatically saves any changes you make to a file, it is important that you regularly save a copy of the file and make periodic backups. This applies to any application that manages important information, not just to FileMaker.

- FileMaker has five main work modes: Define, Browse, Find, Sort, and Layout. Define is used to name the fields and specify their type, entry options, and formulas. Browse is used to view the file, add records, delete records, and modify information stored in the existing records. Find is used to locate records with information that matches a specific criteria. Sort rearranges the file in ascending or descending order based on the contents of one or more sort fields. Layout is used to create a variety of reports and screens for editing, displaying, and printing the contents of the file.

- Six main field types are available in FileMaker: text, number, date, picture, calculation, and summary.

- Entry options are available for automatically entering information, providing a list to choose from, and specifying criteria that FileMaker will check before accepting an entry into a field.

- FileMaker provides the ability to print several types of reports: detail reports, summary reports, labels reports, and field definition reports.

- FileMaker has a variety of tools available for creating and modifying the layout of screens and reports. These tools include: arrow tool, text tool, line tool, rectangle tool, rounded rectangle tool, oval tool, field tool, and part tool.

- The three main parts of a layout are: header, body, and footer. Title parts and summary parts are also available.

- FileMaker provides the capability to preview reports before you commit them to paper.

- FileMaker allows you to create four types of new layouts: standard, columnar, label, and blank.

- FileMaker has the ability to look up information in one file and copy it into another based on a common value stored in a key field.

- You can format fields to change how they display and print their contents.

KEY TERMS

1-up labels	labels report
3-up labels	Layout mode
	line tool
active record indicator	lookup field
arrow tool	
ascending order	number field
backup	oval tool
blank report	
Body part	part tool
book	picture field
Browse mode	
	record
calculation field	rectangle tool
columnar report	repeating field
concatenate	rounded rectangle tool
date field	search criteria
Define	slide control handle
descending order	Sliding objects left
detail report	Sliding objects up
	Sliding part up
field tool	Sort
field	sort field
file	status area
Find	string literal
Footer part	Sub-summary part
footer	summary field
Header part	T-squares
header	text tool
	text field
key field	

FILEMAKER II COMMAND KEYS AND SHORTCUTS

Apple Menu
Help   ⌘ -/

File Menu
Close   ⌘ -W
Preview   ⌘ -U
Print   ⌘ -P
Quit   ⌘ -Q

Edit Menu   (Browse Mode)
Undo   ⌘ -Z
Cut   ⌘ -X
Copy   ⌘ -C
Paste   ⌘ -V
Select All   ⌘ -Y
New Record   ⌘ -N
Duplicate Record   ⌘ -D
Delete Record   ⌘ -E

Select Menu
Browse   ⌘ -B
Find   ⌘ -F
Refind   ⌘ -R
Find All   ⌘ -G
Sort   ⌘ -S
Layout   ⌘ -L

Gadgets Menu
T-Squares   ⌘ -T
Invisible Grid   ⌘ -Y

ADDITIONAL PROJECTS

The following project is accompanied by briefer instructions than those you have previously completed in this chapter. If necessary, refer to the previous projects in this chapter for information and step-by-step instructions for any command that you don't remember how to use. Also, FileMaker's Help file contains valuable and easily accessed information. You will not be reminded to save your work—by now you should be thinking of that on your own.

Project 4: Creating Summary Reports

In Project 4 you will learn to create a summary report that organizes all sales transactions by customer, lists information about each sales invoice, summarizes total sales by customer, and provides final summaries about all the sales invoices as a group.

You will learn to create two new parts: a sub-summary part that summarizes information for each customer when the file is sorted by customer number and a grand summary part that provides information about all the transactions as a group.

You will learn to create a new layout by duplicating layout number 2 that you created in Project 3 and then modifying it for this project.

You will also learn how to select sales invoices that fall within a range of dates. This gives you the ability to display or print a summary for a particular month, quarter, or year in addition to summarizing all of the transactions in the file.

INVOICE

1417 South Jonquil St.
Smyrna, GA 30829
(404) 555-7283

Fax: (404) 555-6284

NAME		CUST NO	MONTHLY	INVOICES
SALES DATE	INVOICE #	SUB TOTAL	SALES TAX	SHIPPING COST
Ms. Sandra M. Hardin		1001		$16.88
Oct 29, 1990	90002	$14.58	$0.80	$1.50
Mr. Jim Bell		1003		$23.03
Oct 29, 1990	90004	$20.41	$1.12	$1.50
Ms. Kay B. Kusunoki		1004		$119.20
Oct 29, 1990	90001	$110.85	$6.10	$2.25
Ms. Faye Mauney		1005		$28.98
Oct 29, 1990	90006	$26.05	$1.43	$1.50
Mrs. Mattie L. Dilbeccio		1006		$2,016.41
Oct 29, 1990	90005	$1,194.63	$65.70	$56.25
Oct 29, 1990	90007	$593.68	$32.65	$73.50
Mr. Gary H. Westmoreland		1008		$64.69
Oct 29, 1990	90003	$58.47	$3.22	$3.00

Average Sale	$288.38	Monthly Invoices	$2,269.19
Largest Sale	$1,194.63	Total Sales Tax	$111.02
Smallest Sale	$14.58	Total Shipping Cost	$139.50

Private and Confidential   Internal Use Only

Page 1

Figure 11-134   Final output of Project 4

DUPLICATING A LAYOUT

To begin this project, open FileMaker and save a copy of the file.

If you have been experimenting with the Sales Invoices file, check the status area to see that the file is not sorted and that all records are currently being browsed.

⌘-S   ➡   You can be sure the file is not sorted by choosing **Sort** and then clicking **Unsort** in the dialog box.

⌘-G   ➡   All records can be browsed by choosing **Find All** from the Select menu.

⌘-L   ➡   Change to Layout mode, and scroll to layout 2.

You will now be looking at the layout you created in Project 3. Let's duplicate this layout.

⌘-D   ➡   Choose **Duplicate Layout** from the Edit menu.

MODIFYING A LAYOUT

You will now see that there are three layouts associated with the Sales Invoices file.

Let's delete all the fields, text, and graphics objects that won't be used in this report.

➡   Select the fields and text labels shown in Figure 11-135. You can use Shift-click to add objects to the selection. Press Backspace (or Delete) to delete these objects.

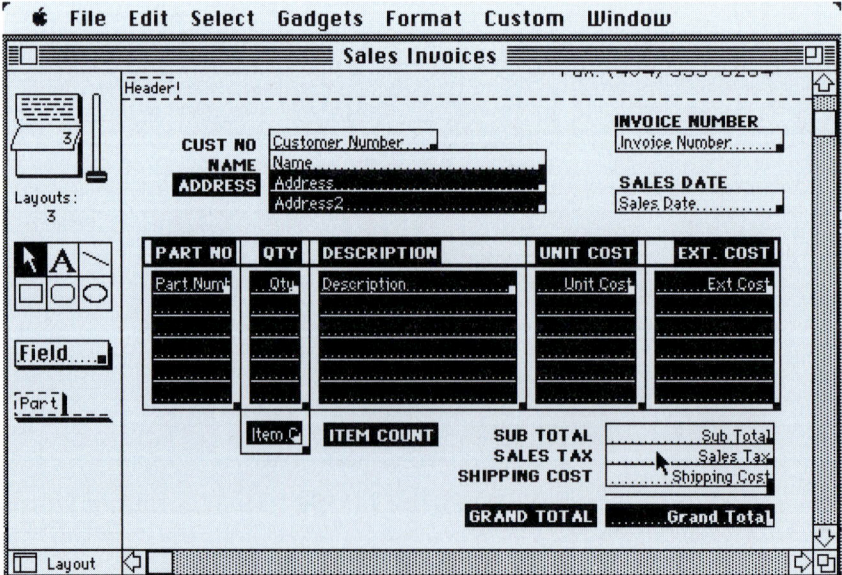

Figure 11-135   Selecting the objects to be deleted

➡   Now delete the rectangles and lines that are not needed in this layout.

You will be left with a layout that contains most of the fields and text you will use for this project (see Figure 11-136).

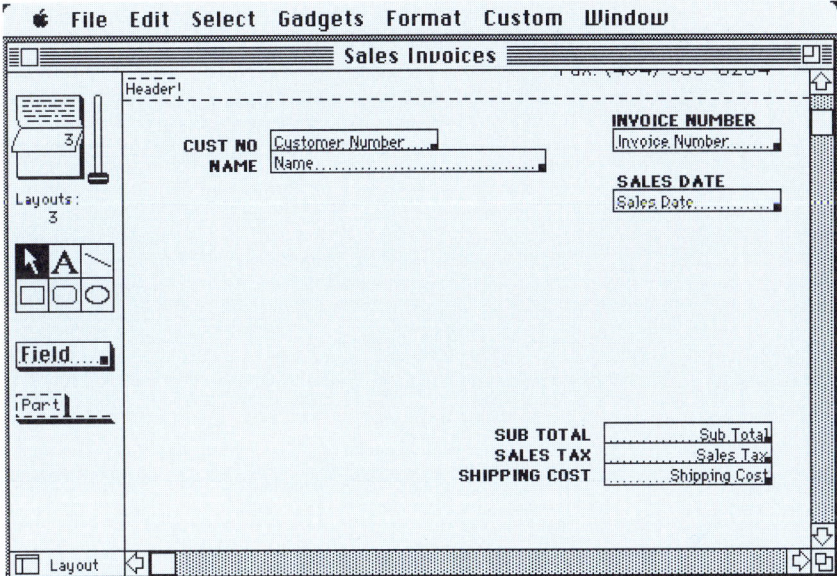

Figure 11-136   The layout after deleting unnecessary objects

The body section will be much smaller in this layout, and you need to make more room in the footer for later use.

➡   Scroll down in the layout until you can see the Body part icon. Drag it back up to just below the Shipping Cost field. Drag the Footer part to about 2 inches below the Body part (see Figure 11-137).

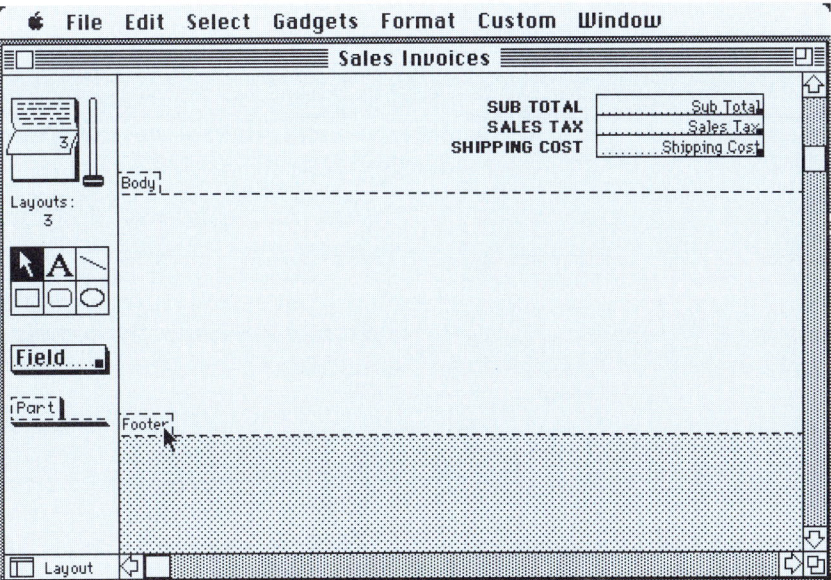

Figure 11-137   Adjusting the Body and Footer parts

You need to make the header about an inch larger. You will put two rows of column headings in the header and add a line above and below these headings.

➡ Drag the Header part down about an inch or so (see Figure 11-138).

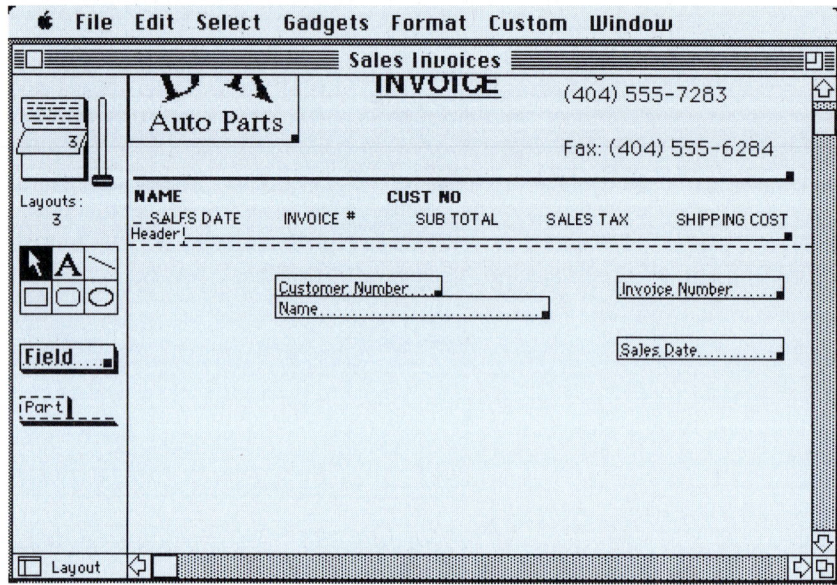

Figure 11-138   Adjusting the objects in the header

➡ Now you need to drag the text labels from the body area into the header area, as shown in Figure 11-138. Don't forget that you can use the T-squares to make this process easier and neater.

➡ Change Invoice Number to Invoice # to make more room for the other column headings.

Since every customer in the summary report will have at least two lines of information, you can make the first line bold and the second line plain to help differentiate them and make it more obvious which headings refer to which data items.

➡ Change the second row of headings (starting with Sales Date) to plain text.

➡ Add a 2-point horizontal line below the fax number and a 1-point horizontal line under the column headings and completely inside the header.

➡ Drag the Header part up to just below the second line you just added.

You now have the header for this report completed. In Project 3, there were only three parts to the layout: the header, the body, and the footer. In this layout, two more parts will be added: a sub-summary and a grand summary.

ADDING A SUB-SUMMARY PART

In this report, you will list each customer one time and, below that, important information about each transaction completed by that customer. You want the customer name to only show once, and you want to show the customer number and the total of all transactions that are listed for that customer. To do this, you will add a *sub-summary part* that will be used in the report when the file is sorted by customer number. Then, you will list the transactions in the body section of the report.

➠ Drag a new part onto the layout about an inch or so below the header.

A dialog box will appear to let you select which body part you want this one to represent.

➠ Click **Sub-summary when sorted by:**, and then click on **Customer Number** in the scrolling list to the right (see Figure 11-139).

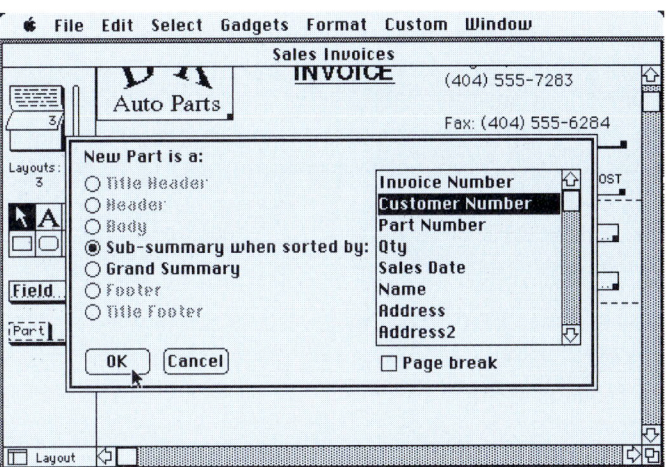

Figure 11-139   Adding a sub-summary and sort requirement

➠ Move the Name and Customer Number fields into this sub-summary area (see Figure 11-140).

You can use the T-squares gadget to help in aligning objects in the layout. Resizing and moving the fields and text labels will also be necessary to get good use of the space available.

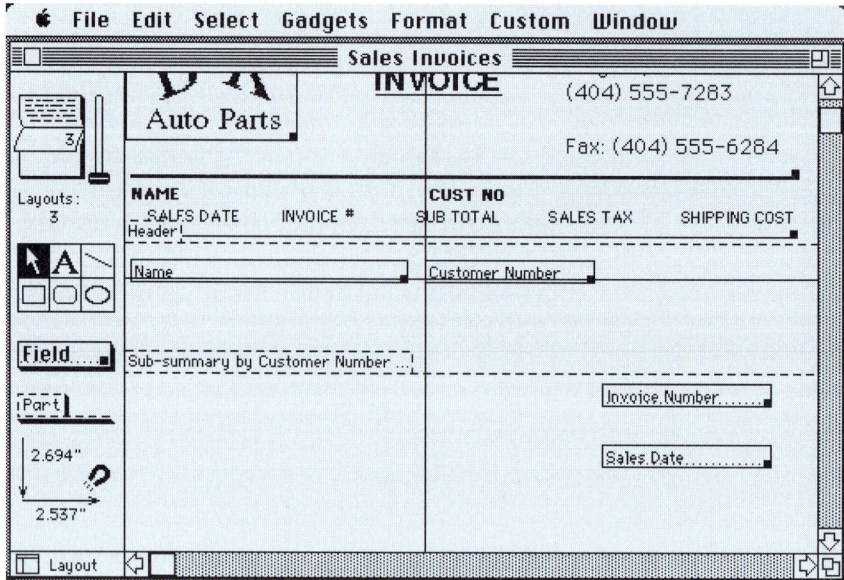

Figure 11-140 Moving fields into the sub-summary part

➡ Add a 1-point horizontal line at the top of the sub-summary area to separate each customer.

Now you need to move the fields that will be in the body into a row just below the sub-summary.

➡ Move the Sales Date, Invoice Number, Sub Total, Sales Tax, and Shipping Cost fields into a row in the body of the layout (see Figure 11-141).

➡ Drag the Body part up just below this row of five fields.

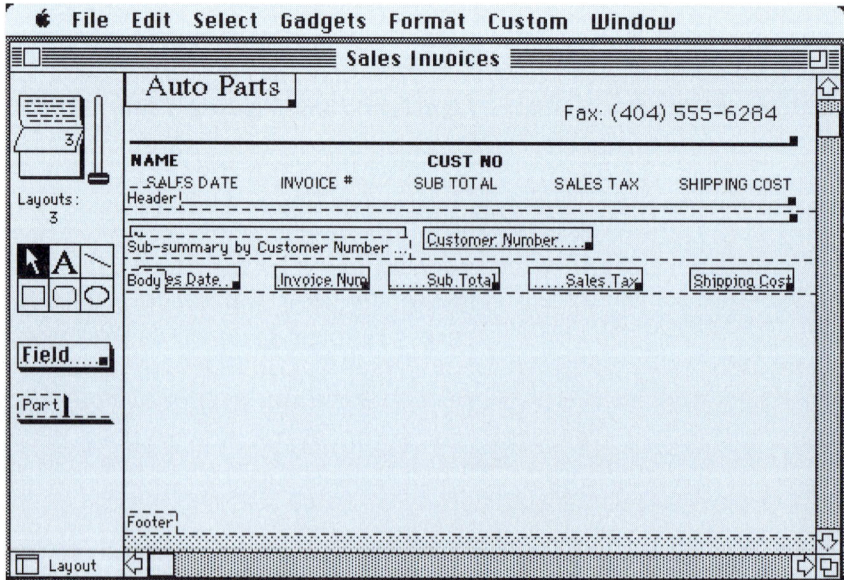

Figure 11-141 Placing fields in the body area of the layout

DEFINING SUMMARY FIELDS

At the end of the report, you want some information to be presented about the records in the file as a group. When you are managing a business, it is useful to know basic statistical information about your sales. Let's calculate the average amount of all the sales and determine the largest and smallest purchases, the total amount for all transactions, the total sales tax collected, and the total amount collected to cover shipping costs.

You want this information to print just once, and you want to reflect summary information about the file as a whole, so you need to define six summary fields, create a summary part, and place the fields into that part.

Let's define the summary fields first.

⇒ Choose **Define** from the Select menu.

⌘-S ⇒ Click **Summary** to designate the type of field, and name the first field Monthly Invoices. Click **OK** or press Return.

A dialog box will appear on the screen (see Figure 11-142), and you should click **Total of** and select **Grand Total** in the scrolling list of fields.

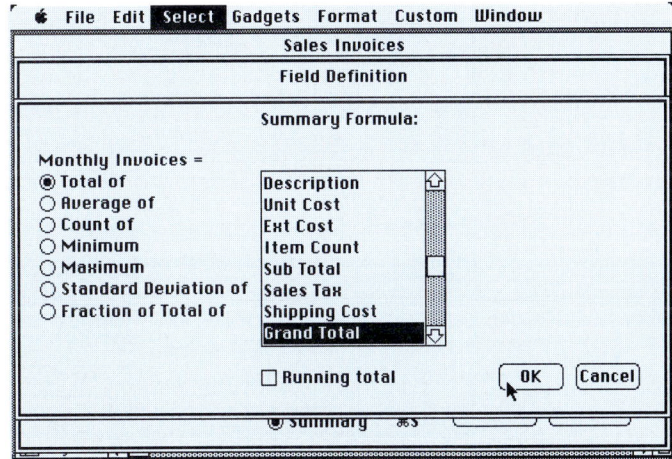

Figure 11-142   Defining the Monthly Invoices summary field

⇒ Using this method, define the other five summary fields (Average Sale, Largest Sale, Smallest Sale, Total Sales Tax, and Total Shipping Cost) as shown in Figure 11-143.

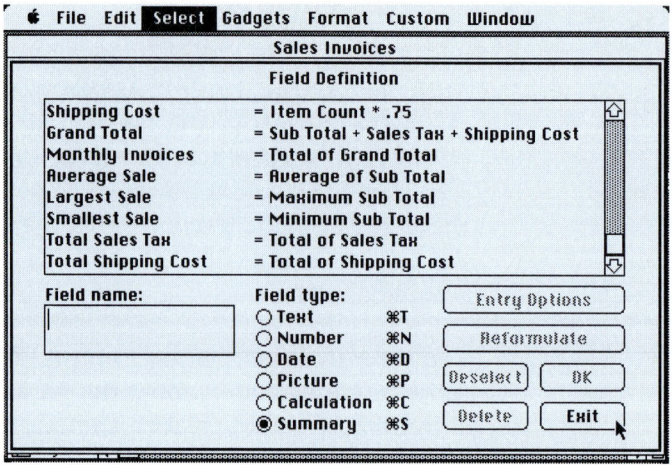

Figure 11-143   Formulas for all the summary fields

When you exit from the Field Definition dialog box, FileMaker adds these new fields into the body of the layout and makes the body large enough to hold them (see Figure 11-144).

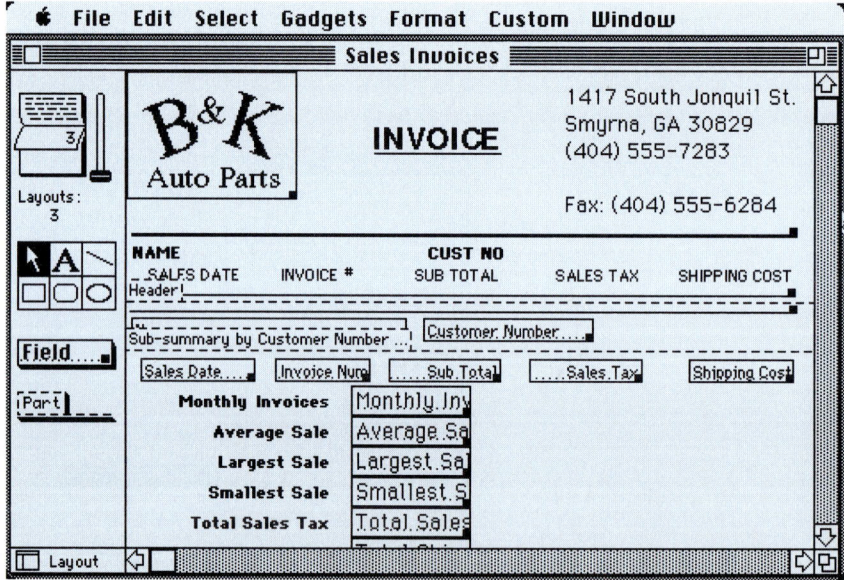

Figure 11-144   FileMaker adds the new fields to the layout.

⟹ Select these fields, and format them as Geneva, 9-point, plain text, and align right.

⟹ Format the summary fields to display currency with commas, dollar signs, and 2 digits to the right of the decimal point.

You want to use the Monthly Invoices field in two different ways in this layout. If you put this field into the sub-summary section of the report, it will show the total amount of all purchases by that particular customer. If you put this field into the grand summary section, it will show the total amount of all purchases made by all customers.

You will duplicate this field (and its text label) and place one Monthly Invoices field in the sub-summary area. Then you will create the Grand Summary part and put the other Monthly Invoices field into the grand summary area.

⇒ Deselect the fields, and then select just the Monthly Invoices field and its associated text label, copy them, and paste them back into the layout. Move the new objects to any white area where you can see them.

⇒ Move the Monthly Invoices field into the sub-summary area and the text label into the header, as shown in Figure 11-145.

⇒ Format the Monthly Invoices field in the sub-summary area to display bold text.

⇒ Rearrange the remaining six summary fields and their text and drag them into the footer. Then drag the Body part up to just below the Sales Date field.

ADDING A GRAND SUMMARY PART

Now you need to create the Grand Summary part and place the summary fields inside it.

⇒ Drag a new part into the footer below the six summary fields, and when the dialog box appears, click **Grand Summary**.

⇒ Arrange the fields and their text labels as shown in Figure 11-145. Add a 2-point line at the top of the grand summary area to separate this section from the last customer.

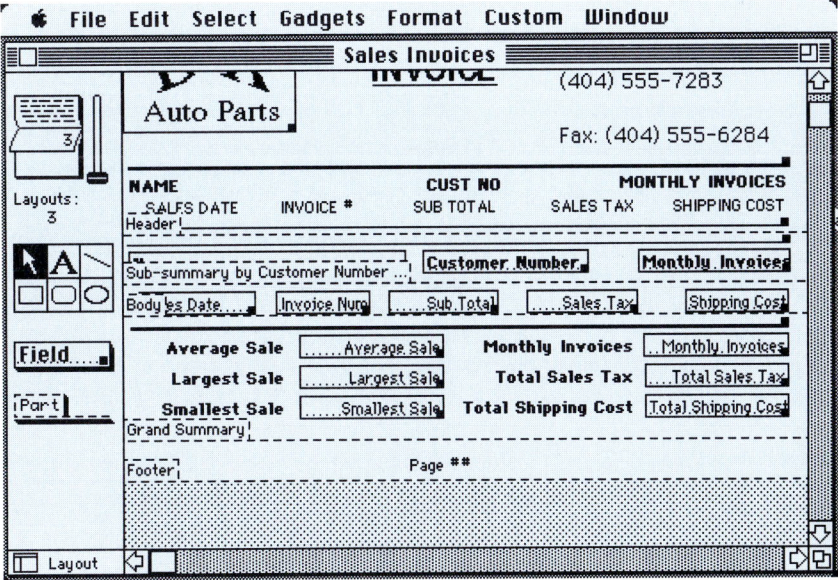

Figure 11-145   Placing a grand summary part and its fields

⇒ Add a page number placeholder in the footer, as shown in Figure 11-145.

This report is for your use only, so it should be labeled as private.

⇒ Make the footer a little larger, and add two text blocks. The first text object should say Private and Confidential, and the other should say Internal Use Only.

Your layout should now look like the one shown in Figure 11-146.

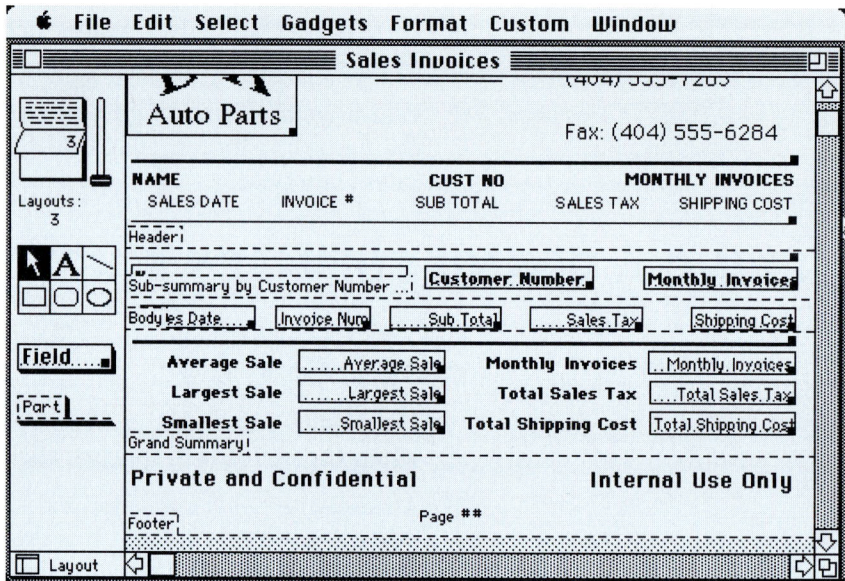

Figure 11-146   The last text objects have been placed.

You have completed designing the layout form, so let's see what it looks like when you browse and preview this report.

BROWSING AND PREVIEWING THE REPORT

⌘-B   ⇒ Choose **Browse** from the Select menu.

Your screen should look like the one shown in Figure 11-147.

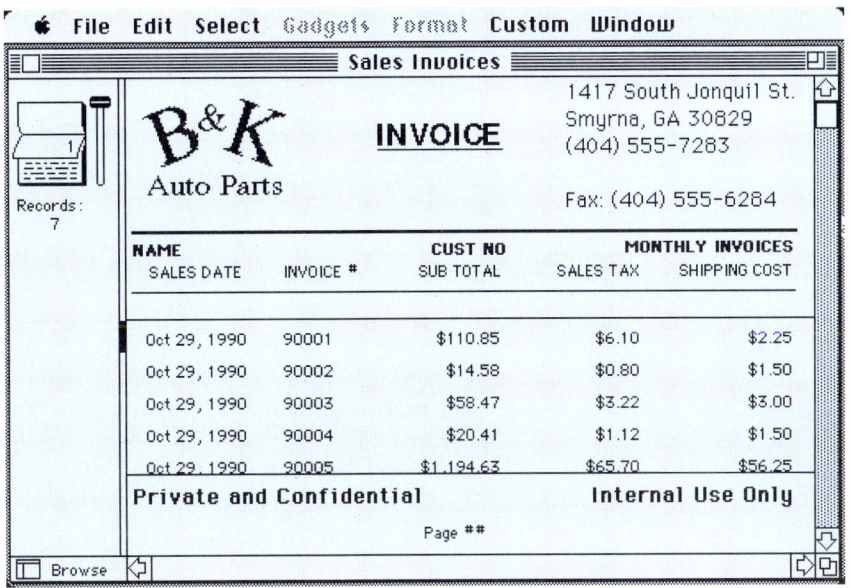

Figure 11-147   Browsing the Sales Invoices report

Where are the customer names, customer numbers, and total invoice amounts?

The sub-summary part will only take effect when the report is sorted by customer number.

⌘-S   ➡   Sort the file by customer number.

⌘-U   ➡   Preview the report (see Figure 11-148).

You can see that the report is working like you wanted.

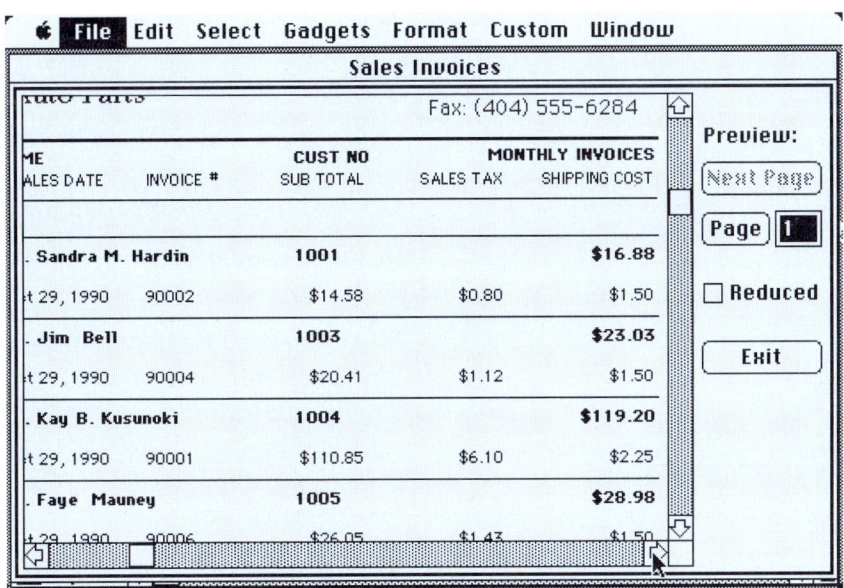

Figure 11-148   Previewing your summary report

➡   Now you can exit the preview.

PRINTING THE REPORT

This report layout is completed. Now is a good time to print the report and the field definitions for the file.

⌘-P ➡ Print the summary report, and then print the field definitions.

SELECTING INVOICES WITHIN A RANGE OF DATES

You now have a report that will give you summary information about the entire file, but it would be more useful if you could tell FileMaker to summarize all transactions for a particular period of time.

FileMaker provides the capability to produce this type of summary report. You will use the report layout you just designed, and all you have to do is select all the records that match specific criteria.

You can choose a summary of all transactions by one customer by using the Find command. If you select **Find**, a report appears on the screen showing rectangles where the field information would normally be. If you type the customer number into the Customer Number field and click **Find**, all the transactions for that customer appear. (You would still have to remember to sort by customer number after finding the records so the sub-summary section would be activated.)

Another use for the Find command is to select all transactions within a particular range of dates. For instance, you can tell FileMaker to find all sales invoices with sales dates that are between 10/1/90 and 10/31/90. This would select the records you entered in Project 3.

Let's record some sales transactions for July 1991.

⌘-L ⌘-B ➡ Switch to layout 2 and choose **Browse** mode.

Enter the following four sales transactions.

7/14/91, Customer #1002 purchased 2 #1017 headlights and 1 #1019 battery.

7/15/91, Customer #1005 purchased 1 #1020 fuel pump.

7/18/91, Customer #1007 purchased 1 #1018 voltage regulator and 1 #1019 battery.

7/22/91, Customer #1009 purchased 2 #1017 headlights, 1 #1018 voltage regulator, and 1 #1020 fuel pump.

⌘-L ➡ Switch to layout 3.

Let's find all sales transactions for July 1991.

⌘-F ➡ Choose **Find** from the Select menu. Type **7/1/91...7/31/91** into the Sales Date field.

Don't worry if it doesn't all show. Just type carefully, or change to the layout and make the sales date longer.

⇒   Click **Find**.

⌘-S   ⇒   Sort the found records by customer number.

When you preview the report, you should see a screen like the one shown in Figure 11-149 (when you scroll a little).

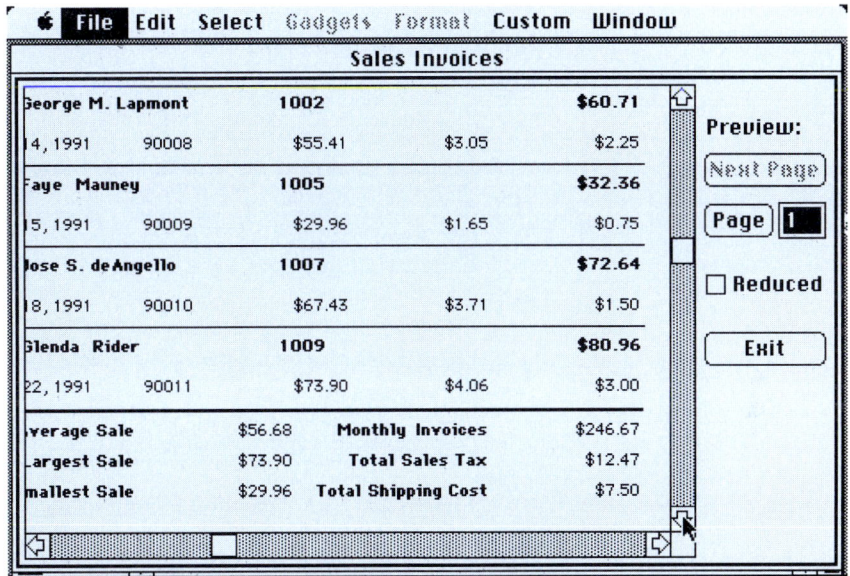

Figure 11-149   Previewing the summary report for July sales

⇒   Exit the preview when you are ready. Print the report if you want.

If you want to see a summary for all the records in the file, you can easily do so.

⌘-G   ⌘-S   ⇒   Choose **Find All** from the Select menu, and then sort by customer number.

When you preview this report, your screen should look similar to the one shown in Figure 11-150.

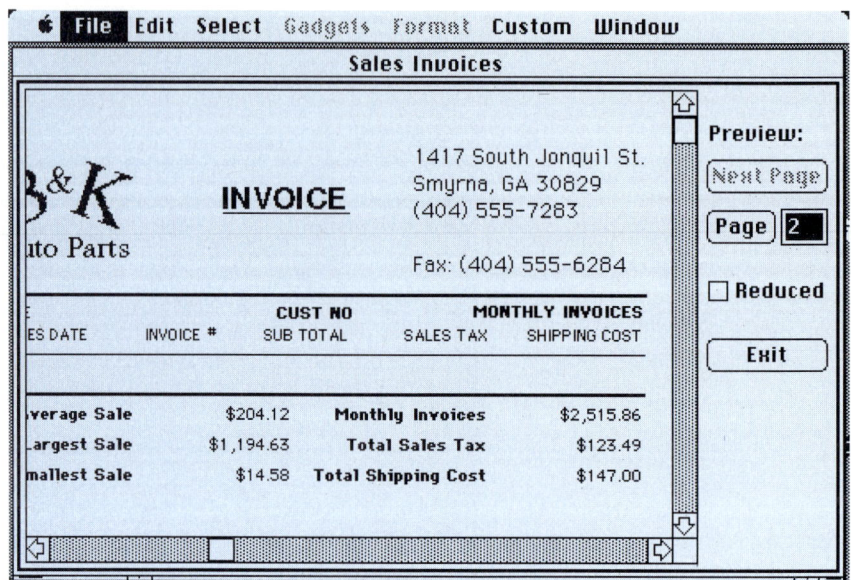

Figure 11-150   Previewing all sales records

➡ Exit from the preview.

You can produce many types of summary reports using this layout. If you want more information about selecting records using the Find command, try looking in the Help file.

You try a report now.

➡ Print a report showing all transactions during the period from July 15, 1991, through July 18, 1991.

You might try adding a few more sales transactions and previewing or printing some more reports.

Congratulations! You have completed all the FileMaker projects.

Chapter 12: HyperCard 1.2

What You Will Learn in This Chapter

After reading this chapter and completing the projects in it, you should be able to:

- Understand what a stack is and how it can be used

- Open stacks and browse through the information in them

- Add and modify the information in stacks

- Create a new stack using HyperCard's authoring features

- Create, modify, and use buttons to control HyperCard's actions

- Create, modify, and use fields to store information

- Use the painting tools to change the appearance of stacks

- Store graphics in stacks

- Add visual effects to your stacks

- Print the cards from a stack

- Print a report based on information stored in the cards of a stack

This chapter introduces you to all these aspects of using HyperCard, but it does not attempt to cover all the features of the program. Several excellent books have been written that cover the entire program, including references to the HyperTalk scripting language and samples of using it.

STARTING HYPERCARD

HyperCard

➠ Start HyperCard by double-clicking on its icon.

When HyperCard opens, it presents you with the *Home* stack, as shown in Figure 12-1. Your *Home* card may look different from the one shown. HyperCard allows you to customize the Home stack.

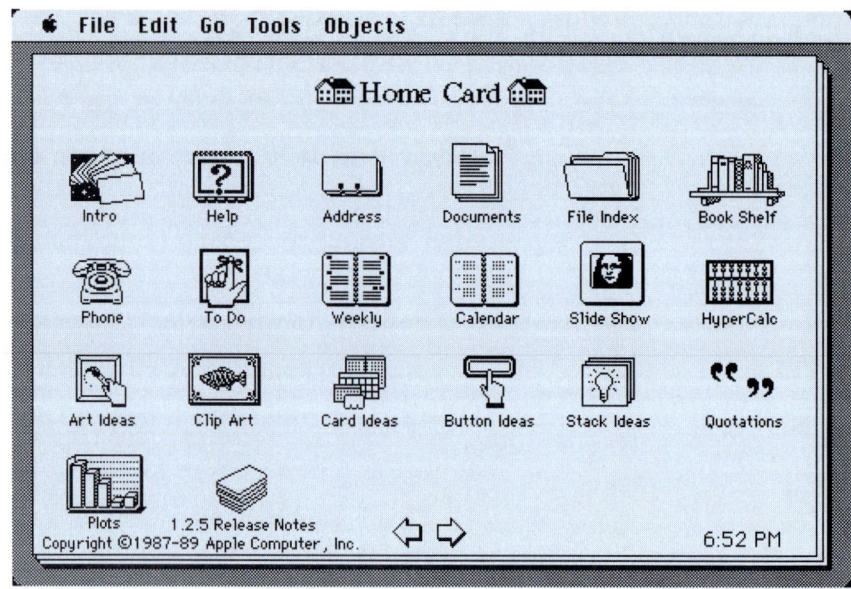

Figure 12-1   HyperCard's Home stack

You can see a number of icons on the Home card. Each is linked to a card in another stack. Unlike icons on the desktop, you don't have to double-click on one to open it. In HyperCard, all you do is click once on the button, and it will then do whatever it is programmed to do. In this case each button is programmed to take you to a specific card or stack.

USING THE GO MENU

Before you start jumping around to the different stacks, you should know how to use the Go menu.

Some stacks allow you to move freely within the stack, and some do not. Since HyperCard is customizable by many people, you can assume certain types of buttons will respond in a particular manner when you click them. However, their response to your click may not always be as you assume.

The first thing to notice is that the Go menu is divided into three groups of commands. The top group is designed to allow movement inside a stack or to other stacks. The middle group is for use in moving inside one stack, and the bottom group is important because it lets you issue commands directly to the stack. These commands may be as varied as the number of people using the stack and can include most of the *HyperTalk* commands.

Back   takes you back to the last card you visited, even if it was in
            a completely different stack.

Home   takes you directly to the Home card.

Help   takes you to the opening card of the Help stack, which
            contains a very large collection of information about
            HyperCard. If you really want to get off to a flying start
            with this program you should become familiar with the
            use of the Help stack. Many people have learned to use
            HyperCard just through the information contained there.

Recent   shows a collection of up to 42 of the last cards you have
            looked at. You can return to one of these cards by clicking
            on its picture.

The next group of commands lets you move around inside the current
stack.

First   takes you to the very first card in the stack, even if it is on
            a different background.

Previous   takes you to the card just before the current card. This is
            generally the same as clicking a left arrow button.

Next   takes you to the next card in the stack, and works the same
            as most right arrow buttons.

Last   takes you to the very last card of the stack.

The last group of commands allows you to do many different things,
depending on what you do after you issue the command.

Find   allows you to find a word, phrase, or even just a few
            characters that appear in any field in the stack. It is a very
            powerful command and searches very quickly to find
            information, even if you can remember only a portion of
            it. For example, if you can only remember a person's first
            name, HyperCard can still find that person in an address
            stack.

Message   shows the Message box and allows you to type one line of
            HyperTalk commands.

EXPLORING THE INTRO STACK

The Intro stack is a friendly introduction to HyperCard. It is not really
a tutorial, but it introduces you to some of the concepts involved in
using HyperCard.

➠   Click the button named Intro.

Figure 12-2   Intro stack opening card

➡ Click the **What is HyperCard?** button.

The Intro stack takes you through a brief introduction to HyperCard. Each card has an arrow pointing to the right. When you have finished reading the card, click on the right arrow to advance to the next one (see Figure 12-3).

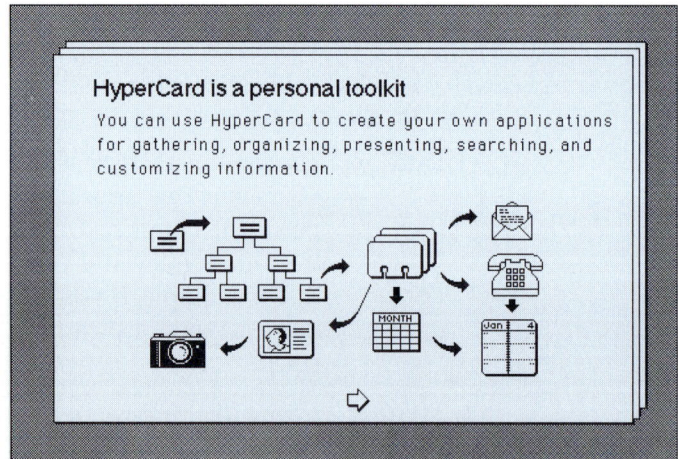

Figure 12-3   The second card in the Intro stack

Continue working through the Intro stack until you come to the last card. In a few minutes you will arrive at the card shown in Figure 12-4, except that the rectangles will not be showing. In fact, it may be a little difficult sometimes to tell where buttons are located since they can be made transparent.

⌘-Option ➡ Press the Command and Option keys at the same time.

You will now see a rectangle drawn around each button on the card (as shown in Figure 12-4).

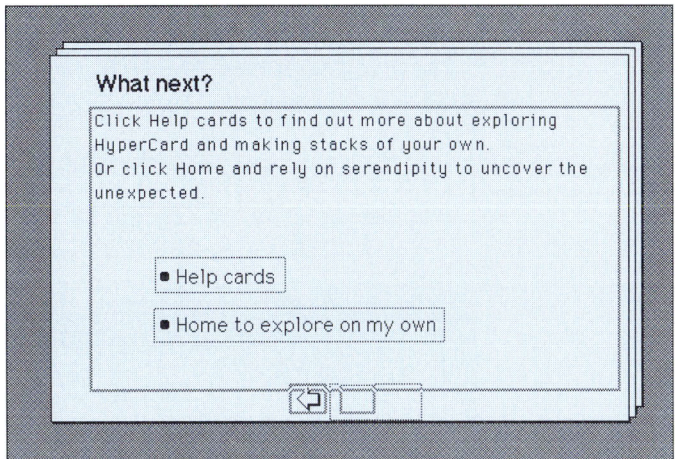

Figure 12-4   Using Command and Option to see the buttons

When you release the two keys, the rectangles will once again disappear, but now you know exactly where the buttons are. This feature is useful whenever you are not sure what buttons are available on a card.

➥ Now that you have found the buttons, click the **Help cards** button.

GETTING HELP

Figure 12-5 shows the first card of the Help stack.

The HyperCard Help stack is a powerful learning tool and will remain a useful reference even when you have become an experienced user.

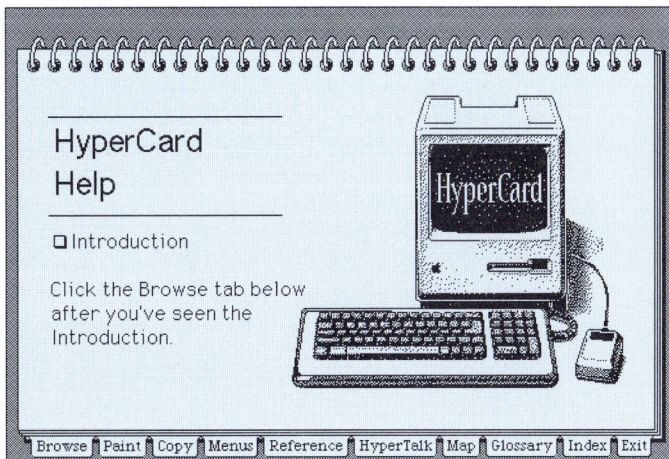

Figure 12-5   The Help stack's opening card

Notice that the Help stack looks like a spiral bound set of flip cards, or a notebook turned sideways. The tabs along the bottom look like and function as index cards. To select the index card of your choice, move the pointer to it and click. (Each tab is a button in disguise.)

You are in the process of learning how to browse through HyperCard, so now would be a good time to see what the Help stack has to say about browsing.

➡ Click the **Browse** tab to go to the first card that has information about browsing (see Figure 12-6).

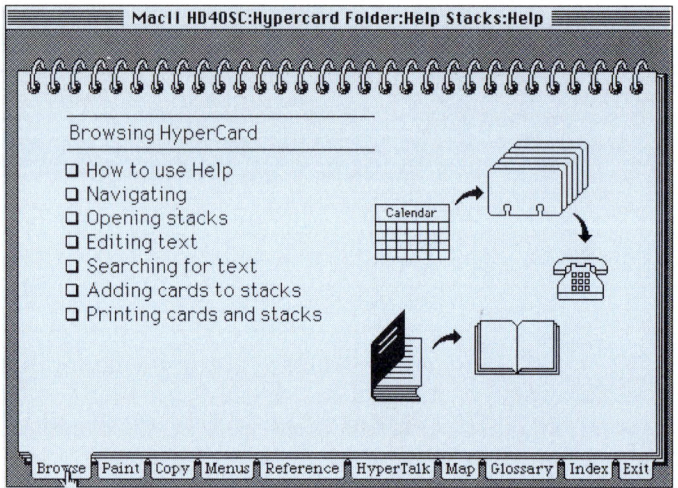

Figure 12-6   Index card for help in browsing through HyperCard

This card is an index to seven topics associated with browsing through HyperCard stacks. By reading each of these sections, you will learn the basics of working with HyperCard. Let's see what this section has to say about using Help.

➡ Click **How to use Help**.

Figure 12-7 shows the card this command will present. It tells you about basic arrow buttons and the shortcut command to get help (pressing Command-?) and provides an introduction to using the Find command.

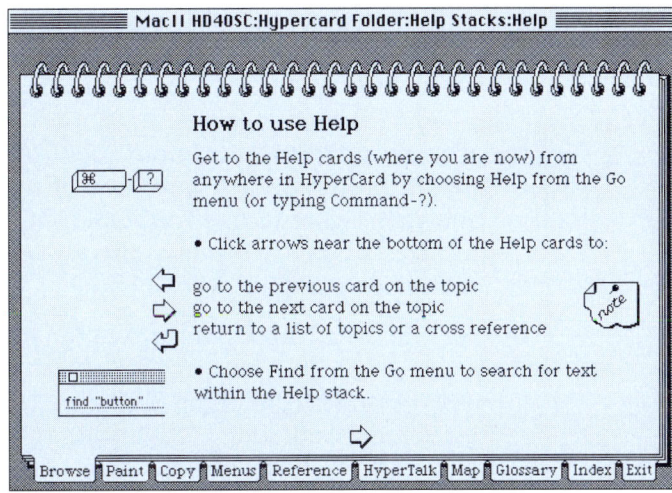

Figure 12-7   First help card of How to use Help topic

The right arrow at the bottom of the card indicates that more information on the same topic is on the next card.

➠   Click on the right arrow to see the next help card on this subject.

This card (see Figure 12-8) tells you about some of the conventions used in the Help stack. It discusses the Glossary and Index features of the Help stack, two parts that are useful for finding information quickly.

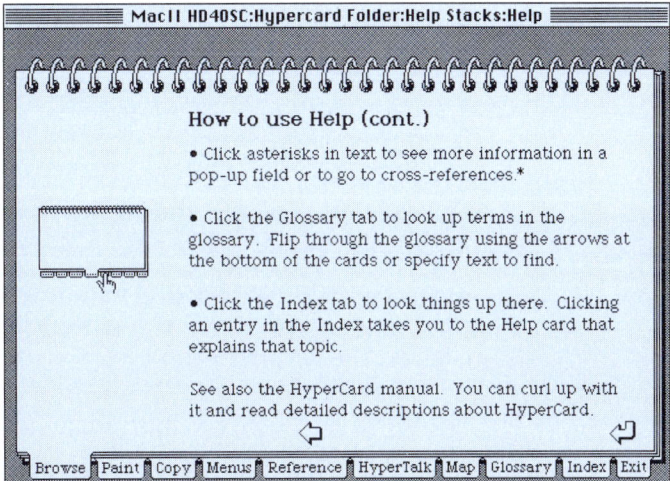

Figure 12-8   Second How to use Help card

The Help stack uses asterisks to indicate that more information is available about a subject. Clicking on the asterisk either shows a hidden field with more information or takes you directly to a card that contains cross-referenced material.

At the bottom of the card you can see two buttons: a left arrow (Previous) button and a Return button. The lack of a right arrow (Next) button indicates that you have reached the end of this branch of information.

If you wanted to learn more about browsing, you could click on the Return button and choose another topic from the index on the card shown in Figure 12-6. If you would like to explore more about this topic, feel free to do so. When you have finished reading about browsing, continue with the next command.

➡ Click the **Index** tab to go to the first card in the Help stack Index.

The first Index card in the Help stack is shown in Figure 12-9. The index gives you several ways of finding more information on HyperCard. Each term to the right of a shadowed square is surrounded by a button. If you click on the term, the button tells HyperCard to take you to the card containing more information about that term.

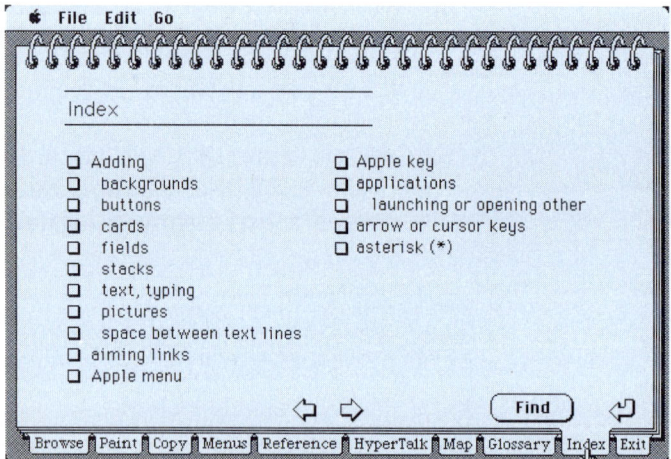

Figure 12-9   The first Index card

You can also look at the previous or next card by clicking on the left or right arrow, respectively. If you don't want to look at the index, you can click on the Return button.

The Index card also has a button named Find located between the right arrow and the Return button. You saw a little about Find on the How to use Help cards. Let's learn more about HyperCard's ability to quickly find text in a stack.

➡ Click **Find**.

As soon as you click the Find button, the Message box appears with the phrase **Find** "" showing in the box (see Figure 12-10). The Find command normally puts this into the Message box, places the insertion point between the quotation marks, and then waits for you to type some characters or one or more words for it to find.

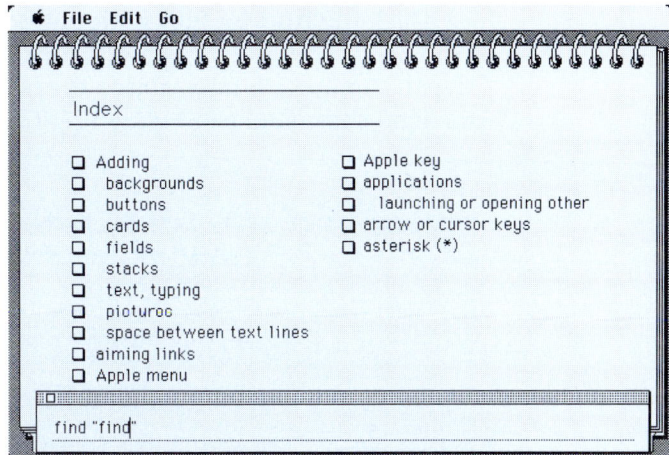

Figure 12-10 Using the Find command

If you type the first few characters of a word, HyperCard searches for any word that begins with those characters in all cards in that stack. If you type one word, it finds any card containing that word. If you type more than one word, it finds only the cards that contain all the words on the same card.

➡ Enter **find** between the quotation marks, and then press the Return key.

HyperCard ignores differences between uppercase and lowercase letters during a find operation.

When you press the Return key, Find looks through all the cards on the Index background and quickly shows the first card containing the word "find" or any word beginning with it (see Figure 12-11).

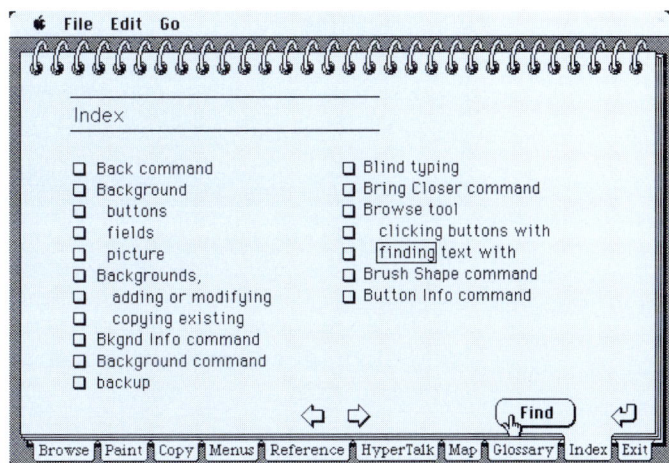

Figure 12-11 The text has been found.

The text found by HyperCard refers to finding text with the browse tool. Now you can click the phrase to take you to that entry in the Help stack.

➥ Click the **finding text with** phrase.

HyperCard quickly takes you to the first card that explains how to use the Find command (see Figure 12-12).

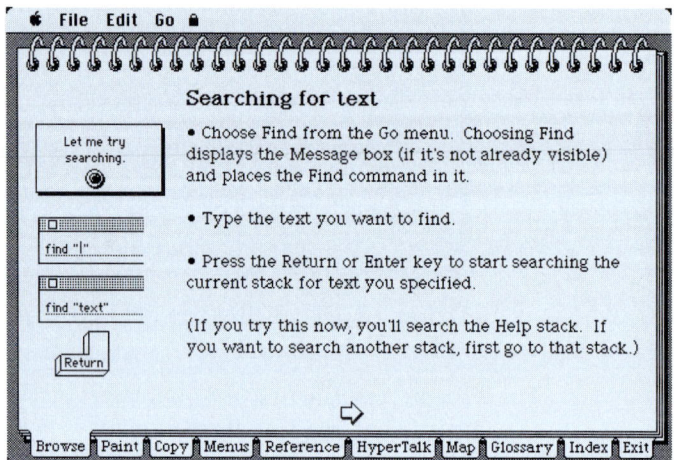

Figure 12-12   Help on searching for text

➥ When you finish reading this card, click on the right arrow.

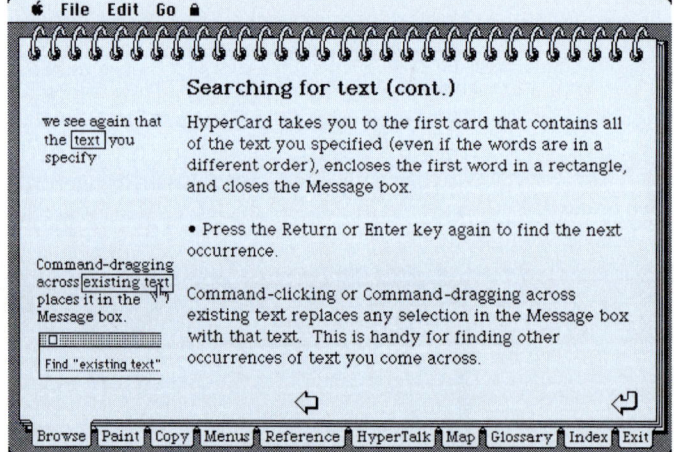

Figure 12-13   Second card on searching for text

You now see the second help card concerning searching for text. You know this is the end of the branch on this topic because there is no right arrow showing.

Depending on the amount of time you have and your interest in exploring the Help stack, you can continue looking through this informative stack. Read at least the Browse information at this point.

➥ When you are ready to leave the Help stack, click the **Exit** tab on the bottom right of the card.

You are returned to the Home card. If you were in a different stack and needed to look up something in the Help stack, you could choose **Help** from the Go menu or type Command-?. Then when you were finished with the Help stack, clicking the Exit tab would return you exactly to where you were before you opened the Help stack.

The Help stack is always available, easy to use, and full of useful information. If you want to learn to use HyperCard to its fullest, you should become familiar with the information in the Help stack and the HyperCard manual.

SAVING YOUR WORK

You do not have to save your work in HyperCard the way you do in other applications. HyperCard is designed to manage information that can change often, so it automatically saves all changes to the disk. These changes are saved almost as soon as they occur, so you stand very little chance of losing any changes you have made.

There is a drawback to this method, however. If you make a big change, involving several operations, that you really did not want to make, you may be forced to return the file to its original state using time-consuming methods.

Also, don't forget that all disks fail eventually. Even HyperCard's dedication to saving your work won't save you if the disk goes bad. Always make a backup of important information on a different disk.

USING HYPERCARD'S TOOLS

Everything in HyperCard in some way involves the use of cards, stacks, fields, and buttons. Whether you are using a stack created by someone else or one that you created, these are HyperCard's basic building blocks.

Essential Elements

Just as the Macintosh operating system is based on the desktop metaphor, HyperCard bases everything on stacks of *cards*.

Cards

You can think of these cards as lying on a table starting at the left and extending to the right, or you can think of them as being piled into a stack. Everything in HyperCard involves at least one card, and most stacks use many cards. HyperCard has a maximum limit of 16,777,216 cards, and a stack can be as large as 512 megabytes, so you shouldn't be too concerned about running out of room.

Unlike a row of cards laid out on a table or a stack of cards piled high on a table, the cards in a HyperCard stack are arranged in a circular fashion. When you reach the last card in a stack and tell HyperCard to go to the next one, it starts over again with the first card. If you are at the first card in the stack and issue a Go Previous command, HyperCard will bring up the last card in the stack.

A card has two layers. There is a *background layer,* which more than one card can share, and there is a *card layer* that belongs to that specific card only. Other objects can be located on one of these layers.

If an object (painting, button, field, and so forth) is located on the background layer, any new cards created with the same background will have this object visible on them as well, and the object will have the same properties and be able to do the same thing on all cards with that background.

If an object is located on the card layer, it will be local to that card only, and if you create a new card with the same background, the object located on the card layer of the original card will not appear on the new card.

It is not uncommon for someone new to HyperCard to mistakenly place an object on the card layer when it should be on the background layer. However, it is easy to cut the object from the card layer, switch to the background layer, and paste the object into its proper layer.

Stacks

This stack of cards, whether you think of it as being located from left to right or top to bottom, has certain features that are common to all stacks.

A stack may be composed of more than one card, as it usually is. A stack can even have multiple backgrounds, with each background containing more than one card. The converse of this is not true: a card cannot be in more than one background or stack.

Regardless of how you picture a stack of cards, each card has a certain relationship to the other cards in the stack. For any given card, except the top or left-most one, there is a card that comes before it known as the previous card. When moving between cards in the same stack, the left arrow means to go to the previous card.

Likewise, for every card (except the bottom or right-most one) there is a next card. The right arrow takes you to the next card.

Cards, by themselves, would not be very interesting, so HyperCard provides two other very important and useful objects.

Fields

A field is also known as a *text field.* It is an area on the card (either on the background or the card layer) that can hold editable text. All text in a field is limited to the same font, size, and style in HyperCard version 1.2.

If a field is in the background layer, then it will appear on every card in that background. But unlike with pictures and buttons, each card can store different information in the field.

A field located on the card layer only exists on that particular card, so it will not have varying contents among different cards.

There can be a maximum of 32,767 fields on a single card (if they would fit), and each field can store up to 30,000 characters. The script associated with each field can be up to 30,000 characters, also.

Buttons

A *button* exists to carry out some type of action. You have already seen a number of buttons. Each icon on the Home card is a button that is linked to a particular card in a different stack. Other buttons, such as the left and right arrows, function the same on every card (although their actions can be customized).

If you are working in the Authoring level, you can link a button to a different card. When you progress to scripting, you can create simple or complex scripts for the button to follow when it is activated.

Buttons in the background layer (known as *background buttons*) appear on every card in that background and have the same capabilities on each of those cards.

Card buttons appear on one card only and are used for special purposes that apply specifically to that card (although they can affect other cards, stacks, and even applications and documents).

Links

If you are in the Authoring or Scripting level, you can establish *links* from an object to another object (such as a button to a card). This involves no programming.

If you were to create a new button, you could double-click on the button (while you are using the button tool), and then tell HyperCard that you want to establish a link. A floating window appears and floats above everything else. You can go to another card or even open a different stack and find a particular card, and then tell HyperCard to link to either the stack or the currently selected card. The next time you click the button using the browse tool, HyperCard will take you to the place you chose for the link.

Home Stack

The *Home stack* is essential for HyperCard to operate. The first card, known as the *Home* card, contains a group of buttons that take you to the stacks distributed by Apple with HyperCard, as shown in Figure 12-1. You are free to delete any buttons you don't use and to add new buttons as you wish. In fact, if one card is not enough, you can add more Home cards to the stack (see Figure 12-14) and put additional buttons on the new cards. The button shown on the card in Figure 12-14 automatically opens Microsoft Word.

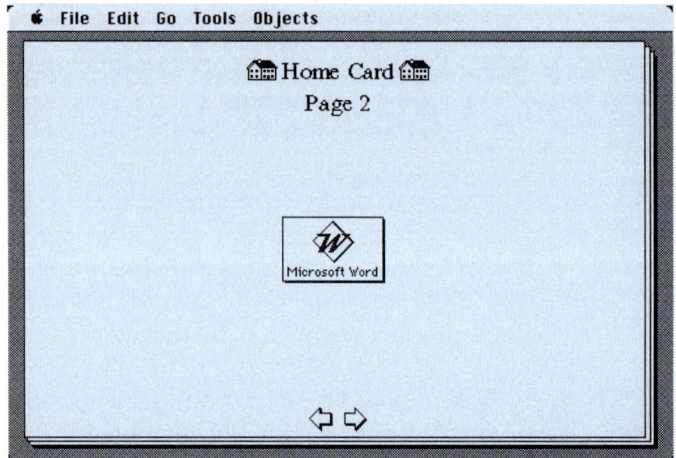

Figure 12-14   Second Home card added to Home stack

The next three cards of the Home stack are where HyperCard stores the paths it follows when looking for other stacks (see Figure 12-15), applications (see Figure 12-16), and documents (see Figure 12-17).

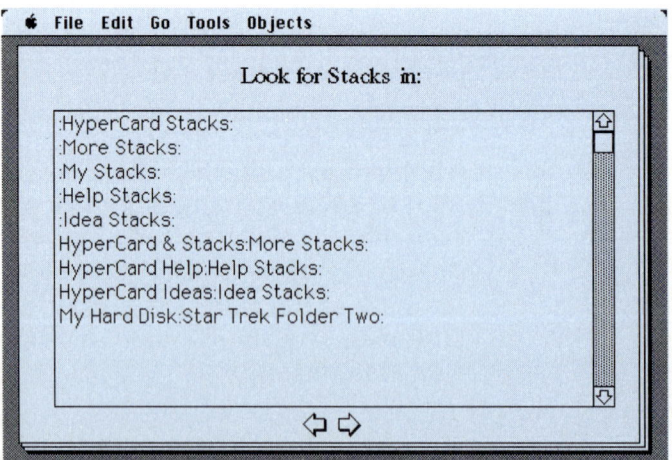

Figure 12-15   Pathnames for finding other stacks

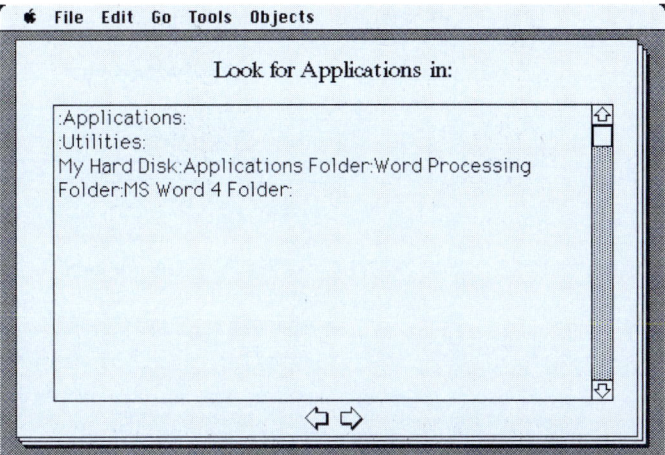

Figure 12-16   Pathnames for finding applications

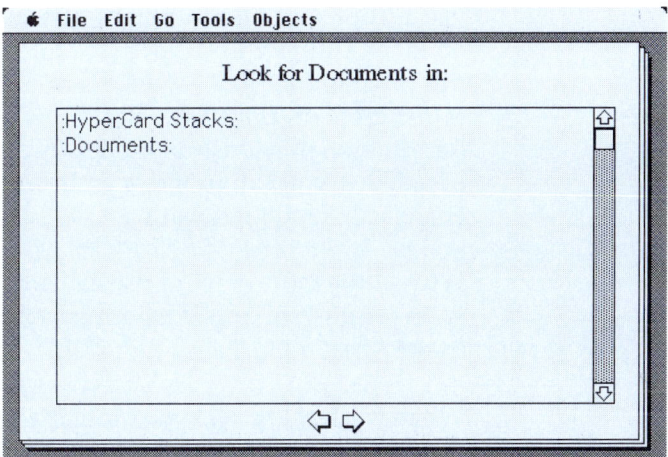

Figure 12-17   Pathnames for finding documents

You don't have to do anything to any of these cards. Whenever you issue the command to open a stack, application, or document, HyperCard looks in the folders listed on the appropriate card. If the file being looked for isn't found in any of the listed folders, HyperCard puts up a standard dialog box for opening a file, allows you to find that file on the disk, and then opens it for you. HyperCard then adds the pathname to the appropriate file, so you won't have to show it where to look the next time.

If you change hard disks or reorganize your disk, you might want to erase the pathnames on these cards that are no longer correct.

User Levels

The last card in the Home stack allows you to set certain preferences for how you like to use HyperCard, to tell it your name, and to choose a *user level* (see Figure 12-18).

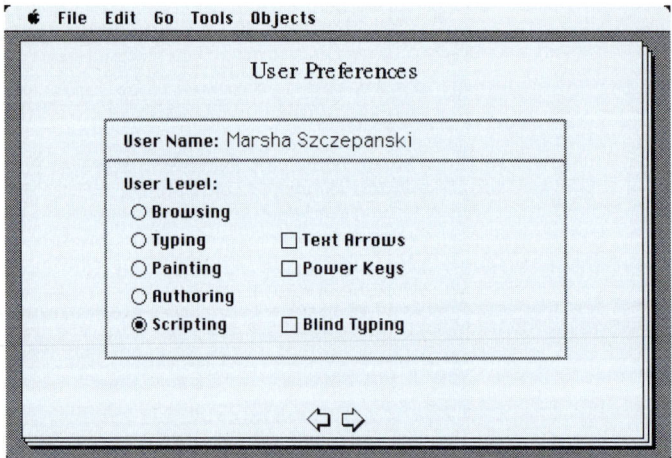

Figure 12-18   User Preferences card in Home stack

Just as the list of descriptions on the last several pages suggests, you can do many things with HyperCard. In fact, there are five levels of using this program, so that—as you learn more about the program—you can access more of its features. Beginners can use the program for *Browsing* information previously compiled by other authors. With a few minutes of practice, you can progress to *Typing*, which is the level that lets you change and add information.

With a little more practice you can progress to *Painting*, which gives you access to the bitmapped Painting tools. These tools work very similarly to the ones in MacPaint.

When you feel like venturing into the world of creating your own stacks, you can choose the *Authoring* user level. Now you can create, copy, paste, and modify buttons and fields. You can create links from a button to a different card in the same stack or a different stack.

If you want to explore HyperTalk programming, you must set the level to *Scripting*. This highest level gives you access to everything HyperCard can do. As you learn to modify existing scripts and then to create your own, you will be able to fully realize the power of this remarkable application.

HyperCard does not restrict you to starting with browsing and then progressing through the user levels in order. Many people use the authoring level before painting, and others paint before typing. You can go directly to the level you need for the job you are doing.

Basic Tools

Everything you do in HyperCard involves using one of four major types of tools. There are 3 *General tools* (browse, button, and field) and 15 *Painting tools*. If you choose the authoring or scripting level, you have access to all 18 tools. The painting level shows all 18 tools, but does not allow access to the button or field tool. In the browsing or typing levels, you have access to the browse tool only.

The tools are shown in Figure 12-19, and a short description for each one follows.

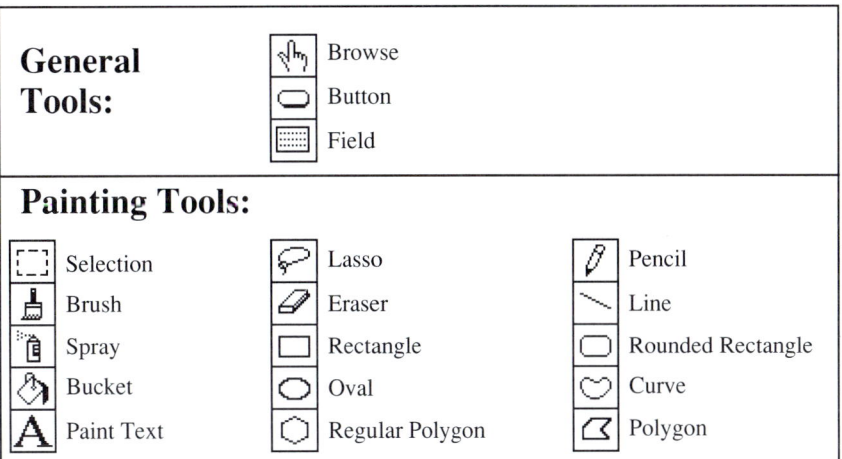

Figure 12-19   Tools available in HyperCard

General Tools

All user levels provide access to the browse tool. The Painting level gives you access to the painting tools, and the Authoring and Scripting levels let you use the button and field tools.

Browse Tool

The *browse tool* is used to click buttons and to select and edit text. When not in a text field, it assumes the appearance of a hand as shown at left. It is the only tool that will activate a button, and it is used for navigating through a stack.

When inside an unlocked text field, the pointer changes to an I-beam to indicate that you may use it to select and edit the text in the field or to add more text.

Button Tool

The *button tool* is used to create new buttons, to see existing buttons (even transparent ones), and to modify buttons if desired.

The button tool is only available if the Authoring or Scripting level has been chosen. When you choose the button tool, all buttons on the card are surrounded by a thin rectangle. If you click a button with the button tool, the button's script is not activated. Instead, the button is selected and then is enclosed by a moving dotted line (sometimes referred to as "marching ants").

You can create a new button by choosing **New Button** from the Objects menu or by holding down the Command key and dragging the button tool diagonally to establish the position of the new button on the card or background.

To select an existing button, make sure you are using the button tool, then point to the button and click.

If you want to place the button on the background so it will be available to all cards with that background, you must choose **Background** from the Edit menu (or press Command-B) and then create the new button. When you change to the background layer, the menu will have diagonal stripes around its outer edges (see Figure 12-20).

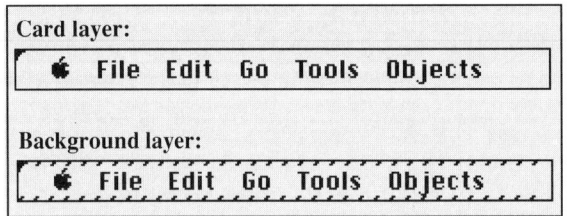

Figure 12-20 Menu appearances for card layer and background layer

You can move buttons to different locations and change their sizes. To move a button, first select it with the button tool, and then place the pointer anywhere inside the button (or exactly on one of the four edges except for a corner) and drag it to its new location. A selected button is resized by dragging any of its corners to make it larger or smaller.

Buttons may be duplicated, copied, cut, cleared, and pasted.

You duplicate a button by selecting it, holding down the Option key, and dragging the new copy to a different location.

You copy a button by selecting it and then choosing **Copy Button** from the Edit menu (or typing Command-C).

A button may be cut by selecting it and then choosing **Cut Button** from the Edit menu (or typing Command-X).

Clear a button by selecting it and then choosing **Clear Button** from the Edit menu (or pressing the Backspace or Delete or Clear key).

Paste a button that has been previously cut or copied by choosing **Paste Button** from the Edit menu (or typing Command-V). A button that is pasted will be in the same location from which it was copied or cut.

If you want more information about a button, or if you want to change its style, show its name, link it to something else, or modify its script, select the button and then choose **Button Info** from the Objects menu (or double-click the button).

For example, if you choose the button tool and then click on the right arrow button on the Home card, HyperCard presents a dialog box similar to the one shown in Figure 12-21.

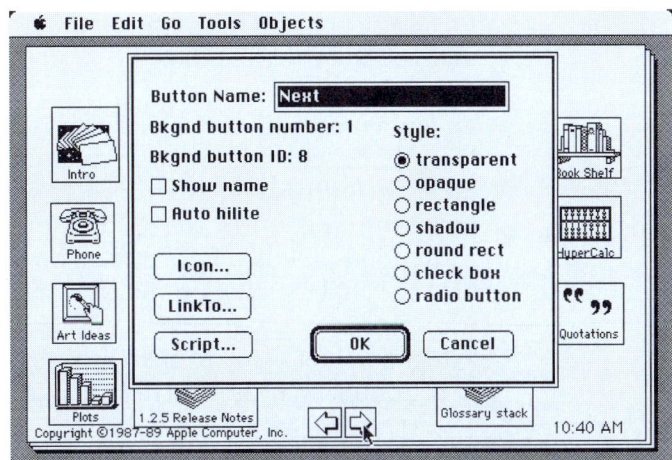

Figure 12-21   Button Info dialog box

When you chose the button tool, each button on the card was outlined to show its size and location. Double-clicking on the right arrow button presented the dialog box that allows you to specify the appearance of the button, its name, and some facts about how it operates.

If you are using the browse tool and want to know where all the buttons on a card are located, and you want to use one of the buttons rather than modify it, hold down the Option and Command keys simultaneously and all the buttons will be outlined in gray. Then when you release the Command and Option keys, you can click the button you want to use.

Field Tool

The *field tool* is used to create new fields, to see existing fields (even transparent ones), and to modify fields if desired.

The field tool is only available if you have chosen the Authoring or Scripting level. When you choose the field tool, all fields on the card are surrounded by a thin rectangle. If you click on a field with the field tool, the field does not allow you to enter or modify text. Instead, it is selected and then is enclosed by a moving dotted line.

You can create a new field by choosing **New Field** from the Objects menu or by holding down the Command key and dragging the field tool diagonally to establish the position of the new field on the card or background.

Notice that the Edit menu changes depending on the tool you are currently using. If you are using the button tool, the Edit menu says New Button, but if you are using the field tool it says New Field.

A *field* is designed to hold text, and the number of lines of text that a field can hold is determined by the font, size, and style chosen for that field. HyperCard allows you to choose only one font, size, and style for a particular field.

Creating a field is done in the same manner as creating a button, except that you use the Field tool.

Thought must go into the placement of a field. If you are creating a field that will be seen on several cards, and each card will hold similar, but different, information, then the field must be placed on the background. If the information in the field is for a particular card and does not correspond to similar information on other cards in the same stack, the field should be placed on the card layer.

Whenever you want to place an object, in this case a field, on the background layer you must first choose **Background** from the Edit menu.

Refer to Figure 12-20 if you want a reminder about how the menus look when the card layer or the background layer is chosen.

CAUTION The most common mistake made when creating a new field is putting it on the card layer when it should have been on the background layer. The easiest way to spot this problem is to go to another card. If the field is also on this card but the contents are blank, the field is on the background. If the field disappears, it was placed on the card layer.

If you put a field on the wrong layer, use the field tool to select the field, cut it, change to the proper layer, and paste the field back into position.

Selecting, duplicating, cutting, copying, clearing, and pasting fields are performed using the same procedures that are used for buttons. The only difference is that you must be using the field tool and it affects only fields. (See the previous section, "Buttons Tool.")

WARNING *Unlike deleting a button, you can lose much valuable information if you delete a background text field. Since a single background field can contain information on hundreds of cards, deleting the field would delete all the information stored on all those cards. HyperCard will ask you to confirm that you want to do this, and if you tell it to continue, there is no way to undo the cut or clear operation. If you actually do this, HyperCard's automatic save feature quickly makes the changes to the stack on the disk. The only way to recover from this mistake would be to reload a backup file if you recently made one.*

Just as you can get information about a button, you can get information about a field. The dialog box that appears when you choose **Field Info** from the Objects menu (or double-click on a field with the field tool) allows you to set the style of the field, give it a name, lock the text so nobody can change it, unlock a field so it can be modified, choose the text characteristics for the field, and even modify its script.

For example, we prepared a Glossary stack (which you will use in Project 1) that lists common terms and definitions associated with using a Macintosh. If you were to open the Glossary stack, choose the field tool, and double-click on the Definition field, you would see the Field Info dialog box as shown in Figure 12-22.

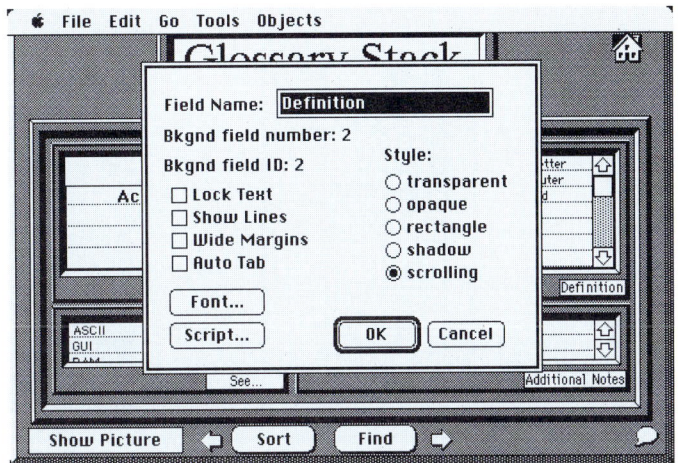

Figure 12-22   Field Info dialog box in Glossary stack

Projects 2 and 3 introduce you to using the button and field tools to create, modify, cut, paste, and further customize both fields and buttons.

Painting Tools

Just as with buttons and fields, the *Painting tools* allow you to paint on the background layer or the card layer. Any picture shown on a background layer appears on all cards that share that background. A picture on a card layer is seen only on that particular card.

The picture on the card layer is on top of the background picture and can obscure portions or all of the background. Painting over a field or button does not deactivate it, but only hides it from view.

HyperCard's Painting tools work similarly to the same tools in MacPaint, but since it is a newer program and is written for computers with more memory, HyperCard extends the power of some of the tools over what is available in MacPaint.

Both the Tools and Patterns menus are known as tear-off menus and may be converted from a menu into a *palette* (see Figure 12-23). These menus are changed into palettes by dragging below the bottom of the menu. When you pass the bottom of the menu, a gray outline of the palette appears. Drag the palette's outline to where you want it and release the mouse button. The palette will "float" on top of everything else on the screen. If you are about to do a lot of painting, it is often beneficial to tear off the menus and select the tools and patterns directly from the palettes.

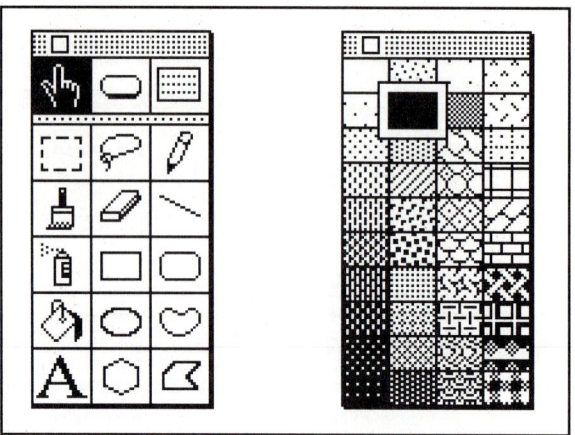

Figure 12-23   The Tools and Patterns palettes

Selection Tool

 The *selection tool* is used to select a rectangular portion of a picture.

Once you have selected something, it can be copied, cut, cleared, resized, rotated, flipped, inverted, outlined, darkened, lightened, and moved on the screen.

If you hold down the Option key while selecting an object with this tool, the tool converts into a lasso and selects only the object, not the surrounding white space.

When you move the pointer into a selected area, it changes from the crosshairs pointer into an arrow pointer. This signifies that you can now drag the object around on the screen.

Double-clicking on the selection tool selects the entire card picture.

Lasso

 The *lasso* is used to select an irregular shaped area of a picture.

Once something is selected, it can be copied, cut, cleared, and moved on the screen. The lasso is similar to the selection tool, but when you draw a loop around the object(s) you want to select, it tightens around the object and only affects it and not the white space surrounding it.

When you move the pointer into a selected area, it changes from the lasso into an arrow pointer. This signifies that you can now drag the object around on the screen.

Brush Tool

The *brush* tool is used to paint with the currently selected pattern.

The shape of the brush can be changed by double-clicking on the brush tool after the Tools menu has been "torn off" and converted into a palette (see Figure 12-24).

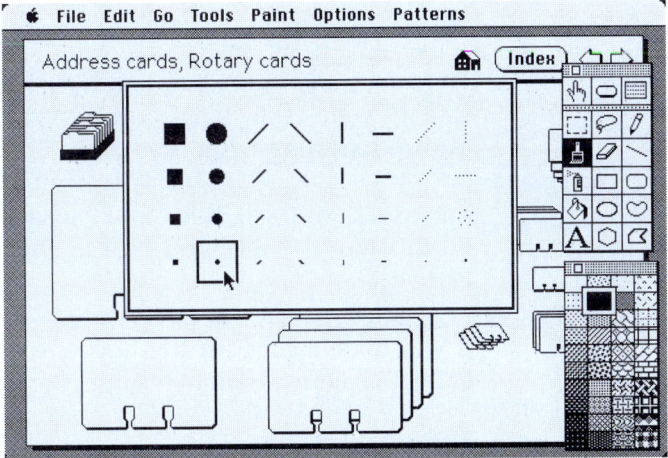

Figure 12-24 Dialog box for choosing new brush shape and size

The brush can be constrained to paint in a straight (horizontal or vertical) line by holding down the Shift key (or locking the Caps Lock key in the down position) while you paint.

Holding down the Command key while you paint with the brush converts it into an eraser with the current brush shape.

Spray Tool

The *spray tool* allows you to spray the current pattern onto the picture. By moving the spray tool back and forth over an area, you add more of the pattern to the picture.

Holding down the Shift key (or the Caps Lock key) while you spray constrains the spray tool to horizontal or vertical movements.

Pressing the Command key while you spray converts it into a spray eraser.

Bucket Tool

The *bucket tool* is used to pour the current pattern into a bounded area.

If the area is not bounded, or if there are any holes (even 1 pixel wide) in the boundary, the paint will spill into the rest of the card.

To recover from a "paint spill," choose **Undo** from the Edit menu immediately after making the mistake. (If you do anything else, the Undo command will not correct the problem.) Then find and correct the hole in the boundary and try again. Sometimes it is easier to repair the hole using the pencil tool and Fat Bits (see the section on the pencil tool).

You can change black areas to other patterns with the bucket tool. In this case the edge of the black area is the boundary; the paint will not spill into surrounding white areas.

You cannot use the bucket tool to change the pattern in a filled area. To do this, use the selection tool or the lasso and choose *Fill* from the Paint menu.

If you double-click on the bucket tool in the palette, you make the Patterns palette alternately appear or disappear.

Paint Text Tool

 The *paint text tool* allows you to add text to your drawing, but painted text is not editable after it has been deselected by clicking somewhere else with the paint text tool or by selecting a different tool. When the text is deselected, it is converted into a bitmapped picture of the text and is no longer editable with the paint text tool. At that point, the only way to change the text is to erase it and re-enter the text as you want it.

If the paint text has not been deselected, you can change any typographical errors by backspacing to the error and retyping the rest of the text. You can also change the font, size, style, line height, and alignment of the text while it is still selected.

When typing text, you can press the Return key to start a new line under the current line. This will not deselect the previous line. The new line will be aligned under the previous line depending upon whether you have selected left, center, or right alignment. Left alignment is the default value.

If you want to change any of the text characteristics, choose **Text Style** from the Edit menu (or double-click on the paint text tool). Figure 12-25 shows the resulting Text Style dialog box, and all of the settings represent the defaults.

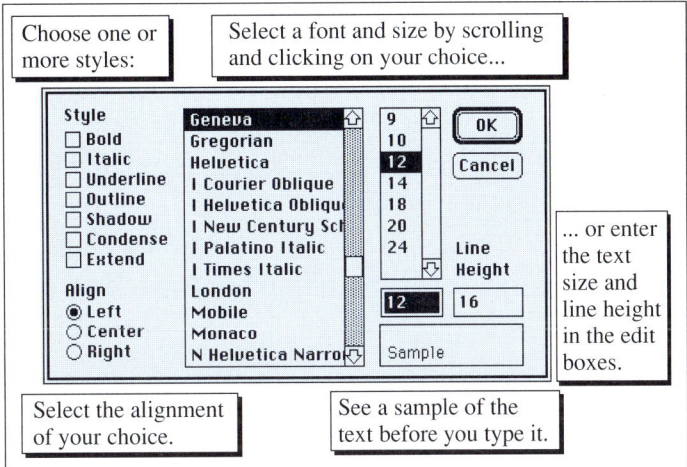

Figure 12-25   Text Style dialog box

If you have just typed and deselected some text and wish to move it to a new position, type Command-S and HyperCard will select it for you.

Paint text is not editable, nor can HyperCard's Find command locate text that was painted. If you want to modify text or be able to have HyperCard find it for you, create a field and enter the text there.

Eraser Tool

 The *eraser* tool is used to eliminate portions of the picture. Erasing a portion of a card picture exposes the background picture underneath, which can be somewhat disconcerting. Instead of erasing parts of a card picture, you may find it easier to paint over something using the brush tool and a white pattern, using the brush tool and the Command key to make the brush into a shaped eraser, or using the eraser tool and the Command key, which makes the eraser paint with white (like using White-Out).

If you want to erase an entire card picture, double-click on the eraser tool in the Tools palette.

Rectangle Tool

 The *rectangle tool* is used to draw rectangles and squares.

To draw a rectangle, press the mouse button when the pointer is where you want one of the corners, and then drag the mouse to the diagonally opposite corner and release the button when the corner is where you want it.

Rectangles may be drawn centered around a point by choosing **Draw Centered** from the Options menu.

Rectangles may be drawn filled with the current pattern by choosing **Draw Filled** from the Options menu (or by double-clicking on the rectangle tool in the palette).

You can change the line thickness of the rectangle tool by choosing **Line Size** from the Options menu (or by double-clicking on the line tool in the palette).

To draw a rectangle with the border lines in the current pattern, hold down the Option key as you draw the rectangle.

To draw a borderless rectangle, choose **Draw Filled** from the Options menu and draw the rectangle with the Option key held down.

To constrain the rectangle to be a square, hold down the Shift key (or Caps Lock key) as you draw.

Oval Tool

 The *oval tool* works like the rectangle tool, except that it draws ovals that fit inside the rectangle you create, instead of drawing the rectangle itself.

All the options listed for the rectangle tool work with the oval tool, except that the Shift key (or Caps Lock key) constrains it to drawing a circle.

Regular Polygon Tool

 The *regular polygon tool* is used to easily create polygons that have regular sides and angles.

Unlike the other tools, the regular polygon tool always draws from the center outward (just as if you had chosen Draw Centered from the Options menu). It makes no difference whether Draw Centered is selected or not.

Also unlike the other shape tools, the regular polygon tool allows you to rotate a shape before it is fixed into place. While you are drawing a shape with this tool, you should normally drag horizontally to the right. If you move the mouse to any other position, the shape will rotate. The rotation can be constrained to 15° increments by holding down the Shift key (or Caps Lock key).

Several shapes are available, and you can select one by double-clicking on the regular polygon tool in the Tools palette and then clicking on the polygon of your choice in the resulting dialog box (see Figure 12-26).

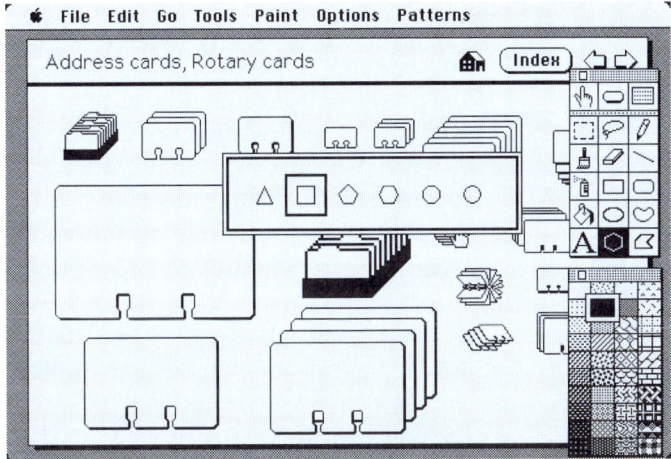

Figure 12-26   Choosing a regular polygon shape

Pencil Tool

The *pencil tool* is used to modify individual pixels in a painting. It can be used to write like a pencil or to erase like one.

If the current pixel is white, the pencil makes it black, and vice versa.

The pencil tool can be constrained to draw only horizontal or vertical lines by holding down the Shift key (or Caps Lock key) while you draw.

Double-clicking on the pencil tool when it is in the Tools palette magnifies the screen eight times and takes you into *Fat Bits* so you can edit individual pixels (see Figure 12-27). The floating window shows the actual-size view of the picture being edited.

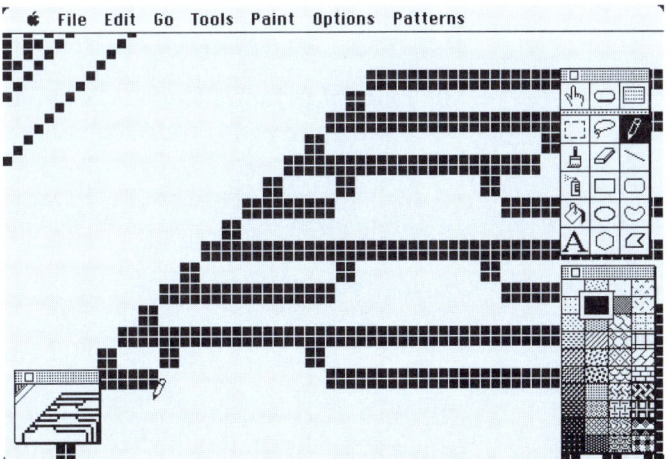

Figure 12-27   Editing with the Pencil tool in Fat Bits

Line Tool

The *line tool* is used to draw lines from one point on the screen to another. Anchor one end of the line by pressing where you want it to start, and then (while continuing to hold the mouse button down) move the mouse to where you want the line to end. The line will continue to be displayed while you move the mouse. When you have the line where you want it, release the mouse button to anchor the second end of the line.

You can constrain the line to 15° increments by holding down the Shift key (or Caps Lock key) while you draw.

Double-clicking on the line tool in the palette allows you to change the thickness of the line (see Figure 12-28).

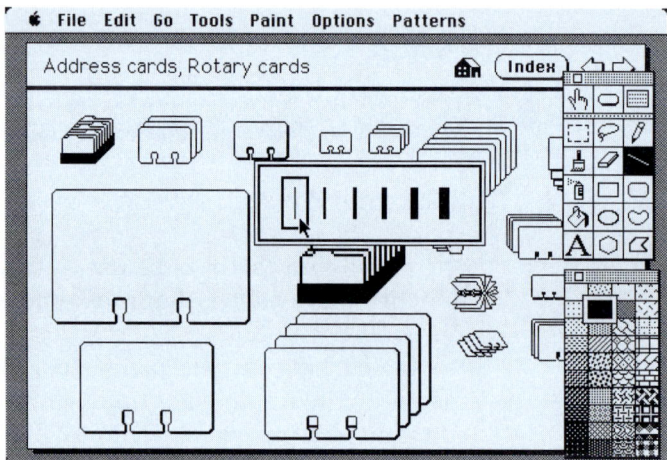

Figure 12-28   Changing the thickness of the line

Rounded Rectangle Tool

The *rounded rectangle tool* works like the rectangle tool, except that it draws rectangles with rounded corners instead of right-angle corners.

All the options listed for the rectangle tool work with the rounded rectangle tool.

Curve Tool

Use the *curve tool* to draw freehand curved shapes.

When Draw Filled is not selected, the curve tool works similarly to the pencil tool. If Draw Filled is selected, the curve tool automatically connects the starting position of the curve to where you release the mouse button at the end of the curve with a straight line. The area bounded by the curve is then filled with the current pattern.

A simple way to toggle Draw Filled on or off is to double-click on the curve tool.

You can modify the width of the line drawn by the curve tool by choosing **Line Size** from the Options menu (or by double-clicking on the line tool).

Holding down the Option key while you draw with the curve tool causes the curve to be drawn using the current pattern.

Polygon Tool

 The *polygon tool* is used to create multi-sided objects with irregular shapes. This is the only shape tool that works as it does. With the other shape tools, you hold down the mouse button until you have completed drawing the object and then release it when the position and size are correct.

The polygon tool works on the principle of drawing a shape with multiple straight lines connected by several vertices (intersections).

To draw a polygon, click where you want the first line to start. Then continue clicking at the location of each of the subsequent vertices. This is like tracing around the edge of the object with a tool that draws multiple connected lines.

Drawing the polygon is completed by double-clicking at the last vertex. This can be at the same point as the starting position or at a different location. If Draw Filled is checked, HyperCard automatically connects the starting and ending points with a line and fills the resulting polygon with the current pattern.

Holding down the Option key while drawing a polygon draws the border in the currently selected pattern.

You can change polygon line widths by double-clicking on the line tool and choosing the line width you prefer.

Holding down the Shift key (or Caps Lock key) constrains the lines that make up the polygon to 15° angles.

Stack Resources

As you get more involved with HyperCard, you will find that you need to do something and there is no button available for that specific purpose. HyperCard allows you to create your own buttons, and you can give the button any icon that is currently available in the Home stack.

When you create a new button, you can tell HyperCard that you want the button to have an icon, and you will be presented with the scrolling list of icons shown in Figure 12-29. Icons are one of the types of resources that HyperCard lets you use in your stacks. You can also add sounds, additional art, and even programming code to extend the commands available in HyperCard.

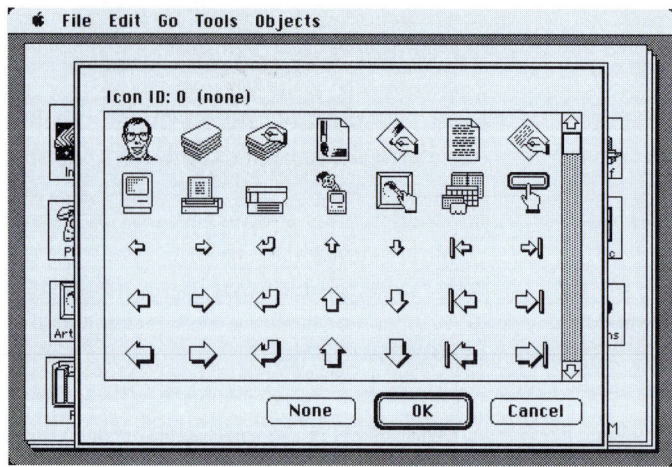

Figure 12-29   Icon resources for buttons

Idea Stacks

HyperCard is distributed with four idea stacks: *Art Ideas*, *Button Ideas*, *Card Ideas*, and *Stack Ideas*.

To open one of these idea stacks, you need only to click the appropriate button on the Home card.

If you look at the Art Ideas stack, you see the index card first (see Figure 12-30). This card has three columns of buttons. Clicking one of these buttons takes you to the card linked to that button. There are also four other buttons just to the right of the stack's title.

Figure 12-30   First index card in Art Ideas stack

The *Tell Me... button* is usually linked to information or help concerning the current stack or card. In this case, clicking on the icon takes you to the card shown in Figure 12-31. This card tells you about the Art Ideas stack. Clicking the Index button takes you back to the first index card. You can also choose **Back** from the Go menu.

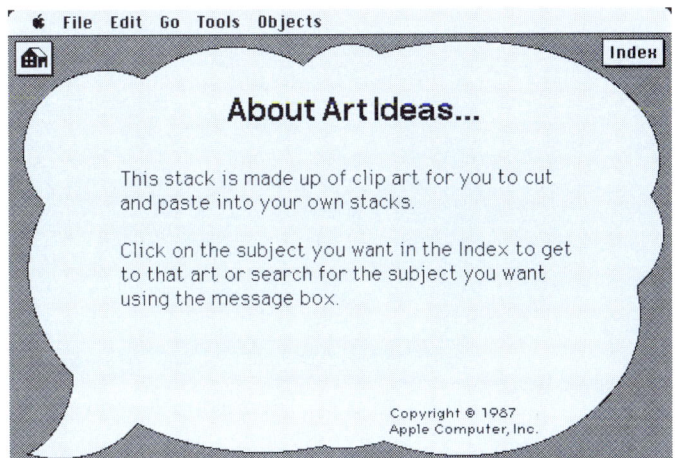

Figure 12-31   Information card for Art Ideas stack

 The *Home* button takes you back to the Home card of the Home stack.

 The left arrow is the Previous button and is used to go to the previous card. If the current card is not the top card on the list, the left arrow takes you to the card just before the current one. You can think of the previous card as being either to the left of or just above the current card. Clicking on the left arrow takes you to the same card (in this case) as pressing the Tell Me... button.

 The right arrow is the Next button and takes you to the next card. If the current card is not the bottom card of the stack, it usually takes you to the card just after the current card. Clicking on the right arrow in this case takes you to the second index card of the Art Ideas stack (see Figure 12-32).

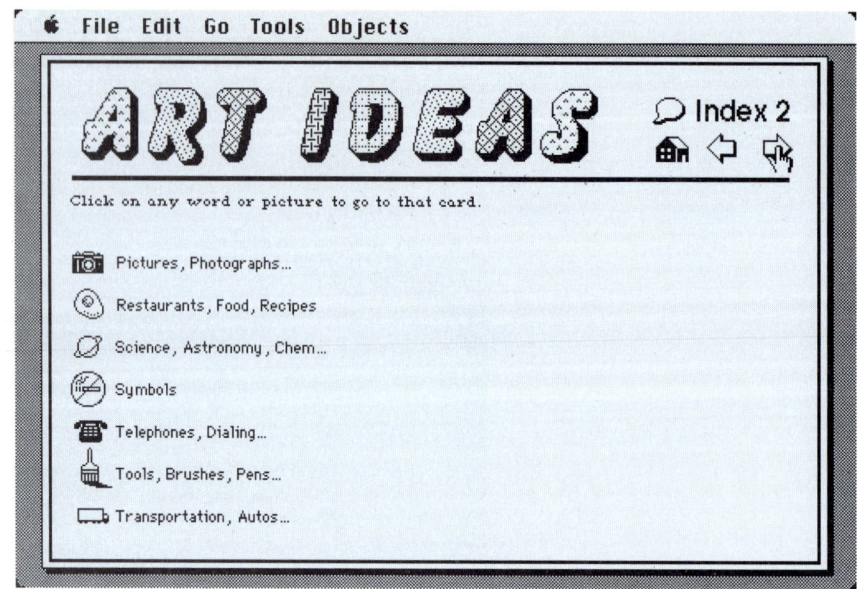

Figure 12-32   Second index card of the Art Ideas stack

Now that you know how to navigate through this stack, let's look at one of the cards in the Art Ideas stack. If you click the button labelled Macintosh, Apple... you go to the card shown in Figure 12-33.

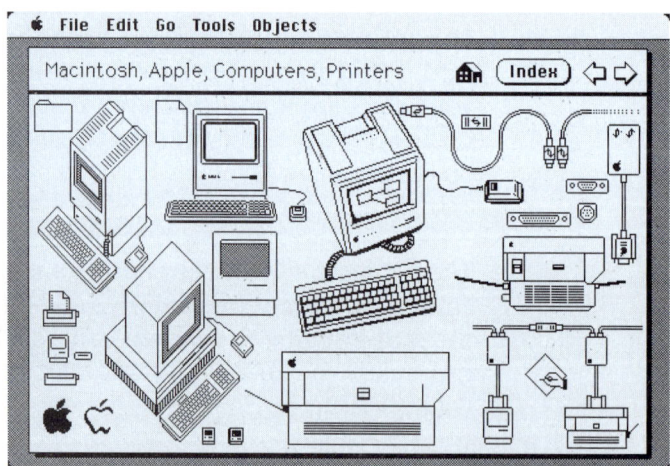

Figure 12-33   Macintosh clip art in Art Ideas stack

This card contains a number of pictures of Macintosh computers, printers, LocalTalk cables, connectors, and Apple Computer logos. All of this art can be copied from the stack and pasted into your stacks whenever you need a picture of a Macintosh computer. (Don't forget, however, that the stack is copyrighted and you have to have Apple's permission to distribute the art in a form that others can copy and reuse.)

You could now click the Home button and return to the Home card. Then, if you click the button labelled Card Ideas, you go to the index card shown in Figure 12-34.

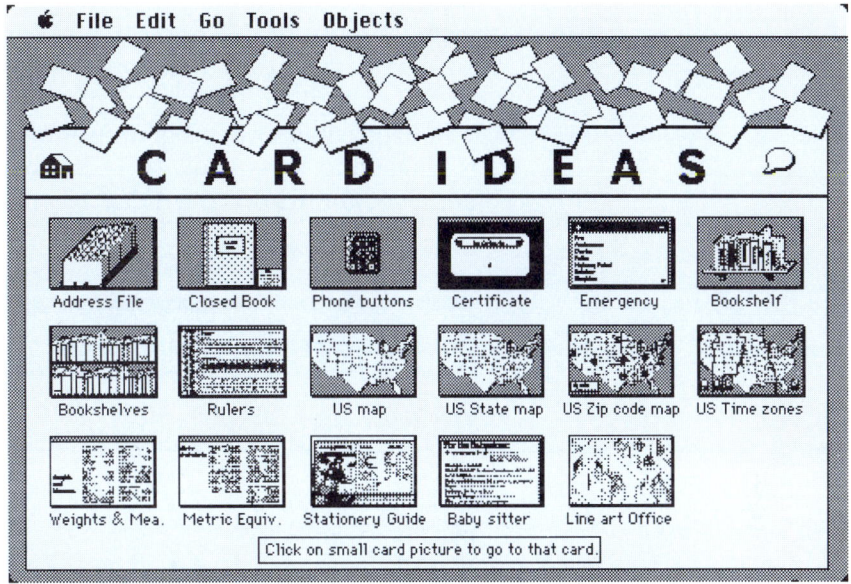

Figure 12-34   Index card to Card Ideas stack

This stack has a number of ideas for cards that can be included in your stacks as you create them. For instance, suppose you were taking a chemistry class and wanted to keep your notes in a HyperCard stack for reviewing before a test. You might decide that you would like a quick reference to metric weights and measurements. You could add this to your stack by clicking the button labelled Metric Equiv., which would take you to the card shown in Figure 12-35.

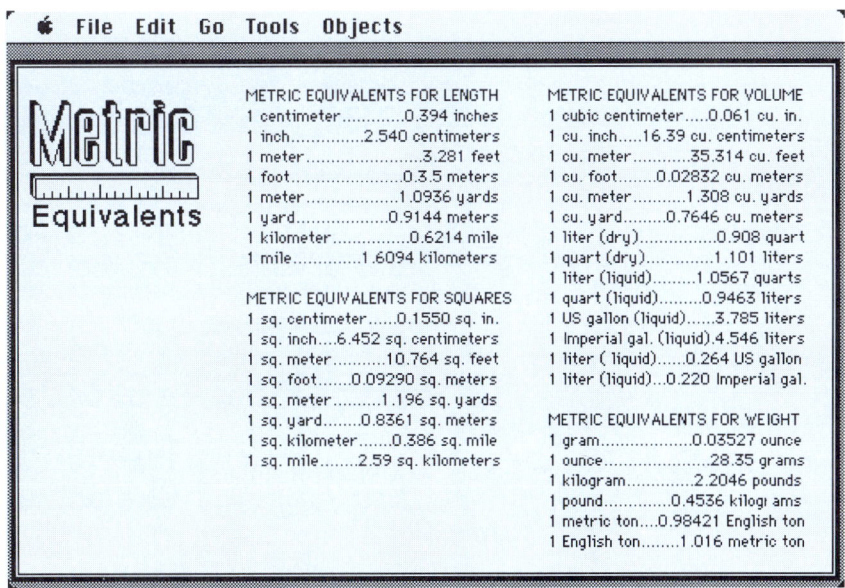

Figure 12-35   Metric Equivalents card in Card Ideas stack

Then, all you have to do is copy the card, go back to your chemistry notes stack, and paste the Metric Equivalents card into the stack.

You could go to the card shown in Figure 12-36, the Button Ideas index card, by clicking on the Button Ideas icon on the Home card. This stack includes seven cards from which you can copy buttons. Most of these buttons have already been programmed to perform a function, and when you copy the button and paste it into your stack it will remember how to do what it was programmed to do in the Button Ideas stack. This is a great time saver and lets you use buttons in your stacks even if you don't yet know how to write scripts in HyperTalk.

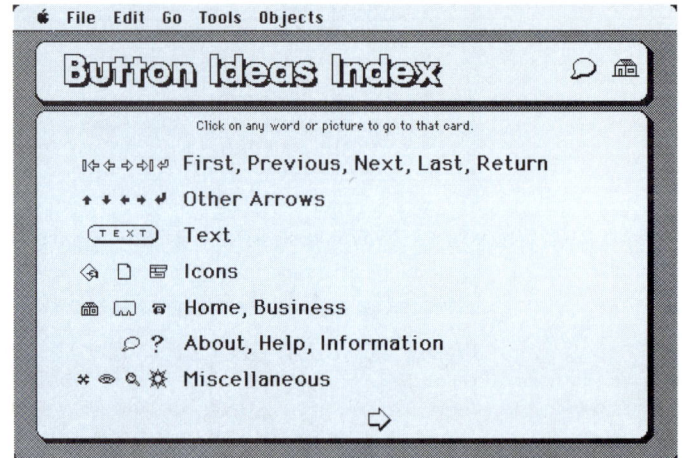

Figure 12-36   Index card for Button Ideas stack

If you click on the Stack Ideas button on the Home card, you go to the card shown in Figure 12-37. This is the first of four index cards in this stack.

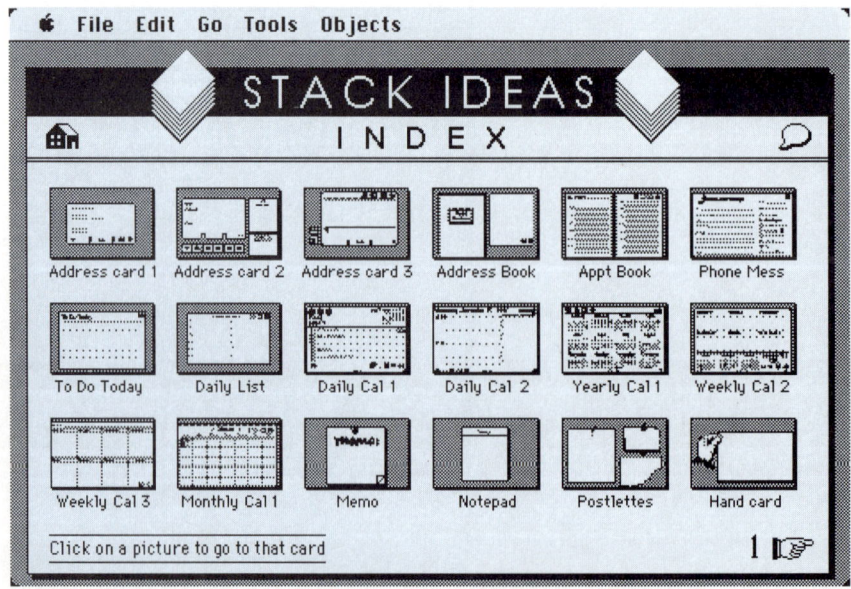

Figure 12-37   Index card for Stack Ideas stack

The third index card is shown in Figure 12-38.

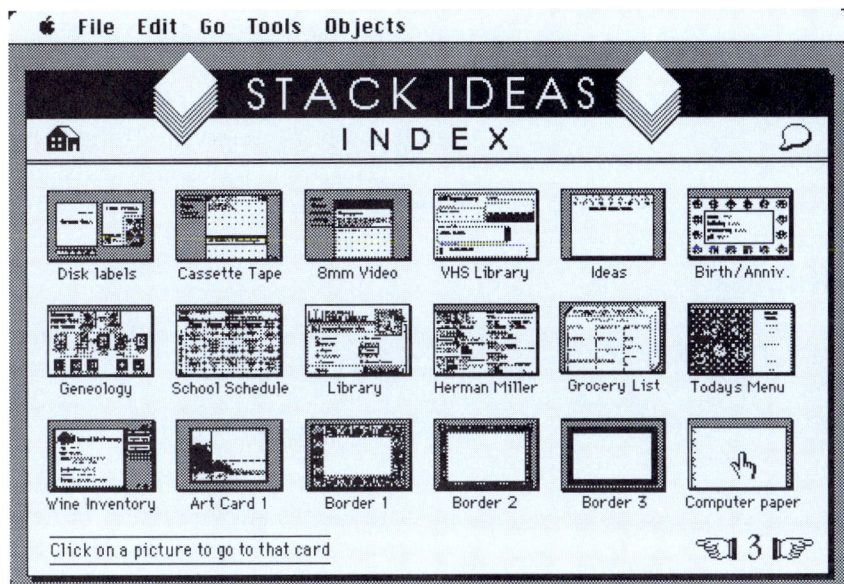

Figure 12-38   Third index card for Stack Ideas stack

If you click the lower right button named "Computer paper," you go to the card shown in Figure 12-39, which you will use as a starting point in Project 3 to hold your class notes.

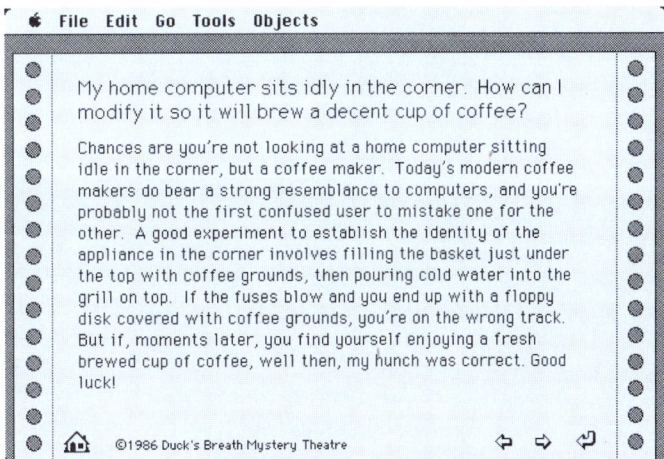

Figure 12-39   The "Computer paper" card

Of course, coffee has little to do with chemistry (except for the night just before the test), so you could copy only the background, which also contains the four buttons shown. You could then add the necessary components for keeping your chemistry notes organized.

 This card introduces a new icon. The Return button takes you back to a previously selected card. You will make use of this button in many stacks.

In this short description of the ideas stacks you have been introduced to some of the ways in which HyperCard's authors have made it easier for you to construct your own stacks and to personalize and customize stacks you get from others.

One of the main reasons that you can put HyperCard to work for you, even if you don't know anything about scripting in HyperTalk, is that the ideas stacks include many cards, buttons, and fields that are already pre-scripted and that can be used directly in your stacks.

Utilities

HyperCard is distributed with several utility stacks that you might find to be useful.

Address Stack

The *Address stack* is designed to work similarly to a rotary card file. You can store names and addresses in this stack (see Figure 12-40). If you need to keep multiple name and address lists you can make several copies of this stack and keep only the names you want in each stack.

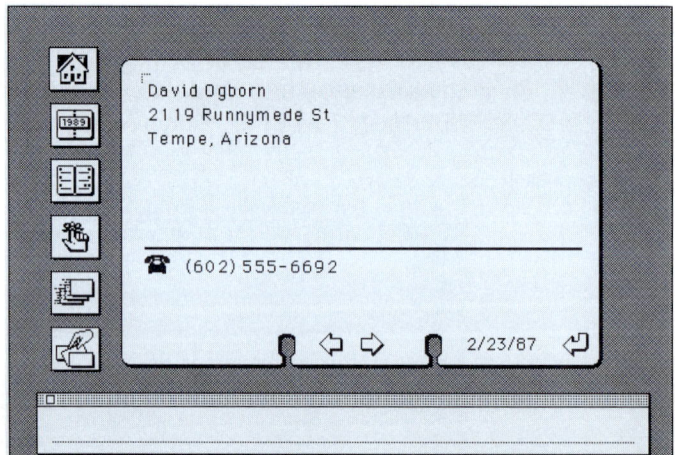

Figure 12-40   Address stack

The Address stack also has the advantage of being linked to the other personal stacks, such as the calendar, phone dialing, and to-do lists. If you want, you can link any of these stacks to other stacks, including the ones you create.

Calendar

HyperCard includes several types of calendars. There is already a *Calendar stack* (see Figure 12-41) linked to the Address stack, and Stack Ideas offers several additional calendars from which to choose. Additionally, you can modify and customize any of these stacks to suit yourself and any special needs you might have.

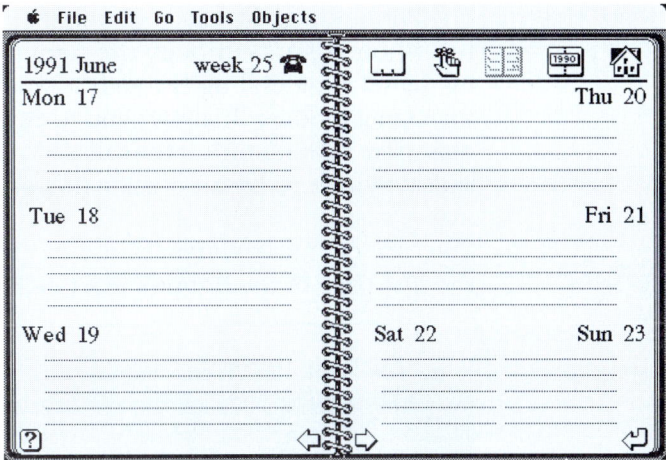

Figure 12-41   Calendar stack

In addition to having a calendar to note future events you must remember, the Calendar stack includes a *to-do list* (see Figure 12-42). You can add, modify, or delete any items on your list. If two pages are not enough, you can add as many as you wish. You can even keep separate to-do lists for personal, business, civic, and other needs.

Figure 12-42   To-do list in the Calendar stack

Phone Dialing

Your Address stack will probably contain many phone numbers, and HyperCard provides a nice feature for dialing them for you. Click on the phone icon, and HyperCard automatically dials the number.

In addition to dialing the numbers in your Address stack, HyperCard provides a *Phone stack* that allows you to customize how the dialing will be done, and it includes the area codes for all of the United States and Canada.

The Phone stack can dial a phone three ways: by creating the phone's touch-tone sounds through the computer's speaker (not very reliable), by digital tone dialing through a modem, or by rotary pulse dialing through a modem. It allows you to enter the local phone prefixes and uses them to determine if the call is a long distance or local call. It is even smart enough to get an outside line or make an international call.

You can set your preferences and local calling information directly on the first page of the Phone stack (see Figure 12-43).

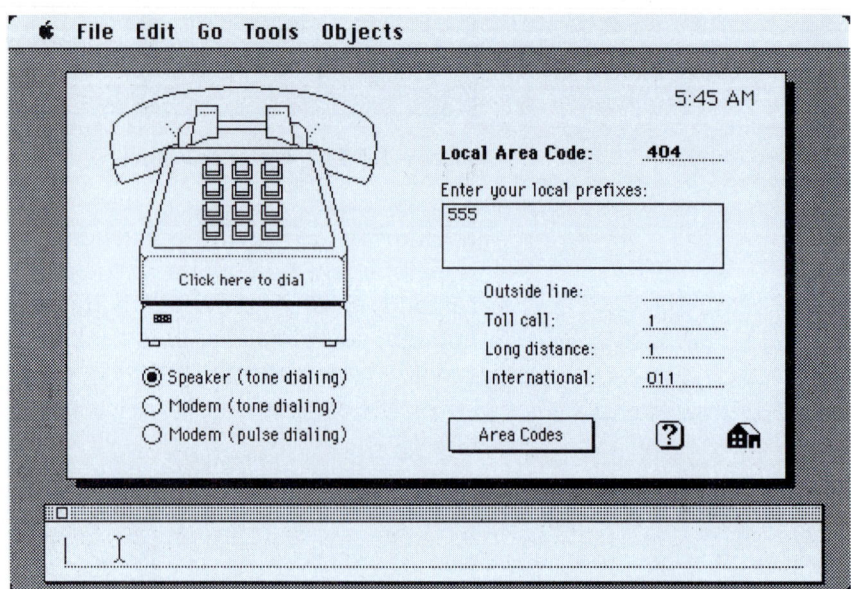

Figure 12-43   Phone stack

If you click the Area Codes button, you will be presented with a stack of area codes, and the Message box will have the Find command already entered with the insertion point located between the quotation marks. To find an area code for a location, type in the name (or part of the name) and HyperCard will find it if it is in the stack. It will find all states and provinces and most larger cities.

If this stack does not contain the places you need to call, search by state or closest city and add the name of the town to the appropriate card. Of course, you are not restricted to just adding towns to the Phone stack. You can also add names of friends and relatives to the appropriate cards and can tell the time difference, nearest cities to visit, or whatever you can think of that would work here. Once you get this stack it is yours to customize as you want.

If you want to find the area codes for Arizona, for example, all you have to do is enter the state's name in the Message box and press the Return key.

You can see (in Figure 12-44) that HyperCard found the appropriate card (which has had some towns added). All of Arizona has a 602 area code.

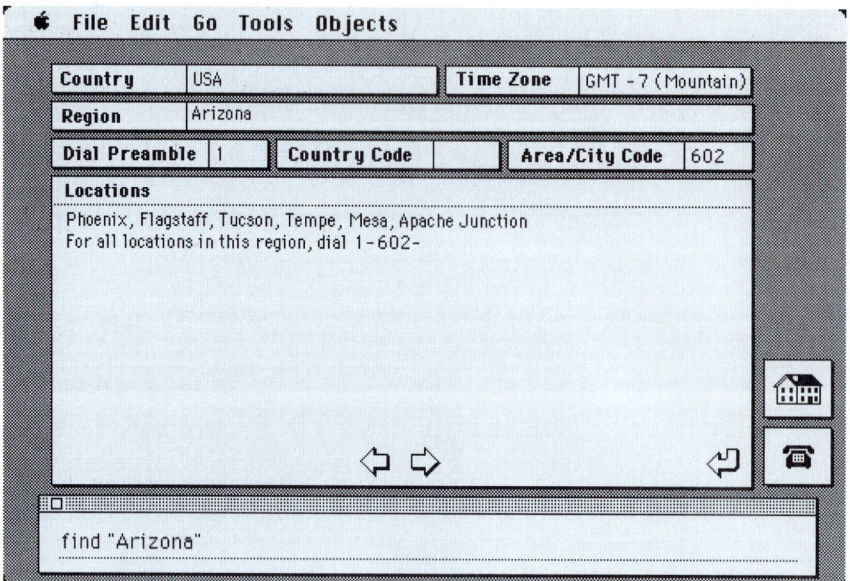

Figure 12-44   Area codes in Phone Stack

This completes the overview of HyperCard. In the projects that follow, you will learn to use some of HyperCard's many powerful—yet surprisingly easy-to-use—features for yourself.

Project 1: Using an Existing Stack

In this project, you will browse through the Glossary stack that was developed for use with this book.

When you complete this project you will know the major concepts and conventions used in browsing through a stack. You will learn to use the Find command, to use the Message box, and how to navigate through dynamic links in the stack.

One of the tasks associated with writing a technical book is producing a glossary of terms used in the book. A glossary for this type of book contains terms relating to computers in general, the Macintosh specifically, desktop publishing, word processing, graphics, information management, spreadsheets, and HyperCard.

Since we used HyperCard to collate and sort this information and then export it to Word to create a text glossary, we thought it would be interesting to demonstrate the dynamic (and some of the graphics) features of HyperCard. We spruced up the stack a little and included it on the *Macintosh Journey Projects* disk.

If you completed Project 1 in Chapter 1, you have already copied the Glossary stack onto your data disk. If not, you need to copy all three HyperCard stacks from the *Projects* disk onto your data disk.

⌘-Q ➡ Quit HyperCard by choosing **Quit HyperCard** from the File menu.

➡ If you haven't already done so, copy the Glossary stack onto your data disk.

➡ Restart HyperCard by double-clicking on the Glossary stack's icon.

Starting HyperCard by double-clicking on a stack icon bypasses the Home card and causes the stack you double-clicked to be loaded (see Figure 12-45).

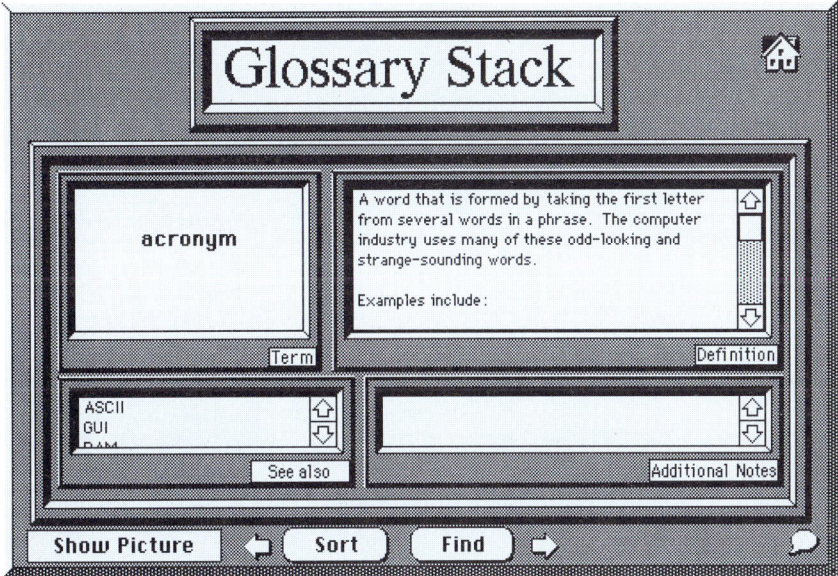

Figure 12-45   The first card containing terms and definitions

The card contains four fields, noted below.

- **Term**   Contains a word or phrase used as a glossary entry

- **Definition**   Contains a definition and possibly a short discussion about the term

- **Additional Notes** Mostly used to inform you when a card contains an explanatory picture

- **See also**   Contains dynamic links to related terms. If you click one of the terms you are taken to a card containing that term.

The background for this card contains nine buttons, some of which are hidden at times depending on your actions.

- **Home**   Shows a closing card, closes the stack, and goes to the Home card

- **Show Picture**   Shows the picture that is hidden on some of the cards. If the Additional Notes field contains "See the Picture" then you can click on this button to show it.

- **Hide Picture**   Hides the picture

- **Previous**   Goes to the previous card and automatically hides the picture before leaving the current card. If you click on the left arrow while on the first card, it shows you the last card.

- **Sort**   Sorts all of the cards on the Terms and Definitions background alphabetically by the contents of the Term field. This is available so you can extend the glossary by adding more terms. Clicking Sort then re-sorts the cards very quickly so you can look through them in alphabetical order.

- **Find**   First determines if you want to find a word or phrase anywhere on a card or just in the Term field. When you answer this question, it lets you enter the word or phrase, and then places the entire Find command into the Message box and finds the first occurrence if it is in the stack. To find any subsequent occurrences, press the Return key. When you are done with this Find command, close the Message box by clicking in its close box.

- **Next**   Goes to the next card and automatically hides the picture before leaving the current card. If you click on the right arrow while on the last card, it shows you the first card.

- **Return**   If you click on a term in the See also field, the Return button appears so you can return to the card from which you jumped.

- **Tell Me**   Displays the copyright notice and authors' names.

As you can see on the first card (see Figure 12-45), it contains the term "acronym", a definition of the term, and some examples. The Additional Notes field of this card is empty, but the See also field contains several items that are acronyms, which also appear as terms in the stack.

NAVIGATING THROUGH DYNAMIC LINKS

The first term in the See also field is "ASCII". You can see the card that contains its definition by clicking the word with the browse tool. The See also field contains locked text, which means that it alone, of the four text fields, contains information that should not be changed. It also contains a short script that remembers that you started on this card and then takes you to the card containing the term that you clicked.

Let's see how the dynamic links in the See also field operate.

➠ Click **ASCII** in the See also field, as shown in Figure 12-46.

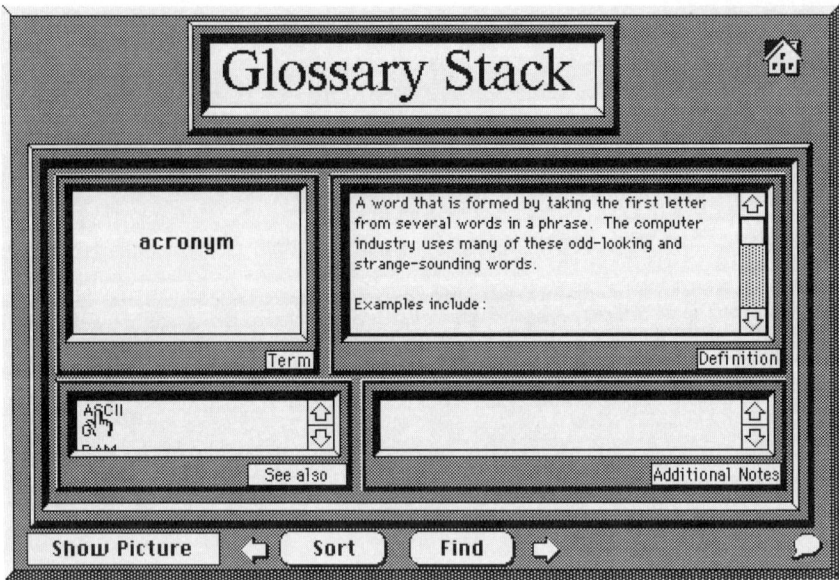

Figure 12-46   Jumping to a related term

When you jump to a related term, a Return arrow appears, and you can use it to return to the original term. This linkage supports jumping to a series of terms through the See also field. Clicking on the Return button will take you back through the series of cards you followed until you reach the original one. If you click the Find, left arrow, or right arrow buttons, this linkage is dissolved and the Return button disappears.

When you click the word in the See also field, HyperCard takes you directly to the card that contains "ASCII" in the Term field. In addition to the definition and other information about "ASCII", this card contains "See the picture" in the Additional Notes field, as shown in Figure 12-47.

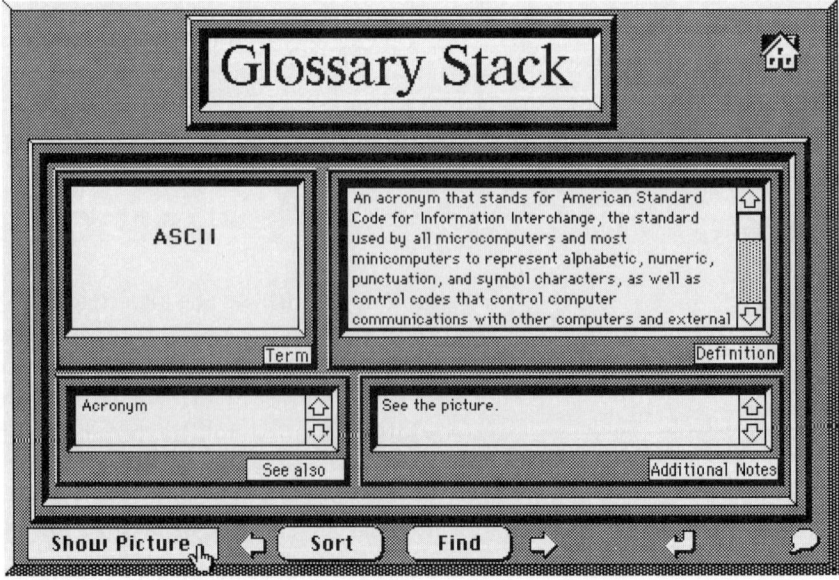

Figure 12-47   Some cards have pictures.

Anytime "See the picture" is showing in the Additional Notes field, you can click Show Picture to see the hidden card picture.

➠ Click **Show Picture.**

This card, which contains the term "ASCII", has a picture showing the entire ASCII character set for the Geneva font (see Figure 12-48).

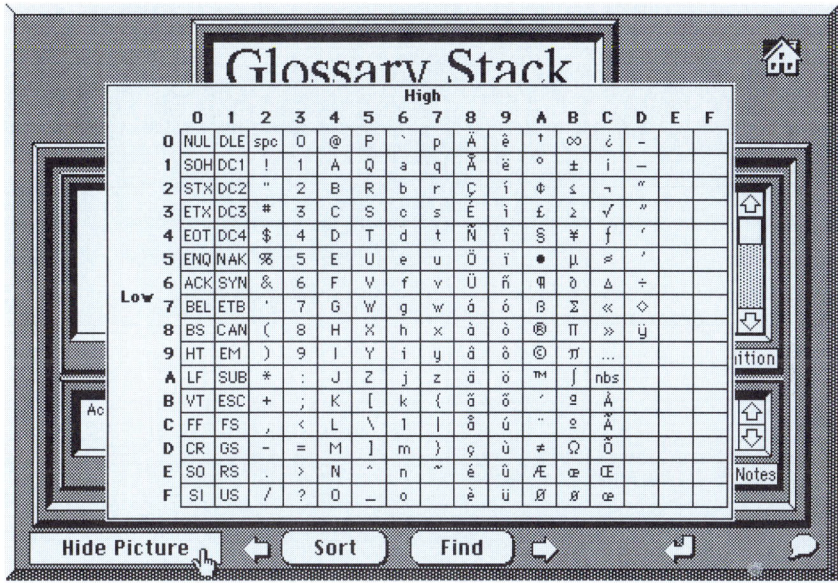

Figure 12-48   Viewing the card picture

Most of you will have little reason to know the actual numbers for each of the characters shown, since you can easily find the characters using the Key Caps desk accessory when you want to type them from the keyboard.

When you are finished looking at the picture, you can click the Hide Picture button or click on any of the arrow buttons. You really don't have to hide the picture, because the stack is programmed to hide the picture automatically whenever you go to a different card.

➠ For practice, click **Hide Picture.**

You originally got to this card by jumping from the card with "acronym" in the Term field. You can now go back to the card from which you originally jumped.

➠ Click on the Return button (see Figure 12-49).

Figure 12-49   Click the Return button to return to the original card

You are now returned to the "acronym" card. Now you know how to navigate through the dynamic links in the See also field. Remember, however, that if you go to a different card using one of the arrow keys, the dynamic link is broken and the Return button disappears. This lets you override the Return link in favor of exploring in a different direction.

USING THE FIND BUTTON

Another way to find information in the Glossary stack is by clicking on the Find button. Unlike choosing **Find** from the Go menu or typing Command-F on the keyboard, this button has a script that offers you two choices of where to look for the term or to cancel if you clicked the button by mistake.

➡ Click **Find**.

When you click the Find button, the Glossary stack asks you where you want it to look (see Figure 12-50). The default is to limit the search to the Term field. You can choose this by clicking on the default button or by pressing Return or Enter.

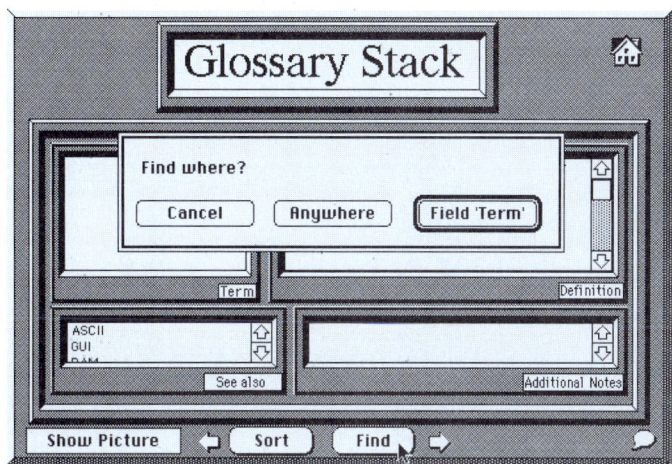

Figure 12-50   Telling the Glossary stack where to look for text

Click the Anywhere button if you want to extend the search to any field in the stack. If you really don't want to find anything, click the Cancel button.

In this case, you will limit the search to finding a word in the Term field only. Two fonts with names that start with "Zapf" are available in LaserWriters that support PostScript. Now you can see how quickly HyperCard will find one of them for you.

➠ Click **Field 'Term'** or press the Return key.

Now that you have told the stack where to look, it is time to enter the word or phrase you want to find (see Figure 12-51).

Figure 12-51   Telling the Glossary stack what to find

➠ Type **Zapf** or **ZAPF** or **zapf** (capitalization does not matter).

In a second or two the card containing "Zapf Chancery" is shown (see Figure 12-52). To aid you in finding other occurrences of the phrase you are finding, the Message box has become visible and a find command has been entered for you.

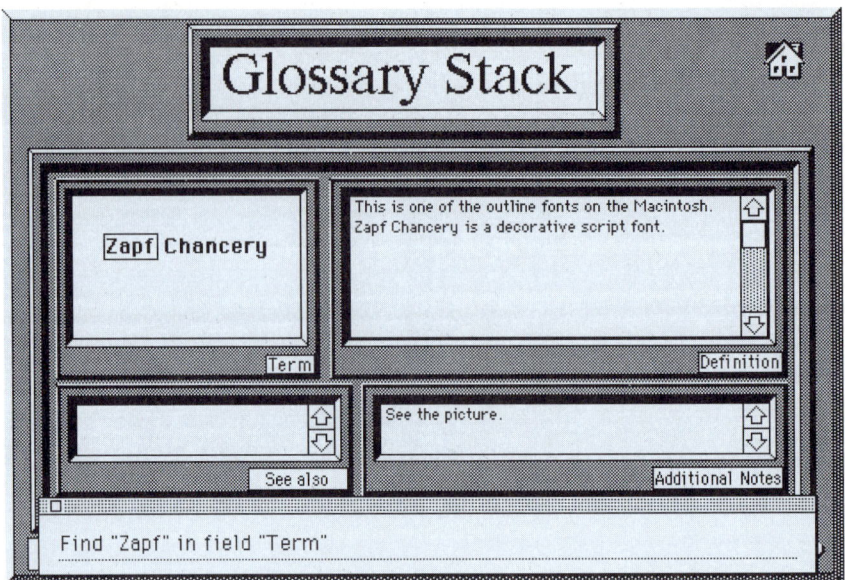

Figure 12-52   Text found in a card

Zapf Chancery is the first of the two cards with the word "Zapf", and you can now find the second very easily. As long as the Message box is showing with the find command, all you have to do is press the Return key to find the next occurrence of the word or phrase being found.

➧ Press the Return key.

The next card containing "Zapf" in the Term field is shown almost immediately (see Figure 12-53).

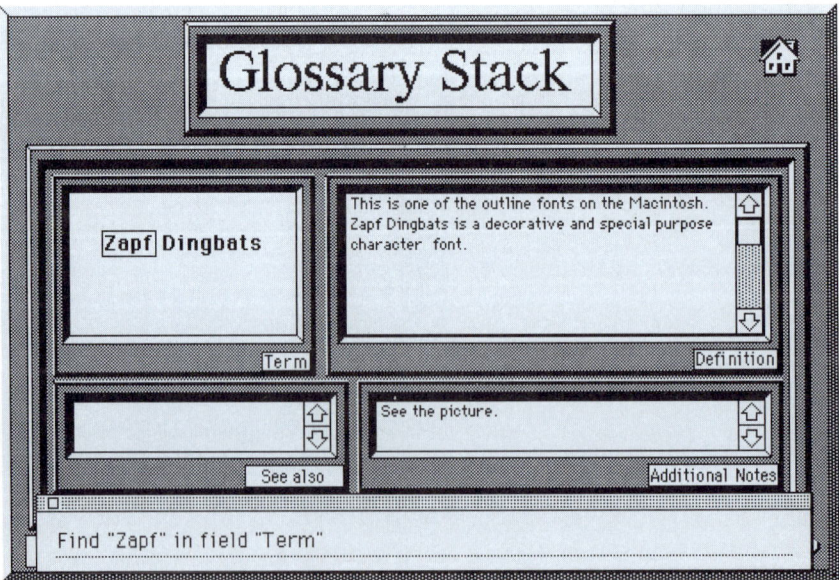

Figure 12-53   Text found in another card

This card (and the preceding one) contains a picture showing a sample of the font. In fact, most of the standard screen and LaserWriter outline fonts are listed in the Glossary, and each has a sample of the font shown on the card picture.

The Zapf Dingbats font contains a number of symbols; if you want to see a sample, click the Show Picture button. A better example of a sample font picture is on the preceding card. Let's look at it.

➡ Click on the left arrow button.

You now see the Zapf Chancery card. Show the picture to see a sample of this font (see Figure 12-54).

➡ Click **Show Picture**.

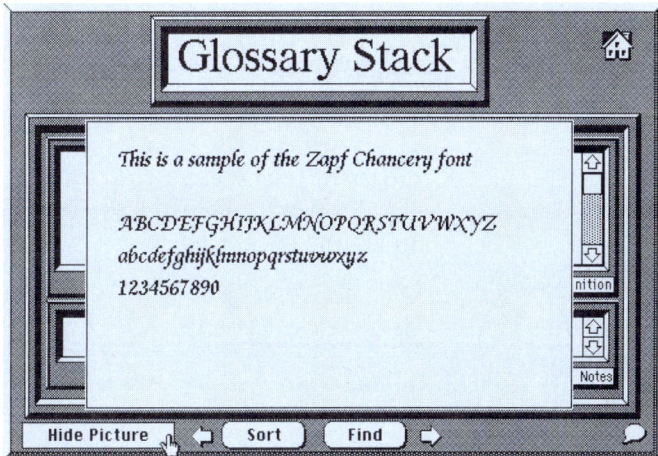

Figure 12-54   A sample of the Zapf Chancery font

Explore the Glossary stack as much as you want. When you are ready to go back to the Home stack, follow the instructions below.

➡ Click on the Home button on the top right of the card.

The stack then shows the closing card, and in a few seconds it fades out and takes you back to the Home card.

You can now continue exploring the other stacks shown on the Home card if you want.

⌘-Q ➡ When you are done, choose **Quit HyperCard** from the File menu.

This completes Project 1. You now know how to move around inside most HyperCard stacks and how to use the Help stack for learning more about HyperCard. The Glossary stack is available for quickly finding definitions and seeing examples of more than 600 terms.

Project 2: Modifying a Stack

In Project 2 you will create a new stack from one of the cards shown in the Card Ideas stack. This stack will allow you to enter, find, and modify names and addresses of your friends and acquaintances. You will see how easily a new stack can be adapted from another one.

In the second part of the stack you will enter a few names and some related information. Then, in the final part of the project you will produce mailing labels and an alphabetical list of all the names in the stack.

SETTING THE USER LEVEL

This project requires that you have access to the authoring capabilities of HyperCard.

➡ Start HyperCard.

➡ Go to the User Preferences card in the Home stack by clicking on the left arrow button and change the user level to Authoring, as shown in Figure 12-55.

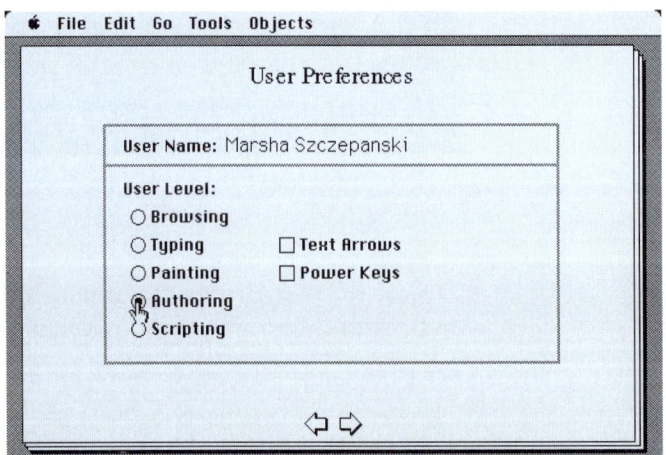

Figure 12-55   Choosing the Authoring user level

➡ If Text Arrows is selected, click it to deselect it. Be sure Power Keys is also deselected.

➡ Go to the Home card by clicking on the right arrow.

When you change the user level to Authoring, you see two new menus added to the menu bar: Tools and Objects.

You now have access to the Tools menu, which allows you to choose the button tool, field tool, and any of the painting tools. The Objects menu allows you to get information about the objects in the stack and to change certain options that control the objects.

COPYING STACK IDEAS ELEMENTS

Instead of creating a new address stack from scratch, you can save yourself a lot of work by creating a new stack based on an existing card. For this project, you will create a new stack from Address card 2 in Stack Ideas.

➡ Click **Stack Ideas**.

This opens Stack Ideas and shows you the index card.

➡ Click **Address card 2**.

You now see the second address card sample (see Figure 12-56). You will use this card to create a new stack. Then you will modify some of the characteristics of the fields on the card and enter information into the fields.

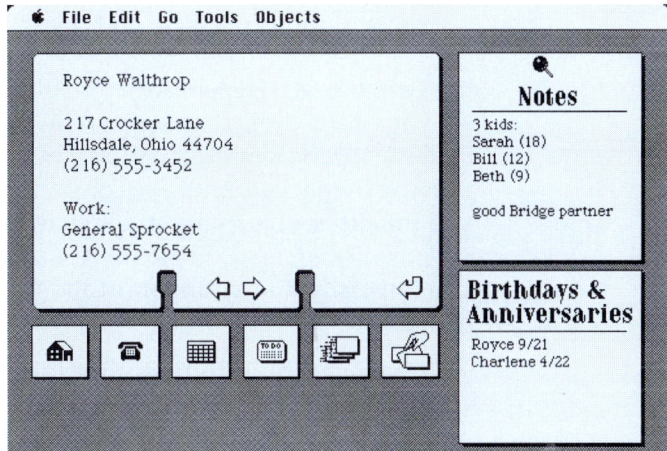

Figure 12-56   The second address card in Stack Ideas

Creating a new stack from an existing card is a fast and easy process.

➡ Choose **New Stack** from the File menu.

You are presented with a dialog box that allows you to name the new stack (see Figure 12-57).

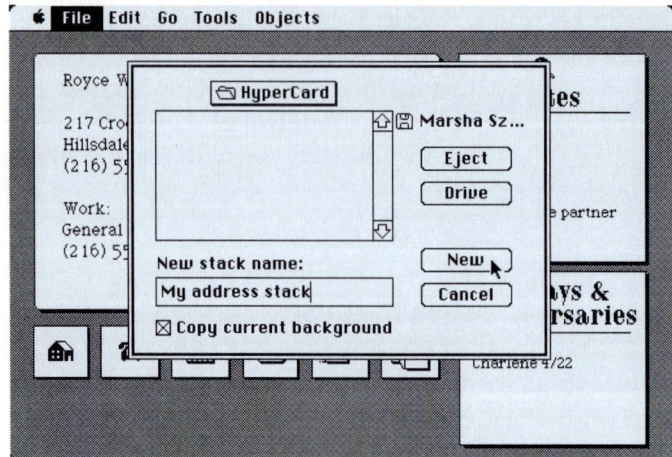

Figure 12-57   Creating a new stack from an existing card

➡ Name the new stack My address stack, be sure Copy current background is selected, and save the new stack on your data disk.

In a few seconds, HyperCard does some work and you have a new stack on your data disk. It is important to copy the current background because it has a number of buttons and fields already in place. By copying the background, you copy not only the graphics on the card but also the other objects and their characteristics and scripts.

You can easily find information about your new stack using the Objects menu.

➡ Choose **Stack Info** from the Objects menu.

A dialog box appears on the screen telling you the name of the stack, where it is located, the number of cards and backgrounds it contains, the current size, and how much space is free in the stack (see Figure 12-58).

This is a new stack with only the one card and one background you just copied. It takes up 8 kilobytes on the disk and has no free space yet.

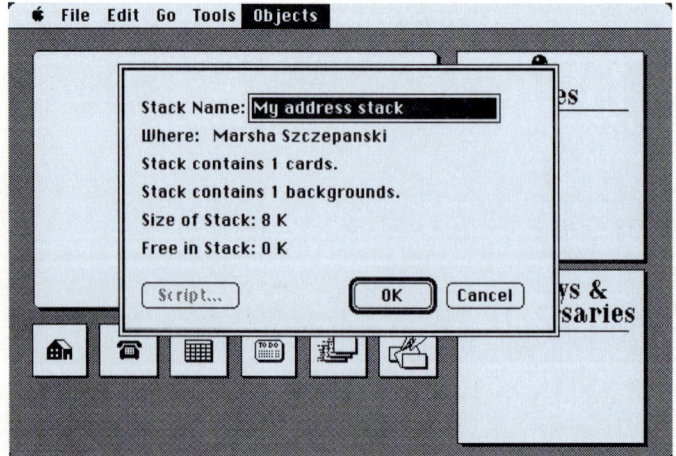

Figure 12-58   Getting information about the stack

⇒   Click **OK** when you have read the information in the dialog box.

Adjusting Background Fields

One of the first changes you will make is to show the outline of the Name and Address field and show the lines in the field. The font for the field is currently 12-point New York, and you will change it to 12-point Geneva.

To make it easier to work with various tools, you can convert the Tools menu into a floating palette. This is a tear-off menu, and all you have to do to move it on the screen is choose the menu and drag it from the menu bar to where you want it.

⇒   Tear off the Tools menu and move the palette to the lower left corner of the card (see Figure 12-59).

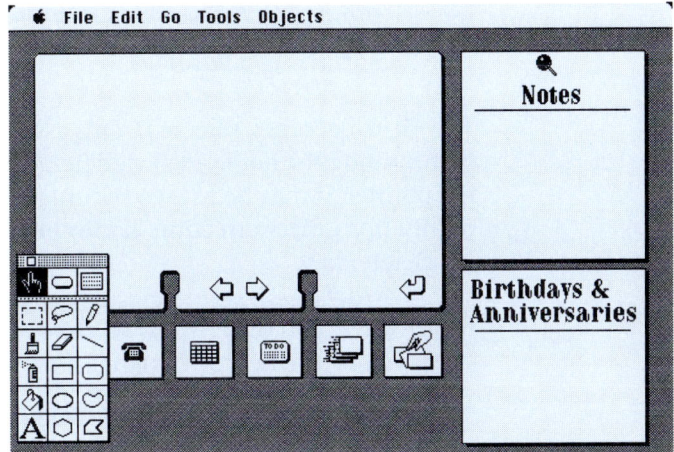

Figure 12-59   Tear off the Tools menu to make it easier to use.

Now that you have the Tools palette where you can use it, you need to choose the field tool so you can modify some of the fields on the background.

⇒   Select the field tool.

When you select the field tool, all the fields on this background become visible. You can see that there are four fields showing on the card (see Figure 12-60).

Figure 12-60   Fields become visible when the field tool is chosen.

Let's examine one of the fields in more detail.

➡ Click in the top left field.

The field becomes selected. This is shown by a moving dotted line surrounding the field. A selected field may be moved by dragging it with the pointer. It may be reduced or enlarged by dragging one of its corners in the appropriate direction. It may be deleted by pressing the Backspace (or Delete) key.

In this case, you don't want to change its size or position or delete it. What you will do next is to change its appearance and font characteristics.

➡ Choose **Field Info** from the Objects menu.

A dialog box similar to a stack information box appears. In this box are the name of the field (Name and Address), its number on the background (1), the style of the field (transparent), and any other chosen characteristics (none).

➡ Change the style to rectangle, and click the **Show Lines** check box.

The dialog box should now look like the one in Figure 12-61.

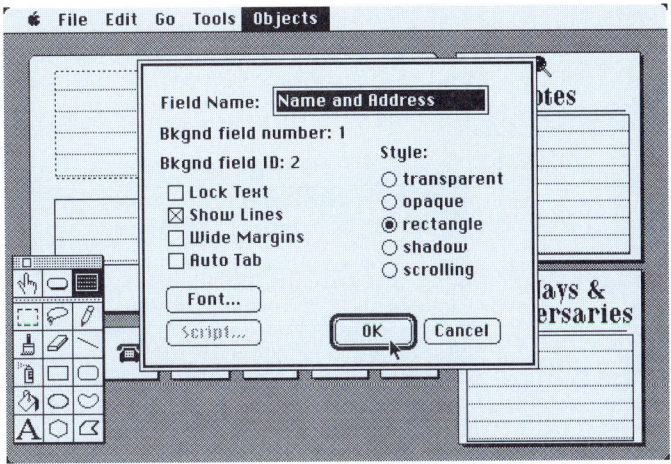

Figure 12-61   Setting characteristics for a field

Before you click the OK button to accept these changes, you can modify some of the text characteristics.

➔   Click **Font**.

Another dialog box appears, replacing the field information box.

Figure 12-62 shows the dialog box just before you click **OK** to accept the new choices.

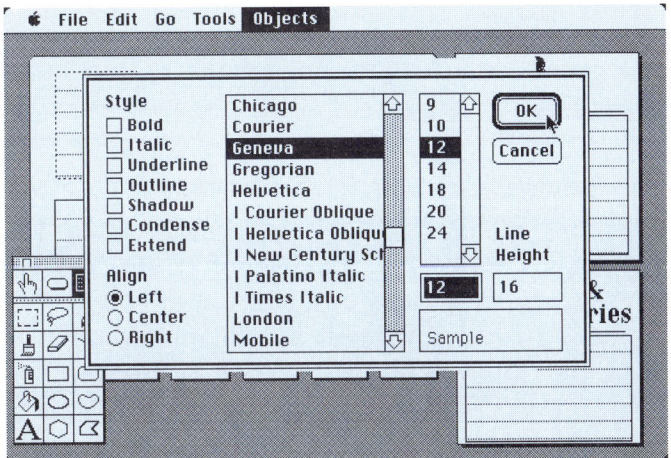

Figure 12-62   Setting font characteristics for a field

➔   Select **Geneva** font, and **12-point** size. Click **OK** to accept the change.

To see the results of the changes you just made to the Name and Address field, choose the browse tool.

➔   Select the browse tool.

The field is now visible on the screen. There is a solid rectangular frame around the field, and dotted lines indicate each line of text the field can contain, based on 12-point Geneva (see Figure 12-63).

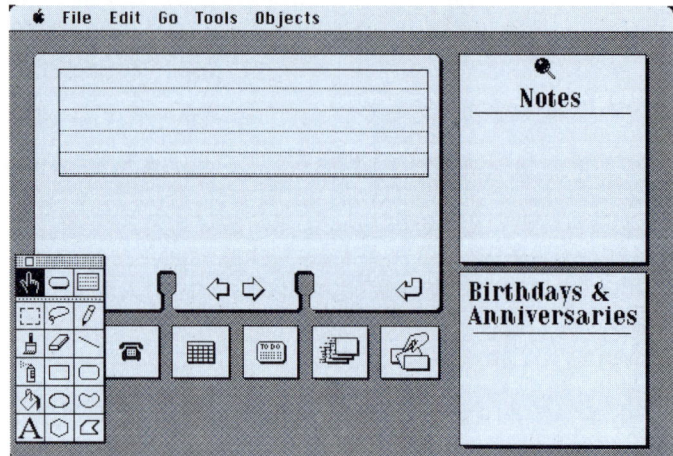

Figure 12-63   The modified Name and Address field

Now that you can see this field, you can modify the field below it.

➡ Select the field tool, and double-click on the lower left field.

You now see a field information dialog box (see Figure 12-64).

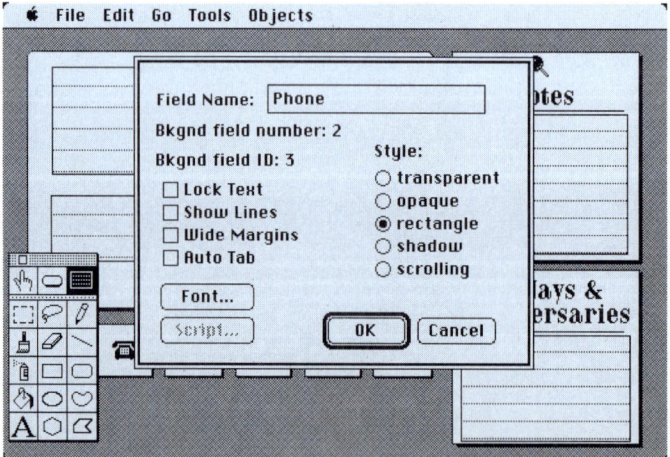

Figure 12-64   Naming the Phone field and changing its style

➡ Name the field Phone, and select the **rectangle** style. Click **OK**.

After you close the dialog box, your address card should look similar to the one shown in Figure 12-65.

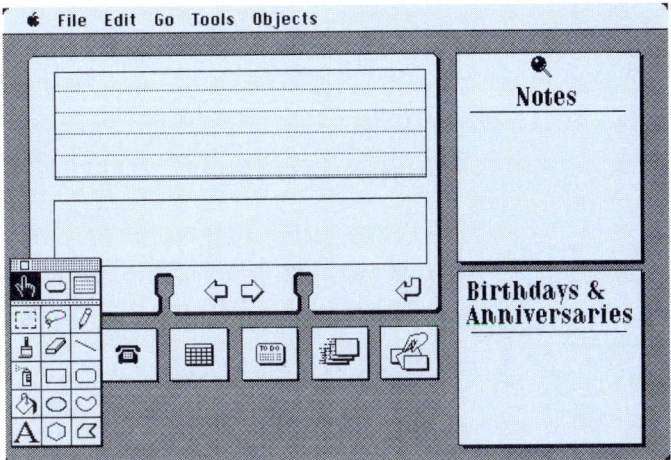

Figure 12-65 The card after changing the two fields

You have now completed all the changes you will be making to the fields in this stack. One of the most appealing aspects of HyperCard is the ability to continually customize and modify stacks to suit your particular needs and aesthetics.

Editing Cards

Now that you have finalized the design of this stack, change back to the browse tool and close the Tools palette.

➡ Choose the browse tool, and close the Tools palette.

You are now ready to enter information into several cards. Entering text in a field is as easy as selecting where you want it and then typing it into the field.

There are several ways to position the text insertion point in the Name and Address field. You can move the pointer to the first line of the field and click the mouse button, or, if no text insertion point is visible in any of the fields, press the Tab key to move the insertion point into the first field on the background.

Since the Name and Address field is the first background field, either method would work in this case. When you are creating new cards and entering information, you may find it easier to use the Tab key method of placing the insertion point.

➡ Press the Tab key.

The insertion point is placed into the first line of the Name and Address field. You are now ready to enter the first person's data in your address stack.

➡ Type **Francesco Cavaliri**, and then press the Return key.

The name appears in the field and the insertion point moves to the start of the next line in the field.

➡ Type **Route 3, Box 149**, and then press Return.

When you type the last line of the address you do not need to press the Return key.

➡ Type **Pagosa Springs**, CO 82032.

This is all the information that needs to go in the first field. Now you can enter the area code and phone number in the Phone field.

➡ Press the Tab key to move the insertion point to the Phone field.

➡ Type **(303) 555-1293**.

You have now entered all the information that will go on this card. Your card should look like the one shown in Figure 12-66.

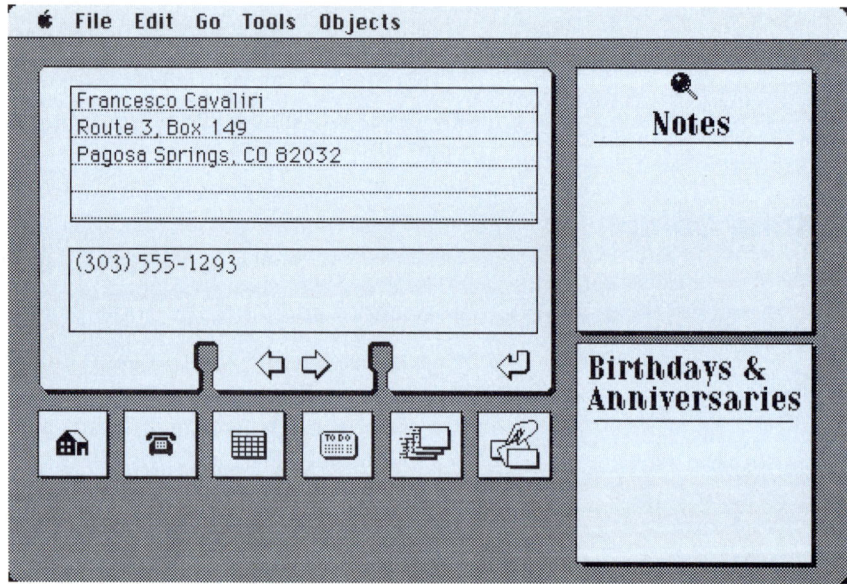

Figure 12-66   The stack's first card with a name and address entered

Adding More Cards

An address stack with only one name and address is not very useful, but how do you add more information to your list? You must create a new card for each person you want to enter in your file.

Let's create a new card and enter another person's data.

➡ Choose **New Card** from the Edit menu.

➡ Type the following information in the appropriate fields:

David Wilson
1429 Denali Drive
Marietta, GA 30922
(404) 555-2916

You should now see a card like the one shown in Figure 12-67.

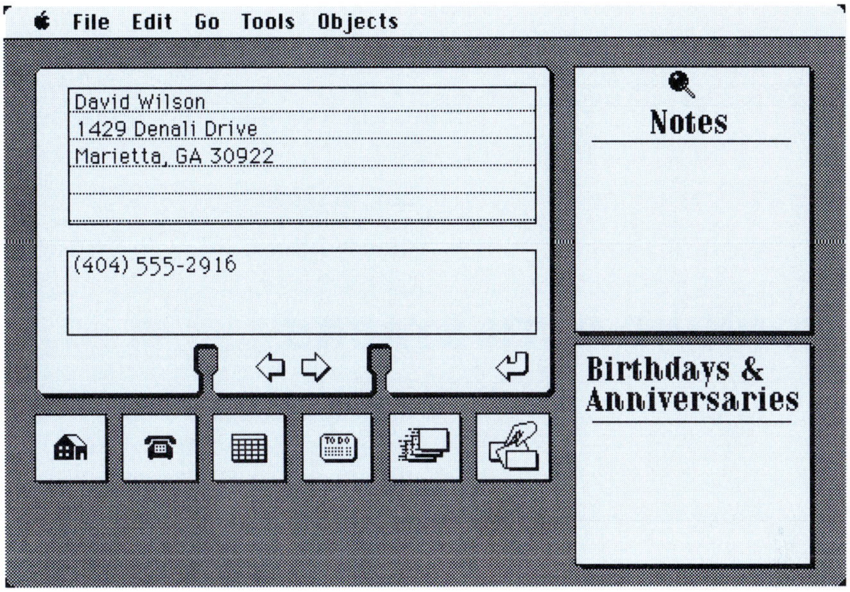

Figure 12-67   The second name and address card

➡ Continue creating new cards, and enter the information for the
following people:

Linda Ammerman   (704) 555-9273
928 Dobie Way
Bellevue, NC 28002

Bill Beck   (704) 555-1092
Route 3, Box 992
Hanging Dog, NC 28982

Larry Wilson   (602) 555-8725
1298 Main Street
Apache Junction, AZ 92778

George Kelischek   (704) 555-2892
112 Via Viol
Brasstown, NC 28672

Ed Smith   (615) 555-2906
Marianne Myers-Smith
8392 Hilltop Lane
Spotted Fawn, TN 27202

David Willie   (404) 555-1296
9289 Rock Road
Auburn, GA 30282

George P. Burdell   (404) 555-9272
1837 Imagination Alley
Atlanta, GA 30003

Printing Cards

HyperCard can print one card or all the cards in the stack, but it does not directly support a command to print only some of the cards. This can be done, but it requires creating a HyperTalk script to accomplish it.

In this case you want to print only one card.

➡ Click on the left arrow or the right arrow until you find a card you want to print.

➡ Choose **Print Card** from the File menu.

WORKING WITH STACKS

You now have an address stack with information on nine people. You can add as many cards as you want to a stack like this, limited only by the amount of disk space available on your system.

The names in this stack were entered in no particular order. One of the main functions of information management software is to organize information.

Sorting the Stack

When you copied the background from Stack Ideas you also copied a number of buttons located on that background. The icons of the buttons and their names are shown in Figure 12-68.

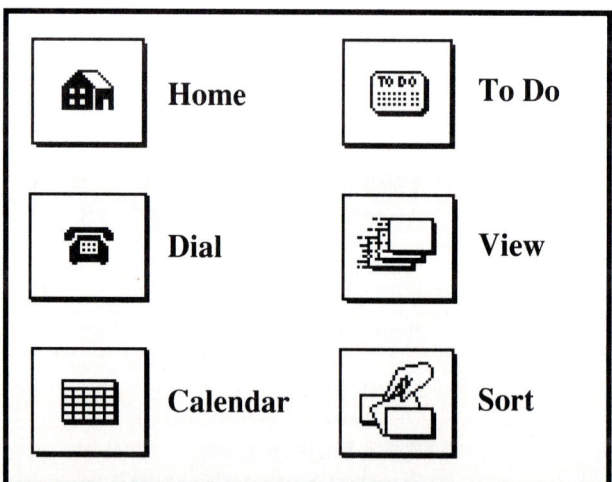

Figure 12-68   Background buttons in the address stack

The Home button does what all Home buttons do: it goes to the Home card.

The Calendar and To Do buttons take you to the previously discussed stacks with the same names. View shows you all the cards in a stack in rapid sequence. To stop View (or almost any other script), type Command-period.

The Sort button was previously programmed to allow you to sort by the first word or the last word of the first line of the Name and Address field. This assumes that you have entered the names on the first line, in first name, middle name or initial, and then last name order.

When you copied the background, the buttons were copied and retained their original position and characteristics, including the scripts they had in their original stack.

Dial allows you to dial a phone number through the Phone stack. Select the number you want to dial, and then click on the Dial button. (Do not do this if you have a modem attached, unless it is a number you really want dialed.)

Now that you know the names of the buttons and a little about what they do, you can put one to work and sort the cards in the stack. Most address lists are sorted alphabetically by last name, with people having the same last name sorted by first name.

You can accomplish this in this stack by sorting first by first name, and then again according to last name. When HyperCard sees two cards with the same sort value it will not change their positions. So, when you sort first by first name, and then by last name, HyperCard will leave the people with the same last name in alphabetical order by first name. Unless you have hundreds of names in the stack, the process goes fairly quickly.

➠ Click **Sort** and choose **First Name**. Then click **Sort** again and choose **Last Name**, as shown in Figure 12-69.

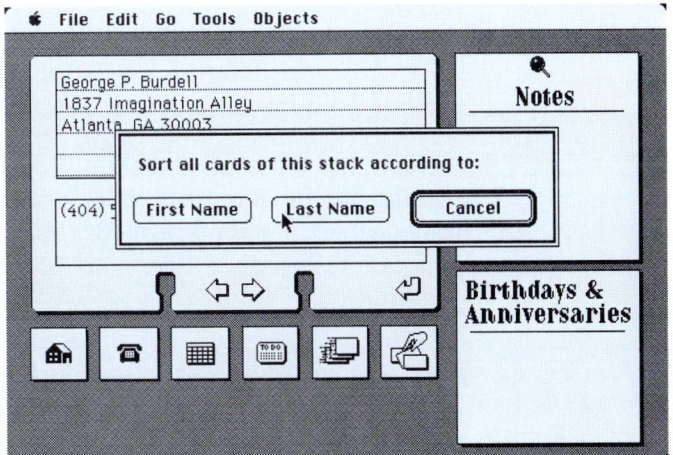

Figure 12-69   Sorting the names in alphabetical order by last name

You have now completed sorting the cards into alphabetical order.

Printing the Stack

With the stack in alphabetical order, it is a good idea to print all the cards in the stack.

HyperCard provides a command to do this: Print Stack. When you choose this command, it allows you to select various options before printing.

➡ Choose **Print Stack** from the File menu.

You are presented with a dialog box like the one shown in Figure 12-70.

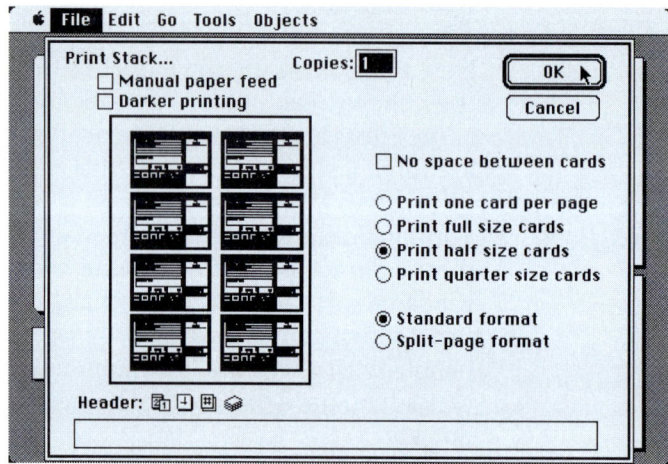

Figure 12-70   The Print Stack dialog box

➡ Select **Print half size cards** and **Standard format**.

The bottom of the dialog box has a box with four icons that lets you create a custom header for the pages on which the stack will be printed.

In order, the icons stand for Date, Time, Page Number, and Stack Name. Clicking on one or more of these will enter the respective data into the header when the stack is printed. You can separate the information with one or more spaces.

➡ Click **OK**.

The stack will print on two pages, with eight cards on the first page and only one on the second page. This is not the fastest or most efficient way to print a report from a stack, but it has the advantage of showing all the graphics stored on each background and on each card. Printing the stack is a good way to document the appearance of a new stack in case you need to create a similar one in the future.

Printing a Report

HyperCard provides three main ways to print reports based on information in the stack. It only processes all cards and will not allow you to select a subset of the data for a report.

The lack of ability to print information that matches specific criteria is one of the problems that inhibits using HyperCard for a database management program. As with most things in HyperCard, however, HyperTalk provides the tools to accomplish this task if you are an accomplished scripter.

To complete this project, you will print each of the three types of reports provided in HyperCard: labels, columns, and rows.

A number of printing options are available when printing HyperCard reports, but this project does not try to exhaustively cover each of the options. Instead, you are presented with an example of how you might produce each of the three types of reports.

Labels

A label report is used to create mailing labels or other labels that are arranged several to a page in a rectangular pattern.

Each label contains information stored in the fields of one card. The information printed in each label is automatically centered on the label. Each label in the report you are about to print will contain left-aligned text, but the left edge of the text in all labels will not be aligned, as HyperCard will adjust the contents of each label so the text will fit as near the center of the label as possible.

This is easier to understand if you print a label report.

➡ Choose **Print Report** from the File menu.

You are presented with a dialog box such as the one in Figure 12-71.

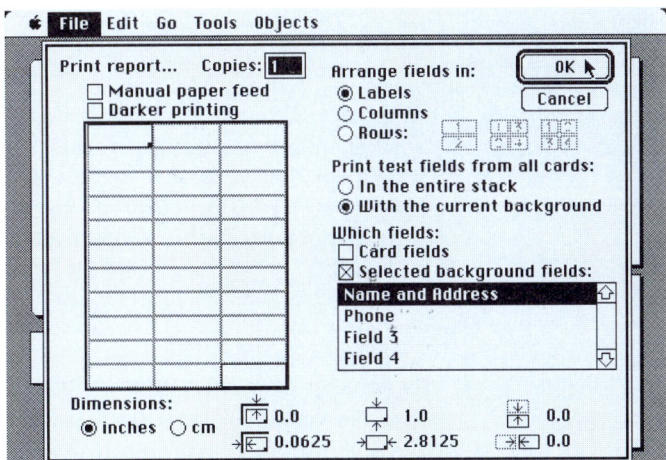

Figure 12-71 The selections for printing a label report

➠ Select **Labels, With the current background, Selected background fields,** and the **Name and Address** field (see Figure 12-71). Then click **OK.**

HyperCard prints the reports to the currently selected printer. If you are printing on an ImageWriter, you must use 3-up labels on 8.5- by 11-inch paper, because HyperCard is not programmed to print on narrower labels.

Columns

A columnar report prints the report in vertical columns. Each field is printed in its own column. If the column is too narrow to hold the entire contents of the field, the text is automatically wrapped within the appropriate column.

In this report, you will print the Name and Address field in the left column and the Phone field in the right column.

➠ Choose **Columns, With the current background, Selected background fields,** and the **Name and Address** and **Phone** fields (see Figure 12-72). Choose to print field names. Click **OK.**

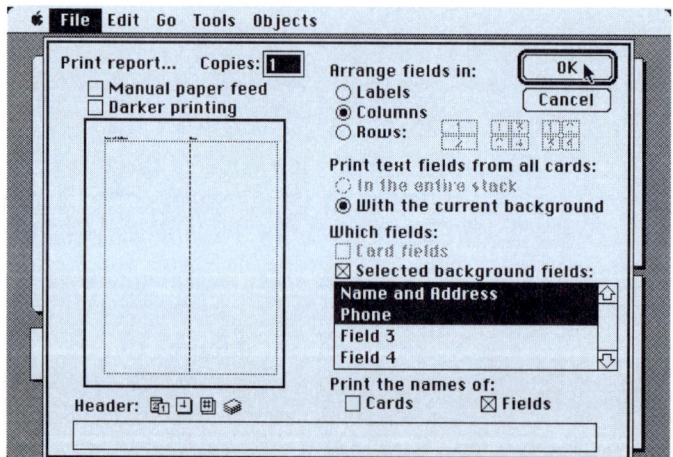

Figure 12-72   Selecting options for a column report

The report consists of a two-column report listing the information in the two fields. The information for a particular card appears side by side.

If you choose to print the names of fields, they appear at the top of each column, while card names appear in their own column on the left side of the report.

Rows

If you choose to print a row report, the information for each card is printed in a vertical format with the name of each field (if the option is chosen) to the left of the first line of the contents of that field.

HyperCard allows you to print row reports in one-column or two-column format. If you choose the one column-format, the information for a single card can go all the way to the right margin. A two-column format causes the information on two cards to be printed side by side.

In this project you will choose a single-column format.

To print a row report, make the same selections as you did for the column report, with one exception:

➠ Choose **Rows** instead of Columns, and then click **OK** (see Figure 12-73).

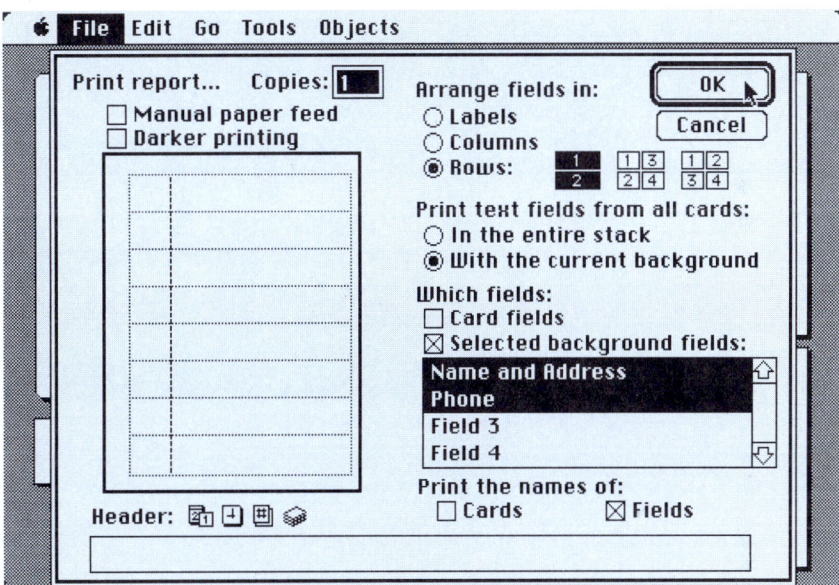

Figure 12-73   Selections for a row report

This completes the three reports for this project.

Dialing a Phone Number

When you copied the background for this stack, you copied an interesting button as well. The Dial button allows you to use your computer to dial the phone automatically based on information in a stack.

Since each of the people in this stack has a phone number listed, you can use the Dial button to call them.

To use this in a real situation, you would open the Phone stack and make any adjustments and customizations necessary for your particular location and computer system.

The Phone stack knows how to dial by generating touch tones from the computer's speaker or by dialing through a modem using pulse or touch tones. If you are doing this in a computer lab or at home without a modem, you can hear the sounds of the computer dialing if the Phone stack is set to generate tones from its speaker.

If your computer is attached to a modem and you have modified the Phone stack to dial through the modem, the following exercise will actually dial your phone. All the numbers are imaginary, so the call shouldn't really go through, but you may want to be aware that it will really dial the phone.

You can use any of the cards in the stack for this exercise.

➡ Select the phone number, and then click on the Dial button (see Figure 12-74).

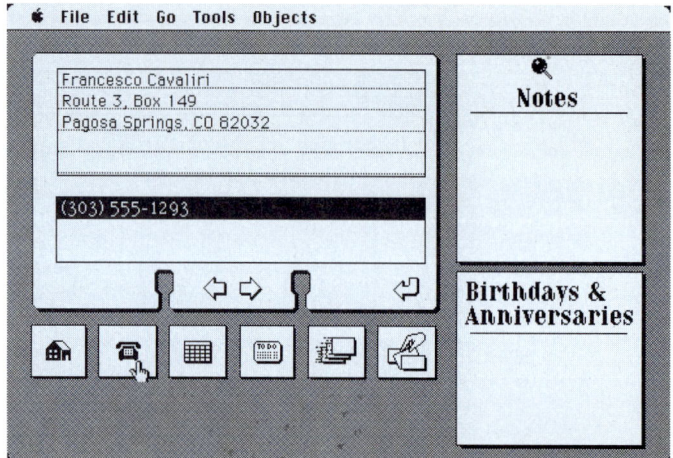

Figure 12-74   Using HyperCard to place a call

HyperCard goes to the Phone stack and attempts to dial the number you selected. If the number has the same area code as that listed in the Phone stack, it asks if this is a local or long-distance call and dials according to the preferences you have listed.

This concludes Project 2.

⌘-Q   ➡ You can choose **Quit HyperCard** or continue with the next project.

Project 3: Creating a New Stack

In Project 3, you create a new stack called Class Notes without copying a card or background. This means that you must draw the background picture, and your new stack will not have the benefit of already having the fields and buttons on the background as you did in Project 2.

When you begin to use HyperCard for automating more tasks, you will want to create stacks that are personalized for the specific task at hand. This project is based on the premise that you will find tasks for which you will not be able to use one of the cards in Stack Ideas. In this project, you will copy a portion of a background picture, paste it into your stack, complete the drawing, add new fields, and import several buttons from other stacks (so you don't have to write the scripts for them).

To make your stack more visually appealing, you will be introduced to *HyperTalk scripting*. Compared to other programming languages, HyperTalk is easy to learn and use, but it is beyond the scope of this book to teach scripting in general.

Most of the buttons in this stack are available in the Button Ideas stack, but you will use a Sort button and a Print Report button that is included in the Class Notes Buttons stack on the *Macintosh Journey Projects* disk. To demonstrate HyperCard's visual effects and how they can be used to add visual appeal to your stacks, we have also included a simple Visual Effects stack on the *Projects* disk.

The Class Notes stack, shown in Figure 12-75, is designed for taking any type of class notes. It can be used for multiple classes and will sort the notes into chronological order within each class. The Print Report button can be used to produce a text file based on a range of dates or a keyword search. The resulting text file may be opened by any word processing application for formatting and printing.

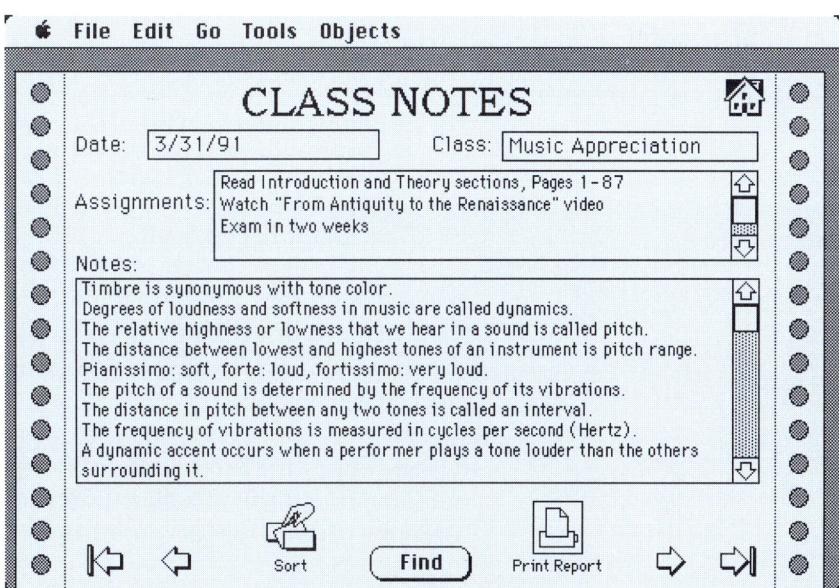

Figure 12-75   The final Class Notes stack

This stack is also useful for making class notes if you teach any type of class or for organizing other notes that may not necessarily be associated with a class. The techniques you will learn in this project will be applicable to many other types of stack creation.

For most of this assignment you can leave the user level set to Authoring. When you add the visual effects to your stack, you will need to (briefly) change the user level to Scripting.

You should also be sure that you have copied the Class Notes Buttons and Visual Effects stacks from the *Macintosh Journey Projects* disk onto your disk. The procedure for doing this was covered in Project 1 in Chapter 1.

If you do not presently have HyperCard open:

➡ Open HyperCard by double-clicking on its icon.

CREATING THE BACKGROUND

When you create a new stack without copying a background, you must create the picture for the background, create all the fields necessary, and create or copy any necessary buttons.

In this case you will create the background picture with minimal help from Stack Ideas.

To begin this project, you need to go to the third index card in Stack Ideas.

➡ Click **Stack Ideas**.

This will take you to the first index card in Stack Ideas.

➡ Click on the right arrow button two times.

The third index card of Stack Ideas contains a miniature picture of a card named Computer paper. This is the card you will use as the basis for creating the background picture of the Class Notes stack.

➡ Click **Computer paper**.

When you do this, HyperCard goes to the card and shows a short story about determining the difference between a coffee maker and a computer. If you would like to take a few moments to read the story before proceeding, go ahead.

It is an interesting method for identifying a coffee maker, but it would not be of much use in a class notes stack. However, the picture of the computer paper in the background might make an interesting background for your new stack.

The picture on the background layer of a stack only serves as a visual analogy for the purpose of the stack and how it operates. In this case, the background picture is not of major importance, and you could have chosen a number of different approaches for the background for a class notes stack.

The background of this stack contains a picture and four buttons you will eventually use on your new stack, and you can accomplish a lot of what you will do in this project by creating a new stack based on this card and copying the background. But, if you do that you won't learn how to create and place all the objects into the background of your new stack.

⌘-B ➡ Change to the background layer by choosing **Background** from the Edit menu.

The Background command is a toggle that switches between the card layer and the background layer.

When you issue this command, HyperCard indicates that you are in the background layer by adding a series of short diagonal stripes at the top and bottom of the menu bar. If the menu bar is not visible, you can make it visible by typing Command-space bar. This is a toggle command and will either hide or display the menu bar. It is very important that the menu bar be visible so you can see in which layer you are currently working.

➡ Tear off the Tools palette, and choose the selection tool.

You will now use this tool to copy the series of pin-feed holes and perforation indicators on the left side of the computer paper.

⌘-C ➡ Select the area of the computer paper shown in Figure 12-76, and then choose **Copy Picture** from the Edit menu.

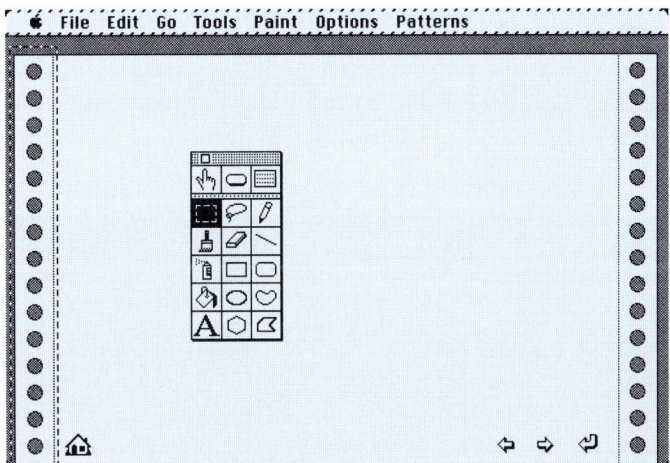

Figure 12-76   Copying the left edge of the computer paper

You will now create a new stack.

➡ Choose **New Stack** from the File menu.

➡ In the dialog box that appears, name the stack Class Notes, and deselect the option **Copy current background**.

This creates a new stack with a blank, white background. You now will paste the picture you copied from the Computer paper card to the background of the only card in the new stack.

⌘-B ➡ Change to the background layer.

⌘-V ➡ Choose **Paste Picture** from the Edit menu (see Figure 12-77). Do not click anywhere to deselect the picture you just pasted into the background layer.

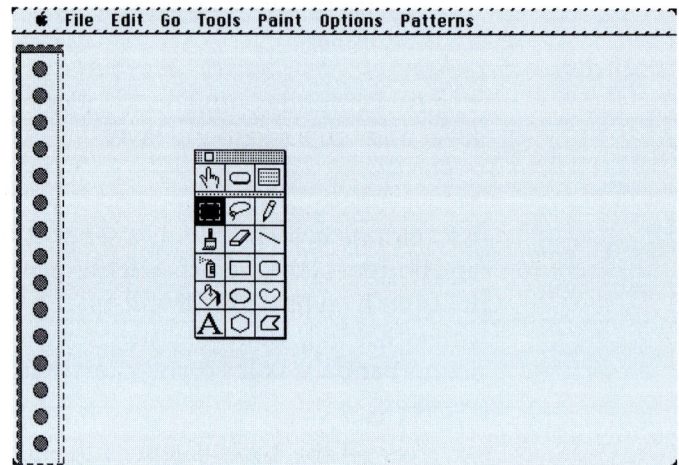

Figure 12-77 Beginning to paint the new background

⌘-V ➡ Paste the picture onto the background again, and be sure to leave it selected.

This puts another (selected) copy of the picture on top of the one you pasted a few seconds ago. Now you will drag the new copy straight to the right and then flip it horizontally to form the right edge of the paper.

➡ Press the Shift key and drag the picture to the right side of the screen (see Figure 12-78).

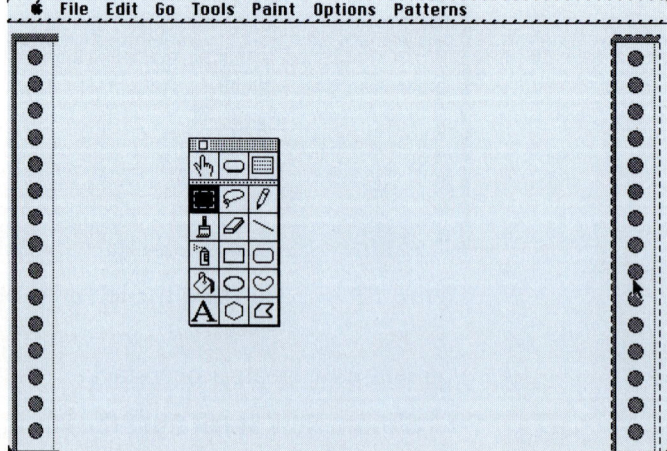

Figure 12-78 The background after dragging the copy of the picture

The second copy of the picture is facing in the wrong direction, so you need to tell HyperCard to flip the picture horizontally.

➡ Choose **Flip Horizontal** from the Paint menu.

This gives the two sides you need for the computer paper you are about to finish painting (see Figure 12-79).

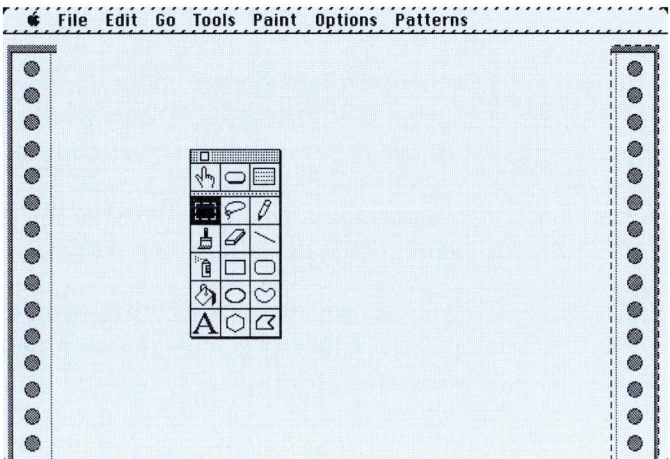

Figure 12-79   Both sides of the paper are in place.

Painting the Background

By holding down the Shift key while you dragged the second copy of the picture to the right side of the card, you constrained the drag to be exactly horizontal. This means that the tops and bottoms of the pictures should match exactly, and you now can easily draw a line across the top and bottom to finish the sheet of paper.

➠   Choose the line tool from the Tools palette.

➠   Press the Shift key to constrain the line tool to horizontal lines only, and draw two horizontal lines to connect the top and bottom of the page (see Figure 12-80).

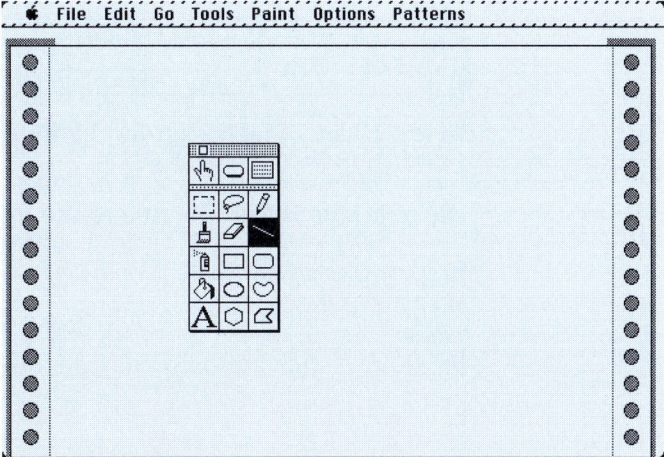

Figure 12-80   The background after the paper is completed

You can now complete the background by pouring a gray pattern around the paper with the bucket tool.

➡ Select the bucket tool and the medium gray pattern, and pour the pattern at the top of the page, above the paper.

Sometimes the pattern you pour might not align properly with the pattern that surrounded the paper when you pasted it onto the screen (see the thin black line above and on the right side of the computer paper's pin-feed holes in Figure 12-81). If you encounter this problem, you can carefully erase the part of the pattern that does not match and then repour the pattern into the area you erased.

Just as the Shift key constrains lines, circles, and squares, you can hold it down while using the eraser tool. This causes the eraser to move only vertically or horizontally, depending on how you first start moving it. This makes it easier to erase a pattern up to the very edge of a straight line such as around the edge of this computer paper.

A pattern is automatically aligned to the top left edge of the card, so the pattern you pour the second time (if you need it) always matches the pattern you poured the first time in any given card.

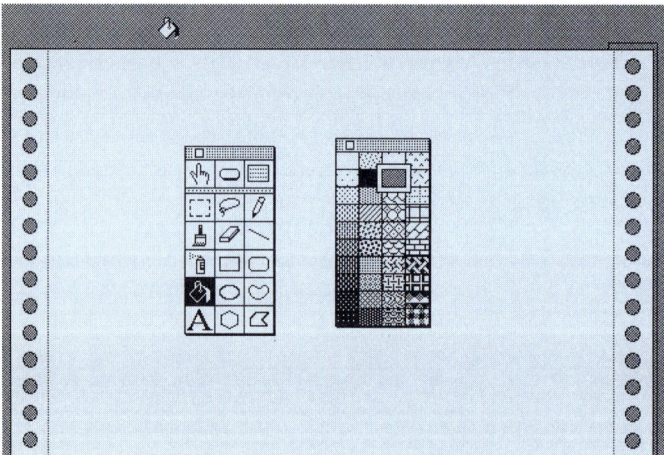

Figure 12-81   The background after pouring a medium gray pattern

The next step is to add a title to the top of the background.

To do this, you will choose a large font and type the name at the center of the top of the computer paper.

➡ Double-click on the paint text tool in the Tools palette.

This opens a dialog box (see Figure 12-82).

➡ Choose **24-point Bookman** (or any similar font available on your system), select **Center** alignment, and click **OK**.

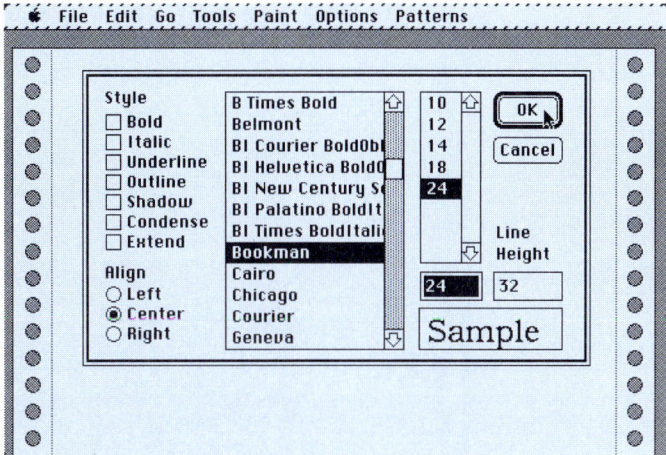

Figure 12-82   Choosing a large font for the title

➧ Click the paint text tool somewhere near the center of the top of the computer paper, and then type **CLASS NOTES** (see Figure 12-83).

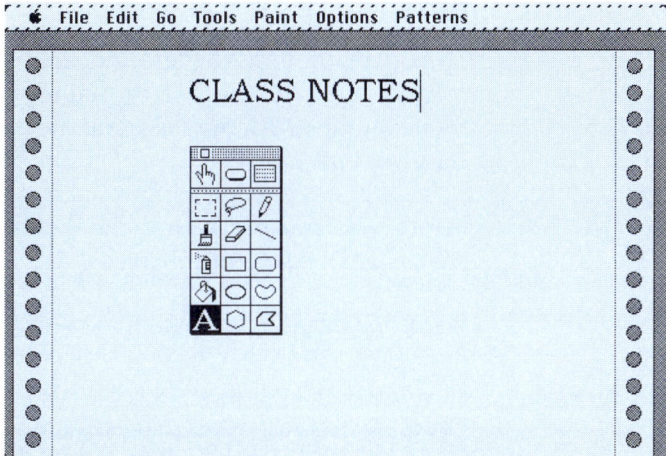

Figure 12-83   Entering the stack's title

It is sometimes difficult to enter the title in an acceptable location the first time. Rather than erasing and typing the title in a new location, you can use the lasso to move it to a better location.

➧ Select the lasso from the Tools palette, and then select the title text by carefully dragging the lasso around it. Drag the title to the location you prefer (see Figure 12-84).

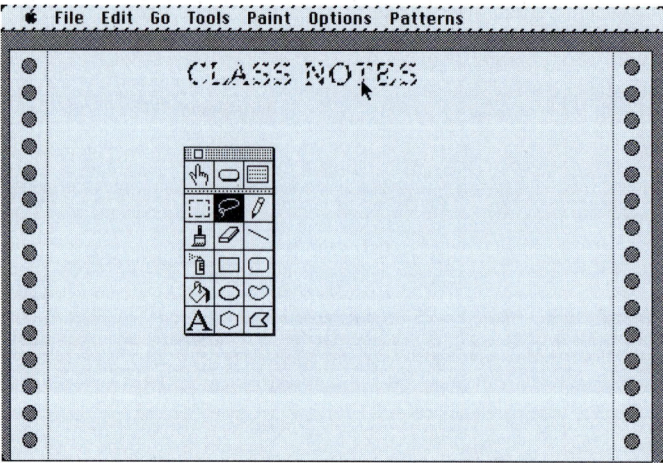

Figure 12-84   Dragging the title to a better location

This completes the painting of the background for the Class Notes stack. You will now add the fields and labels for the fields.

Adding Background Fields

There will be four background fields in the Class Notes stack. One contains the date; another, the name of the class; the third field contains the assignments for the class; and the fourth field holds any notes for the class on that date.

Before you begin creating the fields, be sure that you are still in HyperCard's background layer (hint: look at the menu bar).

Before you begin adding fields, select the field tool from the Tools menu or palette.

There are two easy ways to create a new field. The first is to choose **New Field** from the Objects menu. This places a field somewhere on the card. You can then use the field tool to drag the field to its intended location.

The second way allows you to draw a field in the position where you want it. To do this, move the field tool to one of the four corners of the new field's location, hold the Command key down, and then press the mouse button and drag to the opposite corner of the field's location. The outline of the field is drawn and may be modified until you release the mouse button, at which time the new field will be placed on the card in the location you specified.

A field may be moved by dragging it with the field tool or may be resized by dragging any of the four corners.

Since you can move a field to a new location and easily change its size, it is not critical that you initially place the field exactly in its intended location. If you don't like where it is, you can move it or resize it at will, even after you have typed text into it.

If you move a field after information has been entered into it, the text will reflow based on the new size of the field.

Now it is time for you to try it.

➧ Choose the field tool from the Tools palette.

➧ Using one of the methods you just learned, create a new field on the stack's background.

At this point, it is not important where the field is located, but you should see a field somewhere on the screen similar to the one shown in Figure 12-85.

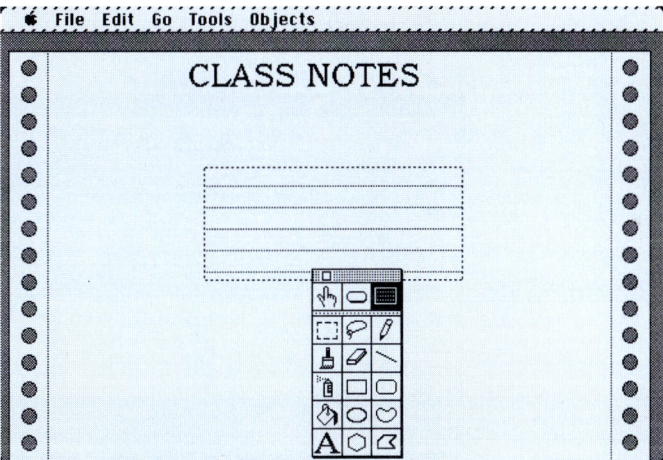

Figure 12-85   Creating your first field

The field is not the right size or in the correct location.

➧ Using the methods previously described, move the field to the location shown in Figure 12-86, and resize it to approximately the size indicated there.

Precise location and sizing are not critical factors in creating this stack.

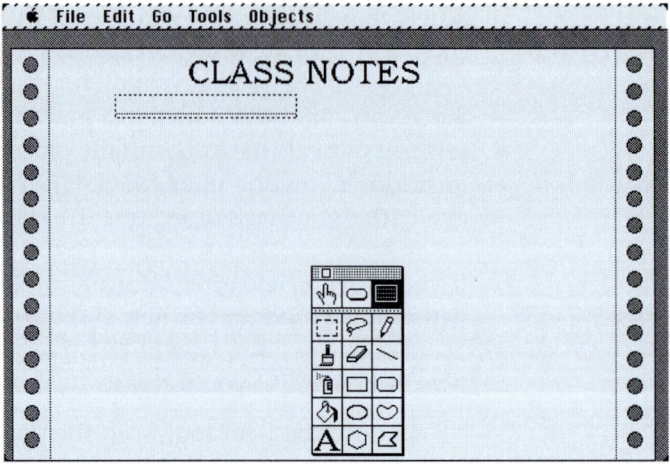

Figure 12-86   The first field in its proper location

➠   Continue adding the other three fields as shown in Figure 12-87.

The style of the fields is not important right now. Just place four fields in approximately the locations shown. You will customize the fields next.

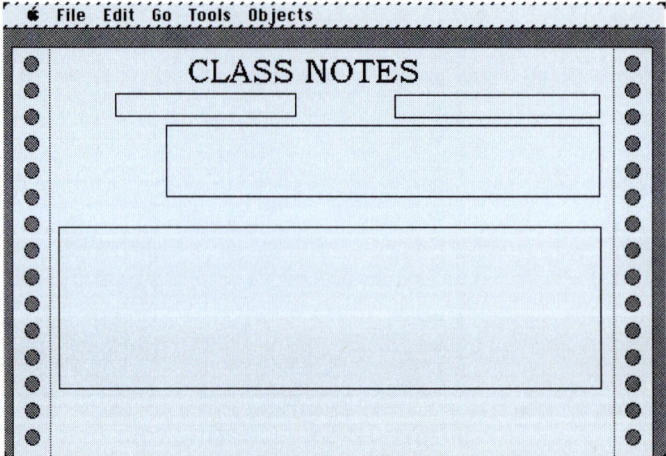

Figure 12-87   The four placed fields

The first field you created becomes the Date field. The second field should be just to the right of the first field and becomes the Class field. The third field is for assignments. The Notes field comes last and is the largest.

➠   Choose the paint text tool and enter the field labels shown in Figure 12-88. The font and style are your choice, but be sure you are in the background layer when you add the text.

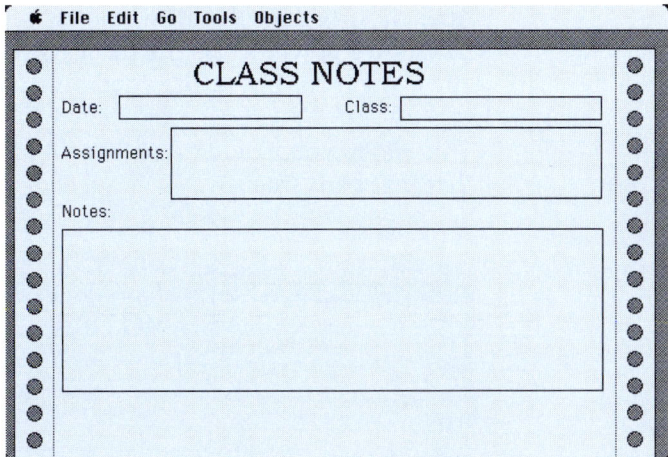

Figure 12-88   The placed fields and text labels

The fields containing assignments and notes will become scrolling fields and allow you to type as much text as you need into the field (up to 30,000 characters). If there is too much text to be visible in the space provided for the field, the text will scroll (similar to a word processor) as you enter more text. Later, you can scroll up or down to see different sections.

You have already learned how to choose fonts, sizes, and styles for the characters to be entered into a field and also how to select the rectangular style for a field.

➡   In this project, you can choose fonts, sizes, and styles of your choice for the four fields. Choose **rectangle** as the style of the Date and Class fields and **scrolling** for the style of the Assignments and Notes fields (see Figure 12-89).

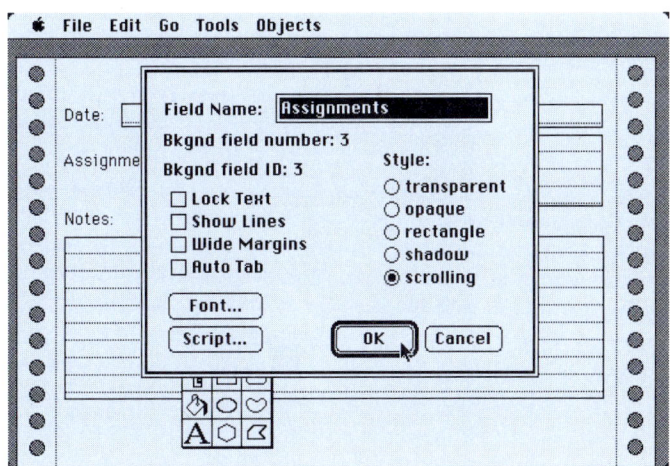

Figure 12-89   Naming a field and selecting its characteristics

After clicking the OK button, you can see the change in the Assignments field (see Figure 12-90). The rectangle outlining this field has changed, and a scroll bar has been added on the right side of the field.

This allows you to add more text than will show in the field and access that text conveniently.

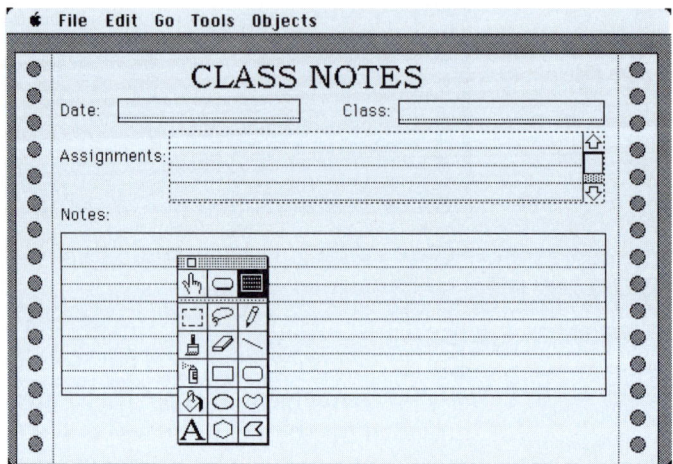

Figure 12-90   The Assignments field has a new scroll bar.

When you finish setting the styles, options, and fonts for the fields, your background should look like the one shown in Figure 12-91. Note that the browse tool is chosen. This automatically takes you from the background layer to the card layer. If you have not properly specified the characteristics of a field it may be apparent at this point.

If you need to make changes, choose the appropriate tool, change to the background layer, and make those changes. Then select the browse tool and see if your card compares to the one in Figure 12-91.

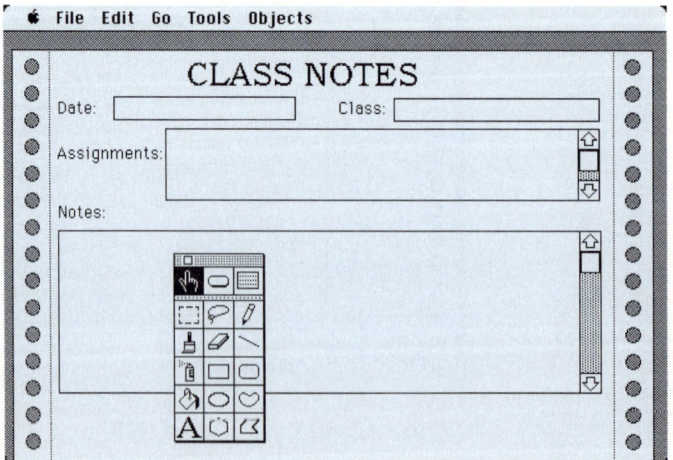

Figure 12-91   Final paint text and fields for the stack

Adding Background Buttons

You can make your stack more convenient by adding a few buttons on the background layer. Moving to the next card, or the previous one, is a common thing to do in stacks. Going to the last card to add a new card would be convenient, and to balance it out you could add a button to go to the first card.

To leave the stack, you probably want a button to go to the Home stack. There will be times when you want to quickly find something, so a Find button also would help.

You will round out the stack's complement of buttons with a button for sorting and one for printing reports. (These reports are different from, and somewhat more flexible than, the ones built into HyperCard, so your stack will have the benefit of being able to print the standard HyperCard reports plus these customized ones.)

You will add the buttons for going to the first, previous, next, and last cards by copying them from the Button Ideas stack. A button contains a HyperTalk script that tells HyperCard what the button can do.

Let's start by copying the button that will be used for going to the first card in the stack.

⌘-H ➠ Choose **Home** from the Go menu.

➠ Click **Button Ideas**, and find the card shown in Figure 12-92.

➠ Select the button tool.

➠ Select the third First button, as shown in Figure 12-92.

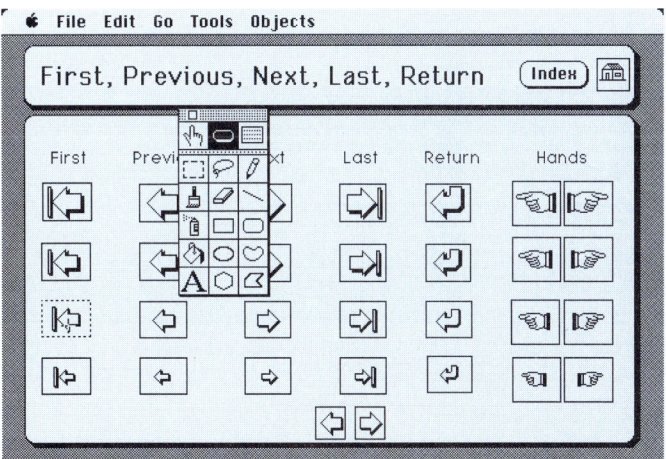

Figure 12-92   Copying a First button

⌘-C ➠ Choose **Copy Button** from the Edit menu.

Now that you have copied this button, you need to go back to the Class Notes stack and place it on the background. The easiest way to get there is to choose the Recent command from the Go menu. This shows you a series (up to 42) of miniature pictures of the cards you have recently visited.

Your list of recent cards depends on which stacks you have opened since starting HyperCard and the manner in which you chose to navigate through those stacks. Figure 12-93 shows a sample list of recent cards. It contains the cards you have seen if you followed these directions carefully and a few others to simulate the condition of other cards possibly being present if you took a different route.

The two important cards shown here are the small picture of the Class Notes stack and the one that represents the current card of the Button Ideas stack (which is outlined and is positioned on the right side of the list of cards).

To go to a recently visited card, click on its picture.

➡ Click on the picture of the Class Notes stack, as shown in Figure 12-93.

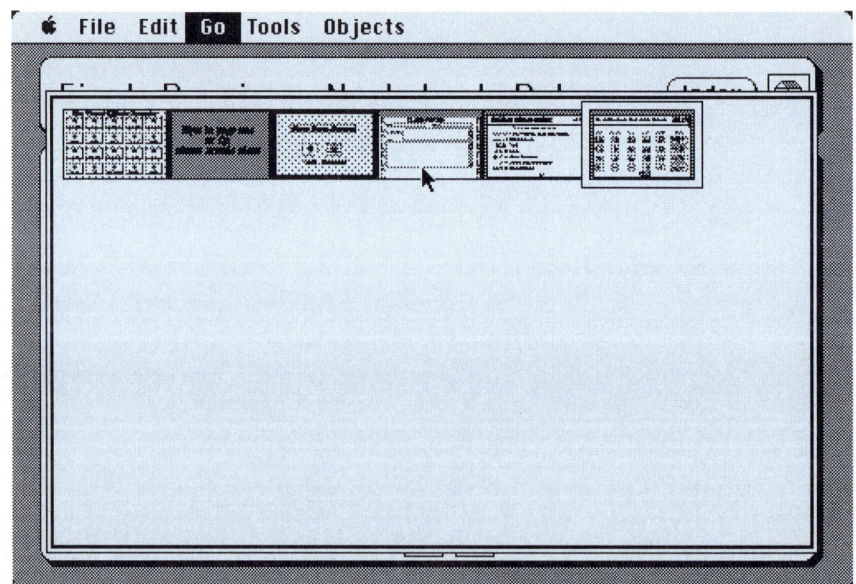

Figure 12-93   A list of recently visited cards

You are immediately returned to the card you chose. If you happened to click on the wrong one, you can choose **Recent** again and click on the proper card.

You will find this a very convenient way to move around in HyperCard. Since some of the stacks you will use will hide the menu bar, you might want to remember that Command-R is the keyboard equivalent for choosing **Recent** from the Go menu.

Now that you have copied the button you need and have returned to the Class Notes stack, you can paste the button onto the background layer. (Make sure you are on the background layer before doing the next step.)

⌘-V ⟹ Choose **Paste Button** from the Edit menu.

This command places the button on this stack's background layer in the same position it occupied in Button Ideas. Moving the button to where you want it is a simple process.

Move the pointer to approximately the center of the button before dragging it. If you are too close to one of the four corners, you tell HyperCard to resize the button, and that is not what you want to do now.

If you do resize the button, before doing anything else choose **Undo** from the Edit menu to return it to its proper size.

⟹ Drag the button to the position indicated in Figure 12-94.

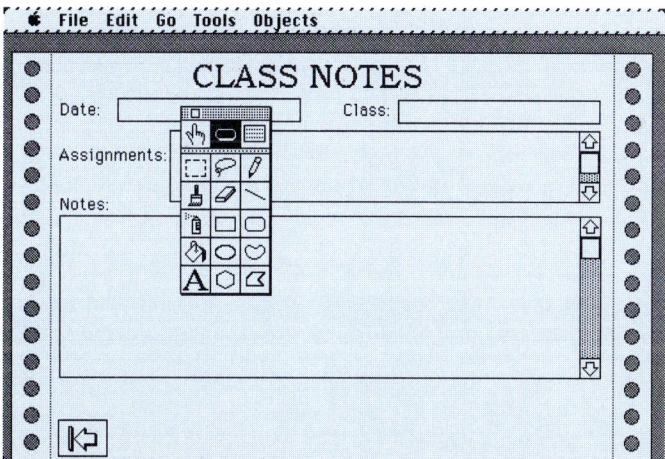

Figure 12-94   The First button pasted into your stack

Now you can copy and paste the other three buttons from that same card in the Button Ideas stack.

⌘-R ⌘-C ⌘-V ⟹ Using what you have learned here, use the Recent command and copy and paste the buttons you need. Drag them to their proper positions (see Figure 12-95).

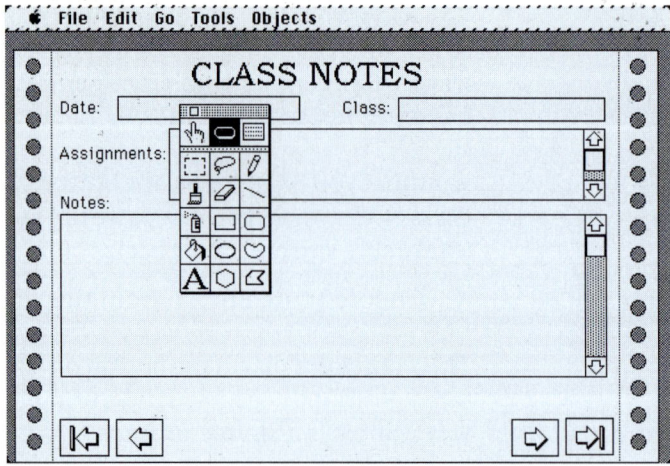

Figure 12-95   The four buttons from Button Ideas pasted into Class
                 Notes

 ⌘-R ⌘-C ⌘-V ➡   Go back to the Button Ideas stack and copy a Home button. Return
                                      to the Class Notes stack and paste it and drag it to the position
                                      shown in Figure 12-96.

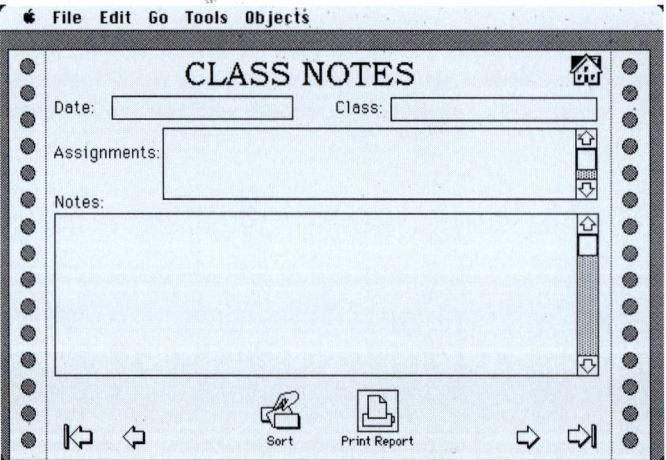

Figure 12-96   The Class Notes stack with all fields and buttons in place

Notice (see Figure 12-96) that two new buttons are at the bottom of the
computer paper. These two buttons have been scripted to sort the class
notes into chronological order, class order, or both and to print custom
reports based on a range of dates or a particular topic.

The Sort button contains a *script* that is not very complex, but the script
of the Print Report button is fairly long and complex. To save you from
having to enter these scripts, we have placed the two buttons (and their
scripts) into a stack named Class Notes Buttons on the *Macintosh Journey
Projects* disk (see Figure 12-97).

Figure 12-97   The Class Notes Buttons stack

If you have a copy of this disk, you can add the two buttons to your Class Notes stack by copying and pasting.

If you do not have a copy of the disk, you can use the scripts that are printed on the last pages of this chapter. Typing them in requires that you change to the Scripting user level, create two new buttons, click on the Script button in the Button Info dialog box, and enter the script.

Be aware that scripting requires absolute accuracy in your typing; you must enter the scripts *exactly* as shown for them to work properly. If you do not have the *Projects* disk, you may skip adding these two buttons to the stack and continue with the rest of the project. Then when you reach an instruction that tells you to do something with one of these buttons you can skip that step.

⌘-C ⌘-V ➠ Copy a button from the Class Notes Buttons stack and paste it into the background of the Class Notes stack. Repeat this process for the other button.

There is one other thing you might want to do to customize the stack to reflect personal preference for going from one card to the next.

Learning to script in HyperTalk usually involves learning something now, then a little more later, and before you know it you are scripting.

One of the easiest things you can do is add a visual effect to a button that changes from one card to another (or one stack to another).

INCLUDING VISUAL EFFECTS

A number of *visual effects* are available in HyperCard, and they can be combined with others for more complex transitions. You can also tell HyperCard to perform the visual effect very slowly, slowly, fast, or very fast.

Since explaining visual effects in print is difficult to do, we created a Visual Effects stack that contains 20 pre-scripted visual effects samples. Figure 12-98 shows the first card of this stack and the 20 buttons on it.

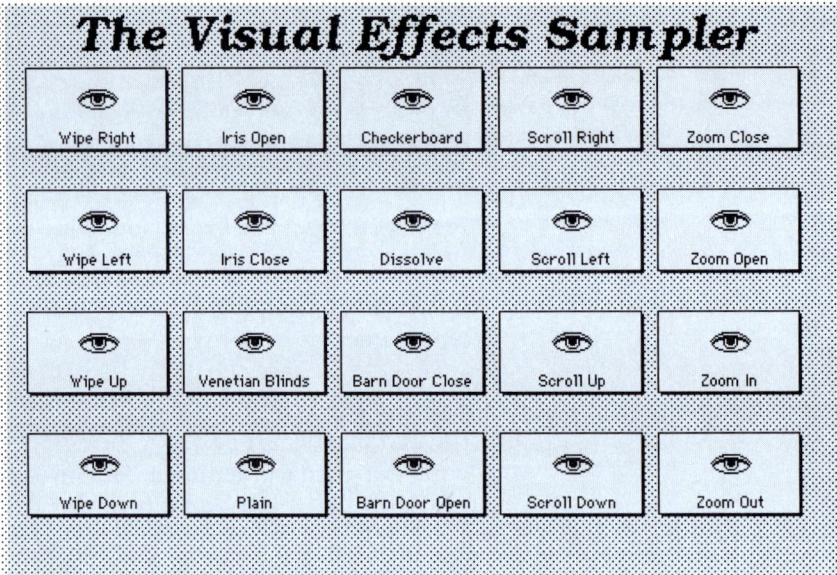

Figure 12-98   The first card of the Visual Effects stack

Visual effects include Wipe, Iris, Venetian Blinds, Checkerboard, Dissolve, Barn Door, Scroll, Zoom, and Plain (which is the same as not using a visual effect).

There are two cards in this stack. The first one does all the work, and the second one (see Figure 12-99) is there for contrast so the effects are easily visible.

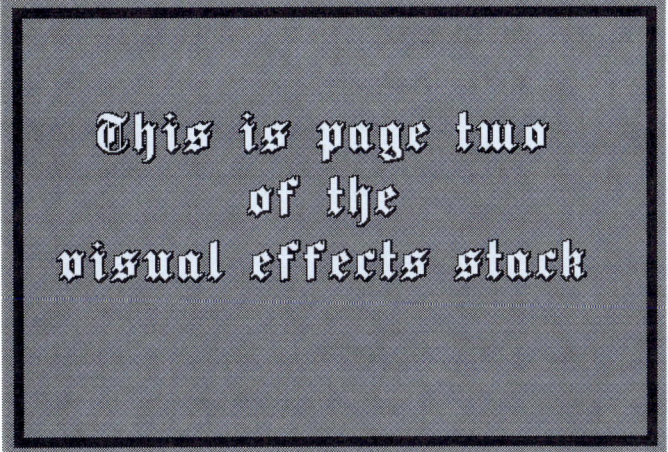

Figure 12-99   The second card of the Visual Effects stack

All of these effects are similar. The script for the Dissolve button, for example, tells HyperCard to use the dissolve effect at a slow speed, go to the next card, wait 30 ticks (this is a half-second—there are 60 ticks per second), use the same visual effect, and go to the next card (see Figure 12-100). Since there are only two cards, this returns you to the first card.

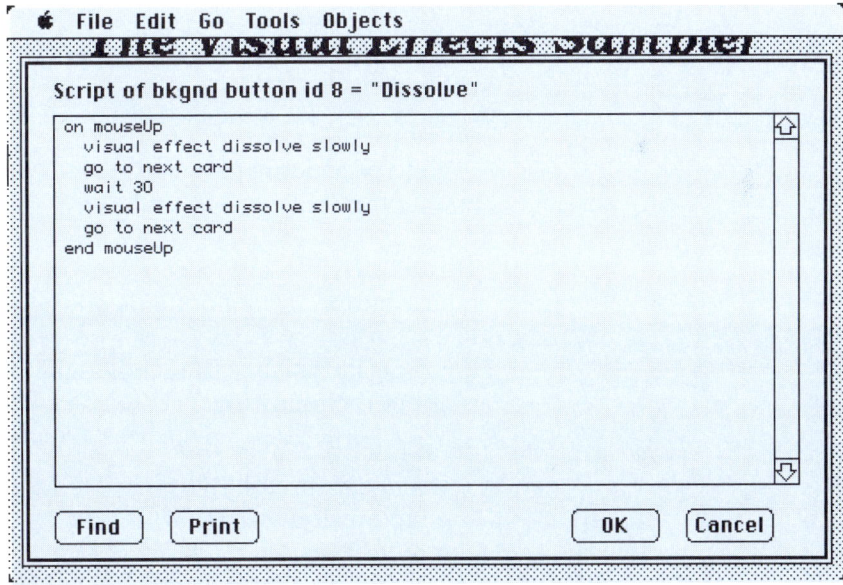

Figure 12-100   The script for the Dissolve button

If you do not have access to the Visual Effects stack, you could create one for yourself by entering this script into a button and then experiment by changing the effects used.

If you do have access to the Visual Effects stack, you can open that stack now and look at the effects available in HyperCard. Pick one that you like and that you want your Class Notes stack to use, and then you can modify the Previous and Next buttons to use the effect of your choice.

⇒ Choose **Open Stack** from the File menu. Locate the Visual Effects stack and then click **Open**.

⌘-R ⇒ Spend as long as you want experimenting with the effects, then use Recent from the Go menu to return to the Class Notes stack.

Remember which effect you liked the most, and you can use it to modify any of the arrow buttons you wish.

To do this, you must choose the Scripting user level. Instead of going back home, you can issue the command directly to HyperCard using the Message box.

⌘-M ⇒ Type **Command-M** to open the Message box, then type **set userlevel to 5** and press the Return key. (Do not enter a space in userlevel, it should be one word for this command.)

This sets the user level to Scripting (Browsing = 1, Typing = 2, Painting = 3, Authoring = 4, and Scripting = 5).

Be sure the button tool is currently selected before doing the following steps.

⇒ Hold down the Command and Option keys, and click on the Previous (left arrow) button.

The scripting dialog box for the left arrow button appears, and should contain this script:

```
on mouseUp
   go to previous card
end mouseUp
```

This tells HyperCard to go to the previous card when you release the mouse button if the pointer is on the left arrow button.

If you decide you like the Scroll Right visual effect, you can change this script to the following:

```
on mouseUp
   visual effect scroll right
   go to previous card
end mouseUp
```

This tells HyperCard to use the effect rather than just jumping to the card. It will look like the previous card comes in from the left of the screen and overlays the current card.

⇒ When you have entered the effects you like, click **OK** to close the dialog box.

If you like, you can add visual effects to any of the arrow buttons or the Home button.

ADDING A FIND BUTTON

Now you will add a button to make finding information in your notes easier.

⌘-C   ➡ Go to the Button Ideas stack and copy the Find button (see Figure 12-101).

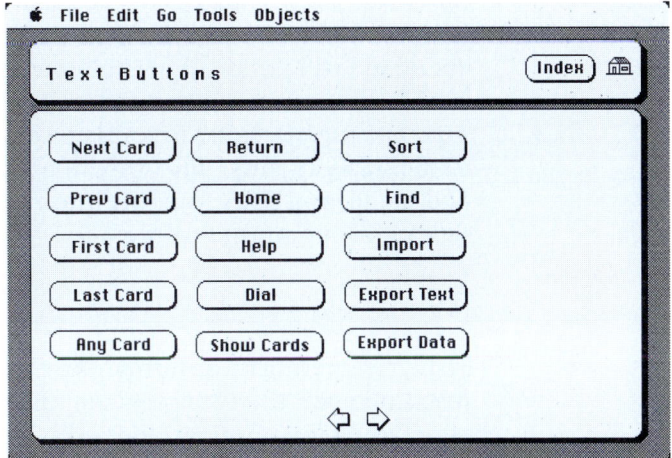

Figure 12-101   Copy the Find button from here.

⌘-R ⌘-V   ➡ Use the Recent command to return to the Class Notes stack, and paste the Find button on the background.

➡ Use the button tool to drag the buttons to their final locations, as shown in Figure 12-102 (or wherever you would prefer them).

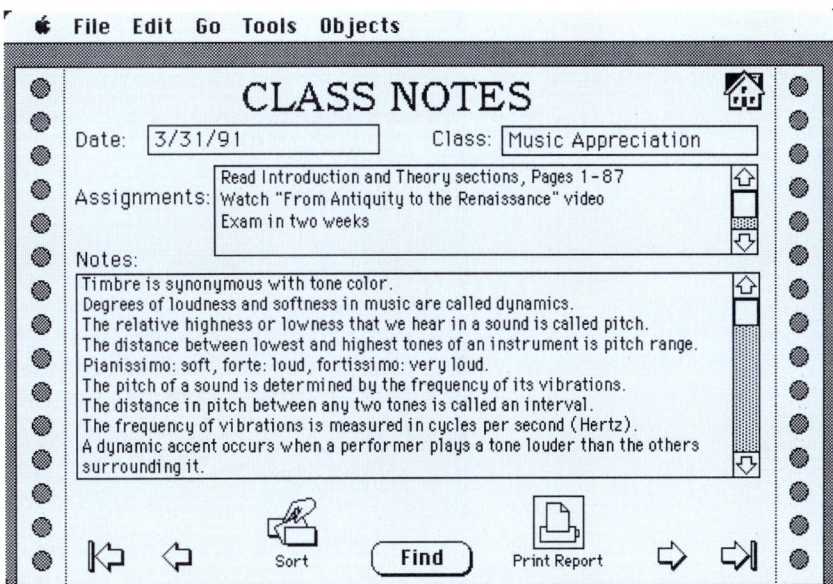

Figure 12-102   Final appearance of the Class Notes stack

If you go to any cards and any of the buttons or fields disappear, go back and use the appropriate tool to cut the object from the card layer and paste it onto the background layer.

ENTERING DATA

A list of 11 notes for 4 classes follows. You will enter all this information into the stack. The dates are chosen at random within a narrow range. It doesn't matter in which order you enter these notes; the Sort command will put them in this order if you sort using the Both option.

You can enter the notes for card one on the card that is already showing in the stack. To enter any other notes, first choose **New Card** from the Edit menu, and then enter the information into the appropriate fields. Be careful typing the information in the Date and Class fields. The information in the other fields is to show how the stack works, and the content is representational only.

To begin entering the information, click in the Date field to put the text insertion point there (or press the Tab key to select the first field). Then, after typing the information for this field, you can select the next field by typing the Tab key or clicking in the next field.

➡ Enter the information for the first card (as shown in Figure 12-103). Refer to the information below the figure for the actual contents.

Card One:

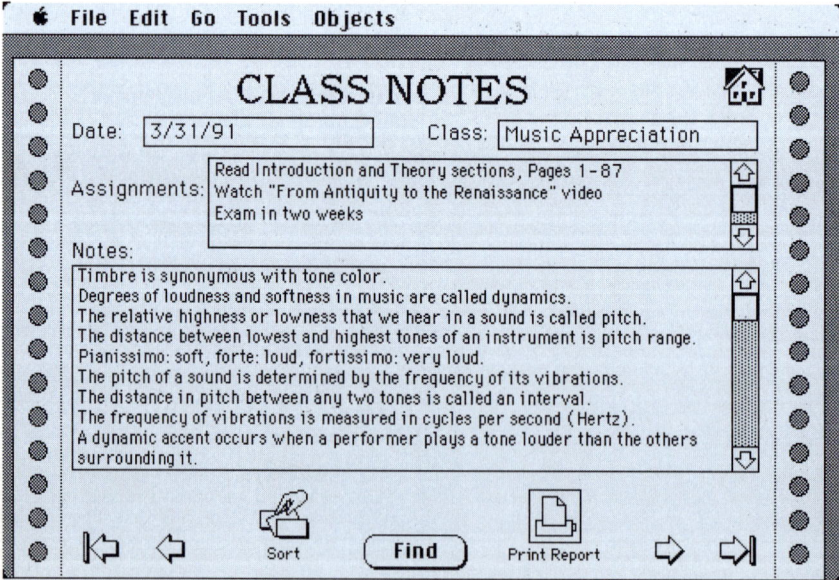

Figure 12-103   First card with data entered

Date:	3/31/91
Class:	**Music Appreciation**
Assignments:	**Read Introduction and Theory sections, Pages 1-87 Watch "From Antiquity to the Renaissance" video Exam in two weeks**
Notes:	**Timbre is synonymous with tone color.**
	Degrees of loudness and softness in music are called dynamics.
	The relative highness or lowness of a sound is called pitch.
	The distance between lowest and highest tones of an instrument is pitch range.
	Pianissimo: soft, forte: loud, fortissimo: very loud.
	The pitch of a sound is determined by the frequency of its vibrations.
	The distance in pitch between any two tones is called an interval.
	The frequency of vibrations is measured in cycles per second (Hertz).
	A dynamic accent occurs when a performer plays a tone louder than the others surrounding it.

⌘-N ➠ Choose **New Card** from the Edit menu. Enter the information for card two. Continue this process until you have entered the information for all 11 cards.

Card Two:	
Date:	4/3/91
Class:	**Music Appreciation**
Notes:	**The lowest instrument in an orchestra is the contrabassoon.**
	A part of an instrument's total range is called a register.
	The highest instrument in the orchestra is the piccolo.
	Vibrato (rocking the left hand to produce small fluctuations) is used by string players to make the tone warmer and more expressive.
	Plucking a string with a finger instead of using a bow is called pizzicato.
	Symphonic bands differ from symphonic orchestras by not having a string section.
	Woodwind instruments are so named because they were originally made of wood.
	The range of a singer's voice depends on both physical makeup and training.

⌘-N   Card Three:

Date: 4/5/91

Class: Music Appreciation

Notes: accent - stress or emphasis on a note.

                   beat - regular, recurrent pulsations that divide music into equal periods of time.

                   downbeat - first, or stressed, beat of a measure.

                   measure - unit or group containing a fixed number of beats.

                   meter - organization of beats into regular groupings

                   metronome - apparatus that produces sounds or light flashes at a desired speed.

                   rhythm - particular arrangement of note lengths in a piece of music.

                   syncopation - putting an accent in music where it is not normally expected.

                   tempo - rate of speed of the beat of music.

                   upbeat - unaccented pulse preceding the downbeat.

⌘-N   Card Four:

Date: 3/31/91

Class: Oral Communications

Assignments: Read chap. 25 - Informative Speaking
                   Informative speech next week - 5 to 7 minutes

Notes: Informative speech - Select subject: What are you interested in? Choose something you already know.

                   Inform: Create understanding; support materials and info should only clarify.

                   Audience: What do they need to know? Select a narrow purpose (more manageable).

                   Formulate bare bones first:

                   • Main idea: points you want to cover

                   • Supporting points

                   • Fill out body of speech with variety of support (summaries, statistics, quotations)

                   • Determine overall pattern (precise order) of speech

                   • Intro (usually best to create this after you have decided what you will say)

                   • Conclusion: tell them what you told them

⌘-N   Card Five:

Date: 4/3/91

Class: **Oral Communications**

Assignments: **Persuasive speech next week**
               5 minutes or less!!!!!

Notes: **Persuasive speech**

               Intro: needs an attention getter, should state main idea, what you want them to do

               Points: should answer question, "Why should I do this?"

               Conclusion: reiterate, sum up, last chance to influence, close neatly

⌘-N   Card Six:

Date: 4/5/91

Class: **Oral Communications**

Assignments: **Prepare that persuasive speech!!**

Notes: **3 types of persuasive speeches:**

               1) logos - reason - logical argument

               2) pathos - appeal to emotion

               3) ethos - how audience sees the speaker; deals with character, how you present yourself, credibility

⌘-N   Card Seven:

Date: 3/29/91

Class: **Sociology II**

Assignments: **Read chapter 10 - Mass Communications**
               First test will cover chapters 10-14

Notes: **Break into groups for discussions. Discuss the following issues:**

               Life before people had TV

               1) How are family holidays different with TV?

               2) How was radio different before TV?

               3) Has TV taken something away from family life?

               4) Give examples of 3 ads on TV that present instant solutions to problems.

               5) Saturday morning TV - what products are pitched to children? How do children respond to those ads?

⌘-N   Card Eight:

     Date: 4/6/91

     Class: Sociology II

     Notes: TV is an addiction for many people - average is 4.5 hours per day per person.

                      Parents spend average of 5 minutes per day really talking to children.

                      "Television violence does have an adverse effect on those children predisposed to violence, and no one knows how many children are predisposed to violence." - U.S. Surgeon General

                      300-500 violent acts per week on network TV. Most people witness over 11,000 "deaths" (on TV) by the time they are 15 years old.

⌘-N   Card Nine:

     Date: 4/8/91

     Class: Sociology II

     Notes: Political leaders have been elected by TV since 1960 (since debates between Kennedy and Nixon). Hundreds of millions of dollars spent on this.

                      News is a network person's VIEW of the news. Even if there is no intent to slant the news, the fact that some events are reported and some aren't has a biasing effect. Bad news and disasters generally make the news. Good news is aired mostly on "slow news days."

                      Newspapers can also slant news - yellow journalism, banner headlines.

⌘-N   Card Ten:

     Date: 3/30/91

     Class: Technical Writing

     Assignments: Read chapters 1-4 by next week

                      Page 39 - do "audience analysis" exercise

                      Page 48 - do "What's wrong with technical writing?" exercise

                      Write paragraph to explain the part writing plays in your job

Notes: **Technical writing - practical writing people do as part of their jobs**

                  What sets technical writing apart? - It's about technical stuff! Usually uses different (technical) vocabulary. Uses sequential thought process. Uses facts, more to the point, meaning must be clear and concise (only one meaning). Uses clear, concise writing to convey one meaning (no ambiguity - only one interpretation possible).

⌘-N   Card Eleven:

Date: **4/2/91**

Class: **Technical Writing**

Assignments: **Write a paragraph about what type of job I want and the type of writing I will have to do in that job.**

Notes: **communication - exchange, dialog**

                  medium - means by which message is conveyed

                  document - (text) - generic term for written object

                  generate - to produce (broader process than writing)

                  Characteristics of technical communication:

                  1) specific audience - only those interested in your subject

                  2) objective language - inform with facts

                  3) clear organization - 3 part form (intro, body, conclusion)

                  4) visual aids - must be integral part of text

You can now check to see if you have a total of 11 cards in this stack.

➡   Choose **Stack Info** from the Objects menu. It should say there are 11 cards in the stack.

If you decide to use this stack for keeping track of notes, you can create a new stack and copy the background so all the buttons and fields are in place. Then all you have to do is enter specific information.

SORTING

HyperCard has the ability to change the order of cards in a stack. This is most easily accomplished by creating a Sort command so HyperCard will rearrange cards automatically in the order you want.

In this stack there are three ways to sort the cards (if you copied the Sort command from the Class Notes Buttons stack).

When you click on the Sort button you see a dialog box that lets you choose to sort the stack by **Date**, **Class**, or **Both**.

Date sorts chronologically by the contents of the Date field. Be sure to enter information consistently in the Date field in the form "mm/dd/yy", without entering leading zeros. For example, the entry for July 1, 1995, would be 7/1/95. It is important that you are consistent and accurate in entering the information in this field if you want the sort to work properly.

Class sorts alphabetically by the contents of the Class field. Again, you need to be consistent when entering the contents of this field. If you were taking Music Appreciation and it had a class number of MUS 101, you would need to use one or the other identifier, but not switch between them for different entries. If you use both names, the Sort script will sort the entries into different classes.

Both sorts first by date and then again by class. This leaves all of the entries for a class sorted in chronological order, and the classes are sorted alphabetically. All your Music Appreciation class notes will appear before the Oral Communications class notes, and inside each class the notes will be sorted by date.

PRINTING REPORTS

HyperCard has some nice reporting capabilities, as you saw in the previous project, but it does not allow you to print a portion of a stack. You can print a single card, the entire stack, or all of the cards on a background.

The Print Report button includes a script that allows you to print a report based on a range of dates or a particular topic. When you enter the starting and ending date, or the topic, the script searches for all cards that match the conditions you specified and prints the entire contents of each card to a text file.

It then asks if you want to open the file with a word processor. If you want to do this, it gives you a choice of MacWrite, Other, or Microsoft Word. They are listed in this order so Microsoft Word will be the default. If you choose Other, you are given the opportunity to type in the name of your word processing application. (If you make use of this stack, you can edit the script so it defaults to the word processor of your choice.)

If the chosen word processing application is not already open, the script opens the application and loads the report file. You can then use the word processor to format and print the report. When you quit the word processor, you are returned to the Class Notes stack.

A useful way to list all your class notes is to sort them using the Both option and then use the Print Report command from the File menu. Make the report a row report and select all four fields. This prints a readable copy of all your class notes sorted chronologically within each class.

SUMMARY

- There must be a Home stack for HyperCard to function correctly. The Home stack is used to open other stacks and applications from HyperCard. There are several buttons on the Home card that represent other stacks. Opening another stack simply requires clicking on its button; you do not double-click as you would from the desktop. The user level may be set from the Home stack.

- There are five user levels: Browsing, Typing, Painting, Authoring, and Scripting. Of these levels, Scripting gives the most access to HyperCard's features and Browsing restricts you to looking at a stack.

- HyperCard automatically saves all changes you make to a stack.

- HyperCard's Go menu allows you to navigate through one or more stacks. The Recent command shows the last 42 cards that were visited and allows you to return to one by clicking on its reduced-size picture.

- Three general tools are available for your use: browse, button, and field. The browse tool is used to activate buttons and select fields for entering or editing data. The button tool is used to create, position, resize, and edit buttons. The field tool is used to create, position, resize, edit, and choose the text attributes for a field.

- Buttons can contain scripts that act like small computer programs. Buttons can also be linked to specific cards or stacks.

- HyperCard has a full set of Painting tools for producing bitmapped pictures. These pictures may be copied and pasted into almost every other Macintosh application.

- There are two layers in every stack: background and card. Background objects are available on every card that shares a background. Card objects are available only on the specific card that contains them.

- HyperCard comes with a Help stack that provides extensive online help.

- Several idea stacks that are included with HyperCard contain resources for creating stacks, cards, buttons, fields, and pictures.

- HyperCard's Find command locates any text in a stack within a few seconds at most. You can decide to search all text or just the text in a specific field. You can choose to find any group of characters that match what you type, or you can restrict HyperCard to finding only words that match the words you entered.

- HyperCard can print reports that are formatted for labels, rows, or columns.

KEY TERMS

Address stack

Authoring level

background button

background layer

browse tool

Browsing level

brush tool

bucket tool

button

button tool

Calendar stack   paint text tool
card   Painting level
card button   Painting tools
card layer   palette
curve tool   pencil tool
                                        Phone stack
dynamic link   polygon tool

eraser tool   rectangle tool
                                        regular polygon tool
Fat Bits   rounded rectangle tool
field
field tool   scripting
                                        Scripting level
General tools   selection tool
                                        spray tool
Home button   stack
Home card
Home stack   tear-off menu
HyperTalk   Tell Me... button
                                        text field
lasso   Typing level
line tool
link   user level

Message box   visual effect

oval tool

HYPERCARD COMMAND KEYS AND SHORTCUTS

File Menu   **Go Menu**
Open   ⌘ -O   Back   ⌘ -~
Print Card   ⌘ -P   Home   ⌘ -H
Quit HyperCard   ⌘ -Q   Help   ⌘ -?
                                            Recent   ⌘ -R
Edit Menu   First   ⌘ -1
Undo   ⌘ -Z   Prev(ious)   ⌘ -2
Cut   ⌘ -X   Next   ⌘ -3
Copy   ⌘ -C   Last   ⌘ -4
Paste   ⌘ -V   Find   ⌘ -F
New Card   ⌘ -N   Message   ⌘ -M
Text Style   ⌘ -T
Background   ⌘ -B   **Objects Menu**
                                            Bring Closer   ⌘ -+
Paint Menu   Send Farther   ⌘ --
Select   ⌘ -S
Select All   ⌘ -A
Keep   ⌘ -K

ADDITIONAL PROJECTS

The following project is accompanied by briefer instructions than those you have previously completed in this chapter. If necessary, refer to the previous projects in this chapter for information and step-by-step instructions for any command that you don't remember how to use. Also, HyperCard's Help file contains valuable and easily accessed information.

Project 4: Creating a Dynamic Company Organization Chart

In this project, you will create an organization chart similar to the second project in the MacDraw chapter. Although the charts look almost alike, there is a big difference in what they do. The chart in MacDraw is static. You create it, print it, and there it sits.

The chart you will create in this project is a dynamic chart. When you click on one of the people represented on the chart, HyperCard takes you to another card that shows more information on that person. You then can return to the chart to obtain information on someone else.

Let's get started.

⟱ Change the user level to Scripting.

⟱ Choose **New Stack**. Name the stack Company Organization and store it on your data disk (see Figure 12-104).

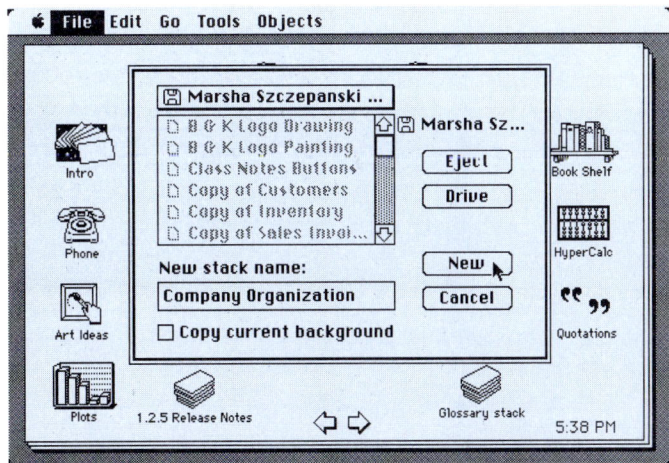

Figure 12-104   Creating the new Company Organization stack

➡ Using the Painting tools, create the organization chart as shown in Figure 12-105. The fonts are Geneva 9-point and 12-point, plain text and bold.

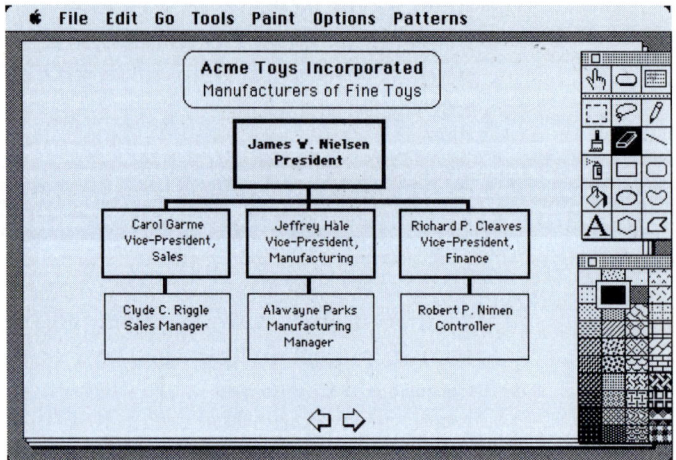

Figure 12-105   Painting the organization chart

➡ Center the chart on the screen using the selection tool (see Figure 12-106).

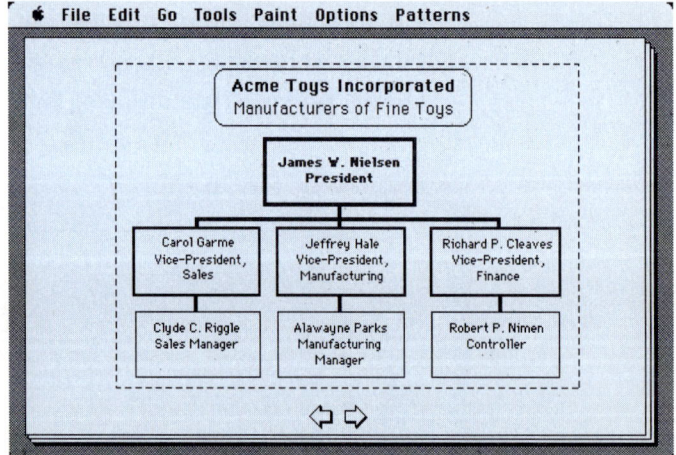

Figure 12-106   Center the chart on the screen

➡ Choose **Bkgnd Info** from the Objects menu.

➡ Name this background Chart, and set it so it can't be deleted (see Figure 12-107).

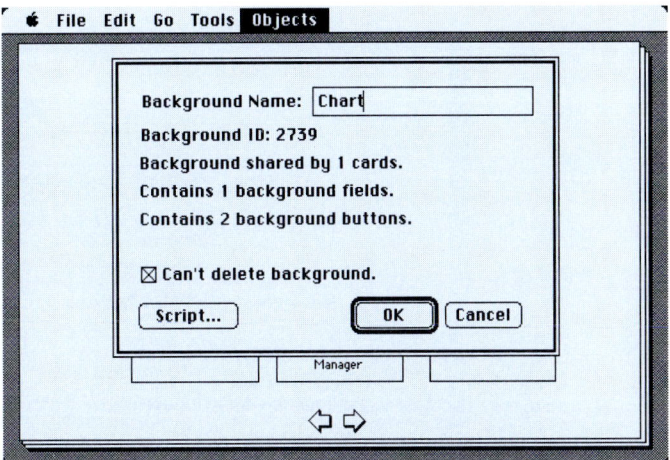

Figure 12-107   Naming and protecting the background

Creating Directory Background

Now that you have completed the organization chart, it is time to create a directory listing for each of the people on the chart.

Let's use the same background painting for the chart and the directory.

⌘-B ⇒ Change to the background layer.

The chart disappears when you change to the background layer, but the picture of a stack of paper is still there.

⇒ Double-click on the selection tool to select the entire background.

⌘-C ⇒ Copy the background.

⇒ Choose **New Background** from the Objects menu.

⌘-V ⇒ Make sure you are in the background layer, and then paste the background picture.

⇒ Choose the field tool, and add the background fields and text for the directory (see Figure 12-108).

The choices of fonts, sizes, and styles are up to you.

⇒ After you create the fields, double-click on each one (with the field tool) and give it a name, such as Title, Name, Address, and so on.

⇒ Name this background Directory.

⇒ Select the browse tool.

⇒ Enter the information for the president (see Figure 12-108).

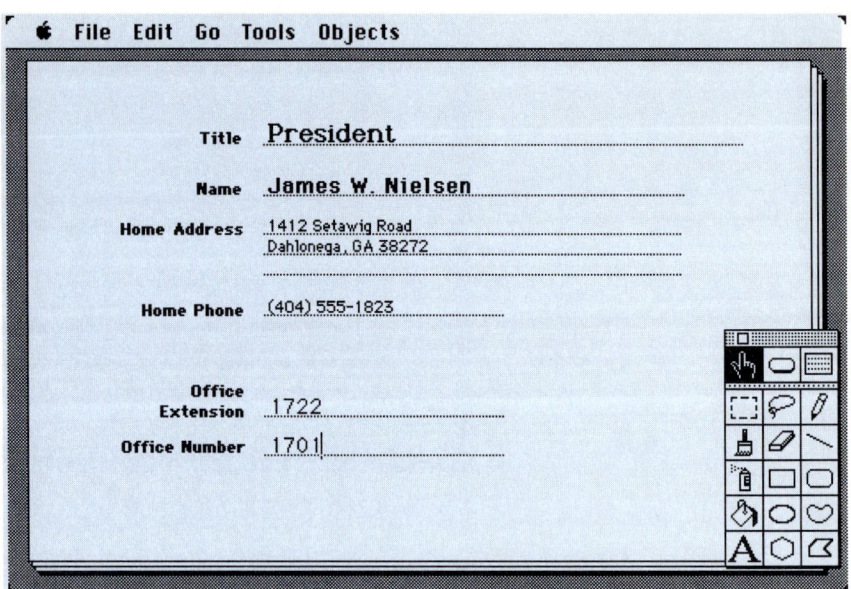

Figure 12-108   The Directory background and president's info

⌘-N   ➡   Create a new card, and enter the information for the vice-president of sales (see Figure 12-109).

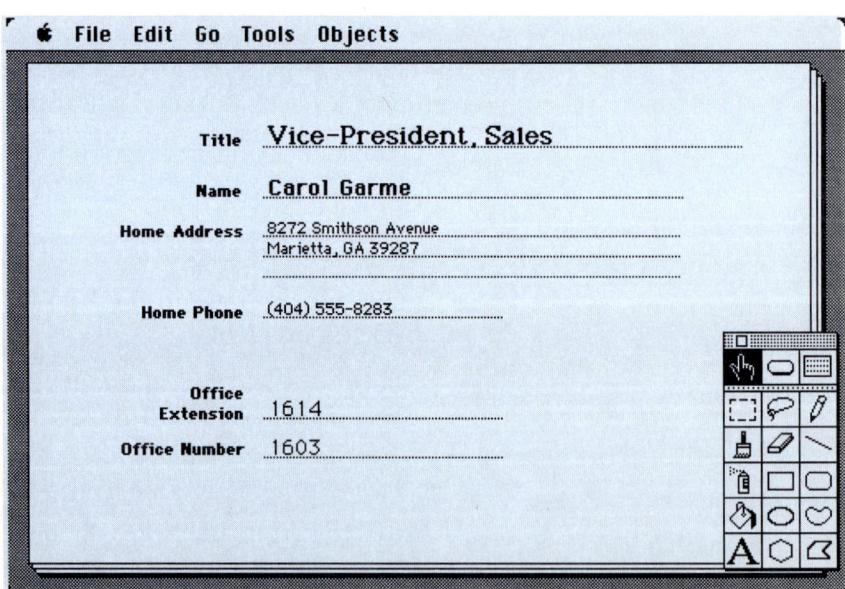

Figure 12-109   Entering information for the V.P. of sales

⌘-N   ➡   Create a new card for each of the other five people on the chart, and make up the information you enter for each of them.

You should now have a background named Chart with one card and a background named Directory with seven cards.

Linking Cards

You created the card with the chart and each person's name. Then you created a separate card in the Directory background for each person on the chart. Now you need to add some buttons to allow navigation around the stack.

➠ Copy a Home button from another stack and paste it onto the bottom right corner of the card containing the organization chart (see Figure 12-110).

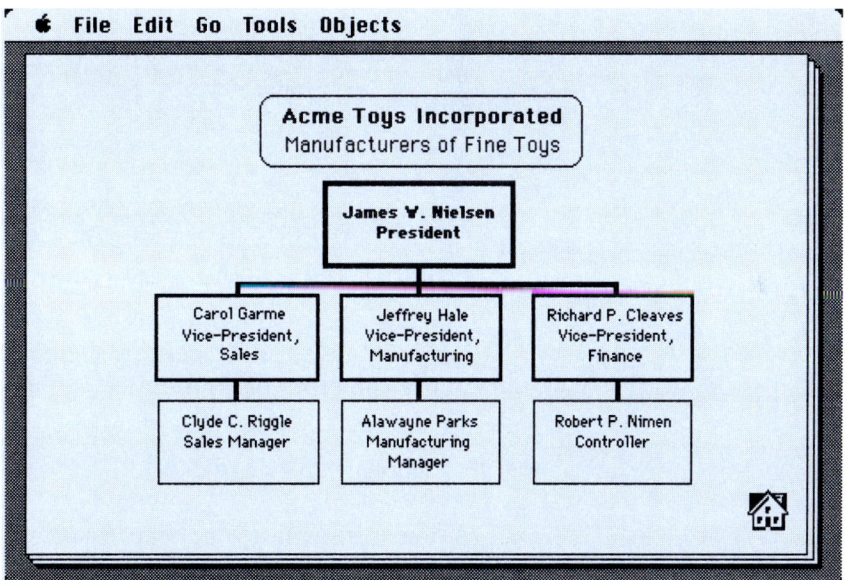

Figure 12-110   Adding a Home button to quit the stack

This button is for going back to the Home stack when you are ready to leave this stack.

Now you will add a transparent button on top of each name in the organization chart. Each of these buttons will be linked to the appropriate card in the Directory background.

➠ Select the button tool. Position the pointer just outside the top-left corner of the president's box.

➠ Press the Command key, and drag a rectangle for a new button that surrounds the president's box.

This is a shortcut method for creating a new button.

➠ Double-click this new button, make it transparent, and deselect the option for showing its name.

Your screen should look like the one in Figure 12-111.

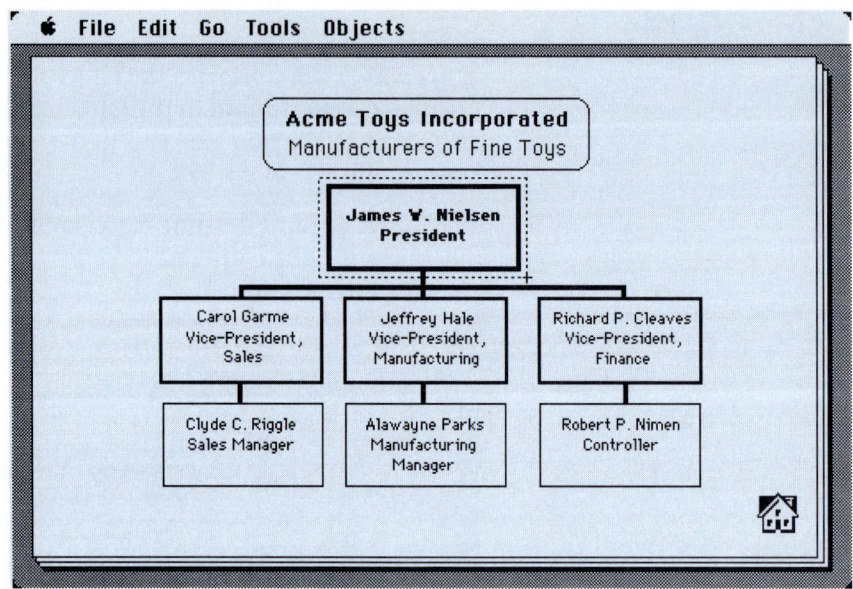

Figure 12-111   Adding a new button on top of the president's box

You are ready to tell HyperCard to link this button to the president's card in the Directory background.

⇒   Double-click the new button and, when its information dialog box appears, click **LinkTo**.

A new mini window appears floating above the card. Most of you are probably unfamiliar with the term mini window. HyperCard introduced a new type of floating window that could be moved and closed, but not resized. Its main characteristic that distinguishes it from a window is that it floats in front of all other windows and has a gray pattern in the title bar rather than horizontal lines. The Message box, LinkTo box, and Tools and Patterns palettes are all mini windows. They are the exception to the rule that all action takes place in the front window. When one or more mini windows are present, all actions will still take place in the active window with the exception of activity directly in the mini window. This way you can use the palette to choose a different tool or pattern, and draw in the active window without forcing any mini windows to go behind the active window. Mini windows are also known as floating windows.

This mini window allows you to link the button you just double-clicked with a specific card in a stack or with the first card of a stack. The stack can be the current one or any other stack.

You want to link to the president's information card.

⇒   Use the arrow keys on the keyboard, the Go menu, or the Command-key equivalents to go to the next card. When the president's card is showing under the linking mini window (see Figure 12-112), click **This Card**.

The link is now completed.

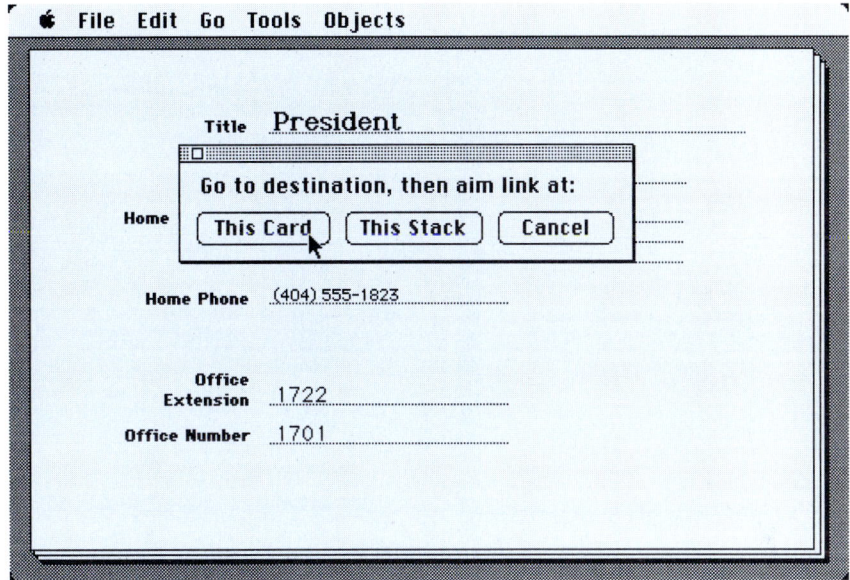

Figure 12-112   Linking a button to this card

Unfortunately, you have not provided a way to get back to the chart card without using the keyboard, the Go menu, or Command-key equivalents. Let's add a button to the Directory background that links to the chart card.

➠   In the lower left corner of the Directory background picture, draw a small picture of the chart. Use Fat Bits to make this easier if you like (see Figure 12-113).

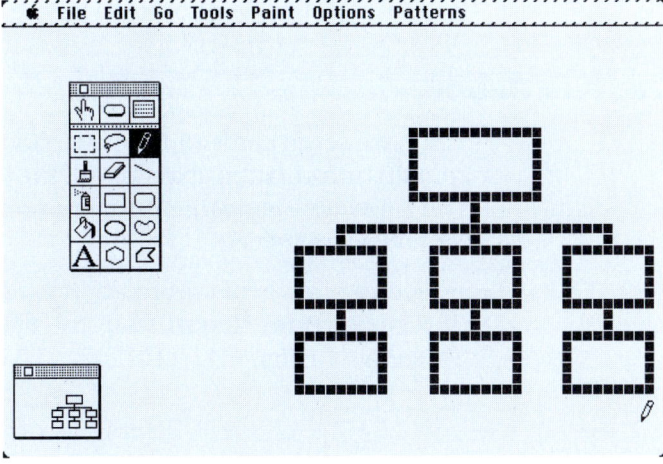

Figure 12-113   Drawing a small picture of the organization chart

➡ When the picture is as you want it, create a transparent button over it, and then link the button to the card containing the organization chart (see Figure 12-114).

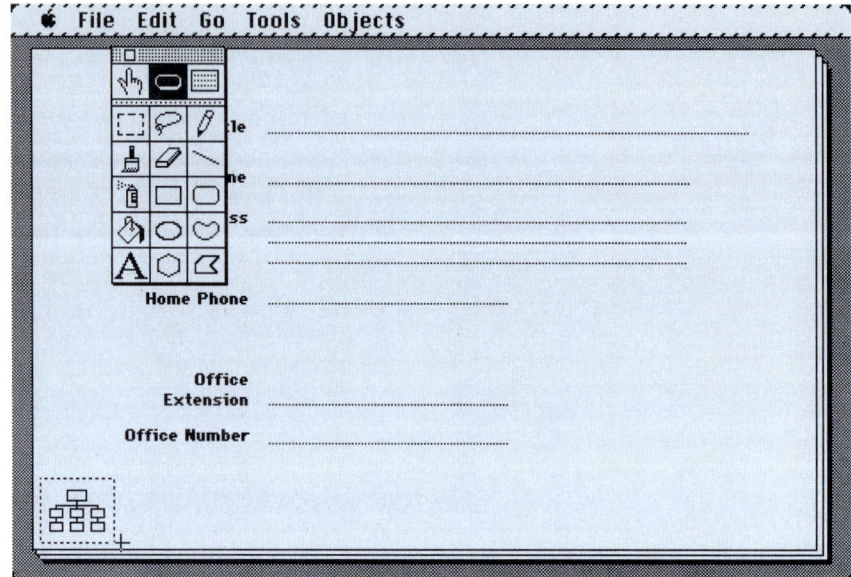

Figure 12-114   Creating a button to link to the chart card

➡ Return to the chart card, and create a button on top of each box in the chart. Link each button to the appropriate card.

When you have completed this, you will be able to click on any name in the chart, and HyperCard will show you information about that person. Then, by clicking on the button at the bottom left corner of the information card, you can return to the chart. When you are finished, you can click the Home button to close the stack (but don't do that yet).

Printing Directory Report

You have seven cards in the Directory background, and each of them contains information about one of the people in the organization chart. This provides a convenient way to print a corporate directory (at least for seven employees).

➡ Go to one of the information cards in the Directory background. Choose **Print Report** from the File menu, and select the options shown in Figure 12-115.

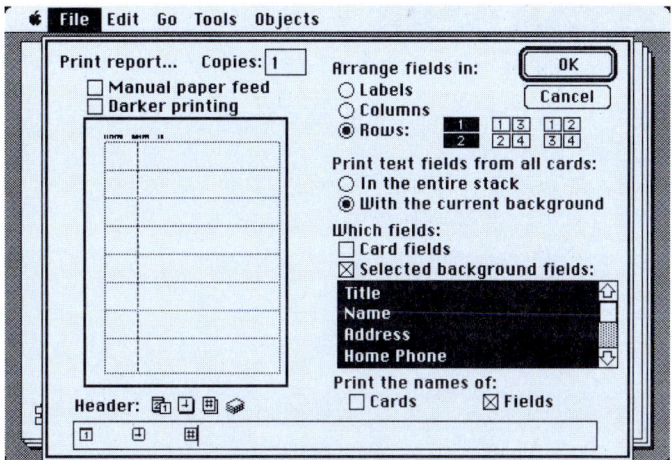

Figure 12-115   Selecting options for printing the directory

By telling HyperCard to print text fields from all cards with the current background, you restrict the printing to the background you were in when you chose the command. This is handy for printing information in a stack with multiple backgrounds when you want only the information in a particular background.

➡ When you have made all the selections, click **OK.**

This creates a two-column report with information about the seven people on the chart.

If you like, you can also tell HyperCard to print all of the cards.

There are a number of ways this stack can be enhanced without too much additional work. It would be easy to copy the Phone button from another stack and paste into this one to automatically dial a person's number. With a little more effort, you could add a map of the company's headquarters and show where the person's office is. A photograph of the person could be scanned into the system and stored with his or her directory card.

If you want to try any of these enhancements, go right ahead. You will find that HyperCard's abilities expand more and more as you learn to make use of them.

Congratulations! You have now completed the last HyperCard project.

SCRIPTS FOR CLASS NOTES BUTTONS STACK

The following scripts may be entered if you do not have the *Macintosh Journey Projects* disk. Be careful typing in the scripts. The character "¬" represents a continued line of HyperTalk code and is entered by holding the Option key down while you press the Return key.

SORT BUTTON SCRIPT

```
on mouseUp
  answer "Sort by what?" with "Date" or "Class" or "Both"
  if it is "Date" then
    Sort datetime by bg field "Date"
  else if it is "Class" then
    Sort by bg field "Class"
  else
    Sort datetime by bg field "Date"
    Sort by bg field "Class"
  end if
end mouseUp
```

PRINT REPORT BUTTON SCRIPT

```
--  © 1990 by John L. Dilbeck, CDP
--  All rights reserved worldwide
on mouseUp
  set cursor to 4
  put the number of cards into cardcount

  put space & return into ret

  get the long name of stack
  delete first word of it
  delete first char of it
  delete last char of it

  repeat while (last char of it <> ":") and (length(it) > 0)
    delete last char of it
  end repeat

  put it into reportfilename

  ask "What do you wish to name the report?" with "Enter Name Here"
  repeat while it is "Enter Name Here"
    beep(1)
    put "You must enter a file name"
    ask "What do you wish to name the report?" with "Enter Name Here"
  end repeat

  put it after reportfilename

  answer "Do you want to produce a report based on" with ¬
  "Cancel" or "Dates" or "Topics"

  if it is "Cancel" then
    exit mouseUp
  end if

  Open file reportfilename
```

```
if it is "Dates" then
  -- produce a report based between two dates
  ask "What is the beginning date" with "mm/dd/yy"
  repeat while it is "mm/dd/yy"
    beep(1)
    put "You must enter a beginning date"
    ask "What is the beginning date" with "mm/dd/yy"
    hide message
  end repeat
  put it into StartDate
  convert StartDate to short date
  put it into startfinddate
  convert startfinddate to short date

  ask "What is the ending date" with "mm/dd/yy"
  repeat while it is "mm/dd/yy"
    beep(1)
    put "You must enter an ending date"
    ask "What is the ending date" with "mm/dd/yy"
    hide message
  end repeat
  put it into EndDate
  convert EndDate to Short date

  write "Class Notes Report between " & quote & ¬
  StartDate & quote & " and " & quote & EndDate & quote ¬
  & return & the long date & tab & the time & ¬
  return & return to file reportfilename

  Sort by bg field "Class"
  Sort datetime by bg field "Date"

  go to card 1 of this background
  put fld "Date" into testdate

  repeat until testdate >= StartDate
    put "Searching..."
    go to next card
    put field "Date" into testdate
  end repeat

  hide msg

  repeat while testdate >= StartDate and testdate <= EndDate
    write "Date:" & tab & field "Date" & return & ¬
    "Class:" & tab & field "Class" & return & return & ¬
    "*** Assignments ***   " & field "Assignments" & ¬
    return & return & ¬
    "*** Notes ****   " & field "Notes" & return & return & ¬
    "-------------------------" & return & return ¬
    to file reportfilename

    if the number of this card = cardcount then
      exit repeat
    end if
```

```
        go to next card
        put field "Date" into testdate
     end repeat

  else
  -- produce a report based on all cards containing a certain topic
  ask "What is the search topic?" with "Enter topic here"
  repeat while it is "Enter topic here"
     beep(1)
     put "You must enter a search topic"
     ask "What is the search topic?" with "Enter topic here"
     hide message
  end repeat
  put it into searchcriteria

  write "Class Notes Report concerning " & quote & ¬
  searchcriteria & quote & return & ¬
  the long date & tab & the time & return & return ¬
  to file reportfilename

  go to card 1 of this background
  find searchcriteria
  if the result is "not found" then
     beep(1)
     put "That topic is not found"
     wait 180
     hide msg
     close file reportfilename
     exit mouseUp
  else
     put the id of this card into startedhere
     put false into foundtwice
  end if

  repeat until (the id of this card = startedhere) and ¬
     foundtwice is true
     put true into foundtwice
     write "Date:" & tab & field "Date" & return & ¬
     "Class:" & tab & field "Class" & return & return & ¬
     "*** Assignments ***   " & field "Assignments" & ¬
     return & return & ¬
     "*** Notes ****   " & field "Notes" & return & return & ¬
     "------------------------" & return & return ¬
     to file reportfilename

     go to next card
     find searchcriteria
  end repeat

  end if
```

```
Close file reportfilename
put "The file has been saved."
wait 60
hide message

answer "Do you want to open the file?" with "No" or "Yes"
if it is "Yes" then
  answer "Which Word Processor?" with "MacWrite" or "Other" ¬
  or "MS Word"

  if it is "MS Word" then
    open reportfilename with "Microsoft Word"
  else
    if it is "MacWrite" then
      open reportfilename with "MacWrite"
    else
      ask "What is the name of your Word Processor" with ¬
      "Enter Name"
      if it is "Enter Name" then
        beep(1)
      else
        open reportfilename with it
      end if
    end if
  end if
end if
end mouseUp
```

Glossary

1-up labels Labels, usually mailing labels, that are one form wide.

3-up labels Labels, usually mailing labels, that have three forms side-by-side on each row.

absolute addressing A method of addressing a cell or a range of cells in a spreadsheet. Absolute addressing does not change if a formula or cell reference is moved, copied or pasted. *(See also relative addressing)*

active cell The cell in a spreadsheet that is marked by a heavy border. Anything typed on the keyboard is entered into the active cell.

active record indicator A small, black vertical line that appears to the left of the current record in FileMaker's Browse mode when records are viewed as a list.

active window The window that is on top of all the other windows; the window in which you may work. The title bar and scroll bars are highlighted. All other windows are inactive and their title bars and scroll bars are white.

actual size A representation that approximates how the output will look when printed. *(See also actual size window)*

actual size window When viewing a MacPaint drawing at 800% size, the actual size window displays the drawing at 100% (actual) size.

Address stack One of the personal utility stacks included with HyperCard. It is useful for storing names, addresses, and phone numbers.

algorithm A step-by-step process used to solve a problem or accomplish a task. A computer program is a group of algorithms coded into a computer language in a form the computer can follow. *(See also program, software)*

alignment How two or more objects line up, whether graphic objects or text. With graphic objects this can include centering one object inside of another or placing objects so that their top edges are at the same horizontal level. Text alignment can include horizontal alignments such as flush left, flush right, justified, and centered, and vertical alignments such as centered between the top and bottom margins.

analytical graphics Charts and graphics useful for analyzing a numeric problem. These graphics are often produced using a spreadsheet program. *(See also presentation graphics)*

Apple menu The menu located on the far left of the menu bar at the top of the screen. Instead of the word "Apple" it has the symbol of an apple. *(See also menu, menu bar)*

application program There are two basic types of programs: application and system programs. An application program is designed and programmed to accomplish a particular task. For instance, Microsoft Word is a word processing application program. Most of the programs advertised for sale are application programs. *(See also software, systems program)*

application software A term that applies to application programs as a group. *(See also application program)*

arc tool A tool in a drawing program used to draw an arc or part of a circle.

area chart A chart, similar to a line chart, that emphasizes the amount of change over a period of time.

arguments Values that are enclosed in parentheses and are used as input to a function in a formula.

arrow pointer The shape the mouse pointer takes when it is possible to use the pointer to select something, such as a command from the menu bar.

arrow tool A tool available in many programs for moving objects.

ascending order An order in which information can be sorted. For text, ascending order is "A" to "Z" and for numbers it is lowest value to highest.

Authoring level One of the five user levels in HyperCard. The authoring level allows you to have full access to all the tools in the program other than scripting in HyperTalk.

Autogrid An option in MacDraw that allows an object to be drawn or moved according to the division increments in a grid.

automatic page break The point where text automatically goes to a new page in Microsoft Word based on the top, bottom, left, and right document margins.

automatic styles   Predefined styles that are built in to Microsoft Word, such as *Normal* and *footer*.

background button   A button, in HyperCard, that is common to all cards sharing the same background.

background layer   A template, in HyperCard, that can be shared by a number of cards. Pictures, fields, buttons, and other objects can be placed in the background layer and accessed from each of the cards that share that background.

backup   Making a copy of your data on more than one disk. The idea is to copy all data on a disk onto another disk at periodic intervals depending on how valuable the information is, and how difficult it would be to recreate it if it were lost.

bar chart A chart that compares items by showing values at a specific time. It is composed of a number of horizontal bars.

baud   The rate at which data is transmitted in serial communications. Common baud rates are 300, 1200, 2400, 9600, and 19200 baud.

bit   An abbreviation of BInary digiT. A bit is a unit of information that can represent one of two states—on or off. Eight bits are defined as a byte.

bitmapped   A method of storing a graphics object or a font by representing each dot as on or off. Since a bit can easily do this, this type of graphic or font is mapped onto a grid of bits, resulting in an area that is bitmapped and easy to reproduce on the screen or printer. *(See also bit, object-oriented)*

blank report   A report in FileMaker in which the user specifies the placement of all fields, text, graphics, and other objects. It is the most flexible report format, but FileMaker helps the least in this report format.

block quote   A quote that is indented on the left and right so as to differentiate it from the rest of the document. It does not require quotation marks.

Body part The main part of a FileMaker report. FileMaker prints one body part for each record, and prints as many as will fit on a page.

book A tool in FileMaker that is used to access other records and layouts.

border palette   The portion of the MacPaint toolbox that is used to change the weight of the outline of an object as it is drawn.

borders   Lines or boxes placed around objects or text.

Browse mode A mode in FileMaker that lets you view, edit, add and delete records.

browse tool The tool used in HyperCard that is shaped like a pointing hand, and is used to click buttons and place the insertion point in fields.

Browsing level The user level in HyperCard that allows you to view a stack but not make any changes to it.

brush shapes   The various sizes and shapes of paint brush available with the paint brush tool in MacPaint and HyperCard.

brush tool   The brush tool is used to paint with a specific shape using the current pattern in MacPaint and HyperCard.

bucket tool   The bucket tool is used to pour the current pattern into an enclosed white area or a continuous black area in MacPaint and HyperCard.

business graphics Business graphics are normally used in business management and presentations to management and they include pie charts, line graphs, bar charts, and others. Many of these graphics are produced by spreadsheet, data base, and presentation programs. Business graphics may also mean pictorial representations and informational screens which can be produced by a wide variety of programs on the Macintosh. *(See also analytical graphics and presentation graphics)*

button   An area on the screen that is a basic component of the Macintosh user interface. A button allows you to start an action by moving the pointer into the area defined by the button and then clicking the mouse.

button tool The tool used in HyperCard to create, select, modify, and delete buttons.

byte A byte is a unit of measurement that is defined to be 8 bits. On the Macintosh we can think of it as being the amount of storage used to store one character, such as an "A" or a "1". *(See also bit, kilobyte, megabyte)*

cable A set of one or more wires used to send information between peripheral devices.

calculation field A type of field in FileMaker that contains a value calculated from other fields in the same record.

Calendar stack One of the personal utility stacks included with HyperCard.

cancel box The small box in the formula bar in Excel. Clicking in this box discards any changes made to the active cell and leaves it as it was.

card A type of HyperCard object that is the basic storage component of a stack. and can hold graphics, buttons, and fields. A card has a background layer and a card (or foreground) layer.

card button A button that appears on a single card in HyperCard.

card layer The storage area of a card where objects such as graphics, fields, and buttons may be placed. These objects are only accessible from the card that contains them.

cell address The combination of column letter and row number that identifies the location of a cell in a spreadsheet program such as Excel.

cell The intersection of a row and a column in an electronic spreadsheet, such as Excel, and in a table, such as created using the Tables feature in Microsoft Word. *(See also column, formula, row, spreadsheet)*

center tab Text is centered around the point at which the center tab stop is placed on the ruler in Microsoft Word.

Central Processing Unit (CPU) The actual computer in a computing system. In microcomputers, the CPU is a single integrated circuit (chip). Larger computers have CPUs that take multiple boards, each of which contains multiple integrated circuits.

character A symbol having a meaning that is standardized and widely recognized. Common characters are the letters you are reading, numbers, punctuation, and other specialized symbols like dollar signs.

chevrons Special pairs of characters («, ») that precede and follow a merge field in a Microsoft Word print merge document. *(See also merge fields)*

click Quickly pressing and releasing the mouse button without moving the mouse. *(See also mouse, mouse button)*

clip art Clip art includes electronic art, saved in a number of formats, that can be pasted into applications. The term derives from books of art which were distributed. You would cut (or clip) the art from the page with scissors or a knife, and paste it onto the pasteup of the document you were creating. Clip art is distributed commercially by a number of vendors.

Clipboard A special file, located in the system folder on the current startup disk, that holds one item. This item may be text, a picture, or any other copyable item on a Macintosh. The Clipboard contains the last item cut or copied in any application or desk accessory. Any time you make a new copy, the old copy on the clipboard is replaced.

close box The small, white square box on the left side of the title bar of the active window. Clicking in this close box closes and deactivates that document, or closes a folder and moves up one level in the file system. Clicking in the close box is the same as choosing Close under the File menu.

column A vertical grouping of cells in an electronic spreadsheet, such as Excel, and in a table, such as is created using the Tables feature in Microsoft Word. *(See also spreadsheet, table)*

column chart A chart used to draw comparisons among several items over a period of time.

columnar report A type of report, available in information management programs, where the fields are listed across the top row of the report, and the data in those fields is listed in columns below the field headings.

combination chart A chart where related information is shown using more than one chart type.

Command key A modifier key on your keyboard that causes a command to be performed when it is depressed along with one or more other keys, or when depressed along with a mouse click. The original name for the key that is also called the Apple key. New keyboards have both the apple symbol and the clover leaf symbol (also referred to as the propeller symbol). Older keyboards only have the clover leaf.

Command-key equivalent Instead of choosing a command from a menu using the mouse, most applications give you the option of pressing a key in combination with the Command key to issue the command. For example, Command-S usually means Save, Command-C is Copy, Command-X is Cut, and Command-V is Paste.

common carrier A standard communications network such as the Bell phone systems.

concatenate The process of joining two or more data items into one longer item by joining the beginning of the second item to the end of the first item.

conditional printing The ability to check the contents of a field in a data file and insert and print different text based on the value of that field.

constrain Using the Shift key while moving or drawing an object in MacPaint, HyperCard and MacDraw limits, or constrains, the movement of the object either vertically or horizontally.

context sensitive help An application help system that can identify the context in which an action occurred. The help program can determine where the pointer is, or what you are trying to do when you ask for help. The system then tries to give you help for the specific task you are performing, or the specific object you are accessing.

copy (1) To make a duplicate of something by selecting it, and choosing Copy from the Edit menu. What you copied is placed on the Clipboard, and may then be pasted one or more times in other locations. (2) To make a duplicate of a file by selecting a file icon and

then choosing Duplicate under the File menu. (3) To make a duplicate of an entire disk by dragging the icon of one disk onto the icon of a second disk. This will destroy what was on the second disk and duplicate all of the files on the first disk onto the second.

corner/center control The control at the bottom of the tools palette in MacDraw that determines the starting point when drawing an object (either from center to corner or from corner to corner).

cross-beam pointer When drawing objects in MacPaint, HyperCard, and MacDraw, the arrow pointer changes to the cross-beam pointer when it is moved into the drawing window.

CRT (cathode ray tube) A television-like device for displaying computer output.

currently selected pattern The fill or line pattern that is shown in the currently selected pattern portion of the patterns menu in MacPaint and the patterns palette in MacDraw. In MacPaint and HyperCard, the currently selected pattern controls the pattern of the objects drawn with the filled shape tools and the pattern used with the paint bucket, paint brush, and spray can. In MacDraw it refers to the fill and line pattern of any object drawn with the shape tools except for the freehand and polygon tools.

curve tool A tool used in HyperCard for drawing free-form shapes.

cut To remove something by selecting it, and choosing Cut from the Edit menu. What you cut is placed on the Clipboard, and may then be pasted one or more times in other locations.

data Raw facts.

data document One of the necessary components of a print merge project in Microsoft Word. It contains the data records to be merged with the main merge document.

data point A category with a corresponding numeric value.

data series A collection of related data points.

database An organized collection of data stored in a group of related files.

date field A type of field in FileMaker that holds a date.

decimal-aligned tab When typing numbers in columns, the method of having the computer automatically align the numbers by lining up the decimal points.

default (1) The initial, predetermined setting for an option in a program. The user has the option of changing this setting, or accepting it as is. An example is the default setting for page margins in a word processing program. These margins are normally set to give standard margins all around the page, but the user may override these defaults and increase or decrease the margin settings. (2) When using buttons in a dialog box, the default button is the one that is highlighted with the larger, darker oval. Default buttons may be chosen by clicking on the button, or by pressing the Return or Enter key.

Define The process of naming a field in FileMaker and specifying its type of contents and entry options.

defined term A term listed in Excel's help file.

delimiter A character that is used to indicate the end of one item and the beginning of another. When used in producing a print merge document in Microsoft Word, all data fields are delimited, or separated, with commas or tabs.

descending order An order in which information can be sorted. For text, descending order is "Z" to "A" and for numbers it is highest value to lowest.

deselect Clicking somewhere on the screen so that a selected object is no longer selected.

desktop publishing The use of microcomputers and page layout programs, or full-featured word processors, to completely design, edit and layout the contents of a document. These programs then allow the user to produce camera ready output when the document is printed on a laser printer or a phototypesetter that is capable of interpreting PostScript output.

desktop The Macintosh interface revolves around the metaphor of items on a desktop. Files, folders, calculators, clocks, notepads, and other items are normally found on desktops. The desktop is the screen you see when you first start the Macintosh. It is normally a gray

area with a menu bar over it, disk drives on the right side and a trash can in the lower right corner. The actual pattern can be changed with the Control Panel desk accessory.

destination disk A disk that receives a file that is being duplicated, copied, or moved.

detail report A report that lists one or more lines of output for each record.

dialog box A box that pops onto the screen and allows the user to interact with the computer. Almost all dialog boxes contain messages to the user, and allow the user to respond. Many dialog boxes also allow the user to select options and perform other commands. All menu choices that end in an ellipsis (...) are followed by a dialog box requesting more input from the user.

dimmed Most commands in a menu appear in black text, but dimmed commands appear in gray text. When the command is dimmed, it means that it may not be chosen at that point. Dimmed icons represent disks, documents, applications or folders that are located on a disk that has been inserted into the system, and then subsequently ejected. The documents may not be opened while the disk is ejected.

direct access A method of accessing data without having to read the preceding data. Usually applies to RAM memory and disk drives.

directory window The window that contains the listing of the contents of a folder or disk.

disk drive The device that contains the disk or diskette. A disk drive is able to read information from a disk, and write information onto a disk.

document Information created and stored on disk by application or system programs. On most computers these are called data files. The Macintosh term "document" may be more descriptive, because each of these files is associated with a document icon in the Finder.

dot leaders A series of dots that lead up to a tab position. Tab leaders make it easier for the eye to follow the area between the tab positions.

dot-matrix printer A type of impact printer that prints by causing small pins to strike the ribbon against the paper. The name is derived from the fact that all characters are made up of a matrix of dots (dots aligned in rows and columns). The printer prints by moving a printhead, containing the pins, left and right across the page and causing the pins to strike as needed. The ImageWriter II from Apple is the standard dot matrix printer for the Macintosh.

double-click The process of placing the cursor where you want it and then clicking the mouse button twice in rapid succession without moving the mouse. Normally, you must click twice in about a half-second to be interpreted as a double-click. The time delay allowed for double-clicking may be changed in the Control Panel desk accessory.

dpi (dots per inch) The number of dots displayed or printed in an inch. The standard Macintosh screen displays 72 dots per inch. The LaserWriter prints at 300 dpi. The higher the dpi, the better the print or screen resolution.

dragging The process of positioning the cursor over some object, pressing the mouse button and holding it down, moving the mouse to reposition the cursor to a new location, and then releasing the mouse button. Dragging has three main uses: (1) to make a large selection by surrounding and selecting all objects in the selection area; (2) to move an icon by dragging it to a new location; (3) to choose a command from a menu by clicking on the menu name, dragging down to the item desired, and releasing the mouse button to select that command.

drawing format The default format for saving a drawing created in MacDraw.

drawing tool The small vertical line to the right of the tab icons on the Microsoft Word ruler. It is used to place a vertical line in a document corresponding to the drawing tool's position on the ruler.

drop-down list A list of options that drop down when you click on the arrow to the right of certain option boxes, such as the underline drop-down list available in the Character dialog box in Microsoft Word.

DSDD disk Double-Sided Double-Density disks. Standard 3.5-inch disks capable of holding 800K.

dummy argument A placeholder argument that indicates the type of argument that should be input to a function.

Duplicate command The command used in MacDraw to create a duplicate of an object in a drawing. It works like a combination copy and paste command in one action.

duplicate An exact copy of the original.

dynamic link An object in HyperCard that links to other objects. It can be a button or a text phrase that is used to take the viewer to a different card or other related information.

Edit menu Most Macintosh programs have an Edit menu following the Apple menu and File menu. Usually the Edit menu will contain at least Undo, Cut, Copy and Paste. It frequently contains Clear as well. The Edit menu is one of the most standardized of the menus used on the Macintosh.

editing Changing or modifying the contents of a document. This includes editing on paper while proofreading, and/or changing a document on the computer.

electronic circuit board A board containing electronic circuits and attached integrated circuit chips. This is also called a card or printed circuit board.

electronic data processing (EDP) The processing of data into information using electronic devices such as computers rather than manual or mechanical methods.

electronic spreadsheet *(See spreadsheet)*

ellipse An oval shape, or a circle.

end-of-cell marker A small black circle that represents the end of a cell in a table in Microsoft Word. The end-of-cell marker is visible only when Show ¶ is active.

end-of-row marker A small black circle that represents the end of a row in a table in Microsoft Word. The end-of-row marker is visible only when Show ¶ is active.

Enter key A key, normally found on the bottom right corner of the Macintosh keyboard, that may be used to accept an entry or confirm a command in a dialog box. Pressing the Enter key or the Return key will select the highlighted (default) button in a dialog box. On many computers, the Enter and Return keys are the same. On the Macintosh, they often have different functions depending on the program being used at the time.

enter box A small box containing a checkmark in Excel's formula bar. Clicking in this box is the same as pressing the Enter key and accepts any changes that have been made in the active cell.

eraser tool A tool used to erase all or part of an item in MacPaint or HyperCard.

exception report A report caused by an exception to anticipated results. This might be a report of sales personnel who did not meet their quotas, or numerical results in an experiment outside the expected range.

expansion port A connector, usually on the outside of the computer, that allows the connection of additional peripheral devices. An example of an expansion port is the SCSI port.

expansion slot A narrow socket located on the main circuit board of the computer into which you can attach a peripheral circuit board or card.

exploded pie chart A pie chart where one or more slices are pulled away (exploded) from the rest of the pie to emphasize what they represent.

FatBits The 800% magnification view in MacPaint and HyperCard, in which you can work with individual pixels.

field (1) A data item used to compose a record. A field is a specific type of information in an information management program. (2) A field in HyperCard is where regular text (as opposed to paint text) may be stored.

field tool The tool used in HyperCard to create, select, modify, and delete text fields.

File menu The second (usually) menu in a Macintosh application. It generally contains commands that affect the entire file, such as Save, Save As, Print, and Quit.

file A single specific collection of information that has a name and is stored on a disk. This information may be a data document, application program, system program, or system data file.

file maintenance The process of keeping information in a file up to date. This can also include making backup copies of files.

file management system A simple information management system where data is organized into discrete files. This is a precursor to database management systems and usually has a limit of only one file open at a time.

fill pattern box The box at the far left of the MacDraw pattern palette that reflects the currently selected fill pattern.

fill The pattern that is inside the borders of an object in a drawing program.

Find A feature available in many applications where you to enter a text phrase and the computer finds that phrase in the current document if it exists.

Finder The application that automatically starts when the Macintosh is turned on. It manages and maintains the desktop, and is used to open applications, organize files and folders on disks, and copy files and folders.

First Page Special An option in the Section dialog box of Microsoft Word that creates a special header and footer that prints on only the first page of a document.

first-line indent The indentation of the first line of a paragraph. The first-line indent setting on Microsoft Word's ruler is used to control this indentation.

flip The process of turning an object vertically or horizontally in a drawing program so that a mirror image is produced.

floppy disk A disk made of flexible plastic. 5.25" disks are encased in paper or plastic envelopes and are floppy when you move them. 3.5" disks are also made of flexible plastic, but are encased in a hard plastic shell. Both are still referred to as a floppy disk.

flush left Alignment where text is aligned on the left margin and ragged on the right.

flush right Alignment where text is aligned on the right margin and ragged on the left.

folder A folder is part of the Macintosh hierarchical file system. The main level of the file system is the disk, which may hold many files and folders. Each folder may also hold many files and folders. On most other computer systems, folders are known as subdirectories.

font A set of characters which includes letters, numbers, punctuation, and other symbols that have a consistent appearance.

footer One or more lines of text and/or graphics that appear on each page of a document in the bottom margin. Footers may include page numbers, dates, times, text, pictures, or other graphics. *(See also header)*

Footer part The part of a FileMaker report that contains the bottom margin. It is printed on every page and can contain page numbers, file names, the date and other similar information.

formatting a disk The process of initializing a disk so that it can store and retrieve data. This process divides the disk into tracks, subdivides the tracks into sectors, and creates a directory structure for accessing the information.

formatting In word processing, the process of determining how text and documents will appear when printed.

formula A formula is a mathematical equation. In a spreadsheet program, you can write a formula that uses values stored in other cells to calculate a value for the current cell. *(See also function)*

formula bar In Excel, an area on the screen just below the menu bar that is used for editing and displaying the contents of the active cell.

freehand tool A tool used in drawing programs, such as MacPaint and MacDraw, that is used to draw freehand shapes.

function A built-in formula in a spreadsheet program or programming language that can be used for calculating commonly used values such as square root, absolute value, average, standard deviation, and so on. *(See also formula)*

Galley View One of the four document views available in Microsoft Word. Galley View gives you the fastest working environment, but does not display the page as it will look when printed. Documents are normally opened in Galley View. *(See also Page View, Print Preview)*

General tools The three HyperCard tools that are not used for painting: Browse, Button and Field.

grabber tool The hand-shaped tool in MacPaint's toolbox that is used to move a different portion of the drawing into view.

graphical user interface The Mac is the premier example of this type of user interface, which consists of icons, windows, and a mouse that controls the movement of a pointer on the screen. Commonly abbreviated GUI.

grid Non-printing guide and control lines in programs that help the user to align objects. MacPaint , HyperCard, MacDraw , and many other graphics programs provide grids that can be used for this purpose.

gridlines Dotted lines that can be displayed and that mark the boundaries of a grid.

grouping In MacDraw, the consolidation of two or more separate objects into one composite object.

guide lines Lines that are created in a drawing to aid in the placement of objects, and that are usually removed before printing.

handle In MacDraw, the small black squares that appear at each corner of a selected object. *(See also selection squares)*

hanging indent When the first line of a paragraph extends (or hangs) to the left of the left margin of the rest of the paragraph.

hard copy When information is printed on paper it is known as hard copy. Soft copy is information presented only on the screen of the computer.

hard disk A disk that is permanently sealed in its disk drive. These are called hard disks because the disk platter is normally made from aluminum, whereas a diskette is normally produced from plastic. Hard disks normally store megabytes of data.

hard return Pressing the Return key creates a hard return in a line of text, and causes the insertion point to move to the next line. A hard return indicates the end of a paragraph.

hardware The part of the computer that you can touch. All physical devices are hardware. This is opposed to software, which is abstract and intangible. *(See also software)*

Header part The part of a FileMaker report that contains the top margin. It is printed on every page and can contain page numbers, file names, the date and other similar information.

header One or more lines of text and/or graphics that appear on each page of a document in the top margin. Headers may include page numbers, dates, times, text, pictures, or other graphics. *(See also footer)*

header record The first record in a print merge data document in Microsoft Word. The header record determines the names of the fields and the order in which they appear in all data records in the data document.

high-density disk The 3.5 inch disks for use in the SuperDrive. It holds 1.4 megabytes (1,400 kilobytes).

highlight A method used to distinguish an object from others of its kind. (1) A highlighted button, also known as the default button, has an additional, darker oval surrounding it. (2) A highlighted menu or menu item is inverted. White pixels become black and vice-versa. (3) Highlighted text is also inverted.

Home button A button with the icon of a house that is used in HyperCard to return to the Home card.

Home card A special card in HyperCard that is used as a pictorial index to other stacks.

Home stack A special stack that is required for using HyperCard. It contains one or more Home cards, cards for storing paths to stacks, documents, and applications, and a preferences card for setting the user level, user name, and other options.

horizontal split bar *(See split bar)*

hot spot The active portion of a MacPaint, HyperCard, or MacDraw tool that actually does the drawing, selecting, or painting. For example, the hot spot of the lasso tool is the straight rope, and the hot spot of the paint bucket tool is the drip. All pointers have a particular hot spot.

HyperTalk The built-in scripting language used to program HyperCard.

hyphenation dictionary A utility file that is used with a word processing program to determine the appropriate hyphenation of words in a document.

I-beam pointer The I-shaped pointer that is used for editing and entering text.

icon A picture that is used to represent something else. Icons may be pictures of disk drives, diskettes, folders, or documents, and are one of the main parts of the Macintosh graphical user interface.

ImageWriter A dot matrix printer introduced and marketed by Apple Computer. *(See also dot matrix printer)*

indentation controls The controls on the Microsoft Word ruler that control the first line, left, and right indentations of a paragraph.

indentation Moving the first line of a paragraph and/or the subsequent lines to the left or right. Sometimes the width of a paragraph will be increased or decreased relative to paragraphs above and below in order to visually set it off from the others.

information Data that has been organized, sorted, collated, and otherwise put into a useful and retrievable form.

initialize The process of preparing a new diskette, hard disk or tape cartridge so that it will be able to store information. This is also known as formatting. *(See also formatting)*

input The information that is transferred into a computer from an external source. Original input is usually supplied through the keyboard. Other input may come from a disk, modem, scanner, mouse, trackball, or tape drive. Input also refers to the process of transferring information into the computer. *(See also output)*

insertion point The place in a text document where the next action will occur. You may move the insertion point by moving the I-beam to a new location and clicking. The insertion point will move to this new location and a short vertical line will blink so that you can easily spot it.

item (1) A synonym for "field" when used in terms of records and files for storing information. (2) One of the words or phrases listed in a menu, known as a menu item.

jaggies The jagged lines of some printed objects that have been created with bit-mapped graphics programs.

jump term A term in Excel's help system that is shown with a solid underline. Clicking a jump term will take you to information associated with that term.

justification The process of aligning text on the left and right by adding extra spacing between words or even between letters. *(See also alignment)*

justified text Text that is flush on both left and right margins. *(See also alignment, justification)*

key field A field around which a file is structured.

keyboard An input device, similar to a typewriter, used for inputting text into a computer.

kilobyte A unit of measurement that is normally thought of as 1,000. However, in computer terminology, this represents 1,024. Kilobyte is normally abbreviated as KB. Although this is a strange number in the decimal number system, it is a round number in the binary number system the computer uses. One kilobyte is 1,024 bytes.

labels report A report format in FileMaker and HyperCard where information is printed on labels, such as mailing labels.

landscape orientation The rotation of a page so that the contents are printed sideways on the page. Rather than the long side of the page being vertical, it will be horizontal. *(See also portrait orientation)*

laser printer A printing device which uses a laser to produce an image on a drum. Then the drum is rotated through tiny bits of plastic called toner. The drum is electrostatically charged and picks up the toner in the areas charged by the laser. A piece of paper which has been charged with the opposite static charge is rotated past the drum, picking up the toner from the drum. The paper then goes through two heated rollers (fusers) that melt the plastic onto the paper and fix it there. Since a laser printer is a non-impact printer it can not successfully print on multi-part forms. *(See also LaserWriter)*

LaserWriter A 300 dot per inch laser printer developed and distributed by Apple Computer. The LaserWriter was one of the four main components that introduced the desktop publishing revolution. The other three were the Macintosh, PageMaker, and PostScript. *(See also desktop publishing, laser printer, PostScript)*

lasso *(See lasso selection tool)*

lasso selection tool The tool in MacPaint and HyperCard that is used to select an object, but that does not select any background around the object. *(See also selection rectangle)*

layer controls The controls at the bottom of the tools palette that enable you to move between named layers in a MacDraw document.

layers MacDraw and HyperCard keep different objects in layers on the screen. Objects created first are behind objects created later. In MacDraw there are layers you can name and view separately or as a group, similar to the way you can view a stack of drawings on transparent film. HyperCard keeps different objects (buttons, fields, pictures, etc.) on different layers on two main layers: background and card.

Layout mode The mode in FileMaker that allows you to arrange fields, text, and graphics for producing on-screen displays and printed reports.

leaks When filling an object with the paint bucket tool in MacPaint or HyperCard, if the border of the object has gaps the pattern "leaks" out the gap and fills the rest of the drawing window.

left indent Where the text in a paragraph is positioned with respect to the left margin of the paper.

left-aligned tab The left side of the first word in the column below this tab on the Microsoft Word ruler will align with the position where the tab is placed on the ruler.

legend Symbols and text that are used to identify the data represented on a chart.

line chart A chart that shows the change in data over a period of time emphasizing direction and rate of change.

line pattern box The box at the far right of the MacDraw pattern palette that reflects the currently selected line pattern.

line spacing The vertical spacing of lines of text. In double spacing, for example, an extra full line of space is placed between each line of text.

line tool The drawing tool in MacPaint, MacDraw, and HyperCard (and other graphics programs) that is used to draw a straight line between a starting and ending point.

line weight The thickness of a line, usually measured in points.

link A relationship between two documents (such as Excel worksheets) that is defined in a formula.

linked terms Terms that are associated with other related terms in Excel's help system.

local area network (LAN) A group of connected computers in a small area (such as a room or building) that share information with each other.

lookup field A field (in FileMaker) into which information is copied from another file based on matching information in both files.

magnify To increase the size of the view of a drawing to allow more detailed work. In MacPaint the Zoom In command allows you to magnify the drawing up to 800% of its actual size. MacDraw enables you to magnify the drawing to 3200% of its original size.

main document One of the two documents used in a print merge project. The main document always contains special print merge commands, the merge fields that hold the data that changes from one document to the next, and the body text that does not change from one document to the next.

management information system (MIS) A computerized system that provides information to management personnel for operational, tactical, and strategic decision making.

manual page break A page break that results from issuing a command that causes the text to go to a new page at a particular place in a document. *(See also automatic page break)*

marching ants A term used to describe the border of a selection made with the selection rectangle in MacPaint and HyperCard. *(See also selection rectangle)*

megabyte A unit of measurement that is normally thought of as 1,000,000. However, in computer terminology, this represents 1,048,576. Megabyte is normally abbreviated as MB. Although this is a strange number in the decimal number system, it is a round number in the binary number system the computer uses. One megabyte is 1,024 kilobytes.

memory Memory Is an electronic device that is capable of storing information. All Macintoshes include two types of memory: RAM and ROM. *(See also RAM, ROM)*

menu A list of commands, or menu items, that are included under the menu title in the menu bar.

menu bar The horizontal bar at the very top of the screen which contains a list of menu titles. Most menu bars are consistent in that the first three menu titles are Apple, File and Edit. Each application has its own distinctive menu bar which contains the specific set of menu titles and commands that are available in that application. *(See also menu, menu item)*

menu item A command that is listed on a menu. To access a menu item, press on the menu bar and drag to the item you want, then release the mouse button to select the highlighted item. All menu items that end in an ellipsis (...) are followed by a dialog box. *(See also dialog box, dragging, highlight, menu bar)*

merge fields Special fields used in the main document of a print merge project that act as place holders for data that comes from the data document. Merge fields in Microsoft Word are enclosed with special characters called chevrons (« and »).

Message box A floating window (or mini window) in HyperCard used to enter commands and show messages.

microprocessor The processor used in a microcomputer, such as the Motorola 68000 or 68030.

modeling The use of a hypothetical representation of a real-world situation. Frequently, modeling refers to using spreadsheets to try to predict future financial events.

modem An abbreviation for modulator/demodulator. A modem is a device that allows computers to communicate to other devices over phone lines. Computers use digital signals internally, and phone lines use analog signals, so a modem has to translate so the computer can communicate over the phone lines. Modulate refers to changing from digital to analog (sound), and demodulate refers to translating from analog (sound) to digital.

monitor (also called CRT or VDT) A television-like device for displaying computer output.

monospace font Fonts where each letter, regardless of its width, is given the same amount of space. Typewriters use monospacing. *(See also proportional font)*

mouse A hand-held device that the user moves on a flat surface next to the computer. As the mouse is moved the cursor on the screen moves in a corresponding manner. Most commands and selections on the Macintosh are made in conjunction with pointing, clicking, dragging and double-clicking with the mouse. *(See also click, double click, dragging)*

mouse button The rectangular button on the top of the mouse that is used in conjunction with moving the mouse (or not moving the mouse) to initiate pointing, clicking, dragging, pressing, and double-clicking. Normally, the user positions the cursor on an object by moving the mouse, and starts an action by pressing the mouse button. Then the action is confirmed by releasing the mouse. *(See also click, double click, dragging)*

nesting folders The process of placing folders inside of other folders. This is the method of organizing the structure of a hard disk into an inverted tree structure. *(See also folder)*

new line command The act of manually moving the insertion point to a new line in a text document without creating a new paragraph. Also called a soft return, in Microsoft Word the new line command is Shift-Return. *(See also insertion point, hard return, soft return)*

number A word, symbol, letter, or combination of symbols used to represent a mathematical quantity.

number field A field in FileMaker that holds a number or a yes/no value.

object-oriented A type of drawing program where each object in the drawing is stored as mathematical information in the computer rather than the collection of dots that bitmapped programs store for each object. *(See also bitmapped)*

Option key A modifier key that is used with a character key to alter its function. In most fonts, there are additional symbols and characters that may be formed other than the ones that are available by using the key by itself or with the Shift key. Two additional combinations—with the Option key, or with the Option key and the Shift key—allow each character key to potentially produce a total of four different characters. The Option key is sometimes used with a tool in an application to change the normal function of the key. For example, in MacPaint, the pencil tool allows you to draw dot by dot, but when the Option key is depressed, the pencil turns into a hand that allows you to move the visible portion of the painting around on the screen.

orphans An orphan line occurs when all of a paragraph is on one page except for the last line which is on the following page.

output Information that is transferred from the computer to an external destination such as the monitor, a printer, modem, or disk drive. Output also refers to the process of transferring described above. *(See also input)*

oval tool The tool in MacPaint and HyperCard used to draw ellipses and circles.

Page View One of four document views in Microsoft Word. Page View allows you to see a full-scale version of a document as it will look when printed and to edit and format text. *(See also Galley View, Print Preview)*

page scale When you click the scale icon on the ruler in Microsoft Word it toggles to page scale, which allows you to modify the margins of the entire document. *(See also table scale)*

paginate The automatic determination of where page breaks will occur in a document based on the margins, size of the font being used, line width, and other pertinent factors. *(See also automatic page break)*

paint brush tool A tool in MacPaint that allows you to draw freehand lines in a variety of shapes and patterns.

paint bucket tool A tool in MacPaint that allows you to fill objects with a pattern.

paint text tool The tool in HyperCard that is used to enter text into a picture. When the text is deselected it is no longer editable as text, but only as a picture of text.

Painting level The user level in HyperCard that allows access to and use of the various painting tools.

Painting tools A HyperCard tool used to make pictures, including the Pencil, Brush, Spray, Lasso, Eraser, and others. Any tool in HyperCard that is not a General tool.

palette A tear-off menu becomes a palette when it is torn off from the menu bar and becomes a floating window. MacPaint and HyperCard support palettes for tools and patterns.

paragraph In word processing, text that is followed by a hard return (pressing Return). A paragraph can consist of one or more characters, words, or sentences.

paragraph spacing settings The settings on the Microsoft Word ruler that control the amount of space between paragraphs.

paragraph text Text used in MacDraw II that is confined to a text box in the drawing window and that uses word wrap to stay within the margins of the text box.

part tool The tool in FileMaker that allows the addition of new parts to the layout.

paste To place a copy of the contents of the Clipboard—whatever was last cut or copied—into the current document at the insertion point. *(See also Clipboard, copy, cut)*

patterns palette, Patterns menu The portion of the drawing window in MacDraw and the menu in MacPaint that contain the available fill and line patterns. *(See also currently selected pattern, fill pattern box, line pattern box)*

Pen menu The menu in the MacDraw menu bar that is used to control the line weights and styles of lines and borders.

pencil tool The tool in MacPaint and HyperCard that is used to draw a freehand one-pixel-wide line.

peripheral An external computer device that is used with the Macintosh, but is not an integral part of it. Peripheral devices include disk drives, tape drives, graphics tablets, scanners, printers, modems and others. These devices are usually attached to the computer by cables, although they may be internally mounted.

Phone stack A stack included with HyperCard that can be used to dial a phone through the Macintosh's speaker or a modem.

picture field A type of field in FileMaker that holds a picture.

pie chart A chart that shows the relationships of the parts comprising a whole. Always contains only one data series.

pixel An abbreviation for picture element, which is one of the dots that can be turned on or off on a screen. A Macintosh screen and an ImageWriter printer have 72 pixels per inch measured horizontally and vertically for a total of 5,184 pixels per square inch. The LaserWriter has 300 pixels per inch for a total of 90,000 pixels per square inch. The higher the density, the finer the resolution and the better the appearance of the output. *(See also bitmapped, dpi)*

pointer A small graphic shape visible on the screen that moves as the mouse moves. Common shapes are arrows (north-east and north-west pointing), I-beams, wrist watches and crossbars. Many other shapes are possible, limited only by the imagination of the programmer. Pointers often change shape over different parts of the screen to indicate that they are capable of doing different things in some areas than in others.

points, point size A point is the smallest unit of measurement in typography and typesetting. There are 12 points in a pica, and 6 picas in an inch. This means that there are 72 points in an inch. Font sizes are measured in points on the Macintosh and different point sizes are available for each font. A 36 point font should be .5 inches high and a 144 point font should be 2 inches tall. *(See also font)*

polygon tool A tool in MacPaint and MacDraw that is used to draw shapes composed of a sequence of connected lines.

portrait orientation The normal page orientation for printing. This means that the long side of the paper is vertical and the short side is horizontal. The other orientation is called landscape. *(See also landscape orientation)*

PostScript A page layout language developed by Adobe Systems, Inc. that is included in the LaserWriter printer and that gives it its special capabilities. In addition to font printing, scaling, and rotating, it also contains many drawing capabilities. PostScript® has become the standard output language for the desktop publishing industry.

presentation graphics Informational graphics produced by a computer application such as a spreadsheet that shows relationships involved in data sets. Presentation graphics are more sophisticated than analytical graphics because they are used to present the information to management and people outside of a company.

Print Preview One of four document views in Microsoft Word. Print Preview allows you to see a scaled-down view of whole pages of a document as it will look when printed. You cannot access text directly while in Print Preview, but it does allow some limited formatting capabilities. *(See also Galley View, Page View)*

print merge A feature in many word processing programs that involves creating a main document that contains the body text, and that contains special fields to mark the parts that will change with each document. A data document is also used that contains the information to be placed in the special fields in the main document. When the print merge command is issued the information from the data document is merged with the main document to create customized form documents. *(See also data document, main document)*

printer A device that produces images on paper, photographic film, or transparencies. Many types of printers are available. The Macintosh primarily uses the ImageWriter dot matrix printer and the LaserWriter laser printer. *(See also dot matrix printer, ImageWriter, LaserWriter)*

printing The process of issuing a print command to send the contents of a document to a printer to produce hard copy output.

program A set of instructions that tells the computer the complex sequence of steps necessary to perform a particular task.

Programs are divided into applications programs and systems programs. Program is synonymous with software. *(See also application program, system program)*

proportional font A font in which different characters are allowed different amounts of space in the line of text depending on their width. A "W" is given more space than an "i" in a proportional font. Most Macintosh fonts are proportionally spaced. *(See also monospace font)*

pull-down menu A menu that is hidden until you press on its title, at which point the list of choices pulls down onto the screen allowing you to select a command. *(See also menu, menu item)*

RAM An acronym that stands for Random Access Memory, and the part of memory that is used to store information that is changeable. RAM holds applications programs, systems programs, documents, and other data. RAM is volatile, which means that the information it contains is lost when the power is removed. *(See also memory, ROM)*

random access A method of accessing a particular record in a file or byte in memory without having to read any preceding information. *(See also direct access and sequential access)*

range (1) In Excel, a group of cells that are acted upon by a command or formula as a unit. (2) In FileMaker, a criterion used for finding information that is between a low value and a high value, either alphabetically, chronologically, or numerically.

record A group of related information that describes one person, place or thing. A record is made up of related fields. A group of related records is known as a file. *(See also file, field)*

rectangle tool A tool used in many graphics programs for drawing rectangles and squares.

redundancy Storing the same data in two or more locations.

reference area The area on the screen to the left of the formula bar in Excel that shows the row number and column letter of the active cell.

reformat To change the format, or the way a document looks when printed. *(See also formatting)*

regular polygon tool A tool in HyperCard for drawing polygons with regular sides. It always draws from the center outwards and allows rotation of the polygon before fixing its location on the card.

relational database A database in which files are organized as tables in rows and columns.

relative addressing A way of defining the location of a cell based on its position relative to the cell containing a formula in Excel.

repeating field A field that has been formatted to allow you to store and display multiple values in one record.

Reshape command A command in MacDraw that enables you to change the shape of objects drawn with the arc tool, the polygon tool, and the freehand tool.

resize To change the size of an object in a drawing program.

resolution A measure of how well a device can produce an image. Higher resolutions produce clearer images. Resolution is applicable to both screen and printer output. A LaserWriter produces better images than the screen or an ImageWriter, because its resolution is a little over 16 times higher. *(See also dpi, pixel)*

Return key A key that normally causes the insertion point to move down to the start of the next line when editing text. Also commonly known as the carriage return key, it is usually used to end a paragraph, or produce a blank line. When used with a dialog box, the Return key can be used as a shortcut to select the highlighted, or default, button. *(See also hard return)*

Revert To Saved command The command in MacPaint that brings back to the drawing window the last version of a document that was saved on disk. It is used to undo errors made to a drawing.

right indent Where the text in a paragraph is positioned with respect to the right margin of the paper.

right-aligned tab The right side of the first word in the column below this tab will align with the position where the tab is placed on the Microsoft Word ruler.

ROM Acronym that stands for Read Only Memory, and the part of memory that is used to store information that is permanent. Information used by the computer system throughout all applications is normally stored in ROM. For instance, the procedures to produce windows, buttons, scroll bars, and other normal parts of the Macintosh interface are stored in ROM. ROM is also used to store the necessary instructions for the computer to follow when the power is first turned on. *(See also memory, RAM)*

rotate To move an object in a drawing program with its center point or corner as an anchor point.

rounded rectangle tool A painting tool available in most graphics programs that is used to draw rectangles and squares with rounded corners.

rounded rectangles Rectangles whose corners are formed by arcs instead of sharp angles.

row In an electronic spreadsheet or in a cell table, a horizontal grouping of cells. *(See also cell, column)*

ruler (1) In a word processing program, a graphic representation of a ruler which allows you to set margins, tab settings, line spacing, indentation and other settings. (2) In drawing and paint programs, a ruler placed along the edge of the window to aid in measuring and placing graphic elements in the image.

ruler settings The margin, tab, line spacing, indentation, and other settings that are controlled by the ruler in a word processing program. *(See ruler)*

scale tool The icon on the Microsoft Word ruler that toggles between the normal scale, page scale, and table scale. *(See also page scale, table scale)*

scatter chart A chart that is used to show the degree of relationship between values in different data series.

Scripting level The highest user level in HyperCard that allows access to programming (or scripting) in HyperTalk. It also allows access to all the other features of HyperCard.

scripting The process of modifying the script of an object in HyperCard. Every item has a script, although some may be empty.

scroll arrow An outline of an arrow located on each end of a scroll bar. Clicking a scroll arrow causes the contents of the window to scroll one line closer to the end of the document to which the arrow points. Pressing a scroll arrow causes the contents of the window to scroll continuously, one line at a time, in the direction pointed to by the arrow. *(See also scroll bar, scroll box)*

scroll bar A rectangular bar that may be oriented vertically along the left or right edge of a window, or horizontally along the top or bottom edge. Normally vertical scroll bars are on the right, and horizontal scroll bars are along the bottom. Clicking or pressing in the scroll bar causes the contents of the window to move a screenfull at a time. The direction of the scroll depends on the location of the scroll box. *(See also scroll arrow, scroll box)*

scroll box The white square box in the scroll bar. The scroll box is also known as the thumb or elevator button. The position of the scroll box in the scroll bar gives a relative indication of where the contents of the window are located in relation to the corresponding edges of the document. For example, in a vertical scroll bar, if the scroll box is approximately in the middle of the scroll bar, then the window is showing approximately the middle of the document from top to bottom (or beginning to end). In order to quickly move to a particular part of the document, you can drag the scroll box to the relative position desired. This is especially useful when going to the top (beginning) or bottom (end) of a long document. *(See also scroll arrow, scroll bar)*

search and replace A feature in many word processing programs that allows you to automatically locate one or all occurrences of a particular word and replace it with a different word.

search criteria The value or phrase entered into a find command that is used to locate any matching data.

section Any part of a document that is designated as separate from another part. A section can be compared to a chapter in a book; a chapter is a part of the whole book, but it is also separate from other chapters. In Microsoft Word, a document can be divided into one or more sections and each section can be formatted differently from other sections in the same document. Sections are separated by section break markers. *(See also section break marker)*

section break marker The double dotted line that runs across the width of a document in Microsoft Word that indicates the division of two sections. The section break command is Command-Enter. *(See also section)*

select When using the Macintosh, you generally select an object and then issue a command which will operate on that object. How something is selected is similar across all applications. Selecting occurs in several ways depending on the program in use. (1) Although not commonly thought of as a selection, positioning the insertion point is the selection of the location where the next action will occur. (2) To select an icon, click on it. (3) To select several icons, click above them and then drag the selection rectangle around all of them. (4) Selecting text can occur by wiping through text, double clicking on a word, dragging through several lines, and other methods, depending on the program. Selected text is highlighted, or inverted. *(See also highlight)*

selection arrow The tool in MacDraw, located at the top of the tools palette, that is used to select objects.

selection bar The area located at the far left of a Microsoft Word document that is about 1/8-inch wide and that enables you to select large blocks of text.

selection rectangle Also called the selection marquee, the MacPaint tool that is used for selecting objects and that also selects the background around the object. *(See also lasso selection tool, marching ants)*

selection squares Small black squares that appear at the corners of a graphic object to indicate the object is selected. *(See also handle)*

sequential access The method of accessing information in a file where all preceding information must be read first. *(See also random access and direct access)*

Shift key A modifier key that affects character keys. When used with an alphabetic key, it produces the upper case letter. When used with a numeric or symbol key, it produces the character shown on the top of the key. This is similar to the Caps Lock key except that it will affect all keys and not just alphabetic keys. *(See also Shift-click)*

Shift-click A selection technique that allows you to extend the area of a selection. (1)When used with text, you click at the first location, scroll to the final position and click the mouse button with the Shift key depressed. This will extend the selection from the first click to the final position. (2)When used with icons or objects, it allows an icon or object to be added to, or removed from, the current group of selected icons or objects.

Show Size command A MacDraw command that displays the size of an object as it is drawn.

slide control handle A tool used for moving to a different record or layout in FileMaker.

Sliding objects left In FileMaker, used to keep fields and punctuation next to preceding fields on the same row.

Sliding objects up In FileMaker, used to eliminate blank lines when fields are empty or the information in a field does not fill the field.

Sliding part up In FileMaker, used to eliminate empty space in a printed report after objects have slid up.

smooth To round the sharp angles in an object into curves.

snap Aligning of an object or text to a grid boundary.

soft copy When information is presented only on the screen of the computer. Hard copy is when information is printed on paper.

soft return A carriage return that causes the insertion point in a word processing program to move to a new line but does not create a new paragraph. In Microsoft Word, a soft return is created with the Shift-Return keys. *(See also hard return, insertion point, new line command)*

software Software is synonymous with program, which is instructions the computer follows when accomplishing a designated task. Software is the intangible part of the computer, as opposed to the physical part which is known as hardware. *(See also application program, hardware, system program)*

sort Placing items in a predetermined alphabetical, chronological, or numerical order.

sort field A field whose contents are used as the basis for sorting a file or stack.

source disk The original disk being copied or moved to a new destination. *(See also destination disk)*

spelling checker A utility program that determines if a word is spelled correctly by comparing each word in a document with the entries in its dictionary. If the word matches a dictionary entry, the spelling checker considers the word correct. If the word is not in the dictionary, that word is considered misspelled.

split bar In Excel, the small black rectangle located at the top of the vertical scroll bar and on the left of the horizontal scroll bar. It is used to split the window into two or four panes so different parts of the worksheet can be seen at the same time.

spray can tool A tool in MacPaint that paints in a "mist" of the currently selected pattern.

spreadsheet A general classification of applications that are used for numeric analysis such as finance, budgeting, and other business uses, as well as other uses such as engineering and scientific calculations. Information in a spreadsheet program is organized into columns and rows. The intersections of these columns and rows are called cells. A spreadsheet application is also known as an electronic spreadsheet program. *(See also cell, column, row)*

stack A HyperCard document containing a group of cards.

stacking order The position of objects in front or behind other objects.

startup disk The disk the computer reads from when the system is first turned on. This disk must have a System file and usually a Finder. It also will contain printing resources, desk accessories, fonts, fkeys, sounds, and other systems software. If more than one of the disks attached to the computer has a system file, the one that is currently active is known as the current startup disk. In the Finder, this disk is the one on the very top right of the screen. All other disk icons will be located below the startup disk. If there is a floppy disk inserted into one of the floppy disk drives, it will take precedence as the startup disk over the hard disk. If you have more than one SCSI hard disk attached to your computer, and if your Macintosh is an SE or Mac II then you can change the startup disk by using the Control Panel desk accessory.

status area An area on the left side of FileMaker's browse screen that shows the number of records in the file, whether or not they are sorted, and the number of records that have been found by the last Find command.

status bar An area at the bottom of the Excel screen that shows information about the current activity or mode.

string literal In programming or scripting, a "string" or group of text enclosed in quotation marks, as opposed to a string variable.

style In word processing programs, a group of formatting characteristics that have been assigned a name. The style name is the name these characteristics have been assigned. Style can also refer to the change in the overall impression of a font, such as bold, italic, underlined, outlined, shadowed, and combinations of these.

style sheet A group of styles attached to a document. Transferring style sheets to other documents enables different documents to have a consistent appearance. *(See also style)*

Sub-summary part A part of a layout used to display or print summary information when a file has been sorted by the contents of a specified field.

summary field A field that contains a numeric summary of all the values in a field across a group of records.

summary report A report that prints only summary information without printing any detail for each record. *(See also detail report)*

System Folder A special folder on the startup disk that contains the System file and any necessary resources to interface with peripherals, such as printers. *(See also peripheral, startup disk)*

system program There are two basic types of programs: application and system programs. A system program is a program which controls the interaction of the hardware devices, or allows the user to control information storage on the system. It is not designed to let the user perform a task like write a letter. Instead, it is designed for tasks the computer must perform. *(See also application program)*

system software The files, resources and applications—normally located in the System folder—which are used by the Macintosh to make itself run.

T-squares A Gadget available in FileMaker's Layout mode for aligning objects horizontally, vertically, or both.

tab leaders A series of characters that lead up to a tab position. Tab leaders make it easier for the eye to follow the area between the tab positions.

tab setting The position to which the insertion point advances when the Tab key is pressed. Also called a tab stop.

table An arrangement of rows and columns of data. In Microsoft Word, the intersection of a row and a vertically aligned column in a table is a cell.

table scale The ruler scale that is displayed in Microsoft Word when the insertion point is in a table and the scale tool is clicked. When in table scale, the width of columns can be modified. *(See also page scale)*

tables feature A feature in Microsoft Word that allows the creation of tables in which each cell can contain text or graphics and can be formatted using any character or paragraph formatting option. *(See also cell, table, table scale)*

tear-off menu A menu that can be detached from the menu bar by dragging past the bottom of the menu. When the menu becomes detached it is known as a palette.

Tell Me... button A button in HyperCard that looks like a cartoon's dialog balloon. Clicking this button generally provides more information about the stack and how to use it.

template A document that contains predefined contents. This can be a word processing template, spreadsheet template, or some other type of template. It is designed to be used for tasks that are often repeated so you don't have to create the document from scratch each time.

text alignment The positioning of text relative to the horizontal and vertical margins in a document. Text alignment can include horizontal alignments such as flush left, flush right, justified, and centered, and vertical alignments such as centered between the top and bottom margins. *(See also alignment, flush left, flush right, justification)*

text entry The process of typing text into a document.

text field A type of field in FileMaker and HyperCard that holds text.

text Information presented in the form of readable characters.

text tool The tool in graphic programs, such as MacPaint and MacDraw, that is used for typing text into a drawing.

title bar The horizontal area at the top of a window that shows the name of the window and is an indicator of whether or not that window is active. When the window is the active window, the title bar has a series of horizontal lines; when the window is not the active window, the lines are not present. A window may be moved on the screen by clicking in the title bar and dragging the window to a new location. *(See also active window)*

toolbox The menu in MacPaint that contains the tools that are used to create lines, shapes, and other drawing elements.

tools palette The group of tools that runs down the left side of the MacDraw drawing window and that are used to create objects in a MacDraw document.

trackball An input device that is used similarly to a mouse, but instead of pushing the mouse on a desk and causing the ball inside to move, the trackball offers a ball that you can move directly. *(See also mouse)*

transparent object An object created in a drawing program that has a transparent fill pattern, making it possible to see other objects beneath the transparent object. *(See also fill)*

Trash An icon located on the lower right corner of the screen that looks like a trash can. When you wish to throw an application or document away, you drag its icon into the trash can. When there is nothing in the trash, the sides of the can are straight; and when there is something in it, the sides appear to bulge. Files may be removed from the trash can and replaced on the desktop until the trash is emptied—either by starting an application, choosing Shut Down from the Special menu, or choosing Empty Trash from the Special Menu.

Typing level A user level in HyperCard that allows browsing the stack and entering and editing text in fields.

Undo command A command in most Macintosh applications that allows you to undo the last action of the mouse or the last command or, in word processing programs, the last typing or formatting action.

unfilled In MacPaint, filled or unfilled shapes can be created depending on the tool selected. A filled shape is filled with the currently selected pattern as it is drawn; an unfilled shape is not filled with a pattern when it is drawn. *(See also currently selected pattern, fill)*

Unsmooth command A MacDraw command that changes a polygon or freehand shape that has been smoothed back to its original form. *(See also freehand tool, polygon tool, smooth)*

user level A setting in the Preferences card in HyperCard's Home stack that lets you set the amount of access you want to HyperCard's tools, commands, and features. The five user levels (from least access to most access) are: Browsing, Typing, Painting, Authoring, and Scripting.

value Generally used to mean a numeric quantity. HyperCard stores all values as text strings, but can still perform mathematical operations on values that represent numbers.

variable The symbol used in a program or script to store text or a numeric value.

vertical split bar *(See split bar)*

video display terminal (VDT) An output device that can receive signals by direct connection to a computer or other video source, but cannot receive transmitted signals.

visual effect A visual transition that takes place on the screen in HyperCard between closing the current card and opening the next card that will appear.

what if... analysis The process of analyzing alternatives using a spreadsheet. This commonly involves changing parameters in the spreadsheet to answer questions that begin with "What if...".

wide area network A system of local area networks that are interconnected over a wide geographical area, usually using the services provided by a common carrier.

widow A widow occurs when the first line of a paragraph appears by itself at the bottom of a page and the rest of the paragraph is on the next page.

window The area on the Macintosh's screen through which you have access to data. Opening a disk causes a window to open which shows the contents of the disk. Opening a document on the desktop opens a window which allows you to edit the contents of that document. Windows may be opened, closed, moved, resized, and the contents of the window may be scrolled, moved and modified.

wiping through text Positioning the I-beam pointer to the left of text and dragging to the right to select the text in the path of the I-beam pointer.

word processing The process of using a computer to enter, edit, format, and print text documents. *(See also editing, formatting, text entry, printing, word wrap)*

word wrap The process of automatically causing a word to drop to the beginning of the next line if it won't fit at the end of the current line. Especially useful in a word processor, it is a common feature of almost all windows, text boxes and other places where text may be edited on the Mac. Word wrap lets you continue typing, without regard to how much text will fit on a particular line. The only time you have to type the Return key is at the end of a paragraph or when you want to create a blank line.

wristwatch pointer The pointer you see on the screen when the Macintosh is performing a lengthy operation. You can interpret it to mean, "Wait a minute, I'm busy."

Zoom In command A MacPaint command that magnifies the view of a drawing in 200% increments, up to 800% of the actual (100%) size. *(See also FatBits, magnify, Zoom Out command)*

Zoom Out command A MacPaint command that reduces the view of a drawing in 200% increments, down to 50% of the actual (100%) size. *(See also FatBits, magnify, Zoom In command)*

zoom box The white square on the right side of many window title bars. Clicking in the zoom box causes the window to expand to fill the screen. Clicking again will resize the window to its original size. *(See also title bar, window)*

zoom controls The controls in the lower left corner of the MacDraw tools palette that reduce and magnify the view of a drawing from 3.12% of the actual size to 3200% of the actual size. *(See also magnify, tools palette, zoom percentage box)*

zoom percentage box The box beneath the zoom controls on the MacDraw tools palette that reflects the current view size of the drawing. *(See also magnify, zoom controls)*

Index

Macintosh Journey Project Disk ○

The **Macintosh Journey Project Disk** is designed to accompany *A Macintosh Journey with Guided Projects* by John Dilbeck and Nicki Fink.

This disk is **not** required for the completion of projects in the book, but it will save time entering data. It includes clip art, several word processing documents with most of the text already entered, an inventory file for use with FileMaker, and three HyperCard stacks (Glossary, Class Notes Buttons, and Visual Effects). This inexpensive disk will help you travel quickly through the projects in *A Macintosh Journey.*

If you are using *A Macintosh Journey* as a text for a course in which you are enrolled, your instructor will already have this disk. You are authorized to make a copy of your instructor's disk to use with our book.

To order, complete the coupon below, and mail it to:

Benjamin/Cummings Publishing Company
ATTN: ORDER DEPT.
1 Jacob Way
Reading, MA   01867-9984

Please allow approximately 10 days for delivery.

- -

Please send me the **Macintosh Journey Project Disk** (31262-5) to accompany the text *A Macintosh Journey with Guided Projects* by John Dilbeck and Nicki Fink.

I understand that the price of the Disk is $2.25 and this covers all costs, including shipping and handling.

Please enclose a check or money order for $2.25 (payable to Benjamin/Cummings Publishing Co).

Name:_____

Organization:_____

Address:_____

City:_____State:_____ Zip:_____

Common Command-Key Shortcuts

Word

⌘ - A	repeat last command
⌘ - B	page view
⌘ - C	copy
⌘ - D	set character formats
⌘ - E	create footnote
⌘ - F	find
⌘ - G	go to page
⌘ - H	change
⌘ - I	page view
⌘ - J	repaginate document
⌘ - K	glossary
⌘ - L	spelling checker
⌘ - M	reformat paragraph
⌘ - N	new (file/folder/ card/record)
⌘ - O	open file
⌘ - P	print document/card
⌘ - Q	quit
⌘ - R	show/hide ruler
⌘ - S	save
⌘ - T	define styles
⌘ - U	enter/leave outlining mode
⌘ - V	paste
⌘ - W	close
⌘ - X	cut
⌘ - Y	show/hide ¶
⌘ - Z	undo
⌘ - ?	help
⌘ - .	stop current action

*You can use the **Word** shortcuts in other applications with the following **common** exceptions:*

FileMaker®

⌘ - /	help
⌘ - U	preview
⌘ - Y	select all
⌘ - D	duplicate record
⌘ - E	delete record
⌘ - B	browse
⌘ - R	refind
⌘ - G	find all
⌘ - S	sort
⌘ - L	layout
⌘ - T	t-squares
⌘ - Y	invisible grid

Excel

⌘ - M	activate next window
⌘ - =	calculate
⌘ - B	clear
⌘ - L	define name
⌘ - K	delete
⌘ - D	fill down
⌘ - J	formula find
⌘ - H	formula find next
⌘ - G	go to
⌘ - I	insert
⌘ - A	select all cells
⌘ - A	select chart
⌘ - U	activate formula bar

Hypercard™

⌘ - T	text style
⌘ - B	background
⌘ - S	select
⌘ - A	select all
⌘ - K	keep
⌘ - ~	back
⌘ - H	home
⌘ - R	recent
⌘ - 1	recent
⌘ - 2	prev(ious)
⌘ - 3	next
⌘ - 4	last
⌘ - M	message
⌘ - +	bring closer
⌘ - -	send farther

MacPaint®

⌘ - T	rotate
⌘ - M	zoom in
⌘ - L	zoom out
⌘ - H	shortcuts
⌘ - B	bold
⌘ - I	italics
⌘ - U	underline

MacDraw® II

⌘ - A	select all
⌘ - D	duplicate
⌘ - E	smooth
⌘ - R	reshape

from *A Macintosh Journey* by John Dilbeck and Nicki Fink
© 1991 The Benjamin/Cummings Publishing Company